Contents

Productivity Apps for School and Work

Corinne Hoisington

Lochlan keeps track of his class notes, football plays, and internship meetings with OneNote.

Zoe is using the annotation features of Microsoft Edge to take and save web notes for her research paper.

Nori is creating a Sway site to highlight this year's activities for the Student Government Association.

Hunter is adding interactive videos and screen recordings to his PowerPoint resume.

© Rawpixel/Shutterstock.com

Being computer literate no longer means mastery of only Word, Excel, PowerPoint, Outlook, and Access. To become technology power users, Hunter, Nori, Zoe, and Lochlan are exploring Microsoft OneNote, Sway, Mix, and Edge in Office 2016 and Windows 10.

In this Module

Learn to use productivity apps!
Links to companion **Sways**, featuring **videos** with hands-on instructions, are located on www.cengagebrain.com.

Introduction to OneNote 2016

notebook | section tab | To Do tag | screen clipping | note | template | Microsoft OneNote Mobile app | sync | drawing canvas | inked handwriting | Ink to Text

Bottom Line

- OneNote is a note-taking app for your academic and professional life.
- Use OneNote to get organized by gathering your ideas, sketches, webpages, photos, videos, and notes in one place.

As you glance around any classroom, you invariably see paper notebooks and notepads on each desk. Because deciphering and sharing handwritten notes can be a challenge, Microsoft OneNote 2016 replaces physical notebooks, binders, and paper notes with a searchable, digital notebook. OneNote captures your ideas and schoolwork on any device so you can stay organized, share notes, and work with others on projects. Whether you are a student taking class notes as shown in **Figure 1** or an employee taking notes in company meetings, OneNote is the one place to keep notes for all of your projects.

Figure 1: OneNote 2016 notebook

Each **notebook** is divided into sections, also called **section tabs**, by subject or topic.

Use **To Do tags**, icons that help you keep track of your assignments and other tasks.

Type on a page to add a **note**, a small window that contains text or other types of information.

Personalize a page with a **template**, or stationery.

Write or draw directly on the page using drawing tools.

Pages can include pictures such as **screen clippings**, images from any part of a computer screen.

Attach files and enter equations so you have everything you need in one place.

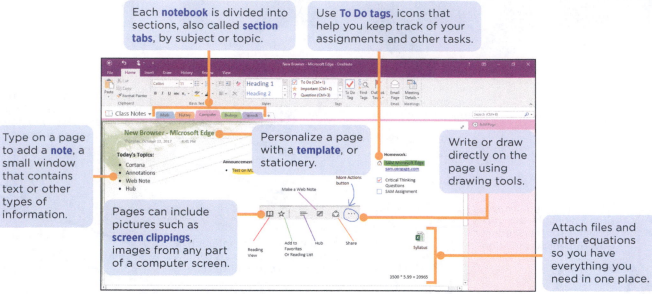

Creating a OneNote Notebook

OneNote is divided into sections similar to those in a spiral-bound notebook. Each OneNote notebook contains sections, pages, and other notebooks. You can use One-Note for school, business, and personal projects. Store information for each type of project in different notebooks to keep your tasks separate, or use any other organization that suits you. OneNote is flexible enough to adapt to the way you want to work.

When you create a notebook, it contains a blank page with a plain white background by default, though you can use templates, or stationery, to apply designs in categories such as Academic, Business, Decorative, and Planners. Start typing or use the buttons on the Insert tab to insert notes, which are small resizable windows that can contain text, equations, tables, on-screen writing, images, audio and video recordings, to-do lists, file attachments, and file printouts. Add as many notes as you need to each page.

Learn to use OneNote!

Links to companion **Sways**, featuring **videos** with hands-on instructions, are located on www.cengagebrain.com.

Syncing a Notebook to the Cloud

OneNote saves your notes every time you make a change in a notebook. To make sure you can access your notebooks with a laptop, tablet, or smartphone wherever you are, OneNote uses cloud-based storage, such as OneDrive or SharePoint. **Microsoft OneNote Mobile app**, a lightweight version of OneNote 2016 shown in **Figure 2**, is available for free in the Windows Store, Google Play for Android devices, and the AppStore for iOS devices.

If you have a Microsoft account, OneNote saves your notes on OneDrive automatically for all your mobile devices and computers, which is called **syncing**. For example, you can use OneNote to take notes on your laptop during class, and then open OneNote on your phone to study later. To use a notebook stored on your computer with your OneNote Mobile app, move the notebook to OneDrive. You can quickly share notebook content with other people using OneDrive.

Figure 2: Microsoft OneNote Mobile app

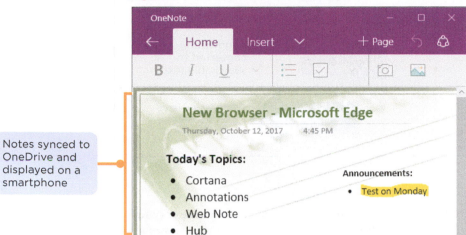

Notes synced to OneDrive and displayed on a smartphone

Taking Notes

Use OneNote pages to organize your notes by class and topic or lecture. Beyond simple typed notes, OneNote stores drawings, converts handwriting to searchable text and mathematical sketches to equations, and records audio and video.

OneNote includes drawing tools that let you sketch freehand drawings such as biological cell diagrams and financial supply-and-demand charts. As shown in **Figure 3**, the Draw tab on the ribbon provides these drawing tools along with shapes so you can insert diagrams and other illustrations to represent your ideas. When you draw on a page, OneNote creates a **drawing canvas**, which is a container for shapes and lines.

On the Job Now

OneNote is ideal for taking notes during meetings, whether you are recording minutes, documenting a discussion, sketching product diagrams, or listing follow-up items. Use a meeting template to add pages with content appropriate for meetings.

Figure 3: Tools on the Draw tab

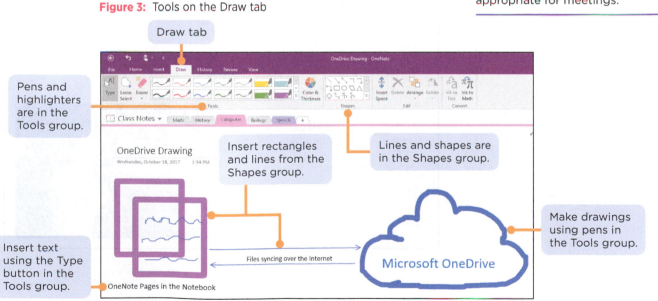

Draw tab

Pens and highlighters are in the Tools group.

Insert rectangles and lines from the Shapes group.

Lines and shapes are in the Shapes group.

Insert text using the Type button in the Tools group.

Make drawings using pens in the Tools group.

Converting Handwriting to Text

When you use a pen tool to write on a notebook page, the text you enter is called **inked handwriting**. OneNote can convert inked handwriting to typed text when you use the **Ink to Text** button in the Convert group on the Draw tab, as shown in **Figure 4**. After OneNote converts the handwriting to text, you can use the Search box to find terms in the converted text or any other note in your notebooks.

Figure 4: Converting handwriting to text

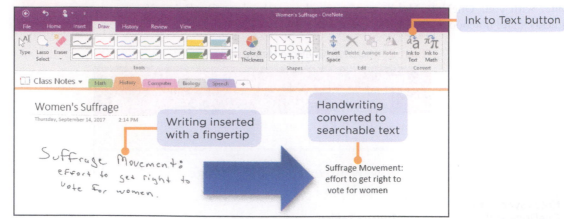

Recording a Lecture

If your computer or mobile device has a microphone or camera, OneNote can record the audio or video from a lecture or business meeting as shown in **Figure 5**. When you record a lecture (with your instructor's permission), you can follow along, take regular notes at your own pace, and review the video recording later. You can control the start, pause, and stop motions of the recording when you play back the recording of your notes.

On the Job Now

Use OneNote as a place to brainstorm ongoing work projects. If a notebook contains sensitive material, you can password-protect some or all of the notebook so that only certain people can open it.

Figure 5: Video inserted in a notebook

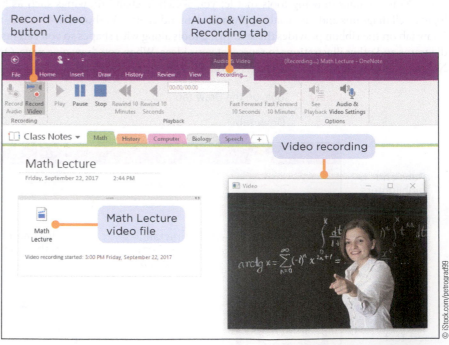

Try This Now

Learn to use OneNote!
Links to companion **Sways**, featuring **videos** with hands-on instructions, are located on www.cengagebrain.com.

1: Taking Notes for a Week

As a student, you can get organized by using OneNote to take detailed notes in your classes. Perform the following tasks:

a. Create a new OneNote notebook on your Microsoft OneDrive account (the default location for new notebooks). Name the notebook with your first name followed by "Notes," as in **Caleb Notes**.

b. Create four section tabs, each with a different class name.

c. Take detailed notes in those classes for one week. Be sure to include notes, drawings, and other types of content.

d. Sync your notes with your OneDrive. Submit your assignment in the format specified by your instructor.

2: Using OneNote to Organize a Research Paper

You have a research paper due on the topic of three habits of successful students. Use OneNote to organize your research. Perform the following tasks:

a. Create a new OneNote notebook on your Microsoft OneDrive account. Name the notebook **Success Research**.

b. Create three section tabs with the following names:

- **Take Detailed Notes**
- **Be Respectful in Class**
- **Come to Class Prepared**

c. On the web, research the topics and find three sources for each section. Copy a sentence from each source and paste the sentence into the appropriate section. When you paste the sentence, OneNote inserts it in a note with a link to the source.

d. Sync your notes with your OneDrive. Submit your assignment in the format specified by your instructor.

3: Planning Your Career

Note: This activity requires a webcam or built-in video camera on any type of device.

Consider an occupation that interests you. Using OneNote, examine the responsibilities, education requirements, potential salary, and employment outlook of a specific career. Perform the following tasks:

a. Create a new OneNote notebook on your Microsoft OneDrive account. Name the notebook with your first name followed by a career title, such as **Kara - App Developer**.

b. Create four section tabs with the names **Responsibilities, Education Requirements, Median Salary**, and **Employment Outlook**.

c. Research the responsibilities of your career path. Using OneNote, record a short video (approximately 30 seconds) of yourself explaining the responsibilities of your career path. Place the video in the Responsibilities section.

d. On the web, research the educational requirements for your career path and find two appropriate sources. Copy a paragraph from each source and paste them into the appropriate section. When you paste a paragraph, OneNote inserts it in a note with a link to the source.

e. Research the median salary for a single year for this career. Create a mathematical equation in the Median Salary section that multiplies the amount of the median salary times 20 years to calculate how much you will possibly earn.

f. For the Employment Outlook section, research the outlook for your career path. Take at least four notes about what you find when researching the topic.

g. Sync your notes with your OneDrive. Submit your assignment in the format specified by your instructor.

Introduction to Sway

Sway site | responsive design | Storyline | card | Creative Commons license | animation emphasis effects | Docs.com

Expressing your ideas in a presentation typically means creating PowerPoint slides or a Word document. Microsoft Sway gives you another way to engage an audience. Sway is a free Microsoft tool available at Sway.com or as an app in Office 365. Using Sway, you can combine text, images, videos, and social media in a website called a **Sway site** that you can share and display on any device. To get started, you create a digital story on a web-based canvas without borders, slides, cells, or page breaks. A Sway site organizes the text, images, and video into a **responsive design**, which means your content adapts perfectly to any screen size as shown in **Figure 6**. You store a Sway site in the cloud on OneDrive using a free Microsoft account.

Figure 6: Sway site with responsive design

You can display a Sway presentation in a web browser.

Sway uses responsive design to make sure pages fit perfectly on any device.

© iStock.com/marinello, © iStock.com/marekuliasz

Creating a Sway Presentation

You can use Sway to build a digital flyer, a club newsletter, a vacation blog, an informational site, a digital art portfolio, or a new product rollout. After you select your topic and sign into Sway with your Microsoft account, a **Storyline** opens, providing tools and a work area for composing your digital story. See **Figure 7**. Each story can include text, images, and videos. You create a Sway by adding text and media content into a Storyline section, or **card**. To add pictures, videos, or documents, select a card in the left pane and then select the Insert Content button. The first card in a Sway presentation contains a title and background image.

Figure 7: Creating a Sway site

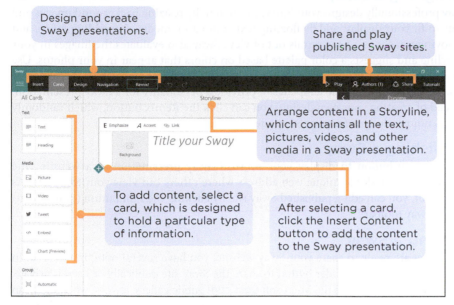

Design and create Sway presentations.

Share and play published Sway sites.

Arrange content in a Storyline, which contains all the text, pictures, videos, and other media in a Sway presentation.

To add content, select a card, which is designed to hold a particular type of information.

After selecting a card, click the Insert Content button to add the content to the Sway presentation.

Adding Content to Build a Story

As you work, Sway searches the Internet to help you find relevant images, videos, tweets, and other content from online sources such as Bing, YouTube, Twitter, and Facebook. You can drag content from the search results right into the Storyline. In addition, you can upload your own images and videos directly in the presentation. For example, if you are creating a Sway presentation about the market for commercial drones, Sway suggests content to incorporate into the presentation by displaying it in the left pane as search results. The search results include drone images tagged with a **Creative Commons license** at online sources as shown in **Figure 8**. A Creative Commons license is a public copyright license that allows the free distribution of an otherwise copyrighted work. In addition, you can specify the source of the media. For example, you can add your own Facebook or OneNote pictures and videos in Sway without leaving the app.

On the Job Now

If you have a Microsoft Word document containing an outline of your business content, drag the outline into Sway to create a card for each topic.

Figure 8: Images in Sway search results

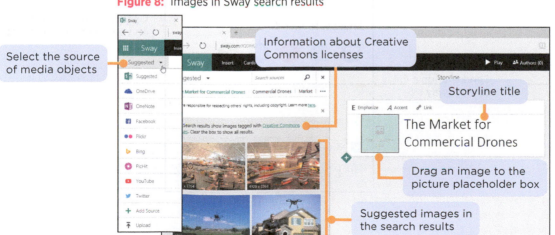

Select the source of media objects

Information about Creative Commons licenses

Storyline title

The Market for Commercial Drones

Drag an image to the picture placeholder box

Suggested images in the search results

On the Job Now

If your project team wants to collaborate on a Sway presentation, click the Authors button on the navigation bar to invite others to edit the presentation.

Designing a Sway

Sway professionally designs your Storyline content by resizing background images and fonts to fit your display, and by floating text, animating media, embedding video, and removing images as a page scrolls out of view. Sway also evaluates the images in your Storyline and suggests a color palette based on colors that appear in your photos. Use the Design button to display tools including color palettes, font choices, **animation emphasis effects**, and style templates to provide a personality for a Sway presentation. Instead of creating your own design, you can click the Remix button, which randomly selects unique designs for your Sway site.

Publishing a Sway

Use the Play button to display your finished Sway presentation as a website. The Address bar includes a unique web address where others can view your Sway site. As the author, you can edit a published Sway site by clicking the Edit button (pencil icon) on the Sway toolbar.

Sharing a Sway

When you are ready to share your Sway website, you have several options as shown in **Figure 9**. Use the Share slider button to share the Sway site publically or keep it private. If you add the Sway site to the Microsoft **Docs.com** public gallery, anyone worldwide can use Bing, Google, or other search engines to find, view, and share your Sway site. You can also share your Sway site using Facebook, Twitter, Google+, Yammer, and other social media sites. Link your presentation to any webpage or email the link to your audience. Sway can also generate a code for embedding the link within another webpage.

Figure 9: Sharing a Sway site

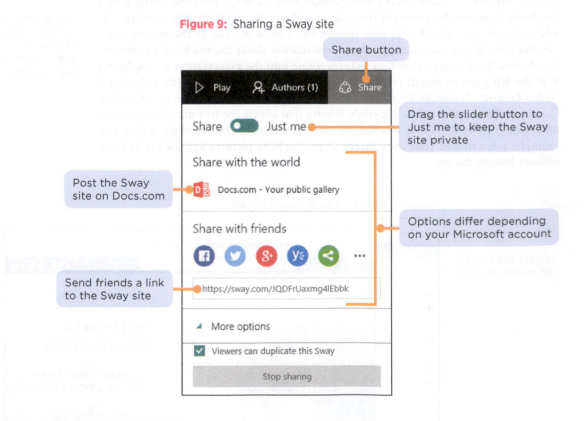

Try This Now

1: Creating a Sway Resume

Sway is a digital storytelling app. Create a Sway resume to share the skills, job experiences, and achievements you have that match the requirements of a future job interest. Perform the following tasks:

a. Create a new presentation in Sway to use as a digital resume. Title the Sway Storyline with your full name and then select a background image.

b. Create three separate sections titled **Academic Background, Work Experience**, and **Skills**, and insert text, a picture, and a paragraph or bulleted points in each section. Be sure to include your own picture.

c. Add a fourth section that includes a video about your school that you find online.

d. Customize the design of your presentation.

e. Submit your assignment link in the format specified by your instructor.

2: Creating an Online Sway Newsletter

Newsletters are designed to capture the attention of their target audience. Using Sway, create a newsletter for a club, organization, or your favorite music group. Perform the following tasks:

a. Create a new presentation in Sway to use as a digital newsletter for a club, organization, or your favorite music group. Provide a title for the Sway Storyline and select an appropriate background image.

b. Select three separate sections with appropriate titles, such as Upcoming Events. In each section, insert text, a picture, and a paragraph or bulleted points.

c. Add a fourth section that includes a video about your selected topic.

d. Customize the design of your presentation.

e. Submit your assignment link in the format specified by your instructor.

3: Creating and Sharing a Technology Presentation

To place a Sway presentation in the hands of your entire audience, you can share a link to the Sway presentation. Create a Sway presentation on a new technology and share it with your class. Perform the following tasks:

a. Create a new presentation in Sway about a cutting-edge technology topic. Provide a title for the Sway Storyline and select a background image.

b. Create four separate sections about your topic, and include text, a picture, and a paragraph in each section.

c. Add a fifth section that includes a video about your topic.

d. Customize the design of your presentation.

e. Share the link to your Sway with your classmates and submit your assignment link in the format specified by your instructor.

Introduction to Office Mix

add-in | clip | slide recording | Slide Notes | screen recording | free-response quiz

Bottom Line

- Office Mix is a free PowerPoint add-in from Microsoft that adds features to PowerPoint.
- The Mix tab on the PowerPoint ribbon provides tools for creating screen recordings, videos, interactive quizzes, and live webpages.

To enliven business meetings and lectures, Microsoft adds a new dimension to presentations with a powerful toolset called Office Mix, a free add-in for PowerPoint. (An **add-in** is software that works with an installed app to extend its features.) Using Office Mix, you can record yourself on video, capture still and moving images on your desktop, and insert interactive elements such as quizzes and live webpages directly into PowerPoint slides. When you post the finished presentation to OneDrive, Office Mix provides a link you can share with friends and colleagues. Anyone with an Internet connection and a web browser can watch a published Office Mix presentation, such as the one in **Figure 10**, on a computer or mobile device.

Figure 10: Office Mix presentation

Adding Office Mix to PowerPoint

Learn to use Office Mix!

Links to companion **Sways**, featuring **videos** with hands-on instructions, are located on www.cengagebrain.com.

To get started, you create an Office Mix account at the website mix.office.com using an email address or a Facebook or Google account. Next, you download and install the Office Mix add-in (see **Figure 11**). Office Mix appears as a new tab named Mix on the PowerPoint ribbon in versions of Office 2013 and Office 2016 running on personal computers (PCs).

Figure 11: Getting started with Office Mix

Capturing Video Clips

A **clip** is a short segment of audio, such as music, or video. After finishing the content on a PowerPoint slide, you can use Office Mix to add a video clip to animate or illustrate the content. Office Mix creates video clips in two ways: by recording live action on a webcam and by capturing screen images and movements. If your computer has a webcam, you can record yourself and annotate the slide to create a **slide recording** as shown in **Figure 12**.

On the Job Now

Companies are using Office Mix to train employees about new products, to explain benefit packages to new workers, and to educate interns about office procedures.

Figure 12: Making a slide recording

Record your voice; also record video if your computer has a camera.

Use the Slide Notes button to display notes for your narration.

For best results, look directly at your webcam while recording video.

Choose a video and audio device to record images and sound.

Use inking tools to write and draw on the slide as you record.

When you are making a slide recording, you can record your spoken narration at the same time. The **Slide Notes** feature works like a teleprompter to help you focus on your presentation content instead of memorizing your narration. Use the Inking tools to make annotations or add highlighting using different pen types and colors. After finishing a recording, edit the video in PowerPoint to trim the length or set playback options.

The second way to create a video is to capture on-screen images and actions with or without a voiceover. This method is ideal if you want to show how to use your favorite website or demonstrate an app such as OneNote. To share your screen with an audience, select the part of the screen you want to show in the video. Office Mix captures everything that happens in that area to create a **screen recording**, as shown in **Figure 13**. Office Mix inserts the screen recording as a video in the slide.

On the Job Now

To make your video recordings accessible to people with hearing impairments, use the Office Mix closed-captioning tools. You can also use closed captions to supplement audio that is difficult to understand and to provide an aid for those learning to read.

Figure 13: Making a screen recording

Record the action on the screen within the red dashed outline.

Record audio while capturing your on-screen actions.

Select Area button

Inserting Quizzes, Live Webpages, and Apps

To enhance and assess audience understanding, make your slides interactive by adding quizzes, live webpages, and apps. Quizzes give immediate feedback to the user as shown in **Figure 14**. Office Mix supports several quiz formats, including a **free-response quiz** similar to a short answer quiz, and true/false, multiple-choice, and multiple-response formats.

Figure 14: Creating an interactive quiz

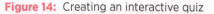
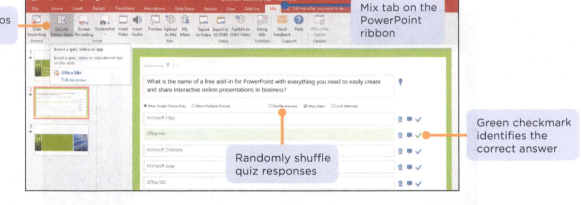

Sharing an Office Mix Presentation

When you complete your work with Office Mix, upload the presentation to your personal Office Mix dashboard as shown in **Figure 15**. Users of PCs, Macs, iOS devices, and Android devices can access and play Office Mix presentations. The Office Mix dashboard displays built-in analytics that include the quiz results and how much time viewers spent on each slide. You can play completed Office Mix presentations online or download them as movies.

Figure 15: Sharing an Office Mix presentation

Try This Now

1: Creating an Office Mix Tutorial for OneNote

Note: This activity requires a microphone on your computer.

Office Mix makes it easy to record screens and their contents. Create PowerPoint slides with an Office Mix screen recording to show OneNote 2016 features. Perform the following tasks:

a. Create a PowerPoint presentation with the Ion Boardroom template. Create an opening slide with the title **My Favorite OneNote Features** and enter your name in the subtitle.
b. Create three additional slides, each titled with a new feature of OneNote. Open OneNote and use the Mix tab in PowerPoint to capture three separate screen recordings that teach your favorite features.
c. Add a fifth slide that quizzes the user with a multiple-choice question about OneNote and includes four responses. Be sure to insert a checkmark indicating the correct response.
d. Upload the completed presentation to your Office Mix dashboard and share the link with your instructor.
e. Submit your assignment link in the format specified by your instructor.

2: Teaching Augmented Reality with Office Mix

Note: This activity requires a webcam or built-in video camera on your computer.

A local elementary school has asked you to teach augmented reality to its students using Office Mix. Perform the following tasks:

a. Research augmented reality using your favorite online search tools.
b. Create a PowerPoint presentation with the Frame template. Create an opening slide with the title **Augmented Reality** and enter your name in the subtitle.
c. Create a slide with four bullets summarizing your research of augmented reality. Create a 20-second slide recording of yourself providing a quick overview of augmented reality.
d. Create another slide with a 30-second screen recording of a video about augmented reality from a site such as YouTube or another video-sharing site.
e. Add a final slide that quizzes the user with a true/false question about augmented reality. Be sure to insert a checkmark indicating the correct response.
f. Upload the completed presentation to your Office Mix dashboard and share the link with your instructor.
g. Submit your assignment link in the format specified by your instructor.

3: Marketing a Travel Destination with Office Mix

Note: This activity requires a webcam or built-in video camera on your computer.

To convince your audience to travel to a particular city, create a slide presentation marketing any city in the world using a slide recording, screen recording, and a quiz. Perform the following tasks:

a. Create a PowerPoint presentation with any template. Create an opening slide with the title of the city you are marketing as a travel destination and your name in the subtitle.
b. Create a slide with four bullets about the featured city. Create a 30-second slide recording of yourself explaining why this city is the perfect vacation destination.
c. Create another slide with a 20-second screen recording of a travel video about the city from a site such as YouTube or another video-sharing site.
d. Add a final slide that quizzes the user with a multiple-choice question about the featured city with five responses. Be sure to include a checkmark indicating the correct response.
e. Upload the completed presentation to your Office Mix dashboard and share your link with your instructor.
f. Submit your assignment link in the format specified by your instructor.

Learn to use Office Mix!
Links to companion **Sways**, featuring **videos** with hands-on instructions, are located on www.cengagebrain.com.

Introduction to Microsoft Edge

Reading view | Hub | Cortana | Web Note | Inking | sandbox

Bottom Line
- Microsoft Edge is the name of the new web browser built into Windows 10.
- Microsoft Edge allows you to search the web faster, take web notes, read webpages without distractions, and get instant assistance from Cortana.

Microsoft Edge is the default web browser developed for the Windows 10 operating system as a replacement for Internet Explorer. Unlike its predecessor, Edge lets you write on webpages, read webpages without advertisements and other distractions, and search for information using a virtual personal assistant. The Edge interface is clean and basic, as shown in **Figure 16**, meaning you can pay more attention to the webpage content.

Figure 16: Microsoft Edge tools

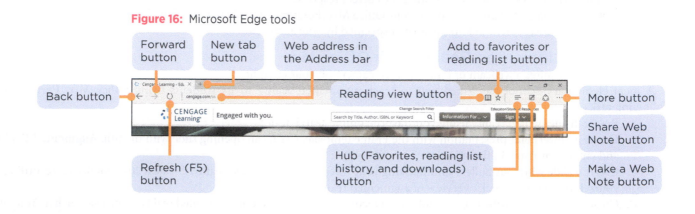

Forward button · New tab button · Web address in the Address bar · Add to favorites or reading list button · Back button · Reading view button · More button · Refresh (F5) button · Hub (Favorites, reading list, history, and downloads) button · Share Web Note button · Make a Web Note button

Learn to use Edge!
Links to companion **Sways**, featuring **videos** with hands-on instructions, are located on www.cengagebrain.com.

Browsing the Web with Microsoft Edge

One of the fastest browsers available, Edge allows you to type search text directly in the Address bar. As you view the resulting webpage, you can switch to **Reading view**, which is available for most news and research sites, to eliminate distracting advertisements. For example, if you are catching up on technology news online, the webpage might be difficult to read due to a busy layout cluttered with ads. Switch to Reading view to refresh the page and remove the original page formatting, ads, and menu sidebars to read the article distraction-free.

Consider the **Hub** in Microsoft Edge as providing one-stop access to all the things you collect on the web, such as your favorite websites, reading list, surfing history, and downloaded files.

On the Job Now

Businesses started adopting Internet Explorer more than 20 years ago simply to view webpages. Today, Microsoft Edge has a different purpose: to promote interaction with the web and share its contents with colleagues.

Locating Information with Cortana

Cortana, the Windows 10 virtual assistant, plays an important role in Microsoft Edge. After you turn on Cortana, it appears as an animated circle in the Address bar when you might need assistance, as shown in the restaurant website in **Figure 17**. When you click the Cortana icon, a pane slides in from the right of the browser window to display detailed information about the restaurant, including maps and reviews. Cortana can also assist you in defining words, finding the weather, suggesting coupons for shopping, updating stock market information, and calculating math.

Figure 17: Cortana providing restaurant information

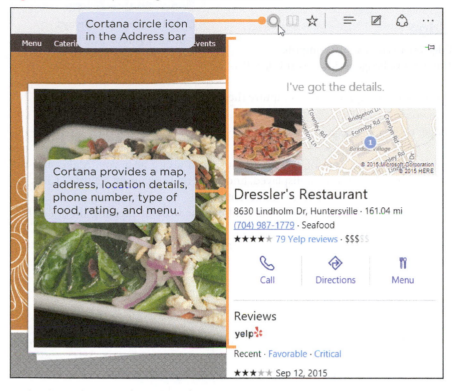

Cortana circle icon in the Address bar

Cortana provides a map, address, location details, phone number, type of food, rating, and menu.

Annotating Webpages

One of the most impressive Microsoft Edge features are the **Web Note** tools, which you use to write on a webpage or to highlight text. When you click the Make a Web Note button, an **Inking** toolbar appears, as shown in **Figure 18**, that provides writing and drawing tools. These tools include an eraser, a pen, and a highlighter with different colors. You can also insert a typed note and copy a screen image (called a screen clipping). You can draw with a pointing device, fingertip, or stylus using different pen colors. Whether you add notes to a recipe, annotate sources for a research paper, or select a product while shopping online, the Web Note tools can enhance your productivity. After you complete your notes, click the Save button to save the annotations to OneNote, your Favorites list, or your Reading list. You can share the inked page with others using the Share Web Note button.

On the Job Now

To enhance security, Microsoft Edge runs in a partial sandbox, an arrangement that prevents attackers from gaining control of your computer. Browsing within the **sandbox** protects computer resources and information from hackers.

Figure 18: Web Note tools in Microsoft Edge

Inking toolbar with Web Note tools for making annotations

Writing and drawing created with the Pen tool

Highlighted text

Save a copy of the webpage with annotations

Typed note

Try This Now

1: Using Cortana in Microsoft Edge

Learn to use Edge!
Links to companion **Sways**, featuring **videos** with hands-on instructions, are located on www.cengagebrain.com.

Note: This activity requires using Microsoft Edge on a Windows 10 computer.

Cortana can assist you in finding information on a webpage in Microsoft Edge. Perform the following tasks:

a. Create a Word document using the Word Screen Clipping tool to capture the following screenshots.

- Screenshot A—Using Microsoft Edge, open a webpage with a technology news article. Right-click a term in the article and ask Cortana to define it.
- Screenshot B—Using Microsoft Edge, open the website of a fancy restaurant in a city near you. Make sure the Cortana circle icon is displayed in the Address bar. (If it's not displayed, find a different restaurant website.) Click the Cortana circle icon to display a pane with information about the restaurant.
- Screenshot C—Using Microsoft Edge, type **10 USD to Euros** in the Address bar without pressing the Enter key. Cortana converts the U.S. dollars to Euros.
- Screenshot D—Using Microsoft Edge, type **Apple stock** in the Address bar without pressing the Enter key. Cortana displays the current stock quote.

b. Submit your assignment in the format specified by your instructor.

2: Viewing Online News with Reading View

Note: This activity requires using Microsoft Edge on a Windows 10 computer.

Reading view in Microsoft Edge can make a webpage less cluttered with ads and other distractions. Perform the following tasks:

a. Create a Word document using the Word Screen Clipping tool to capture the following screenshots.

- Screenshot A—Using Microsoft Edge, open the website **mashable.com**. Open a technology article. Click the Reading view button to display an ad-free page that uses only basic text formatting.
- Screenshot B—Using Microsoft Edge, open the website **bbc.com**. Open any news article. Click the Reading view button to display an ad-free page that uses only basic text formatting.
- Screenshot C—Make three types of annotations (Pen, Highlighter, and Add a typed note) on the BBC article page displayed in Reading view.

b. Submit your assignment in the format specified by your instructor.

3: Inking with Microsoft Edge

Note: This activity requires using Microsoft Edge on a Windows 10 computer.

Microsoft Edge provides many annotation options to record your ideas. Perform the following tasks:

a. Open the website **wolframalpha.com** in the Microsoft Edge browser. Wolfram Alpha is a well-respected academic search engine. Type **US$100 1965 dollars in 2015** in the Wolfram Alpha search text box and press the Enter key.
b. Click the Make a Web Note button to display the Web Note tools. Using the Pen tool, draw a circle around the result on the webpage. Save the page to OneNote.
c. In the Wolfram Alpha search text box, type the name of the city closest to where you live and press the Enter key. Using the Highlighter tool, highlight at least three interesting results. Add a note and then type a sentence about what you learned about this city. Save the page to OneNote. Share your OneNote notebook with your instructor.
d. Submit your assignment link in the format specified by your instructor.

Getting Started with Microsoft Office 2016

CASE This module introduces you to the most frequently used programs in Office, as well as common features they all share.

Module Objectives

After completing this module, you will be able to:

- Understand the Office 2016 suite
- Start an Office app
- Identify Office 2016 screen elements
- Create and save a file
- Open a file and save it with a new name
- View and print your work
- Get Help, close a file, and exit an app

Files You Will Need

OF 1-1.xlsx

Learning Outcomes
- Identify Office suite components
- Describe the features of each app

Understand the Office 2016 Suite

Microsoft Office 2016 is a group of programs—which are also called applications or apps—designed to help you create documents, collaborate with coworkers, and track and analyze information. You use different Office programs to accomplish specific tasks, such as writing a letter or producing a presentation, yet all the programs have a similar look and feel. Microsoft Office 2016 apps feature a common, context-sensitive user interface, so you can get up to speed faster and use advanced features with greater ease. The Office apps are bundled together in a group called a **suite**. The Office suite is available in several configurations, but all include Word, Excel, PowerPoint, and OneNote. Some configurations include Access, Outlook, Publisher, Skype, and OneDrive. **CASE** *As part of your job, you need to understand how each Office app is best used to complete specific tasks.*

DETAILS

The Office apps covered in this book include:

QUICK TIP
In this book, the terms "program" and "app" are used interchangeably.

- **Microsoft Word 2016**

  When you need to create any kind of text-based document, such as a memo, newsletter, or multipage report, Word is the program to use. You can easily make your documents look great by using formatting tools and inserting eye-catching graphics. The Word document shown in **FIGURE 1-1** contains a company logo and simple formatting.

- **Microsoft Excel 2016**

  Excel is the perfect solution when you need to work with numeric values and make calculations. It puts the power of formulas, functions, charts, and other analytical tools into the hands of every user, so you can analyze sales projections, calculate loan payments, and present your findings in a professional manner. The Excel worksheet shown in **FIGURE 1-1** tracks checkbook transactions. Because Excel automatically recalculates results whenever a value changes, the information is always up to date. A chart illustrates how the monthly expenses are broken down.

- **Microsoft PowerPoint 2016**

  Using PowerPoint, it's easy to create powerful presentations complete with graphics, transitions, and even a soundtrack. Using professionally designed themes and clip art, you can quickly and easily create dynamic slide shows such as the one shown in **FIGURE 1-1**.

- **Microsoft Access 2016**

  Access is a relational database program that helps you keep track of large amounts of quantitative data, such as product inventories or employee records. The form shown in **FIGURE 1-1** can be used to generate reports on customer invoices and tours.

Microsoft Office has benefits beyond the power of each program, including:

- **Note-taking made simple; available on all devices**

  Use OneNote to take notes (organized in tabbed pages) on information that can be accessed on your computer, tablet, or phone. Share the editable results with others. Contents can include text, web page clips (using OneNote Clipper), email contents (directly inserted into a default section), photos (using Office Lens), and web pages.

- **Common user interface: Improving business processes**

  Because the Office suite apps have a similar **interface**, your experience using one app's tools makes it easy to learn those in the other apps. Office documents are **compatible** with one another, so you can easily **integrate**, or combine, elements—for example, you can add an Excel chart to a PowerPoint slide, or an Access table to a Word document.

  Most Office programs include the capability to incorporate feedback—called **online collaboration**—across the Internet or a company network.

FIGURE 1-1: Microsoft Office 2016 documents

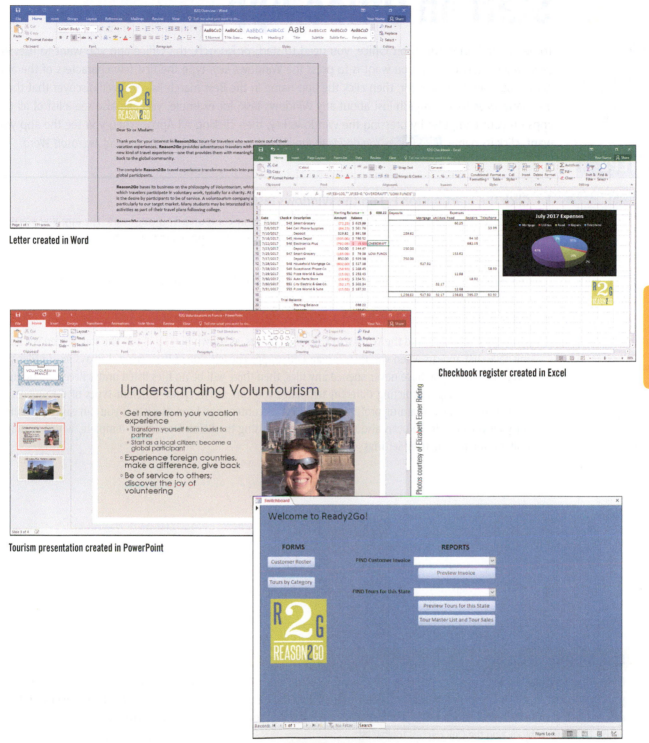

Letter created in Word

Checkbook register created in Excel

Tourism presentation created in PowerPoint

Form created in Access

What is Office 365?

Until recently, most consumers purchased Microsoft Office in a traditional way: by buying a retail package from a store or downloading it from Microsoft.com. You can still purchase Microsoft Office 2016 in this traditional way—but you can also now purchase it as a subscription service called Microsoft Office 365, which is available in a wide variety of configurations.

Depending on which configuration you purchase, you will always have access to the most up-to-date versions of the apps in your package and, in many cases, can install these apps on multiple computers, tablets, and phones. And if you change computers or devices, you can easily uninstall the apps from an old device and install them on a new one.

Start an Office App

Learning Outcomes
- Start an Office app
- Explain the purpose of a template
- Start a new blank document

To get started using Microsoft Office, you need to start, or **launch**, the Office app you want to use. An easy way to start the app you want is to press the Windows key, type the first few characters of the app name you want to search for, then click the app name In the Best match list. You will discover that there are many ways to accomplish just about any Windows task; for example, you can also see a list of all the apps on your computer by pressing the Windows key, then clicking All Apps. When you see the app you want, click its name. **CASE** *You decide to familiarize yourself with Office by starting Microsoft Word.*

STEPS

1. **Click the Start button ⊞ on the Windows taskbar**

   The Start menu opens, listing the most used apps on your computer. You can locate the app you want to open by clicking the app name if you see it, or you can type the app name to search for it.

2. **Type word**

   Your screen now displays "Word 2016" under "Best match", along with any other app that has "word" as part of its name (such as WordPad). See **FIGURE 1-2**.

3. **Click Word 2016**

   Word 2016 launches, and the Word **start screen** appears, as shown in **FIGURE 1-3**. The start screen is a landing page that appears when you first start an Office app. The left side of this screen displays recent files you have opened. (If you have never opened any files, then there will be no files listed under Recent.) The right side displays images depicting different templates you can use to create different types of documents. A **template** is a file containing professionally designed content and formatting that you can easily customize for your own needs. You can also start from scratch using the Blank Document template, which contains only minimal formatting settings.

Enabling touch mode

If you are using a touch screen with any of the Office 2016 apps, you can enable the touch mode to give the user interface a more spacious look, making it easier to navigate with your fingertips. Enable touch mode by clicking the Quick Access toolbar list arrow, then clicking Touch/Mouse Mode to select it. Then you'll see the Touch Mode button 👆 in the Quick Access toolbar. Click 👆, and you'll see the interface spread out.

Using shortcut keys to move between Office programs

You can switch between open apps using a keyboard shortcut. The [Alt][Tab] keyboard combination lets you either switch quickly to the next open program or file or choose one from a gallery. To switch immediately to the next open program or file, press [Alt][Tab]. To choose from all open programs and files, press and hold [Alt], then press and release [Tab] without releasing [Alt]. A gallery opens on screen, displaying the filename and a thumbnail image of each open program and file, as well as of the desktop. Each time you press [Tab] while holding [Alt], the selection cycles to the next open file or location. Release [Alt] when the program, file, or location you want to activate is selected.

FIGURE 1-2: Searching for the Word app

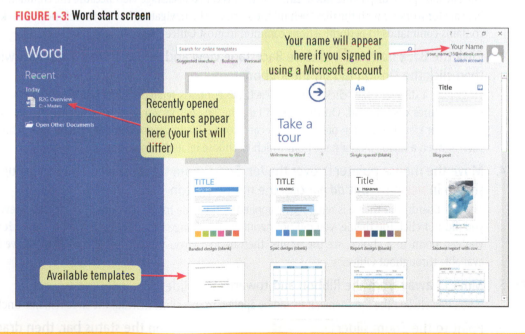

FIGURE 1-3: Word start screen

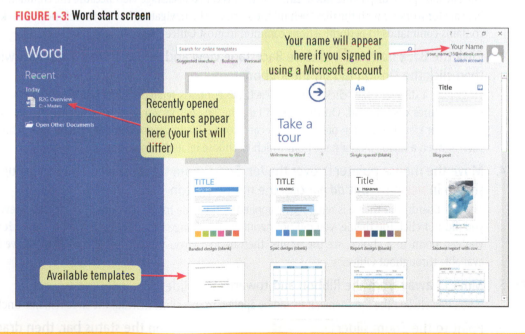

Using the Office Clipboard

You can use the Office Clipboard to cut and copy items from one Office program and paste them into others. The Office Clipboard can store a maximum of 24 items. To access it, open the Office Clipboard task pane by clicking the dialog box launcher ⬚ in the Clipboard group on the Home tab. Each time you copy a selection, it is saved in the Office Clipboard. Each entry in the Office Clipboard includes an icon that tells you the program it was created in. To paste an entry, click in the document where you want it to appear, then click the item in the Office Clipboard. To delete an item from the Office Clipboard, right-click the item, then click Delete.

Identify Office 2016 Screen Elements

Learning Outcomes
- Identify basic components of the user interface
- Display and use Backstage view
- Adjust the zoom level

One of the benefits of using Office is that its apps have much in common, making them easy to learn and making it simple to move from one to another. All Office 2016 apps share a similar user interface, so you can use your knowledge of one to get up to speed in another. A **user interface** is a collective term for all the ways you interact with a software program. The user interface in Office 2016 provides intuitive ways to choose commands, work with files, and navigate in the program window. **CASE** *Familiarize yourself with some of the common interface elements in Office by examining the PowerPoint program window.*

STEPS

1. **Click the Start button ⊞ on the Windows taskbar, type pow, click PowerPoint 2016, then click Blank Presentation**

   PowerPoint starts and opens a new file, which contains a blank slide. Refer to **FIGURE 1-4** to identify common elements of the Office user interface. The **document window** occupies most of the screen. At the top of every Office program window is a **title bar** that displays the document name and program name. Below the title bar is the **Ribbon**, which displays commands you're likely to need for the current task. Commands are organized onto **tabs**. The tab names appear at the top of the Ribbon, and the active tab appears in front. The **Share button** in the upper-right corner lets you invite other users to view your cloud-stored Word, Excel, or Powerpoint file.

   QUICK TIP
   The Ribbon in every Office program includes tabs specific to the program, but all Office programs include a File tab and Home tab on the left end of the Ribbon. Just above the File tab is the **Quick Access toolbar**, which also includes buttons for common Office commands.

2. **Click the File tab**

   The File tab opens, displaying **Backstage view**. It is called Backstage view because the commands available here are for working with the files "behind the scenes." The navigation bar on the left side of Backstage view contains commands to perform actions common to most Office programs.

3. **Click the Back button ⊙ to close Backstage view and return to the document window, then click the Design tab on the Ribbon**

   To display a different tab, click its name. Each tab contains related commands arranged into **groups** to make features easy to find. On the Design tab, the Themes group displays available design themes in a **gallery**, or visual collection of choices you can browse. Many groups contain a **launcher**, which you can click to open a dialog box or pane from which to choose related commands.

4. **Move the mouse pointer ⇲ over the Ion Boardroom theme in the Themes group as shown in FIGURE 1-5, but *do not click* the mouse button**

   The Ion Boardroom theme is temporarily applied to the slide in the document window. However, because you did not click the theme, you did not permanently change the slide. With the **Live Preview** feature, you can point to a choice, see the results, then decide if you want to make the change. Live Preview is available throughout Office.

   TROUBLE
   If you accidentally click a theme, click the Undo button on the Quick Access toolbar.

5. **Move ⇲ away from the Ribbon and towards the slide**

   If you had clicked the Ion theme, it would be applied to this slide. Instead, the slide remains unchanged.

   QUICK TIP
   You can also use the Zoom button in the Zoom group on the View tab to enlarge or reduce a document's appearance.

6. **Point to the Zoom slider ▭ ─────┃─────── + 100% on the status bar, then drag to the right until the Zoom level reads 166%**

   The slide display is enlarged. Zoom tools are located on the status bar. You can drag the slider or click the Zoom In or Zoom Out buttons to zoom in or out on an area of interest. **Zooming in** (a higher percentage), makes a document appear bigger on screen but less of it fits on the screen at once; **zooming out** (a lower percentage) lets you see more of the document at a reduced size.

7. **Click the Zoom Out button ▭ on the status bar to the left of the Zoom slider until the Zoom level reads 120%**

FIGURE 1-4: PowerPoint program window

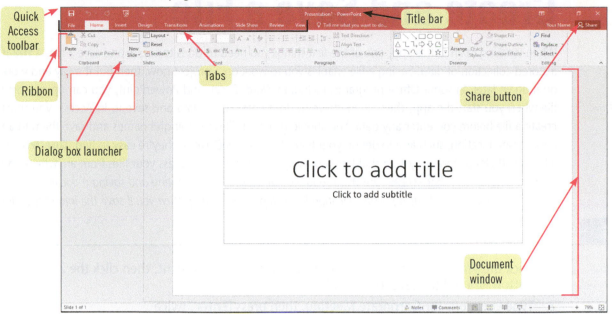

Quick Access toolbar

Title bar

Ribbon

Tabs

Share button

Dialog box launcher

Click to add title

Click to add subtitle

Document window

FIGURE 1-5: Viewing a theme with Live Preview

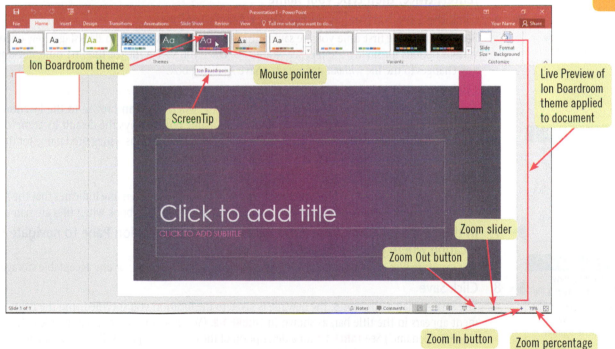

Ion Boardroom theme

Mouse pointer

Live Preview of Ion Boardroom theme applied to document

ScreenTip

Click to add title

CLICK TO ADD SUBTITLE

Zoom slider

Zoom Out button

Zoom In button

Zoom percentage

Using Backstage view

Backstage view in each Microsoft Office app offers "one stop shopping" for many commonly performed tasks, such as opening and saving a file, printing and previewing a document, defining document properties, sharing information, and exiting a program. Backstage view opens when you click the File tab in any Office app, and while features such as the Ribbon, Mini toolbar, and Live Preview all help you work *in* your documents, the File tab and Backstage view help you work *with* your documents. You can click commands in the navigation pane to open different places for working with your documents, such as the Open place, the Save place, and so on. You can return to your active document by clicking the Back button.

Create and Save a File

Learning Outcomes
• Create a file
• Save a file
• Explain OneDrive

When working in an Office app, one of the first things you need to do is to create and save a file. A **file** is a stored collection of data. Saving a file enables you to work on a project now, then put it away and work on it again later. In some Office programs, including Word, Excel, and PowerPoint, you can open a new file when you start the app, then all you have to do is enter some data and save it. In Access, you must create a file before you enter any data. You should give your files meaningful names and save them in an appropriate location, such as a folder on your hard drive or OneDrive so they're easy to find. **OneDrive** is a Microsoft cloud storage system that lets you easily save, share, and access your files from anywhere you have Internet access. **CASE** *Use Word to familiarize yourself with creating and saving a document. First you'll type some notes about a possible location for a corporate meeting, then you'll save the information for later use.*

STEPS

1. **Click the Word button 🗗 on the taskbar, click Blank document, then click the Zoom In button ➕ until the level is 120%, if necessary**

2. **Type Locations for Corporate Meeting, then press [Enter] twice**
   The text appears in the document window, and the **insertion point** blinks on a new blank line. The insertion point indicates where the next typed text will appear.

QUICK TIP

A filename can be up to 255 characters, including a file extension, and can include upper- or lowercase characters and spaces, but not ?, ", /, \, <, >, *, |, or :.

3. **Type Las Vegas, NV, press [Enter], type Chicago, IL, press [Enter], type Seattle, WA, press [Enter] twice, then type your name**

4. **Click the Save button 🖫 on the Quick Access toolbar**
   Because this is the first time you are saving this new file, the Save place in Backstage view opens, showing various options for saving the file. See **FIGURE 1-6**. Once you save a file for the first time, clicking 🖫 saves any changes to the file *without* opening the Save As dialog box.

5. **Click Browse**
   The Save As dialog box opens, as shown in **FIGURE 1-7**, where you can browse to the location where you want to save the file. The Address bar in the Save As dialog box displays the default location for saving the file, but you can change it to any location. The File name field contains a suggested name for the document based on text in the file, but you can enter a different name.

QUICK TIP

Saving a file to the Desktop creates a desktop icon that you can double-click to both launch a program and open a document.

6. **Type OF 1-Possible Corporate Meeting Locations**
   The text you type replaces the highlighted text. (The "OF 1-" in the filename indicates that the file is created in Office Module 1. You will see similar designations throughout this book when files are named.)

QUICK TIP

To create a new blank file when a file is open, click the File tab, click New on the navigation bar, then choose a template.

7. **In the Save As dialog box, use the Address bar or Navigation Pane to navigate to the location where you store your Data Files**
   You can store files on your computer, a network drive, your OneDrive, or any acceptable storage device.

8. **Click Save**
   The Save As dialog box closes, the new file is saved to the location you specified, and the name of the document appears in the title bar, as shown in **FIGURE 1-8**. (You may or may not see the file extension ".docx" after the filename.) See **TABLE 1-1** for a description of the different types of files you create in Office, and the file extensions associated with each.

TABLE 1-1: Common filenames and default file extensions

file created in	is called a	and has the default extension
Word	document	.docx
Excel	workbook	.xlsx
PowerPoint	presentation	.pptx
Access	database	.accdb

FIGURE 1-6: Save place in Backstage view

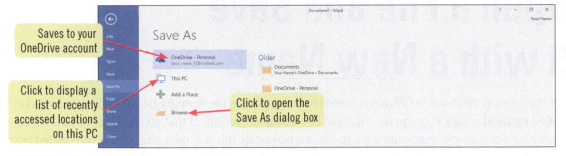

Saves to your OneDrive account

Click to display a list of recently accessed locations on this PC

Click to open the Save As dialog box

FIGURE 1-7: Save As dialog box

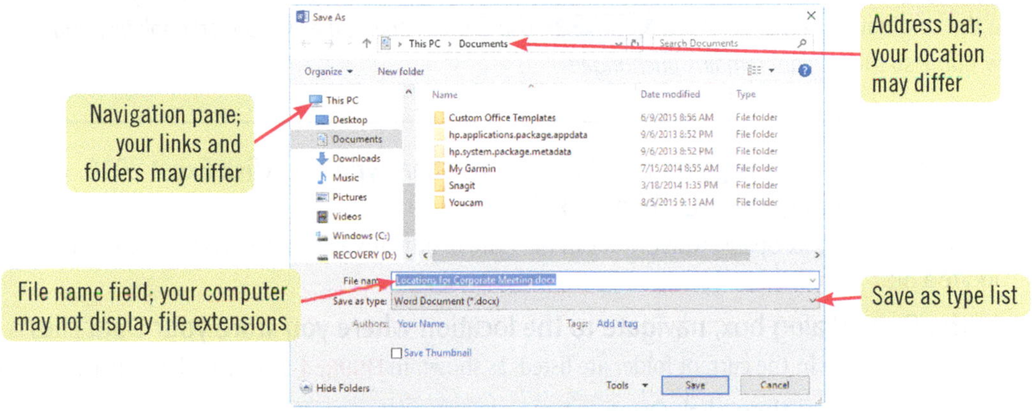

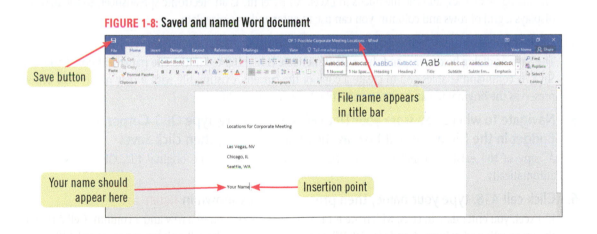

Address bar; your location may differ

Navigation pane; your links and folders may differ

File name field; your computer may not display file extensions

Save as type list

FIGURE 1-8: Saved and named Word document

Save button

File name appears in title bar

Your name should appear here

Insertion point

Saving files to OneDrive

All Office programs include the capability to incorporate feedback—called **online collaboration**—across the Internet or a company network. Using **cloud computing** (work done in a virtual environment), you can store your work in the cloud. Using OneDrive, a file storage service from Microsoft, you and your colleagues can create and store documents in the cloud and make the documents available anywhere there is Internet access to whomever you choose. To use OneDrive, you need a Microsoft Account, which you obtain at onedrive.live.com. Pricing and storage plans vary based on the type of Microsoft account you have. When you are logged into your Microsoft account and you save a file in any of the Office apps, the first option in the Save As screen is your OneDrive. Double-click your OneDrive option, and the Save As dialog box opens displaying a location in the address bar unique to your OneDrive account. Type a name in the File name text box, then click Save and your file is saved to your OneDrive. To sync your files with OneDrive, you'll need to download and install the OneDrive for Windows app. Then, when you open Explorer, you'll notice a new folder called OneDrive has been added to your folder. In this folder is a sub-folder called Documents. This means if your Internet connection fails, you can work on your files offline.

Office 2016

Learning
Outcomes
• Open an existing
file
• Save a file with a
new name

Open a File and Save It with a New Name

In many cases as you work in Office, you need to use an existing file. It might be a file you or a coworker created earlier as a work in progress, or it could be a complete document that you want to use as the basis for another. For example, you might want to create a budget for this year using the budget you created last year; instead of typing in all the categories and information from scratch, you could open last year's budget, save it with a new name, and just make changes to update it for the current year. By opening the existing file and saving it with the Save As command, you create a duplicate that you can modify to suit your needs, while the original file remains intact. **CASE** ▶ *Use Excel to open an existing workbook file, and save it with a new name so the original remains unchanged.*

STEPS

1. **Click the Start button ⊞ on the Windows taskbar, type exc, click Excel 2016, click Open Other Workbooks, This PC, then click Browse**

   The Open dialog box opens, where you can navigate to any drive or folder accessible to your computer to locate a file.

2. **In the Open dialog box, navigate to the location where you store your Data Files**

   The files available in the current folder are listed, as shown in FIGURE 1-9. This folder displays one file.

3. **Click OF 1-1.xlsx, then click Open**

   The dialog box closes, and the file opens in Excel. An Excel file is an electronic spreadsheet, so the new file displays a grid of rows and columns you can use to enter and organize data.

4. **Click the File tab, click Save As on the navigation bar, then click Browse**

   The Save As dialog box opens, and the current filename is highlighted in the File name text box. Using the Save As command enables you to create a copy of the current, existing file with a new name. This action preserves the original file and creates a new file that you can modify.

5. **Navigate to where you store your Data Files if necessary, type OF 1-Corporate Meeting Budget in the File name text box, as shown in FIGURE 1-10, then click Save**

   A copy of the existing workbook is created with the new name. The original file, OF 1-1.xlsx, closes automatically.

6. **Click cell A18, type your name, then press [Enter], as shown in FIGURE 1-11**

   In Excel, you enter data in cells, which are formed by the intersection of a row and a column. Cell A18 is at the intersection of column A and row 18. When you press [Enter], the cell pointer moves to cell A19.

7. **Click the Save button 🖫 on the Quick Access toolbar**

   Your name appears in the workbook, and your changes to the file are saved.

Exploring File Open options

You might have noticed that the Open button in the Open dialog box includes a list arrow to the right of the button. In a dialog box, if a button includes a list arrow you can click the button to invoke the command, or you can click the list arrow to see a list of related commands that you can apply to the currently selected file. The Open list arrow includes several related commands, including Open Read-Only and Open as Copy.

Clicking Open Read-Only opens a file that you can only save with a new name; you cannot make changes to the original file. Clicking Open as Copy creates and opens a copy of the selected file and inserts the word "Copy" in the file's title. Like the Save As command, these commands provide additional ways to use copies of existing files while ensuring that original files do not get changed by mistake.

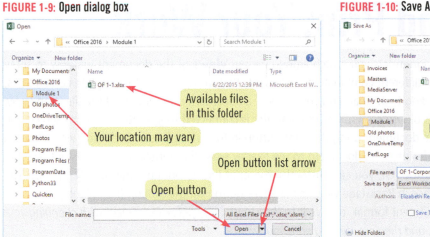

FIGURE 1-9: Open dialog box

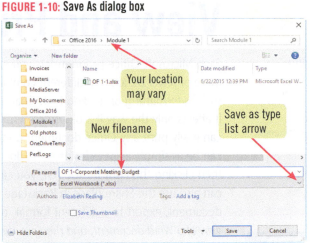

FIGURE 1-10: Save As dialog box

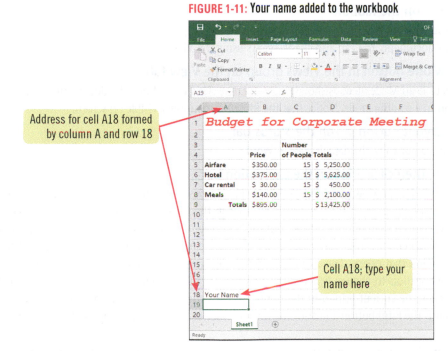

FIGURE 1-11: Your name added to the workbook

Working in Compatibility Mode

Not everyone upgrades to the newest version of Office. As a general rule, new software versions are **backward compatible**, meaning that documents saved by an older version can be read by newer software. To open documents created in older Office versions, Office 2016 includes a feature called Compatibility Mode. When you use Office 2016 to open a file created in an earlier version of Office, "Compatibility Mode" appears in the title bar, letting you know the file was created in an earlier but usable version of the program. If you are working with someone who may not be using the newest version of the software, you can avoid possible incompatibility problems by saving your file in another, earlier format. To do this in an Office program, click the File tab, click Save As on the navigation bar, then click Browse. In the Save As dialog box, click the Save as type list arrow in the Save As dialog box, then click an option in the list. For example, if you're working in Excel, click Excel 97-2003 Workbook format in the Save as type list to save an Excel file so it can be opened in Excel 97 or Excel 2003.

View and Print Your Work

Each Microsoft Office program lets you switch among various **views** of the document window to show more or fewer details or a different combination of elements that make it easier to complete certain tasks, such as formatting or reading text. Changing your view of a document does not affect the file in any way, it affects only the way it looks on screen. If your computer is connected to a printer or a print server, you can easily print any Office document using the Print button in the Print place in Backstage view. Printing can be as simple as **previewing** the document to see exactly what the printed version will look like and then clicking the Print button. Or, you can customize the print job by printing only selected pages. You can also use the Share place in Backstage view or the Share button on the Ribbon (if available) to share a document, export to a different format, or save it to the cloud. **CASE** *Experiment with changing your view of a Word document, and then preview and print your work.*

STEPS

1. **Click the Word program button 🗔 on the taskbar**

   Word becomes active, and the program window fills the screen.

2. **Click the View tab on the Ribbon**

   In most Office programs, the View tab on the Ribbon includes groups and commands for changing your view of the current document. You can also change views using the View buttons on the status bar.

3. **Click the Read Mode button in the Views group on the View tab**

   The view changes to Read Mode view, as shown in **FIGURE 1-12**. This view shows the document in an easy-to-read, distraction-free reading mode. Notice that the Ribbon is no longer visible on screen.

4. **Click the Print Layout button 🗎 on the Status bar**

   You return to Print Layout view, the default view in Word.

5. **Click the File tab, then click Print on the navigation bar**

   The Print place opens. The preview pane on the right displays a preview of how your document will look when printed. Compare your screen to **FIGURE 1-13**. Options in the Settings section enable you to change margins, orientation, and related options before printing. To change a setting, click it, and then click a new setting. For instance, to change from Letter paper size to Legal, click Letter in the Settings section, then click Legal on the menu that opens. The document preview updates as you change the settings. You also can use the Settings section to change which pages to print. If your computer is connected to multiple printers, you can click the current printer in the Printer section, then click the one you want to use. The Print section contains the Print button and also enables you to select the number of copies of the document to print.

6. **If your school allows printing, click the Print button in the Print place (otherwise, click the Back button ⬅)**

   If you chose to print, a copy of the document prints, and Backstage view closes.

Customizing the Quick Access toolbar

You can customize the Quick Access toolbar to display your favorite commands. To do so, click the Customize Quick Access Toolbar button ⬇ in the title bar, then click the command you want to add. If you don't see the command in the list, click More Commands to open the Quick Access Toolbar tab of the current program's Options dialog box. In the Options dialog box, use the Choose commands from list to choose a category, click the desired command in the list on the left, click Add to add it to the Quick Access toolbar, then click OK. To remove a button from the toolbar, click the name in the list on the right in the Options dialog box, then click Remove. To add a command to the Quick Access toolbar as you work, simply right-click the button on the Ribbon, then click Add to Quick Access Toolbar on the shortcut menu. To move the Quick Access toolbar below the Ribbon, click the Customize Quick Access Toolbar button, and then click Show Below the Ribbon.

FIGURE 1-12: Read Mode view

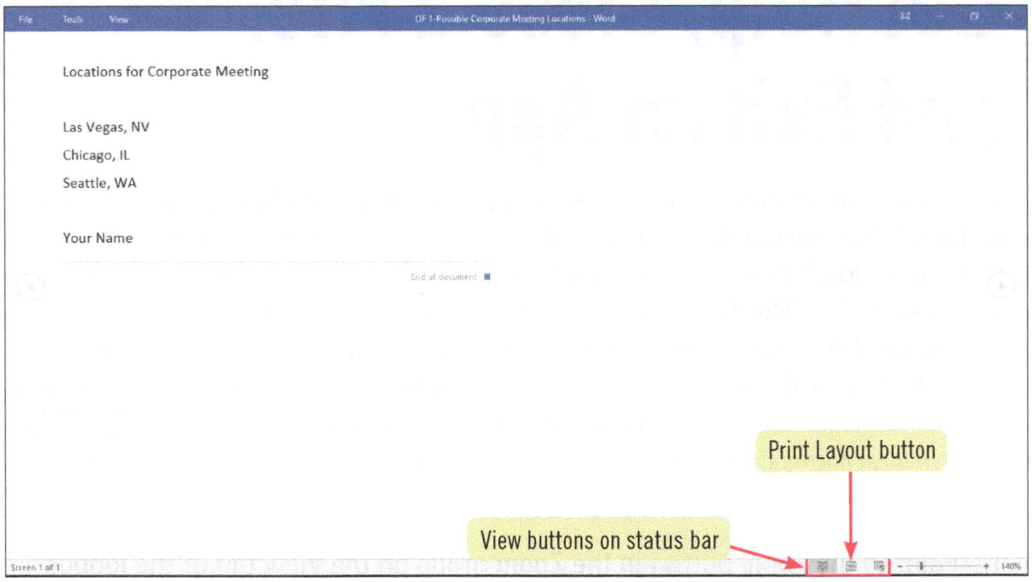

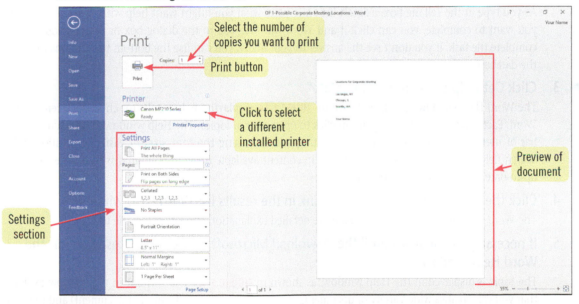

Print Layout button

View buttons on status bar

FIGURE 1-13: Print settings on the File tab

Select the number of copies you want to print

Print button

Click to select a different installed printer

Settings section

Preview of document

Creating a screen capture

A **screen capture** is a digital image of your screen, as if you took a picture of it with a camera. For instance, you might want to take a screen capture if an error message occurs and you want a Technical Support person to see exactly what's on the screen. You can create a screen capture using the Snipping Tool, an accessory designed to capture whole screens or portions of screens. To open the Snipping Tool, click the Start button on the Windows taskbar, type "sni", then click the Snipping Tool when it appears in the left panel. On the Snipping Tool toolbar, click New, then drag the pointer on the screen to select the area of the screen you want to capture. When you release the mouse button, the screen capture opens in the Snipping Tool window, and you can

save, copy, or send it in an email. In Word, Excel, and PowerPoint 2016, you can capture screens or portions of screens and insert them in the current document using the Screenshot button in the Illustrations group on the Insert tab. Alternatively, you can create a screen capture by pressing [PrtScn]. (Keyboards differ, but you may find the [PrtScn] button in or near your keyboard's function keys.) Pressing this key places a digital image of your screen in the Windows temporary storage area known as the **Clipboard**. Open the document where you want the screen capture to appear, click the Home tab on the Ribbon (if necessary), then click the Paste button in the Clipboard group on the Home tab. The screen capture is pasted into the document.

Get Help, Close a File, and Exit an App

Learning Outcomes
• Display a ScreenTip
• Use Help
• Close a file
• Exit an app

You can get comprehensive help at any time by pressing [F1] in an Office app or clicking the Help button on the title bar. You can also get help in the form of a ScreenTip by pointing to almost any icon in the program window. When you're finished working in an Office document, you have a few choices for ending your work session. You close a file by clicking the File tab, then clicking Close; you exit a program by clicking the Close button on the title bar. Closing a file leaves a program running, while exiting a program closes all the open files in that program as well as the program itself. In all cases, Office reminds you if you try to close a file or exit a program and your document contains unsaved changes. **CASE** *Explore the Help system in Microsoft Office, and then close your documents and exit any open programs.*

STEPS

1. **Point to the Zoom button in the Zoom group on the View tab of the Ribbon**

   A ScreenTip appears that describes how the Zoom button works and explains where to find other zoom controls.

2. **Click the Tell me box above the Ribbon, then type Choose a template**

   As you type in the Tell me box, a Smart list anticipates what you might want help with. If you see the task you want to complete, you can click it and Word will take you to the dialog box or options you need to complete the task. If you don't see the answer to your query, you can use the bottom two options to search the database.

3. **Click Get Help on "choose a template"**

   The Word Help window opens, as shown in **FIGURE 1-14**, displaying help results for choosing a template in Word. Each entry is a hyperlink you can click to open a list of topics. The Help window also includes a toolbar of useful Help commands such as printing and increasing the font size for easier readability, and a Search field. Office.com supplements the help content available on your computer with a wide variety of up-to-date topics, templates, and training.

4. **Click the Where do I find templates link in the results list Word Help window**

   The Word Help window changes, and a more detailed explanation appears below the topic.

5. **If necessary, scroll down until the Download Microsoft Office templates topic fills the Word Help window**

   The topic is displayed in the Help window, as shown in **FIGURE 1-15**. The content in the window explains that you can create a wide variety of documents using a template (a pre-formatted document) and that you can get many templates free of charge.

6. **Click the Keep Help on Top button 📌 in the lower-right corner of the window**

   The Pin Help button rotates so the pin point is pointed towards the bottom of the screen: this allows you to read the Help window while you work on your document.

7. **Click the Word document window, notice the Help window remains visible**

8. **Click a blank area of the Help window, click 📌 to Unpin Help, click the Close button ✕ in the Help window, then click the Close button ✕ in the Word program window**

   Word closes, and the Excel program window is active.

9. **Click the Close button ✕ in the Excel program window, click the PowerPoint app button 📊 on the taskbar if necessary, then click the Close button ✕ to exit PowerPoint**

   Excel and PowerPoint both close.

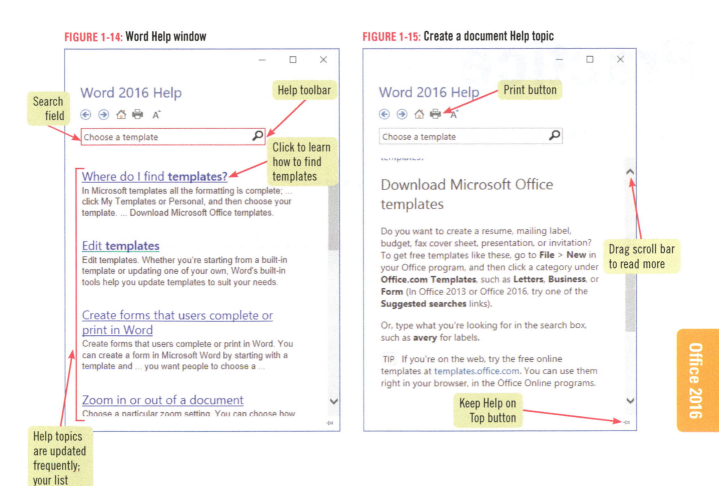

FIGURE 1-14: Word Help window

Search field

Word 2016 Help

Help toolbar

Choose a template

Click to learn how to find templates

Where do I find **templates?**
In Microsoft templates all the formatting is complete; ... click My Templates or Personal, and then choose your template. ... Download Microsoft Office templates.

Edit **templates**
Edit templates. Whether you're starting from a built-in template or updating one of your own, Word's built-in tools help you update templates to suit your needs.

Create forms that users complete or print in Word
Create forms that users complete or print in Word. You can create a form in Microsoft Word by starting with a template and ... you want people to choose a ...

Zoom in or out of a document
Choose a particular zoom setting. You can choose how

Help topics are updated frequently; your list may differ

FIGURE 1-15: Create a document Help topic

Word 2016 Help

Print button

Choose a template

Download Microsoft Office templates

Do you want to create a resume, mailing label, budget, fax cover sheet, presentation, or invitation? To get free templates like these, go to **File** > **New** in your Office program, and then click a category under **Office.com Templates**, such as **Letters**, **Business**, or **Form** (In Office 2013 or Office 2016, try one of the **Suggested searches** links).

Or, type what you're looking for in the search box, such as **avery** for labels.

TIP   If you're on the web, try the free online templates at templates.office.com. You can use them right in your browser, in the Office Online programs.

Drag scroll bar to read more

Keep Help on Top button

Using sharing features and co-authoring capabilities

If you are using Word, Excel, or PowerPoint, you can take advantage of the Share feature, which makes it easy to share your files that have been saved to OneDrive. When you click the Share button, you will be asked to invite others to share the file. To do this, type in the name or email addresses in the Invite people text box. When you invite others, you have the opportunity to give them different levels of permission. You might want some people to have read-only privileges; you might want others to be able to make edits. Also available in Word, Excel, and PowerPoint is real-time co-authoring capabilities for files stored on OneDrive. Once a file on OneDrive is opened and all the users have been given editing privileges, all the users can make edits simultaneously. On first use, each user will be prompted to automatically share their changes.

Recovering a document

Each Office program has a built-in recovery feature that allows you to open and save files that were open at the time of an interruption such as a power failure. When you restart the program(s) after an interruption, the Document Recovery task pane opens on the left side of your screen displaying both original and recovered versions of the files that were open. If you're not sure which file to open (original or recovered), it's usually better to open the recovered file because it will contain the latest information. You can, however, open and review all versions of the file that were recovered and save the best one. Each file listed in the Document Recovery task pane displays a list arrow with options that allow you to open the file, save it as is, delete it, or show repairs made to it during recovery.

Practice

Concepts Review

Label the elements of the program window shown in FIGURE 1-16.

FIGURE 1-16

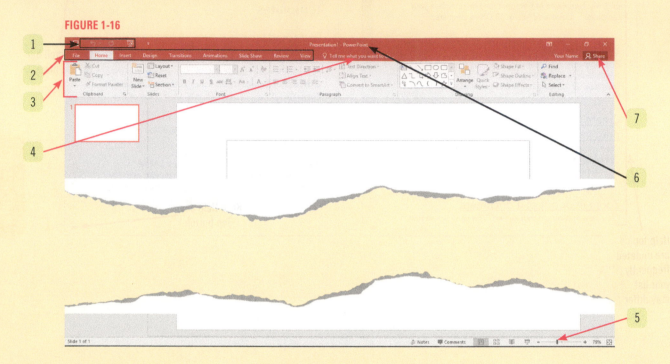

Match each project with the program for which it is best suited.

8. Microsoft PowerPoint
9. Microsoft Word
10. Microsoft Excel
11. Microsoft Access

a. Corporate convention budget with expense projections
b. Presentation for city council meeting
c. Business cover letter for a job application
d. Department store inventory

Independent Challenge 1

You just accepted an administrative position with a local independently owned insurance agent who has recently invested in computers and is now considering purchasing a subscription to Office 365. You have been asked to think of uses for the apps and you put your ideas in a Word document.

a. Start Word, create a new Blank document, then save the document as **OF 1-Microsoft Office Apps Uses** in the location where you store your Data Files.

b. Change the zoom factor to 120%, type **Microsoft Access**, press [Enter] twice, type **Microsoft Excel**, press [Enter] twice, type **Microsoft PowerPoint**, press [Enter] twice, type **Microsoft Word**, press [Enter] twice, then type your name.

c. Click the line beneath each program name, type at least two tasks you can perform using that program (each separated by a comma), then press [Enter].

d. Save the document, then submit your work to your instructor as directed.

e. Exit Word.

Getting Started with Excel 2016

CASE ▶ You have been hired as an assistant at Reason2Go (R2G), a company that allows travelers to make a difference in the global community through voluntourism, while having a memorable vacation experience. You report to Yolanda Lee, the vice president of finance. As Yolanda's assistant, you create worksheets to analyze data from various divisions of the company, so you can help her make sound decisions on company expansion, investments, and new voluntourism opportunities.

Module Objectives

After completing this module, you will be able to:

- Understand spreadsheet software
- Identify Excel 2016 window components
- Understand formulas
- Enter labels and values and use the AutoSum button
- Edit cell entries
- Enter and edit a simple formula
- Switch worksheet views
- Choose print options

Files You Will Need

EX 1-1.xlsx   EX 1-4.xlsx

EX 1-2.xlsx   EX 1-5.xlsx

EX 1-3.xlsx

Learning
Outcomes
• Describe the
uses of Excel
• Define key spread-
sheet terms

Understand Spreadsheet Software

Microsoft Excel is the electronic spreadsheet program within the Microsoft Office suite. An **electronic spreadsheet** is an app you use to perform numeric calculations and to analyze and present numeric data. One advantage of a spreadsheet program over pencil and paper is that your calculations are updated automatically, so you can change entries without having to manually recalculate. **TABLE 1-1** shows some of the common business tasks people accomplish using Excel. In Excel, the electronic spreadsheet you work in is called a **worksheet**, and it is contained in a file called a **workbook**, which has the file extension .xlsx. **CASE** ▷ *At R2G, you use Excel extensively to track finances and manage corporate data.*

DETAILS

When you use Excel, you have the ability to:

QUICK TIP
You can also use the **Quick Analysis tool** to easily create charts and other elements that help you visualize how data is distributed.

- ### Enter data quickly and accurately

  With Excel, you can enter information faster and more accurately than with pencil and paper. **FIGURE 1-1** shows a payroll worksheet created using pencil and paper. **FIGURE 1-2** shows the same worksheet created using Excel. Equations were added to calculate the hours and pay. You can use Excel to recreate this information for each week by copying the worksheet's structure and the information that doesn't change from week to week, then entering unique data and formulas for each week.

- ### Recalculate data easily

  Fixing typing errors or updating data is easy in Excel. In the payroll example, if you receive updated hours for an employee, you just enter the new hours and Excel recalculates the pay.

QUICK TIP
Power users can perform more complex analysis using **Business Intelligence tools** such as Power Query and new forecasting functions.

- ### Perform what-if analysis

  The ability to change data and quickly view the recalculated results gives you the power to make informed business decisions. For instance, if you're considering raising the hourly rate for an entry-level tour guide from $12.50 to $15.00, you can enter the new value in the worksheet and immediately see the impact on the overall payroll as well as on the individual employee. Any time you use a worksheet to ask the question "What if?" you are performing **what-if analysis**. Excel also includes a Scenario Manager where you can name and save different what-if versions of your worksheet.

- ### Change the appearance of information

  Excel provides powerful features, such as the Quick Analysis tool, for making information visually appealing and easier to understand. Format text and numbers in different fonts, colors, and styles to make it stand out.

- ### Create charts

  Excel makes it easy to create charts based on worksheet information. Charts are updated automatically in Excel whenever data changes. The worksheet in **FIGURE 1-2** includes a 3-D pie chart.

- ### Share information

  It's easy for everyone at R2G to collaborate in Excel using the company intranet, the Internet, or a network storage device. For example, you can complete the weekly payroll that your boss, Yolanda Lee, started creating. You can also take advantage of collaboration tools such as shared workbooks so that multiple people can edit a workbook simultaneously.

QUICK TIP
The **flash fill** feature makes it easy to fill a range of text based on examples that are already in your worksheet. Simply type [Ctrl][E] if Excel correctly matches the information you want, and it will be entered in a cell for you.

- ### Build on previous work

  Instead of creating a new worksheet for every project, it's easy to modify an existing Excel worksheet. When you are ready to create next week's payroll, you can open the file for last week's payroll, save it with a new filename, and modify the information as necessary. You can also use predesigned, formatted files called **templates** to create new worksheets quickly. Excel comes with many templates that you can customize.

FIGURE 1-1: Traditional paper worksheet

Reason2Go
Project Leader Divison Payroll Calculator

Name	Hours	O/T Hrs	Hrly Rate	Reg Pay	O/T Pay	Gross Pay
Brucker, Pieter	40	4	16.75	670	134	804
Cucci, Lucia	35	0	12	420	0	420
Klimt, Gustave	40	2	13.25	530	53	583
Lafontaine, Jeanne	29	0	15.25	442.25	0	442.25
Martinez, Juan	37	0	13.2	488.4	0	488.4
Mioshi, Keiko	39	0	21	819	0	819
Shernwood, Burt	40	0	16.75	670	0	670
Strano, Riccardo	40	8	16.25	650	260	910
Wadsworth, Alice	40	5	13.25	530	132.5	662.5
Yamamoto, Johji	38	0	15.5	589	0	589

FIGURE 1-2: Excel worksheet

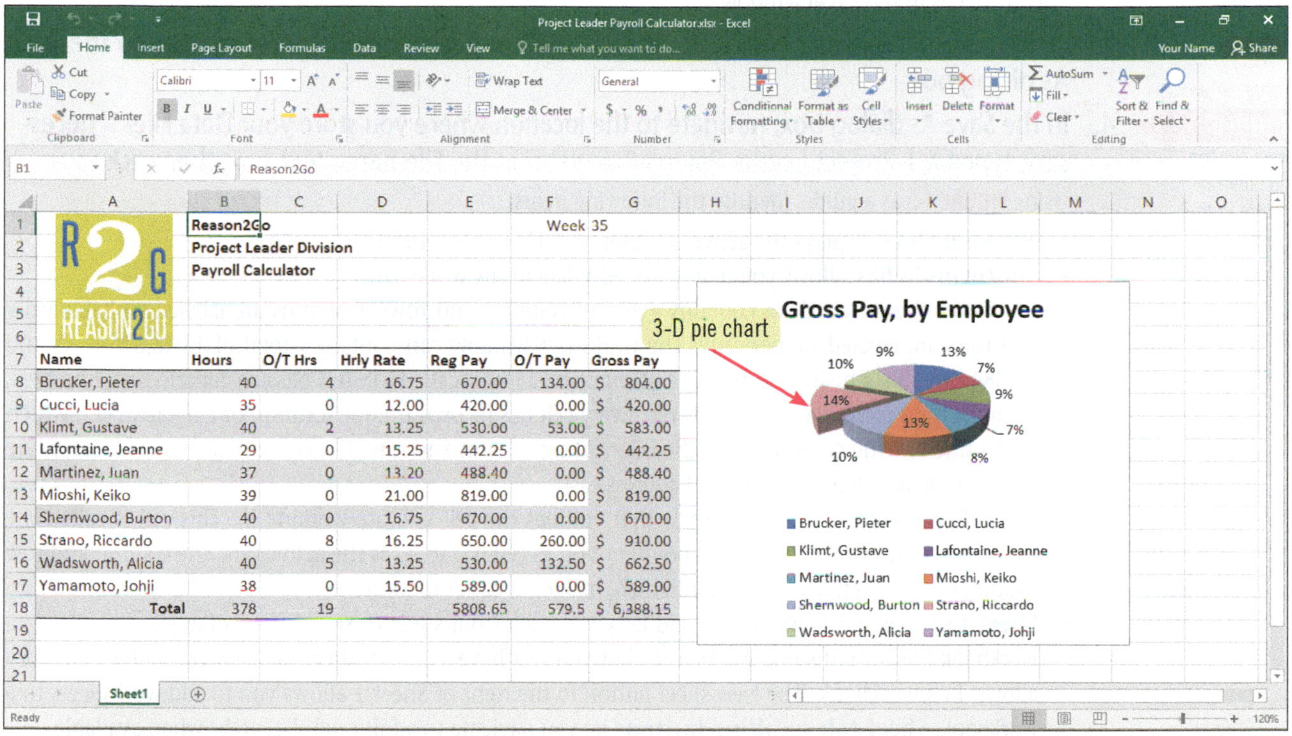

TABLE 1-1: Business tasks you can accomplish using Excel

you can use spreadsheets to	by
Perform calculations	Adding formulas and functions to worksheet data; for example, adding a list of sales results or calculating a car payment
Represent values graphically	Creating charts based on worksheet data; for example, creating a chart that displays expenses
Generate reports	Creating workbooks that combine information from multiple worksheets, such as summarized sales information from multiple stores
Organize data	Sorting data in ascending or descending order; for example, alphabetizing a list of products or customer names, or prioritizing orders by date
Analyze data	Creating data summaries and short lists using PivotTables or AutoFilters; for example, making a list of the top 10 customers based on spending habits
Create what-if data scenarios	Using variable values to investigate and sample different outcomes, such as changing the interest rate or payment schedule on a loan

Excel 2016

Identify Excel 2016 Window Components

Learning Outcomes
• Open and save an Excel file
• Identify Excel window elements

To start Excel, Microsoft Windows must be running. Similar to starting any app in Office, you can use the Start button on the Windows taskbar, the Start button on your keyboard, or you may have a shortcut on your desktop you prefer to use. If you need additional assistance, ask your instructor or technical support person. **CASE** ▶ *You decide to start Excel and familiarize yourself with the worksheet window.*

STEPS

1. **Start Excel, click Open Other Workbooks on the navigation bar, click This PC, then click Browse to open the Open dialog box**

2. **In the Open dialog box, navigate to the location where you store your Data Files, click EX 1-1.xlsx, then click Open**

   The file opens in the Excel window.

3. **Click the File tab, click Save As on the navigation bar, then click Browse to open the Save As dialog box**

4. **In the Save As dialog box, navigate to the location where you store your Data Files if necessary, type EX 1-Project Leader Payroll Calculator in the File name text box, then click Save**

   Using **FIGURE 1-3** as a guide, identify the following items:

   • The **Name box** displays the active cell address. "A1" appears in the Name box.
   • The **formula bar** allows you to enter or edit data in the worksheet.
   • The **worksheet window** contains a grid of columns and rows. Columns are labeled alphabetically and rows are labeled numerically. The worksheet window can contain a total of 1,048,576 rows and 16,384 columns. The intersection of a column and a row is called a **cell**. Cells can contain text, numbers, formulas, or a combination of all three. Every cell has its own unique location or **cell address**, which is identified by the coordinates of the intersecting column and row. The column and row indicators are shaded to make identifying the cell address easy.
   • The **cell pointer** is a dark rectangle that outlines the cell you are working in. This cell is called the **active cell**. In **FIGURE 1-3**, the cell pointer outlines cell A1, so A1 is the active cell. The column and row headings for the active cell are highlighted, making it easier to locate.
   • **Sheet tabs** below the worksheet grid let you switch from sheet to sheet in a workbook. By default, a workbook file contains one worksheet—but you can have as many sheets as your computer's memory allows, in a workbook. The New sheet button to the right of Sheet 1 allows you to add worksheets to a workbook. **Sheet tab scrolling buttons** let you navigate to additional sheet tabs when available.
   • You can use the **scroll bars** to move around in a worksheet that is too large to fit on the screen at once.
   • The **status bar** is located at the bottom of the Excel window. It provides a brief description of the active command or task in progress. **The mode indicator** in the lower-left corner of the status bar provides additional information about certain tasks.

5. **Click cell A4**

   Cell A4 becomes the active cell. To activate a different cell, you can click the cell or press the arrow keys on your keyboard to move to it.

6. **Click cell B5, press and hold the mouse button, drag ✛ to cell B14, then release the mouse button**

   You selected a group of cells and they are highlighted, as shown in **FIGURE 1-4**. A selection of two or more cells such as B5:B14 is called a **range**; you select a range when you want to perform an action on a group of cells at once, such as moving them or formatting them. When you select a range, the status bar displays the average, count (or number of items selected), and sum of the selected cells as a quick reference.

FIGURE 1-3: Open workbook

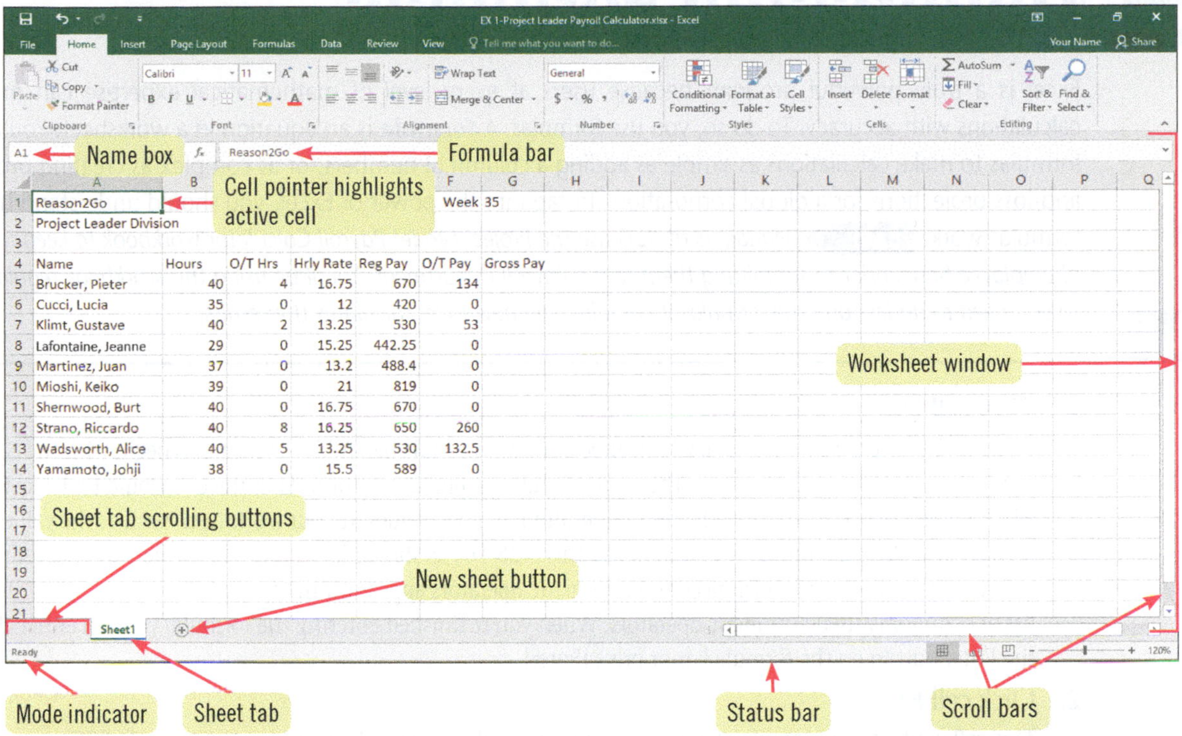

FIGURE 1-4: Selected range

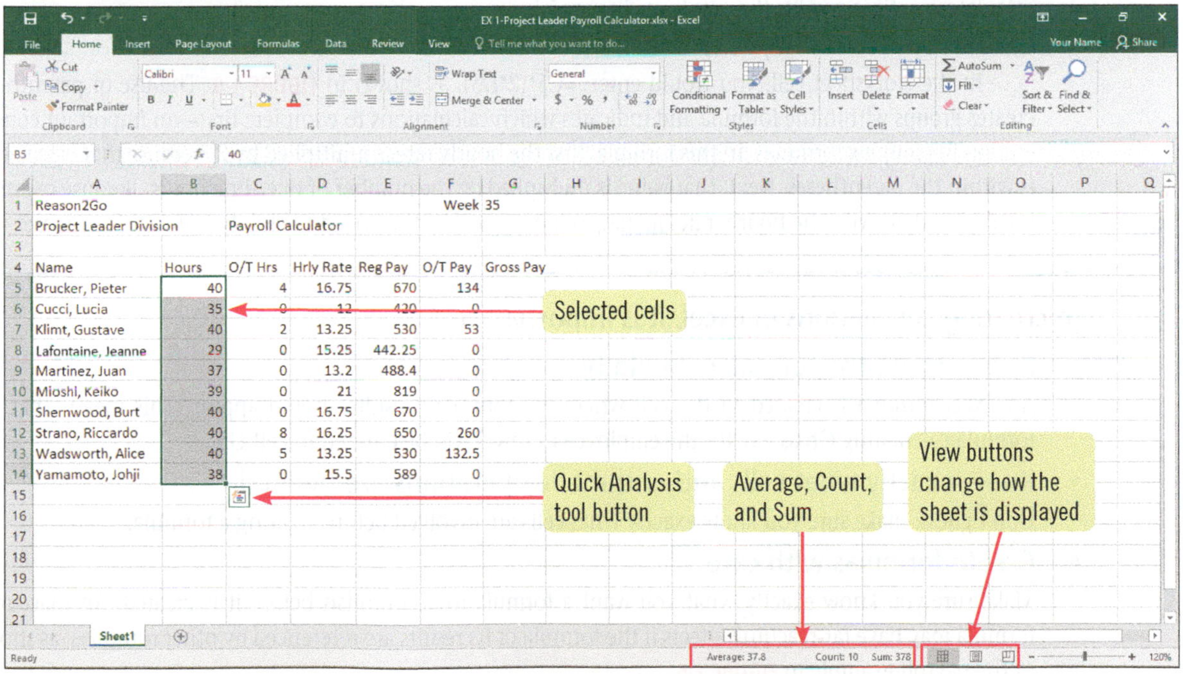

Using OneDrive and Office Online

If you have a Microsoft account, you can save your Excel files and photos in OneDrive, a cloud-based service from Microsoft. When you save files in OneDrive, you can access them on other devices—such as a tablet or smartphone. OneDrive is available as an app on smartphones and tablets, making access simple. You can open files to view them on any device, and you can even make edits to them using **Office Online**, which includes simplified versions of the apps found in the Office 2016 suite. Because Office Online is web-based, the apps take up no computer disk space and you can use them on any Internet-connected device.

Understand Formulas

Learning Outcomes
- Explain how a formula works
- Identify Excel arithmetic operators

Excel is a truly powerful program because users at every level of mathematical expertise can make calculations with accuracy. To do so, you use formulas. A **formula** is an equation in a worksheet. You use formulas to make calculations as simple as adding a column of numbers, or as complex as creating profit-and-loss projections for a global corporation. To tap into the power of Excel, you should understand how formulas work. **CASE** ▶ *Managers at R2G use the Project Leader Payroll Calculator workbook to keep track of employee hours prior to submitting them to the Payroll Department. You'll be using this workbook regularly, so you need to understand the formulas it contains and how Excel calculates the results.*

STEPS

1. **Click cell E5**

   The active cell contains a formula, which appears on the formula bar. All Excel formulas begin with the equal sign (=). If you want a cell to show the result of adding 4 plus 2, the formula in the cell would look like this: =4+2. If you want a cell to show the result of multiplying two values in your worksheet, such as the values in cells B5 and D5, the formula would look like this: =B5*D5, as shown in **FIGURE 1-5**. While you're entering a formula in a cell, the cell references and arithmetic operators appear on the formula bar. See **TABLE 1-2** for a list of commonly used arithmetic operators. When you're finished entering the formula, you can either click the Enter button on the formula bar or press [Enter].

2. **Click cell F5**

   This cell contains an example of a more complex formula, which calculates overtime pay. At R2G, overtime pay is calculated at twice the regular hourly rate times the number of overtime hours. The formula used to calculate overtime pay for the employee in row 5 is:

   O/T Hrs times (2 times Hrly Rate)

   In the worksheet cell, you would enter: =C5*(2*D5), as shown in **FIGURE 1-6**. The use of parentheses creates groups within the formula and indicates which calculations to complete first—an important consideration in complex formulas. In this formula, first the hourly rate is multiplied by 2, because that calculation is within the parentheses. Next, that value is multiplied by the number of overtime hours. Because overtime is calculated at twice the hourly rate, managers are aware that they need to closely watch this expense.

DETAILS

In creating calculations in Excel, it is important to:

- **Know where the formulas should be**

   An Excel formula is created in the cell where the formula's results should appear. This means that the formula calculating Gross Pay for the employee in row 5 will be entered in cell G5.

- **Know exactly what cells and arithmetic operations are needed**

   Don't guess; make sure you know exactly what cells are involved before creating a formula.

- **Create formulas with care**

   Make sure you know exactly what you want a formula to accomplish before it is created. An inaccurate formula may have far-reaching effects if the formula or its results are referenced by other formulas, as shown in the payroll example in **FIGURE 1-6**.

- **Use cell references rather than values**

   The beauty of Excel is that whenever you change a value in a cell, any formula containing a reference to that cell is automatically updated. For this reason, it's important that you use cell references in formulas, rather than actual values, whenever possible.

- **Determine what calculations will be needed**

   Sometimes it's difficult to predict what data will be needed within a worksheet, but you should try to anticipate what statistical information may be required. For example, if there are columns of numbers, chances are good that both column and row totals should be present.

FIGURE 1-5: Viewing a formula

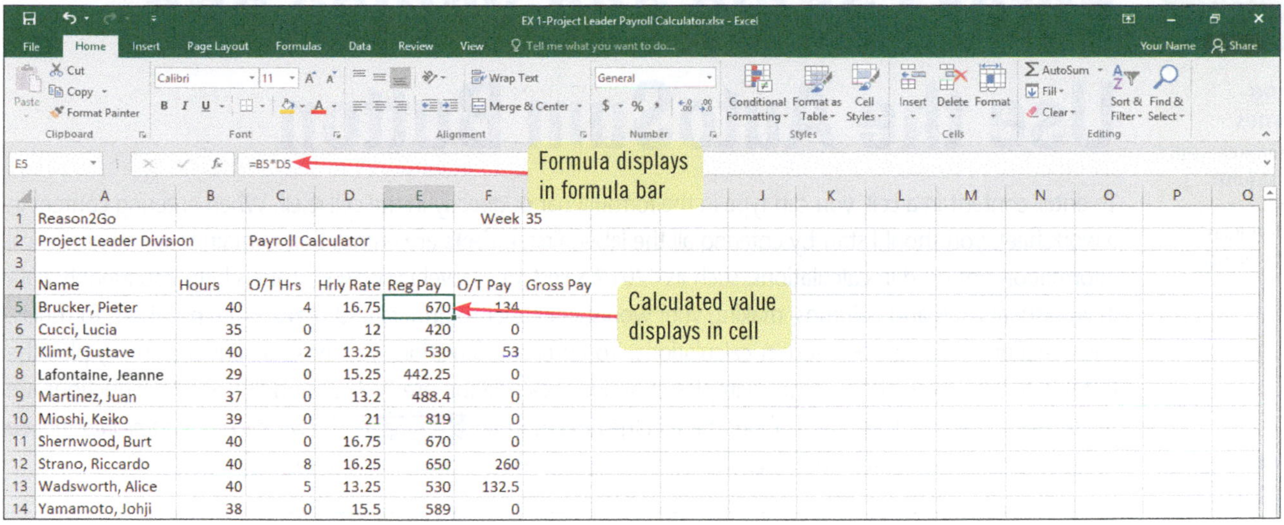

Formula displays in formula bar

Calculated value displays in cell

FIGURE 1-6: Formula with multiple operators

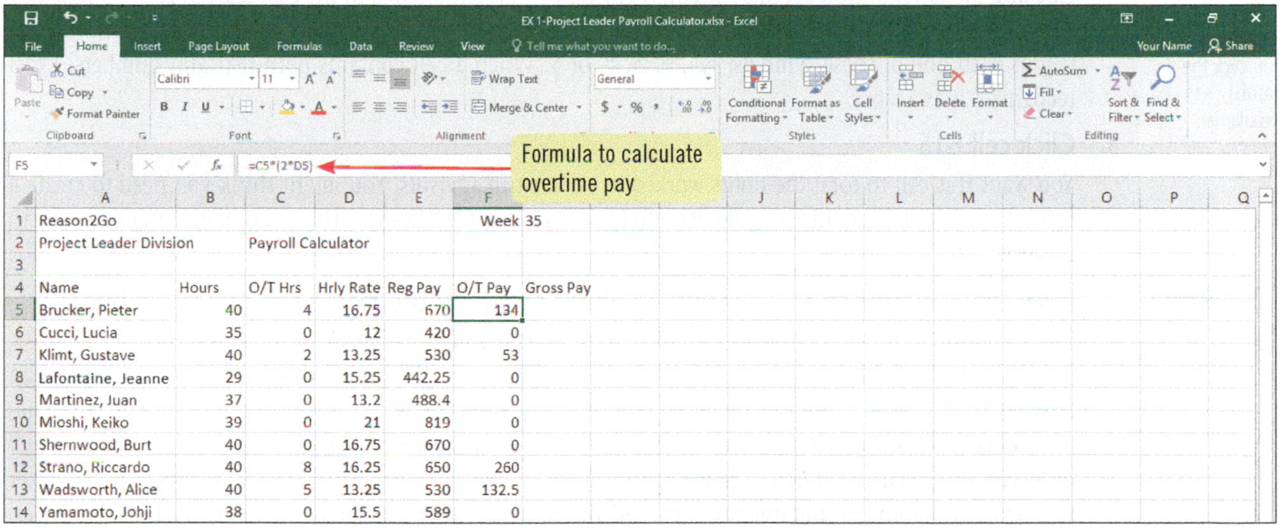

Formula to calculate overtime pay

TABLE 1-2: Excel arithmetic operators

operator	purpose	example
+	Addition	=A5+A7
-	Subtraction or negation	=A5-10
*	Multiplication	=A5*A7
/	Division	=A5/A7
%	Percent	=35%
^ (caret)	Exponent	=6^2 (same as 6^2)

Learning Outcomes
- Build formulas with the AutoSum button
- Copy formulas with the fill handle

Enter Labels and Values and Use the AutoSum Button

To enter content in a cell, you can type in the formula bar or directly in the cell itself. When entering content in a worksheet, you should start by entering all the labels first. **Labels** are entries that contain text and numerical information not used in calculations, such as "2019 Sales" or "Travel Expenses". Labels help you identify data in worksheet rows and columns, making your worksheet easier to understand. **Values** are numbers, formulas, and functions that can be used in calculations. To enter a calculation, you type an equal sign (=) plus the formula for the calculation; some examples of an Excel calculation are "=2+2" and "=C5+C6". Functions are built-in formulas; you learn more about them in the next module. **CASE** *You want to enter some information in the Project Leader Payroll Calculator workbook and use a very simple function to total a range of cells.*

STEPS

1. **Click cell A15, then click in the formula bar**

   Notice that the **mode indicator** on the status bar now reads "Edit," indicating you are in Edit mode. You are in Edit mode any time you are entering or changing the contents of a cell.

   > **QUICK TIP**
   > If you change your mind and want to cancel an entry in the formula bar, click the Cancel button ✕ on the formula bar.

2. **Type Totals, then click the Enter button ✓ on the formula bar**

   Clicking the Enter button accepts the entry. The new text is left-aligned in the cell. Labels are left-aligned by default, and values are right-aligned by default. Excel recognizes an entry as a value if it is a number or it begins with one of these symbols: +, -, =, @, #, or $. When a cell contains both text and numbers, Excel recognizes it as a label.

3. **Click cell B15**

   You want this cell to total the hours worked by all the trip advisors. You might think you need to create a formula that looks like this: =B5+B6+B7+B8+B9+B10+B11+B12+B13+B14. However, there's an easier way to achieve this result.

   > **QUICK TIP**
   > The AutoSum button is also referred to as the Sum button because clicking it inserts the SUM function.

4. **Click the AutoSum button ∑ in the Editing group on the Home tab on the Ribbon**

   The SUM function is inserted in the cell, and a suggested range appears in parentheses, as shown in **FIGURE 1-7**. A **function** is a built-in formula; it includes the **arguments** (the information necessary to calculate an answer) as well as cell references and other unique information. Clicking the AutoSum button sums the adjacent range (that is, the cells next to the active cell) above or to the left, although you can adjust the range if necessary by selecting a different range before accepting the cell entry. Using the SUM function is quicker than entering a formula, and using the range B5:B14 is more efficient than entering individual cell references.

   > **QUICK TIP**
   > You can create formulas in a cell even before you enter the values to be calculated.

5. **Click ✓ on the formula bar**

   Excel calculates the total contained in cells B5:B14 and displays the result, 378, in cell B15. The cell actually contains the formula =SUM(B5:B14), and the result is displayed.

6. **Click cell C13, type 6, then press [Enter]**

   The number 6 replaces the cell's contents, the cell pointer moves to cell C14, and the value in cell F13 changes.

   > **QUICK TIP**
   > You can also press [Tab] to complete a cell entry and move the cell pointer to the right.

7. **Click cell C18, type Average Gross Pay, then press [Enter]**

   The new label is entered in cell C18. The contents appear to spill into the empty cells to the right.

8. **Click cell B15, position the pointer on the lower-right corner of the cell (the fill handle) so that the pointer changes to ✛, drag ✛ to cell G15, then release the mouse button**

   Dragging the fill handle across a range of cells copies the contents of the first cell into the other cells in the range. In the range B15:G15, each filled cell now contains a function that sums the range of cells above, as shown in **FIGURE 1-8**.

9. **Save your work**

FIGURE 1-7: Creating a formula using the AutoSum button

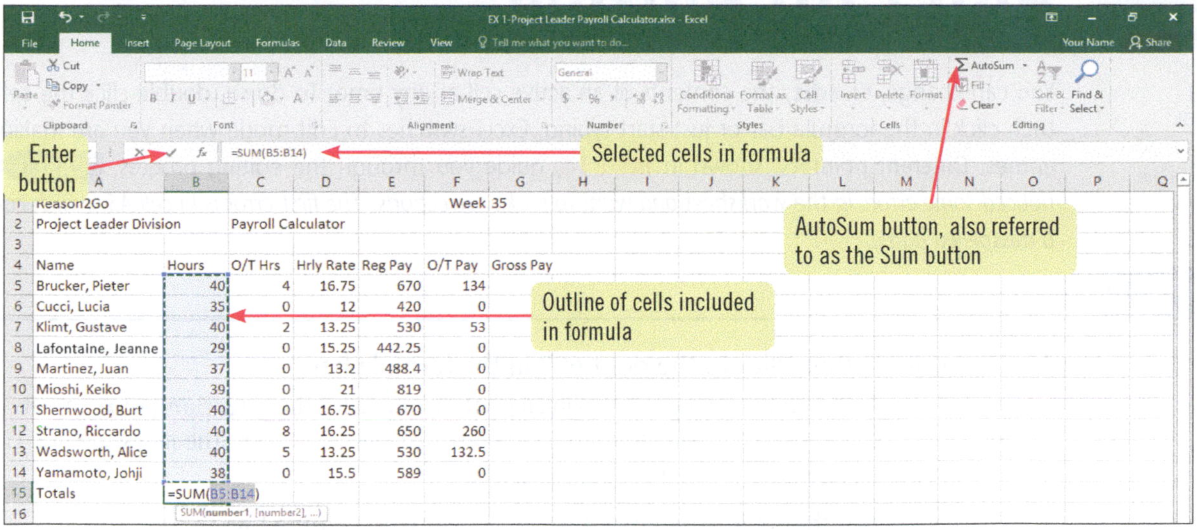

FIGURE 1-8: Results of copied SUM functions

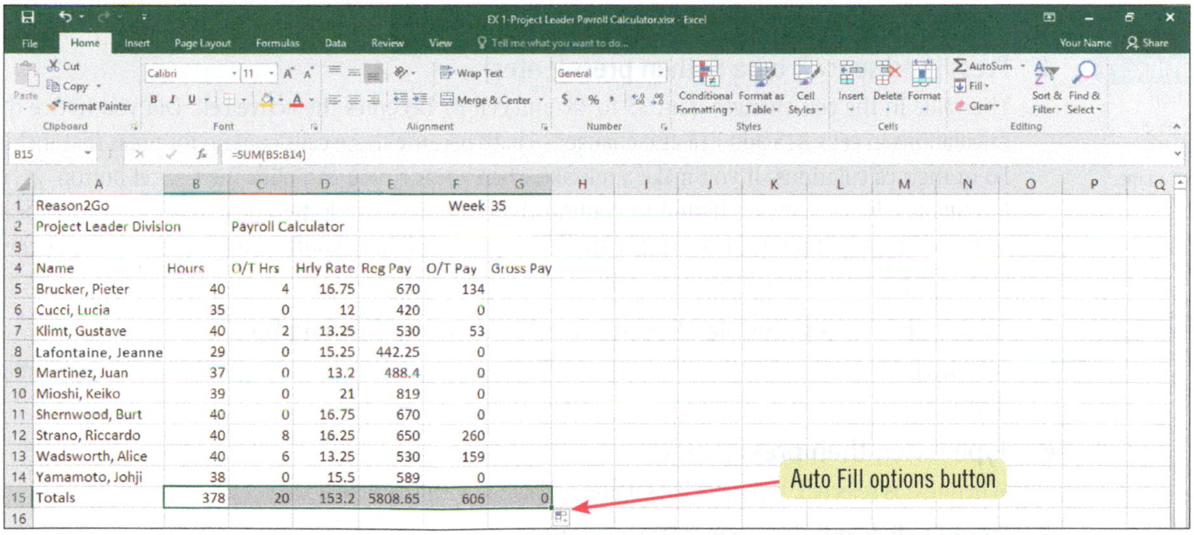

Navigating a worksheet

With over a million cells available in a worksheet, it is important to know how to move around in, or **navigate**, a worksheet. You can use the arrow keys on the keyboard ↑, ↓, →, or ← to move one cell at a time, or press [Page Up] or [Page Down] to move one screen at a time. To move one screen to the left, press [Alt][Page Up]; to move one screen to the right, press [Alt][Page Down]. You can also use the mouse pointer to click the desired cell. If the desired cell is not visible in the worksheet window, use the scroll bars or use the Go To command by clicking the Find & Select button in the Editing group on the Home tab on the Ribbon. To quickly jump to the first cell in a worksheet, press [Ctrl][Home]; to jump to the last cell, press [Ctrl][End].

Edit Cell Entries

Learning Outcomes
• Edit cell entries in the formula bar
• Edit cell entries in the cell

You can change, or **edit**, the contents of an active cell at any time. To do so, double-click the cell, and then click in the formula bar or just start typing. Excel switches to Edit mode when you are making cell entries. Different pointers, shown in **TABLE 1-3**, guide you through the editing process. **CASE** *You noticed some errors in the worksheet and want to make corrections. The first error is in cell A5, which contains a misspelled name.*

STEPS

1. **Click cell A5, then click to the right of P in the formula bar**

   As soon as you click in the formula bar, a blinking vertical line called the **insertion point** appears on the formula bar at the location where new text will be inserted. See **FIGURE 1-9**. The mouse pointer changes to I when you point anywhere in the formula bar.

2. **Press [Delete], then click the Enter button ✓ on the formula bar**

   Clicking the Enter button accepts the edit, and the spelling of the employee's first name is corrected. You can also press [Enter] or [Tab] to accept an edit. Pressing [Enter] to accept an edit moves the cell pointer down one cell, and pressing [Tab] to accept an edit moves the cell pointer one cell to the right.

   QUICK TIP
   On some keyboards, you might need to press an [F-Lock] key to enable the function keys.

3. **Click cell B6, then press [F2]**

   Excel switches to Edit mode, and the insertion point blinks in the cell. Pressing [F2] activates the cell for editing directly in the cell instead of the formula bar. Whether you edit in the cell or the formula bar is simply a matter of preference; the results in the worksheet are the same.

   QUICK TIP
   The Undo button allows you to reverse up to 100 previous actions, one at a time.

4. **Press [Backspace], type 8, then press [Enter]**

   The value in the cell changes from 35 to 38, and cell B7 becomes the active cell. Did you notice that the calculations in cells B15 and E15 also changed? That's because those cells contain formulas that include cell B6 in their calculations. If you make a mistake when editing, you can click the Cancel button ✕ on the formula bar *before* pressing [Enter] to confirm the cell entry. The Enter and Cancel buttons appear only when you're in Edit mode. If you notice the mistake *after* you have confirmed the cell entry, click the Undo button ↶ ▾ on the Quick Access toolbar.

   QUICK TIP
   You can use the keyboard to select all cell contents by clicking to the right of the cell contents in the cell or formula bar, pressing and holding [Shift], then pressing [Home].

5. **Click cell A9, then double-click the word Juan in the formula bar**

   Double-clicking a word in a cell selects it. When you selected the word, the Mini toolbar automatically displayed.

6. **Type Javier, then press [Enter]**

   When text is selected, typing deletes it and replaces it with the new text.

7. **Double-click cell C12, press [Delete], type 4, then click ✓**

   Double-clicking a cell activates it for editing directly in the cell. Compare your screen to **FIGURE 1-10**.

8. **Save your work**

Recovering unsaved changes to a workbook file

You can use Excel's AutoRecover feature to automatically save (Autosave) your work as often as you want. This means that if you suddenly lose power or if Excel closes unexpectedly while you're working, you can recover all or some of the changes you made since you saved it last. (Of course, this is no substitute for regularly saving your work: this is just added insurance.) To customize the AutoRecover settings, click the File tab, click Options, then click

Save. AutoRecover lets you decide how often and into which location it should Autosave files. When you restart Excel after losing power, a Document Recovery pane opens and provides access to the saved and Autosaved versions of the files that were open when Excel closed. You can also click the File tab, click Open on the navigation bar, then click any file in the Recover Unsaved Workbooks list to open Autosaved workbooks.

FIGURE 1-9: Worksheet in Edit mode

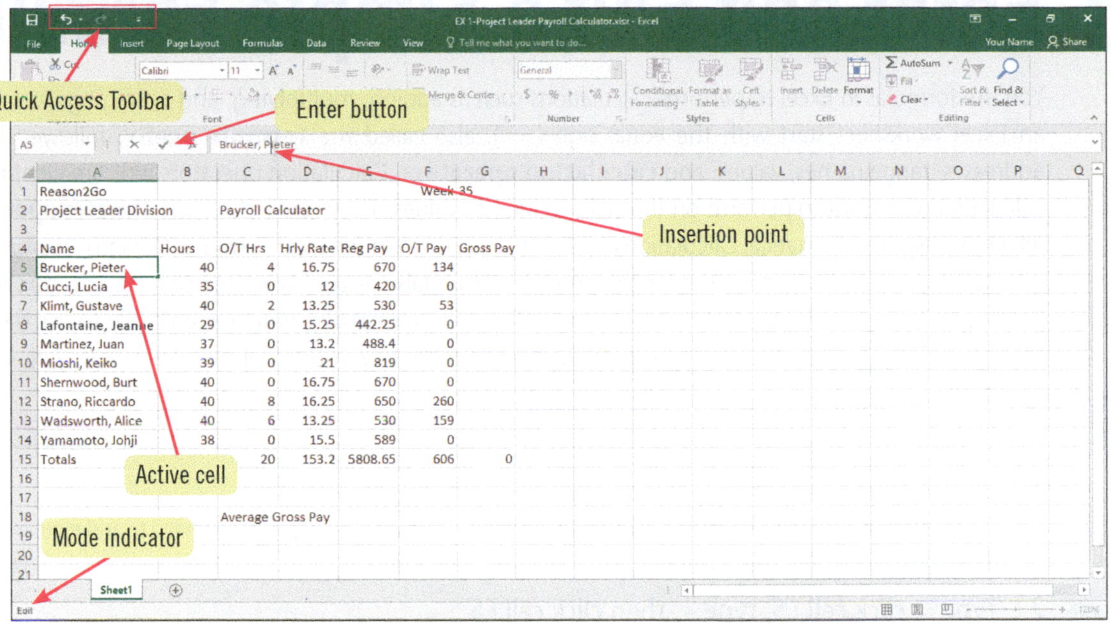

Quick Access Toolbar

Enter button

Insertion point

Active cell

Mode indicator

FIGURE 1-10: Edited worksheet

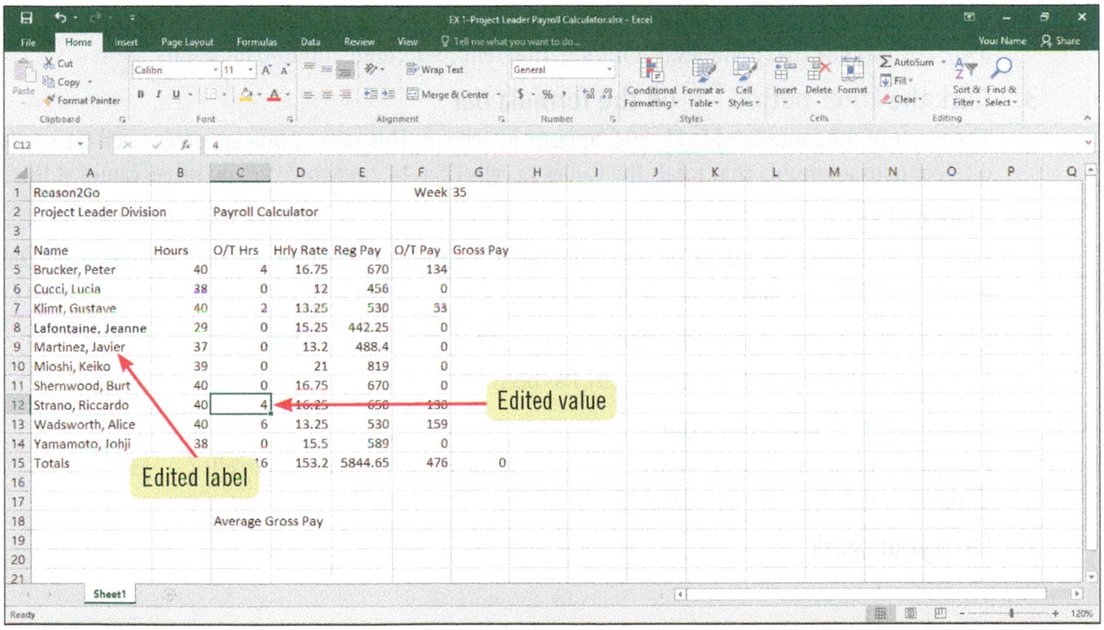

Edited value

Edited label

TABLE 1-3: Common pointers in Excel

name	pointer	use to	visible over the
Normal	⊹	Select a cell or range; indicates Ready mode	Active worksheet
Fill handle	+	Copy cell contents to adjacent cells	Lower right corner of the active cell or range
I-beam	I	Edit cell contents in active cell or formula bar	Active cell in Edit mode or over the formula bar
Move	⊹	Change the location of the selected cell(s)	Perimeter of the active cell(s)
Copy	⊹⁺	Create a duplicate of the selected cell(s)	Perimeter of the active cell(s) when [Ctrl] is pressed
Column resize	⊹⊹	Change the width of a column	Border between column heading indicators

Enter and Edit a Simple Formula

Learning
Outcomes
• Enter a formula
• Use cell references
  to create a formula

You use formulas in Excel to perform calculations such as adding, multiplying, and averaging. Formulas in an Excel worksheet start with the equal sign (=), also called the **formula prefix**, followed by cell addresses, range names, values, and **calculation operators**. Calculation operators indicate what type of calculation you want to perform on the cells, ranges, or values. They can include **arithmetic operators**, which perform mathematical calculations (see TABLE 1-2 in the "Understand Formulas" lesson); **comparison operators**, which compare values for the purpose of true/false results; **text concatenation operators**, which join strings of text in different cells; and **reference operators**, which enable you to use ranges in calculations. CASE ▶ *You want to create a formula in the worksheet that calculates gross pay for each employee.*

STEPS

1. Click cell G5

This is the first cell where you want to insert the formula. To calculate gross pay, you need to add regular pay and overtime pay. For employee Peter Brucker, regular pay appears in cell E5 and overtime pay appears in cell F5.

QUICK TIP

You can reference a cell in a formula either by typing the cell reference or clicking the cell in the worksheet; when you click a cell to add a reference, the Mode indicator changes to "Point."

2. Type =, click cell E5, type +, then click cell F5

Compare your formula bar to FIGURE 1-11. The blue and red cell references in cell G5 correspond to the colored cell outlines. When entering a formula, it's a good idea to use cell references instead of values whenever you can. That way, if you later change a value in a cell (if, for example, Peter's regular pay changes to 690), any formula that includes this information reflects accurate, up-to-date results.

3. Click the Enter button ☑ on the formula bar

The result of the formula =E5+F5, 804, appears in cell G5. This same value appears in cell G15 because cell G15 contains a formula that totals the values in cells G5:G14, and there are no other values at this time.

4. Click cell F5

The formula in this cell calculates overtime pay by multiplying overtime hours (C5) times twice the regular hourly rate (2*D5). You want to edit this formula to reflect a new overtime pay rate.

5. Click to the right of 2 in the formula bar, then type .5 as shown in FIGURE 1-12

The formula that calculates overtime pay has been edited.

6. Click ☑ on the formula bar

Compare your screen to FIGURE 1-13. Notice that the calculated values in cells G5, F15, and G15 have all changed to reflect your edits to cell F5.

7. Save your work

Understanding named ranges

It can be difficult to remember the cell locations of critical information in a worksheet, but using cell names can make this task much easier. You can name a single cell or range of contiguous, or touching, cells. For example, you might name a cell that contains data on average gross pay "AVG_GP" instead of trying to remember the cell address C18. A named range must begin with a letter or an underscore. It cannot contain any spaces or be the same as a built-in name, such as a function or another object (such as a different named range) in the workbook. To name a range, select the cell(s) you want to name, click the Name box in the formula bar, type the name you want to use, then press

[Enter]. You can also name a range by clicking the Formulas tab, then clicking the Define Name button in the Defined Names group. Type the new range name in the Name text box in the New Name dialog box, verify the selected range, then click OK. When you use a named range in a formula, the named range appears instead of the cell address. You can also create a named range using the contents of a cell already in the range. Select the range containing the text you want to use as a name, then click the Create from Selection button in the Defined Names group. The Create Names from Selection dialog box opens. Choose the location of the name you want to use, then click OK.

FIGURE 1-11: Simple formula in a worksheet

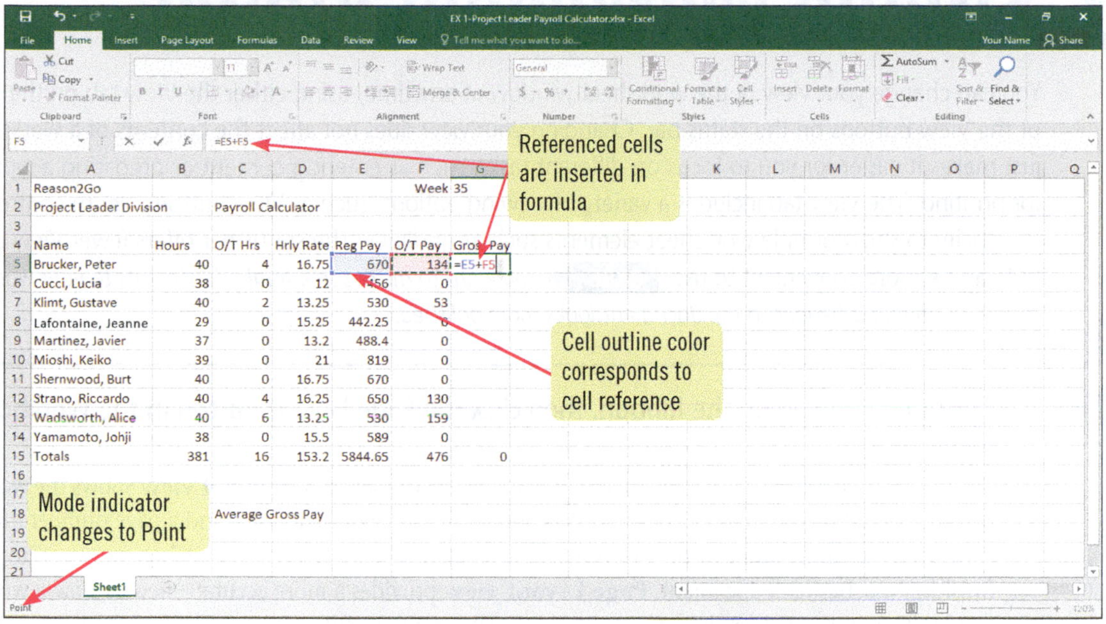

Referenced cells are inserted in formula

Cell outline color corresponds to cell reference

Mode indicator changes to Point

FIGURE 1-12: Edited formula in a worksheet

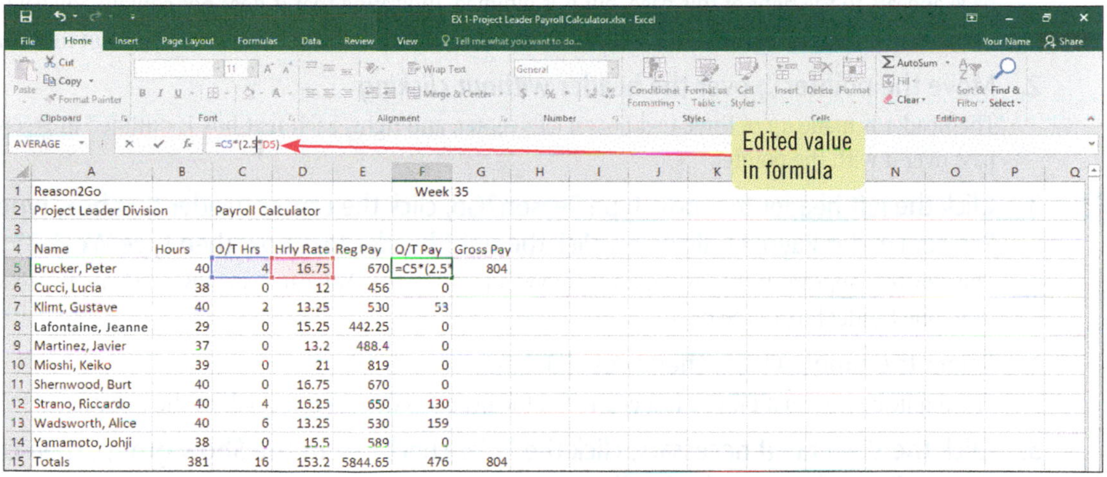

Edited value in formula

FIGURE 1-13: Edited formula with changes

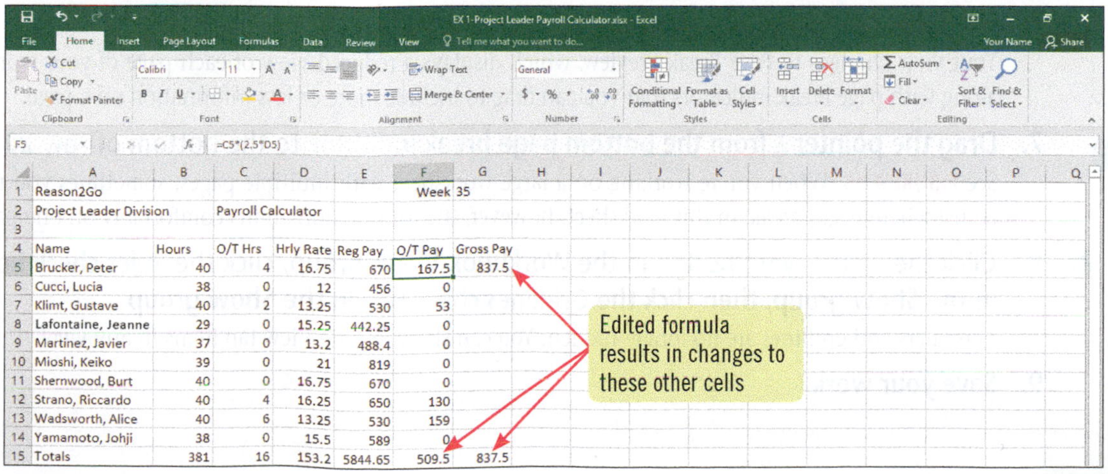

Edited formula results in changes to these other cells

Switch Worksheet Views

You can change your view of the worksheet window at any time, using either the View tab on the Ribbon or the View buttons on the status bar. Changing your view does not affect the contents of a worksheet; it just makes it easier for you to focus on different tasks, such as entering content or preparing a worksheet for printing. The View tab includes a variety of viewing options, such as View buttons, zoom controls, and the ability to show or hide worksheet elements such as gridlines. The status bar offers fewer View options but can be more convenient to use. **CASE** *You want to make some final adjustments to your worksheet, including adding a header so the document looks more polished.*

STEPS

QUICK TIP

Although a worksheet can contain more than a million rows and thousands of columns, the current document contains only as many pages as necessary for the current project.

1. **Click the View tab on the Ribbon, then click the Page Layout button in the Workbook Views group**

   The view switches from the default view, Normal, to Page Layout view. **Normal view** shows the worksheet without including certain details like headers and footers, or tools like rulers and a page number indicator; it's great for creating and editing a worksheet, but may not be detailed enough when you want to put the finishing touches on a document. **Page Layout view** provides a more accurate view of how a worksheet will look when printed, as shown in **FIGURE 1-14**. The margins of the page are displayed, along with a text box for the header. A footer text box appears at the bottom of the page, but your screen may not be large enough to view it without scrolling. Above and to the left of the page are rulers. Part of an additional page appears to the right of this page, but it is dimmed, indicating that it does not contain any data. A page number indicator on the status bar tells you the current page and the total number of pages in this worksheet.

2. **Move the pointer over the header *without clicking***

   The header is made up of three text boxes: left, center, and right. Each text box is outlined in green as you pass over it with the pointer.

QUICK TIP

You can change header and footer information using the Header & Footer Tools Design tab that opens on the Ribbon when a header or footer is active. For example, you can insert the date by clicking the Current Date button in the Header & Footer Elements group, or insert the time by clicking the Current Time button.

3. **Click the left header text box, type Reason2Go, click the center header text box, type Project Leader Payroll Calculator, click the right header text box, then type Week 35**

   The new text appears in the text boxes, as shown in **FIGURE 1-15**. You can also press the [Tab] key to advance from one header box to the next.

4. **Select the range A1:G2, then press [Delete]**

   The duplicate information you just entered in the header is deleted from cells in the worksheet.

5. **Click the View tab if necessary, click the Ruler check box in the Show group, then click the Gridlines check box in the Show group**

   The rulers and the gridlines are hidden. By default, gridlines in a worksheet do not print, so hiding them gives you a more accurate image of your final document.

6. **Click the Page Break Preview button on the status bar**

   Your view changes to Page Break Preview, which displays a reduced view of each page of your worksheet, along with page break indicators that you can drag to include more or less information on a page.

QUICK TIP

Once you view a worksheet in Page Break Preview, the page break indicators appear as dotted lines after you switch back to Normal view or Page Layout view.

7. **Drag the pointer from the bottom page break indicator to the bottom of row 20**

   See **FIGURE 1-16**. When you're working on a large worksheet with multiple pages, sometimes you need to adjust where pages break; in this worksheet, however, the information all fits comfortably on one page.

8. **Click the Page Layout button in the Workbook Views group, click the Ruler check box in the Show group, then click the Gridlines check box in the Show group**

   The rulers and gridlines are no longer hidden. You can show or hide View tab items in any view.

9. **Save your work**

FIGURE 1-14: Page Layout view

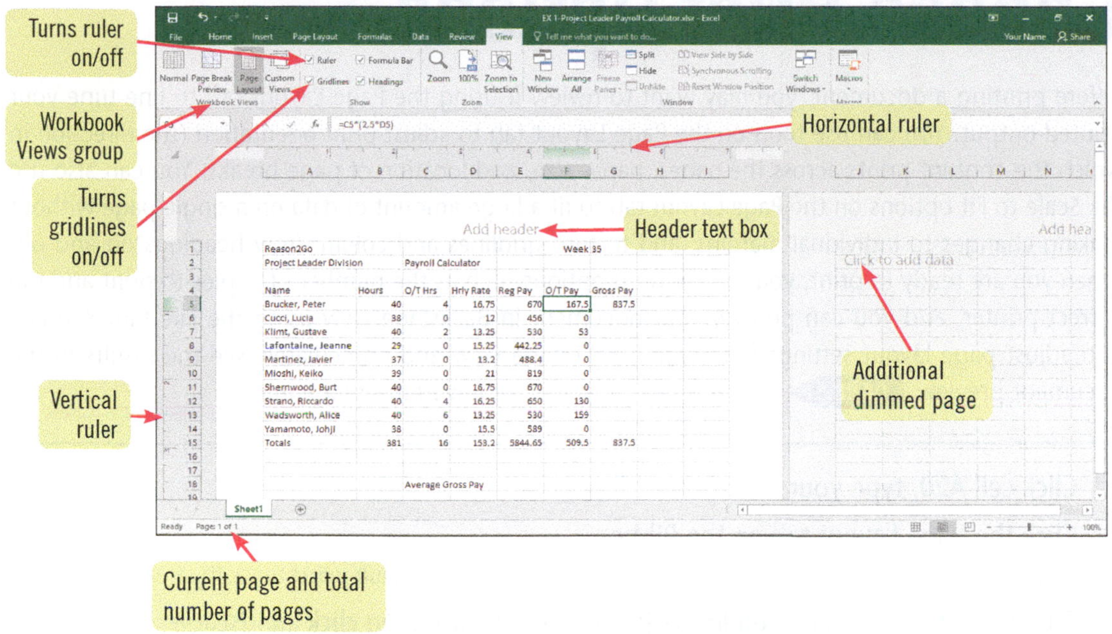

Turns ruler on/off

Workbook Views group

Turns gridlines on/off

Vertical ruler

Horizontal ruler

Header text box

Additional dimmed page

Current page and total number of pages

FIGURE 1-15: Header text entered

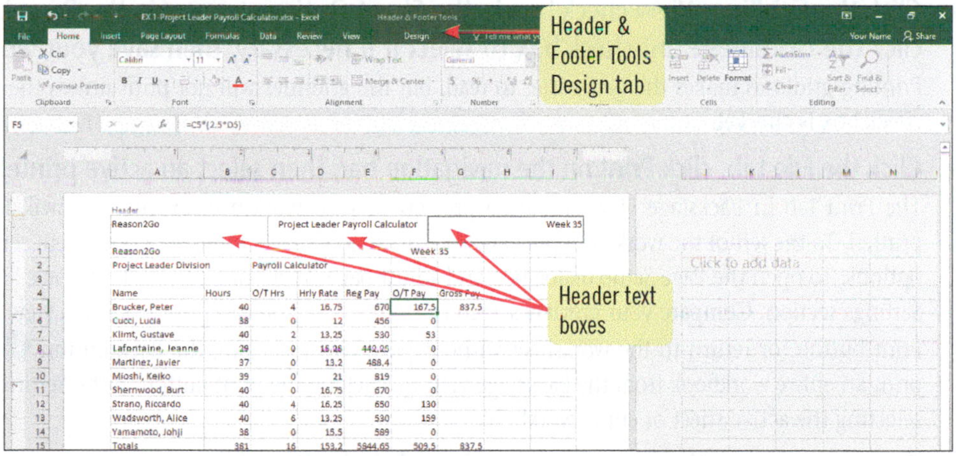

Header & Footer Tools Design tab

Header text boxes

FIGURE 1-16: Page Break Preview

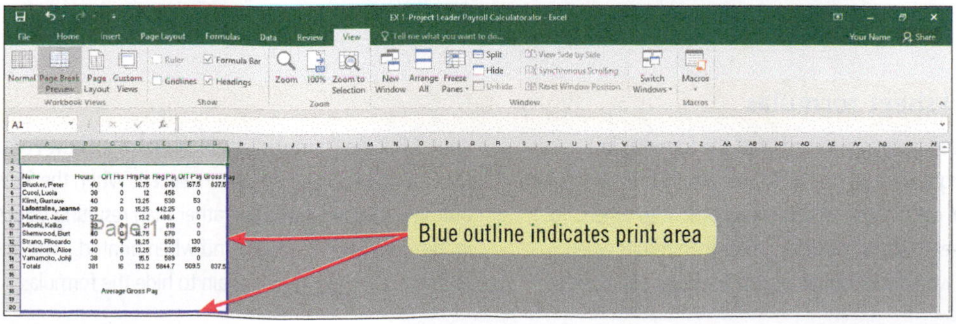

Blue outline indicates print area

Getting Started with Excel 2016

Choose Print Options

Before printing a document, you may want to review it using the Page Layout tab to fine-tune your printed output. You can use tools on the Page Layout tab to adjust print orientation (the direction in which the content prints across the page), paper size, and location of page breaks. You can also use the Scale to Fit options on the Page Layout tab to fit a large amount of data on a single page without making changes to individual margins, and to turn gridlines and column/row headings on and off. When you are ready to print, you can set print options such as the number of copies to print and the correct printer, and you can preview your document in Backstage view using the File tab. You can also adjust page layout settings from within Backstage view and immediately see the results in the document preview. **CASE** *You are ready to prepare your worksheet for printing.*

STEPS

1. **Click cell A20, type your name, then click ✓**

2. **Click the Page Layout tab on the Ribbon**

   Compare your screen to FIGURE 1-17. The solid outline indicates the default **print area**, the area to be printed.

3. **Click the Orientation button in the Page Setup group, then click Landscape**

   The paper orientation changes to **landscape**, so the contents will print across the length of the page instead of across the width. Notice how the margins of the worksheet adjust.

4. **Click the Orientation button in the Page Setup group, then click Portrait**

   The orientation returns to **portrait**, so the contents will print across the width of the page.

5. **Click the Gridlines View check box in the Sheet Options group on the Page Layout tab, click the Gridlines Print check box to select it if necessary, then save your work**

   Printing gridlines makes the data easier to read, but the gridlines will not print unless the Gridlines Print check box is checked.

6. **Click the File tab, click Print on the navigation bar, then select an active printer if necessary**

   The Print tab in Backstage view displays a preview of your worksheet exactly as it will look when it is printed. To the left of the worksheet preview, you can also change a number of document settings and print options. To open the Page Setup dialog box and adjust page layout options, click the Page Setup link in the Settings section. Compare your preview screen to FIGURE 1-18. You can print from this view by clicking the Print button, or return to the worksheet without printing by clicking the Back button ←. You can also print an entire workbook from the Backstage view by clicking the Print button in the Settings section, then selecting the active sheet or entire workbook.

7. **Compare your settings to FIGURE 1-18, then click the Print button**

   One copy of the worksheet prints.

8. **Submit your work to your instructor as directed, then exit Excel**

Printing worksheet formulas

Sometimes you need to keep a record of all the formulas in a worksheet. You might want to do this to see exactly how you came up with a complex calculation, so you can explain it to others. To prepare a worksheet to show formulas rather than results when printed, open the workbook containing the formulas you want to print. Click the Formulas tab, then click the Show Formulas button in the Formula Auditing group to select it. When the Show Formulas button is selected, formulas rather than resulting values are displayed in the worksheet on screen and when printed. (The Show Formulas button is a toggle: click it again to hide the formulas.)

FIGURE 1-17: Worksheet with Portrait orientation

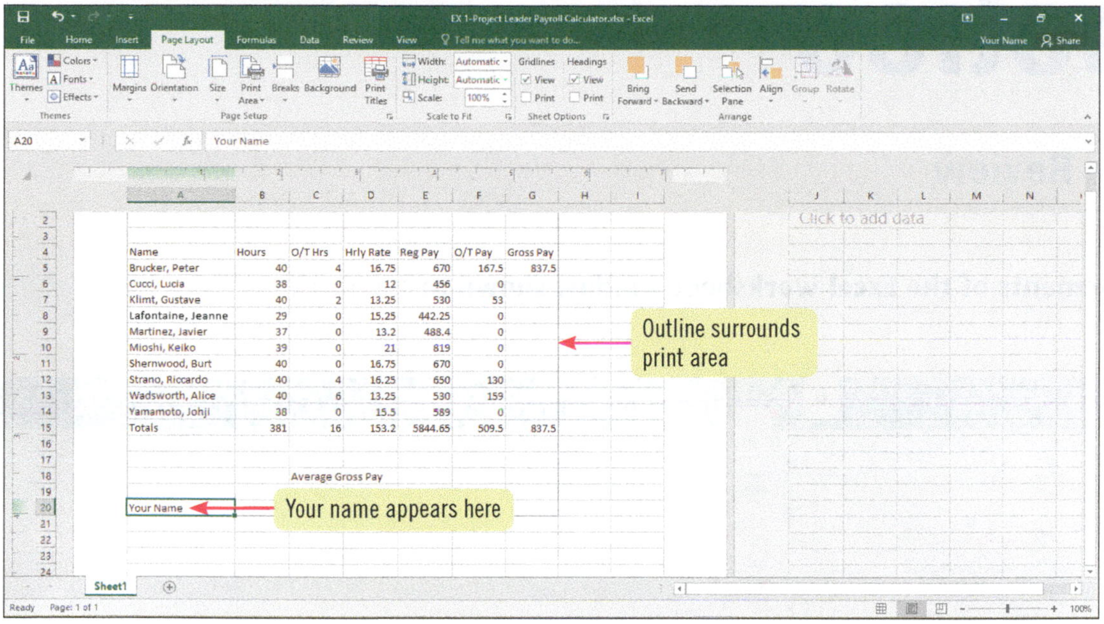

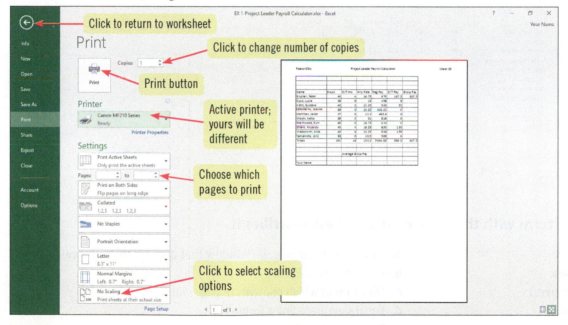

Outline surrounds print area

Your name appears here

FIGURE 1-18: Worksheet in Backstage view

Click to return to worksheet

Print

Click to change number of copies

Print button

Active printer; yours will be different

Choose which pages to print

Click to select scaling options

Scaling to fit

If you have a large amount of data that you want to fit to a single sheet of paper, but you don't want to spend a lot of time trying to adjust the margins and other settings, you have several options. You can easily print your work on a single sheet by clicking the No Scaling list arrow in the Settings section on the Print place in Backstage view, then clicking Fit Sheet in One Page. Another method for fitting worksheet content onto one page is to click the Page Layout tab, then change the Width and Height settings in the Scale to Fit group each to 1 Page. You can also use the Fit to option in the Page Setup dialog box to fit a worksheet on one page. To open the Page Setup dialog box, click the dialog box launcher in the Scale to Fit group on the Page Layout tab, or click the Page Setup link in the Print place in Backstage view. Make sure the Page tab is selected in the Page Setup dialog box, then click the Fit to option button.

Practice

Concepts Review

Label the elements of the Excel worksheet window shown in FIGURE 1-19.

FIGURE 1-19

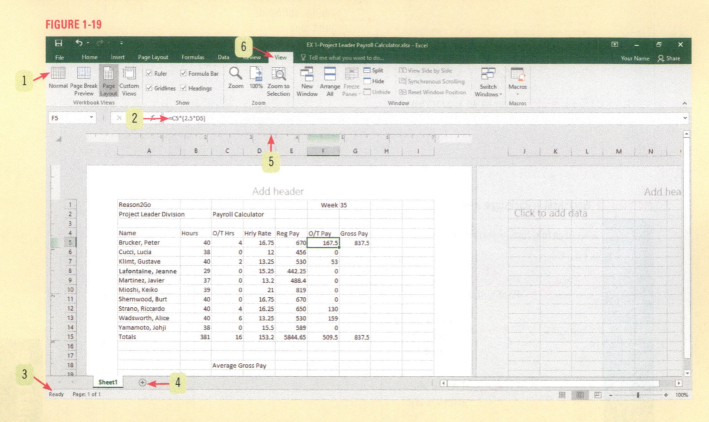

Match each term with the statement that best describes it.

7. **Name box**   a. Part of the Excel program window that displays the active cell address
8. **Workbook**   b. Default view in Excel
9. **Formula prefix**   c. Direction in which contents of page will print
10. **Orientation**   d. Equal sign preceding a formula
11. **Cell**   e. File consisting of one or more worksheets
12. **Normal view**   f. Intersection of a column and a row

Select the best answer from the list of choices.

13. **Which feature could be used to print a very long worksheet on a single sheet of paper?**
    a. Show Formulas
    b. Scale to Fit
    c. Page Break Preview
    d. Named Ranges

14. **In which area can you see a preview of your worksheet?**
    a. Page Setup
    b. Backstage view
    c. Printer Setup
    d. View tab

15. **A selection of multiple cells is called a:**
    a. Group.
    b. Range.
    c. Reference.
    d. Package.

16. **Using a cell address in a formula is known as:**
    a. Formularizing.
    b. Prefixing.
    c. Cell referencing.
    d. Cell mathematics.

17. **Which worksheet view shows how your worksheet will look when printed?**
    a. Page Layout
    b. Data
    c. Review
    d. View

18. **Which key can you press to switch to Edit mode?**
    a. [F1]
    b. [F2]
    c. [F4]
    d. [F6]

19. **In which view can you see the header and footer areas of a worksheet?**
    a. Normal view
    b. Page Layout view
    c. Page Break Preview
    d. Header/Footer view

20. **Which view shows you a reduced view of each page of your worksheet?**
    a. Normal
    b. Page Layout
    c. Thumbnail
    d. Page Break Preview

21. **The maximum number of worksheets you can include in a workbook is:**
    a. 3.
    b. 250.
    c. 255.
    d. Unlimited.

Skills Review

1. **Understand spreadsheet software.**
   a. What is the difference between a workbook and a worksheet?
   b. Identify five common business uses for electronic spreadsheets.
   c. What is what-if analysis?

2. **Identify Excel 2016 window components.**
   a. Start Excel.
   b. Open EX 1-2.xlsx from the location where you store your Data Files, then save it as **EX 1-Weather Data**.
   c. Locate the formula bar, the Sheet tabs, the mode indicator, and the cell pointer.

3. **Understand formulas.**
   a. What is the average high temperature of the listed cities? (*Hint*: Select the range B5:G5 and use the status bar.)
   b. What formula would you create to calculate the difference in altitude between Atlanta and Dallas? Enter your answer (as an equation) in cell D13.

Skills Review (continued)

4. **Enter labels and values and use the AutoSum button.**
   a. Click cell H8, then use the AutoSum button to calculate the total snowfall.
   b. Click cell H7, then use the AutoSum button to calculate the total rainfall.
   c. Save your changes to the file.

5. **Edit cell entries.**
   a. Use [F2] to correct the spelling of SanteFe in cell G3 (the correct spelling is Santa Fe).
   b. Click cell A17, then type your name.
   c. Save your changes.

6. **Enter and edit a simple formula.**
   a. Change the value 41 in cell C8 to **52**.
   b. Change the value 37 in cell D6 to **35.4**.
   c. Select cell J4, then use the fill handle to copy the formula in cell J4 to cells J5:J8.
   d. Save your changes.

7. **Switch worksheet views.**
   a. Click the View tab on the Ribbon, then switch to Page Layout view.
   b. Add the header **Average Annual Weather Data** to the center header text box.
   c. Add your name to the right header box.
   d. Delete the contents of cell A17.
   e. Delete the contents of cell A1.
   f. Save your changes.

8. **Choose print options.**
   a. Use the Page Layout tab to change the orientation to Portrait.
   b. Turn off gridlines by deselecting both the Gridlines View and Gridlines Print check boxes (if necessary) in the Sheet Options group.
   c. Scale the worksheet so all the information fits on one page. If necessary, scale the worksheet so all the information fits on one page. (*Hint*: Click the Width list arrow in the Scale to Fit group, click 1 page, click the Height list arrow in the Scale to Fit group, then click 1 page.) Compare your screen to **FIGURE 1-20**.
   d. Preview the worksheet in Backstage view, then print the worksheet.
   e. Save your changes, submit your work to your instructor as directed, then close the workbook and exit Excel.

FIGURE 1-20

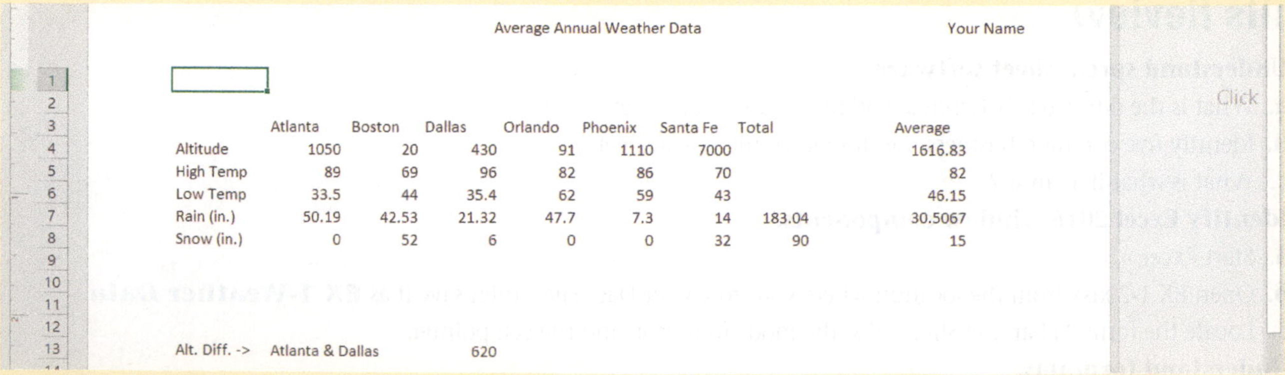

	Atlanta	Boston	Dallas	Orlando	Phoenix	Santa Fe	Total		Average
			Average Annual Weather Data					Your Name	
Altitude	1050	20	430	91	1110	7000			1616.83
High Temp	89	69	96	82	86	70			82
Low Temp	33.5	44	35.4	62	59	43			46.15
Rain (in.)	50.19	42.53	21.32	47.7	7.3	14	183.04		30.5067
Snow (in.)	0	52	6	0	0	32	90		15
Alt. Diff. ->	Atlanta & Dallas		620						

Independent Challenge 1

A real estate development company has hired you to help them make the transition to using Excel in their office. They would like to list properties they are interested in acquiring in a workbook. You've started a worksheet for this project that contains labels but no data.

a. Open the file EX 1-3.xlsx from the location where you store your Data Files, then save it as **EX 1-Real Estate Acquisitions**.

b. Enter the data shown in **TABLE 1-4** in columns A, C, D, and E (the property address information should spill into column B).

TABLE 1-4

Property Address	Price	Bedrooms	Bathrooms	Area
1507 Pinon Lane	575000	4	2.5	NE
32 Zanzibar Way	429000	3	4	SE
60 Pottery Lane	526500	2	2	NE
902 Excelsior Drive	315000	4	3	NW

c. Use Page Layout view to create a header with the following components: the title **Real Estate Acquisitions** in the center and your name on the right.

d. Create formulas for totals in cells C6:E6.

e. Save your changes, then compare your worksheet to **FIGURE 1-21**.

f. Submit your work to your instructor as directed.

g. Close the worksheet and exit Excel.

FIGURE 1-21

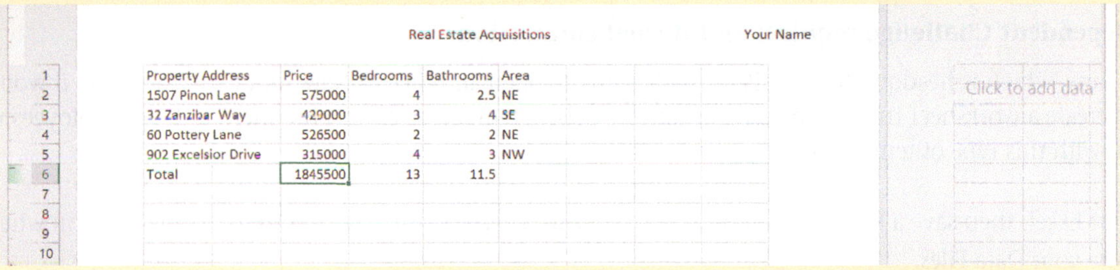

Independent Challenge 2

You are the general manager for Luxury Motors, a high-end auto reseller. Although the company is just five years old, it is expanding rapidly, and you are continually looking for ways to save time. You recently began using Excel to manage and maintain data on inventory and sales, which has greatly helped you to track information accurately and efficiently.

a. Start Excel.

b. Save a new workbook as **EX 1-Luxury Motors** in the location where you store your Data Files.

c. Switch to an appropriate view, then add a header that contains your name in the left header text box and the title **Luxury Motors** in the center header text box.

Independent Challenge 2 (continued)

d. Using **FIGURE 1-22** as a guide, create labels for at least seven car manufacturers and sales for three months. Include other labels as appropriate. The car make should be in column A and the months should be in columns B, C, and D. A Total row should be beneath the data, and a Total column should be in column E.

FIGURE 1-22

	A	B	C	D	E
	Your Name				Luxury Motors
1	Sales for Quarter 1				
2	Make	January	February	March	Total
3					
4	Acura	16650	16000	16500	49150
5	Honda	13220	15500	19000	47720
6	Integra	16000	20000	20500	56500
7	Lexus	19000	26500	23000	68500
8	Mercedes	20000	24000	24750	68750
9	Nissan	22500	26000	26750	75250
10	Toyota	24000	28000	28750	80750
11	Total	131370	156000	159250	446620

Your formulas go here

e. Enter values of your choice for the monthly sales for each make.

f. Add formulas in the Total column to calculate total quarterly sales for each make. Add formulas at the bottom of each column of values to calculate the total for that column. Remember that you can use the AutoSum button and the fill handle to save time.

g. Save your changes, preview the worksheet in Backstage view, then submit your work to your instructor as directed.

h. Close the workbook and exit Excel.

Independent Challenge 3

This Independent Challenge requires an Internet connection.

Your company, which is headquartered in Paris, is planning to open an office in New York City. You think it would be helpful to create a worksheet that can be used to convert Celsius temperatures to Fahrenheit, to help employees who are unfamiliar with this type of temperature measurement.

a. Start Excel, then save a blank workbook as **EX 1-Temperature Conversions** in the location where you store your Data Files.

b. Create column headings using **FIGURE 1-23** as a guide. (*Hint*: You can widen column B by clicking cell B1, clicking the Format button in the Cells group on the Home tab, then clicking AutoFit Column Width.)

FIGURE 1-23

	A	B	C
		Temperature Conversions	Your Name
1	Season	Celsius	Fahrenheit
2	Spring	16	60.8
3	Winter	23	73.4
4	Summer	24	75.2
5	Fall	20	68
6			

Your formulas go here

c. Create row labels for each of the seasons.

d. In the appropriate cells, enter what you determine to be a reasonable indoor temperature for each season.

e. Use your web browser to find out the conversion rate for Fahrenheit to Celsius. (*Hint*: Use your favorite search engine to search on a term such as **temperature conversion formula**.)

Independent Challenge 3 (continued)

f. In the appropriate cells, create a formula that calculates the conversion of the Fahrenheit temperature you entered into a Celsius temperature.

g. In Page Layout View, add your name and the title **Temperature Conversions** to the header.

h. Save your work, then submit your work to your instructor as directed.

i. Close the file, then exit Excel.

Independent Challenge 4: Explore

You've been asked to take over a project started by a co-worker whose Excel skills are not as good as your own. The assignment was to create a sample invoice for an existing client. The invoice will include personnel hours, supplies, and sales tax. Your predecessor started the project, including layout and initial calculations, but she has not made good use of Excel features and has made errors in her calculations. Complete the worksheet by correcting the errors and improving the design. Be prepared to discuss what is wrong with each of the items in the worksheet that you change.

a. Start Excel, open the file EX 1-4.xlsx from the location where you store your Data Files, then save it as **EX 1-Improved Invoice**.

b. There is an error in cell E5: please use the Help feature to find out what is wrong. If you need additional assistance, search Help on *overview of formulas*.

c. Correct the error in the formula in cell E5, then copy the corrected formula into cells E6:E7.

d. Correct the error in the formula in cell E11, then copy the corrected formula into cells E12 and E13.

e. Cells E8 and E14 also contain incorrect formulas. Cell E8 should contain a formula that calculates the total personnel expense, and cell E14 should calculate the total supplies used.

f. Cell G17 should contain a formula that adds the Invoice subtotal (total personnel and total supplies).

g. Cell G18 should calculate the sales tax by multiplying the Subtotal (G17) and the sales tax (cell G18).

h. The Invoice Total (cell G19) should contain a formula that adds the Invoice subtotal (cell G17) and Sales tax (cell G18).

i. Add the following to cell A21: **Terms**, then add the following to cell B21: **Net 10**.

j. Switch to Page Layout view and make the following changes to the Header: Improved Invoice for Week 22 (in the left header box), Client ABC (in the center header box), and your name (in the right header box).

k. Delete the contents of A1:A2, switch to Normal view, then compare your worksheet to FIGURE 1-24.

l. Save your work.

FIGURE 1-24

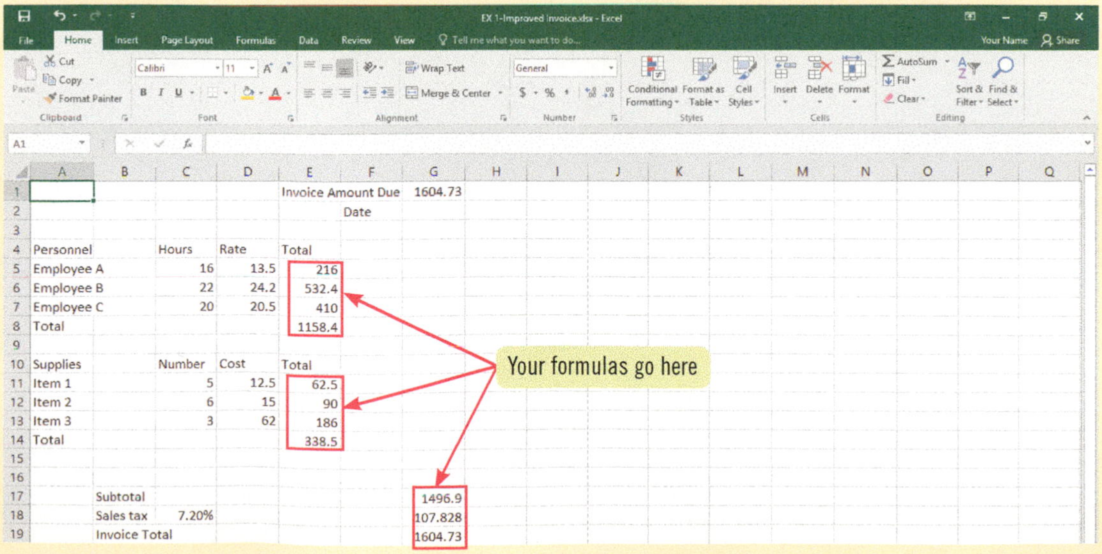

Visual Workshop

Open the file EX 1-5.xlsx from the location where you store your Data Files, then save it as **EX 1-Project Tools**. Using the skills you learned in this module, modify your worksheet so it matches **FIGURE 1-25**. Enter formulas in cells D4 through D13 and in cells B14 and C14. Use the AutoSum button and fill handle to make entering your formulas easier. Add your name in the left header text box, then print one copy of the worksheet with the formulas displayed.

FIGURE 1-25

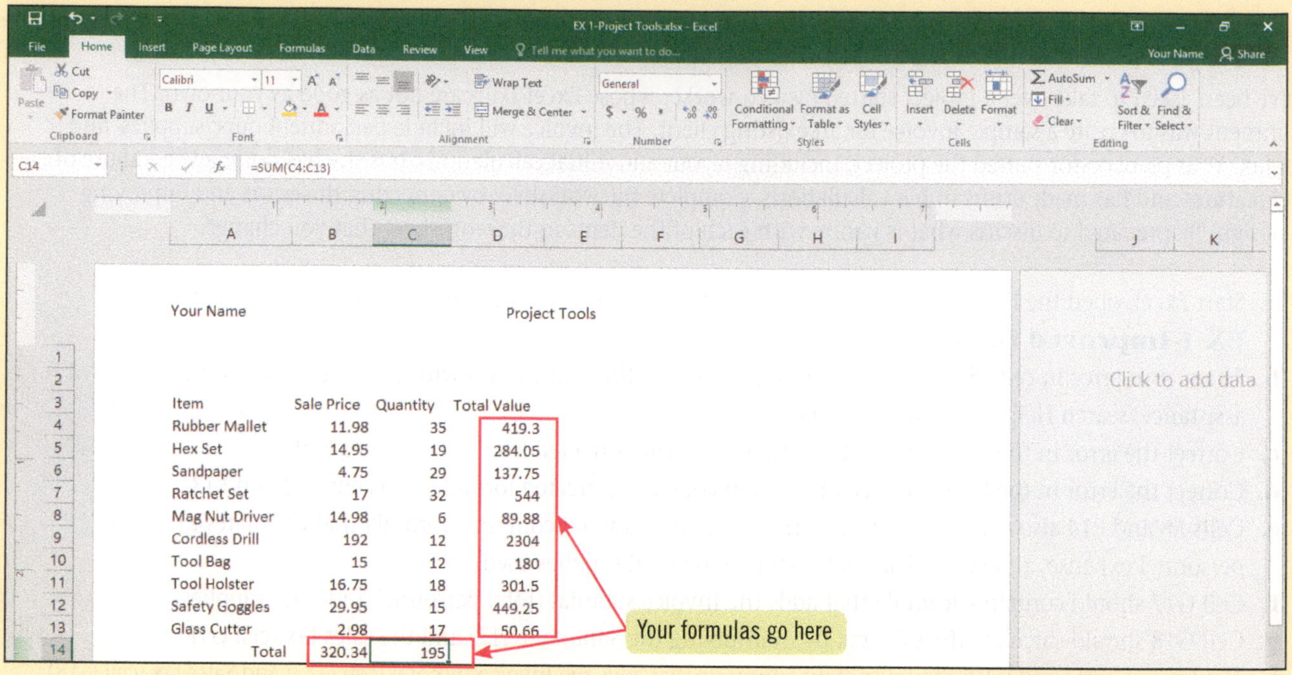

EX 1-Project Tools.xlsx - Excel
File
Home
Insert
Page Layout
Formulas
Data
Review
View
Tell me what you want to do...
Your Name
Share
C14
=SUM(C4:C13)
Your Name
Project Tools
Item
Sale Price
Quantity
Total Value
Rubber Mallet 11.98 35 419.3
Hex Set 14.95 19 284.05
Sandpaper 4.75 29 137.75
Ratchet Set 17 32 544
Mag Nut Driver 14.98 6 89.88
Cordless Drill 192 12 2304
Tool Bag 15 12 180
Tool Holster 16.75 18 301.5
Safety Goggles 29.95 15 449.25
Glass Cutter 2.98 17 50.66
Total 320.34 195
Click to add data
Your formulas go here

Working with Formulas and Functions

CASE ▶ Yolanda Lee, the vice president of finance at Reason2Go, needs to analyze tour expenses for the current year. She has asked you to prepare a worksheet that summarizes this expense data and includes some statistical analysis. She would also like you to perform some what-if analysis, to see what quarterly expenses would look like with various projected increases.

Module Objectives

After completing this module, you will be able to:

- Create a complex formula
- Insert a function
- Type a function
- Copy and move cell entries
- Understand relative and absolute cell references
- Copy formulas with relative cell references
- Copy formulas with absolute cell references
- Round a value with a function

Files You Will Need

EX 2-1.xlsx	EX 2-3.xlsx
EX 2-2.xlsx	EX 2-4.xlsx

Create a Complex Formula

A **complex formula** is one that uses more than one arithmetic operator. You might, for example, need to create a formula that uses addition and multiplication. In formulas containing more than one arithmetic operator, Excel uses the standard **order of precedence** rules to determine which operation to perform first. You can change the order of precedence in a formula by using parentheses around the part you want to calculate first. For example, the formula =4+2*5 equals 14, because the order of precedence dictates that multiplication is performed before addition. However, the formula =(4+2)*5 equals 30, because the parentheses cause 4+2 to be calculated first. **CASE** *You want to create a formula that calculates a 20% increase in tour expenses.*

STEPS

1. **Start Excel, open the file EX 2-1.xlsx from the location where you store your Data Files, then save it as EX 2-R2G Tour Expense Analysis**

2. **Select the range B4:B11, click the Quick Analysis tool 📊 that appears below the selection, then click the Totals tab**

   The Totals tab in the Quick Analysis tool displays commonly used functions, as seen in **FIGURE 2-1**.

3. **Click the AutoSum button Σ in the Quick Analysis tool**

   The newly calculated value displays in cell B12 and has bold formatting automatically applied, helping to set it off as a sum. This shading is temporary, and will not appear after you click a cell.

4. **Click cell B12, then drag the fill handle to cell E12**

   The formula in cell B12, as well as the bold formatting, is copied to cells C12:E12.

5. **Click cell B14, type =, click cell B12, then type +**

   In this first part of the formula, you are inserting a reference to the cell that contains total expenses for Quarter 1.

6. **Click cell B12, then type *.2**

   The second part of this formula adds a 20% increase (B12*.2) to the original value of the cell (the total expenses for Quarter 1).

7. **Click the Enter button ✓ on the formula bar**

   The result, 42749.58, appears in cell B14.

8. **Press [Tab], type =, click cell C12, type +, click cell C12, type *.2, then click ✓**

   The result, 42323.712, appears in cell C14.

9. **Drag the fill handle from cell C14 to cell E14, then save your work**

   The calculated values appear in the selected range, as shown in **FIGURE 2-2**. Dragging the fill handle on a cell copies the cell's contents or continues a series of data (such as Quarter 1, Quarter 2, etc.) into adjacent cells. This option is called **Auto Fill**.

Using Add-ins to improve worksheet functionality

Excel has more functionality than simple and complex math computations. Using the My Add-ins feature (found in the Add-ins group in the Insert tab), you can insert an add-in into your worksheet that accesses the web and adds functionality. Many of the add-ins are free or available for a small fee and can be used to create an email, appointment, meeting, contact, or task, or be a reference source, such as the Mini Calendar or Date Picker. When you click the My Add-ins button list arrow, you'll see any Recently Used Add-ins. Click See All to display the featured Add-ins for Office and to go to the Store to view available add-ins. When you find one you want, make sure you're logged in to Office.com, click the add-in, click Trust It, and the add-in will be installed. Click the My Add-ins button and your add-in should display under Recently Used Add-ins. Click it, then click Insert. The add-in will display in the Recently Used Add-ins pane when you click the My Add-ins button.

FIGURE 2-1: Totals tab in the Quick Analysis tool

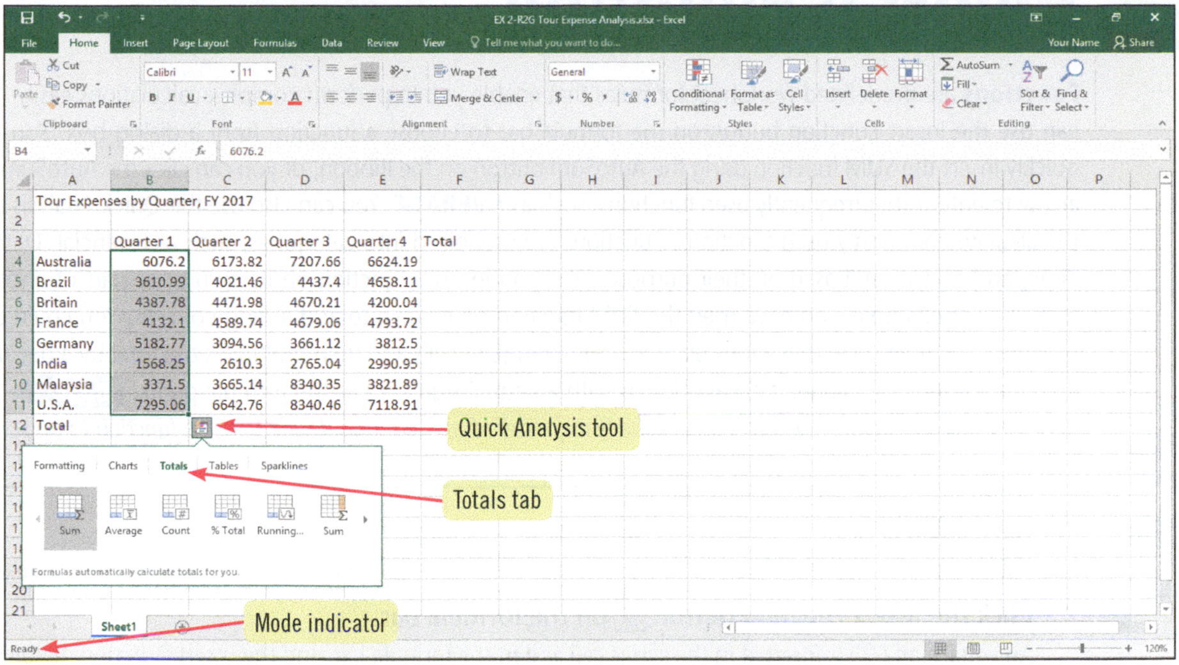

FIGURE 2-2: Results of copied formulas

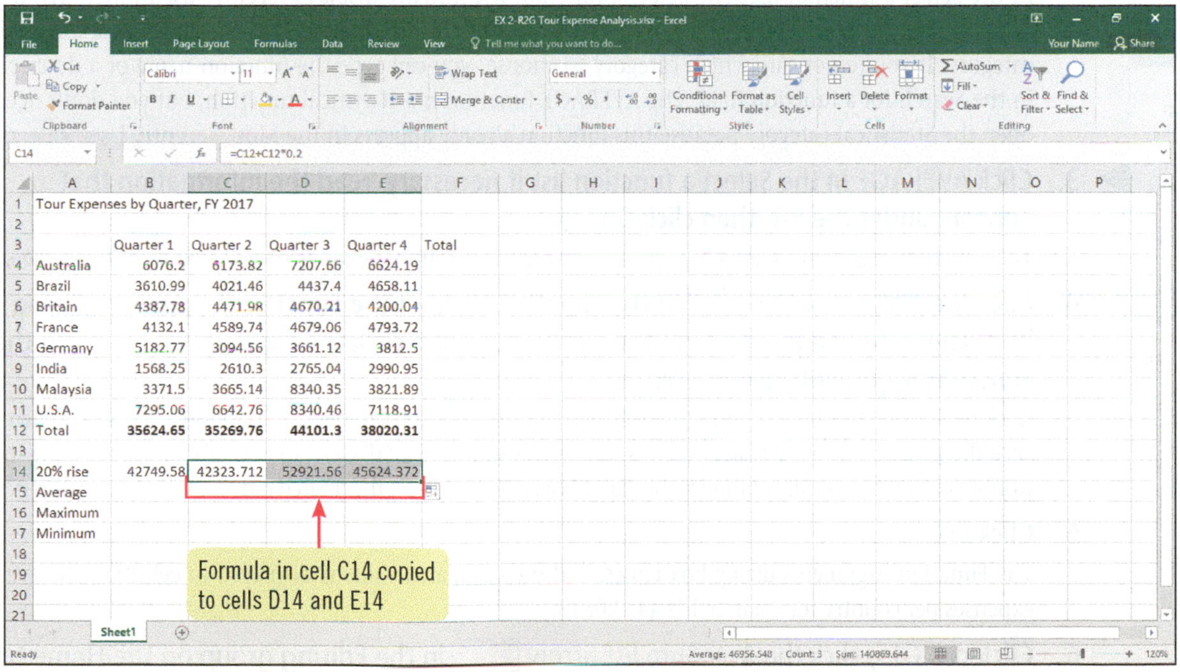

Reviewing the order of precedence

When you work with formulas that contain more than one operator, the order of precedence is very important because it affects the final value. If a formula contains two or more operators, such as 4+.55/4000*25, Excel performs the calculations in a particular sequence based on the following rules: Operations inside parentheses are calculated before any other operations. Reference operators (such as ranges) are calculated first. Exponents are calculated next, then any multiplication and division—progressing from left to right. Finally, addition and subtraction are calculated from left to right. In the example 4+.55/4000*25, Excel performs the arithmetic operations by first dividing .55 by 4000, then multiplying the result by 25, then adding 4. You can change the order of calculations by using parentheses. For example, in the formula (4+.55)/4000*25, Excel would first add 4 and .55, then divide that amount by 4000, then finally multiply by 25.

Working with Formulas and Functions

Insert a Function

Learning Outcomes
- Use the Insert Function button
- Select a range for use in a function
- Select a function from the AutoSum list arrow

Functions are predefined worksheet formulas that enable you to perform complex calculations easily. You can use the Insert Function button on the formula bar to choose a function from a dialog box. You can quickly insert the SUM function using the AutoSum button on the Ribbon, or you can click the AutoSum list arrow to enter other frequently used functions, such as **AVERAGE**. You can also use the Quick Analysis tool to calculate commonly used functions. Functions are organized into categories, such as Financial, Date & Time, and Statistical, based on their purposes. You can insert a function on its own or as part of another formula. For example, you have used the SUM function on its own to add a range of cells. You could also use the SUM function within a formula that adds a range of cells and then multiplies the total by a decimal. If you use a function alone, it always begins with an equal sign (=) as the formula prefix. **CASE** *You need to calculate the average expenses for the first quarter of the year and decide to use a function to do so.*

STEPS

QUICK TIP

When using the Insert Function button or the AutoSum list arrow, it is not necessary to type the equal sign (=); Excel adds it as necessary.

1. **Click cell B15**

   This is the cell where you want to enter a calculation that averages expenses per country for the first quarter.

2. **Click the Insert Function button 𝑓ₓ on the formula bar**

   An equal sign (=) is inserted in the active cell and in the formula bar, and the Insert Function dialog box opens, as shown in **FIGURE 2-3**. In this dialog box, you specify the function you want to use by clicking it in the Select a function list. The Select a function list initially displays recently used functions. If you don't see the function you want, you can click the Or select a category list arrow to choose the desired category. If you're not sure which category to choose, you can type the function name or a description in the Search for a function field. The AVERAGE function is a statistical function, but you don't need to open the Statistical category because this function already appears in the Most Recently Used category.

QUICK TIP

To learn about a function, click it in the Select a function list. The arguments and format required for the function appear below the list.

3. **Click AVERAGE in the Select a function list if necessary, read the information that appears under the list, then click OK**

   The Function Arguments dialog box opens, in which you define the range of cells you want to average.

QUICK TIP

When selecting a range, remember to select all the cells between and including the two references in the range.

4. **Click the Collapse button 📉 in the Number1 field of the Function Arguments dialog box, select the range B4:B11 in the worksheet, then click the Expand button 📈 in the Function Arguments dialog box**

   Clicking the Collapse button minimizes the dialog box so that you can select cells in the worksheet. When you click the Expand button, the dialog box is restored, as shown in **FIGURE 2-4**. You can also begin dragging in the worksheet to automatically minimize the dialog box; after you select the desired range, the dialog box is restored.

5. **Click OK**

   The Function Arguments dialog box closes, and the calculated value is displayed in cell B15. The average expenses per country for Quarter 1 is 4453.0813.

6. **Click cell C15, click the AutoSum list arrow Σ ▾ in the Editing group on the Home tab, then click Average**

   A ScreenTip beneath cell C15 displays the arguments needed to complete the function. The text "number1" is in boldface, telling you that the next step is to supply the first cell in the group you want to average.

7. **Select the range C4:C11 in the worksheet, then click the Enter button ✓ on the formula bar**

   The average expenses per country for the second quarter appear in cell C15.

8. **Drag the fill handle from cell C15 to cell E15**

   The formula in cell C15 is copied to the rest of the selected range, as shown in **FIGURE 2-5**.

9. **Save your work**

FIGURE 2-3: Insert Function dialog box

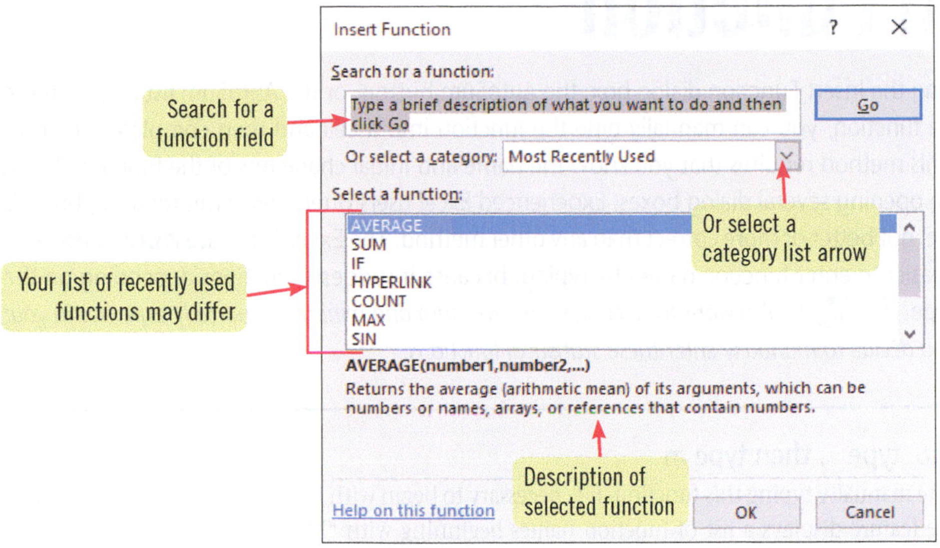

Search for a function field →

Your list of recently used functions may differ →

Or select a category list arrow

Description of selected function

FIGURE 2-4: Expanded Function Arguments dialog box

Function in formula bar

Insert Function button

Argument

Sum list arrow

Drag title bar of dialog box to move it if necessary

Collapse button

Description of function and arguments

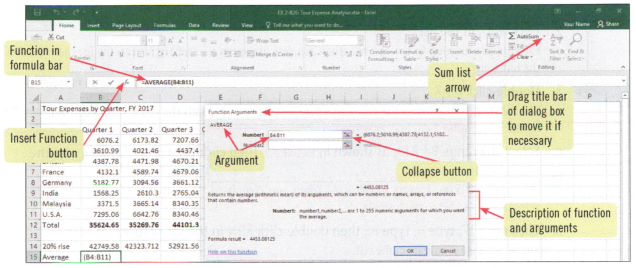

FIGURE 2-5: Average functions used in worksheet

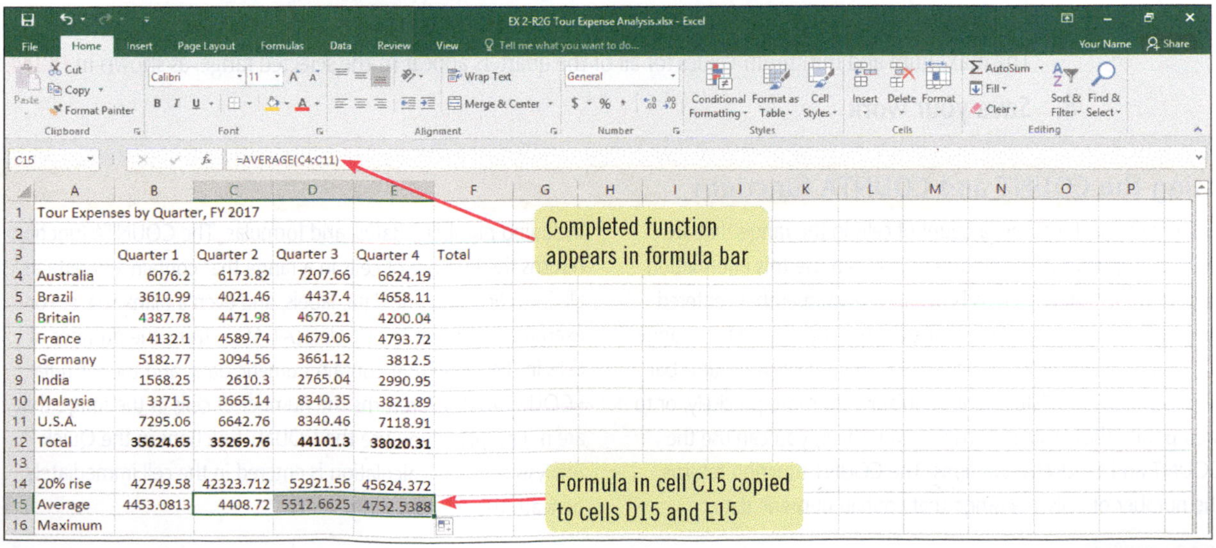

Completed function appears in formula bar

Formula in cell C15 copied to cells D15 and E15

Excel 2016

Learning Outcomes
- Select a function by typing
- Use AutoComplete to copy formulas

Type a Function

In addition to using the Insert Function dialog box, the AutoSum button, or the AutoSum list arrow on the Ribbon to enter a function, you can manually type the function into a cell and then complete the arguments needed. This method requires that you know the name and initial characters of the function, but it can be faster than opening several dialog boxes. Experienced Excel users often prefer this method, but it is only an alternative, not better or more correct than any other method. The Excel **Formula AutoComplete** feature makes it easier to enter function names by typing, because it suggests functions depending on the first letters you type. **CASE** *You want to calculate the maximum and minimum quarterly expenses in your worksheet, and you decide to manually enter these statistical functions.*

STEPS

1. **Click cell B16, type =, then type m**

   Because you are manually typing this function, it is necessary to begin with the equal sign (=). The Formula AutoComplete feature displays a list of function names beginning with "M" beneath cell B16. Once you type an equal sign in a cell, each letter you type acts as a trigger to activate the Formula AutoComplete feature. This feature minimizes the amount of typing you need to do to enter a function and reduces typing and syntax errors.

2. **Click MAX in the list**

   Clicking any function in the Formula AutoComplete list opens a ScreenTip next to the list that describes the function.

3. **Double-click MAX**

   The function is inserted in the cell, and a ScreenTip appears beneath the cell to help you complete the formula. See **FIGURE 2-6**.

4. **Select the range B4:B11, as shown in FIGURE 2-7, then click the Enter button ☑ on the formula bar**

   The result, 7295.06, appears in cell B16. When you completed the entry, the closing parenthesis was automatically added to the formula.

5. **Click cell B17, type =, type m, then double-click MIN in the list of function names**

   The MIN function appears in the cell.

6. **Select the range B4:B11, then press [Enter]**

   The result, 1568.25, appears in cell B17.

7. **Select the range B16:B17, then drag the fill handle from cell B17 to cell E17**

   The maximum and minimum values for all of the quarters appear in the selected range, as shown in **FIGURE 2-8**.

8. **Save your work**

Using the COUNT and COUNTA functions

When you select a range, a count of cells in the range that are not blank appears in the status bar. You can use this information to determine things such as how many team members entered project hours in a worksheet. For example, if you select the range A1:A5 and only cells A1, A4, and A5 contain data, the status bar displays "Count: 3." To count nonblank cells more precisely, or to incorporate these calculations in a worksheet, you can use the COUNT and COUNTA functions. The COUNT function returns the number of cells in a range that contain numeric data, including numbers, dates, and formulas. The COUNTA function returns the number of cells in a range that contain any data at all, including numeric data, labels, and even a blank space. For example, the formula =COUNT(A1:A5) returns the number of cells in the range that contain numeric data, and the formula =COUNTA(A1:A5) returns the number of cells in the range that are not empty. If you use the COUNT functions in the Quick Analysis tool, the calculation is entered in the cell immediately beneath the selected range.

FIGURE 2-6: MAX function in progress

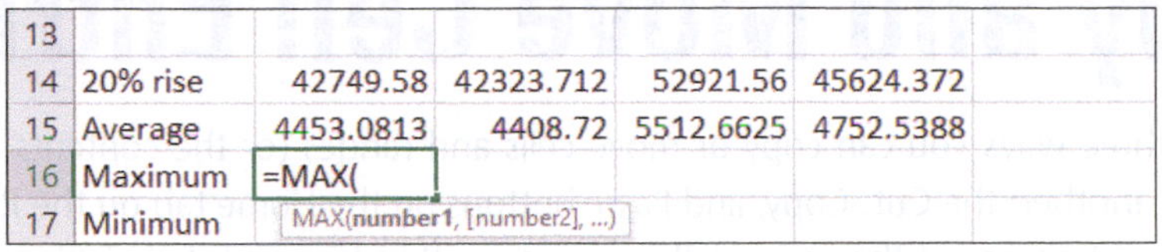

13					
14	20% rise	42749.58	42323.712	52921.56	45624.372
15	Average	4453.0813	4408.72	5512.6625	4752.5388
16	Maximum	=MAX(			
17	Minimum	MAX(**number1**, [number2], ...)			

FIGURE 2-7: Completing the MAX function

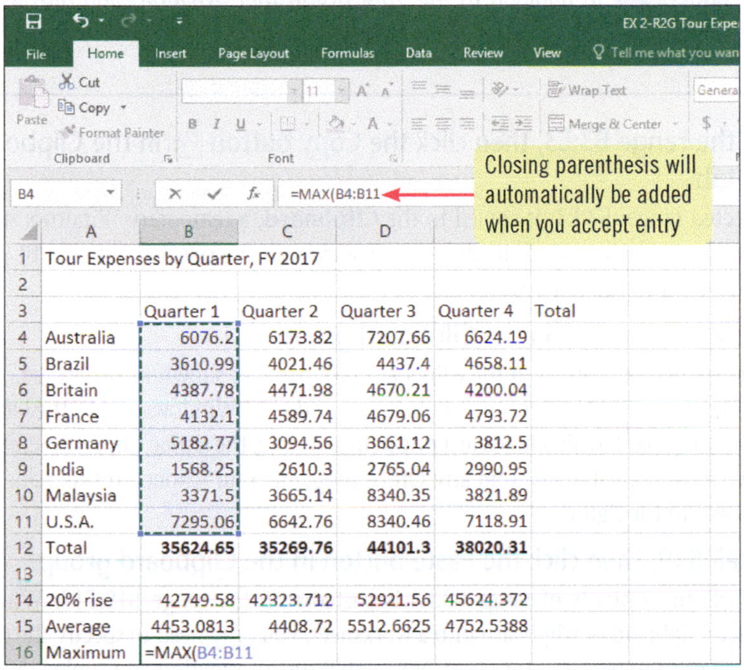

Closing parenthesis will automatically be added when you accept entry

B4 ... =MAX(B4:B11

1	Tour Expenses by Quarter, FY 2017					
	A	B	C	D		
1	Tour Expenses by Quarter, FY 2017					
2						
3		Quarter 1	Quarter 2	Quarter 3	Quarter 4	Total
4	Australia	6076.2	6173.82	7207.66	6624.19	
5	Brazil	3610.99	4021.46	4437.4	4658.11	
6	Britain	4387.78	4471.98	4670.21	4200.04	
7	France	4132.1	4589.74	4679.06	4793.72	
8	Germany	5182.77	3094.56	3661.12	3812.5	
9	India	1568.25	2610.3	2765.04	2990.95	
10	Malaysia	3371.5	3665.14	8340.35	3821.89	
11	U.S.A.	7295.06	6642.76	8340.46	7118.91	
12	Total	35624.65	35269.76	44101.3	38020.31	
13						
14	20% rise	42749.58	42323.712	52921.56	45624.372	
15	Average	4453.0813	4408.72	5512.6625	4752.5388	
16	Maximum	=MAX(B4:B11				

FIGURE 2-8: Completed MAX and MIN functions

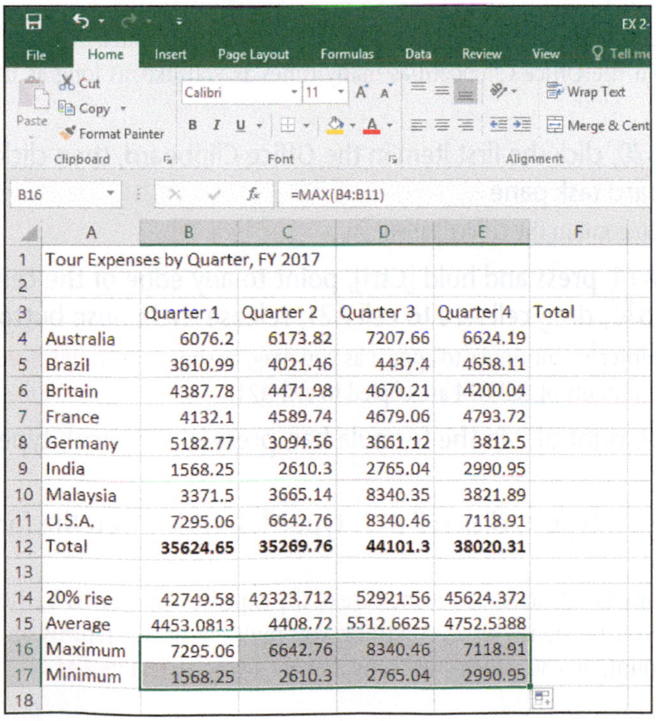

B16 ... =MAX(B4:B11)

	A	B	C	D	E	F
1	Tour Expenses by Quarter, FY 2017					
2						
3		Quarter 1	Quarter 2	Quarter 3	Quarter 4	Total
4	Australia	6076.2	6173.82	7207.66	6624.19	
5	Brazil	3610.99	4021.46	4437.4	4658.11	
6	Britain	4387.78	4471.98	4670.21	4200.04	
7	France	4132.1	4589.74	4679.06	4793.72	
8	Germany	5182.77	3094.56	3661.12	3812.5	
9	India	1568.25	2610.3	2765.04	2990.95	
10	Malaysia	3371.5	3665.14	8340.35	3821.89	
11	U.S.A.	7295.06	6642.76	8340.46	7118.91	
12	Total	35624.65	35269.76	44101.3	38020.31	
13						
14	20% rise	42749.58	42323.712	52921.56	45624.372	
15	Average	4453.0813	4408.72	5512.6625	4752.5388	
16	Maximum	7295.06	6642.76	8340.46	7118.91	
17	Minimum	1568.25	2610.3	2765.04	2990.95	
18						

Copy and Move Cell Entries

Learning
Outcomes
• Copy a range to
  the Clipboard
• Paste a Clipboard
  entry
• Empty cell contents
• Copy cell contents

There are three ways you can copy or move cells and ranges (or the contents within them) from one location to another: the Cut, Copy, and Paste buttons on the Home tab on the Ribbon; the fill handle in the lower-right corner of the active cell or range; or the drag-and-drop feature. When you copy cells, the original data remains in the original location; when you cut or move cells, the original data is deleted from its original location. You can also cut, copy, and paste cells or ranges from one worksheet to another. **CASE** ➤ *In addition to the 20% rise in tour expenses, you also want to show a 30% rise. Rather than retype this information, you copy and move selected cells.*

STEPS

1. **Select the range B3:E3, then click the Copy button 📋 in the Clipboard group on the Home tab**

   The selected range (B3:E3) is copied to the **Clipboard**, a temporary Windows storage area that holds the selections you copy or cut. A moving border surrounds the selected range until you press [Esc] or copy an additional item to the Clipboard.

2. **Click the launcher 🔽 in the Clipboard group**

   The Office Clipboard opens in the Clipboard task pane, as shown in **FIGURE 2-9**. When you copy or cut an item, it is cut or copied both to the Clipboard provided by Windows and to the Office Clipboard. Unlike the Windows Clipboard, which holds just one item at a time, the Office Clipboard contains up to 24 of the most recently cut or copied items from any Office program. Your Clipboard task pane may contain more items than shown in the figure.

3. **Click cell B19, then click the Paste button in the Clipboard group**

   A copy of the contents of range B3:E3 is pasted into the range B19:E19. When pasting an item from the Office Clipboard or Clipboard into a worksheet, you only need to specify the upper left cell of the range where you want to paste the selection. Notice that the information you copied remains in the original range B3:E3; if you had cut instead of copied, the information would have been deleted from its original location once it was pasted.

4. **Press [Delete]**

   The selected cells are empty. You have decided to paste the cells in a different row. You can repeatedly paste an item from the Office Clipboard as many times as you like, as long as the item remains in the Office Clipboard.

5. **Click cell B20, click the first item in the Office Clipboard, then click the Close button ❌ on the Clipboard task pane**

   Cells B20:E20 contain the copied labels.

6. **Click cell A14, press and hold [Ctrl], point to any edge of the cell until the pointer changes to ▷, drag cell A14 to cell A21, release the mouse button, then release [Ctrl]**

   The copy pointer ▷ continues to appear as you drag, as shown in **FIGURE 2-10**. When you release the mouse button, the contents of cell A14 are copied to cell A21.

7. **Click to the right of 2 in the formula bar, press [Backspace], type 3, then click the Enter button ✓**

8. **Click cell B21, type =, click cell B12, type *1.3, click ✓ on the formula bar, then save your work**

   This new formula calculates a 30% increase of the expenses for Quarter 1, though using a different method from what you previously used. Anything you multiply by 1.3 returns an amount that is 130% of the original amount, or a 30% increase. Compare your screen to **FIGURE 2-11**.

FIGURE 2-9: Copied data in Office Clipboard

FIGURE 2-9: Copied data in Office Clipboard

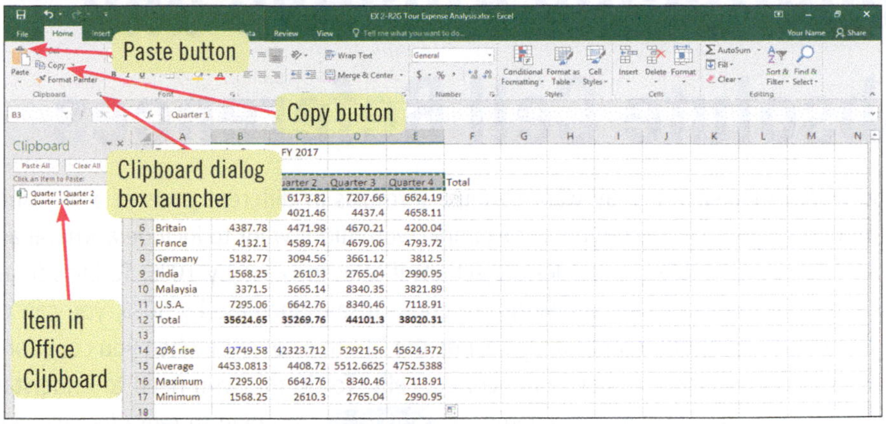

FIGURE 2-10: Copying cell contents with drag-and-drop

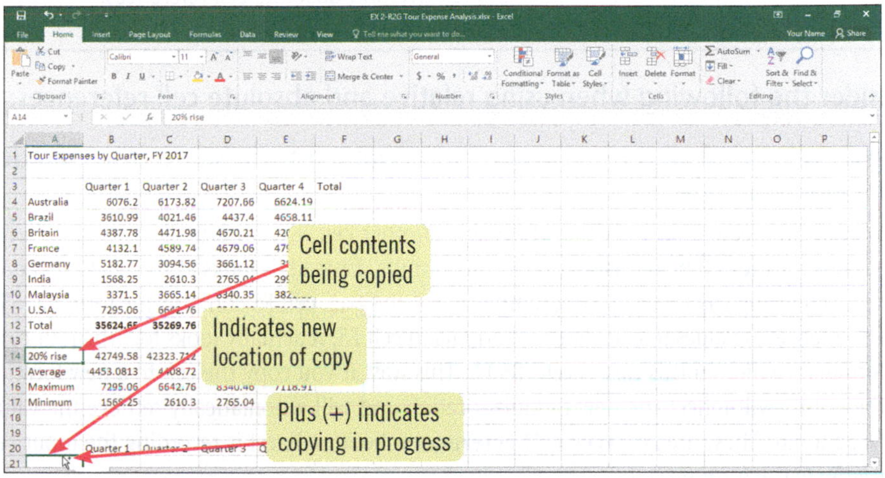

FIGURE 2-11: Formula entered to calculate a 30% increase

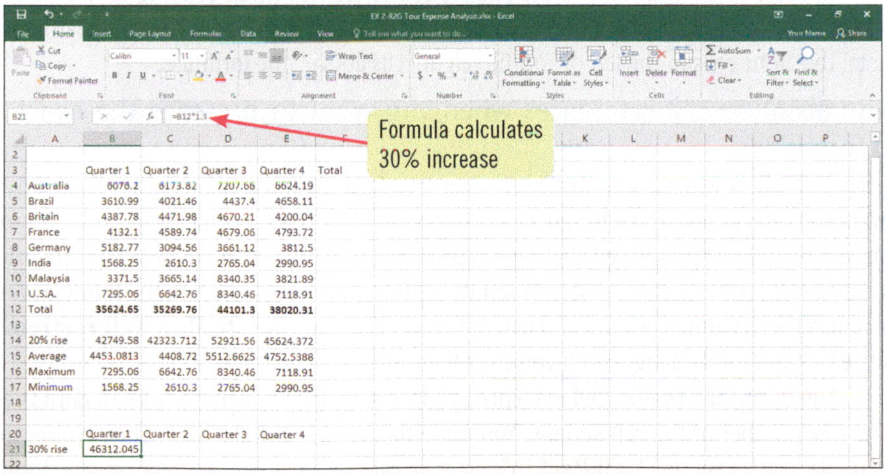

Inserting and deleting selected cells

As you add formulas to your workbook, you may need to insert or delete cells. When you do this, Excel automatically adjusts cell references to reflect their new locations. To insert cells, click the Insert list arrow in the Cells group on the Home tab, then click Insert Cells. The Insert dialog box opens, asking if you want to insert a cell and move the current active cell down or to the right of the new one. To delete one or more selected cells, click the Delete list arrow in the Cells group, click Delete Cells, and in the Delete dialog box, indicate which way you want to move the adjacent cells. When using this option, be careful not to disturb row or column alignment that may be necessary to maintain the accuracy of cell references in the worksheet. Click the Insert button or Delete button in the Cells group to insert or delete a single cell.

Learning
Outcomes
• Identify cell
  referencing
• Identify when to
  use absolute or
  relative cell
  references

Understand Relative and Absolute Cell References

As you work in Excel, you may want to reuse formulas in different parts of a worksheet to reduce the amount of data you have to retype. For example, you might want to include a what-if analysis in one part of a worksheet showing a set of sales projections if sales increase by 10%. To include another analysis in another part of the worksheet showing projections if sales increase by 50%, you can copy the formulas from one section to another and simply change the "1" to a "5". But when you copy formulas, it is important to make sure that they refer to the correct cells. To do this, you need to understand the difference between relative and absolute cell references. **CASE** ▶ *You plan to reuse formulas in different parts of your worksheets, so you want to understand relative and absolute cell references.*

DETAILS

Consider the following when using relative and absolute cell references:

• **Use relative references when you want to preserve the relationship to the formula location**

When you create a formula that references another cell, Excel normally does not "record" the exact cell address for the cell being referenced in the formula. Instead, it looks at the relationship that cell has to the cell containing the formula. For example, in **FIGURE 2-12**, cell F5 contains the formula: =SUM(B5:E5). When Excel retrieves values to calculate the formula in cell F5, it actually looks for "the four cells to the left of the formula," which in this case is cells B5:E5. This way, if you copy the cell to a new location, such as cell F6, the results will reflect the new formula location and will automatically retrieve the values in cells B6, C6, D6, and E6. These are **relative cell references**, because Excel is recording the input cells *in relation to* or *relative to* the formula cell.

In most cases, you want to use relative cell references when copying or moving, so this is the Excel default. In **FIGURE 2-12**, the formulas in cells F5:F12 and cells B13:F13 contain relative cell references. They total the "four cells to the left of" or the "eight cells above" the formulas.

• **Use absolute cell references when you want to preserve the exact cell address in a formula**

There are times when you want Excel to retrieve formula information from a specific cell, and you don't want the cell address in the formula to change when you copy it to a new location. For example, you might have a price in a specific cell that you want to use in all formulas, regardless of their location. If you use relative cell referencing, the formula results would be incorrect, because the formula would reference a different cell every time you copy it. Therefore, you need to use an **absolute cell reference**, which is a reference that does not change when you copy the formula.

You create an absolute cell reference by placing a $ (dollar sign) in front of both the column letter and the row number of the cell address. You can either type the dollar sign when typing the cell address in a formula (for example, "=C12*$B$16") or you can select a cell address on the formula bar and then press [F4], and the dollar signs are added automatically. **FIGURE 2-13** shows formulas containing both absolute and relative references. The formulas in cells B19 to E26 use absolute cell references to refer to a potential sales increase of 50%, shown in cell B16.

FIGURE 2-12: Formulas containing relative references

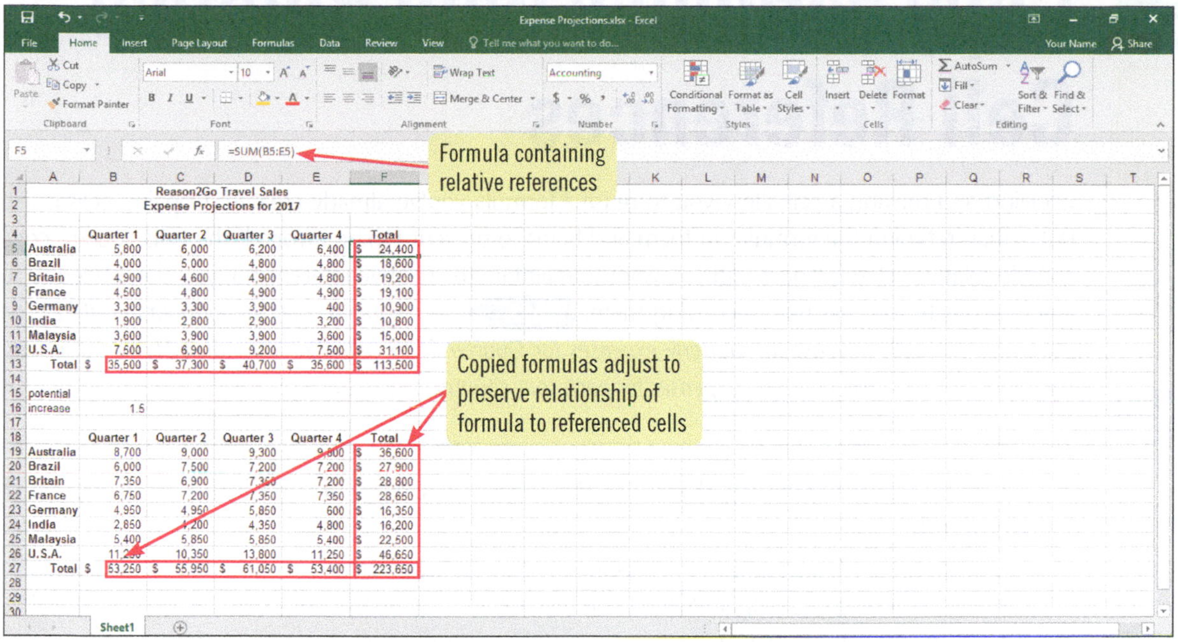

FIGURE 2-13: Formulas containing absolute and relative references

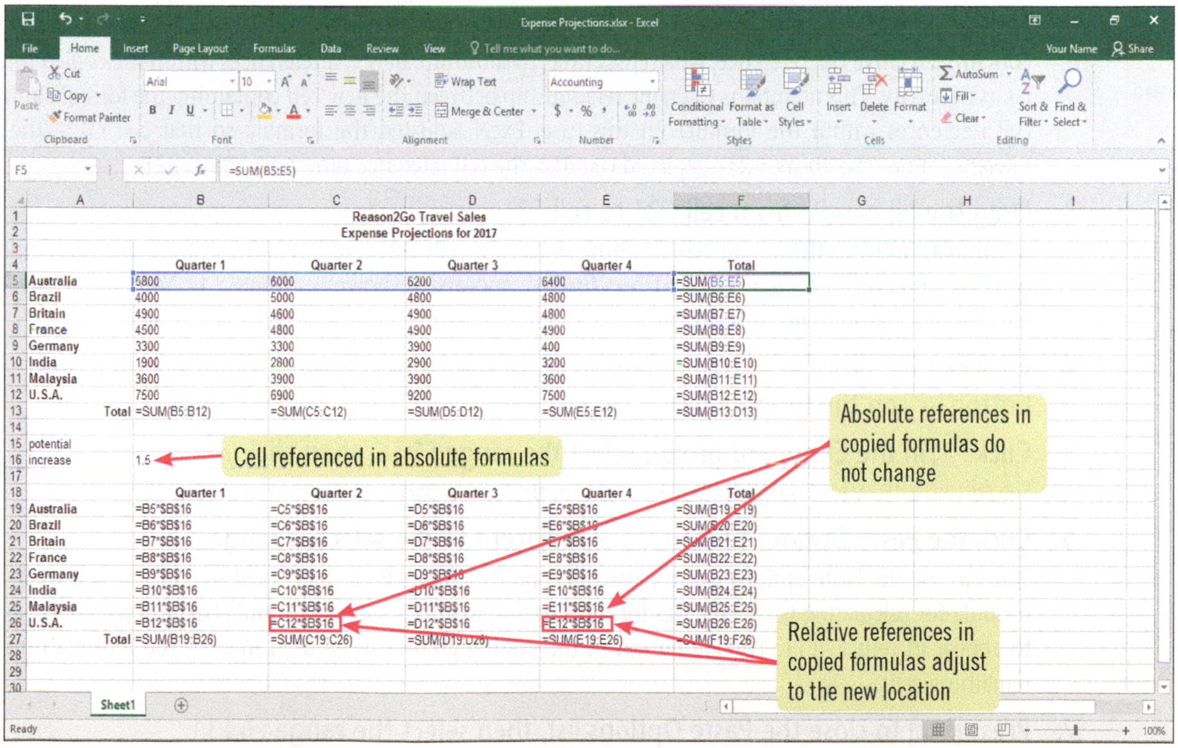

Using a mixed reference

Sometimes when you copy a formula, you want to change the row reference, but keep the column reference the same. This type of cell referencing combines elements of both absolute and relative referencing and is called a **mixed reference**. For example, when copied, a formula containing the mixed reference C$14 would change the column letter relative to its new location, but not the row number. In the mixed reference $C14, the column letter would not change, but the row number would be updated relative to its location. Like an absolute reference, a mixed reference can be created by pressing the [F4] function key with the cell reference selected. With each press of the [F4] key, you cycle through all the possible combinations of relative, absolute, and mixed references (C14, $C$14, C$14, and $C14).

Copy Formulas with Relative Cell References

Learning Outcomes
• Copy and Paste formulas with relative cell references
• Examine Auto Fill and Paste Options
• Use the Fill button

Copying and moving a cell allow you to reuse a formula you've already created. Copying cells is usually faster than retyping the formulas in them and helps to prevent typing errors. If the cells you are copying contain relative cell references and you want to maintain the relative referencing, you don't need to make any changes to the cells before copying them. **CASE** ▶ *You want to copy the formula in cell B21, which calculates the 30% increase in quarterly expenses for Quarter 1, to cells C21 through E21. You also want to create formulas to calculate total expenses for each tour country.*

STEPS

1. **Click cell B21 if necessary, then click the Copy button 📋 in the Clipboard group on the Home tab**

   The formula for calculating the 30% expense increase during Quarter 1 is copied to the Clipboard. Notice that the formula =B12*1.3 appears in the formula bar, and a moving border surrounds the active cell.

QUICK TIP

To paste only specific components of a copied cell or range, click the Paste list arrow in the Clipboard group, then click Paste Special. You can selectively copy formats, formulas, values, comments, and validation rules; transpose columns and rows; paste a link; or add, subtract, multiply, or divide using the Paste Special dialog box.

2. **Click cell C21, then click the Paste button 📋** *(not the list arrow)* **in the Clipboard group**

   The formula from cell B21 is copied into cell C21, where the new result of 45850.688 appears. Notice in the formula bar that the cell references have changed so that cell C12 is referenced instead of B12. This formula contains a relative cell reference, which tells Excel to substitute new cell references within the copied formulas as necessary. This maintains the same relationship between the new cell containing the formula and the cell references within the formula. In this case, Excel adjusted the formula so that cell C12—the cell reference nine rows above C21—replaced cell B12, the cell reference nine rows above B21.

3. **Drag the fill handle from cell C21 to cell E21**

   A formula similar to the one in cell C21 now appears in cells D21 and E21. After you use the fill handle to copy cell contents, the **Auto Fill Options button** appears, as shown in **FIGURE 2-14**. You can use the Auto Fill Options button to fill the cells with only specific elements of the copied cell if you wish.

4. **Click cell F4, click the AutoSum button Σ in the Editing group, then click the Enter button ✓ on the formula bar**

5. **Click 📋 in the Clipboard group, select the range F5:F6, then click 📋**

   See **FIGURE 2-15**. After you click the Paste button, the **Paste Options button** appears.

6. **Click the Paste Options button 📋 (Ctrl)▾ adjacent to the selected range**

   You can use the Paste options list to paste only specific elements of the copied selection if you wish. The formula for calculating total expenses for tours in Britain appears in the formula bar. You would like totals to appear in cells F7:F11. The Fill button in the Editing group can be used to copy the formula into the remaining cells.

7. **Press [Esc] to close the Paste Options list, then select the range F6:F11**

8. **Click the Fill button 🔽 in the Editing group, then click Down**

   The formulas containing relative references are copied to each cell. Compare your worksheet to **FIGURE 2-16**.

9. **Save your work**

FIGURE 2-14: Formula copied using the fill handle

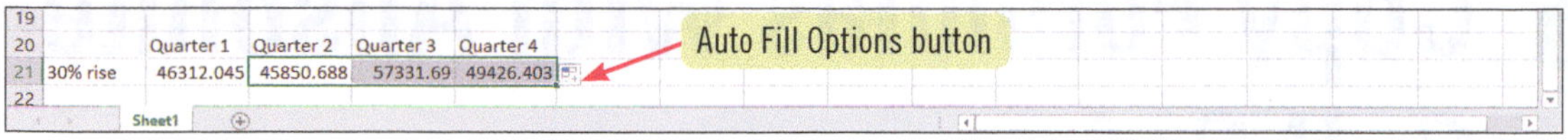

	Quarter 1	Quarter 2	Quarter 3	Quarter 4	
19					
20					
21 30% rise	46312.045	45850.688	57331.69	49426.403	⟵ Auto Fill Options button
22					

FIGURE 2-15: Formulas pasted in the range F5:F6

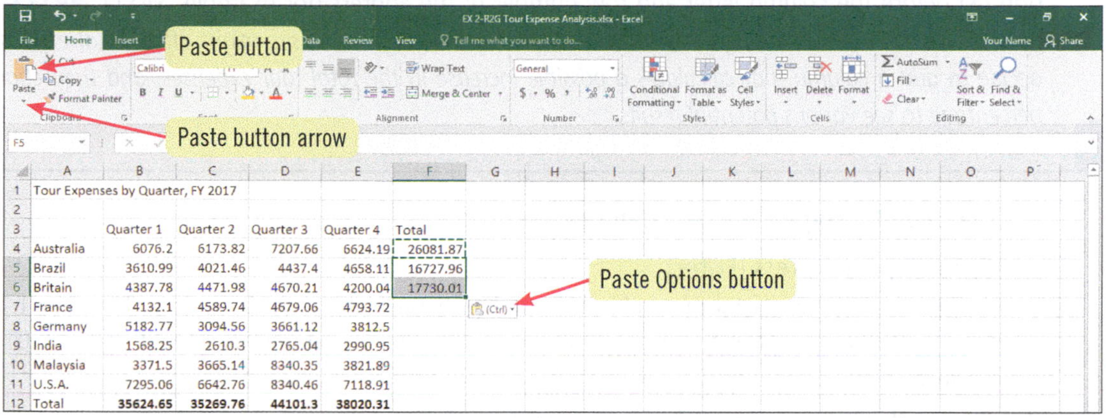

Paste button

Paste button arrow

Paste Options button

FIGURE 2-16: Formula copied using Fill Down

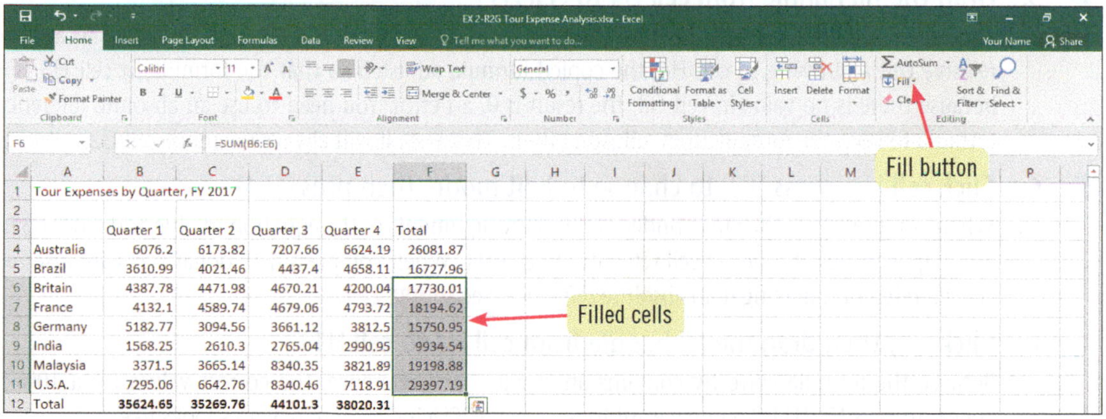

Fill button

Filled cells

Using Paste Preview

You can selectively copy formulas, values, or other choices using the Paste list arrow, and you can see how the pasted contents will look using the Paste Preview feature. When you click the Paste list arrow, a gallery of paste option icons opens. When you point to an icon, a preview of how the content will be pasted using that option is shown in the worksheet. Options include pasting values only, pasting values with number formatting, pasting formulas only, pasting formatting only, pasting transposed data so that column data appears in rows and row data appears in columns, and pasting with no borders (to remove any borders around pasted cells).

Copy Formulas with Absolute Cell References

Learning Outcomes
• Create an absolute cell reference
• Use the fill handle to copy absolute cell references

When copying cells, you might want one or more cell references in a formula to remain unchanged. In such an instance, you need to apply an absolute cell reference before copying the formula to preserve the specific cell address when the formula is copied. You create an absolute reference by placing a dollar sign ($) before the column letter and row number of the address (for example, $A$1). **CASE** *You need to do some what-if analysis to see how various percentage increases might affect total expenses. You decide to add a column that calculates a possible increase in the total tour expenses, and then change the percentage to see various potential results.*

STEPS

1. **Click cell G1, type Change, then press [Enter]**

2. **Type 1.1, then press [Enter]**

   You store the increase factor that will be used in the what-if analysis in this cell (G2). The value 1.1 can be used to calculate a 10% increase: anything you multiply by 1.1 returns an amount that is 110% of the original amount.

3. **Click cell H3, type What if?, then press [Enter]**

4. **In cell H4, type =, click cell F4, type *, click cell G2, then click the Enter button ☑ on the formula bar**

   The result, 28690.1, appears in cell H4. This value represents the total annual expenses for Australia if there is a 10% increase. You want to perform a what-if analysis for all the tour countries.

5. **Drag the fill handle from cell H4 to cell H11**

   The resulting values in the range H5:H11 are all zeros, which is not the result you wanted. Because you used relative cell addressing in cell H4, the copied formula adjusted so that the formula in cell H5 is =F5*G3; because there is no value in cell G3, the result is 0, an error. You need to use an absolute reference in the formula to keep the formula from adjusting itself. That way, it will always reference cell G2.

6. **Click cell H4, press [F2] to change to Edit mode, then press [F4]**

   When you press [F2], the range finder outlines the arguments of the equation in blue and red. The insertion point appears next to the G2 cell reference in cell H4. When you press [F4], dollar signs are inserted in the G2 cell reference, making it an absolute reference. See **FIGURE 2-17**.

7. **Click ☑, then drag the fill handle from cell H4 to cell H11**

   Because the formula correctly contains an absolute cell reference, the correct values for a 10% increase appear in cells H4:H11. You now want to see what a 20% increase in expenses looks like.

8. **Click cell G2, type 1.2, then click ☑**

   The values in the range H4:H11 change to reflect the 20% increase. Compare your worksheet to **FIGURE 2-18**.

9. **Save your work**

FIGURE 2-17: Absolute reference created in formula

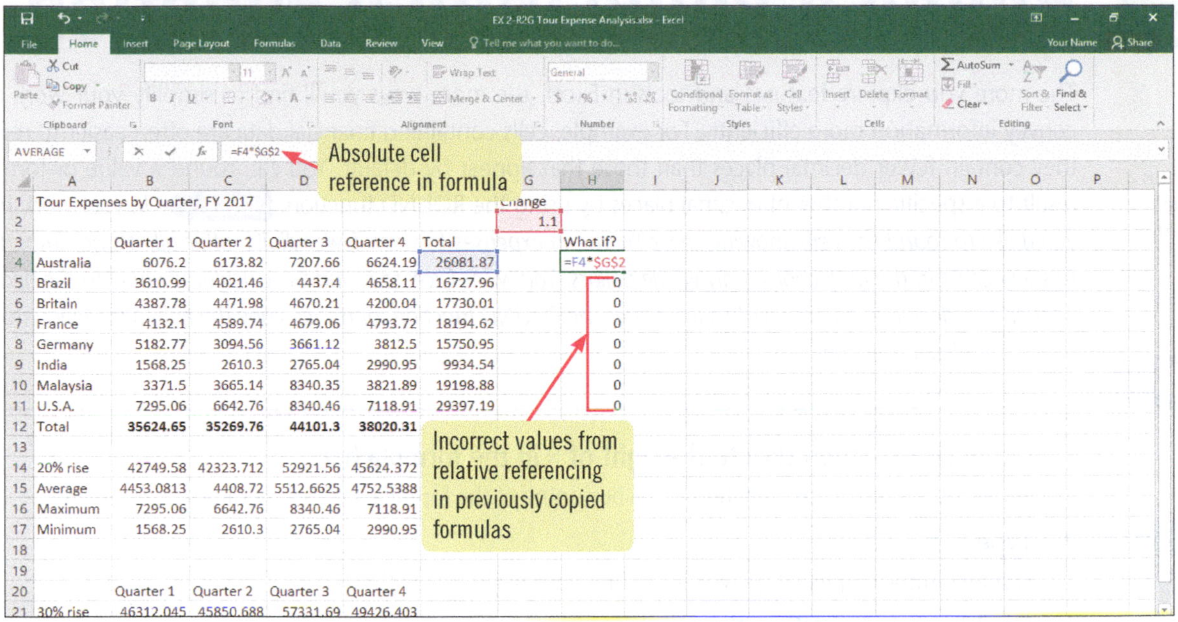

Absolute cell reference in formula

Incorrect values from relative referencing in previously copied formulas

FIGURE 2-18: What-if analysis with modified change factor

Modified change factor

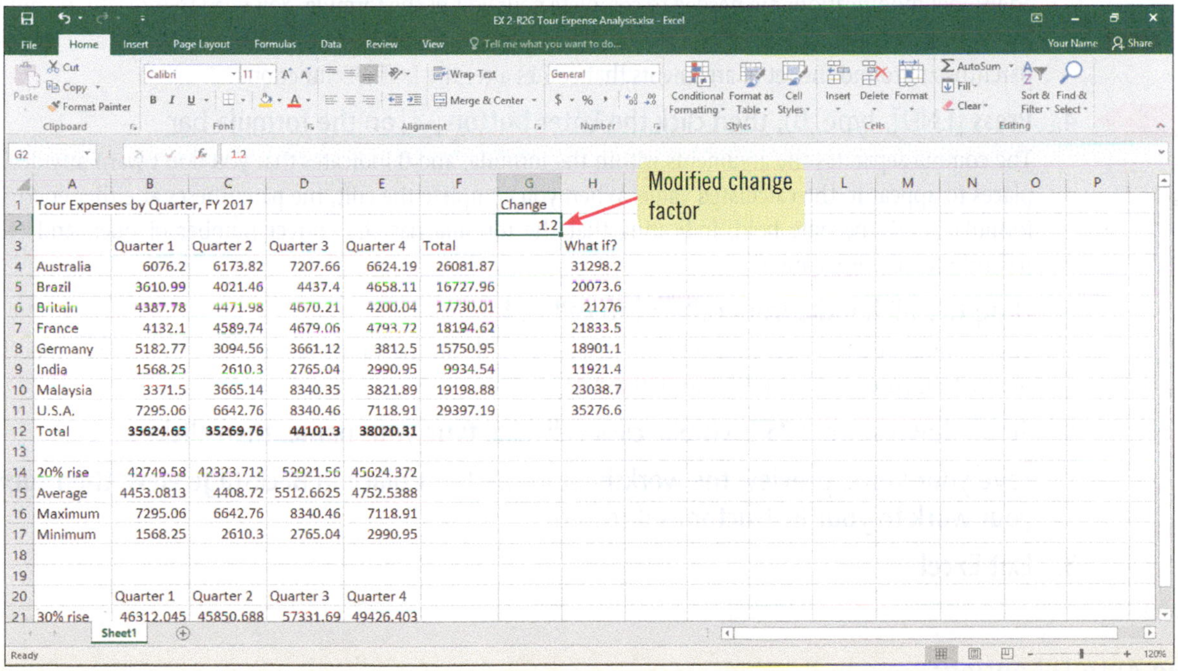

Using the fill handle for sequential text or values

Often, you need to fill cells with sequential text: months of the year, days of the week, years, or text plus a number (Quarter 1, Quarter 2,...). For example, you might want to create a worksheet that calculates data for every month of the year. Using the fill handle, you can quickly and easily create labels for the months of the year just by typing "January" in a cell. Drag the fill handle from the cell containing "January" until you have all the monthly labels you need. You can also easily fill cells with a date sequence by dragging the fill handle on a single cell containing a date. You can fill cells with a number sequence (such as 1, 2, 3,...) by dragging the fill handle on a selection of two or more cells that contain the sequence. To create a number sequence using the value in a single cell, press and hold [Ctrl] as you drag the fill handle of the cell. As you drag the fill handle, Excel automatically extends the existing sequence into the additional cells. (The content of the last filled cell appears in the ScreenTip.) To choose from all the fill series options for the current selection, click the Fill button in the Editing group on the Home tab, then click Series to open the Series dialog box.

Round a Value with a Function

Learning Outcomes
- Use Formula AutoComplete to insert a function
- Copy an edited formula

The more you explore features and tools in Excel, the more ways you'll find to simplify your work and convey information more efficiently. For example, cells containing financial data are often easier to read if they contain fewer decimal places than those that appear by default. You can round a value or formula result to a specific number of decimal places by using the ROUND function. **CASE** ▶ *In your worksheet, you'd like to round the cells showing the 20% rise in expenses to show fewer digits; after all, it's not important to show cents in the projections, only whole dollars. You want Excel to round the calculated value to the nearest integer. You decide to edit cell B14 so it includes the ROUND function, and then copy the edited formula into the other formulas in this row.*

STEPS

1. **Click cell B14, then click to the right of = in the formula bar**

   You want to position the function at the beginning of the formula, before any values or arguments.

QUICK TIP

In the Insert Function dialog box, the ROUND function is in the Math & Trig category.

2. **Type RO**

   Formula AutoComplete displays a list of functions beginning with RO beneath the formula bar.

3. **Double-click ROUND in the functions list**

   The new function and an opening parenthesis are added to the formula, as shown in **FIGURE 2-19**. A few additional modifications are needed to complete your edit of the formula. You need to indicate the number of decimal places to which the function should round numbers, and you also need to add a closing parenthesis around the set of arguments that comes after the ROUND function.

TROUBLE

If you have too many or too few parentheses, the extraneous parenthesis is displayed in red, or a warning dialog box opens with a suggested solution to the error.

4. **Press [END], type ,0), then click the Enter button ☑ on the formula bar**

   The comma separates the arguments within the formula, and 0 indicates that you don't want any decimal places to appear in the calculated value. When you complete the edit, the parentheses at either end of the formula briefly become bold, indicating that the formula has the correct number of open and closed parentheses and is balanced.

5. **Drag the fill handle from cell B14 to cell E14**

   The formula in cell B14 is copied to the range C14:E14. All the values are rounded to display no decimal places. Compare your worksheet to **FIGURE 2-20**.

6. **Scroll down so row 25 is visible, click cell A25, type your name, then click ☑**

7. **Save your work, preview the worksheet in the Print place in Backstage view, then submit your work to your Instructor as directed**

8. **Exit Excel**

Using Auto Fill options

When you use the fill handle to copy cells, the Auto Fill Options button appears. Auto Fill options differ depending on what you are copying. If you had selected cells containing a series (such as "Monday" and "Tuesday") and then used the fill handle, you would see options for continuing the series (such as "Wednesday" and "Thursday") or for simply pasting the copied cells. Clicking the Auto Fill Options button opens a list that lets you choose from the following options: Copy Cells, Fill Series (if applicable), Fill Formatting Only, Fill Without Formatting, or Flash Fill. Choosing Copy Cells means that the cell's contents and its formatting will be copied. The Fill Formatting Only option copies only the formatting attributes, but not cell contents. The Fill Without Formatting option copies the cell contents, but no formatting attributes. Copy Cells is the default option when using the fill handle to copy a cell, so if you want to copy the cell's contents and its formatting, you can ignore the Auto Fill Options button. The Flash Fill option allows you to create customized fill ranges on the fly, such as 2, 4, 6, 8, 10, by entering at least two values in a pattern: Excel automatically senses the pattern.

FIGURE 2-19: ROUND function added to an existing formula

AVERAGE   =ROUND(B12+B12*0.2-

ROUND(number, num_digits)

> **ROUND function and opening parenthesis inserted in formula**

> **ScreenTip indicates needed arguments**

	A	B	C	D	E	F	G	H
1	Tour Expenses by Quarter, FY 2017						Change	
2								1.2
3		Quarter 1	Quarter 2	Quarter 3	Quarter 4	Total		What if?
4	Australia	6076.2	6173.82	7207.66	6624.19	26081.87		31298.2
5	Brazil	3610.99	4021.46	4437.4	4658.11	16727.96		20073.6
6	Britain	4387.78	4471.98	4670.21	4200.04	17730.01		21276
7	France	4132.1	4589.74	4679.06	4793.72	18194.62		21833.5
8	Germany	5182.77	3094.56	3661.12	3812.5	15750.95		18901.1
9	India	1568.25	2610.3	2765.04	2990.95	9934.54		11921.4
10	Malaysia	3371.5	3665.14	8340.35	3821.89	19198.88		23038.7
11	U.S.A.	7295.06	6642.76	8340.46	7118.91	29397.19		35276.6
12	Total	35624.65	35269.76	44101.3	38020.31			
13								
14	20% rise	=ROUND(B1	42323.712	52921.56	45624.372			
15	Average	4453.0813	4408.72	5512.6625	4752.5388			
16	Maximum	7295.06	6642.76	8340.46	7118.91			
17	Minimum	1568.25	2610.3	2765.04	2990.95			
18								
19								
20		Quarter 1	Quarter 2	Quarter 3	Quarter 4			
21	30% rise	46312.045	45850.688	57331.69	49426.403			

FIGURE 2-20: Completed worksheet

B14   =ROUND(B12+B12*0.2,0)

> **Function surrounds existing formula**

	A	B	C	D	E	F	G
1	Tour Expenses by Quarter, FY 2017						
2							
3		Quarter 1	Quarter 2	Quarter 3	Quarter 4	Total	What if?
4	Australia	6076.2	6173.82	7207.66	6624.19	26081.87	31298.2
5	Brazil	3610.99	4021.46	4437.4	4658.11	16727.96	20073.6
6	Britain	4387.78	4471.98	4670.21	4200.04	17730.01	21276
7	France	4132.1	4589.74	4679.06	4793.72	18194.62	21833.5
8	Germany	5182.77	3094.56	3661.12	3812.5	15750.95	18901.1
9	India	1568.25	2610.3	2765.04	2990.95	9934.54	11921.4
10	Malaysia	3371.5	3665.14	8340.35	3821.89	19198.88	23038.7
11	U.S.A.	7295.06	6642.76	8340.46	7118.91	29397.19	35276.6
12	Total	35624.65	35269.76	44101.3	38020.31		
13							
14	20% rise	42750	42324	52922	45624		
15	Average	4453.0813	4408.72	5512.6625	4752.5388		
16	Maximum	7295.06	6642.76	8340.46	7118.91		
17	Minimum	1568.25	2610.3	2765.04	2990.95		
18							
19							
20		Quarter 1	Quarter 2	Quarter 3	Quarter 4		
21	30% rise	46312.045	45850.688	57331.69	49426.403		

> **Calculated values with no decimals**

Creating a new workbook using a template

Excel **templates** are predesigned workbook files intended to save time when you create common documents such as balance sheets, budgets, or time cards. Templates contain labels, values, formulas, and formatting, so all you have to do is customize them with your own information. Excel comes with many templates, and you can also create your own or find additional templates on the web. Unlike a typical workbook, which has the file extension .xlsx, a template has the extension .xltx. To create a workbook using a template, click the File tab, then click New on the navigation bar. The New place in Backstage view displays thumbnails of some of the many templates available. The Blank workbook template is selected by default and is used to create a blank workbook with no content or special formatting. To select a different template, click one of the selections in the New place, view the preview, then click Create. **FIGURE 2-21** shows an example. (Your available templates may differ.) When you click

Create, a new workbook is created based on the template; when you save the new file in the default format, it has the regular .xlsx extension. To save a workbook of your own as a template, open the Save As dialog box, click the Save as type list arrow, then change the file type to Excel Template.

FIGURE 2-21: Previewing the Budget Planner template

Working with Formulas and Functions

Practice

Concepts Review

Label each element of the Excel worksheet window shown in FIGURE 2-22.

FIGURE 2-22

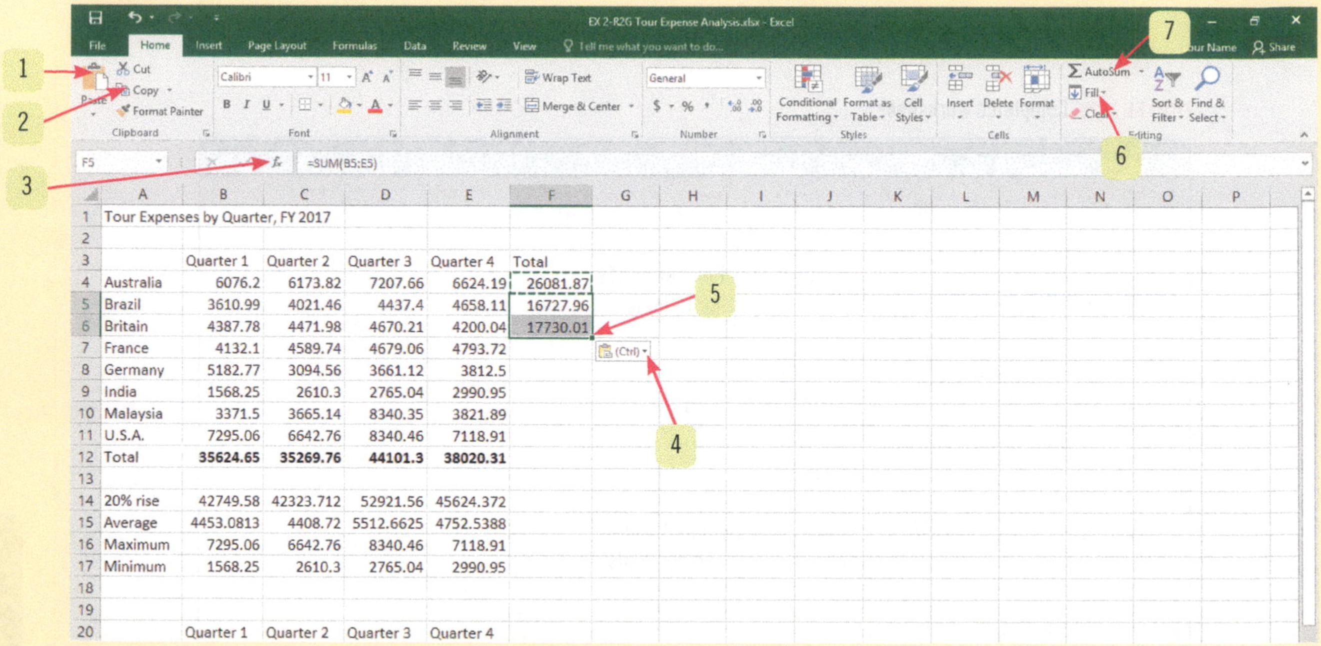

Match each term or button with the statement that best describes it.

8. Launcher
9. Fill handle
10. Drag-and-drop method
11. Formula AutoComplete
12. [Delete] key

a. Clears the contents of selected cells
b. Item on the Ribbon that opens a dialog box or task pane
c. Lets you move or copy data from one cell to another without using the Clipboard
d. Displays an alphabetical list of functions from which you can choose
e. Lets you copy cell contents or continue a series of data into a range of selected cells

Select the best answer from the list of choices.

13. You can use any of the following features to enter a new function *except*:

   a. Insert Function button.

   b. Formula AutoComplete.

   c. AutoSum list arrow.

   d. Clipboard.

14. Which key do you press and hold to copy while dragging and dropping selected cells?

   a. [Alt]

   b. [Ctrl]

   c. [F2]

   d. [Tab]

15. What type of cell reference is C$19?

   a. Relative

   b. Absolute

   c. Mixed

   d. Certain

16. Which key do you press to convert a relative cell reference to an absolute cell reference?

   a. [F2]

   b. [F4]

   c. [F5]

   d. [F6]

17. What type of cell reference changes when it is copied?

   a. Circular

   b. Absolute

   c. Relative

   d. Specified

Skills Review

1. Create a complex formula.

   a. Open EX 2-2.xlsx from the location where you store your Data Files, then save it as **EX 2-Construction Supply Company Inventory**.

   b. Select the range B4:B8, click the Totals tab in the Quick Analysis tool, then click the AutoSum button.

   c. Use the fill handle to copy the formula in cell B9 to cells C9:E9.

   d. In cell B11, create a complex formula that calculates a 30% decrease in the total number of cases of pylons.

   e. Use the fill handle to copy this formula into cell C11 through cell E11.

   f. Save your work.

2. Insert a function.

   a. Use the AutoSum list arrow to create a formula in cell B13 that averages the number of cases of pylons in each storage area.

   b. Use the Insert Function button to create a formula in cell B14 that calculates the maximum number of cases of pylons in a storage area.

   c. Use the AutoSum list arrow to create a formula in cell B15 that calculates the minimum number of cases of pylons in a storage area.

   d. Save your work.

Skills Review (continued)

3. Type a function.

   a. In cell C13, type a formula that includes a function to average the number of cases of bricks in each storage area. (*Hint*: Use Formula AutoComplete to enter the function.)

   b. In cell C14, type a formula that includes a function to calculate the maximum number of cases of bricks in a storage area.

   c. In cell C15, type a formula that includes a function to calculate the minimum number of cases of bricks in a storage area.

   d. Save your work.

4. Copy and move cell entries.

   a. Select the range B3:F3.

   b. Copy the selection to the Clipboard.

   c. Open the Clipboard task pane, then paste the selection into cell B17.

   d. Close the Clipboard task pane, then select the range A4:A9.

   e. Use the drag-and-drop method to copy the selection to cell A18. (*Hint*: The results should fill the range A18:A23.)

   f. Save your work.

5. Understand relative and absolute cell references.

   a. Write a brief description of the difference between relative and absolute references.

   b. List at least three situations in which you think a business might use an absolute reference in its calculations. Examples can include calculations for different types of worksheets, such as time cards, invoices, and budgets.

6. Copy formulas with relative cell references.

   a. Calculate the total in cell F4.

   b. Use the Fill button to copy the formula in cell F4 down to cells F5:F8.

   c. Select the range C13:C15.

   d. Use the fill handle to copy these cells to the range D13:F15.

   e. Save your work.

7. Copy formulas with absolute cell references.

   a. In cell H1, change the existing value to **1.575**.

   b. In cell H4, create a formula that multiplies F4 and an absolute reference to cell H1.

   c. Use the fill handle to copy the formula in cell H4 to cells H5 and H6.

   d. Use the Copy and Paste buttons to copy the formula in cell H4 to cells H7 and H8.

   e. Change the amount in cell H1 to **2.5**.

   f. Save your work.

Skills Review (continued)

8. **Round a value with a function.**
   a. Click cell H4.
   b. Edit this formula to include the ROUND function showing zero decimal places.
   c. Use the fill handle to copy the formula in cell H4 to the range H5:H8.
   d. Enter your name in cell A25, then compare your work to FIGURE 2-23.
   e. Save your work, preview the worksheet in Backstage view, then submit your work to your instructor as directed.
   f. Close the workbook, then exit Excel.

FIGURE 2-23

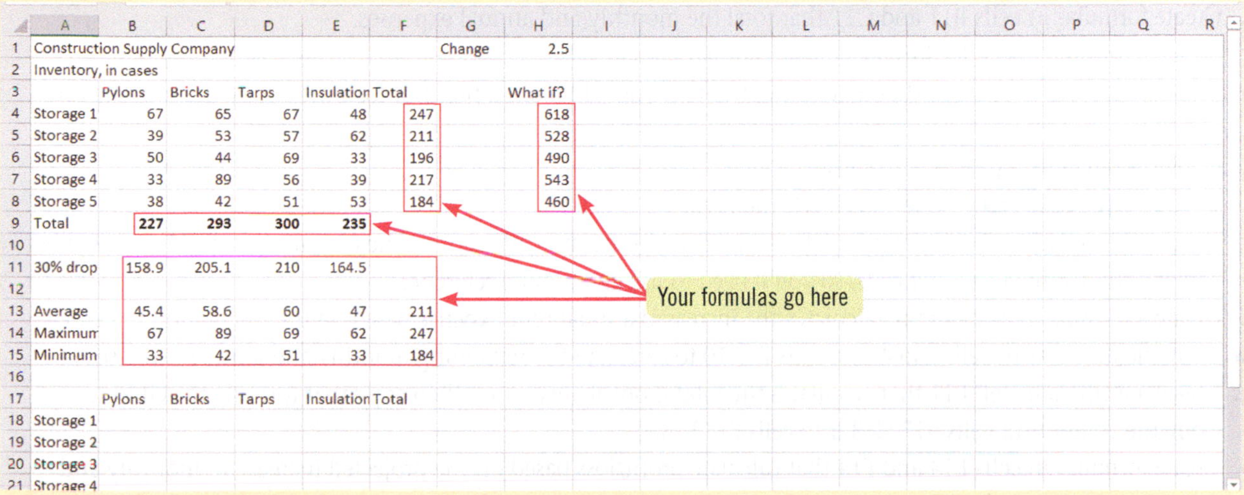

	A	B	C	D	E	F	G	H
1	Construction Supply Company						Change	2.5
2	Inventory, in cases							
3		Pylons	Bricks	Tarps	Insulation	Total		What if?
4	Storage 1	67	65	67	48	247		618
5	Storage 2	39	53	57	62	211		528
6	Storage 3	50	44	69	33	196		490
7	Storage 4	33	89	56	39	217		543
8	Storage 5	38	42	51	53	184		460
9	Total	**227**	**293**	**300**	**235**			
10								
11	30% drop	158.9	205.1	210	164.5			
12								
13	Average	45.4	58.6	60	47	211		
14	Maximum	67	89	69	62	247		
15	Minimum	33	42	51	33	184		
16								
17		Pylons	Bricks	Tarps	Insulation	Total		
18	Storage 1							
19	Storage 2							
20	Storage 3							
21	Storage 4							

Your formulas go here

Independent Challenge 1

You are thinking of starting a small coffee shop where locals can gather. Before you begin, you need to evaluate what you think your monthly expenses will be. You've started a workbook, but need to complete the entries and add formulas.

a. Open EX 2-3.xlsx from the location where you store your Data Files, then save it as **EX 2-Coffee Shop Expenses**.

b. Make up your own expense data, and enter it in cells B4:B10. (Monthly sales are already included in the worksheet.)

c. Create a formula in cell C4 that calculates the annual rent.

d. Copy the formula in cell C4 to the range C5:C10.

e. Move the label in cell A15 to cell A14.

f. Create formulas in cells B11 and C11 that total the monthly and annual expenses.

g. Create a formula in cell C13 that calculates annual sales.

h. Create a formula in cell B14 that determines whether you will make a profit or loss, then copy the formula into cell C14.

i. Copy the labels in cells B3:C3 to cells E3:F3.

j. Type **Projected Increase** in cell G1, then type **.2** in cell H2.

k. Create a formula in cell E4 that calculates an increase in the monthly rent by the amount in cell H2. You will be copying this formula to other cells, so you'll need to use an absolute reference.

l. Create a formula in cell F4 that calculates the increased annual rent expense based on the calculation in cell E4.

m. Copy the formulas in cells E4:F4 into cells E5:F10 to calculate the remaining monthly and annual expenses.

n. Create a formula in cell E11 that calculates the total monthly expenses, then copy that formula to cell F11.

o. Copy the contents of cells B13:C13 into cells E13:F13.

p. Create formulas in cells E14 and F14 that calculate profit/loss based on the projected increase in monthly and annual expenses.

q. Change the projected increase to **.17**, then compare your work to the sample in FIGURE 2-24.

r. Enter your name in a cell in the worksheet.

s. Save your work, preview the worksheet in Backstage view, submit your work to your instructor as directed, close the workbook, and exit Excel.

FIGURE 2-24

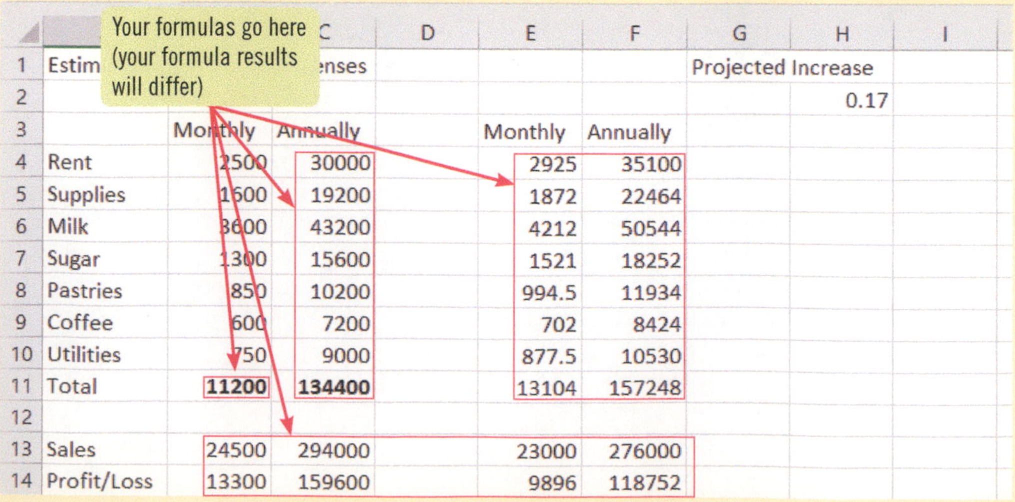

	A	B	C	D	E	F	G	H	I
1	Estim	Your formulas go here (your formula results will differ)	enses				Projected Increase		
2								0.17	
3		Monthly	Annually		Monthly	Annually			
4	Rent	2500	30000		2925	35100			
5	Supplies	1600	19200		1872	22464			
6	Milk	3600	43200		4212	50544			
7	Sugar	1300	15600		1521	18252			
8	Pastries	850	10200		994.5	11934			
9	Coffee	600	7200		702	8424			
10	Utilities	750	9000		877.5	10530			
11	Total	11200	134400		13104	157248			
12									
13	Sales	24500	294000		23000	276000			
14	Profit/Loss	13300	159600		9896	118752			

Independent Challenge 2

The Office Specialists Center is a small, growing business that rents small companies space and provides limited business services. They have hired you to organize their accounting records using Excel. The owners want you to track the company's expenses. Before you were hired, one of the bookkeepers began entering last year's expenses in a workbook, but the analysis was never completed.

a. Start Excel, open EX 2-4.xlsx from the location where you store your Data Files, then save it as **EX 2-Office Specialists Center Finances**. The worksheet includes labels for functions such as the average, maximum, and minimum amounts of each of the expenses in the worksheet.

b. Think about what information would be important for the bookkeeping staff to know.

c. Using the Quick Analysis tool, create a formula in the Quarter 1 column that uses the SUM function, then copy that formula into the Total row for the remaining quarters.

d. Use the SUM function to create formulas for each expense in the Total column.

e. Create formulas for each expense and each quarter in the Average, Maximum, and Minimum columns and rows using the method of your choice.

f. Compare your worksheet to the sample shown in FIGURE 2-25.

g. Enter your name in cell A25, then save your work.

h. Preview the worksheet, then submit your work to your instructor as directed.

i. Close the workbook and exit Excel.

FIGURE 2-25

	A	B	C	D	E	F	G	H	I	J
1	Office Specialists Center									
2										
3	Operating Expenses for 2017									
4										
5	Expense	Quarter 1	Quarter 2	Quarter 3	Quarter 4	Total	Average	Maximum	Minimum	
6	Rent	10240	10240	10240	10240	40960	10240	10240	10240	
7	Utilities	9500	8482	7929	8596	34507	8626.75	9500	7929	
8	Payroll	24456	27922	26876	30415	109669	27417.3	30415	24456	
9	Insurance	9000	8594	8472	8523	34589	8647.25	9000	8472	
10	Education	4000	4081	7552	5006	20639	5159.75	7552	4000	
11	Inventory	15986	14115	14641	15465	60207	15051.8	15986	14115	
12	Total	73182	73434	75710	78245					
13										
14	Average	12197	12239	12618.3	13040.8			Your formulas go here		
15	Maximum	24456	27922	26876	30415					
16	Minimum	4000	4081	7552	5006					

Excel 2016

Independent Challenge 3

As the accounting manager of a locally owned food co-op with multiple locations, it is your responsibility to calculate accrued sales tax payments on a monthly basis and then submit the payments to the state government. You've decided to use an Excel workbook to make these calculations.

a. Start Excel, then save a new, blank workbook to the drive and folder where you store your Data Files as **EX 2-Food Co-op Sales Tax Calculations**.

b. Decide on the layout for all columns and rows. The worksheet will contain data for six stores, which you can name by store number, neighborhood, or another method of your choice. For each store, you will calculate total sales tax based on the local sales tax rate. You'll also calculate total tax owed for all six locations.

c. Make up sales data for all six stores.

d. Enter the rate to be used to calculate the sales tax, using your own local rate.

e. Create formulas to calculate the sales tax owed for each location. If you don't know the local tax rate, use **6.5%**.

f. Create a formula to total all the accrued sales tax.

g. Use the ROUND function to eliminate any decimal places in the sales tax figures for each location and in the total due.

h. Add your name to the header, then compare your work to the sample shown in **FIGURE 2-26**.

i. Save your work, preview the worksheet, and submit your work to your instructor as directed.

j. Close the workbook and exit Excel.

FIGURE 2-26

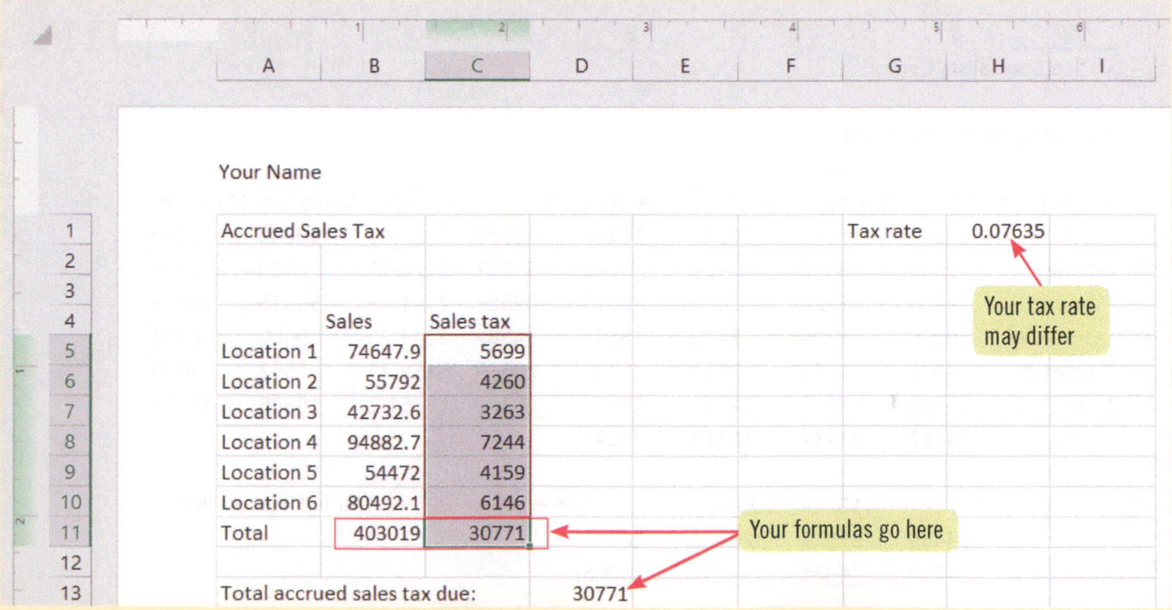

Independent Challenge 4: Explore

So many friends have come to you for help in understanding the various fees associated with purchasing a home that you've decided to create a business that specializes in helping first-time home-buyers. Your first task is to create a worksheet that clearly shows all the information a home buyer will need. Some fees are based on a percentage of the purchase price, and others are a flat fee; overall, they seem to represent a substantial amount above the purchase prices you see listed. A client has seen five houses so far that interest her; one is easily affordable, and the remaining four are all nice, but increasingly more expensive. You decide to create an Excel workbook to help her figure out the real cost of each home.

- **a.** Find out the typical cost or percentage rate of at least three fees that are usually charged when buying a home and taking out a mortgage. (*Hint*: If you have access to the Internet, you can research the topic of home buying on the web, or you can ask friends about standard rates or percentages for items such as title insurance, credit reports, and inspection fees.)
- **b.** Start Excel, then save a new, blank workbook to the location where you store your Data Files as **EX 2-Home Purchase Fees Worksheet**.
- **c.** Create labels and enter data for at least five homes. If you enter this information across the columns in your worksheet, you should have one column for each house, with the purchase price in the cell below each label. Be sure to enter a different purchase price for each house.
- **d.** Create labels for the Fees column and for an Amount or Rate column. Enter the information for each of the fees you have researched.
- **e.** In each house column, enter formulas that calculate the fee for each item. The formulas (and use of absolute or relative referencing) will vary depending on whether the charges are a flat fee or based on a percentage of the purchase price. Make sure that the formulas for items that are based on a percentage of the purchase price (such as the fees for the Title Insurance Policy, Loan Origination, and Underwriter) contain absolute references. A sample of what your workbook might look like is shown in FIGURE 2-27.
- **f.** Total the fees for each house, then create formulas that add the total fees to the purchase price.
- **g.** Enter a title for the worksheet and include your client's name (or use Client 1) in the header.
- **h.** Enter your name in the header, save your work, preview the worksheet, then submit your work to your instructor as directed.
- **i.** Close the file and exit Excel.

FIGURE 2-27

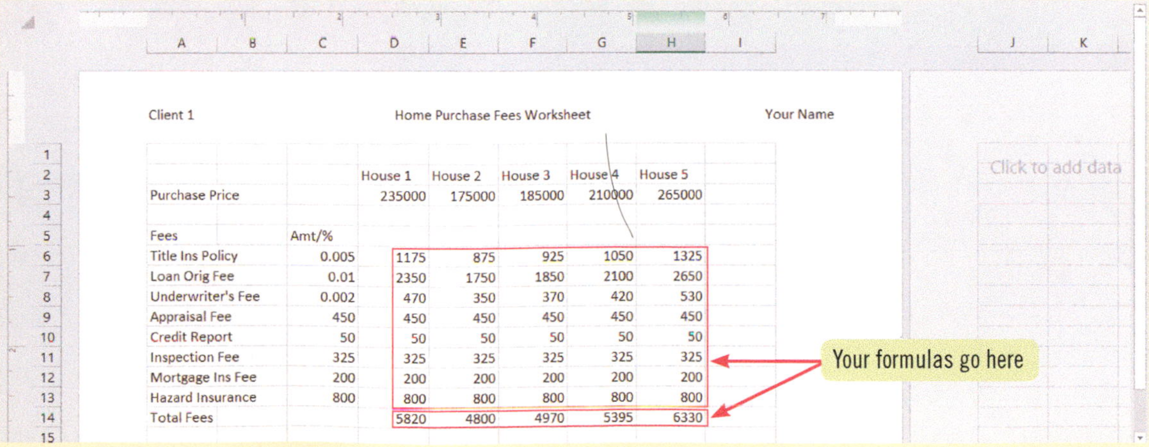

Client 1 | Home Purchase Fees Worksheet | Your Name

1							
2			House 1	House 2	House 3	House 4	House 5
3	Purchase Price		235000	175000	185000	210000	265000
4							
5	Fees	Amt/%					
6	Title Ins Policy	0.005	1175	875	925	1050	1325
7	Loan Orig Fee	0.01	2350	1750	1850	2100	2650
8	Underwriter's Fee	0.002	470	350	370	420	530
9	Appraisal Fee	450	450	450	450	450	450
10	Credit Report	50	50	50	50	50	50
11	Inspection Fee	325	325	325	325	325	325
12	Mortgage Ins Fee	200	200	200	200	200	200
13	Hazard Insurance	800	800	800	800	800	800
14	Total Fees		5820	4800	4970	5395	6330
15							

Visual Workshop

Create the worksheet shown in **FIGURE 2-28** using the skills you learned in this module. Save the workbook as
EX 2-Monthly Expenses to the location where you store your Data Files. Enter your name and worksheet title in
the header as shown, hide the gridlines, preview the worksheet, and then submit your work to your instructor as directed.
(*Hint:* Change the Zoom factor to 90% by using the Zoom out button.)

FIGURE 2-28

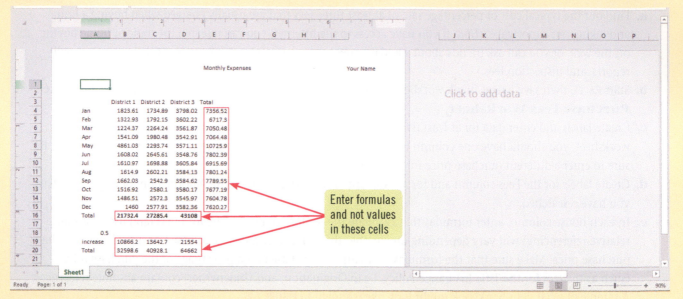

	District 1	District 2	District 3	Total
Jan	1823.61	1734.89	3798.02	7356.52
Feb	1322.93	1792.15	3602.22	6717.3
Mar	1224.37	2264.24	3561.87	7050.48
Apr	1541.09	1980.48	3542.91	7064.48
May	4861.03	2293.74	3571.11	10725.9
Jun	1608.02	2645.61	3548.76	7802.39
Jul	1610.97	1698.88	3605.84	6915.69
Aug	1614.9	2602.21	3584.13	7801.24
Sep	1662.03	2542.9	3584.62	7789.55
Oct	1516.92	2580.1	3580.17	7677.19
Nov	1486.51	2572.3	3545.97	7604.78
Dec	1460	2577.91	3582.36	7620.27
Total	21732.4	27285.4	43108	

0.5

	District 1	District 2	District 3
increase	10866.2	13642.7	21554
Total	32598.6	40928.1	64662

Monthly Expenses   Your Name

Enter formulas and not values in these cells

Formatting a Worksheet

CASE The marketing managers at Reason2Go have requested data from all R2G locations for advertising expenses incurred during the first quarter of this year. Mary Watson has created a worksheet listing this information. She asks you to format the worksheet to make it easier to read and to call attention to important data.

Module Objectives

After completing this module, you will be able to:

- Format values
- Change font and font size
- Change font styles and alignment
- Adjust column width
- Insert and delete rows and columns
- Apply colors, patterns, and borders
- Apply conditional formatting
- Rename and move a worksheet
- Check spelling

Files You Will Need

EX 3-1.xlsx	EX 3-4.xlsx
EX 3-2.xlsx	EX 3-5.xlsx
EX 3-3.xlsx	

Format Values

Learning Outcomes
- Format a number
- Format a date
- Increase/decrease decimals

The **format** of a cell determines how the labels and values look—for example, whether the contents appear boldfaced, italicized, or with dollar signs and commas. Formatting changes only the appearance of a value or label; it does not alter the actual data in any way. To format a cell or range, first you select it, then you apply the formatting using the Ribbon, Mini toolbar, or a keyboard shortcut. You can apply formatting before or after you enter data in a cell or range. **CASE** *Mary has provided you with a worksheet that details advertising expenses, and you're ready to improve its appearance and readability. You start by formatting some of the values so they are displayed as currency, percentages, and dates.*

STEPS

1. **Start Excel, open the file EX 3-1.xlsx from the location where you store your Data Files, then save it as EX 3-R2G Advertising Expenses**

   This worksheet is difficult to interpret because all the information is crowded and looks the same. In some columns, the contents appear cut off because there is too much data to fit given the current column width. You decide not to widen the columns yet, because the other changes you plan to make might affect column width and row height. The first thing you want to do is format the data showing the cost of each ad.

   QUICK TIP
   You can use a different type of currency, such as Euros or British pounds, by clicking the Accounting Number Format list arrow, then clicking a different currency type.

2. **Select the range D4:D32, then click the Accounting Number Format button $ in the Number group on the Home tab**

   The default Accounting **number format** adds dollar signs and two decimal places to the data, as shown in **FIGURE 3-1**. Formatting this data in Accounting format makes it clear that its values are monetary values. Excel automatically resizes the column to display the new formatting. The Accounting and Currency number formats are both used for monetary values, but the Accounting format aligns currency symbols and decimal points of numbers in a column.

   QUICK TIP
   Select any range of contiguous cells by clicking the upper-left cell of the range, pressing and holding [Shift], then clicking the lower-right cell of the range. Add a column to the selected range by continuing to hold down [Shift] and pressing →; add a row by pressing ↓.

3. **Select the range F4:H32, then click the Comma Style button in the Number group**

   The values in columns F, G, and H display the Comma Style format, which does not include a dollar sign but can be useful for some types of accounting data.

4. **Select the range J4:J32, click the Number Format list arrow, click Percentage, then click the Increase Decimal button in the Number group**

   The data in the % of Total column is now formatted with a percent sign (%) and three decimal places. The Number Format list arrow lets you choose from popular number formats and shows an example of what the selected cell or cells would look like in each format (when multiple cells are selected, the example is based on the first cell in the range). Each time you click the Increase Decimal button, you add one decimal place; clicking the button twice would add two decimal places.

5. **Click the Decrease Decimal button in the Number group twice**

   Two decimal places are removed from the percentage values in column J.

6. **Select the range B4:B31, then click the launcher in the Number group**

   The Format Cells dialog box opens with the Date category already selected on the Number tab.

   QUICK TIP
   Make sure you examine formatted data to confirm that you have applied the appropriate formatting; for example, dates should not have a currency format, and monetary values should not have a date format.

7. **Select the first 14-Mar-12 format in the Type list box as shown in FIGURE 3-2, then click OK**

   The dates in column B appear in the 14-Mar-12 format. The second 14-Mar-12 format in the list (visible if you scroll down the list) displays all days in two digits (it adds a leading zero if the day is only a single-digit number), while the one you chose displays single-digit days without a leading zero.

8. **Select the range C4:C31, right-click the range, click Format Cells on the shortcut menu, click 14-Mar in the Type list box in the Format Cells dialog box, then click OK**

   Compare your worksheet to **FIGURE 3-3**.

9. **Press [Ctrl][Home], then save your work**

FIGURE 3-1: Accounting number format applied to range

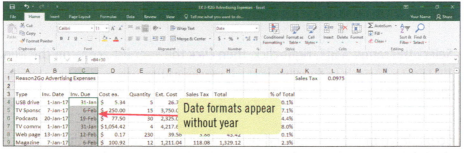

Number Format list arrow

Accounting Number Format button

Number group buttons change the appearance of a value

Decrease Decimal button

Increase Decimal button

Cells formatted with Accounting number format

FIGURE 3-2: Format Cells dialog box

Format Cells

Number | Alignment | Font | Border | Fill | Protection

Category:
General
Number
Currency
Accounting
Date
Time
Percentage
Fraction
Scientific
Text
Special
Custom

Sample
1-Jan-20

Type:
*3/14/2012
*Wednesday, March 14, 2012
3/14
3/14/12
03/14/12
14-Mar
14-Mar-12

Locale (location):
English (United States)

Sample of selected type

Number categories

Date format types

In Step 7, click this format

date and time serial numbers as date values. Date formats that begin with to changes in regional date and time settings that are specified for the mats without an asterisk are not affected by operating system settings.

OK | Cancel

FIGURE 3-3: Worksheet with formatted values

	A	B	C	D	E	F	G	H	I	J	K	L
1	Reason2Go Advertising Expenses									Sales Tax	0.0975	
2												
3	Type	Inv. Date	Inv. Due	Cost ea.	Quantity	Ext. Cost	Sales Tax	Total		% of Total		
4	USB drive	1-Jan-17	31-Jan	$ 5.34	5	26.7				0.1%		
5	TV Sponsc	7-Jan-17	6-Feb	$ 250.00	15	3,750.0				7.1%		
6	Podcasts	20-Jan-17	19-Feb	$ 77.50	30	2,325.0				4.4%		
7	TV comm	1-Jan-17	31-Jan	$1,054.42	4	4,217.6				8.0%		
8	Web page	13-Jan-17	12-Feb	$ 0.17	230	39.56	3.86	43.42		0.1%		
9	Magazine	7-Jan-17	6-Feb	$ 100.92	12	1,211.04	118.08	1,329.12		2.3%		

Date formats appear without year

Formatting as a table

Excel includes 60 predefined **table styles** to make it easy to format selected worksheet cells as a table. You can apply table styles to any range of cells that you want to format quickly, or even to an entire worksheet, but they're especially useful for those ranges with labels in the left column and top row, and totals in the bottom row or right column. To apply a table style, select the data to be formatted or click anywhere within the intended range (Excel can automatically detect a range of cells filled with data), click the Format as Table button in the Styles group on the Home tab, then click a style in the gallery, as shown in **FIGURE 3-4**. Table styles are organized in three categories: Light, Medium, and Dark. Once you click a style, Excel asks you to confirm the range selection, then applies the style. Once you have formatted a range as a table, you can use Live Preview to preview the table in other styles by pointing to any style in the Table Styles gallery.

FIGURE 3-4: Table Styles gallery

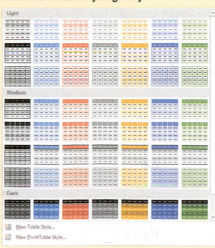

Light

Medium

Dark

New Table Style...
New PivotTable Style...

Formatting a Worksheet

Change Font and Font Size

Learning Outcomes
• Change a font
• Change a font size
• Use the Mini toolbar

A **font** is the name for a collection of characters (letters, numbers, symbols, and punctuation marks) with a similar, specific design. The **font size** is the physical size of the text, measured in units called points. A **point** is equal to 1/72 of an inch. The default font and font size in Excel is 11-point Calibri. **TABLE 3-1** shows several fonts in different font sizes. You can change the font and font size of any cell or range using the Font and Font Size list arrows. The Font and Font Size list arrows appear on the Home tab on the Ribbon and on the Mini toolbar, which opens when you right-click a cell or range. **CASE** *You want to change the font and font size of the labels and the worksheet title so that they stand out more from the data.*

STEPS

QUICK TIP

When you point to an option in the Font or Font Size list, Live Preview shows the selected cells with the option temporarily applied.

1. **Click the Font list arrow in the Font group on the Home tab, scroll down in the Font list to see an alphabetical listing of the fonts available on your computer, then click Times New Roman, as shown in FIGURE 3-5**

   The font in cell A1 changes to Times New Roman. Notice that the font names on the list are displayed in the font they represent.

QUICK TIP

You can format an entire row by clicking the row indicator button to select the row before formatting (or select an entire column by clicking the column indicator button before formatting).

2. **Click the Font Size list arrow in the Font group, then click 20**

   The worksheet title appears in 20-point Times New Roman, and the Font and Font Size list boxes on the Home tab display the new font and font size information.

3. **Click the Increase Font Size button A˙ in the Font group twice**

   The font size of the title increases to 24 point.

4. **Select the range A3:J3, right-click, then click the Font list arrow on the Mini toolbar**

   The Mini toolbar includes the most commonly used formatting tools, so it's great for making quick formatting changes.

QUICK TIP

To quickly move to a font in the Font list, type the first few characters of its name.

5. **Scroll down in the Font list and click Times New Roman, click the Font Size list arrow on the Mini toolbar, then click 14**

   The Mini toolbar closes when you move the pointer away from the selection. Compare your worksheet to **FIGURE 3-6**. Notice that some of the column labels are now too wide to appear fully in the column. Excel does not automatically adjust column widths to accommodate cell formatting; you have to adjust column widths manually. You'll learn to do this in a later lesson.

6. **Save your work**

TABLE 3-1: Examples of fonts and font sizes

font	12 point	24 point	
Calibri	Excel	Excel	
Playbill	Excel	Excel	
Comic Sans MS	Excel	Excel	
Times New Roman	Excel	Excel	

FIGURE 3-5: Font list

Font size list arrow

Font list arrow

Click a font to apply it to the selected cell

Active cell displays selected font

FIGURE 3-6: Worksheet with formatted title and column labels

Font and font size of active cell or range

Title appears in 24-point Times New Roman

Reason2Go Advertising Expenses

Column headings are now 14-point Times New Roman

Inserting and adjusting online pictures and other images

You can illustrate your worksheets using online pictures and other images. Office.com makes many photos and animations available for your use. To add a picture to a worksheet, click the Online Pictures button in the Illustrations group on the Insert tab. The Insert Pictures window opens. Here you can search for online pictures (or Clip Art) from a variety of popular sources such as Facebook and Flickr, through the Bing search engine, or on OneDrive. To search, type one or more **keywords** (words related to your subject) in the appropriate Search text box, then press [Enter]. For example, pictures that relate to the keyword house in a search of Office.com appear in the Office.com window, as shown in **FIGURE 3-7**. When you double-click the image you want in the window, the image is inserted at the location of the active cell. To add images on your computer (or computers on your network) to a worksheet, click the Insert tab on the Ribbon, then click the Pictures button in the Illustrations group. Navigate to

the file you want, then click Insert. To resize an image, drag any corner sizing handle. To move an image, point inside the clip until the pointer changes to ⁺⇤, then drag it to a new location.

FIGURE 3-7: Results of Online Picture search

Type keyword(s) here, then press [Enter] to begin search

Your displayed images may differ

Change Font Styles and Alignment

Font styles are formats such as bold, italic, and underlining that you can apply to affect the way text and numbers look in a worksheet. You can also change the **alignment** of labels and values in cells to position them in relation to the cells' edges—such as left-aligned, right-aligned, or centered. You can apply font styles and alignment options using the Home tab, the Format Cells dialog box, or the Mini toolbar. See **TABLE 3-2** for a description of common font style and alignment buttons that are available on the Home tab and the Mini toolbar. Once you have formatted a cell the way you want it, you can "paint" or copy the cell's formats into other cells by using the Format Painter button in the Clipboard group on the Home tab. This is similar to using copy and paste, but instead of copying cell contents, it copies only the cell's formatting. **CASE** *You want to further enhance the worksheet's appearance by adding bold and underline formatting and centering some of the labels.*

STEPS

1. **Press [Ctrl][Home], then click the Bold button** ⒷⒷ **in the Font group on the Home tab**
   The title in cell A1 appears in bold.

2. **Click cell A3, then click the Underline button** Ⓤ **in the Font group**
   The column label is now underlined.

3. **Click the Italic button** Ⓘ **in the Font group, then click** ⒷⒷ
   The heading now appears in boldface, underlined, italic type. Notice that the Bold, Italic, and Underline buttons in the Font group are all selected.

4. **Click the Italic button** Ⓘ **to deselect it**
   The italic font style is removed from cell A3, but the bold and underline font styles remain.

5. **Click the Format Painter button** 🖌 **in the Clipboard group, then select the range B3:J3**
   The formatting in cell A3 is copied to the rest of the column labels. To paint the formats on more than one selection, double-click the Format Painter button to keep it activated until you turn it off. You can turn off the Format Painter by pressing [Esc] or by clicking 🖌. You decide the title would look better if it were centered over the data columns.

6. **Select the range A1:H1, then click the Merge & Center button** 🔲 **in the Alignment group**
   The Merge & Center button creates one cell out of the eight cells across the row, then centers the text in that newly created, merged cell. The title "Reason2Go Advertising Expenses" is centered across the eight columns you selected. To split a merged cell into its original components, select the merged cell, then click the Merge & Center button to deselect it. Occasionally, you may find that you want cell contents to wrap within a cell. You can do this by selecting the cells containing the text you want to wrap, then clicking the Wrap Text button 📄 in the Alignment group on the Home tab on the Ribbon.

7. **Select the range A3:J3, right-click, then click the Center button** ☰ **on the Mini toolbar**
   Compare your screen to **FIGURE 3-8**. Although they may be difficult to read, notice that all the headings are centered within their cells.

8. **Save your work**

FIGURE 3-8: Worksheet with font styles and alignment applied

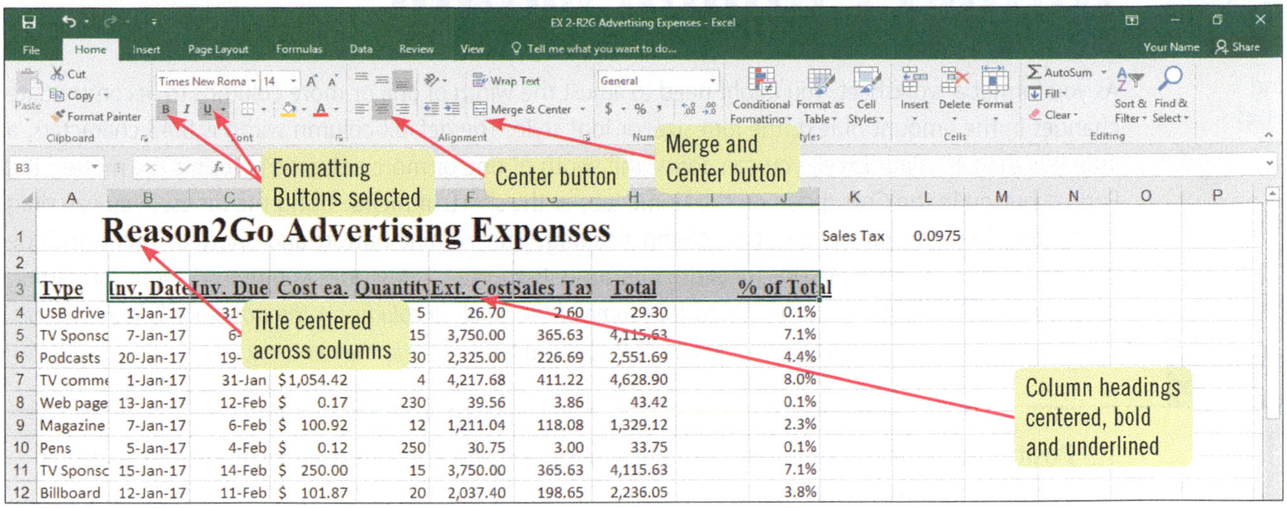

TABLE 3-2: Common font style and alignment buttons

button	description
B	Bolds text
I	Italicizes text
U	Underlines text
⊟	Centers text across columns, and combines two or more selected, adjacent cells into one cell
≡	Aligns text at the left edge of the cell
≡	Centers text horizontally within the cell
≡	Aligns text at the right edge of the cell
⊟	Wraps long text into multiple lines

Rotating and indenting cell entries

In addition to applying fonts and font styles, you can rotate or indent data within a cell to further change its appearance. You can rotate text within a cell by altering its alignment. Click the Home tab, select the cells you want to modify, then click the launcher in the Alignment group to open the Alignment tab of the Format Cells dialog box. Click a position in the Orientation box or type a number in the Degrees text box to rotate text from its default horizontal orientation, then click OK. You can indent cell contents using the Increase Indent button in the Alignment group, which moves cell contents to the right one space, or the Decrease Indent button, which moves cell contents to the left one space.

Adjust Column Width

Learning Outcomes
- Change a column width by dragging
- Resize a column with AutoFit
- Change the width of multiple columns

As you format a worksheet, you might need to adjust the width of one or more columns to accommodate changes in the amount of text, the font size, or font style. The default column width is 8.43 characters, a little less than 1". With Excel, you can adjust the width of one or more columns by using the mouse, the Format button in the Cells group on the Home tab, or the shortcut menu. Using the mouse, you can drag or double-click the right edge of a column heading. The Format button and shortcut menu include commands for making more precise width adjustments. **TABLE 3-3** describes common column formatting commands. **CASE** *You have noticed that some of the labels in columns A through J don't fit in the cells. You want to adjust the widths of the columns so that the labels appear in their entirety.*

STEPS

1. **Position the mouse pointer on the line between the column A and column B headings until it changes to ↔**

   See **FIGURE 3-9**. The **column heading** is the box at the top of each column containing a letter. Before you can adjust column width using the mouse, you need to position the pointer on the right edge of the column heading for the column you want to adjust. The cell entry "TV commercials" is the widest in the column.

2. **Click and drag the ↔ to the right until the column displays the "TV commercials" cell entries fully (approximately 15.29 characters, 1.23", or 112 pixels)**

   As you change the column width, a ScreenTip is displayed listing the column width. In Normal view, the ScreenTip lists the width in characters and pixels; in Page Layout view, the ScreenTip lists the width in inches and pixels.

3. **Position the pointer on the line between columns B and C until it changes to ↔, then double-click**

   Double-clicking the right edge of a column heading activates the **AutoFit** feature, which automatically resizes the column to accommodate the widest entry in the column. Column B automatically widens to fit the widest entry, which is the column label "Inv. Date".

4. **Use AutoFit to resize columns C, D, and J**

5. **Select the range E5:H5**

   You can change the width of multiple columns at once, by first selecting either the column headings or at least one cell in each column.

6. **Click the Format button in the Cells group, then click Column Width**

   The Column Width dialog box opens. Column width measurement is based on the number of characters that will fit in the column when formatted in the Normal font and font size (in this case, 11-point Calibri).

7. **Drag the dialog box by its title bar if its placement obscures your view of the worksheet, type 11 in the Column width text box, then click OK**

   The widths of columns E, F, G, and H change to reflect the new setting. See **FIGURE 3-10**.

8. **Save your work**

TABLE 3-3: Common column formatting commands

command	description	available using
Column Width	Sets the width to a specific number of characters	Format button; shortcut menu
AutoFit Column Width	Fits to the widest entry in a column	Format button; mouse
Hide & Unhide	Hides or displays hidden column(s)	Format button; shortcut menu
Default Width	Resets column to worksheet's default column width	Format button

FIGURE 3-9: Preparing to change the column width

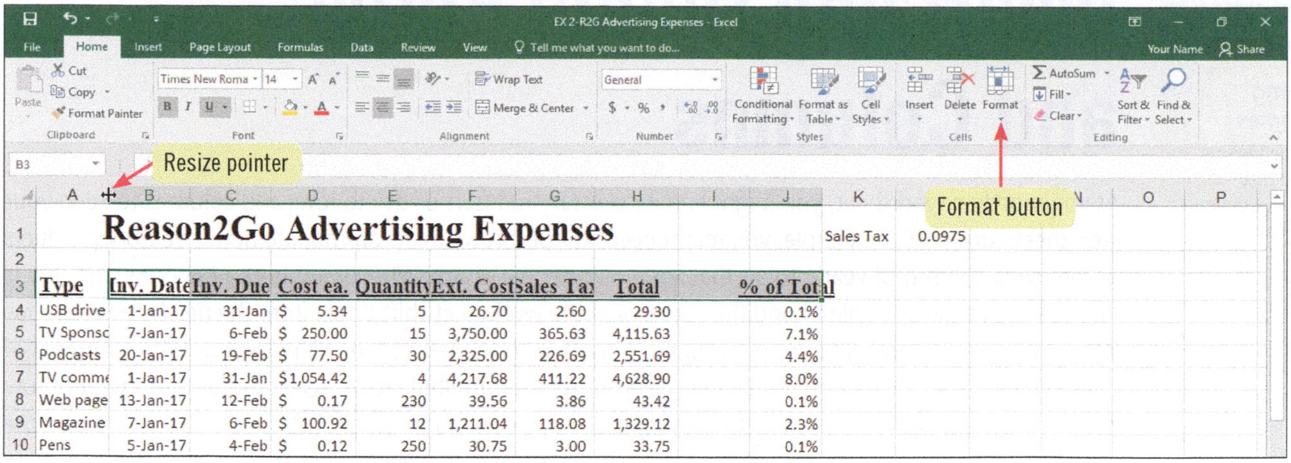

FIGURE 3-10: Worksheet with column widths adjusted

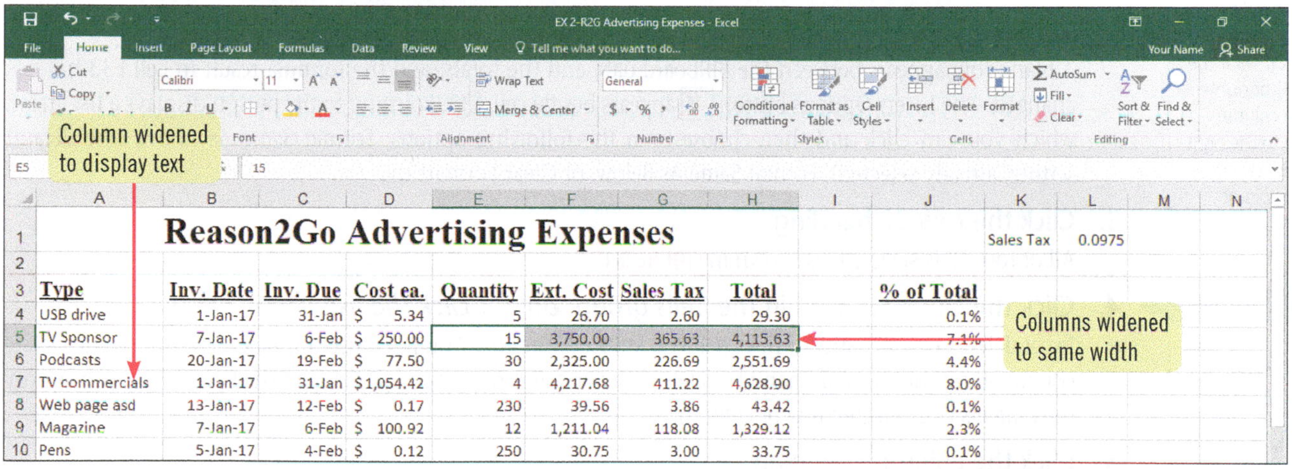

Excel 2016

Changing row height

Changing row height is as easy as changing column width. Row height is calculated in points, the same units of measure used for fonts. The row height must exceed the size of the font you are using. Normally, you don't need to adjust row heights manually, because row heights adjust automatically to accommodate font size changes. If you format something in a row to be a larger point size, Excel adjusts the row to fit the largest point size in the row. However, you have just as many options for changing row

height as you do column width. Using the mouse, you can place the ✛ pointer on the line dividing a row heading from the heading below, and then drag to the desired height; double-clicking the line AutoFits the row height where necessary. You can also select one or more rows, then use the Row Height command on the shortcut menu, or click the Format button on the Home tab and click the Row Height or AutoFit Row Height command.

Formatting a Worksheet

Excel 59

Insert and Delete Rows and Columns

Learning Outcomes
• Use the Insert dialog box
• Use column and row heading buttons to insert and delete

As you modify a worksheet, you might find it necessary to insert or delete rows and columns to keep your worksheet current. For example, you might need to insert rows to accommodate new inventory products or remove a column of yearly totals that are no longer necessary. When you insert a new row, the row is inserted above the cell pointer and the contents of the worksheet shift down from the newly inserted row. When you insert a new column, the column is inserted to the left of the cell pointer and the contents of the worksheet shift to the right of the new column. To insert multiple rows, select the same number of row headings as you want to insert before using the Insert command. **CASE** *You want to improve the overall appearance of the worksheet by inserting a row between the last row of data and the totals. Also, you have learned that row 27 and column J need to be deleted from the worksheet.*

STEPS

1. **Right-click cell A32, then click Insert on the shortcut menu**

   The Insert dialog box opens. See **FIGURE 3-11**. You can choose to insert a column or a row; insert a single cell and shift the cells in the active column to the right; or insert a single cell and shift the cells in the active row down. An additional row between the last row of data and the totals will visually separate the totals.

2. **Click the Entire row option button, then click OK**

   A blank row appears between the Billboard data and the totals, and the formula result in cell E33 has not changed. The Insert Options button [icon] appears beside cell A33. Pointing to the button displays a list arrow, which you can click and then choose from the following options: Format Same As Above (the default setting, already selected), Format Same As Below, or Clear Formatting.

3. **Click the row 27 heading**

   All of row 27 is selected, as shown in **FIGURE 3-12**.

4. **Click the Delete button in the Cells group; *do not click the list arrow***

   Excel deletes row 27, and all rows below it shift up one row. You must use the Delete button or the Delete command on the shortcut menu to delete a row or column; pressing [Delete] on the keyboard removes only the *contents* of a selected row or column.

5. **Click the column J heading**

   The percentage information is calculated elsewhere and is no longer necessary in this worksheet.

6. **Click the Delete button in the Cells group**

   Excel deletes column J. The remaining columns to the right shift left one column.

7. **Use AutoFit to resize columns F and H, then save your work**

Hiding and unhiding columns and rows

When you don't want data in a column or row to be visible, but you don't want to delete it, you can hide the column or row. To hide a selected column, click the Format button in the Cells group on the Home tab, point to Hide & Unhide, then click Hide Columns. A hidden column is indicated by a dark green vertical line in its original position. This green line disappears when you click elsewhere in the worksheet. You can display a hidden column by selecting the columns on either side of the hidden column, clicking the Format button in the Cells group, pointing to Hide & Unhide, and then clicking Unhide Columns. (To hide or unhide one or more rows, substitute Hide Rows and Unhide Rows for the Hide Columns and Unhide Columns commands.)

FIGURE 3-11: Insert dialog box

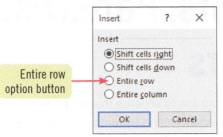

Entire row option button → Entire **r**ow

FIGURE 3-12: Worksheet with row 27 selected

	A	B	C	D	E	F	G	H	I	J	K	L	M	N
16	TV commercials	1-Feb-17	3-Mar	$1,054.42	4	4,217.68	411.22	4,628.90		8.0%				
17	USB drive	1-Mar-17	31-Mar	$ 23.91	2	47.82	4.66	52.48		0.1%				
18	Web page ads	28-Feb-17	30-Mar	$ 0.17	275	47.30	4.61	51.91		0.1%				
19	Magazine	27-Feb-17	29-Mar	$ 100.92	12	1,211.04	118.08	1,329.12		2.3%				
20	Podacsts	22-Feb-17	24-Mar	$ 77.50	30	2,325.00	226.69	2,551.69		4.4%				
21	TV Sponsor	1-Feb-17	3-Mar	$ 250.00	30	7,500.00	731.25	8,231.25		14.2%				
22	USB drive	25-Feb-17	27-Mar	$ 5.34	6	32.04	3.12	35.16		0.1%				
23	W	Mar-17	9-Apr	$ 0.17	275	47.30	4.61	51.91		0.1%				
24	T	Feb-17	17-Mar	$ 250.00	25	6,250.00	609.38	6,859.38		11.8%				
25	Pens	15-Mar-17	14-Apr	$ 0.12	250	30.75	3.00	33.75		0.1%				
26	TV commercials	1-Mar-17	31-Mar	$1,054.44	4	4,217.76	411.23	4,628.99		8.0%				
27	Hats	20-Mar-17	19-Apr	$ 7.20	250	1,800.00	175.50	1,975.50		3.4%				
28	Podcasts	20-Mar-17	19-Apr	$ 75.50	30	2,265.00	220.84	2,485.84		4.3%				
29	USB drive	21-Mar-17	20-Apr	$ 5.34	2	10.68	1.04	11.72		0.0%				
30	Podcasts	23-Mar-17	22-Apr	$ 77.50	30	2,325.00	226.69	2,551.69		4.4%				
31	Billboard	28-Mar-17	27-Apr	$ 101.87	20	2,037.40	198.65	2,236.05		3.8%				
32														
33				$4,941.10	2034	52,929.62	5,160.64	58,090.26		100.0%				
34														
35														
36														

Delete button

Row 27 heading

Inserted row — Insert Options button

EX 2-R2G Advertising Expenses - Excel

A27 — Hats

Excel 2016

Adding and editing comments

Much of your work in Excel may be in collaboration with teammates with whom you share worksheets. You can share ideas with other worksheet users by adding comments within selected cells. To include a comment in a worksheet, click the cell where you want to place the comment, click the Review tab on the Ribbon, then click the New Comment button in the Comments group. You can type your comments in the resizable text box that opens containing the computer user's name. A small, red triangle appears in the upper-right corner of a cell containing a comment. If comments are not already displayed in a workbook, other users can point to the triangle to display the comment. To see all worksheet comments, as shown in **FIGURE 3-13**, click the Show All Comments button in the Comments group. To edit a comment, click the cell containing the comment, then click the Edit Comment button in the Comments

group. To delete a comment, click the cell containing the comment, then click the Delete button in the Comments group.

FIGURE 3-13: Comments displayed in a worksheet

21	TV Sponsor	1-Feb-16	2-Mar	Food Network
22	Newspaper	25-Feb-16	26-Mar	Village Reader
23	Web page ads	10-Mar-16	9-Apr	Advertising Concepts
24	TV Sponsor	15-Feb-16	16-Mar	Food Network
25	Pens	15-Mar-16	14-Apr	Mass Appeal, Inc.
26	TV commercials	1-Mar-16	31-Mar	Discovery Channel
27	Podcasts	20-Mar-16	19-Apr	iPodAds
28	Newspaper	1-Apr-16	1-May	University Voice
29	Podcasts	10-Apr-16	10-May	iPodAds
30	Billboard	28-Mar-16	27-Apr	Advertising Concepts

Harriet McDonald: I think this will turn out to be a very good decision.

Will Moss: Should we continue with this market, or expand to other types of publications?

Formatting a Worksheet

Excel 61

Apply Colors, Patterns, and Borders

You can use colors, patterns, and borders to enhance the overall appearance of a worksheet and make it easier to read. You can add these enhancements by using the Borders, Font Color, and Fill Color buttons in the Font group on the Home tab of the Ribbon and on the Mini toolbar, or by using the Fill tab and the Border tab in the Format Cells dialog box. You can open the Format Cells dialog box by clicking the dialog box launcher in the Font, Alignment, or Number group on the Home tab, or by right-clicking a selection, then clicking Format Cells on the shortcut menu. You can apply a color to the background of a cell or a range or to cell contents (such as letters and numbers), and you can apply a pattern to a cell or range. You can apply borders to all the cells in a worksheet or only to selected cells to call attention to selected information. To save time, you can also apply **cell styles**, predesigned combinations of formats. **CASE** ▶ *You want to add a pattern, a border, and color to the title of the worksheet to give the worksheet a more professional appearance.*

STEPS

1. **Select cell A1, click the Fill Color list arrow 🖌 in the Font group, then hover the pointer over the Turquoise, Accent 2 color (first row, sixth column from the left)**
   See **FIGURE 3-14**. Live Preview shows you how the color will look *before* you apply it. (Remember that cell A1 spans columns A through H because the Merge & Center command was applied.)

2. **Click the Turquoise, Accent 2 color**
   The color is applied to the background (or fill) of this cell. When you change fill or font color, the color on the Fill Color or Font Color button changes to the last color you selected.

3. **Right-click cell A1, then click Format Cells on the shortcut menu**
   The Format Cells dialog box opens.

4. **Click the Fill tab, click the Pattern Style list arrow, click the 6.25% Gray style (first row, sixth column from the left), then click OK**

5. **Click the Borders list arrow ⊞ in the Font group, then click Thick Bottom Border**
   Unlike underlining, which is a text-formatting tool, borders extend to the width of the cell, and can appear at the bottom of the cell, at the top, on either side, or on any combination of the four sides. It can be difficult to see a border when the cell is selected.

6. **Select the range A3:H3, click the Font Color list arrow 🅰 in the Font group, then click the Blue, Accent 1 color (first Theme Colors row, fifth column from the left) on the palette**
   The new color is applied to the labels in the selected range.

7. **Select the range J1:K1, click the Cell Styles button in the Styles group, click the Neutral cell style (first row, fourth column from the left) in the gallery, then AutoFit column J**
   The font and color change in the range, as shown in **FIGURE 3-15**.

8. **Save your work**

FIGURE 3-14: Live Preview of fill color

Fill Color list arrow

Turquoise, Accent 2

Standard Colors

No Fill

More Colors...

Click to apply styles to selected cells

Live Preview shows cell A1 with Turquoise, Accent 2 background

Reason2Go Advertising Expenses

Sales Tax   0.0975

Type	Inv. Date	In...		Quantity	Ext. Cost	Sales Tax	Total
USB drive	1-Jan-17	31-Jan	$ 5.34	5	26.70	2.60	29.30
TV Sponsor	7-Jan-17	6-Feb	$ 250.00	15	3,750.00	365.63	4,115.63
Podcasts	20-Jan-17	19-Feb	$ 77.50	30	2,325.00	226.69	2,551.69
TV commercials	1-Jan-17	31-Jan	$1,054.42	4	4,217.68	411.22	4,628.90
Web page asd	13-Jan-17	12-Feb	$ 0.17	230	39.56	3.86	43.42
Magazine	7-Jan-17	6-Feb	$ 100.92	12	1,211.04	118.08	1,329.12

FIGURE 3-15: Worksheet with color, patterns, border, and style applied

J1   Sales Tax

Reason2Go Advertising Expenses

Sales Tax   0.0975

Type	Inv. Date	Inv. Due	Cost ea.	Quantity	Ext. Cost	Sales Tax	Total
USB drive	1-Jan-17	31-Jan	$ 5.34	5	26.70	2.60	29.30
TV Sponsor	7-Jan-17	6-Feb	$ 250.00	15	3,750.00	365.63	4,115.63
Podcasts	20-Jan-17	19-Feb	$ 77.50	30	2,325.00	226.69	2,551.69
TV commercials	1-Jan-17	31-Jan	$1,054.42	4	4,217.68	411.22	4,628.90
Web page asd	13-Jan-17	12-Feb	$ 0.17	230	39.56	3.86	43.42
Magazine	7-Jan-17	6-Feb	$ 100.92	12	1,211.04	118.08	1,329.12
Pens	5-Jan-17	4-Feb	$ 0.12	250	30.75	3.00	33.75
TV Sponsor	15-Jan-17	14-Feb	$ 250.00	15	3,750.00	365.63	4,115.63
Billboard	12-Jan-17	11-Feb	$ 101.87	20	2,037.40	198.65	2,236.05
USB drive	25-Jan-17	24-Feb	$ 5.34	6	32.04	3.12	35.16
USB drive	1-Feb-17	3-Mar	$ 5.34	2	10.68	1.04	11.72
T-Shirts	3-Feb-17	5-Mar	$ 5.67	200	1,134.00	110.57	1,244.57

Excel 2016

Working with themes and cell styles

Using themes and cell styles makes it easier to ensure that your worksheets are consistent. A **theme** is a predefined set of formats that gives your Excel worksheet a professional look. Formatting choices included in a theme are colors, fonts, and line and fill effects. To apply a theme, click the Themes button in the Themes group on the Page Layout tab to open the Themes gallery, as shown in **FIGURE 3-16**, then click a theme in the gallery. **Cell styles** are automatically updated if you change a theme. For example, if you apply the 20% - Accent1 cell style to cell A1 in a worksheet that has no theme applied, the fill color changes to light blue with no pattern, and the font changes to Calibri. If you change the theme of the worksheet to Ion Boardroom, cell A1's fill color changes to red and the font changes to Century Gothic, because these are the new theme's associated formats.

FIGURE 3-16: Themes gallery

Apply Conditional Formatting

Learning Outcomes
• Create conditional formatting in a range
• Change formatting and parameters in conditional formatting

So far, you've used formatting to change the appearance of different types of data, but you can also use formatting to highlight important aspects of the data itself. For example, you can apply formatting that changes the font color to red for any cells where the value is greater than $100 and to green where the value is below $50. This is called **conditional formatting** because Excel automatically applies different formats to data if the data meets conditions you specify. The formatting is updated if you change data in the worksheet. You can also copy conditional formats the same way you copy other formats. **CASE** ▸ *Mary is concerned about advertising costs exceeding the yearly budget. You decide to use conditional formatting to highlight certain trends and patterns in the data so that it's easy to spot the most expensive advertising.*

STEPS

1. **Select the range H4:H30, click the Conditional Formatting button in the Styles group on the Home tab, point to Data Bars, then point to the Light Blue Data Bar (second row, second from left)**

   Data bars are colored horizontal bars that visually illustrate differences between values in a range of cells. Live Preview shows how this formatting will appear in the worksheet, as shown in **FIGURE 3-17**.

2. **Point to the Green Data Bar (first row, second from left), then click it**

3. **Select the range F4:F30, click the Conditional Formatting button in the Styles group, then point to Highlight Cells Rules**

   The Highlight Cells Rules submenu displays choices for creating different formatting conditions. For example, you can create a rule for values that are greater than or less than a certain amount, or between two amounts.

4. **Click Between on the submenu**

   The Between dialog box opens, displaying input boxes you can use to define the condition and a default format (Light Red Fill with Dark Red Text) selected for cells that meet that condition. Depending on the condition you select in the Highlight Cells Rules submenu (such as "Greater Than" or "Less Than"), this dialog box displays different input boxes. You define the condition using the input boxes and then assign the formatting you want to use for cells that meet that condition. Values used in input boxes for a condition can be constants, formulas, cell references, or dates.

5. **Type 2000 in the first text box, type 4000 in the second text box, click the with list arrow, click Light Red Fill, compare your settings to FIGURE 3-18, then click OK**

   All cells with values between 2000 and 4000 in column F appear with a light red fill.

6. **Click cell E7, type 3, then press [Enter]**

   When the value in cell E7 changes, the formatting also changes because the new value meets the condition you set. Compare your results to **FIGURE 3-19**.

7. **Press [Ctrl][Home] to select cell A1, then save your work**

FIGURE 3-17: Previewing data bars in a range

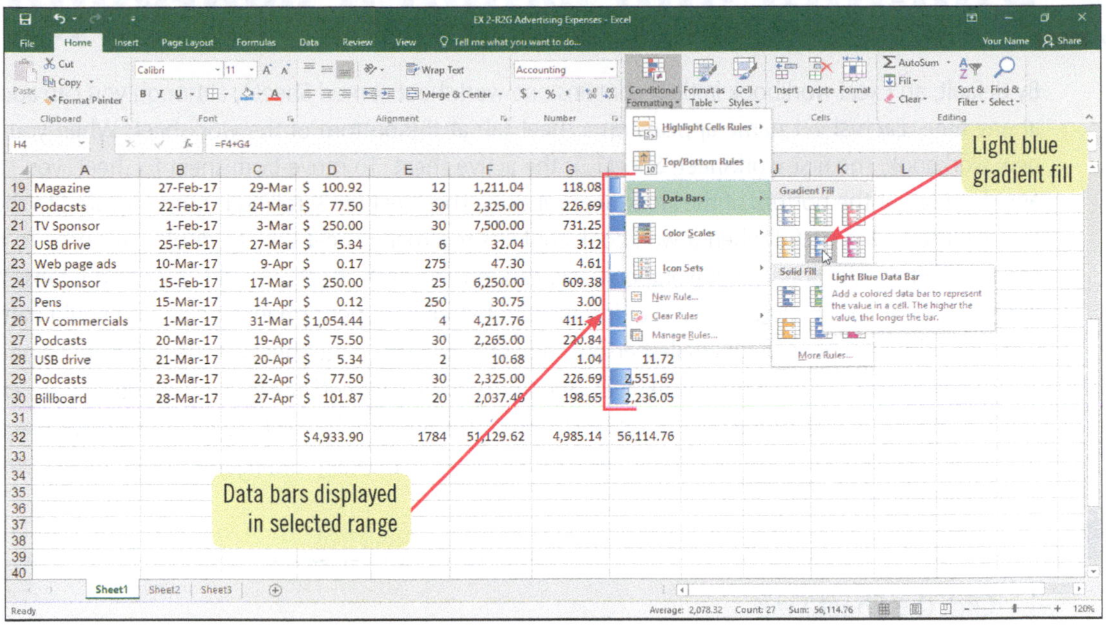

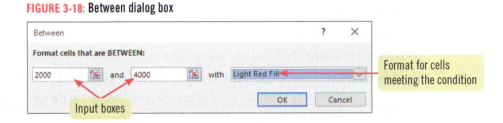

FIGURE 3-18: Between dialog box

FIGURE 3-19: Worksheet with conditional formatting

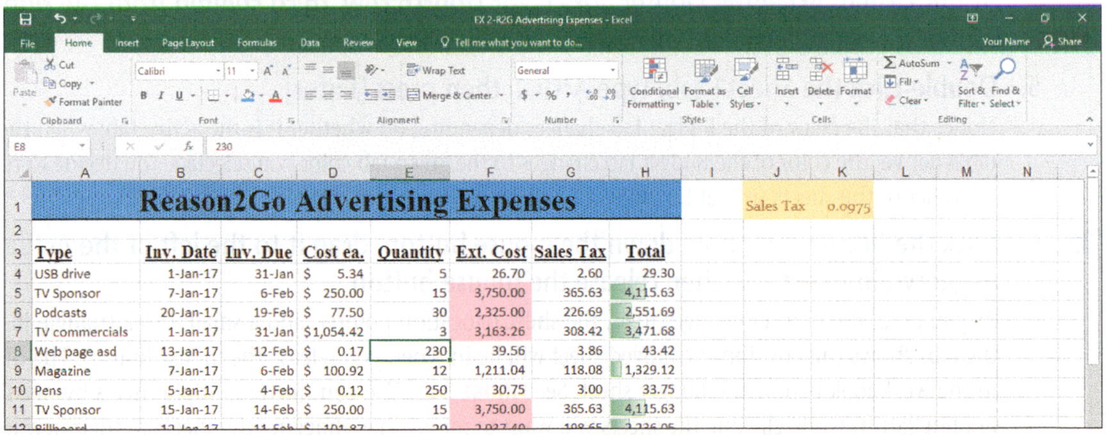

Managing conditional formatting rules

If you create a conditional formatting rule and then want to change a condition, you don't need to create a new rule; instead, you can modify the rule using the Rules Manager. Click the Conditional Formatting button in the Styles group, then click Manage Rules. The Conditional Formatting Rules Manager dialog box opens. Select the rule you want to edit, click Edit Rule, and then modify the settings in the Edit the Rule Description area in the Edit Formatting Rule dialog box. To change the formatting for a rule, click the Format Style button in the Edit the Rule Description area, select the formatting styles you want the text to have, then click OK three times to close the Format Cells dialog box, the Edit Formatting Rule dialog box, and the Conditional Formatting Rules Manager dialog box. The rule is modified, and the new conditional formatting is applied to the selected cells. To delete a rule, select the rule in the Conditional Formatting Rules Manager dialog box, then click the Delete Rule button.

Rename and Move a Worksheet

Learning
Outcomes
• Rename a sheet
• Apply color to a
  sheet tab
• Reorder sheets in
  a workbook

By default, an Excel workbook initially contains one worksheet named Sheet1, although you can add sheets at any time. Each sheet name appears on a sheet tab at the bottom of the worksheet. When you open a new workbook, the first worksheet, Sheet1, is the active sheet. To move from sheet to sheet, you can click any sheet tab at the bottom of the worksheet window. The sheet tab scrolling buttons, located to the left of the sheet tabs, are useful when a workbook contains too many sheet tabs to display at once. To make it easier to identify the sheets in a workbook, you can rename each sheet and add color to the tabs. You can also organize them in a logical way. For instance, to better track performance goals, you could name each workbook sheet for an individual salesperson, and you could move the sheets so they appear in alphabetical order. **CASE** *In the current worksheet, Sheet1 contains information about actual advertising expenses. Sheet2 contains an advertising budget, and Sheet3 contains no data. You want to rename the two sheets in the workbook to reflect their contents, add color to a sheet tab to easily distinguish one from the other, and change their order.*

STEPS

1. **Click the Sheet2 tab**

   Sheet2 becomes active, appearing in front of the Sheet1 tab; this is the worksheet that contains the budgeted advertising expenses. See **FIGURE 3-20**.

QUICK TIP
You can also rename a sheet by right-clicking the tab, clicking Rename on the shortcut menu, typing the new name, then pressing [Enter].

2. **Click the Sheet1 tab**

   Sheet1, which contains the actual advertising expenses, becomes active again.

3. **Double-click the Sheet2 tab, type Budget, then press [Enter]**

   The new name for Sheet2 automatically replaces the default name on the tab. Worksheet names can have up to 31 characters, including spaces and punctuation.

QUICK TIP
To delete a sheet, click its tab, click the Delete list arrow in the Cells group, then click Delete Sheet. To insert a worksheet, click the New sheet button ⊕ to the right of the sheet tabs.

4. **Right-click the Budget tab, point to Tab Color on the shortcut menu, then click the Bright Green, Accent 4, Lighter 40% color (fourth row, third column from the right) as shown in FIGURE 3-21**

5. **Double-click the Sheet1 tab, type Actual, then press [Enter]**

   Notice that the color of the Budget tab changes depending on whether it is the active tab; when the Actual tab is active, the color of the Budget tab changes to the green tab color you selected. You decide to rearrange the order of the sheets so that the Budget tab is to the left of the Actual tab.

QUICK TIP
If you have more sheet tabs than are visible, you can move between sheets by using the tab scrolling buttons to the left of the sheet tabs: the Previous Worksheet button ◄ and the Next Worksheet button ►.

6. **Click the Budget tab, hold down the mouse button, drag it to the left of the Actual tab, as shown in FIGURE 3-22, then release the mouse button**

   As you drag, the pointer changes to ⧉, the sheet relocation pointer, and a small, black triangle just above the tabs shows the position the moved sheet will be in when you release the mouse button. The first sheet in the workbook is now the Budget sheet. See **FIGURE 3-23**. You can move multiple sheets by pressing and holding [Shift] while clicking the sheets you want to move, then dragging the sheets to their new location.

7. **Click the Actual sheet tab, click the Page Layout button ▣ on the status bar to open Page Layout view, enter your name in the left header text box, then click anywhere in the worksheet to deselect the header**

8. **Click the Page Layout tab on the Ribbon, click the Orientation button in the Page Setup group, then click Landscape**

9. **Right-click the Sheet3 tab, click Delete on the shortcut menu, press [Ctrl][Home], then save your work**

FIGURE 3-20: Sheet tabs in workbook

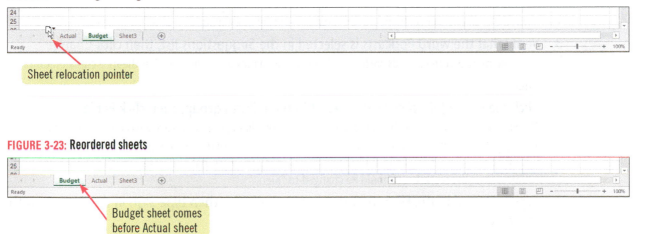

Sheet1 tab   Sheet2 tab

FIGURE 3-21: Tab Color palette

Sheet2 renamed

FIGURE 3-22: Moving the Budget sheet

Sheet relocation pointer

FIGURE 3-23: Reordered sheets

Budget sheet comes
before Actual sheet

Excel 2016

Copying, adding, and deleting worksheets

There are times when you may want to copy a worksheet. For example, a workbook might contain a sheet with Quarter 1 expenses, and you want to use that sheet as the basis for a sheet containing Quarter 2 expenses. To copy a sheet within the same workbook, press and hold [Ctrl], drag the sheet tab to the desired tab location, release the mouse button, then release [Ctrl]. A duplicate sheet appears with the same name as the copied sheet followed by "(2)" indicating that it is a copy. You can then rename the sheet to a more meaningful name. To copy a sheet to a different workbook, both the source and destination workbooks must be open. Select the sheet to copy or move, right-click the sheet tab, then click Move or Copy in the shortcut menu. Complete the information in the Move or Copy dialog

box. Be sure to click the Create a copy check box if you are copying rather than moving the worksheet. Carefully check your calculation results whenever you move or copy a worksheet. You can add multiple worksheets to a workbook by clicking the Home tab on the Ribbon, pressing and holding [Shift], then clicking the number of existing worksheet tabs that correspond with the number of sheets you want to add, clicking the Insert list arrow in the Cells group on the Home tab, then clicking Insert Sheet. You can delete multiple worksheets from a workbook by clicking the Home tab, pressing and holding [Shift], clicking the sheet tabs of the worksheets you want to delete, clicking the Delete list arrow in the Cells group on the Home tab, then clicking Delete Sheet.

Check Spelling

Excel includes a spell checker to help you ensure that the words in your worksheet are spelled correctly. The spell checker scans your worksheet, displays words it doesn't find in its built-in dictionary, and suggests replacements when they are available. To check all of the sheets in a multiple-sheet workbook, you need to display each sheet individually and run the spell checker for each one. Because the built-in dictionary cannot possibly include all the words that anyone needs, you can add words to the dictionary, such as your company name, an acronym, or an unusual technical term. Once you add a word or term, the spell checker no longer considers that word misspelled. Any words you've added to the dictionary using Word, Access, or PowerPoint are also available in Excel. **CASE** Before you distribute this workbook to Mary, you check the spelling.

STEPS

QUICK TIP
The Spelling dialog box lists the name of the language currently being used in its title bar.

1. **Click the Review tab on the Ribbon, then click the Spelling button in the Proofing group**

   The Spelling: English (United States) dialog box opens, as shown in **FIGURE 3-24**, with "asd" selected as the first misspelled word in the worksheet, and with "ads" selected in the Suggestions list as a possible replacement. For any word, you have the option to Ignore this case of the flagged word, Ignore All cases of the flagged word, Change the word to the selected suggestion, Change All instances of the flagged word to the selected suggestion, or add the flagged word to the dictionary using Add to Dictionary.

2. **Click Change**

   Next, the spell checker finds the word "Podacsts" and suggests "Podcasts" as an alternative.

3. **Verify that the word Podcasts is selected in the Suggestions list, then click Change**

   When no more incorrect words are found, Excel displays a message indicating that the spell check is complete.

4. **Click OK**

5. **Click the Home tab, click Find & Select in the Editing group, then click Replace**

   The Find and Replace dialog box opens. You can use this dialog box to replace a word or phrase. It might be a misspelling of a proper name that the spell checker didn't recognize as misspelled, or it could simply be a term that you want to change throughout the worksheet. Mary has just told you that each instance of "Billboard" in the worksheet should be changed to "Sign."

6. **Type Billboard in the Find what text box, press [Tab], then type Sign in the Replace with text box**

   Compare your dialog box to **FIGURE 3-25**.

7. **Click Replace All, click OK to close the Microsoft Excel dialog box, then click Close to close the Find and Replace dialog box**

   Excel has made two replacements.

8. **Click the File tab, click Print on the navigation bar, click the No Scaling setting in the Settings section on the Print tab, then click Fit Sheet on One Page**

9. **Click the Return button ⬅ to return to your worksheet, save your work, submit it to your instructor as directed, close the workbook, then exit Excel**

   The completed worksheet is shown in **FIGURE 3-26**.

Emailing a workbook

You can send an entire workbook from within Excel using your installed email program, such as Microsoft Outlook. To send a workbook as an email message attachment, open the workbook, click the File tab, then click Share on the navigation bar. With the Email option selected in the Share section in Backstage view, click Send as Attachment in the right pane. An email message opens in your default email program with the workbook automatically attached; the filename appears in the Attached field. Complete the To and optional Cc fields, include a message if you wish, then click Send.

FIGURE 3-24: Spelling: English (United States) dialog box

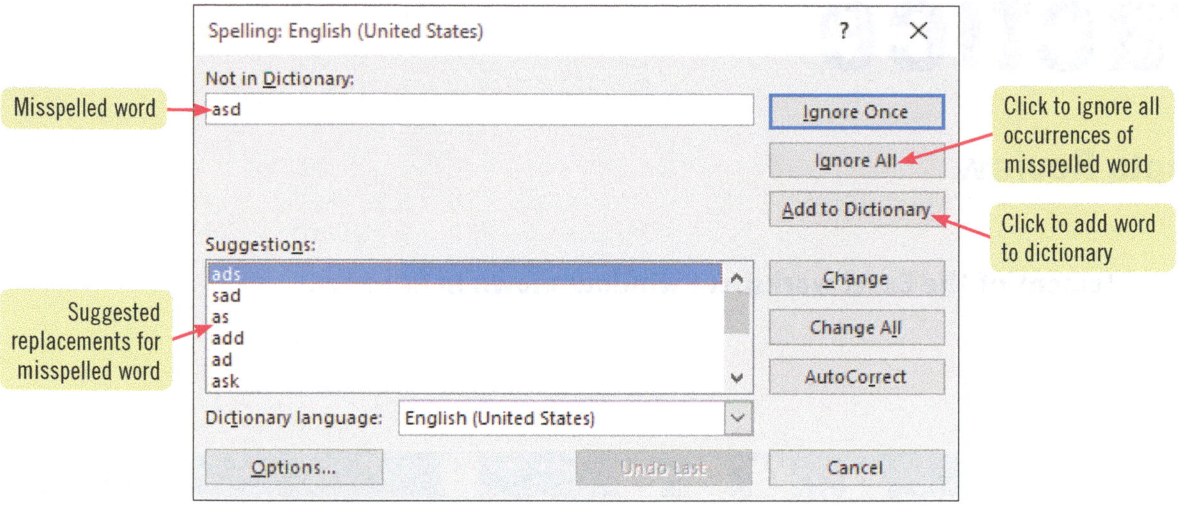

Misspelled word →

Suggested replacements for misspelled word →

Click to ignore all occurrences of misspelled word

Click to add word to dictionary

Spelling: English (United States)

Not in Dictionary:
asd

Suggestions:
ads
sad
as
add
ad
ask

Dictionary language: English (United States)

Ignore Once
Ignore All
Add to Dictionary
Change
Change All
AutoCorrect

Options...   Undo Last   Cancel

FIGURE 3-25: Find and Replace dialog box

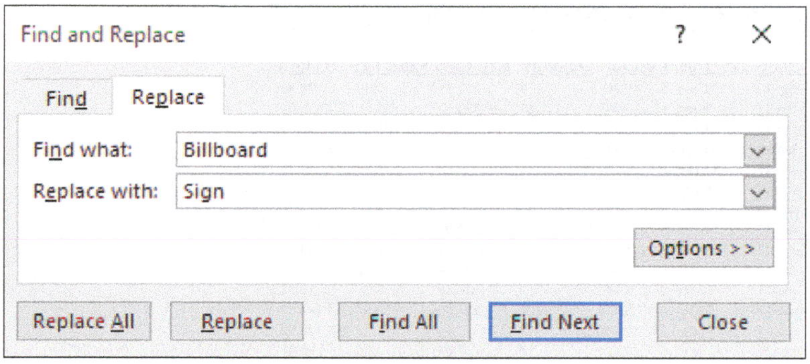

Find and Replace

Find   Replace

Find what: Billboard

Replace with: Sign

Options >>

Replace All   Replace   Find All   Find Next   Close

FIGURE 3-26: Completed worksheet

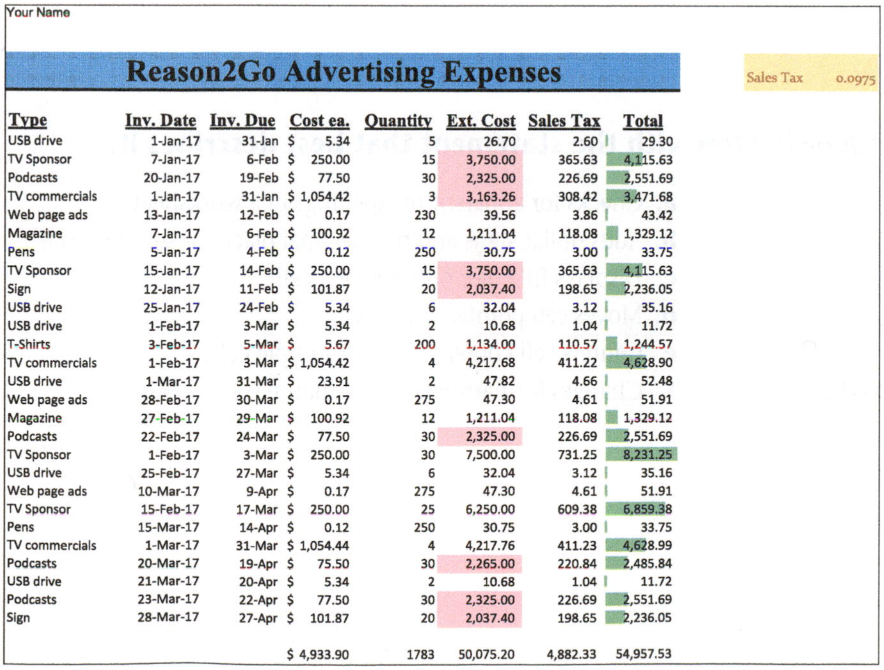

Your Name

Reason2Go Advertising Expenses

Sales Tax   0.0975

Type	Inv. Date	Inv. Due	Cost ea.	Quantity	Ext. Cost	Sales Tax	Total
USB drive	1-Jan-17	31-Jan	$ 5.34	5	26.70	2.60	29.30
TV Sponsor	7-Jan-17	6-Feb	$ 250.00	15	3,750.00	365.63	4,115.63
Podcasts	20-Jan-17	19-Feb	$ 77.50	30	2,325.00	226.69	2,551.69
TV commercials	1-Jan-17	31-Jan	$ 1,054.42	3	3,163.26	308.42	3,471.68
Web page ads	13-Jan-17	12-Feb	$ 0.17	230	39.56	3.86	43.42
Magazine	7-Jan-17	6-Feb	$ 100.92	12	1,211.04	118.08	1,329.12
Pens	5-Jan-17	4-Feb	$ 0.12	250	30.75	3.00	33.75
TV Sponsor	15-Jan-17	14-Feb	$ 250.00	15	3,750.00	365.63	4,115.63
Sign	12-Jan-17	11-Feb	$ 101.87	20	2,037.40	198.65	2,236.05
USB drive	25-Jan-17	24-Feb	$ 5.34	6	32.04	3.12	35.16
USB drive	1-Feb-17	3-Mar	$ 5.34	2	10.68	1.04	11.72
T-Shirts	3-Feb-17	5-Mar	$ 5.67	200	1,134.00	110.57	1,244.57
TV commercials	1-Feb-17	3-Mar	$ 1,054.42	4	4,217.68	411.22	4,628.90
USB drive	1-Mar-17	31-Mar	$ 23.91	2	47.82	4.66	52.48
Web page ads	28-Feb-17	30-Mar	$ 0.17	275	47.30	4.61	51.91
Magazine	27-Feb-17	29-Mar	$ 100.92	12	1,211.04	118.08	1,329.12
Podcasts	22-Feb-17	24-Mar	$ 77.50	30	2,325.00	226.69	2,551.69
TV Sponsor	1-Feb-17	3-Mar	$ 250.00	30	7,500.00	731.25	8,231.25
USB drive	25-Feb-17	27-Mar	$ 5.34	6	32.04	3.12	35.16
Web page ads	10-Mar-17	9-Apr	$ 0.17	275	47.30	4.61	51.91
TV Sponsor	15-Feb-17	17-Mar	$ 250.00	25	6,250.00	609.38	6,859.38
Pens	15-Mar-17	14-Apr	$ 0.12	250	30.75	3.00	33.75
TV commercials	1-Mar-17	31-Mar	$ 1,054.44	4	4,217.76	411.23	4,628.99
Podcasts	20-Mar-17	19-Apr	$ 75.50	30	2,265.00	220.84	2,485.84
USB drive	21-Mar-17	20-Apr	$ 5.34	2	10.68	1.04	11.72
Podcasts	23-Mar-17	22-Apr	$ 77.50	30	2,325.00	226.69	2,551.69
Sign	28-Mar-17	27-Apr	$ 101.87	20	2,037.40	198.65	2,236.05
			$ 4,933.90	1783	50,075.20	4,882.33	54,957.53

Practice

Concepts Review

Label each element of the Excel worksheet window shown in FIGURE 3-27.

FIGURE 3-27

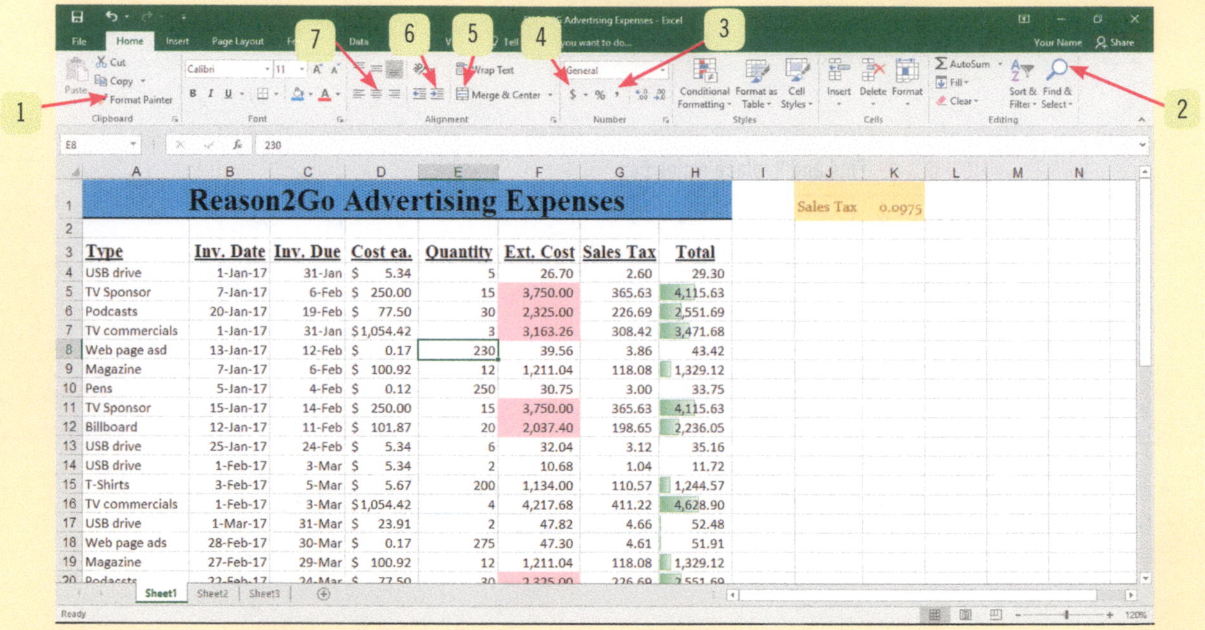

Match each command or button with the statement that best describes it.

8. Spelling button
9. $
10.  (fill color icon)
11. [Ctrl][Home]
12. (merge icon)
13. Conditional formatting

a. Checks for apparent misspellings in a worksheet
b. Adds dollar signs and two decimal places to selected data
c. Displays fill color options for a cell
d. Moves cell pointer to cell A1
e. Centers cell contents across multiple cells
f. Changes formatting of a cell that meets a certain rule

Select the best answer from the list of choices.

14. **Which of the following is an example of Accounting number format?**
    a. 5555
    b. $5,555.55
    c. 55.55%
    d. 5,555.55

15. **What is the name of the feature used to resize a column to accommodate its widest entry?**
    a. AutoFormat
    b. AutoFit
    c. AutoResize
    d. AutoRefit

16. **Which button copies multiple formats from selected cells to other cells?**
    a. [icon]
    b. [icon]
    c. [icon]
    d. [icon]

17. **Which button increases the number of decimal places in selected cells?**
    a. [icon]
    b. [icon]
    c. [icon]
    d. [icon]

18. **Which button removes the italic font style from selected cells?**
    a. [I icon]
    b. [B icon]
    c. [I icon]
    d. [U icon]

19. **What feature is used to delete a conditional formatting rule?**
    a. Rules Reminder
    b. Conditional Formatting Rules Manager
    c. Condition Manager
    d. Format Manager

Skills Review

1. **Format values.**
   a. Start Excel, open the file EX 3-2.xlsx from the location where you store your Data Files, then save it as **EX 3-Health Insurance Premiums**.
   b. Use the Sum function to enter a formula in cell B10 that totals the number of employees.
   c. Create a formula in cell C5 that calculates the monthly insurance premium for the accounting department. (*Hint*: Make sure you use the correct type of cell reference in the formula. To calculate the department's monthly premium, multiply the number of employees by the monthly premium in cell B14.)
   d. Copy the formula in cell C5 to the range C6:C10.
   e. Format the range C5:C10 using Accounting number format.
   f. Change the format of the range C6:C9 to the Comma Style.
   g. Reduce the number of decimals in cell B14 to 0 using a button in the Number group on the Home tab.
   h. Save your work.

2. **Change font and font sizes.**
   a. Select the range of cells containing the column labels (in row 4).
   b. Change the font of the selection to Times New Roman.
   c. Increase the font size of the selection to 12 points.
   d. Increase the font size of the label in cell A1 to 14 points.
   e. Save your changes.

3. **Change font styles and alignment.**
   a. Apply the bold and italic font styles to the worksheet title in cell A1.
   b. Use the Merge & Center button to center the Health Insurance Premiums label over columns A–C.
   c. Apply the italic font style to the Health Insurance Premiums label.
   d. Add the bold font style to the labels in row 4.
   e. Use the Format Painter to copy the format in cell A4 to the range A5:A10.
   f. Apply the format in cell C10 to cell B14.
   g. Change the alignment of cell A10 to Align Right using a button in the Alignment group.

Skills Review (continued)

   h. Select the range of cells containing the column labels, then center them.

   i. Remove the italic font style from the Health Insurance Premiums label, then increase the font size to 14.

   j. Move the Health Insurance Premiums label to cell A3, remove the Merge & Center format, then add the bold and underline font styles.

   k. Save your changes.

4. **Adjust column width.**

   a. Resize column C to a width of 10.71 characters.

   b. Use the AutoFit feature to resize columns A and B.

   c. Clear the contents of cell A13 (do not delete the cell).

   d. Change the text in cell A14 to **Monthly Premium**, then change the width of the column to 25 characters.

   e. Save your changes.

5. **Insert and delete rows and columns.**

   a. Insert a new row between rows 5 and 6.

   b. Add a new department, **Donations**, in the newly inserted row. Enter **6** as the number of employees in the department.

   c. Copy the formula in cell C7 to C6.

   d. Add the following comment to cell A6: **New department**. Display the comment, then drag to move it out of the way, if necessary.

   e. Add a new column between the Department and Employees columns with the title **Family Coverage**, then resize the column using AutoFit.

   f. Delete the Legal row from the worksheet.

   g. Move the value in cell C14 to cell B14.

   h. Save your changes.

6. **Apply colors, patterns, and borders.**

   a. Add Outside Borders around the range A4:D10.

   b. Add a Bottom Double Border to cells C9 and D9 (above the calculated employee and premium totals).

   c. Apply the Aqua, Accent 5, Lighter 80% fill color to the labels in the Department column (do not include the Total label).

   d. Apply the Orange, Accent 6, Lighter 60% fill color to the range A4:D4.

   e. Change the color of the font in the range A4:D4 to Red, Accent 2, Darker 25%.

   f. Add a 12.5% Gray pattern style to cell A1.

   g. Format the range A14:B14 with a fill color of Dark Blue, Text 2, Lighter 40%, change the font color to White, Background 1, then apply the bold font style.

   h. Save your changes.

7. **Apply conditional formatting.**

   a. Select the range D5:D9, then create a conditional format that changes cell contents to green fill with dark green text if the value is between 150 and 275.

   b. Select the range C5:C9, then create a conditional format that changes cell contents to red text if the number of employees exceeds 10.

   c. Apply a purple gradient-filled data bar to the range C5:C9. (*Hint*: Click Purple Data Bar in the Gradient Fill section.)

   d. Use the Rules Manager to modify the conditional format in cells C5:C9 to display values greater than 10 in bold dark red text.

   e. Save your changes.

8. **Rename and move a worksheet.**

   a. Name the Sheet1 tab **Insurance Data**.

   b. Add a sheet to the workbook, then name the new sheet **Employee Data**.

   c. Change the Insurance Data tab color to Red, Accent 2, Lighter 40%.

Skills Review (continued)

d. Change the Employee Data tab color to Aqua, Accent 5, Lighter 40%.

e. Move the Employee Data sheet so it comes before (to the left of) the Insurance Data sheet.

f. Make the Insurance Data sheet active, enter your name in cell A20, then save your work.

9. Check spelling.

a. Move the cell pointer to cell A1.

b. Use the Find & Select feature to replace the Accounting label with **Accounting/Legal**.

c. Check the spelling in the worksheet using the spell checker, and correct any spelling errors if necessary.

d. Save your changes, then compare your Insurance Data sheet to FIGURE 3-28.

e. Preview the Insurance Data sheet in Backstage view, submit your work to your instructor as directed, then close the workbook and exit Excel.

FIGURE 3-28

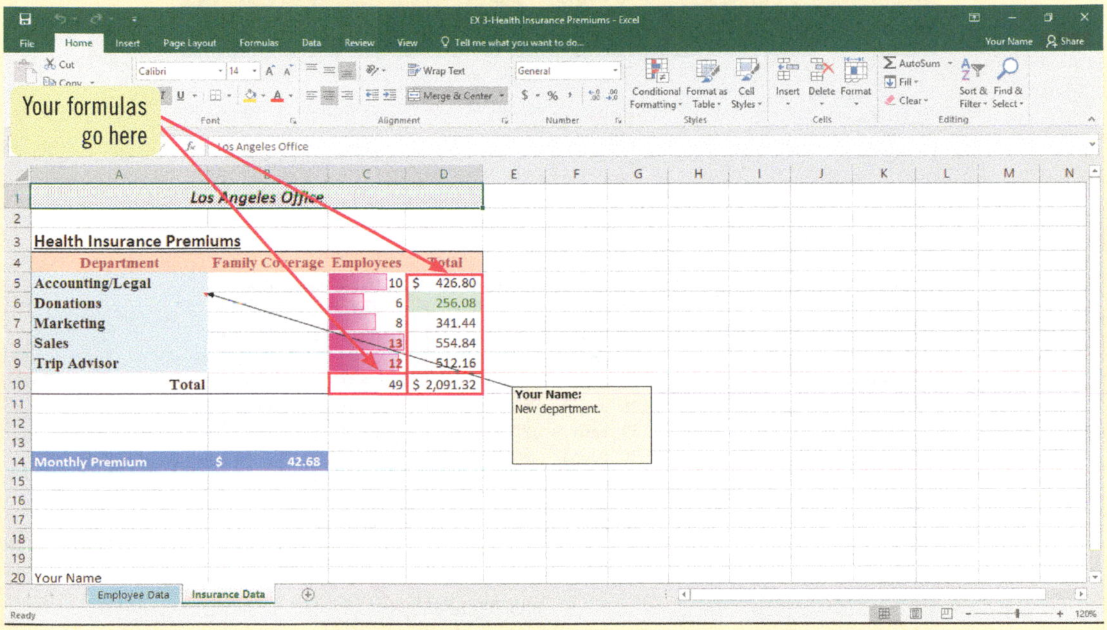

Independent Challenge 1

You run a freelance accounting business, and one of your newest clients is Fresh To You, a small local grocery store. Now that you've converted the store's accounting records to Excel, the manager would like you to work on an analysis of the inventory. Although more items will be added later, the worksheet has enough items for you to begin your modifications.

a. Start Excel, open the file EX 3-3.xlsx from the location where you store your Data Files, then save it as **EX 3-Fresh To You Inventory**.

b. Create a formula in cell E4 that calculates the value of the items in stock based on the price paid per item in cell B4. Format the cell in the Comma Style.

c. In cell F4, calculate the sale value of the items in stock using an absolute reference to the markup value shown in cell H1.

d. Copy the formulas created above into the range E5:F14; first convert any necessary cell references to absolute so that the formulas work correctly.

e. Apply bold to the column labels, and italicize the inventory items in column A.

f. Make sure that all columns are wide enough to display the data and labels.

g. Format the values in the Sale Value column as Accounting number format with two decimal places.

h. Format the values in the Price Paid column as Comma Style with two decimal places.

Independent Challenge 1 (continued)

i. Add a row under Cheddar Cheese for **Whole Wheat flour**, price paid **0.95**, sold by weight (**pound**), with **23** on hand. Copy the appropriate formulas to cells E7:F7.

j. Verify that all the data in the worksheet is visible and formulas are correct. Adjust any items as needed, and check the spelling of the entire worksheet.

k. Use conditional formatting to apply yellow fill with dark yellow text to items with a quantity of less than 25 on hand.

l. Use an icon set of your choosing in the range D4:D14 to illustrate the relative differences between values in the range.

m. Add an outside border around the data in the Item column (*do not* include the Item column label).

n. Delete the row containing the Resource Coffee - decaf entry.

o. Enter your name in an empty cell below the data, then save the file. Compare your worksheet to the sample in FIGURE 3-29.

p. Preview the worksheet in Backstage view, submit your work to your instructor as directed, close the workbook, then exit Excel.

FIGURE 3-29

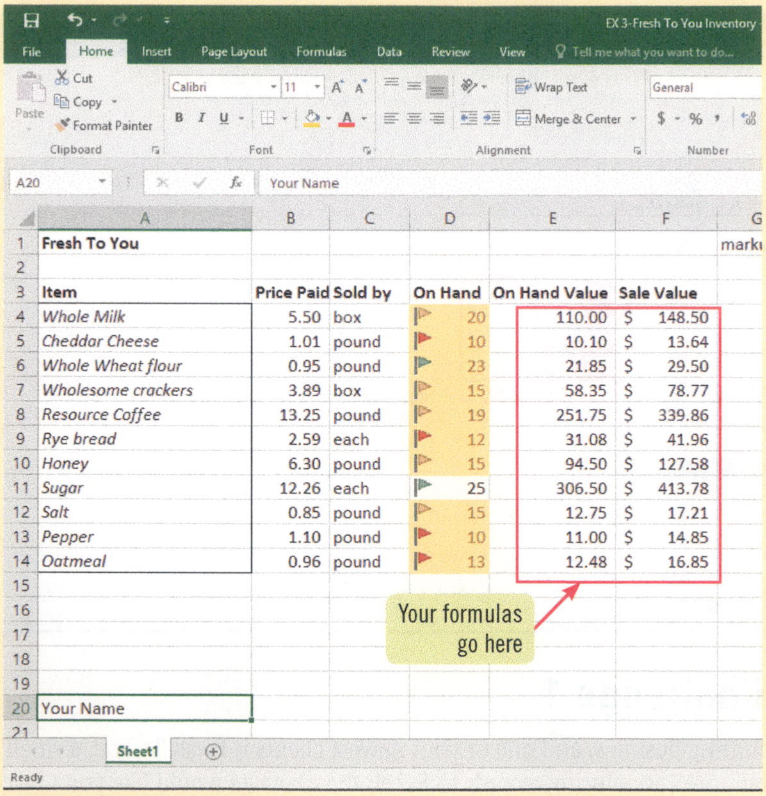

Independent Challenge 2

You volunteer several hours each week with the Assistance League of San Antonio, and you are in charge of maintaining the membership list. You're currently planning a mailing campaign to members in certain regions of the city. You also want to create renewal letters for members whose membership expires soon. You decide to format the list to enhance the appearance of the worksheet and make your upcoming tasks easier to plan.

a. Start Excel, open the file EX 3-4.xlsx from the location where you store your Data Files, then save it as **EX 3-Memphis Assistance League**.

b. Remove any blank columns.

c. Create a conditional format in the Zip Code column so that entries greater than 38249 appear in light red fill with dark red text.

d. Make all columns wide enough to fit their data and labels. (*Hint*: You can use any method to size the columns.)

e. Use formatting enhancements, such as fonts, font sizes, font styles, and fill colors, to make the worksheet more attractive.

Independent Challenge 2 (continued)

f. Center the column labels.

g. Use conditional formatting so that entries for Year of Membership Expiration that are between 2021 and 2023 appear in green fill with bold black text. (*Hint*: Create a custom format for cells that meet the condition.)

h. Adjust any items as necessary, then check the spelling.

i. Change the name of the Sheet1 tab to one that reflects the sheet's contents, then add a tab color of your choice.

j. Enter your name in an empty cell, then save your work.

k. Preview the worksheet, make any final changes you think necessary, then submit your work to your instructor as directed. Compare your work to the sample shown in FIGURE 3-30.

l. Close the workbook, then exit Excel.

FIGURE 3-30

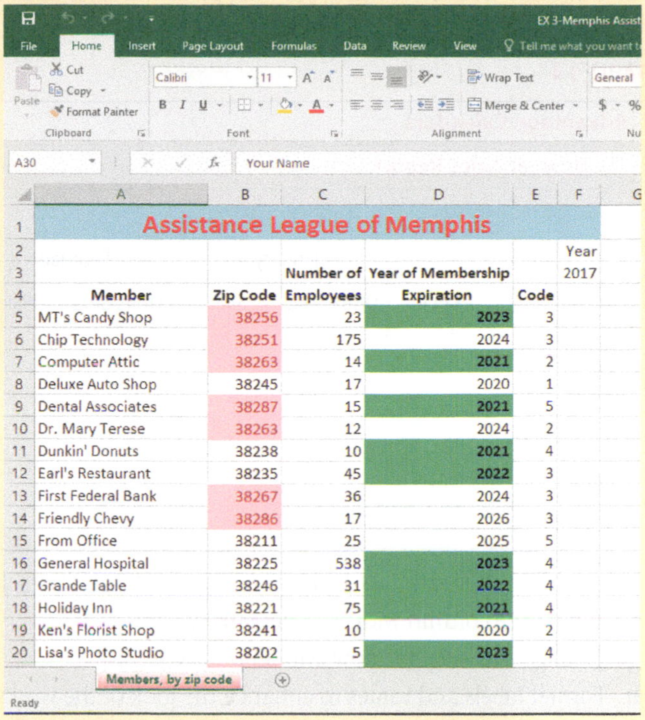

Independent Challenge 3

Advantage Calendars is a Dallas-based printer that prints and assembles calendars. As the finance manager for the company, one of your responsibilities is to analyze the monthly reports from the five district sales offices. Your boss, Joanne Bennington, has just asked you to prepare a quarterly sales report for an upcoming meeting. Because several top executives will be attending this meeting, Joanne reminds you that the report must look professional. In particular, she asks you to highlight the fact that the Northeastern district continues to outpace the other districts.

a. Plan a worksheet that shows the company's sales during the first quarter. Assume that all calendars are the same price. Make sure you include the following:

- The number of calendars sold (units sold) and the associated revenues (total sales) for each of the five district sales offices. The five sales districts are Northeastern, Midwestern, Southeastern, Southern, and Western.
- Calculations that show month-by-month totals for January, February, and March, and a 3-month cumulative total.
- Calculations that show each district's share of sales (percent of Total Sales).
- Labels that reflect the month-by-month data as well as the cumulative data.
- Formatting enhancements such as data bars that emphasize the recent month's sales surge and the Northeastern district's sales leadership.

b. Ask yourself the following questions about the organization and formatting of the worksheet: What worksheet title and labels do you need, and where should they appear? How can you calculate the totals? What formulas can you copy to save time and keystrokes? Do any of these formulas need to use an absolute reference? How do you show dollar amounts? What information should be shown in bold? Do you need to use more than one font? Should you use more than one point size?

c. Start Excel, then save a new, blank workbook as **EX 3-Advantage Calendars** to the location where you store your Data Files.

Excel 2016

Independent Challenge 3 (continued)

d. Build the worksheet with your own price and sales data. Enter the titles and labels first, then enter the numbers and formulas. You can use the information in **TABLE 3-4** to get started.

TABLE 3-4

Advantage Calendars										
1st Quarter Sales Report										
		January		February		March		Total		
Office	Price	Units Sold	Sales	Units Sold	Sales	Units Sold	Sales	Units Sold	Sales	Total % of Sales
Northeastern										
Midwestern										
Southeastern										
Southern										
Western										

e. Add a row beneath the data containing the totals for each column.

f. Adjust the column widths as necessary.

g. Change the height of row 1 to 33 points.

h. Format labels and values to enhance the look of the worksheet, and change the font styles and alignment if necessary.

i. Resize columns and adjust the formatting as necessary.

j. Add data bars for the monthly Units Sold columns.

k. Add a column that calculates a 25% increase in total sales dollars. Use an absolute cell reference in this calculation. (*Hint*: Make sure that the current formatting is applied to the new information.)

l. Delete the contents of cells J4:K4 if necessary, then merge and center cell I4 over column I:K.

m. Add a bottom double border to cells I10:L10.

n. Enter your name in an empty cell.

o. Check the spelling in the workbook, change to a landscape orientation, save your work, then compare your work to **FIGURE 3-31**.

p. Preview the worksheet in Backstage view, then submit your work to your instructor as directed.

q. Close the workbook file, then exit Excel.

FIGURE 3-31

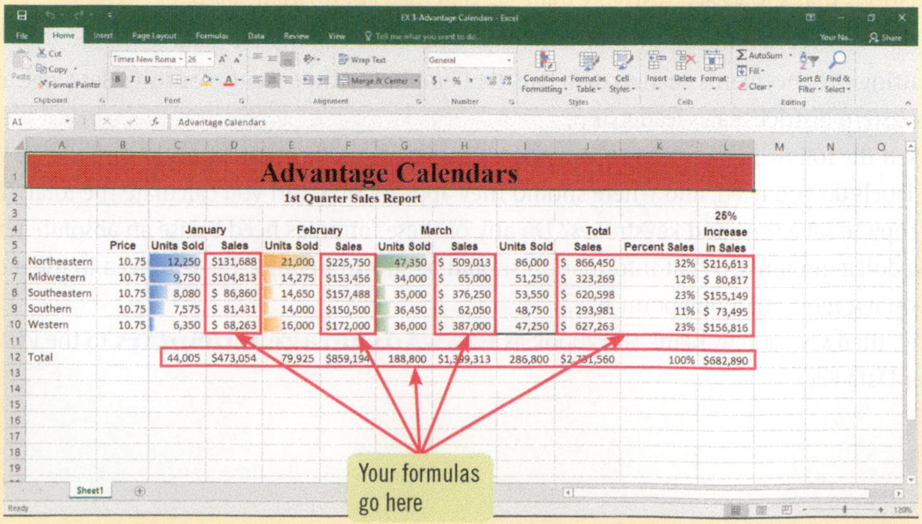

Independent Challenge 4: Explore

This Independent Challenge requires an Internet connection.

Your corporate relocation company helps employees to settle quickly and easily into new cities around the world. Your latest client plans to send employees to seven different countries. All employees will receive the same weekly budget in American currency. You need to create a worksheet to help all the employees understand the currency conversion rates in the different countries so that they can plan their spending effectively.

a. Start Excel, then save a new, blank workbook as **EX 3-Foreign Currency Rates** to the location where you store your Data Files.

b. Add a title at the top of the worksheet.

c. Think of seven countries that each use a different currency, then enter column and row labels for your worksheet. (*Hint*: You may wish to include row labels for each country, plus column labels for the country, the $1 equivalent in native currency, the total amount of native currency employees will have in each country, and the name of each country's monetary unit.)

d. Decide how much money employees will bring to each country (for example, $1,000), and enter that in the worksheet.

e. Use your favorite search engine to find your own information sources on currency conversions for the countries you have listed.

f. Enter the cash equivalent to $1 in U.S. dollars for each country in your list.

g. Create an equation that calculates the amount of native currency employees will have in each country, using an absolute cell reference in the formula.

h. Format the entries in the column containing the native currency $1 equivalent as Number number format with three decimal places, and format the column containing the total native currency budget with two decimal places, using the correct currency number format for each country. (*Hint*: Use the Number tab in the Format cells dialog box; choose the appropriate currency number format from the Symbol list.)

i. Create a conditional format that changes the font style and color of the calculated amount in the $1,000 US column to light red fill with dark red text if the amount exceeds **1000** units of the local currency.

j. Merge and center the worksheet title over the column headings.

k. Add any formatting you want to the column headings, and resize the columns as necessary.

l. Add a background color to the title and change the font color if you choose.

m. Enter your name in the header of the worksheet.

n. Spell check the worksheet, save your changes, compare your work to **FIGURE 3-32**, then preview the worksheet, and submit your work to your instructor as directed.

o. Close the workbook and exit Excel.

FIGURE 3-32

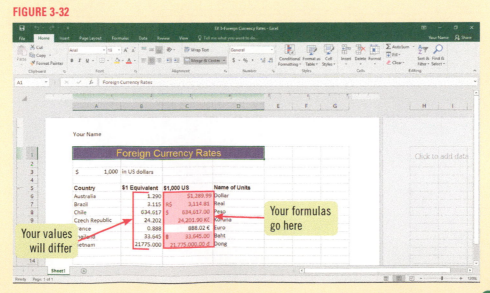

Visual Workshop

Open the file EX 3-5.xlsx from the location where you store your Data Files, then save it as **EX 3-London Employees**. Use the skills you learned in this module to format the worksheet so it looks like the one shown in FIGURE 3-33. Create a conditional format in the Level column so that entries greater than 3 appear in light red fill with dark red text. Create an additional conditional format in the Review Cycle column so that any value equal to 3 appears in black fill with white bold text. Replace the Accounting department label with **Legal**. (*Hint*: The only additional font used in this exercise is 18-point Times New Roman in row 1.) Enter your name in the upper-right part of the header, check the spelling in the worksheet, save your changes, then submit your work to your instructor as directed. (*Hint*: To match the figure exactly, remember to match the zoom level.)

FIGURE 3-33

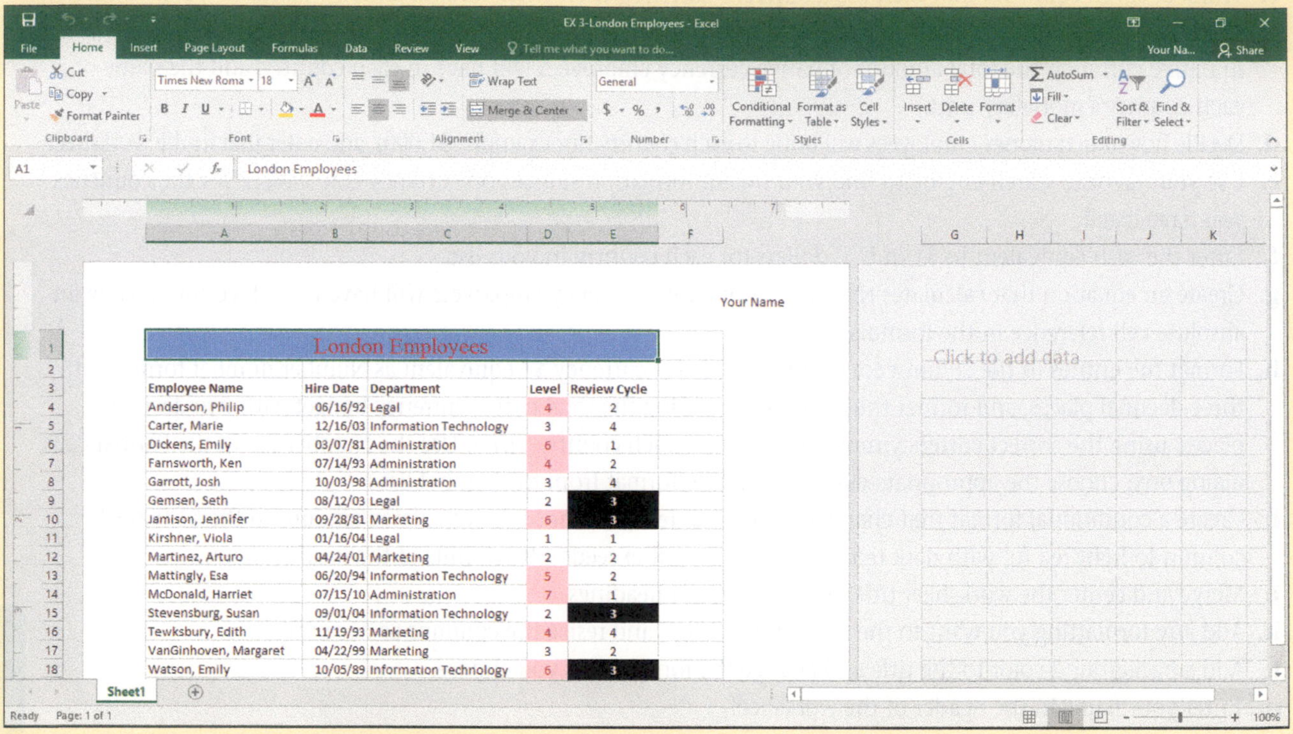

Working with Charts

CASE At the upcoming annual meeting, Yolanda Lee wants to discuss spending patterns at Reason2Go. She asks you to create a chart showing the trends in company expenses over the past four quarters.

Module Objectives

After completing this module, you will be able to:

- Plan a chart
- Create a chart
- Move and resize a chart
- Change the chart design
- Change the chart format
- Format a chart
- Annotate and draw on a chart
- Create a pie chart

Files You Will Need

EX 4-1.xlsx	EX 4-4.xlsx
EX 4-2.xlsx	EX 4-5.xlsx
EX 4-3.xlsx	EX 4-6.xlsx

Plan a Chart

Before creating a chart, you need to plan the information you want your chart to show and how you want it to look. Planning ahead helps you decide what type of chart to create and how to organize the data. Understanding the parts of a chart makes it easier to format and change specific elements so that the chart best illustrates your data. **CASE** ▶ *In preparation for creating the chart for Yolanda's presentation, you identify your goals for the chart and plan its layout.*

DETAILS

Use the following guidelines to plan the chart:

• **Determine the purpose of the chart, and identify the data relationships you want to communicate graphically**

   You want to create a chart that shows quarterly tour expenses for each country where Reason2Go provides tours. This worksheet data is shown in **FIGURE 4-1**. You also want the chart to illustrate whether the quarterly expenses for each country increased or decreased from quarter to quarter.

• **Determine the results you want to see, and decide which chart type is most appropriate**

   Different chart types display data in distinctive ways. For example, a pie chart compares parts to the whole, so it's useful for showing what proportion of a budget amount was spent on tours in one country relative to what was spent on tours in other countries. A line chart, in contrast, is best for showing trends over time. To choose the best chart type for your data, you should first decide how you want your data displayed and interpreted. **TABLE 4-1** describes several different types of charts you can create in Excel and their corresponding buttons on the Insert tab on the Ribbon. Because you want to compare R2G tour expenses in multiple countries over a period of four quarters, you decide to use a column chart.

• **Identify the worksheet data you want the chart to illustrate**

   Sometimes you use all the data in a worksheet to create a chart, while at other times you may need to select a range within the sheet. The worksheet from which you are creating your chart contains expense data for each of the past four quarters and the totals for the past year. You will need to use all the quarterly data except the quarterly totals.

• **Understand the elements of a chart**

   The chart shown in **FIGURE 4-2** contains basic elements of a chart. In the figure, R2G tour countries are on the horizontal axis (also called the **x-axis**) and expense dollar amounts are on the vertical axis (also called the **y-axis**). The horizontal axis is also called the **category axis** because it often contains the names of data groups, such as locations, months, or years. The vertical axis is also called the **value axis** because it often contains numerical values that help you interpret the size of chart elements. (3-D charts also contain a **z-axis**, for comparing data across both categories and values.) The area inside the horizontal and vertical axes is the **plot area**. The **tick marks**, on the vertical axis, and **gridlines** (extending across the plot area) create a scale of measure for each value. Each value in a cell you select for your chart is a **data point**. In any chart, a **data marker** visually represents each data point, which in this case is a column. A collection of related data points is a **data series**. In this chart, there are four data series (Quarter 1, Quarter 2, Quarter 3, and Quarter 4). Each is made up of column data markers of a different color, so a **legend** is included to make it easy to identify them.

FIGURE 4-1: Worksheet containing expense data

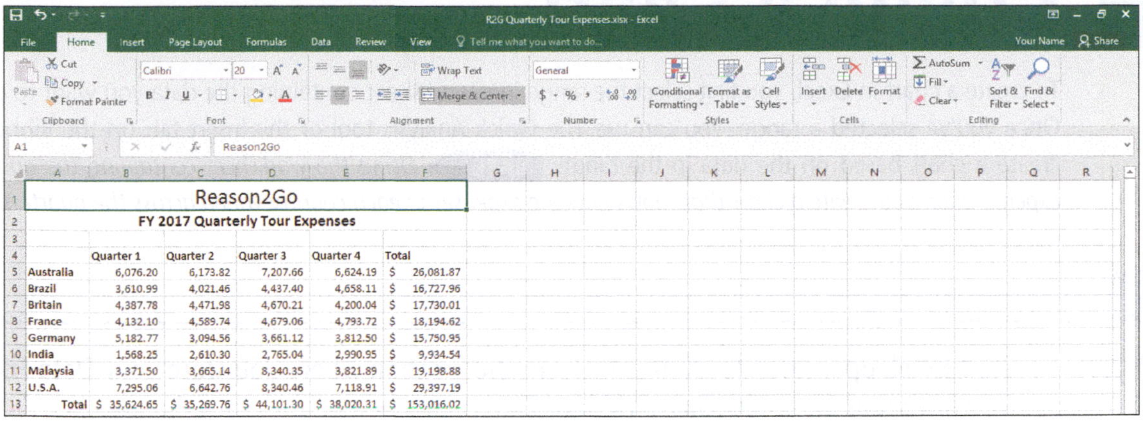

FIGURE 4-2: Chart elements

TABLE 4-1: Common chart types

type	button	description
Column		Compares data using columns; the Excel default; sometimes referred to as a bar chart in other spreadsheet programs
Line		Compares trends over even time intervals; looks similar to an area chart, but does not emphasize total
Pie		Compares sizes of pieces as part of a whole; used for a single series of numbers
Bar		Compares data using horizontal bars; sometimes referred to as a horizontal bar chart in other spreadsheet programs
Area		Shows how individual volume changes over time in relation to total volume
Scatter		Compares trends over uneven time or measurement intervals; used in scientific and engineering disciplines for trend spotting and extrapolation
Combo		Displays two or more types of data using different chart types; illustrates mixed or widely varying types of data

Excel 2016

Create a Chart

To create a chart in Excel, you first select the range in a worksheet containing the data you want to chart. Once you've selected a range, you can use The Quick Analysis tool or the Insert tab on the Ribbon to create a chart based on the data in the range. **CASE** ▶ *Using the worksheet containing the quarterly expense data, you create a chart that shows how the expenses in each country varied across the quarters.*

STEPS

QUICK TIP

When charting data for a particular time period, make sure that all series are for the same time period.

1. **Start Excel, open the file EX 4-1.xlsx from the location where you store your Data Files, then save it as EX 4-R2G Quarterly Tour Expenses**

   You want the chart to include the quarterly tour expenses values, as well as quarter and country labels. You don't include the Total column and row because the figures in these cells would skew the chart.

2. **Select the range A4:E12, click the Quick Analysis tool 📧 in the lower-right corner of the range, then click Charts**

   The Charts tab on the Quick Analysis tool recommends commonly used chart types based on the range you have selected. The Charts tab also includes a More Charts button for additional chart types, such as stock charts for charting stock market data.

QUICK TIP

To base a chart on data in nonadjacent ranges, press and hold [Ctrl] while selecting each range, then use the Insert tab to create the chart.

3. **On the Charts tab, verify that Clustered Column is selected, as shown in FIGURE 4-3, then click Clustered Column**

   The chart is inserted in the center of the worksheet, and two contextual Chart Tools tabs appear on the Ribbon: Design and Format. On the Design tab, which is currently active, you can quickly change the chart type, chart layout, and chart style, and you can swap how the columns and rows of data in the worksheet are represented in the chart. When seen in the Normal view, three tools display to the right of the chart: these enable you to add, remove, or change chart elements ➕, set a style and color scheme 🖌, and filter the results shown in a chart ▼. Currently, the countries are charted along the horizontal x-axis, with the quarterly expense dollar amounts charted along the y-axis. This lets you easily compare the quarterly expenses for each country.

4. **Click the Switch Row/Column button in the Data group on the Chart Tools Design tab**

   The quarters are now charted along the x-axis. The expense amounts per country are charted along the y-axis, as indicated by the updated legend. See FIGURE 4-4.

5. **Click the Undo button 🔄 ▾ on the Quick Access Toolbar**

   The chart returns to its original design.

QUICK TIP

You can also triple-click to select the chart title text.

6. **Click the Chart Title placeholder to show the text box, click anywhere in the Chart Title text box, press [Ctrl][A] to select the text, type R2G Quarterly Tour Expenses, then click anywhere in the chart to deselect the title**

   Adding a title helps identify the chart. The border around the chart and the **sizing handles**, the small series of dots at the corners and sides of the chart's border, indicate that the chart is selected. See FIGURE 4-5. Your chart might be in a different location on the worksheet and may look slightly different; you will move and resize it in the next lesson. Any time a chart is selected, as it is now, a blue border surrounds the worksheet data range on which the chart is based, a purple border surrounds the cells containing the category axis labels, and a red border surrounds the cells containing the data series labels. This chart is known as an **embedded chart** because it is inserted directly in the current worksheet and doesn't exist in a separate file. Embedding a chart in the current sheet is the default selection when creating a chart, but you can also embed a chart on a different sheet in the workbook, or on a newly created chart sheet. A **chart sheet** is a sheet in a workbook that contains only a chart that is linked to the workbook data.

7. **Save your work**

FIGURE 4-3: Charts tab in Quick Analysis tool

| 12 | U.S.A. | 7,295.06 | 6,642.76 | 8,340.46 | 7,118.91 | $ | 29,397.19 |
| 13 | **Total** | $ 35,624.65 | $ 35,269.76 | $ 44,101.30 | $ 38,020.31 | | 153,016.02 |

Quick Analysis tool

Charts tab selected

Formatting **Charts** Totals Tables Sparklines

Clustere... Stacked... Clustere... Scatter Scatter More...

Recommended Charts help you visualize data.

Clustered Column

Sheet1

Ready   Ave

FIGURE 4-4: Clustered Column chart with different configuration of rows and columns

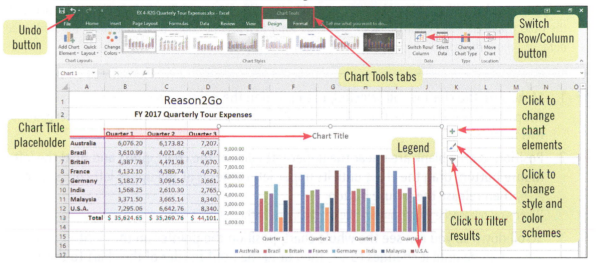

Undo button

Switch Row/Column button

Chart Tools tabs

Chart Title placeholder

Chart Title

Legend

Click to change chart elements

Click to change style and color schemes

Click to filter results

FIGURE 4-5: Chart with original configuration restored and title added

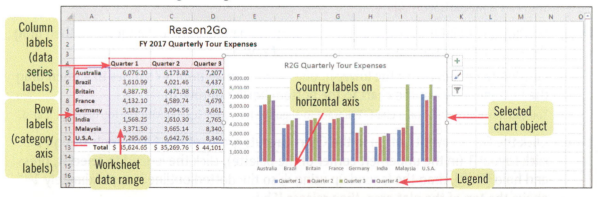

Column labels (data series labels)

Row labels (category axis labels)

Worksheet data range

Country labels on horizontal axis

Selected chart object

Legend

Creating sparklines

You can quickly create a miniature chart called a **sparkline** that serves as a visual indicator of data trends. You can create a sparkline by selecting a range of data, clicking the Quick Analysis tool, clicking the Sparklines tab, then clicking the type of sparkline you want. (The sparkline appears in the cell immediately adjacent to the selected range.) You can also select a range, click the Insert tab, then click the Line, Column, or Win/Loss button in the Sparklines group. In the Create Sparklines dialog box that opens, enter the cell in which you want the sparkline to appear,

then click OK. **FIGURE 4-6** shows a sparkline created in a cell. Any changes to data in the range are reflected in the sparkline. To delete a selected sparkline from a cell, click the Clear button in the Group group on the Sparkline Tools Design tab.

FIGURE 4-6: Sparklines in a cell

Move and Resize a Chart

A chart is an **object,** or an independent element on a worksheet, and is not located in a specific cell or range. You can select an object by clicking it; sizing handles around the object indicate it is selected. (When a chart is selected in Excel, the Name box, which normally tells you the address of the active cell, tells you the chart number.) You can move a selected chart anywhere on a worksheet without affecting formulas or data in the worksheet. Any data changed in the worksheet is automatically updated in the chart. You can even move a chart to a different sheet in the workbook, and it will still reflect the original data. You can resize a chart to improve its appearance by dragging its sizing handles. You can reposition chart objects (such as a title or legend) to predefined locations using commands using the Chart Elements button or the Add Chart Element button on the Chart Tools Design tab, or you can freely move any chart object by dragging it or by cutting and pasting it to a new location. When you point to a chart object, the name of the object appears as a ScreenTip. **CASE** *You want to resize the chart, position it below the worksheet data, and move the legend.*

STEPS

QUICK TIP
To delete a selected chart, press [Delete].

1. **Make sure the chart is still selected, then position the pointer over the chart**
   The pointer shape ⁺↖ indicates that you can move the chart. For a table of commonly used object pointers, refer to **TABLE 4-2**.

TROUBLE
Dragging a chart element instead of a blank area moves the element instead of the chart; if this happens, undo the action and try again.

2. **Position ⁺↖ on a blank area near the upper-left edge of the chart, press and hold the left mouse button, drag the chart until its upper-left corner is at the upper-left corner of cell A16, then release the mouse button**
   When you release the mouse button, the chart appears in the new location.

3. **Scroll down so you can see the whole chart, position the pointer on the right-middle sizing handle until it changes to ↔, then drag the right border of the chart to the right edge of column G**
   The chart is widened. See **FIGURE 4-7**.

QUICK TIP
To resize a selected chart to an exact size, click the Chart Tools Format tab, then enter the desired height and width in the Size group.

4. **Position the pointer over the upper-middle sizing handle until it changes to ↕, then drag the top border of the chart to the top edge of row 15**

5. **Position the pointer over the lower-middle sizing handle until it changes to ↕, then drag the bottom border of the chart to the bottom border of row 26**
   You can move any object on a chart. You want to align the top of the legend with the top of the plot area.

QUICK TIP
You can move a legend to the right, top, left, or bottom of a chart by clicking Legend in the Add Chart Element button in the Chart Layouts group on the Chart Tools Design tab, then clicking a location option.

6. **Click the Quick Layout button in the Chart Layouts group of the Chart Tools Design tab, click Layout 1 (in the upper-left corner of the palette), click the legend to select it, press and hold [Shift], drag the legend up using ⁺↖ so the dotted outline is approximately 1/4" above the top of the plot area, then release [Shift]**
   When you click the legend, sizing handles appear around it and "Legend" appears as a ScreenTip when the pointer hovers over the object. As you drag, a dotted outline of the legend border appears. Pressing and holding the [Shift] key holds the horizontal position of the legend as you move it vertically. Although the sizing handles on objects within a chart look different from the sizing handles that surround a chart, they function the same way.

7. **Click cell A12, type United States, click the Enter button ✓ on the formula bar, use AutoFit to resize column A, then save your work**
   The axis label changes to reflect the updated cell contents, as shown in **FIGURE 4-8**. Changing any data in the worksheet modifies corresponding text or values in the chart. Because the chart is no longer selected, the Chart Tools tabs no longer appear on the Ribbon.

FIGURE 4-7: Moved and resized chart

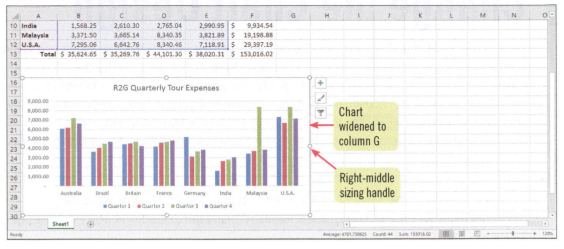

Chart widened to column G

Right-middle sizing handle

FIGURE 4-8: Worksheet with modified legend and label

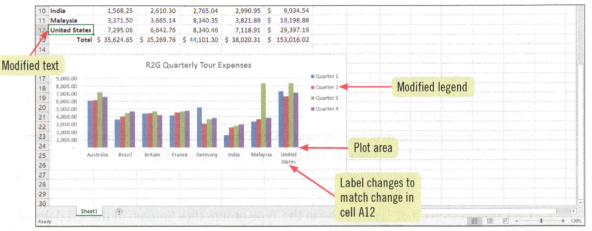

Modified text

Modified legend

Plot area

Label changes to match change in cell A12

TABLE 4-2: Common object pointers

name	pointer	use	name	pointer	use
Diagonal resizing	↖ or ↘	Change chart shape from corners	I-beam	I	Edit object text
Draw	+	Draw an object	Move	✛	Move object
Horizontal resizing	⟺	Change object width	Vertical resizing	↕	Change object height

Moving an embedded chart to a sheet

Suppose you have created an embedded chart that you decide would look better on a chart sheet or in a different worksheet. You can make this change without recreating the entire chart. To do so, first select the chart, click the Chart Tools Design tab, then click the Move Chart button in the Location group. The Move Chart dialog box opens. To move the chart to its own chart sheet, click the New sheet option button, type a name for the new sheet if desired, then click OK. If the chart is already on its own sheet or you want to move it to a different existing sheet, click the Object in option button, click the desired worksheet, then click OK.

Change the Chart Design

**Learning
Outcomes**
• Change the chart
design
• Change the chart
type
• Apply a chart style

Once you've created a chart, you can change the chart type, modify the data range and column/row configuration, apply a different chart style, and change the layout of objects in the chart. The layouts in the Chart Layouts group on the Chart Tools Design tab offer arrangements of objects in your chart, such as its legend, title, or gridlines; choosing one of these layouts is an alternative to manually changing how objects are arranged in a chart. **CASE** ▶ *You discovered that the data for Malaysia and the United States in Quarter 3 is incorrect. After the correction, you want to see how the data looks using different chart layouts and types.*

STEPS

1. **Click cell D11, type 5568.92, press [Enter], type 7107.09, then press [Enter]**
   In the chart, the Quarter 3 data markers for Malaysia and the United States reflect the adjusted expense figures. See **FIGURE 4-9**.

QUICK TIP

You can see more layout choices by clicking the More button ⬇ in the Chart Styles group.

2. **Select the chart by clicking a blank area within the chart border, click the Chart Tools Design tab on the Ribbon, click the Quick Layout button in the Chart Layouts group, then click Layout 3**
   The legend moves to the bottom of the chart. You prefer the original layout.

3. **Click the Undo button 🔙 on the Quick Access Toolbar, then click the Change Chart Type button in the Type group**
   The Change Chart Type dialog box opens, as shown in **FIGURE 4-10**. The left pane of the dialog box lists the available categories, and the right pane shows the individual chart types. A pale gray border surrounds the currently selected chart type.

4. **Click Bar in the left pane of the Change Chart Type dialog box, confirm that the first Clustered Bar chart type is selected in the right pane, then click OK**
   The column chart changes to a clustered bar chart. See **FIGURE 4-11**. You decide to see how the data looks in a three-dimensional column chart.

5. **Click the Change Chart Type button in the Type group, click Column in the left pane of the Change Chart Type dialog box, click 3-D Clustered Column (fourth from the left in the top row) in the right pane, verify that the left-most 3-D chart is selected, then click OK**
   A three-dimensional column chart appears. You notice that the three-dimensional column format gives you a sense of volume, but it is more crowded than the two-dimensional column format.

QUICK TIP

If you plan to print a chart on a black-and-white printer, you may wish to apply a black-and-white chart style to your chart so you can see how the output will look as you work.

6. **Click the Change Chart Type button in the Type group, click Clustered Column (first from the left in the top row) in the right pane of the Change Chart Type dialog box, then click OK**

7. **Click the Style 3 chart style in the Chart Styles group**
   The columns change to lighter shades of color. You prefer the previous chart style's color scheme.

8. **Click 🔙 on the Quick Access Toolbar, then save your work**

Creating a combo chart

A **combo chart** presents two or more charts in one; a column chart with a line chart, for example. This type of chart is helpful when charting dissimilar but related data. For example, you can create a combo chart based on home price and home size data, showing home prices in a column chart and related home sizes in a line chart. Here a **secondary axis** (such as a vertical axis on the right side of the chart) would supply the scale for the home sizes.

To create a combo chart, select all the data you want to plot, click the Combo chart button 📊 in the Charts group in the Insert tab, click a suggested type or Create Custom Combo Chart, supply additional series information if necessary, then click OK. To change an existing chart to a combo chart, select the chart, click Change Chart Type in the Type group on the Chart Tools Design tab, then follow the same procedure.

FIGURE 4-9: Worksheet with modified data

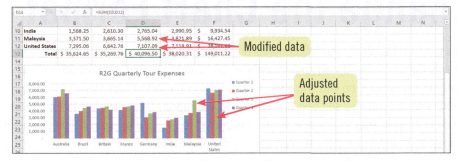

Modified data

Adjusted data points

FIGURE 4-10: Change Chart Type dialog box

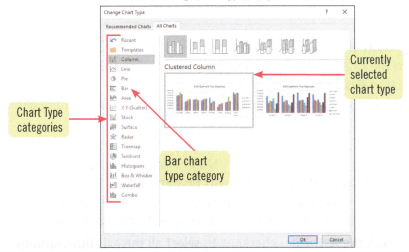

Currently selected chart type

Chart Type categories

Bar chart type category

FIGURE 4-11: Column chart changed to bar chart

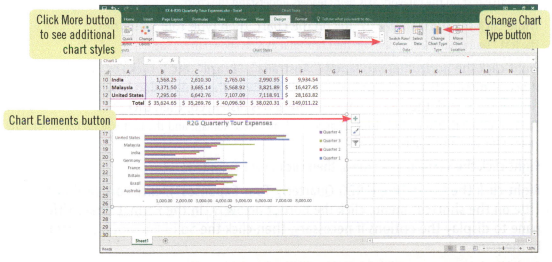

Click More button to see additional chart styles

Change Chart Type button

Chart Elements button

Working with a 3-D chart

Excel includes two kinds of 3-D chart types. In a true 3-D chart, a third axis, called the **z-axis**, lets you compare data points across both categories and values. The z-axis runs along the depth of the chart, so it appears to advance from the back of the chart. To create a true 3-D chart, look for chart types that begin with "3-D," such as 3-D Column. In a 3-D chart, data series can sometimes obscure other columns or bars in the same chart, but you can rotate the chart to obtain a better view. Right-click the chart, then click 3-D Rotation. The Format Chart Area pane opens with the 3-D Rotation category active. The 3-D Rotation options let you change the orientation and perspective of the chart area, plot area, walls, and floor. The 3-D Format category lets you apply three-dimensional effects to selected chart objects. (Not all 3-D Rotation and 3-D Format options are available on all charts.)

Change the Chart Format

**Learning
Outcomes**
• Change the
gridlines display
• Add axis titles
• Change the
border color
• Add a shadow
to an object

While the Chart Tools Design tab contains preconfigured chart layouts you can apply to a chart, the Chart Elements button makes it easy to add, remove, and modify individual chart objects such as a chart title or legend. Using options on this shortcut menu (or using the Add Chart Element button on the Chart Tools Design tab), you can also add text to a chart, add and modify labels, change the display of axes, modify the fill behind the plot area, create titles for the horizontal and vertical axes, and eliminate or change the look of gridlines. You can format the text in a chart object using the Home tab or the Mini toolbar, just as you would the text in a worksheet. **CASE** *You want to change the layout of the chart by creating titles for the horizontal and vertical axes. To improve the chart's appearance, you'll add a drop shadow to the chart title.*

STEPS

1. **With the chart still selected, click the Add Chart Element button in the Chart Layouts group on the Chart Tools Design tab, point to Gridlines, then click Primary Major Horizontal to deselect it**

   The gridlines that extend from the value axis tick marks across the chart's plot area are removed as shown in **FIGURE 4-12**.

2. **Click the Chart Elements button** ⊞ **in the upper-right corner *outside* the chart border, click the Gridlines arrow, click Primary Major Horizontal, click Primary Minor Horizontal, then click** ⊞ **to close the Chart Elements fly-out menu**

   Both major and minor gridlines now appear in the chart. **Major gridlines** represent the values at the value axis tick marks, and **minor gridlines** represent the values between the tick marks.

   QUICK TIP
   You can move any title to a new position by clicking one of its edges, then dragging it.

3. **Click** ⊞**, click the Axis Titles checkbox to select all the axis titles options, triple-click the vertical axis title on the chart, then type Expenses (in $)**

   Descriptive text on the category axis helps readers understand the chart.

   QUICK TIP
   You can also edit text in a chart or axis title by positioning the pointer over the selected title until it changes to I, clicking the title, then editing the text.

4. **Triple-click the horizontal axis title on the chart, then type Tour Countries**

   The text "Tour Countries" appears on the horizontal axis, as shown in **FIGURE 4-13**.

5. **Right-click the horizontal axis labels ("Australia", "Brazil", etc.), click Font on the shortcut menu, click the Latin text font list arrow in the Font dialog box, click Times New Roman, click the Size down arrow until 8 is displayed, then click OK**

   The font of the horizontal axis labels changes to Times New Roman, and the font size decreases, making more of the plot area visible.

   QUICK TIP
   You can also apply a border to a selected chart object by clicking the Shape Outline list arrow on the Chart Tools Format tab, and then selecting from the available options.

6. **Right-click the vertical axis labels, then click Reset to Match**

7. **Right-click the Chart Title ("R2G Quarterly Tour Expenses"), click Format Chart Title on the shortcut menu, click the Border arrow** ▶ **in the Format Chart Title pane to display the options if necessary, then click the Solid line option button in the pane**

   A solid border appears around the chart title with the default blue color.

   QUICK TIP
   You can also apply a shadow to a selected chart object by clicking the Shadow arrow, then clicking a shadow effect.

8. **Click the Effects button** ⬠ **in the Format Chart Title pane, click Shadow, click the Presets list arrow, click Offset Diagonal Bottom Right in the Outer group (first row, first from the left), click the Format Chart Title pane Close button** ✖**, then save your work**

   A blue border with a drop shadow surrounds the title. Compare your work to **FIGURE 4-14**.

FIGURE 4-12: Gridlines removed from chart

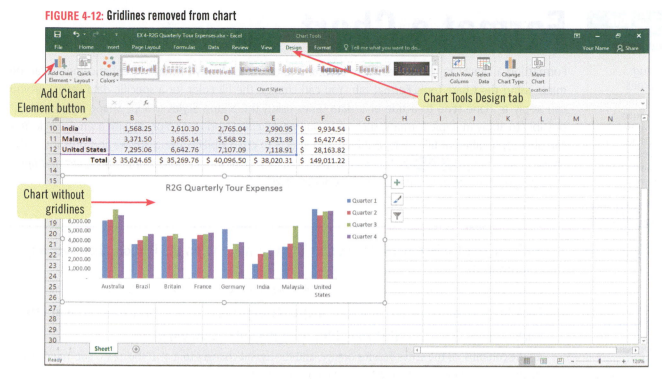

Add Chart Element button

Chart Tools Design tab

Chart without gridlines

FIGURE 4-13: Axis titles added to chart

Chart title

Vertical axis title

Vertical axis labels

Horizontal axis title

Horizontal axis labels

FIGURE 4-14: Enhanced chart

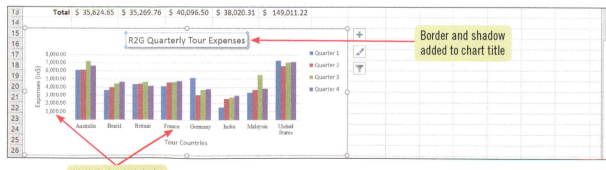

Border and shadow added to chart title

Modified axis labels

Adding data labels to a chart

There are times when your audience might benefit by seeing data labels on a chart. These labels appear next to the data markers in the chart and can indicate the series name, category name, and/or the value of one or more data points. Once your chart is selected, you can add this information to your chart by clicking the Chart Elements button in the upper-right corner outside the selected chart, clicking the Data Labels arrow, and then clicking a display option for the data labels. Once you have added the data labels, you can format them or delete individual data labels. To delete a data label, select it and then press [Delete].

Excel 2016

Format a Chart

Formatting a chart can make it easier to read and understand. Many formatting enhancements can be made using the Chart Tools Format tab. You can change the fill color for a specific data series, or you can apply a shape style to a title or a data series using the Shape Styles group. Shape styles make it possible to apply multiple formats, such as an outline, fill color, and text color, all with a single click. You can also apply different fill colors, outlines, and effects to chart objects using arrows and buttons in the Shape Styles group. **CASE** *You want to use a different color for one data series in the chart and apply a shape style to another, to enhance the look of the chart.*

STEPS

1. **With the chart selected, click the Chart Tools Format tab on the Ribbon, then click any column in the Quarter 4 data series**

   Handles appear on each column in the Quarter 4 data series, indicating that the entire series is selected.

2. **Click the Shape Fill list arrow in the Shape Styles group on the Chart Tools Format tab**

3. **Click Orange, Accent 6 (first row, 10th from the left) as shown in FIGURE 4-15**

   All the columns for the series become orange, and the legend changes to match the new color. You can also change the color of selected objects by applying a shape style.

4. **Click any column in the Quarter 3 data series**

   Handles appear on each column in the Quarter 3 data series.

5. **Click the More button ▼ on the Shape Styles gallery, then *hover the pointer* over the Moderate Effect – Olive Green, Accent 3 shape style (fifth row, fourth from the left) in the gallery, as shown in FIGURE 4-16**

   Live Preview shows the data series in the chart with the shape style applied.

6. **Click the Subtle Effect – Olive Green, Accent 3 shape style**

   The style for the data series changes, as shown in FIGURE 4-17.

7. **Save your work**

Previewing a chart

To print or preview just a chart, select the chart (or make the chart sheet active), click the File tab, then click Print on the navigation bar. To reposition a chart by changing the page's margins, click the Show Margins button ⊞ in the lower-right corner of the Print tab to display the margins in the preview. You can drag the margin lines to the exact settings you want; as the margins change, the size and placement of the chart on the page change too.

FIGURE 4-15: New shape fill applied to data series

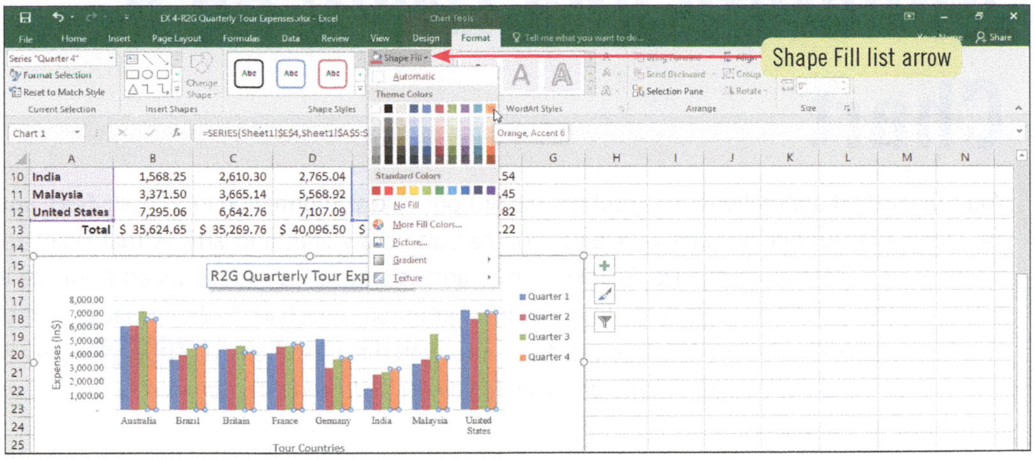

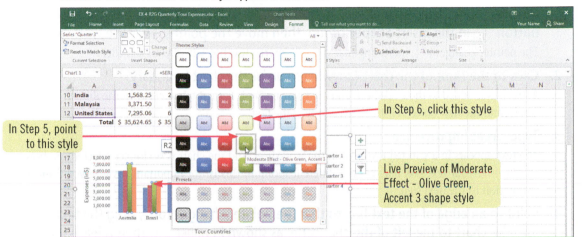

FIGURE 4-16: Live Preview of new style applied to data series

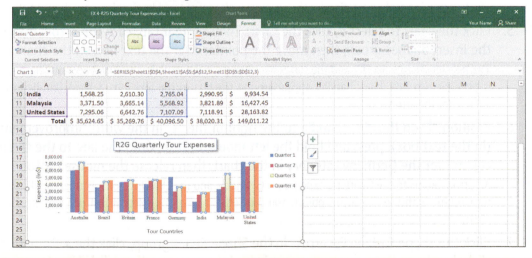

FIGURE 4-17: Style of data series changed

![Figure 4-17 screenshot showing style of data series changed]

Changing alignment and angle in axis labels and titles

The buttons on the Chart Tools Design tab provide a few options for positioning axis labels and titles, but you can customize their position and rotation to exact specifications using the Format Axis pane or Format Axis Title pane. With a chart selected, right-click the axis text you want to modify, then click Format Axis or Format Axis Title on the shortcut menu. In the pane that opens, click the Size & Properties button, then select the appropriate option. You can also create a custom angle by clicking the Custom angle up and down arrows. When you have made the desired changes, close the pane.

Annotate and Draw on a Chart

Learning
Outcomes
• Type text in a text box
• Draw an arrow on a chart
• Modify a drawn object

You can use text annotations and graphics to point out critical information in a chart. **Text annotations** are labels that further describe your data. You can also draw lines and arrows that point to the exact locations you want to emphasize. Shapes such as arrows and boxes can be added from the Illustrations group on the Insert tab or from the Insert Shapes group on the Chart Tools Format tab on the Ribbon. The Insert group is also used to insert pictures into worksheets and charts. **CASE** *You want to call attention to the Germany tour expense decrease, so you decide to add a text annotation and an arrow to this information in the chart.*

STEPS

1. **With the chart selected and the Chart Tools Format tab active, click the Text Box button in the Insert Shapes group, then move the pointer over the worksheet**
   The pointer changes to ↓, indicating that you will insert a text box where you next click.

2. **Click to the right of the chart (anywhere *outside* the chart boundary)**
   A text box is added to the worksheet, and the Drawing Tools Format tab appears on the Ribbon so that you can format the new object. First you need to type the text.

3. **Type Great Improvement**
   The text appears in a selected text box on the worksheet, and the chart is no longer selected, as shown in **FIGURE 4-18**. Your text box may be in a different location; this is not important because you'll move the annotation in the next step.

4. **Point to an edge of the text box so that the pointer changes to ⬚, drag the text box into the chart to the left of the chart title, as shown in FIGURE 4-19, then release the mouse button**
   The text box is a text annotation for the chart. You also want to add a simple arrow shape in the chart.

5. **Click the chart to select it, click the Chart Tools Format tab, click the Arrow button in the Insert Shapes group, then move the pointer over the text box on the chart**
   The pointer changes to ✛, and the status bar displays "Click and drag to insert an AutoShape." When ✛ is over the text box, black handles appear around the text in the text box. A black handle can act as an anchor for the arrow.

6. **Position ✛ on the black handle to the right of the "t" in the word "improvement" (in the text box), press and hold the left mouse button, drag the line to the Quarter 2 column for the Germany category in the chart, then release the mouse button**
   An arrow points to the Quarter 2 expense for Germany, and the Drawing Tools Format tab displays options for working with the new arrow object. You can resize, format, or delete it just like any other object in a chart.

7. **Click the Shape Outline list arrow in the Shape Styles group, click the Automatic color, click the Shape Outline list arrow again, point to Weight, then click 1½ pt**
   Compare your finished chart to **FIGURE 4-20**.

8. **Save your work**

FIGURE 4-18: Text box added

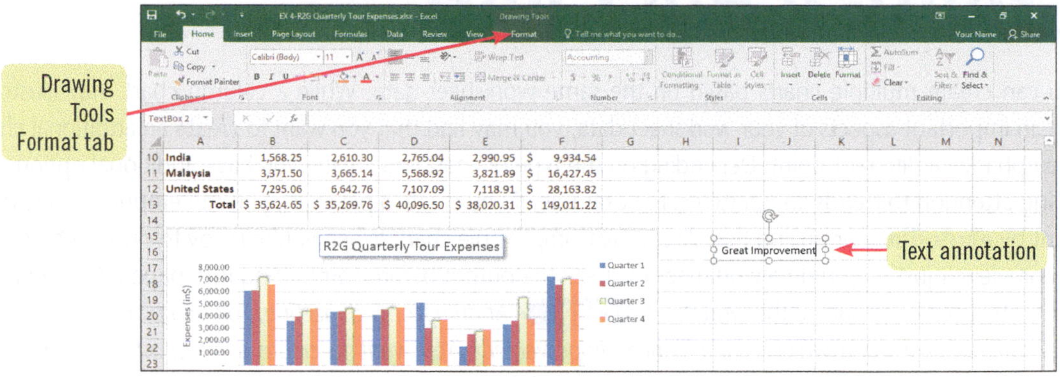

Drawing
Tools
Format tab

Text annotation

FIGURE 4-19: Text annotation on the chart

Text annotation

FIGURE 4-20: Arrow shape added to chart

Arrow drawn
and formatted

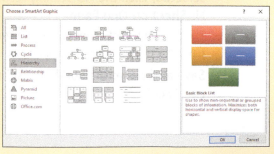

Adding SmartArt graphics

In addition to charts, annotations, and drawn objects, you can create a variety of diagrams using SmartArt graphics. **SmartArt graphics** are available in List, Process, Cycle, Hierarchy, Relationship, Matrix, Pyramid, Picture, and Office.com categories. To insert SmartArt, click the Insert a SmartArt Graphic button in the Illustrations group on the Insert tab to open the Choose a SmartArt Graphic dialog box. Click a SmartArt category in the left pane, then click a layout for the graphic in the right pane. The right pane shows sample layouts for the selected SmartArt, as shown in **FIGURE 4-21**. The SmartArt graphic appears in the worksheet as an embedded object with sizing handles. Depending on the type of SmartArt graphic you selected, a text pane opens next to the graphic; you can enter text into the graphic using the text pane or by typing directly in the shapes in the diagram.

FIGURE 4-21: Choose a SmartArt Graphic dialog box

Create a Pie Chart

You can create multiple charts based on the same worksheet data. While a column chart may illustrate certain important aspects of your worksheet data, you may find that you want to create an additional chart to emphasize a different point. Depending on the type of chart you create, you have additional options for calling attention to trends and patterns. For example, if you create a pie chart, you can emphasize one data point by **exploding**, or pulling that slice away from, the pie chart. When you're ready to print a chart, you can preview it just as you do a worksheet to check the output before committing it to paper. You can print a chart by itself or as part of the worksheet. **CASE** ▶ *At an upcoming meeting, Yolanda plans to discuss the total tour expenses and which countries need improvement. You want to create a pie chart she can use to illustrate total expenses. Finally, you want to fit the worksheet and the charts onto one worksheet page.*

STEPS

1. **Select the range A5:A12, press and hold [Ctrl], select the range F5:F12, click the Insert tab, click the Insert Pie or Doughnut Chart button in the Charts group, then click 3-D Pie in the chart gallery**

   The new chart appears in the center of the worksheet. You can move the chart and quickly format it using a chart layout.

2. **Drag the chart so its upper-left corner is at the upper-left corner of cell G1, click the Quick Layout button in the Chart Layouts group of the Chart Tools Design tab, then click Layout 2**

   The chart is repositioned on the page, and its layout changes so that a chart title is added, the percentages display on each slice, and the legend appears just below the chart title.

3. **Select the Chart Title text, then type R2G Total Expenses, by Country**

4. **Click the slice for the India data point, click it again so it is the only slice selected, right-click it, then click Format Data Point**

   The Format Data Point pane opens, as shown in **FIGURE 4-22**. You can use the Point Explosion slider to control the distance a pie slice moves away from the pie, or you can type a value in the Point Explosion text box.

5. **Double-click 0 in the Point Explosion text box, type 40, then click the Close button ✕**

   Compare your chart to **FIGURE 4-23**. You decide to preview the chart and data before you print.

6. **Click cell A1, switch to Page Layout view, type your name in the left header text box, then click cell A1**

   You decide the chart and data would fit better on the page if they were printed in landscape orientation.

7. **Click the Page Layout tab, click the Orientation button in the Page Setup group, then click Landscape**

8. **Click the File tab, click Print on the navigation bar, verify that the correct printer is selected, click the No Scaling setting in the Settings section on the Print tab, then click Fit Sheet on One Page**

   The data and chart are positioned horizontally on a single page, as shown in **FIGURE 4-24**. The printer you have selected may affect the appearance of your preview screen.

9. **Save and close the workbook, submit your work to your instructor as directed, then exit Excel**

FIGURE 4-22: Format Data Point pane

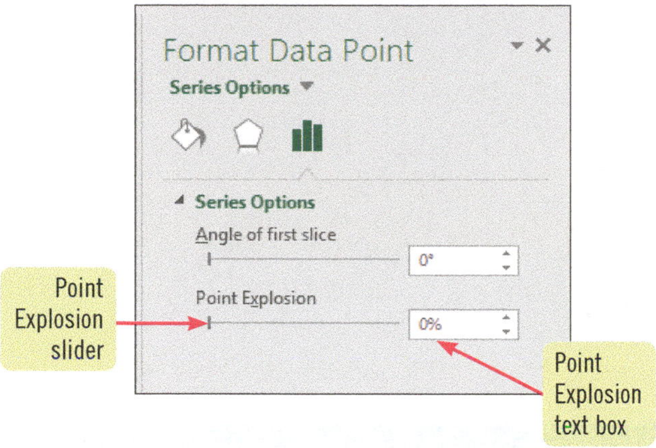

FIGURE 4-23: Exploded pie slice

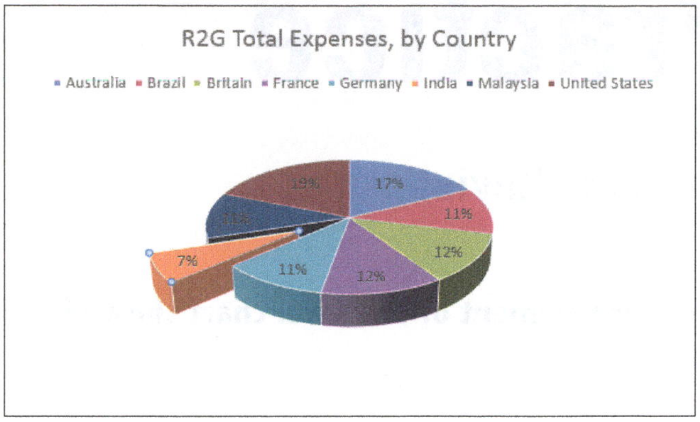

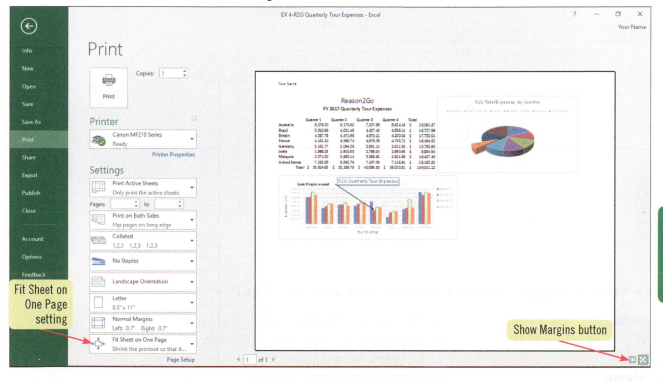

FIGURE 4-24: Preview of worksheet with charts in Backstage view

Using the Insert Chart dialog box to discover new chart types

Excel 2016 includes five new chart types. You can explore these charts by clicking the Insert tab on the Ribbon, clicking Recommended Charts, then clicking the All Charts tab in the Insert Chart dialog box. Near the bottom of the list in the left panel are the new chart types: Treemap (which has nine variations), Sunburst, Histogram, Box & Whisker, and Waterfall. If cells are selected prior to opening the Insert Chart dialog box, you will see a sample of the chart type when you click each chart type; the sample will be magnified when you hover the mouse over the sample. The Treemap and Sunburst charts both offer visual comparisons of relative sizes. The Histogram looks like a column chart, but each column (or bin) represents a range of values. The Box & Whisker chart shows distribution details as well as the mean, quartiles, and outliers. The Waterfall chart shows results above and below an imaginary line.

Practice

Concepts Review

Label each element of the Excel chart shown in FIGURE 4-25.

FIGURE 4-25

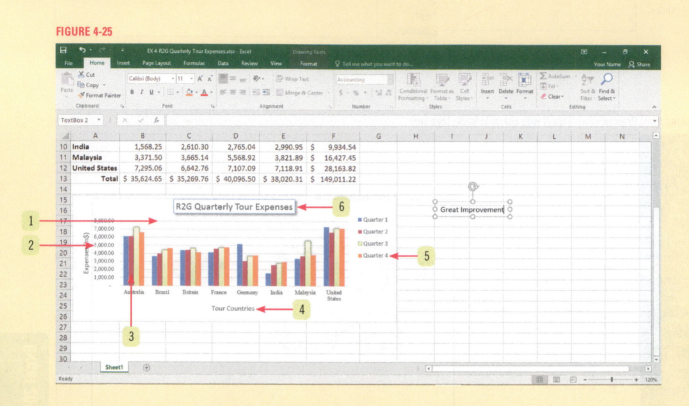

Match each chart type with the statement that best describes it.

7. **Combo**   a. Displays different chart types within one chart
8. **Pie**   b. Compares trends over even time intervals
9. **Area**   c. Compares data using columns
10. **Column**   d. Compares data as parts of a whole
11. **Line**   e. Shows how volume changes over time

Select the best answer from the list of choices.

12. **Which tab on the Ribbon do you use to create a chart?**
    a. Design
    b. Insert
    c. Page Layout
    d. Format

13. **A collection of related data points in a chart is called a:**
    a. Data series.
    b. Data tick.
    c. Cell address.
    d. Value title.

14. **The object in a chart that identifies the colors used for each data series is a(n):**
    a. Data marker.
    b. Data point.
    c. Organizer.
    d. Legend.

15. **How do you move an embedded chart to a chart sheet?**
    a. Click a button on the Chart Tools Design tab.
    b. Drag the chart to the sheet tab.
    c. Delete the chart, switch to a different sheet, then create a new chart.
    d. Use the Copy and Paste buttons on the Ribbon.

16. **Which is *not* an example of a SmartArt graphic?**
    a. Sparkline
    b. Basic Matrix
    c. Organization Chart
    d. Basic Pyramid

17. **Which tab appears only when a chart is selected?**
    a. Insert
    b. Chart Tools Format
    c. Review
    d. Page Layout

Skills Review

1. **Plan a chart.**
    a. Start Excel, open the Data File EX 4-2.xlsx from the location where you store your Data Files, then save it as **EX 4-Software Usage Polling Results**.
    b. Describe the type of chart you would use to plot this data.
    c. What chart type would you use to compare the number of Excel users in each type of business?

2. **Create a chart.**
    a. In the worksheet, select the range containing all the data and headings.
    b. Click the Quick Analysis tool.
    c. Create a Clustered Column chart, then add the chart title **Software Usage, by Business** above the chart.
    d. If necessary, click the Switch Row/Column button so the business type (Accounting, Advertising, etc.) appears as the x-axis.
    e. Save your work.

Skills Review (continued)

3. Move and resize a chart.

   a. Make sure the chart is still selected, and close any open panes if necessary.

   b. Move the chart beneath the worksheet data.

   c. Widen the chart so it extends to the right edge of column H.

   d. Use the Quick Layout button in the Chart Tools Design tab to move the legend to the right of the charted data. (*Hint*: Use Layout 1.)

   e. Resize the chart so its bottom edge is at the top of row 25.

   f. Save your work.

4. Change the chart design.

   a. Change the value in cell B3 to **8**. Observe the change in the chart.

   b. Select the chart.

   c. Use the Quick Layout button in the Chart Layouts group on the Chart Tools Design tab to apply the Layout 10 layout to the chart, then undo the change.

   d. Use the Change Chart Type button on the Chart Tools Design tab to change the chart to a Clustered Bar chart.

   e. Change the chart to a 3-D Clustered Column chart, then change it back to a Clustered Column chart.

   f. Save your work.

5. Change the chart layout.

   a. Use the Chart Elements button to turn off the primary major horizontal gridlines in the chart.

   b. Change the font used in the horizontal and vertical axis labels to Times New Roman.

   c. Turn on the primary major gridlines for both the horizontal and vertical axes.

   d. Change the chart title's font to Times New Roman if necessary, with a font size of 20.

   e. Insert **Business** as the primary horizontal axis title.

   f. Insert **Number of Users** as the primary vertical axis title.

   g. Change the font size of the horizontal and vertical axis titles to 10 and the font to Times New Roman, if necessary.

   h. Change "Personnel" in the worksheet column heading to **Human Resources**, then AutoFit column D, and any other columns as necessary.

   i. Change the font size of the legend to 14.

   j. Add a solid line border in the default color and a (preset) Offset Diagonal Bottom Right shadow to the chart title.

   k. Save your work.

6. Format a chart.

   a. Make sure the chart is selected, then select the Chart Tools Format tab, if necessary.

   b. Change the shape fill of the Excel data series to Dark Blue, Text 2.

   c. Change the shape style of the Excel data series to Subtle Effect – Orange, Accent 6.

   d. Save your work.

7. Annotate and draw on a chart.

   a. Make sure the chart is selected, then create the text annotation **Needs more users**.

   b. Position the text annotation so the word "Needs" is just below the word "Software" in the chart title.

   c. Select the chart, then use the Chart Tools Format tab to create a 1½ pt weight dark blue arrow that points from the bottom center of the text box to the Excel users in the Human Resources category.

   d. Deselect the chart.

   e. Save your work.

Skills Review (continued)

8. Create a pie chart.

    a. Select the range A1:F2, then create a 3-D Pie chart.

    b. Drag the 3-D pie chart beneath the existing chart.

    c. Change the chart title to **Excel Users**.

    d. Apply the Style 7 chart style to the chart, then apply Layout 6 using the Quick Layout button.

    e. Explode the Law Firm slice from the pie chart at **25%**.

    f. In Page Layout view, enter your name in the left section of the worksheet header.

    g. Preview the worksheet and charts in Backstage view, make sure all the contents fit on one page, then submit your work to your instructor as directed. When printed, the worksheet should look like **FIGURE 4-26**. (Note that certain elements such as the title may look slightly different when printed.)

    h. Save your work, close the workbook, then exit Excel.

FIGURE 4-26

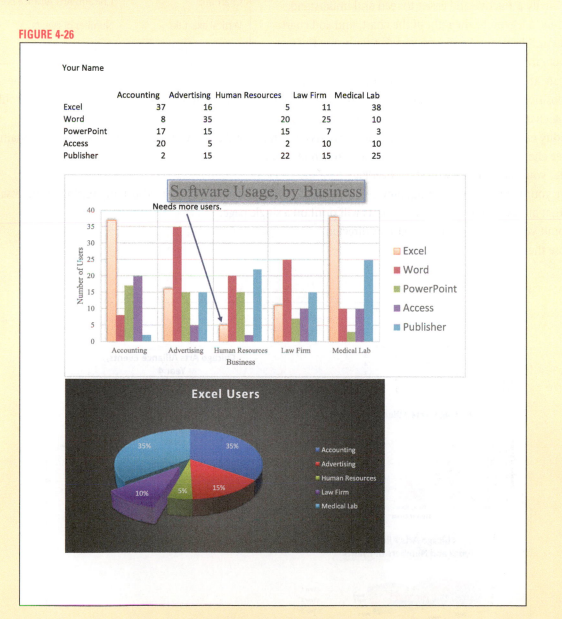

Independent Challenge 1

You are the operations manager for the Chicago Arts Alliance. Each year the group revisits the number and types of activities they support to better manage their budgets. For this year's budget, you need to create charts to document the number of events in previous years.

a. Start Excel, open the file EX 4-3.xlsx from the location where you store your Data Files, then save it as **EX 4-Chicago Arts Alliance**.

b. Take some time to plan your charts. Which type of chart or charts might best illustrate the information you need to display? What kind of chart enhancements do you want to use? Will a 3-D effect make your chart easier to understand?

c. Create a Clustered Column chart for the data.

d. Change at least one of the colors used in a data series.

e. Make the appropriate modifications to the chart to make it visually attractive and easier to read and understand. Include a legend to the right of the chart, and add chart titles and horizontal and vertical axis titles using the text shown in **TABLE 4-3**.

TABLE 4-3

title	text
Chart title	Chicago Arts Alliance Events
Vertical axis title	Number of Events
Horizontal axis title	Types of Events

f. Create at least two additional charts for the same data to show how different chart types display the same data. Reposition each new chart so that all charts are visible in the worksheet. One of the additional charts should be a pie chart for an appropriate data set; the other is up to you.

g. Modify each new chart as necessary to improve its appearance and effectiveness. A sample worksheet containing three charts based on the worksheet data is shown in **FIGURE 4-27**.

h. Enter your name in the worksheet header.

i. Save your work. Before printing, preview the worksheet in Backstage view, then adjust any settings as necessary so that all the worksheet data and charts will print on a single page.

j. Submit your work to your instructor as directed.

k. Close the workbook, then exit Excel.

FIGURE 4-27

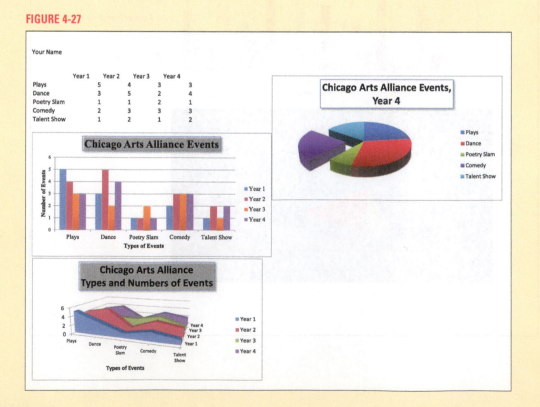

Independent Challenge 2

You work at Canine Companions, a locally owned dog obedience school. One of your responsibilities at the school is to manage the company's sales and expenses using Excel. As part of your efforts, you want to help the staff better understand and manage the school's largest sources of both expenses and sales. To do this, you've decided to create charts using current operating expenses including rent, utilities, and payroll. The manager will use these charts at the next monthly meeting.

a. Start Excel, open EX 4-4.xlsx from the location where you store your Data Files, then save it as **EX 4-Canine Companions Expense Analysis**.

b. Decide which data in the worksheet should be charted. What chart types are best suited for the information you need to show? What kinds of chart enhancements are necessary?

c. Create a 3-D Clustered Column chart in the worksheet showing the expense data for all four quarters. (*Hint*: The expense categories should appear on the x-axis. Do not include the totals.)

d. Change the vertical axis labels (Expenses data) so that no decimals are displayed. (*Hint*: Use the Number category in the Format Axis pane.)

e. Using the sales data, create two charts on this worksheet that compare the sales amounts. (*Hint*: Move each chart to a new location on the worksheet, then deselect it before creating the next one.)

f. In one chart of the sales data, add data labels, then add chart titles as you see fit.

g. Make any necessary formatting changes to make the charts look more attractive, then enter your name in a worksheet cell.

h. Save your work.

i. Preview each chart in Backstage view, and adjust any items as needed. Fit the worksheet to a single page, then submit your work to your instructor as directed. A sample of a printed worksheet is shown in FIGURE 4-28.

j. Close the workbook, then exit Excel.

FIGURE 4-28

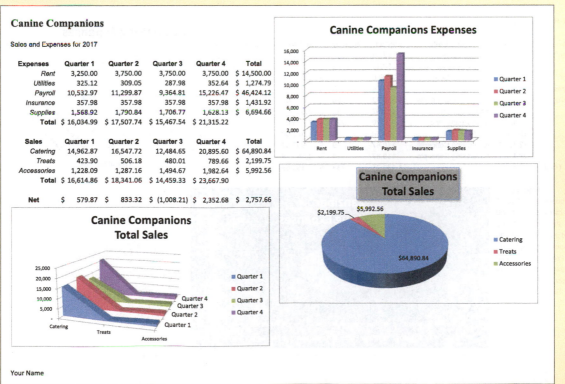

Independent Challenge 3

You are working as an account representative at a clothing store called Zanzibar. You have been examining the advertising expenses incurred recently. The CEO wants to examine expenses designed to increase sales and has asked you to prepare charts that can be used in this evaluation. In particular, you want to see how dollar amounts compare among the different expenses, and you also want to see how expenses compare with each other proportional to the total budget.

a. Start Excel, open the Data File EX 4-5.xlsx from the location where you store your Data Files, then save it as **EX 4-Zanzibar Advertising Expenses**.

b. Identify three types of charts that seem best suited to illustrate the data in the range A16:B24. What kinds of chart enhancements are necessary?

c. Create at least two different types of charts that show the distribution of advertising expenses. (*Hint*: Move each chart to a new location on the same worksheet.) One of the charts should be a 3-D pie chart.

d. In at least one of the charts, add annotated text and arrows highlighting important data, such as the largest expense.

e. Change the color of at least one data series in at least one of the charts.

f. Add chart titles and category and value axis titles where appropriate. Format the titles with a font of your choice. Apply a shadow to the chart title in at least one chart.

g. Add your name to a section of the header, then save your work.

h. Explode a slice from the 3-D pie chart.

i. Add a data label to the exploded pie slice.

j. Preview the worksheet in Backstage view. Adjust any items as needed. Be sure the charts are all visible on one page. Compare your work to the sample in FIGURE 4-29.

k. Submit your work to your instructor as directed, close the workbook, then exit Excel.

FIGURE 4-29

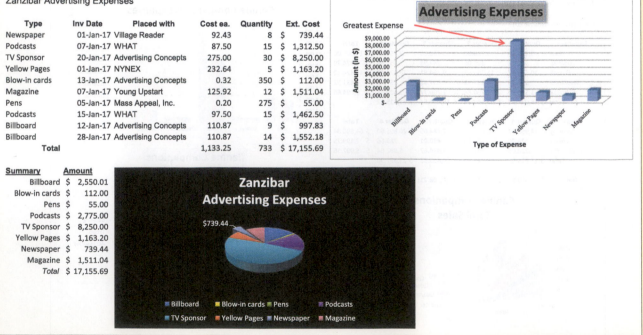

Independent Challenge 4: Explore

This Independent Challenge requires an Internet connection.

All the years of hard work and saving money have paid off, and you have decided to purchase a home. You know where you'd like to live, and you decide to use the web to find out more about houses that are currently available. A worksheet would be a great place to compare the features and prices of potential homes.

a. Start Excel, then save a new, blank workbook as **EX 4-My New House** to the location where you save your Data Files.

b. Decide on where you would like to live, and use your favorite search engine to find information sources on homes for sale in that area. (*Hint*: Try using realtor.com or other realtor-sponsored sites.)

c. Determine a price range and features within the home. Find data for at least five homes that meet your location and price requirements, and enter them in the worksheet. See **TABLE 4-4** for a suggested data layout.

TABLE 4-4

suggested data layout					
Location					
Price range					
	House 1	House 2	House 3	House 4	House 5
Asking price					
Bedrooms					
Bathrooms					
Year built					
Size (in sq. ft.)					

d. Format the data so it looks attractive and professional.

e. Create any type of column chart using only the House and Asking Price data. Place it on the same worksheet as the data. Include a descriptive title.

f. Change the colors in the chart using the chart style of your choice.

g. Enter your name in a section of the header.

h. Create an additional chart: a combo chart that plots the asking price on one axis and the size of the home on the other axis. (*Hint*: Use the Tell me what you want to do text box above the Ribbon to get more guidance on creating a Combo Chart.)

i. Save the workbook. Preview the worksheet in Backstage view and make adjustments if necessary to fit all of the information on one page. See **FIGURE 4-30** for an example of what your worksheet might look like.

j. Submit your work to your instructor as directed.

k. Close the workbook, then exit Excel.

FIGURE 4-30

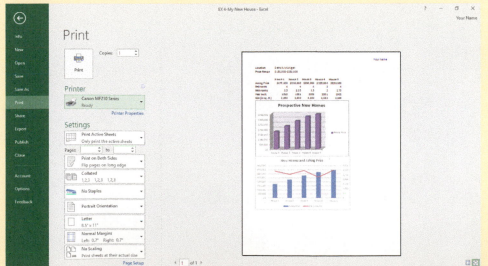

Working with Charts

Visual Workshop

Open the Data File EX 4-6.xlsx from the location where you store your Data Files, then save it as **EX 4-Estimated Cost Center Expenses**. Format the worksheet data so it looks like **FIGURE 4-31**, then create and modify two charts to match the ones shown in the figure. You will need to make formatting, layout, and design changes once you create the charts. (*Hint*: The shadow used in the 3-D pie chart title is made using the Outer Offset Diagonal Top Right shadow.) Enter your name in the left text box of the header, then save and preview the worksheet. Submit your work to your instructor as directed, then close the workbook and exit Excel.

FIGURE 4-31

Your Name

Estimated Cost Center Expenses

	Quarter 1	Quarter 2	Quarter 3	Quarter 4	Total
Cost Center 1	1,925.00	1,935.00	2,035.00	2,600.00	8,495
Cost Center 2	2,800.00	2,590.00	2,500.00	2,250.00	10,140
Cost Center 3	2,950.00	2,940.00	3,290.00	3,600.00	12,780
Cost Center 4	1,672.00	1,572.00	1,572.00	1,810.00	6,626
Cost Center 5	2,390.00	2,160.00	6,500.00	2,900.00	13,950
Cost Center 6	2,990.00	3,650.00	3,835.00	3,540.00	14,015
Total	14,727	14,847	19,732	16,700	

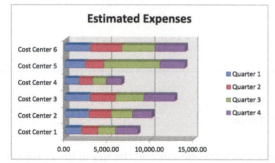

Analyzing Data Using Formulas

CASE Mary Watson, Reason2Go's vice president of sales and marketing, uses Excel formulas and functions to analyze sales data for the U.S. region and to consolidate sales data from branch offices. Because management is considering adding a new regional branch, Mary asks you to estimate the loan costs for a new office facility and to compare sales in the existing U.S. offices.

Module Objectives

After completing this module, you will be able to:

- Format data using text functions
- Sum a data range based on conditions
- Consolidate data using a formula
- Check formulas for errors
- Construct formulas using named ranges
- Build a logical formula with the IF function
- Build a logical formula with the AND function
- Calculate payments with the PMT function

Files You Will Need

EX 5-1.xlsx	EX 5-5.xlsx
EX 5-2.xlsx	EX 5-6.xlsx
EX 5-3.xlsx	EX 5-7.xlsx
EX 5-4.xlsx	

Format Data Using Text Functions

Learning Outcomes
• Separate text data using Flash Fill
• Format text data using the PROPER function
• Format text data using the CONCATENATE function

Often, you need to import data into Excel from an outside source, such as another program or the Internet. Sometimes you need to reformat this data to make it understandable and attractive. Instead of handling these formatting tasks manually in each cell, you can use Excel text functions to perform them automatically for an entire range. The Flash Fill feature can be used to break data fields in one column into separate columns. The text function PROPER capitalizes the first letter in a string of text as well as any text following a space. You can use the CONCATENATE function to join two or more strings into one text string. **CASE** ▸ *Mary has received the U.S. sales representatives' data from the Human Resources Department, and has imported it into Excel. She asks you to use text formulas to format the data into a more useful layout.*

STEPS

1. **Start Excel, open EX 5-1.xlsx from the location where you store your Data Files, then save it as EX 5-Sales**

2. **On the Sales Reps sheet, click cell B4, type troy silva, press [Tab], type new york, press [Tab], type 5, then click the Enter button ☑ on the formula bar**
   You are manually separating the data in cell A4 into the adjacent cells, as shown in **FIGURE 5-1**. You will let Excel follow your pattern for the rows below using Flash Fill. **Flash Fill** uses worksheet data you have entered as an example to predict what should be entered into similar column cells.

3. **With cell D4 selected, click the Data tab, then click the Flash Fill button in the Data Tools group**
   The years of service number is copied from cell D4 into the range D5:D15. You will use Flash Fill to fill in the names and cities.

QUICK TIP
You can move the Function Arguments dialog box if it overlaps a cell or range that you need to click. You can also click the Collapse Dialog box button 📑, select the cell or range, then click the Expand Dialog box button 📑 to return to the Function Arguments dialog box.

4. **Click cell B4, click the Flash Fill button in the Data Tools group, click cell C4, then click the Flash Fill button again**
   The column A data is separated into columns B, C and D. You want to format the letters in the names and cities to the correct cases.

5. **Click cell E4, click the Formulas tab, click the Text button in the Function Library group, click PROPER, with the insertion point in the Text text box click cell B4, then click OK**
   The name is copied from cell B4 to cell E4 with the correct uppercase letters for proper names. The name is formatted in green, taking on the column's previously applied formatting.

6. **Drag the fill handle to copy the formula in cell E4 to cell F4, then copy the formulas in cells E4:F4 into the range E5:F15**
   You want to format the years data to be more descriptive.

QUICK TIP
Excel automatically inserts quotation marks to enclose the space and the Years text.

7. **Click cell G4, click the Text button in the Function Library group, click CONCATENATE, with the insertion point in the Text1 text box click cell D4, press [Tab], with the insertion point in the Text2 text box press [Spacebar], type Years, then click OK**

8. **Copy the formula in cell G4 into the range G5:G15, click cell A1, compare your work to FIGURE 5-2, click the Insert tab, click the Header & Footer button in the Text group, click the Go to Footer button in the Navigation group, enter your name in the center text box, click on the worksheet, scroll up and click cell A1, then click the Normal button ▦ in the Workbook Views group on the View tab**

9. **Save your file, then preview the worksheet**

FIGURE 5-1: Worksheet with data separated into columns

▲	A	B	C	D	E	F	G
1						R2G	
2						Sales Representatives	
3					**Name**	**Office**	**Years of Service**
4	troy silva, new york, 5	troy silva	new york	5			
5	tony collins, new york, 3						
6	keith bradley, new york, 5						
7	linanne lu, new york, 10						
8	jacki kearny, new york, 2						
9	garrett coleson, new york, 7						
10	kris jaques, los angeles, 4						
11	alyssa mello, los angeles, 4						
12	keri tadka, los angeles, 3						
13	jose cruz, los angeles, 7						
14	jean hanley, los angeles, 2						
15	spring regan, los angeles, 7						

Data separated into three columns

FIGURE 5-2: Worksheet with data formatted in columns

▲	A	B	C	D	E	F	G
1						R2G	
2						Sales Representatives	
3					**Name**	**Office**	**Years of Service**
4	troy silva, new york, 5	troy silva	new york	5	Troy Silva	New York	5 Years
5	tony collins, new york, 3	tony collins	new york	3	Tony Collins	New York	3 Years
6	keith bradley, new york, 5	keith bradley	new york	5	Keith Bradley	New York	5 Years
7	linanne lu, new york, 10	linanne lu	new york	10	Linanne Lu	New York	10 Years
8	jacki kearny, new york, 2	jacki kearny	new york	2	Jacki Kearny	New York	2 Years
9	garrett coleson, new york, 7	garrett coleson	new york	7	Garrett Coleson	New York	7 Years
10	kris jaques, los angeles, 4	kris jaques	los angeles	4	Kris Jaques	Los Angeles	4 Years
11	alyssa mello, los angeles, 4	alyssa mello	los angeles	4	Alyssa Mello	Los Angeles	4 Years
12	keri tadka, los angeles, 3	keri tadka	los angeles	3	Keri Tadka	Los Angeles	3 Years
13	jose cruz, los angeles, 7	jose cruz	los angeles	7	Jose Cruz	Los Angeles	7 Years
14	jean hanley, los angeles, 2	jean hanley	los angeles	2	Jean Hanley	Los Angeles	2 Years
15	spring regan, los angeles, 7	spring regan	los angeles	7	Spring Regan	Los Angeles	7 Years
16							

Working with text in other ways

Other useful text functions include UPPER, LOWER, and SUBSTITUTE. The UPPER function converts text to all uppercase letters, the LOWER function converts text to all lowercase letters, and SUBSTITUTE replaces text in a text string. For example, if cell A1 contains the text string "Today is Wednesday", then =LOWER(A1) would produce "today is wednesday"; =UPPER(A1) would produce "TODAY IS WEDNESDAY"; and =SUBSTITUTE(A1, "Wednesday", "Tuesday") would result in "Today is Tuesday". You can also use functions to display one or more characters at certain locations within a string. Use the RIGHT function to find the last characters with the syntax =RIGHT(string, # characters), the LEFT function to find the first characters with the syntax =LEFT(string, # characters), or the MID function to display the middle characters with the syntax =MID(string, starting character, # characters). You can separate text data stored in one column into multiple columns by clicking the Data tab, clicking the Text to Columns button in the Data Tools group, and specifying the delimiter for your data. A **delimiter** is a separator, such as a space, comma, or semicolon, that should separate your data. Excel then separates your data into columns at the delimiter.

Sum a Data Range Based on Conditions

You can also use Excel functions to sum, count, and average data in a range based on criteria, or conditions, you set. The SUMIF function totals only the cells in a range that meet given criteria. The COUNTIF function counts cells and the AVERAGEIF function averages values in a range based on a specified condition. The format for the SUMIF function appears in **FIGURE 5-3**. **CASE** *Mary asks you to analyze the New York branch's January sales data to provide her with information about each experience.*

STEPS

1. **Click the NY sheet tab, click cell G7, click the Formulas tab, click the More Functions button in the Function Library group, point to Statistical, scroll down the list of functions if necessary, then click COUNTIF**

   You want to count the number of times Wildlife Care appears in the Experience Category column. The formula you use will say, in effect, "Examine the range I specify, then count the number of cells in that range that contain "Wildlife Care."" You will specify absolute addresses for the range so you can copy the formula later on in the worksheet when the same range will be used.

2. **With the insertion point in the Range text box select the range A6:A25, press [F4], press [Tab], with the insertion point in the Criteria text box, click cell F7, then click OK**

   Your formula, as shown in the formula bar in **FIGURE 5-4**, asks Excel to search the range A6:A25, and where it finds the value shown in cell F7 (that is, when it finds the value "Wildlife Care"), to add one to the total count. The number of Wildlife Care experiences, 4, appears in cell G7. You want to calculate the total sales revenue for the Wildlife Care experiences.

3. **Click cell H7, click the Math & Trig button in the Function Library group, scroll down the list of functions, then click SUMIF**

   The Function Arguments dialog box opens. You want to enter two ranges and a criterion; the first range is the one where you want Excel to search for the criteria entered. The second range contains the corresponding cells that Excel will total when it finds the criterion you specify in the first range.

4. **With the insertion point in the Range text box, select the range A6:A25, press [F4], press [Tab], with the insertion point in the Criteria text box click cell F7, press [Tab], with the insertion point in the Sum_range text box select the range B6:B25, press [F4], then click OK**

   Your formula asks Excel to search the range A6:A25, and where it finds Wildlife Care to add the corresponding amounts from column B. The revenue for the Wildlife Care experiences, $4,603, appears in cell H7. You want to calculate the average price paid for the Wildlife Care experiences.

5. **Click cell I7, click the More Functions button in the Function Library group, point to Statistical, then click AVERAGEIF**

6. **With the insertion point in the Range text box select the range A6:A25, press [F4], press [Tab], with the insertion point in the Criteria text box click cell F7, press [Tab], with the insertion point in the Average_range text box select the range B6:B25, press [F4], then click OK**

   The average price paid for the Wildlife Care experiences, $1,151, appears in cell I7.

7. **Select the range G7:I7, then drag the fill handle to fill the range G8:I10**

   Compare your results with those in **FIGURE 5-5**.

8. **Add your name to the center of the footer, save the workbook, then preview the sheet**

FIGURE 5-3: Format of SUMIF function

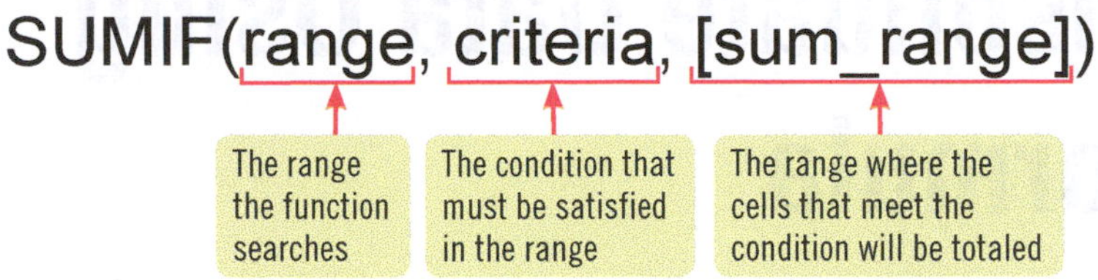

SUMIF(range, criteria, [sum_range])

| The range the function searches | The condition that must be satisfied in the range | The range where the cells that meet the condition will be totaled |

FIGURE 5-4: COUNTIF function in the formula bar

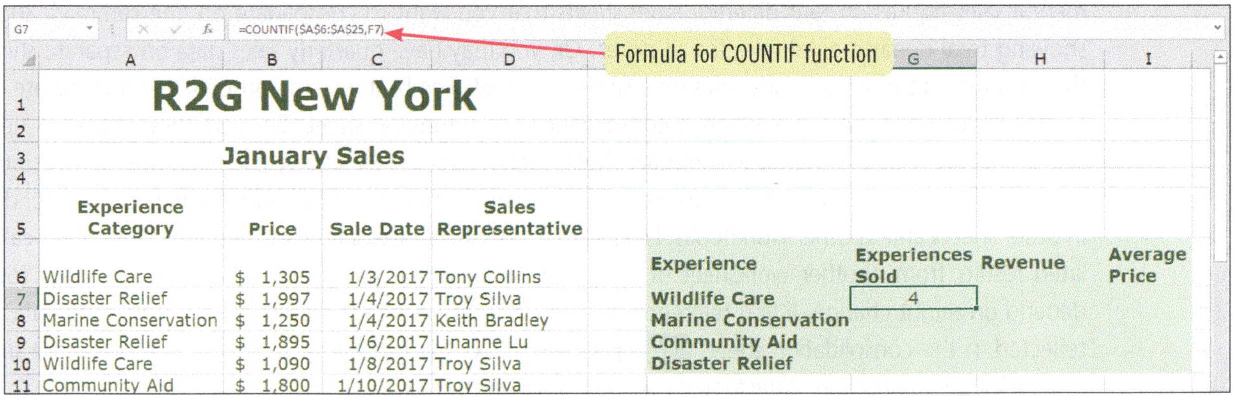

Formula for COUNTIF function

=COUNTIF($A$6:$A$25,F7)

R2G New York

January Sales

Experience Category	Price	Sale Date	Sales Representative		Experience	Experiences Sold	Revenue	Average Price
Wildlife Care	$ 1,305	1/3/2017	Tony Collins		Wildlife Care	4		
Disaster Relief	$ 1,997	1/4/2017	Troy Silva		Marine Conservation			
Marine Conservation	$ 1,250	1/4/2017	Keith Bradley		Community Aid			
Disaster Relief	$ 1,895	1/6/2017	Linanne Lu		Disaster Relief			
Wildlife Care	$ 1,090	1/8/2017	Troy Silva					
Community Aid	$ 1,800	1/10/2017	Troy Silva					

FIGURE 5-5: Worksheet with conditional statistics

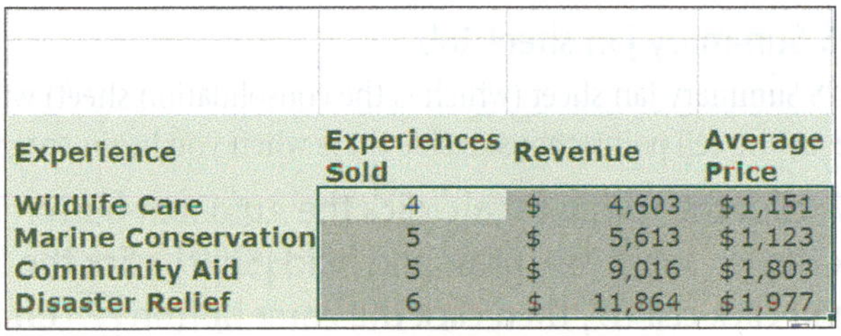

Experience	Experiences Sold	Revenue	Average Price
Wildlife Care	4	$ 4,603	$1,151
Marine Conservation	5	$ 5,613	$1,123
Community Aid	5	$ 9,016	$1,803
Disaster Relief	6	$ 11,864	$1,977

Entering date and time functions

Microsoft Excel stores dates as sequential serial numbers and uses them in calculations. January 1, 1900 is assigned serial number 1 and numbers are represented as the number of days following that date. You can see the serial number of a date by using the DATE function. For example, to see the serial number of January, 1, 2017 you would enter =DATE(2017,1,1). The result would be in date format, but if you formatted the cell as Number, it would display the serial number 42736 for this date. Because Excel uses serial numbers, you can perform calculations that include dates and times using the Excel date and time functions. To enter a date or time function, click the Formulas tab on the Ribbon, click the Date & Time button in the Function Library group, then click the Date or Time function you want. All of the date and time functions will be displayed as dates and times unless you change the formatting to Number. See TABLE 5-1 for some of the available Date and Time functions in Excel.

TABLE 5-1: Date and Time functions

function	calculates	example
TODAY	The current date	=TODAY()
NOW	The current date and time	=NOW()
DATE	Displays a date you enter	=DATE(2017,1,2)
TIME	A serial number from hours, minutes, and seconds	=TIME(5,12,20)
YEAR	A year portion of a date	=YEAR(1/20/2017)
HOUR	The hour portion of a time	=HOUR("15:30:30")
MINUTE	The minute portion of a time	=MINUTE("15:30:30")

Excel 2016

Consolidate Data Using a Formula

When you want to summarize similar data that exists in different sheets or workbooks, you can **consolidate**, or combine and display, the data in one sheet. For example, you might have entered departmental sales figures on four different store sheets that you want to consolidate on one summary sheet, showing total departmental sales for all stores. Or, you may have quarterly sales data on separate sheets that you want to total for yearly sales on a summary sheet. The best way to consolidate data is to use cell references to the various sheets on a consolidation, or summary, sheet. Because they reference other sheets that are usually behind the summary sheet, such references effectively create another dimension in the workbook and are called **3-D references**, as shown in FIGURE 5-6. You can reference, or **link** to, data in other sheets and in other workbooks. Linking to a worksheet or workbook is better than retyping calculated results from another worksheet or workbook because the data values that the calculated totals depend on might change. If you reference the cells, any changes to the original values are automatically reflected in the consolidation sheet. **CASE** *Mary asks you to prepare a January sales summary sheet comparing the total U.S. revenue for the experiences sold in the month.*

STEPS

1. **Click the US Summary Jan sheet tab**

   Because the US Summary Jan sheet (which is the consolidation sheet) will contain references to the data in the other sheets, the cell pointer must reside there when you begin entering the reference.

2. **Click cell B7, click the Formulas tab, click the AutoSum button in the Function Library group, click the NY sheet tab, press and hold [Shift], click the LA sheet tab, scroll up if necessary and click cell G7, then click the Enter button ✓ on the formula bar**

   The US Summary Jan sheet becomes active, and the formula bar reads =SUM(NY:LA!G7), as shown in FIGURE 5-7. "NY:LA" references the NY and LA sheets. The exclamation point (!) is an **external reference indicator**, meaning that the cells referenced are outside the active sheet; G7 is the actual cell reference you want to total in the external sheets. The result, 7, appears in cell B7 of the US Summary Jan sheet; it is the sum of the number of Wildlife Care experiences sold and referenced in cell G7 of the NY and LA sheets. Because the Revenue data is in the column to the right of the Experiences Sold column on the NY and LA sheets, you can copy the experiences sold summary formula, with its relative addresses, into the cell that holds the revenue summary information.

3. **Drag the fill handle to copy the formula in cell B7 to cell C7, click the Auto Fill Options list arrow 🖳▾, then click the Fill Without Formatting option button**

   The result, $8,004, appears in cell C7 of the US Summary Jan sheet, showing the sum of the Wildlife Care experience revenue referenced in cell H7 of the NY and LA sheets.

4. **In the US Summary Jan sheet, with the range B7:C7 selected, drag the fill handle to fill the range B8:C10**

   You can test a consolidation reference by changing one cell value on which the formula is based and seeing if the formula result changes.

5. **Click the LA sheet tab, edit cell A6 to read Wildlife Care, then click the US Summary Jan sheet tab**

   The number of Wildlife Care experiences sold is automatically updated to 8, and the revenue is increased to $9,883, as shown in FIGURE 5-8.

6. **Save the workbook, then preview the worksheet**

FIGURE 5-6: Consolidating data from two worksheets

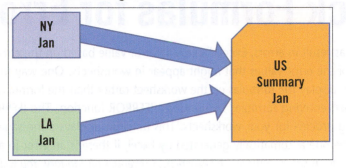

FIGURE 5-7: Worksheet showing total Wildlife Care experiences sold

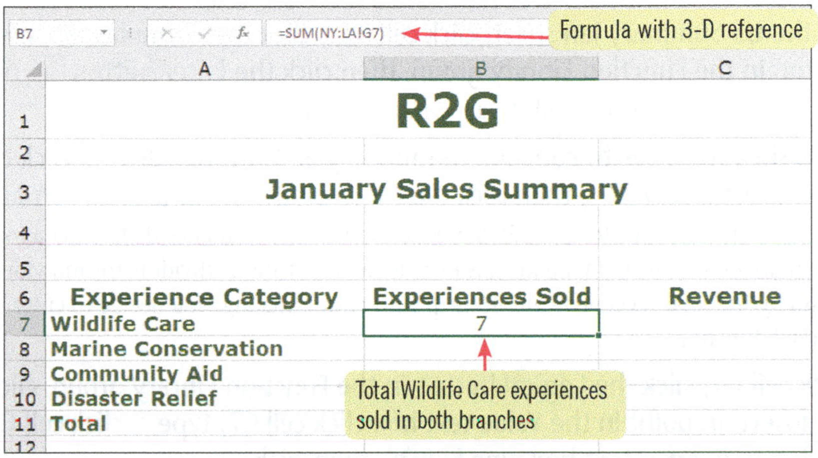

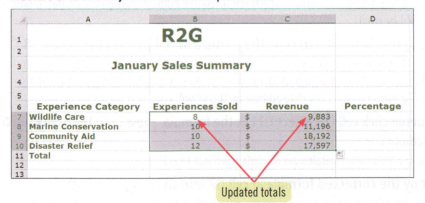

FIGURE 5-8: US Summary Jan worksheet with updated totals

Linking data between workbooks

Just as you can link data between cells in a worksheet and between sheets in a workbook, you can link workbooks so that changes made in referenced cells in one workbook are reflected in the consolidation sheet in the other workbook. To link a single cell between workbooks, open both workbooks, select the cell to receive the linked data, type the equal sign (=), select the cell in the other workbook containing the data to be linked, then press [Enter]. Excel automatically inserts the name of the referenced workbook in the cell reference. For example, if the linked data is contained in cell C7 of the Sales worksheet in the Product workbook, the cell entry reads =[Product.xlsx]Sales!$C$7. To perform calculations, enter formulas on the consolidation sheet using cells in the supporting sheets.

Check Formulas for Errors

When formulas result in errors, Excel displays an error value based on the error type. See **TABLE 5-2** for an explanation of the error values that might appear in worksheets. One way to check worksheet formulas for errors is to display the formulas on the worksheet rather than the formula results. You can also check for errors when entering formulas by using the IFERROR function. The IFERROR function simplifies the error-checking process for your worksheets. This function displays a message or value that you specify, rather than the one automatically generated by Excel, if there is an error in a formula. **CASE** *Mary asks you to use formulas to compare the experiences revenues for January. You will use the IFERROR function to help catch formula errors.*

STEPS

1. **On the US Summary Jan sheet, click cell B11, click the Formulas tab, click the AutoSum button in the Function Library group, then click the Enter button ☑ on the formula bar**

   The number of experiences sold, 40, appears in cell B11.

2. **Drag the fill handle to copy the formula in cell B11 into cell C11, click the Auto Fill options list arrow 📑▾, then click the Fill Without Formatting option button**

   The experience revenue total of $56,868 appears in cell C11. You decide to enter a formula to calculate the percentage of revenue the Wildlife Care experience represents by dividing the individual experience revenue figures by the total revenue figure. To help with error checking, you decide to enter the formula using the IFERROR function.

3. **Click cell D7, click the Logical button in the Function Library group, click IFERROR, with the insertion point in the Value text box click cell C7, type /, click cell C11, press [Tab], in the Value_if_error text box type ERROR, then click OK**

   The Wildlife Care experience revenue percentage of 17.38% appears in cell D7. You want to be sure that your error message will be displayed properly, so you decide to test it by intentionally creating an error. You copy and paste the formula—which has a relative address in the denominator, where an absolute address should be used.

4. **Drag the fill handle to copy the formula in cell D7 into the range D8:D10**

   The ERROR value appears in cells D8:D10, as shown in **FIGURE 5-9**. The errors are a result of the relative address for C11 in the denominator of the copied formula. Changing the relative address of C11 in the copied formula to an absolute address of $C$11 will correct the errors.

5. **Double-click cell D7, select C11 in the formula, press [F4], then click ☑ on the formula bar**

   The formula now contains an absolute reference to cell C11.

6. **Copy the corrected formula in cell D7 into the range D8:D10**

   The experience revenue percentages now appear in all four cells, without error messages, as shown in **FIGURE 5-10**. You want to check all of your worksheet formulas by displaying them on the worksheet.

7. **Click the Show Formulas button in the Formula Auditing group**

   The formulas appear in columns B, C, and D. You want to display the formula results again. The Show Formulas button works as a toggle, turning the feature on and off with each click.

8. **Click the Show Formulas button in the Formula Auditing group**

   The formula results appear on the worksheet.

9. **Add your name to the center section of the footer, save the workbook, preview the worksheet, close the workbook, then submit the workbook to your instructor**

Analyzing Data Using Formulas

FIGURE 5-9: Worksheet with error codes

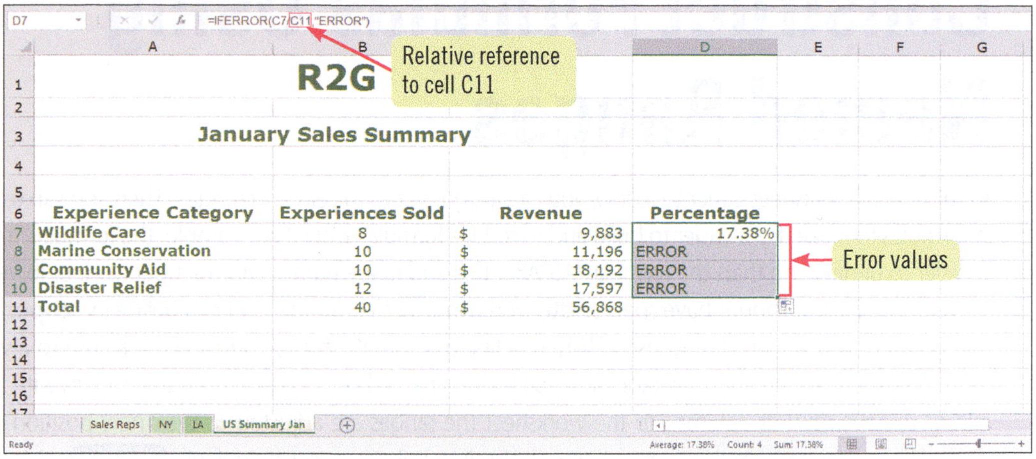

FIGURE 5-10: Worksheet with experience percentages

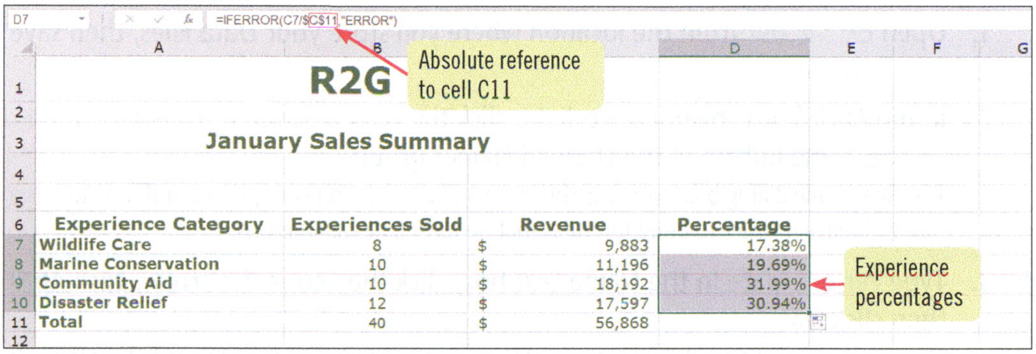

TABLE 5-2: Understanding error values

error value	cause of error	error value	cause of error
#DIV/0!	A number is divided by 0	#NAME?	Formula contains text error
#NA	A value in a formula is not available	#NULL!	Invalid intersection of areas
#NUM!	Invalid use of a number in a formula	#REF!	Invalid cell reference
#VALUE!	Wrong type of formula argument or operand	#####	Column is not wide enough to display data

Correcting circular references

A cell with a circular reference contains a formula that refers to its own cell location. If you accidentally enter a formula with a circular reference, a warning box opens, alerting you to the problem. Click Help to open a Help window explaining how to find the circular reference. In simple formulas, a circular reference is easy to spot. To correct it, edit the formula to remove any reference to the cell where the formula is located.

If the circular reference is intentional, you can avoid this error by enabling the iteration feature. Excel then recalculates the formula for the number of times you specify. To enable iterative calculations, click the File tab on the Ribbon, click Options, click Formulas to view the options for calculations, click the Enable iterative calculation check box in the Calculation options group, enter the maximum number of iterations in the Maximum Iterations text box, enter the maximum amount of change between recalculation results in the Maximum Change text box, then click OK.

Construct Formulas Using Named Ranges

Learning Outcomes
- Assign names to cells
- Assign names to cell ranges
- Build formulas using names

To make your worksheet easier to follow, you can assign names to cells and ranges. Then you can use the names in formulas to make them easier to build and to reduce formula errors. For example, the formula "revenue-cost" is easier to understand than the formula "A5-A8". Cell and range names can use uppercase or lowercase letters as well as digits, but cannot have spaces. After you name a cell or range, you can define its **scope**, or the worksheets where you will be able to use it. When defining a name's scope, you can limit its use to a worksheet or make it available to the entire workbook. If you move a named cell or range, its name moves with it, and if you add or remove rows or columns to the worksheet the ranges are adjusted to their new position in the worksheet. When used in formulas, names become absolute cell references by default. **CASE** *Mary asks you to calculate the number of days before each experience departs. You will use range names to construct the formula.*

STEPS

QUICK TIP

You can also create range names by selecting a cell or range, typing a name in the Name Box, then pressing [Enter]. By default, its scope will be the workbook.

1. **Open EX 5-2.xlsx from the location where you store your Data Files, then save it as EX 5-Experiences**

2. **In the April Sales sheet, click cell B4, click the Formulas tab if necessary, then click the Define Name button in the Defined Names group**

   The New Name dialog box opens, as shown in FIGURE 5-11. You can give a cell that contains a date a name that will make it easier to build formulas that perform date calculations.

QUICK TIP

Because range names cannot contain spaces, underscores are often used between words to replace spaces.

3. **Type current_date in the Name text box, click the Scope list arrow, click April Sales, then click OK**

   The name assigned to cell B4, current_date, appears in the Name Box. Because its scope is the April Sales worksheet, the range name current_date will appear on the name list only on that worksheet.

4. **Select the range B7:B13, click the Define Name button in the Defined Names group, enter experience_date in the Name text box, click the Scope list arrow, click April Sales, then click OK**

   Now you can use the named cell and named range in a formula. The formula =experience_date–current_date is easier to understand than =B7-$B$4.

QUICK TIP

Named cells and ranges can be used as a navigational tool in a worksheet by selecting the name in the Name box.

5. **Click cell C7, type =, click the Use in Formula button in the Defined Names group, click experience_date, type –, click the Use in Formula button, click current_date, then click the Enter button ✓ on the formula bar**

   The number of days before the elephant conservation experience departs, 6, appears in cell C7. You can use the same formula to calculate the number of days before the other experiences depart.

6. **Drag the fill handle to copy the formula in cell C7 into the range C8:C13, then compare your formula results with those in FIGURE 5-12**

7. **Save the workbook**

Consolidating data using named ranges

You can consolidate data using named cells and ranges. For example, you might have entered team sales figures using the names team1, team2, and team3 on different sheets that you want to consolidate on one summary sheet. As you enter the summary formula you can click the Formulas tab, click the Use in Formula button in the Defined Names group, and select the cell or range name.

FIGURE 5-11: New Name dialog box

New Name

Name: _4_1_2017

Scope: Workbook

Comment:

Enter cell or range name here

Refers to: ='April Sales'!$B$4

OK   Cancel

FIGURE 5-12: Worksheet with days before departure

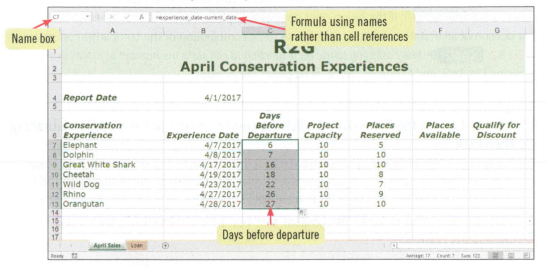

Name box

Formula using names rather than cell references

C7   =experience_date-current_date

R2G

April Conservation Experiences

	A	B	C		D	E	F	G
4	Report Date	4/1/2017						
6	Conservation Experience	Experience Date	Days Before Departure		Project Capacity	Places Reserved	Places Available	Qualify for Discount
7	Elephant	4/7/2017	6		10	5		
8	Dolphin	4/8/2017	7		10	10		
9	Great White Shark	4/17/2017	16		10	10		
10	Cheetah	4/19/2017	18		10	8		
11	Wild Dog	4/23/2017	22		10	7		
12	Rhino	4/27/2017	26		10	9		
13	Orangutan	4/28/2017	27		10	10		

Days before departure

April Sales   Loan

Ready   Average: 17   Count: 7   Sum: 122

Managing workbook names

You can use the Name Manager to create, delete, and edit names in a workbook. Click the Name Manager button in the Defined Names group on the Formulas tab to open the Name Manager dialog box, shown in **FIGURE 5-13**. Click the New button to create a new named cell or range, click Delete to remove a highlighted name, and click Filter to see options for displaying specific criteria for displaying names. Clicking Edit opens the Edit Name dialog box where you can change a highlighted cell name, edit or add comments, and change the cell or cells that the name refers to on the worksheet.

FIGURE 5-13: Name Manager dialog box

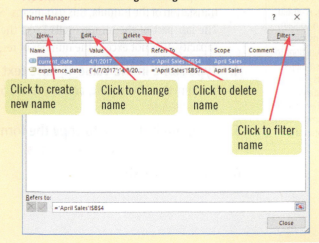

Name Manager

New...   Edit...   Delete   Filter

Name	Value	Refers To	Scope	Comment
current_date	4/1/2017	='April Sales'!$B$4	April Sales	
experience_date	{"4/7/2017";"4/8/20...	='April Sales'!$B$7...	April Sales	

Click to create new name

Click to change name

Click to delete name

Click to filter name

Refers to:

='April Sales'!$B$4

Close

Build a Logical Formula with the IF Function

You can build a logical formula using an IF function. A **logical formula** makes calculations based on criteria that you create, called **stated conditions**. For example, you can build a formula to calculate bonuses based on a person's performance rating. If a person is rated a 5 (the stated condition) on a scale of 1 to 5, with 5 being the highest rating, he or she receives an additional 10% of his or her salary as a bonus; otherwise, there is no bonus. A condition that can be answered with a true or false response is called a **logical test**. The IF function has three parts, separated by commas: a condition or logical test, an action to take if the logical test or condition is true, and an action to take if the logical test or condition is false. Another way of expressing this is: IF(test_cond,do_this,else_this). Translated into an Excel IF function, the formula to calculate bonuses might look like this: IF(Rating=5,Salary*0.10,0). In other words, if the rating equals 5, multiply the salary by 0.10 (the decimal equivalent of 10%), then place the result in the selected cell; if the rating does not equal 5, place a 0 in the cell. When entering the logical test portion of an IF statement, you typically use some combination of the comparison operators listed in **TABLE 5-3**. **CASE** *Mary asks you to use an IF function to calculate the number of places available for each experience in April, and to display "None" if no places are available.*

STEPS

1. **Click cell F7, on the Formulas tab click the Logical button in the Function Library group, then click IF**

   The Function Arguments dialog box opens. You want the function to do the following: If the project capacity is greater than the number of places reserved, calculate the number of places that are available (capacity minus number reserved), and place the result in cell F7; otherwise, place the text "None" in the cell.

2. **With the insertion point in the Logical_test text box, click cell D7, type >, click cell E7, then press [Tab]**

   The symbol (>) represents "greater than." So far, the formula reads "If the project capacity is greater than the number of reserved places,". The next part of the function tells Excel the action to take if the capacity exceeds the reserved number of places.

3. **With the insertion point in the Value_if_true text box, click cell D7, type –, click cell E7, then press [Tab]**

   This part of the formula tells the program what you want it to do if the logical test is true. Continuing the translation of the formula, this part means "Subtract the number of reserved places from the project capacity." The last part of the formula tells Excel the action to take if the logical test is false (that is, if the project capacity does not exceed the number of reserved places).

4. **Type None in the Value_if_false text box, then click OK**

   The function is complete, and the result, 5 (the number of available places), appears in cell F7, as shown in **FIGURE 5-14**.

5. **Drag the fill handle to copy the formula in cell F7 into the range F8:F13**

   Compare your results with **FIGURE 5-15**.

6. **Save the workbook**

FIGURE 5-14: Worksheet with IF function

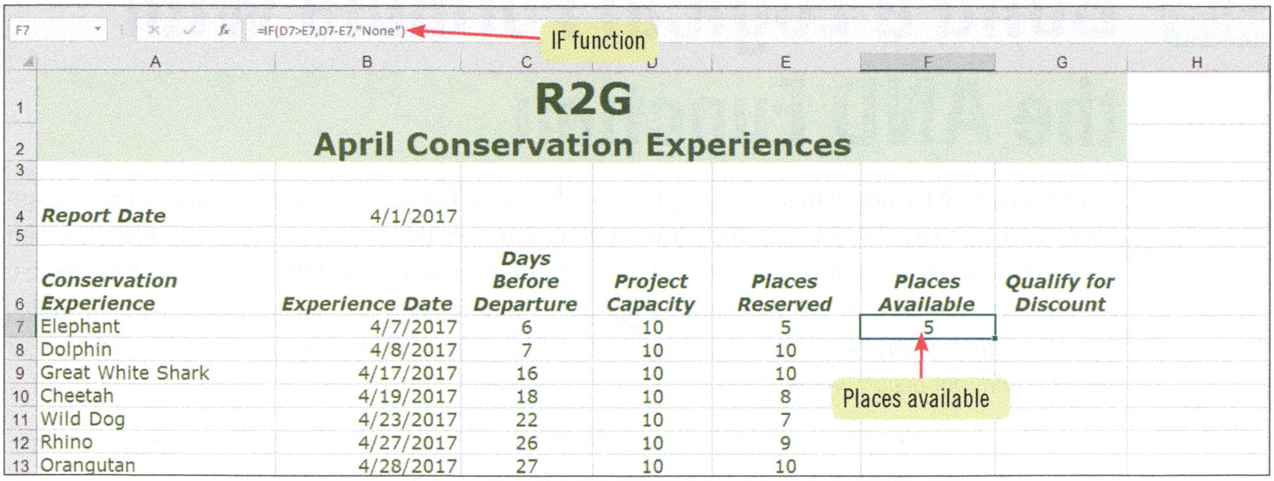

	A	B	C	D	E	F	G	H
F7			=IF(D7>E7,D7-E7,"None") ← IF function					
1			**R2G**					
2			**April Conservation Experiences**					
3								
4	**Report Date**	4/1/2017						
5								
6	**Conservation Experience**	**Experience Date**	**Days Before Departure**	**Project Capacity**	**Places Reserved**	**Places Available**	**Qualify for Discount**	
7	Elephant	4/7/2017	6	10	5	5		
8	Dolphin	4/8/2017	7	10	10			
9	Great White Shark	4/17/2017	16	10	10			
10	Cheetah	4/19/2017	18	10	8		Places available	
11	Wild Dog	4/23/2017	22	10	7			
12	Rhino	4/27/2017	26	10	9			
13	Orangutan	4/28/2017	27	10	10			

FIGURE 5-15: Worksheet showing places available

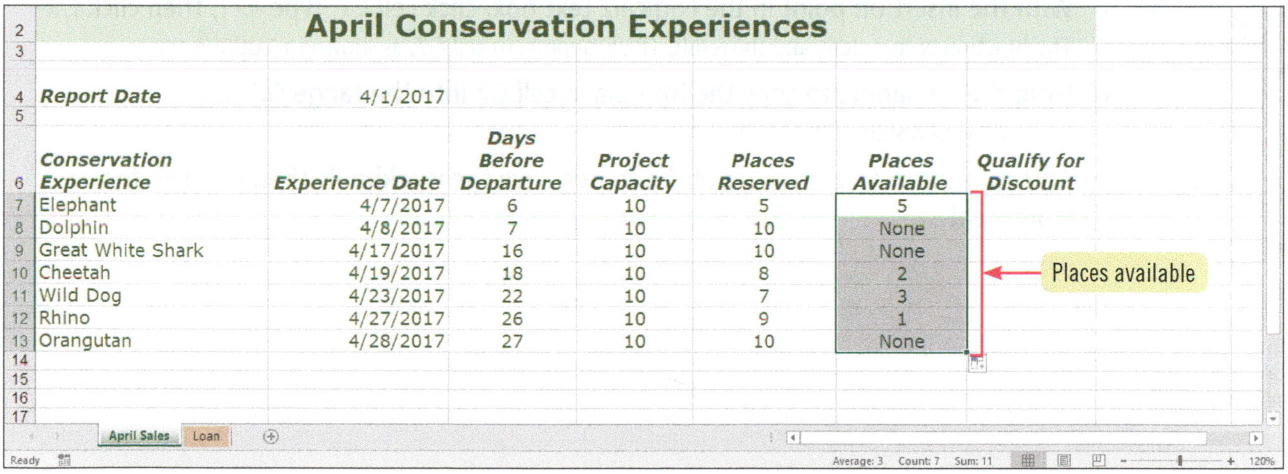

	A	B	C	D	E	F	G	
2			**April Conservation Experiences**					
3								
4	**Report Date**	4/1/2017						
5								
6	**Conservation Experience**	**Experience Date**	**Days Before Departure**	**Project Capacity**	**Places Reserved**	**Places Available**	**Qualify for Discount**	
7	Elephant	4/7/2017	6	10	5	5		
8	Dolphin	4/8/2017	7	10	10	None		
9	Great White Shark	4/17/2017	16	10	10	None	Places available	
10	Cheetah	4/19/2017	18	10	8	2		
11	Wild Dog	4/23/2017	22	10	7	3		
12	Rhino	4/27/2017	26	10	9	1		
13	Orangutan	4/28/2017	27	10	10	None		
14								
15								
16								
17								

April Sales Loan

Ready   Average: 3 Count: 7 Sum: 11   120%

TABLE 5-3: Comparison operators

operator	meaning	operator	meaning
<	Less than	<=	Less than or equal to
>	Greater than	>=	Greater than or equal to
=	Equal to	<>	Not equal to

Build a Logical Formula with the AND Function

Learning Outcomes
- Select the AND function
- Apply logical tests using text

You can also build a logical function using the AND function. The AND function evaluates all of its arguments and **returns**, or displays, TRUE if every logical test in the formula is true. The AND function returns a value of FALSE if one or more of its logical tests is false. The AND function arguments can include text, numbers, or cell references. **CASE** *Mary wants you to analyze the sales data to find experiences that qualify for discounting. You will use the AND function to check for experiences with places available and that depart within 21 days.*

STEPS

TROUBLE

If you get a formula error, check to be sure that you typed the quotation marks around None.

1. **Click cell G7, click the Logical button in the Function Library group, then click AND**

   The Function Arguments dialog box opens. You want the function to evaluate the discount qualification as follows: There must be places available, and the experience must depart within 21 days.

QUICK TIP

Functions can be placed inside of an IF function. For example, the formula in cell G7 could be replaced by the formula =IF(AND(F7<> "None", C7<21), "TRUE", "FALSE")

2. **With the insertion point in the Logical1 text box, click cell F7, type < >, type "None", then press [Tab]**

   The symbol (<>) represents "not equal to." So far, the formula reads "If the number of places available is not equal to None"—in other words, if it is an integer. The next logical test checks the number of days before the experience departs.

3. **With the insertion point in the Logical2 text box, click cell C7, type <21, then click OK**

   The function is complete, and the result, TRUE, appears in cell G7, as shown in **FIGURE 5-16**.

4. **Drag the fill handle to copy the formula in cell G7 into the range G8:G13**

   Compare your results with **FIGURE 5-17**.

QUICK TIP

You can fit your worksheet on one page to print by clicking the Page Layout tab, clicking the Width list arrow in the Scale to Fit group, then clicking 1 page.

5. **Add your name to the center of the footer, save the workbook, then preview the worksheet**

Using the OR and NOT logical functions

The OR logical function has the same syntax as the AND function, but rather than returning TRUE if every argument is true, the OR function will return TRUE if any of its arguments are true. It will only return FALSE if all of its arguments are false. The NOT logical function reverses the value of its argument. For example NOT(TRUE) reverses its argument of TRUE and returns FALSE. This can be used in a worksheet to ensure that a cell is not equal to a particular value. See **TABLE 5-4** for examples of the AND, OR, and NOT functions.

TABLE 5-4: Examples of AND, OR, and NOT functions with cell values A1=10 and B1=20

function	formula	result
AND	=AND(A1>5,B1>25)	FALSE
OR	=OR(A1>5,B1>25)	TRUE
NOT	=NOT(A1=0)	TRUE

FIGURE 5-16: Worksheet with AND function

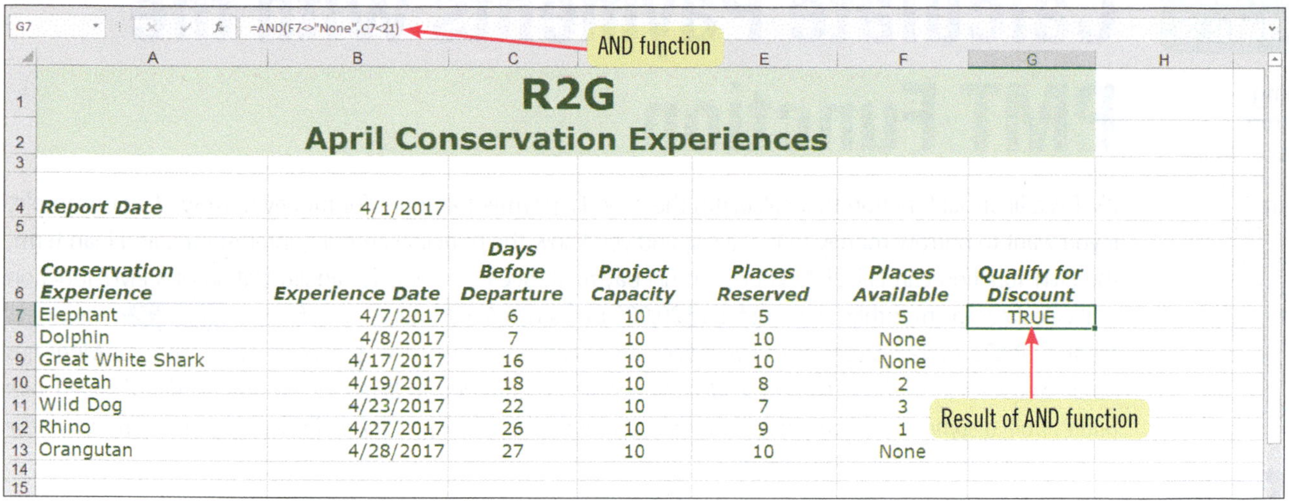

FIGURE 5-17: Worksheet with discount status evaluated

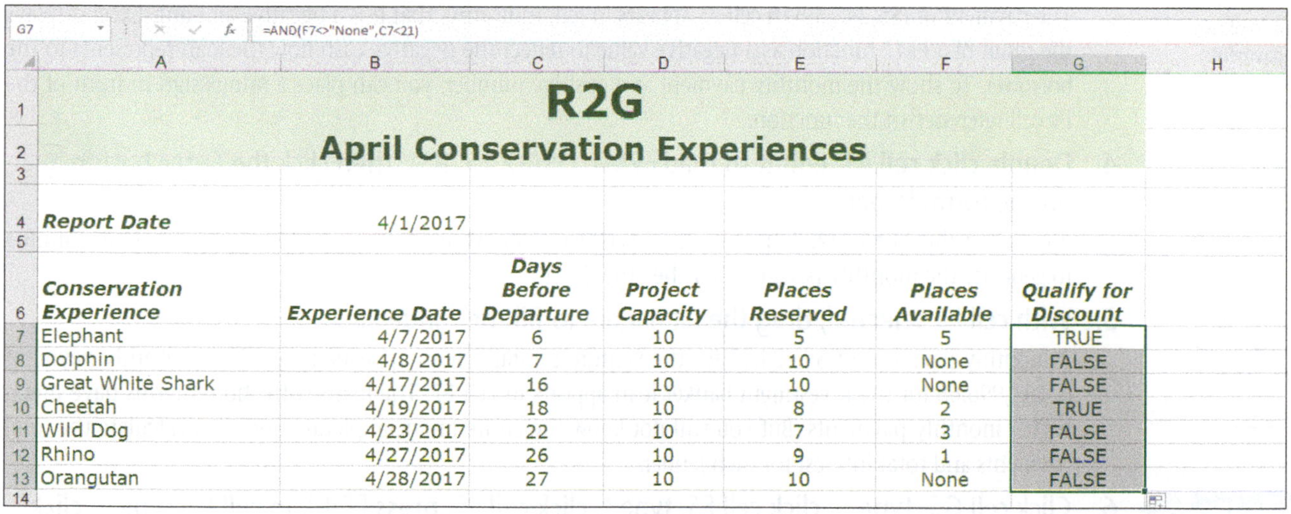

Calculate Payments with the PMT Function

PMT is a financial function that calculates the periodic payment amount for money borrowed. For example, if you want to borrow money to buy a car, and you know the principal amount, interest rate, and loan term, the PMT function can calculate your monthly payment. See **FIGURE 5-18** for an illustration of a PMT function that calculates the monthly payment for a $20,000 car loan at 6.5% interest over 5 years. **CASE** ▸ *For several months, R2G's United States region has been discussing opening a new branch in San Francisco. Mary has obtained quotes from three different lenders on borrowing $500,000 to begin the expansion. She obtained loan quotes from a commercial bank, a venture capitalist, and an investment banker. She wants you to summarize the information using the Excel PMT function.*

STEPS

1. **Click the Loan sheet tab, click cell F5, click the Formulas tab, click the Financial button in the Function Library group, scroll down the list of functions, then click PMT**

2. **With the insertion point in the Rate text box, click cell D5 on the worksheet, type /12, then press [Tab]**

   You must divide the annual interest by 12 because you are calculating monthly, not annual, payments. You need to be consistent about the units you use for rate and nper. If you express nper as the number of monthly payments, then you must express the interest rate as a monthly rate.

3. **With the insertion point in the Nper text box click cell E5, click the Pv text box, click cell B5, then click OK**

   The payment of ($5,242.39) in cell F5 appears in red, indicating that it is a negative amount. Excel displays the result of a PMT function as a negative value to reflect the negative cash flow the loan represents to the borrower. To show the monthly payment as a positive number, you can place a minus sign in front of the Pv cell reference in the function.

4. **Double-click cell F5, edit it to read =PMT(D5/12,E5,-B5), then click the Enter button ☑ on the formula bar**

   A positive value of $5,242.39 now appears in cell F5, as shown in **FIGURE 5-19**. You can use the same formula to generate the monthly payments for the other loans.

5. **With cell F5 selected, drag the fill handle to fill the range F6:F7**

   A monthly payment of $9,424.17 for the venture capitalist loan appears in cell F6. A monthly payment of $14,996.68 for the investment banker loan appears in cell F7. The loans with shorter terms have much higher monthly payments. But you will not know the entire financial picture until you calculate the total payments and total interest for each lender.

6. **Click cell G5, type =, click cell E5, type *, click cell F5, press [Tab], in cell H5 type =, click cell G5, type –, click cell B5, then click ☑**

7. **Copy the formulas in cells G5:H5 into the range G6:H7, then click cell A1**

   You can experiment with different interest rates, loan amounts, or terms for any one of the lenders; the PMT function generates a new set of values automatically.

8. **Add your name to the center section of the footer, save the workbook, preview the worksheet, submit the workbook to your instructor, close the workbook, then exit Excel**

   Your worksheet appears as shown in **FIGURE 5-20**.

FIGURE 5-18: Example of PMT function for car loan

$$PMT(0.065/12, \ 60, \ 20000) = \$391.32$$

Interest rate per month (rate)

Number of monthly payments

Present value of loan amount (pv)

Monthly payment calculated

FIGURE 5-19: PMT function calculating monthly loan payment

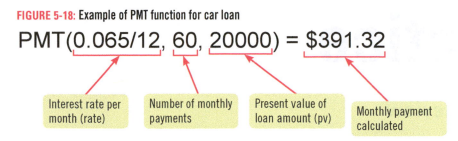

F5   fx   =PMT(D5/12,E5,-B5)

R2G
Expansion Loan Summary

Lender	Loan Amount	Term (Years)	Interest Rate	Term (Months)	Monthly Payment	Total Payments	Total Interest
Commercial Bank	$ 500,000	10	4.75%	120	$5,242.39		
Venture Capitalist	$ 500,000	5	4.95%	60			
Investment Banker	$ 500,000	3	5.05%	36			

Minus sign before present value displays payment as a positive amount

FIGURE 5-20: Completed worksheet

R2G
Expansion Loan Summary

Lender	Loan Amount	Term (Years)	Interest Rate	Term (Months)	Monthly Payment	Total Payments	Total Interest
Commercial Bank	$ 500,000	10	4.75%	120	$5,242.39	$629,086.46	$ 129,086.46
Venture Capitalist	$ 500,000	5	4.95%	60	$9,424.17	$565,450.05	$ 65,450.05
Investment Banker	$ 500,000	3	5.05%	36	$14,996.68	$539,880.32	$ 39,880.32

Excel 2016

Calculating future value with the FV function

You can use the FV (Future Value) function to determine the amount of money a given monthly investment will amount to, at a given interest rate, after a given number of payment periods. The syntax is similar to that of the PMT function: FV(rate,nper,pmt,pv,type). The rate is the interest paid by the financial institution, the nper is the number of periods, and the pmt is the amount that you deposit. For example, suppose you want to invest $1,000 every month for the next 12 months into an account that pays 2% a year, and you want to know how much you will have at the end of 12 months (that is, its future value). You enter the function FV(.02/12,12,-1000), and Excel returns the value $12,110.61 as the future value of your investment. As with the PMT function, the units for the rate and nper must be consistent.

Practice

Concepts Review

FIGURE 5-21

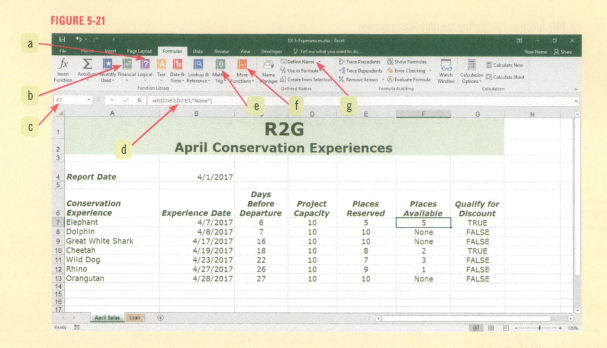

1. **Which element do you click to name a cell or range and define its scope?**
2. **Which element do you click to add a statistical function to a worksheet?**
3. **Which element points to a logical formula?**
4. **Which element points to the area where the name of a selected cell or range appears?**
5. **Which element do you click to add a SUMIF function to a worksheet?**
6. **Which element do you click to insert a PMT function into a worksheet?**
7. **Which element do you click to add an IF function to a worksheet?**

Match each term with the statement that best describes it.

8. FV	a. Function used to change the first letter of a string to uppercase
9. PV	b. Function used to determine the future amount of an investment
10. SUMIF	c. Part of the PMT function that represents the loan amount
11. PROPER	d. Part of the IF function that the conditions are stated in
12. test_cond	e. Function used to conditionally total cells

Select the best answer from the list of choices.

13. **To express conditions such as less than or equal to, you can use a:**
    a. Text formula.
    b. Comparison operator.
    c. PMT function.
    d. Statistical function.

14. **When you enter the rate and nper arguments in a PMT function, you must:**
    a. Be consistent in the units used.
    b. Multiply both units by 12.
    c. Divide both values by 12.
    d. Always use annual units.

15. Which of the following is an external reference indicator in a formula?

   a.   **c.** !

   b. :   **d.** =

16. Which of the following statements is false?

   a. When used in formulas, names become relative cell references by default.

   b. Names cannot contain spaces.

   c. Named ranges make formulas easier to build.

   d. If you move a named cell or range, its name moves with it.

17. Which function joins text strings into one text string?

   a. Proper   **c.** Combine

   b. Join   **d.** Concatenate

18. When using text in logical tests, the text must be enclosed in:

   a. " "   **c.** !

   b. ()   **d.** < >

Skills Review

1. Format data using text functions.

   a. Start Excel, open EX 5-3.xlsx from the location where you store your Data Files, then save it as **EX 5-North Systems**.

   b. On the Managers worksheet, select cell B4 and use the Flash Fill button on the Data tab to enter the names into column B.

   c. In cell D2, use a text function to convert the first letter of the department in cell C2 to uppercase, then copy the formula in cell D2 into the range D3:D9.

   d. In cell E2, use a text function to convert all letters of the department in cell C2 to uppercase, then copy the formula in cell E2 into the range E3:E9. Widen column E to fit the uppercase entries.

   e. In cell F2, use a text function to convert all letters of the department in cell C2 to lowercase, then copy the formula in cell F2 into the range F3:F9.

   f. In cell G2, use a text function to substitute "IT" for "operations" if that text exists in cell F2. (*Hint*: In the Function Arguments dialog box, Text is F2, Old_text is "operations", and New_text is "IT".) Copy the formula in cell G2 into the range G3:G9 to change any cells containing "operations" to "IT."

   g. Save your work, then enter your name in the worksheet footer. Switch back to Normal view, then compare your screen to FIGURE 5-22.

   h. Display the formulas in the worksheet.

   i. Redisplay the formula results.

FIGURE 5-22

	A	B	C	D	E	F	G
1		Name	Department	Proper	Upper	Lower	Substitute
2	JasonSears@company.com	Jason Sears	service	Service	SERVICE	service	service
3	CarolTaft@company.com	Carol Taft	sALES	Sales	SALES	sales	sales
4	LucyKnoll@company.com	Lucy Knoll	OperaTions	Operations	OPERATIONS	operations	IT
5	MiaMeng@company.com	Mia Meng	service	Service	SERVICE	service	service
6	RobertDally@company.com	Robert Dally	saLEs	Sales	SALES	sales	sales
7	CareyDegual@company.com	Carey Degual	saleS	Sales	SALES	sales	sales
8	JodyWolls@company.com	Jody Wolls	service	Service	SERVICE	service	service
9	MaryAllen@company.com	Mary Allen	OpErations	Operations	OPERATIONS	operations	IT
10							

2. Sum a data range based on conditions.

   a. Make the Service sheet active.

   b. In cell B20, use the COUNTIF function to count the number of employees with a rating of 5.

   c. In cell B21, use the AVERAGEIF function to average the salaries of those with a rating of 5.

   d. In cell B22, enter the SUMIF function that totals the salaries of employees with a rating of 5.

   e. Format cells B21 and B22 with the Number format using commas and no decimals. Save your work, then compare your formula results to FIGURE 5-23.

FIGURE 5-23

18	Department Statistics	
19	Top Rating	
20	Number	4
21	Average Salary	58,110
22	Total Salary	232,440
23		

Skills Review (continued)

3. Consolidate data using a formula.

  a. Make the Summary sheet active.

  b. In cell B4, use the AutoSum function to total cell F15 on the Service and Accounting sheets.

  c. Format cell B4 with the Accounting Number format with two decimal places.

  d. Enter your name in the worksheet footer, then save your work. Return to Normal view, then compare your screen to **FIGURE 5-24**.

  e. Display the formula in the worksheet, then redisplay the formula results in the worksheet.

4. Check formulas for errors.

  a. Make the Service sheet active.

  b. In cell I6, use the IFERROR function to display "ERROR" in the event that the formula F6/F15 results in a formula error. (*Note*: This formula will generate an intentional error after the next step, which you will correct in a moment.)

  c. Copy the formula in cell I6 into the range I7:I14.

  d. Correct the formula in cell I6 by making the denominator, F15, an absolute address.

  e. Copy the new formula in cell I6 into the range I7:I14, then save your work.

5. Construct formulas using named ranges.

  a. On the Service sheet, name the range C6:C14 **review_date**, and limit the scope of the name to the Service worksheet.

  b. In cell E6, enter the formula **=review_date+183**, using the Use in Formula button to enter the cell name.

  c. Copy the formula in cell E6 into the range E7:E14.

  d. Use the Name Manager to add a comment of **Date of last review** to the review_date name. (*Hint*: In the Name Manager dialog box, click the review_date name, then click Edit to enter the comment.) Widen the worksheet columns to display all of the data as necessary, then save your work.

6. Build a logical formula with the IF function.

  a. In cell G6, use the Function Arguments dialog box to enter the formula **=IF(D6=5,F6*0.05,0)**.

  b. Copy the formula in cell G6 into the range G7:G14.

  c. In cell G15, use AutoSum to total the range G6:G14.

  d. Save your work.

7. Build a logical formula with the AND function.

  a. In cell H6, use the Function Arguments dialog box to enter the formula **=AND(G6>0,B6>6)**.

  b. Copy the formula in cell H6 into the range H7:H14.

  c. Enter your name in the footers of the Service and Accounting sheets, save your work, then return to Normal view and compare your Service worksheet to **FIGURE 5-25**.

FIGURE 5-24

	A	B
1	**Salary Summary**	
2		
3		**Salary**
4	**TOTAL**	$ 852,035.00
5		

FIGURE 5-25

	A	B	C	D	E	F	G	H	I
1	**Service Department**								
2	**Bonus Pay**								
3									
4									
5	Last Name	Professional Development Hours	Review Date	Rating	Next Review	Salary	Bonus	Pay Bonus	Percentage of Total
6	Boady	5	1/7/2017	5	7/9/2017	$ 59,740.00	$2,987.00	FALSE	13.73%
7	Cane	9	4/1/2017	4	10/1/2017	$ 66,800.00	$0.00	FALSE	15.35%
8	Dugal	1	6/1/2017	4	12/1/2017	$ 33,400.00	$0.00	FALSE	7.67%
9	Hennely	7	4/1/2017	5	10/1/2017	$ 45,500.00	$2,275.00	TRUE	10.45%
10	Krones	10	3/1/2017	4	8/31/2017	$ 37,500.00	$0.00	FALSE	8.62%
11	Malone	4	5/15/2017	3	11/14/2017	$ 36,500.00	$0.00	FALSE	8.39%
12	Mercy	4	6/1/2017	5	12/1/2017	$ 57,500.00	$2,875.00	FALSE	13.21%
13	Stone	6	8/1/2017	3	1/31/2018	$ 28,600.00	$0.00	FALSE	6.57%
14	Storey	8	7/23/2017	5	1/22/2018	$ 69,700.00	$3,485.00	TRUE	16.01%
15	Totals					$ 435,240.00	$11,622.00		

Skills Review (continued)

8. **Calculate payments with the PMT function.**

   a. Make the Loan sheet active.

   b. In cell B9, determine the monthly payment using the loan information shown: Use the Function Arguments dialog box to enter the formula **=PMT(B5/12,B6,-B4)**.

   c. In cell B10, enter a formula that multiplies the number of payments by the monthly payment.

   d. In cell B11, enter the formula that subtracts the loan amount from the total payment amount, then compare your screen to **FIGURE 5-26**.

   e. Enter your name in the worksheet footer, save the workbook, then submit your workbook to your instructor.

   f. Close the workbook, then exit Excel.

FIGURE 5-26

	A	B	C	D	E	F
1	**Service Department**					
2	Equipment Loan Quote					
3						
4	*Loan Amount*	$ 125,000.00				
5	*Interest Rate*	4.75%				
6	*Term in Months*	48				
7						
8						
9	Monthly Payment:	$2,864.53				
10	Total Payments: $	137,497.31				
11	Total Interest: $	12,497.31				
12						
13						

Independent Challenge 1

As the accounting manager of Ace Floors, a carpet and flooring company, you are reviewing the accounts payable information for your advertising accounts and prioritizing the overdue invoices for your collections service. You will analyze the invoices and use logical functions to emphasize priority accounts.

   a. Start Excel, open EX 5-4.xlsx from the location where you store your Data Files, then save it as **EX 5-Ace**.

   b. Name the range B7:B13 **invoice_date**, and give the name a scope of the accounts payable worksheet.

   c. Name the cell B4 **current_date**, and give the name a scope of the accounts payable worksheet.

   d. Enter a formula using the named range invoice_date in cell E7 that calculates the invoice due date by adding 30 to the invoice date.

   e. Copy the formula in cell E7 to the range E8:E13.

   f. In cell F7, enter a formula using the named range invoice_date and the named cell current_date that calculates the invoice age by subtracting the invoice date from the current date.

   g. Copy the formula in cell F7 to the range F8:F13.

   h. In cell G7, enter an IF function that calculates the number of days an invoice is overdue, assuming that an invoice must be paid in 30 days. (*Hint*: The Logical_test should check to see if the age of the invoice is greater than 30, the Value_if_true should calculate the current date minus the invoice due date, and the Value_if_false should be 0.) Copy the IF function into the range G8:G13.

   i. In cell H7, enter an AND function to prioritize the overdue invoices that are more than $1,000 for collection services. (*Hint*: The Logical1 condition should check to see if the number of days overdue is more than 0, and the Logical2 condition should check if the amount is more than 1,000.) Copy the AND function into the range H8:H13.

   j. Use the Name Manager to name the range H7:H13 **Priority** and give the name a scope of the accounts payable worksheet. (*Hint*: In the Name Manager dialog box, click New to enter the range name.)

   k. Enter your name in the worksheet footer, save the workbook, preview the worksheet, then submit the workbook to your instructor.

   l. Close the workbook, then exit Excel.

Independent Challenge 2

You are an auditor with a certified public accounting firm. Boston Paper, an online seller of office products, has contacted you to audit its first-quarter sales records. The management is considering expanding and needs its sales records audited to prepare the business plan. Specifically, they want to show what percent of annual sales each category represents. You will use a formula on a summary worksheet to summarize the sales for January, February, and March and to calculate the overall first-quarter percentage of the sales categories.

a. Start Excel, open EX 5-5.xlsx from the location where you store your Data Files, then save it as **EX 5-Paper**.

b. In cell B10 of the Jan, Feb, and Mar sheets, enter the formulas to calculate the sales totals for the month.

c. For each month, in cell C5, create a formula calculating the percent of sales for the Equipment sales category. Use a function to display "INCORRECT" if there is a mistake in the formula. Verify that the percent appears with two decimal places. Copy this formula as necessary to complete the % of sales for all sales categories on all sheets. If any cells display "INCORRECT", fix the formulas in those cells.

d. In column B of the Summary sheet, use formulas to total the sales categories for the Jan, Feb, and Mar worksheets.

e. Enter the formula to calculate the first quarter sales total in cell B10 using the sales totals on the Jan, Feb, and Mar worksheets.

f. Calculate the percent of each sales category on the Summary sheet. Use a function to display "MISCALCULATION" if there is a mistake in the formula. Copy this formula as necessary. If any cells display "MISCALCULATION", fix the formulas in those cells.

g. Enter your name in the Summary worksheet footer, save the workbook, preview the worksheet, then submit it to your instructor.

FIGURE 5-27

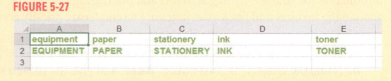

h. On the Products sheet, separate the product list in cell A1 into separate columns of text data. (*Hint*: With cell A1 as the active cell, use the Text to Columns button in the Data Tools group of the Data tab. The products are delimited with commas.) Use the second row to display the products in uppercase, as shown in FIGURE 5-27. Widen the columns as necessary.

i. Enter your name in the Products worksheet footer, save the workbook, preview the worksheet, then submit the workbook to your instructor.

Independent Challenge 3

As the owner of GWW, an advertising firm, you are planning to expand your business. Because you will have to purchase additional equipment and hire a new part-time accounts manager, you decide to take out a $100,000 loan to finance your expansion expenses. You check three loan sources: the Small Business Administration (SBA), your local bank, and a consortium of investors. The SBA will lend you the money at 4.5% interest, but you have to pay it off in 4 years. The local bank offers you the loan at 5.75% interest over 5 years. The consortium offers you a 8.25% loan, and they require you to pay it back in 2 years. To analyze all three loan options, you decide to build a loan summary worksheet. Using the loan terms provided, build a worksheet summarizing your options.

a. Start Excel, open a new workbook, save it as **EX 5-Options**, then rename Sheet1 **Loan Summary**.

b. Using FIGURE 5-28 as a guide, enter labels and worksheet data for the three loan sources in columns A through D. Use the formatting of your choice.

FIGURE 5-28

	A	B	C	D	E	F	G
1				GWW			
2				Loan Options			
3							
4	Loan Source	Loan Amount	Interest Rate	# Payments	Monthly Payment	Total Payments	Total Interest
5	SBA	$100,000.00	4.50%	48	$ 2,280.35	$ 109,456.73	$ 9,456.73
6	Bank	$100,000.00	5.75%	60	$ 1,921.68	$ 115,300.61	$ 15,300.61
7	Investors	$100,000.00	8.25%	24	$ 4,534.14	$ 108,819.35	$ 8,819.35
8							

Independent Challenge 3 (continued)

   c. Enter the monthly payment formula for your first loan source (making sure to show the payment as a positive amount), copy the formula as appropriate, then name the range containing the monthly payment formulas **Monthly_Payment** with a scope of the workbook.

   d. Name the cell range containing the number of payments **Number_Payments** with the scope of the workbook.

   e. Enter the formula for total payments for your first loan source using the named ranges Monthly_Payment and Number_Payments, then copy the formula as necessary.

   f. Name the cell range containing the formulas for Total payments **Total_Payments**. Name the cell range containing the loan amounts **Loan_Amount**. Each name should have the workbook as its scope.

   g. Enter the formula for total interest for your first loan source using the named ranges Total_Payments and Loan_Amount, then copy the formula as necessary.

   h. Format the worksheet using appropriate formatting, then enter your name in the worksheet footer.

   i. Save the workbook, preview the worksheet and change it to landscape orientation on a single page, then submit the workbook to your instructor.

   j. Close the workbook, then exit Excel.

Independent Challenge 4: Explore

As the physical therapist at NE Rehab, you are using a weekly worksheet to log and analyze the training for each of your patients. As part of this therapy, you record daily walking, biking, swimming, and weight training data and analyze it on a weekly basis.

   a. Start Excel, open EX 5-6.xlsx from the location where you store your Data Files, then save it as **EX 5-Activity**.

   b. Use SUMIF functions in cells G5:G8 to calculate the total minutes spent on each corresponding activity in cells F5:F8.

   c. Use AVERAGEIF functions in cells H5:H8 to calculate the average number of minutes spent on each corresponding activity in cells F5:F8.

   d. Use COUNTIF functions in cells I5:I8 to calculate the number of times each activity in cells F5:F8 was performed. (*Hint*: The Range of cells to count is $B$4:$B$15.)

   e. Use the SUMIFS function in cell G9 to calculate the total number of minutes spent walking outdoors.

   f. Use the AVERAGEIFS function in cell H9 to calculate the average number of minutes spent walking outdoors.

   g. Use the COUNTIFS function in cell I9 to calculate the number of days spent walking outdoors. Compare your worksheet to **FIGURE 5-29** and adjust your cell formatting as needed to match the figure.

   h. Enter your name in the worksheet footer, save the workbook, preview the worksheet, then submit it to your instructor.

   i. Close the workbook, then exit Excel.

FIGURE 5-29

	A	B	C	D	E	F	G	H	I
1					NE Rehab				
2	Client Name:	Karl Logan							
3	Date	Activity	Minutes	Location			Week of January 2nd		
4	1/2/2017	Walk	40	Gym		Activity	Total Minutes	Average Minutes	Number of Workouts
5	1/2/2017	Swim	30	Aquatics Center		Walk	172	43.00	4
6	1/3/2017	Walk	50	Outdoors		Swim	125	41.67	3
7	1/3/2017	Bike	25	Outdoors		Bike	80	26.67	3
8	1/4/2017	Walk	42	Outdoors		Weights	60	30.00	2
9	1/4/2017	Weights	30	Gym		Walk Outdoors	92	46	2
10	1/5/2017	Swim	50	Aquatics Center					
11	1/6/2017	Weights	30	Gym					
12	1/6/2017	Bike	30	Outdoors					
13	1/7/2017	Walk	40	Gym					
14	1/7/2017	Swim	45	Aquatics Center					
15	1/8/2017	Bike	25	Gym					
16									

Visual Workshop

Open EX 5-7.xlsx from the location where you store your Data Files, then save it as **EX 5-Bonus**. Create the worksheet shown in FIGURE 5-30 using the data in columns B, C, and D along with the following criteria:

- The employee is eligible for a bonus if:
  - The employee has sales that exceed the sales quota.
    AND
  - The employee has a performance rating of seven or higher.
- If the employee is eligible for a bonus, the bonus amount is calculated as three percent of the sales amount. Otherwise the bonus amount is 0. (*Hint:* Use an AND formula to determine if a person is eligible for a bonus, and use an IF formula to check eligibility and to enter the bonus amount.) Enter your name in the worksheet footer, save the workbook, preview the worksheet, then submit the worksheet to your instructor.

FIGURE 5-30

	A	B	C	D	E	F
1			Fitness Unlimited			
2			Bonus Pay Summary			
3	Last Name	Quota	Sales	Performance Rating	Eligible	Bonus Amount
4	Andrews	$145,000	$157,557	7	TRUE	$4,727
5	Lee	$78,587	$91,588	3	FALSE	$0
6	Atkinson	$113,984	$125,474	9	TRUE	$3,764
7	Halley	$135,977	$187,255	5	FALSE	$0
8	Pratt	$187,900	$151,228	8	FALSE	$0
9	Balla	$128,744	$152,774	5	FALSE	$0
10	Cruz	$129,855	$160,224	7	TRUE	$4,807
11	Yanck	$94,000	$87,224	3	FALSE	$0
12	Green	$79,500	$86,700	9	TRUE	$2,601
13						

Managing Workbook Data

CASE ▶ Mary Watson, the vice president of sales and marketing at Reason2Go, asks for your help in analyzing yearly sales data from the U.S. branches. When the analysis is complete, she will distribute the workbook for branch managers to review.

Module Objectives

After completing this module, you will be able to:

- View and arrange worksheets
- Protect worksheets and workbooks
- Save custom views of a worksheet
- Add a worksheet background

- Prepare a workbook for distribution
- Insert hyperlinks
- Save a workbook for distribution
- Group worksheets

Files You Will Need

EX 6-1.xlsx	EX 6-8.jpg
EX 6-2.xlsx	EX 6-Classifications.xlsx
EX 6-3.jpg	EX 6-Equipment.xlsx
EX 6-4.xlsx	EX 6-Expenses.xlsx
EX 6-5.xlsx	EX 6-Information.xlsx
EX 6-6.xlsx	EX 6-LA Sales.xlsx
EX 6-7.xlsx	EX 6-Logo.jpg

View and Arrange Worksheets

Learning Outcomes
- Compare worksheet data by arranging worksheets
- View and hide instances of a workbook

As you work with workbooks made up of multiple worksheets, you might need to compare data in the various sheets. To do this, you can view each worksheet in its own workbook window, called an **instance**, and display the windows in an arrangement that makes it easy to compare data. When you work with worksheets in separate windows, you are working with different views of the same workbook; the data itself remains in one file. **CASE** *Mary asks you to compare the monthly store sales totals for the Los Angeles and New York branches. Because the sales totals are on different worksheets, you want to arrange the worksheets side by side in separate windows.*

STEPS

1. **Start Excel, open EX 6-1.xlsx from the location where you store your Data Files, then save it as EX 6-Store Sales**

2. **With the Los Angeles sheet active, click the View tab, then click the New Window button in the Window group**

   There are now two instances of the Store Sales workbook open. You can see them when you place the mouse pointer over the Excel icon on the task bar: EX 6-Store Sales.xlsx:1 and EX 6-Store Sales.xlsx:2. The EX 6-Store Sales.xlsx:2 window appears in front, indicating that it's the active instance.

3. **Click the New York sheet tab, click the View tab, click the Switch Windows button in the Window group, then click EX 6-Store Sales.xlsx:1**

   The EX 6-Store Sales.xlsx:1 instance moves to the front. The Los Angeles sheet is active in the EX 6-Store Sales.xlsx:1 workbook, and the New York sheet is active in the EX 6-Store Sales.xlsx:2 workbook.

4. **Click the Arrange All button in the Window group**

   The Arrange Windows dialog box, shown in **FIGURE 6-1**, lets you choose how to display the instances. You want to view the workbooks next to each other.

5. **Click the Vertical option button to select it, then click OK**

   The windows are arranged next to each other, as shown in **FIGURE 6-2**. The second instance of the workbook opens at a zoom of 100%, not the 120% zoom of the workbook. You can activate a workbook by clicking one of its cells. You can also view only one of the workbooks by hiding the one you do not wish to see.

6. **Scroll horizontally to view the data in the EX 6-Store Sales.xlsx:1 workbook, click anywhere in the EX 6-Store Sales.xlsx:2 workbook, scroll horizontally to view the data in it, then click the Hide Window button in the Window group**

   When you hide the second instance, only the EX 6-Store Sales.xlsx:1 workbook is visible.

7. **In the EX 6-Store Sales.xlsx:1 window, click the Unhide Window button in the Window group; click EX 6-Store Sales.xlsx:2 if necessary in the Unhide dialog box, then click OK**

   The EX 6-Store Sales.xlsx:2 instance appears.

8. **Click the Close Window button ☒ in the title bar to close the EX 6-Store Sales.xlsx:2 instance, then maximize the Los Angeles worksheet in the EX 6-Store Sales.xlsx workbook**

   Closing the EX 6-Store Sales.xlsx:2 instance leaves only the first instance open. Its name in the title bar returns to EX 6-Store Sales.xlsx. When closing an instance of a workbook, it is important to use the close button and not the Close command on the File menu, which closes the workbook.

FIGURE 6-1: Arrange Windows dialog box

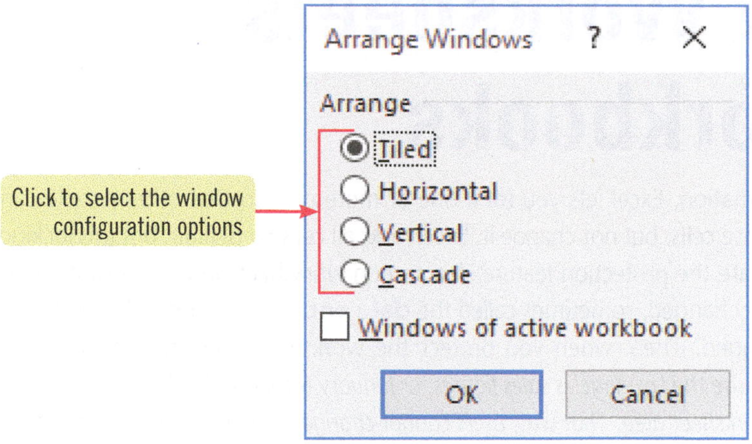

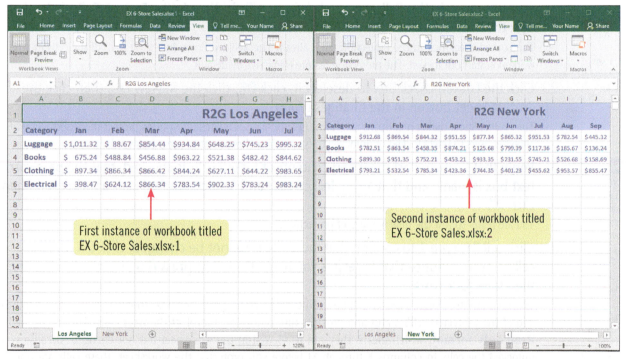

Click to select the window configuration options
Arrange Windows
Arrange
Tiled
Horizontal
Vertical
Cascade
Windows of active workbook
OK
Cancel

FIGURE 6-2: Windows instances displayed vertically

R2G Los Angeles
R2G New York
First instance of workbook titled EX 6-Store Sales.xlsx:1
Second instance of workbook titled EX 6-Store Sales.xlsx:2

Splitting the worksheet into multiple panes

Excel lets you split the worksheet area into vertical and/or horizontal panes, so that you can click inside any one pane and scroll to locate information in that pane while the other panes remain in place, as shown in FIGURE 6-3. To split a worksheet area into multiple panes, click a cell below and to the right of where you want the split to appear, click the View tab, then click the Split button in the Window group. You can also split a worksheet into only two panes by selecting the row or column below or to the right of where you want the split to appear, clicking the View tab, then clicking Split in the Window group. To remove a split, click the View tab, then click Split in the Window group.

FIGURE 6-3: Worksheet split into four panes

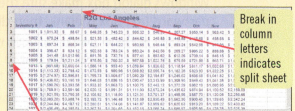

Break in column letters indicates split sheet
Break in row numbers indicates split sheet

Protect Worksheets and Workbooks

Learning Outcomes
- Protect worksheet data by locking cells
- Create a data entry area on a worksheet by unlocking cells
- Protect a workbook using Read-only format

To protect sensitive information, Excel lets you **lock** one or more cells so that other people can view the values and formulas in those cells, but not change it. Excel locks all cells by default, but this locking does not take effect until you activate the protection feature. A common worksheet protection strategy is to unlock cells in which data will be changed, sometimes called the **data entry area**, and to lock cells in which the data should not be changed. Then, when you protect the worksheet, the unlocked areas can still be changed. **CASE** ▶ *Because the Los Angeles sales figures for January through March have been finalized, Mary asks you to protect that worksheet area. That way, users cannot change the figures for those months.*

STEPS

QUICK TIP

You can also lock a cell by clicking the Format button in the Cells group of the Home tab, then clicking Lock Cell on the Format menu.

1. **On the Los Angeles sheet, select the range E3:M6, click the Home tab, click the Format button in the Cells group, click Format Cells, then in the Format Cells dialog box click the Protection tab**

   The Locked check box in the Protection tab is already checked, as shown in **FIGURE 6-4**. All the cells in a new workbook start out locked. The protection feature is inactive by default.

2. **Click the Locked check box to deselect it, click OK, click the Review tab, then click the Protect Sheet button in the Changes group**

   The Protect Sheet dialog box opens, as shown in **FIGURE 6-5**. The default options protect the worksheet while allowing users to select locked or unlocked cells only. You choose not to use a password.

QUICK TIP

To hide any formulas that you don't want to be visible, select the cells that contain formulas that you want to hide, open the Format Cells dialog box, then click the Hidden check box on the Protection tab to select it. The formula will be hidden after the worksheet is protected.

3. **Verify that Protect worksheet and contents of locked cells is checked, that the password text box is blank, and that Select locked cells and Select unlocked cells are checked, then click OK**

   You are ready to test the new worksheet protection.

4. **Click cell B3, type 1 to confirm that locked cells cannot be changed, click OK, click cell F3, type 1, notice that Excel lets you begin the entry, press [Esc] to cancel the entry, then save your work**

   When you try to change a locked cell on a protected worksheet, a dialog box, shown in **FIGURE 6-6**, reminds you of the protected cell's status and provides instructions to unprotect the worksheet. These cells are in **Read-only format**, which means they can be viewed in the worksheet but not changed. Because you unlocked the cells in columns E through M before you protected the worksheet, these cells are not in read-only format and you can change these cells. You want to add more protection by protecting the workbook from changes to the workbook's structure, but decide not to require a password.

5. **Click the Protect Workbook button in the Changes group, in the Protect Structure and Windows dialog box make sure the Structure check box is selected, verify that the password text box is blank, then click OK**

   The Protect Workbook button is a toggle, which means it's like an on/off switch. When it is highlighted, the workbook is protected. Clicking it again removes the highlighting indicating the protection is removed from the workbook. You are ready to test the new workbook protection.

6. **Right-click the Los Angeles sheet tab**

   The Insert, Delete, Rename, Move or Copy, Tab Color, Hide, and Unhide menu options are not available because the structure is protected. You decide to remove the workbook and worksheet protections.

7. **Click the Protect Workbook button in the Changes group to turn off the protection, click the Unprotect Sheet button, then save your changes**

FIGURE 6-4: Protection tab in Format Cells dialog box

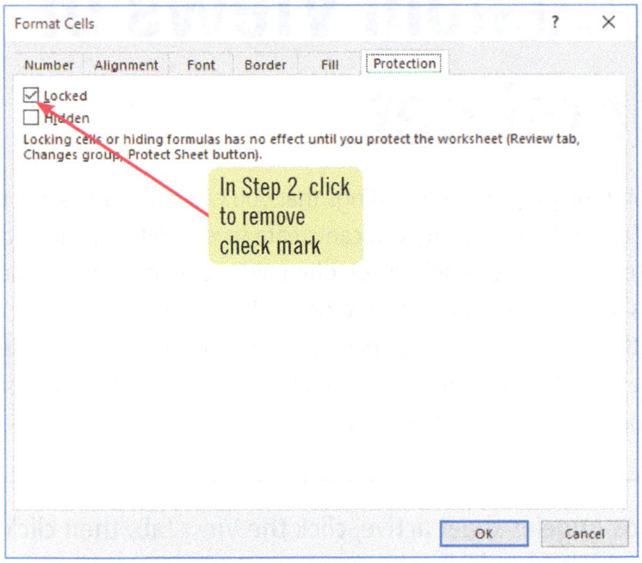

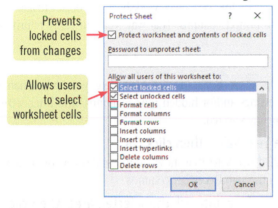

In Step 2, click to remove check mark

FIGURE 6-5: Protect Sheet dialog box

Prevents locked cells from changes

Allows users to select worksheet cells

FIGURE 6-6: Reminder of protected worksheet status

Freezing rows and columns

As the rows and columns of a worksheet fill up with data, you might want to Freeze panes to hold headers in place so you can see them as you scroll through the worksheet. Freezing panes is similar to splitting panes except that the panes do not move, so you can keep column or row labels in view as you scroll. **Panes** are the columns and rows that **freeze**, or remain in place, while you scroll through your worksheet. To freeze panes, click the first cell in the area you want to scroll, click the View tab, click the Freeze Panes button in the Window group, then click Freeze Panes. Excel freezes the columns to the left and the rows above the selected cell, as shown in **FIGURE 6-7**. You can also select Freeze Top Row or Freeze First Column to freeze the top row or left worksheet column. To unfreeze panes, click the View tab, click Freeze panes, then click Unfreeze Panes.

FIGURE 6-7: Worksheet with top row and left column frozen

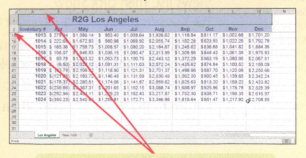

Break in column letters and row numbers indicates first column and first two rows are frozen

Managing Workbook Data

Save Custom Views of a Worksheet

Learning Outcomes
• Create different views of worksheet data using custom views
• Display different views of worksheet data using custom views

A **view** is a set of display and/or print settings that you can name and save, then access at a later time. By using the Excel Custom Views feature, you can create several different views of a worksheet without having to create separate sheets. For example, if you often hide columns in a worksheet, you can create two views, one that displays all of the columns and another with the columns hidden. You set the worksheet display first, then name the view. Then you can open the view whenever you want. **CASE** ▶ *Because Mary wants to generate a sales report from the final sales data for January through March, she asks you to create a custom view that shows only the first-quarter sales data.*

STEPS

1. **With the Los Angeles sheet active, click the View tab, then click the Custom Views button in the Workbook Views group**

   The Custom Views dialog box opens. Any previously defined views for the active worksheet appear in the Views box. No views are defined for the Los Angeles worksheet. You decide to add a named view for the current view, which shows all the worksheet columns. That way, you can easily return to it from any other views you create.

   QUICK TIP
   To delete views from the active worksheet, select the view in the Custom Views dialog box, then click Delete.

2. **Click Add**

   The Add View dialog box opens, as shown in **FIGURE 6-8**. Here, you enter a name for the view and decide whether to include print settings and/or hidden rows, columns, and filter settings. You want to include these options, which are already selected.

3. **In the Name box, type Year Sales, then click OK**

   You have created a view called Year Sales that shows all the worksheet columns. You want to set up another view that will hide the April through December columns.

4. **Select columns E through M, right-click the selected area, then click Hide on the shortcut menu**

   You are ready to create a custom view of the January through March sales data.

5. **Click cell A1, click the Custom Views button in the Workbook Views group, click Add, in the Name box type First Quarter, then click OK**

   You are ready to test the two custom views.

   TROUBLE
   If you receive the message "Some view settings could not be applied", turn off worksheet protection by clicking the Unprotect Sheet button in the Changes group of the Review tab.

6. **Click the Custom Views button in the Workbook Views group, click Year Sales in the Views list, then click Show**

   The Year Sales custom view displays all of the months' sales data.

7. **Click the Custom Views button in the Workbook Views group, then with First Quarter in the Custom Views dialog box selected, click Show**

   Only the January through March sales figures appear on the screen, as shown in **FIGURE 6-9**.

8. **Return to the Year Sales view, then save your work**

Managing Workbook Data

FIGURE 6-8: Add View dialog box

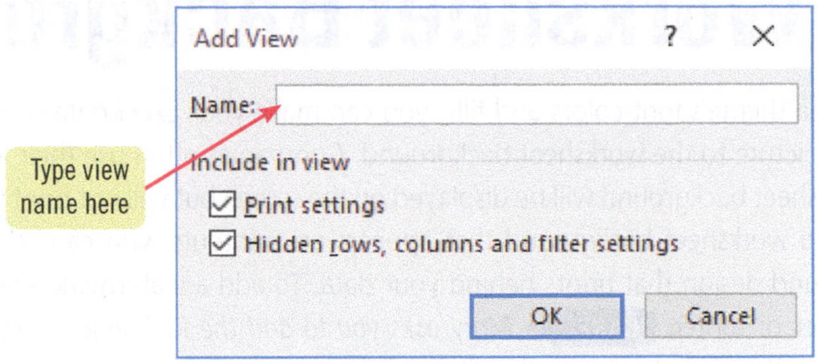

Add View

Name: [   ]

[Type view name here →]

Include in view
☑ Print settings
☑ Hidden rows, columns and filter settings

[OK] [Cancel]

FIGURE 6-9: First Quarter view

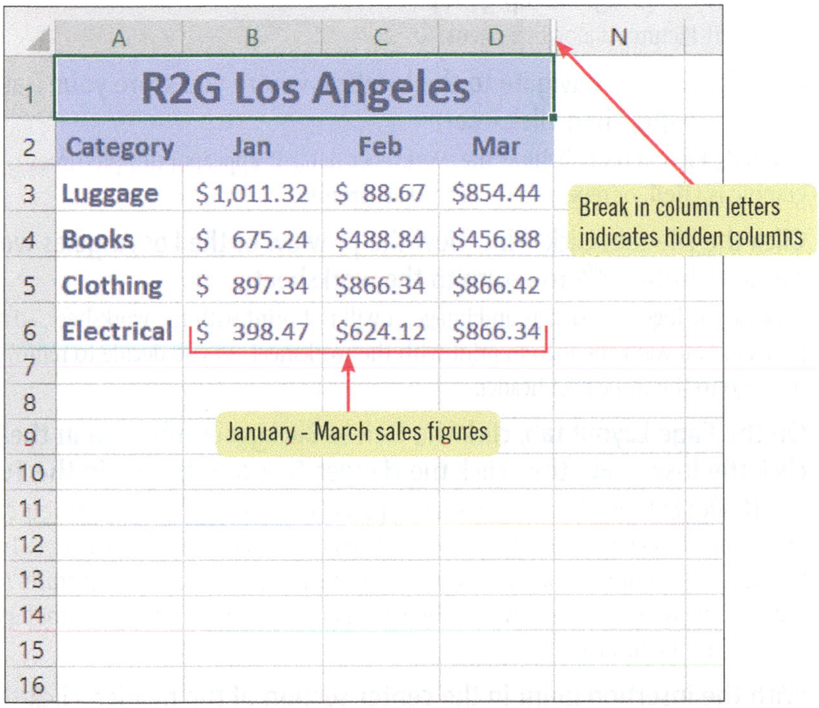

	A	B	C	D	N
1	**R2G Los Angeles**				
2	Category	Jan	Feb	Mar	
3	Luggage	$1,011.32	$ 88.67	$854.44	
4	Books	$ 675.24	$488.84	$456.88	
5	Clothing	$ 897.34	$866.34	$866.42	
6	Electrical	$ 398.47	$624.12	$866.34	
7					
8					
9					
10					
11					
12					
13					
14					
15					
16					

[Break in column letters indicates hidden columns]

[January - March sales figures]

Excel 2016

Using Page Break Preview

The vertical and horizontal dashed lines in the Normal view of worksheets represent page breaks. Excel automatically inserts a page break when your worksheet data doesn't fit on one page. These page breaks are **dynamic**, which means they adjust automatically when you insert or delete rows and columns and when you change column widths or row heights. Everything to the left of the first vertical dashed line and above the first horizontal dashed line is printed on the first page. You can manually add or remove page breaks by clicking the Page Layout tab, clicking the Breaks button in the Page Setup group, then clicking the appropriate command. You can also view and change page breaks manually by clicking the View tab, then clicking the Page Break Preview button in the Workbook Views group, or by clicking the Page Break Preview button 🔲 on the status bar. You can drag the blue page break lines to the desired location. Some cells may temporarily display ##### while you are in Page Break Preview. If you drag a page break to the right to include more data on a page, Excel shrinks the type to fit the data on that page. To exit Page Break Preview, click the Normal button in the Workbook Views group.

Add a Worksheet Background

Learning Outcomes
- Add a background to a worksheet
- Add a watermark to a worksheet

In addition to using a theme's font colors and fills, you can make your Excel data more attractive on the screen by adding a picture to the worksheet background. Companies often use their logo as a worksheet background. A worksheet background will be displayed on the screen but will not print with the worksheet. If you want to add a worksheet background that appears on printouts, you can add a **watermark**, a translucent background design that prints behind your data. To add a watermark, you add the image to the worksheet header or footer. **CASE** ▶ *Mary asks you to add the R2G logo to the background of the Los Angeles worksheet. You want to explore the difference between adding it as a worksheet background and adding it as a watermark.*

STEPS

1. **With the Los Angeles sheet active, click the Page Layout tab, then click the Background button in the Page Setup group**

   The Insert Pictures dialog box opens.

2. **Click From a file, navigate to the location where you store your Data Files, click EX 6-Logo.jpg, then click Insert**

   The R2G logo appears behind the worksheet data. It appears multiple times on your screen because the graphic is **tiled**, or repeated, to fill the background.

3. **Click the File tab, click Print, view the preview of the Los Angeles worksheet, then click the Back button ⊙ to return to the worksheet**

   Because the logo is a background image, it will not print with the worksheet, so it is not visible in the Print preview. You want the logo to print with the worksheet, so you decide to remove the background and add the logo to the worksheet header.

4. **On the Page Layout tab, click the Delete Background button in the Page Setup group, click the Insert tab, then click the Header & Footer button in the Text group**

   The Header & Footer Tools Design tab appears, as shown in **FIGURE 6-10**. You can use the buttons in this group to add preformatted headers and footers to a worksheet. The Header & Footer Elements buttons let you add page numbers, the date, the time, the file location, names, and pictures to the header or footer. The Navigation group buttons move the insertion point from the header to the footer and back. You want to add a picture to the header.

5. **With the insertion point in the center section of the header, click the Picture button in the Header & Footer Elements group, click Browse, navigate to where you store your Data Files, click EX 6-Logo.jpg, then click Insert**

   A code representing a picture, "&[Picture]", appears in the center of the header.

6. **Click cell A1, click the Page Layout tab, click the Width list arrow in the Scale to Fit group, click 1 page, click the Height list arrow in the Scale to Fit group, click 1 page, then preview the worksheet**

   Your worksheet should look like **FIGURE 6-11**, with all the data fitting on one page.

7. **Return to the worksheet, switch to Normal view, click the Home tab, then save the workbook**

FIGURE 6-10: Header & Footer Tools Design tab

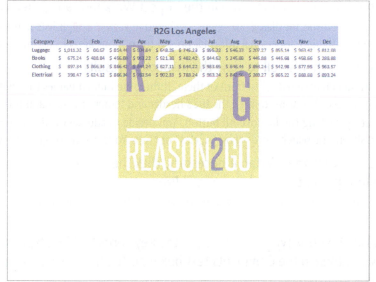

FIGURE 6-11: Preview of Los Angeles worksheet with logo in the background

Working with screenshots in Excel

You can paste an image of an open file, called a **screenshot**, into an Excel workbook or another Office document. The pasted screenshot is an image that you can move, copy, or edit. To do so, click the Insert tab, click the Take a Screenshot button in the Illustrations group to see a gallery of other available open windows, then click one of the windows in the gallery. This pastes a screenshot of the window you clicked into the current Excel document. You can also click the Screen Clipping button in the gallery to select and paste an area from an open window. Once you have created a screenshot and positioned it in your worksheet, you can modify it using tools on the Picture Tools Format tab. You can change the overall visual style of the image by clicking the More button in the Picture Styles group, then clicking a style. In the Picture Styles group you can also use the Picture Effects button to apply a visual effect to the image, the Picture Border button to enhance the border surrounding the image, and the Picture Layout button to convert the image to a SmartArt Graphic. The Picture Tools tab also has other tools to correct images. For example, you can sharpen and soften an image and make corrections for brightness and contrast by clicking the Corrections button in the Adjust group. Clicking a choice in the Sharpen/Soften section allows you to change the visual acuity of the image and choosing an option in the Brightness/Contrast section adjusts the lightness of an image.

Prepare a Workbook for Distribution

Learning Outcomes
- Add keywords to a worksheet using the Document Panel
- Review a file for problems using the Inspect Document feature
- Protect a workbook by using Mark as Final status

If you are collaborating with others and want to share a workbook with them, you might want to remove sensitive information before distributing the file. On the other hand, you might want to add helpful information, called **properties**, to a file to help others identify, understand, and locate it. Properties might include keywords, the author's name, a title, the status, and comments. **Keywords** are terms users can search for that will help them locate your workbook. Properties are a form of **metadata**, information that describes data and is used in Microsoft Windows document searches. In addition, to ensure that others do not make unauthorized changes to your workbook, you can mark a file as final. This makes it a read-only file, which others can open but not change. **CASE** *Mary wants you to protect the workbook and prepare it for distribution.*

STEPS

1. **Click the File tab**

   Backstage view opens, and displays the Info place. It shows you information about your file. It also includes tools you can use to check for security issues.

2. **Click the Check for Issues button in the Inspect Workbook area, then click Inspect Document**

   The Document Inspector dialog box opens, as shown in **FIGURE 6-12**. It lists items from which you can have Excel evaluate hidden or personal information. All the options are selected by default.

3. **Click Inspect, then scroll to view the inspection results**

   Areas with data have a red "**!**" in front of them. If there are hidden names they will be flagged. Headers and footers is flagged. You want to keep the file's header and footer. If personal information is flagged, you can remove it by clicking the Remove All button. You decide to add keywords to help the sales managers find the worksheet. The search words "Los Angeles" or "New York" would be good keywords for this workbook.

4. **Click Close, click the File tab if necessary, click the Properties list arrow on the right side of the Info place, then click Advanced Properties**

   The file's properties dialog box opens, as shown in **FIGURE 6-13**. You decide to add a title, keywords, and comments.

5. **In the Title text box type Store Sales, in the Keywords text box type Los Angeles New York store sales, then in the Comments text box type The first-quarter figures are final., then click OK**

   You are ready to mark the workbook as final.

6. **Click the Protect Workbook button in the Info place, click Mark as Final, click OK, then click OK again**

   "[Read-Only]" appears in the title bar indicating the workbook is saved as a read-only file. A yellow bar also appears below the tabs indicating the workbook is marked as final. The yellow bar also has an Edit Anyway button.

7. **Click the Home tab, click cell B3, type 1 to confirm that the cell cannot be changed, click the Edit Anyway button above the formula bar, then save the workbook**

   Marking a workbook as final is not a strong form of workbook protection because a workbook recipient can remove this Final status. By clicking Edit Anyway, you remove the read-only status, which makes the workbook editable again.

FIGURE 6-12: Document Inspector Properties dialog box

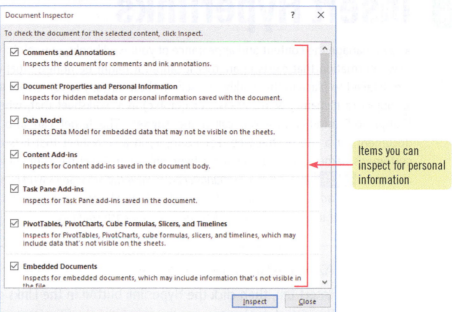

Items you can inspect for personal information

FIGURE 6-13: Document Properties panel

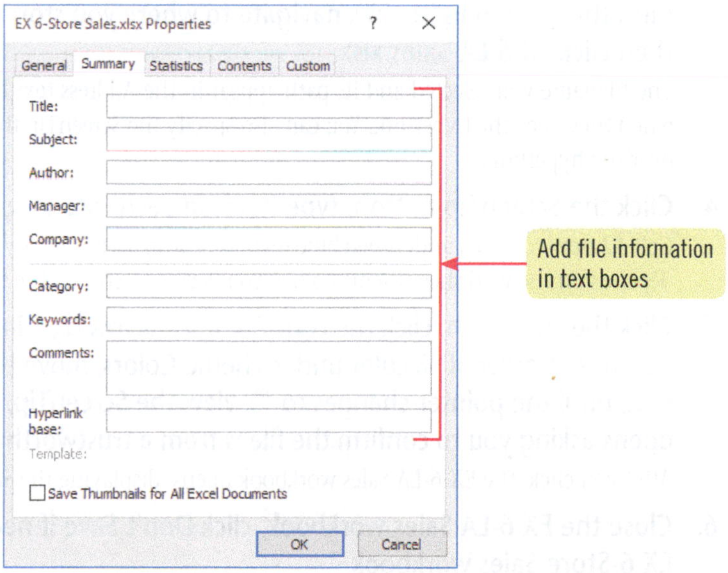

Add file information in text boxes

Sharing a workbook using OneDrive

Once you set up a Windows Live account you can save your Excel files to the cloud using OneDrive. This allows you to access your Excel files from any computer and share Excel files with others. When saving an Excel file to the cloud, click the File tab, click Save As, then click OneDrive, which is the default location. After you save an Excel file to your OneDrive, you can share it by clicking the File tab, clicking Share, clicking Share with People, entering the email addresses of the people you wish to invite to share the file in the Invite people text box, and then clicking Share. An email with a link to the Excel file on your OneDrive will be sent to the addresses you entered. The recipients can view or edit the file using the Excel web app.

Insert Hyperlinks

Learning Outcomes
- Link to workbooks and websites by adding hyperlinks
- Add screentips to a hyperlink

As you manage the content and appearance of your workbooks, you might want the workbook user to view information that exists in another location. It might be nonessential information or data that is too detailed to place in the workbook itself. In these cases, you can create a hyperlink. A **hyperlink** is an object (a filename, word, phrase, or graphic) in a worksheet that, when you click it, displays, or "jumps to," another location, called the **target**. The target can also be a worksheet, another document, or a site on the web. For example, in a worksheet that lists customer invoices, at each customer's name, you might create a hyperlink to an Excel file containing payment terms for each customer. **CASE** *Mary wants managers who view the Store Sales workbook to be able to view the item totals for each sales category in the Los Angeles sheet. She asks you to create a hyperlink at the Category heading so that users can click it to view the items for each category.*

STEPS

1. **Click cell A2 on the Los Angeles worksheet**

2. **Click the Insert tab, then click the Hyperlink button in the Links group**

   The Insert Hyperlink dialog box opens, as shown in **FIGURE 6-14**. The icons under "Link to" on the left side of the dialog box let you select the type of location to where you want the link to jump: an existing file or webpage, a place in the same document, a new document, or an e-mail address. Because you want the link to display an already existing document, the selected first icon, Existing File or webpage, is correct, so you won't have to change it.

3. **Click the Look in list arrow, navigate to where you store your Data Files if necessary, then click EX 6-LA Sales.xlsx**

   The filename you selected and its path appear in the Address text box. This is the document users will see when they click the hyperlink. You can also specify the ScreenTip that users see when they hold the pointer over the hyperlink.

QUICK TIP

To remove a hyperlink or change its target, right-click it, then click Remove Hyperlink or Edit Hyperlink.

4. **Click the ScreenTip button, type Items in each category, click OK, then click OK again**

   Cell A2 now contains underlined blue text, indicating that it is a hyperlink. The default color of a hyperlink depends on the worksheet theme colors. You decide to change the text color of the hyperlink.

5. **Click the Home tab, click the Font Color list arrow [A] in the Font group, click the Green, Accent 6, Darker 50% color under Theme Colors, move the pointer over the Category text, until the pointer changes to 🖑, view the ScreenTip, then click once; if a dialog box opens asking you to confirm the file is from a trustworthy source, click OK**

   After you click, the EX 6-LA Sales workbook opens, displaying the Sales sheet, as shown in **FIGURE 6-15**.

6. **Close the EX 6-LA Sales workbook, click Don't Save if necessary, then save the EX 6-Store Sales workbook**

Working with Headers and Footers

You may want to add a different header or footer to the first page of your worksheet. You can do this by clicking the Insert tab on the Ribbon, clicking the Header & Footer button in the Text group, then clicking the Different First Page check box in the Options group of the Header & Footer Tools Design tab to select it. You can also have different headers or footers on odd and even pages of your worksheet by clicking the Different Odd & Even Pages check box to select it. In the Options group of the Header & Footer Tools Design tab, you can also adjust the header and footer size relative to the rest of the document by using the Scale with Document check box. You can use the Align with Page Margins check box to place the header or footer at the margins of the worksheet. You can also add the name of the worksheet by clicking the Sheet Name button in the Header and Footer Elements group of the Header & Footer Tools Design tab.

FIGURE 6-14: Insert Hyperlink dialog box

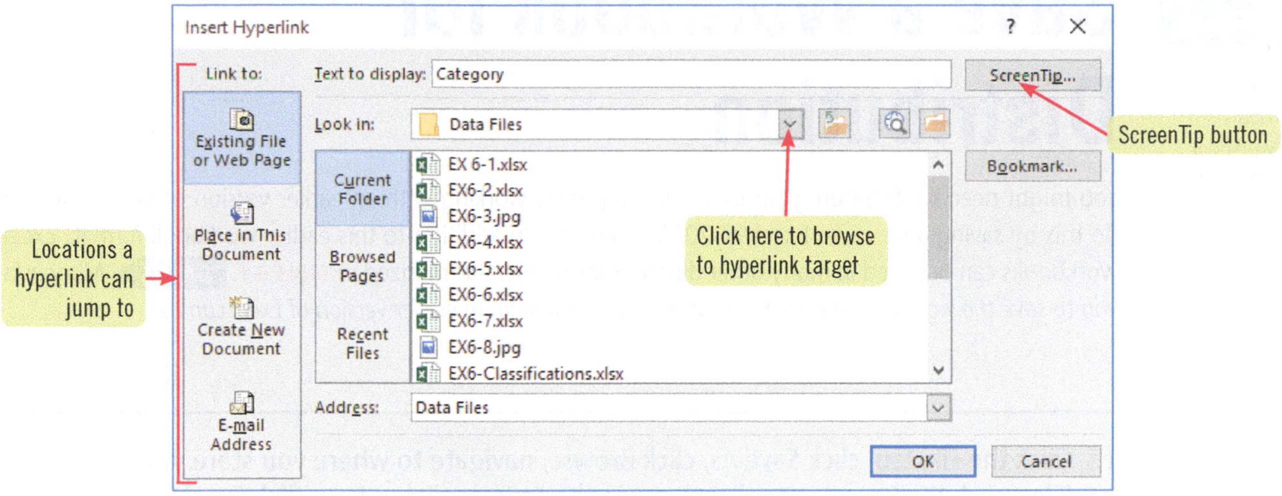

Locations a hyperlink can jump to

Click here to browse to hyperlink target

ScreenTip button

FIGURE 6-15: Target document

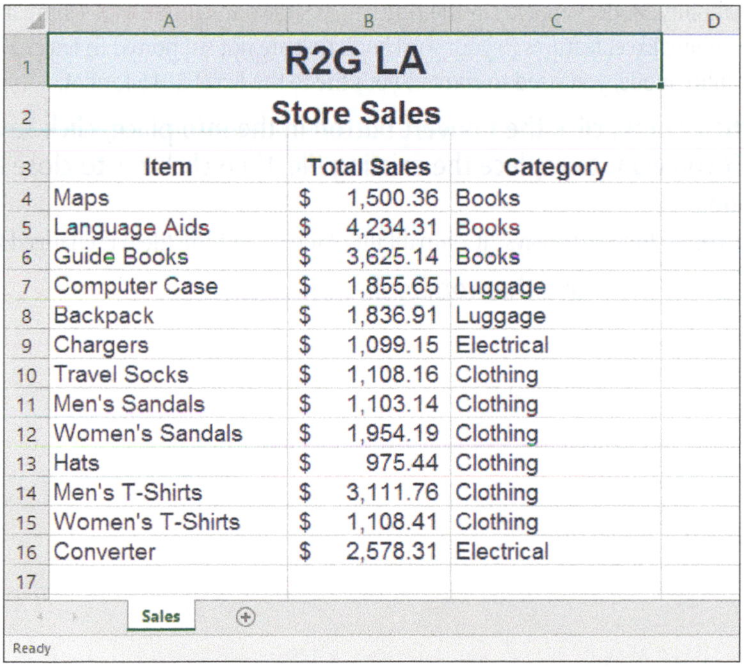

	A	B	C	D
1	**R2G LA**			
2	**Store Sales**			
3	**Item**	**Total Sales**	**Category**	
4	Maps	$ 1,500.36	Books	
5	Language Aids	$ 4,234.31	Books	
6	Guide Books	$ 3,625.14	Books	
7	Computer Case	$ 1,855.65	Luggage	
8	Backpack	$ 1,836.91	Luggage	
9	Chargers	$ 1,099.15	Electrical	
10	Travel Socks	$ 1,108.16	Clothing	
11	Men's Sandals	$ 1,103.14	Clothing	
12	Women's Sandals	$ 1,954.19	Clothing	
13	Hats	$ 975.44	Clothing	
14	Men's T-Shirts	$ 3,111.76	Clothing	
15	Women's T-Shirts	$ 1,108.41	Clothing	
16	Converter	$ 2,578.31	Electrical	
17				

Sales

Ready

Using research tools

You can access resources online and locally on your computer using the Insights task pane. The research results are based on selected data on your Excel worksheet. To open the Insights task pane, click the Review tab, then click the Smart Lookup button in the Insights group. The Insights pane shows results for your selected data in the Explore and Define areas. The Explore area displays Wikipedia information, images, maps, and web searches. The Define pane displays definitions and pronunciation help.

Save a Workbook for Distribution

Learning Outcomes
- Save a workbook in earlier formats of Excel
- Convert an Excel 97-2003 workbook to the 2016 format

You might need to distribute your Excel files to people working with an earlier version of Excel. You can do this by saving a file as an Excel 97-2003 workbook. In addition to this earlier workbook format, Excel workbooks can be saved in many other different formats as summarized in **TABLE 6-1**. **CASE** *Mary asks you to save the workbook in a format that managers running an earlier version of Excel can use.*

STEPS

QUICK TIP
You can also export an Excel file into another format by clicking the File tab, clicking Export, clicking Change File Type, then clicking a file type.

1. **Click the File tab, click Save As, click Browse, navigate to where you store your Data Files, click the Save as type list arrow in the Save As dialog box, click Excel 97-2003 Workbook (*.xls), then click Save**

   The Compatibility Checker dialog box opens as shown in **FIGURE 6-16**. It alerts you to the features that will be lost or converted by saving in the earlier format. Some Excel 2016 features are not available in earlier versions of Excel.

2. **Click Continue, close the workbook, then reopen the EX 6-Store Sales.xls workbook**

   "[Compatibility Mode]" appears in the title bar, as shown in **FIGURE 6-17**. Compatibility mode prevents you from including Excel features in your workbook that are not supported in Excel 97-2003 workbooks. To exit compatibility mode, you need to convert your file to the Excel 2016 format.

3. **Click the File tab, click the Convert button in the Info place, click Save, click Yes if you are asked if you want to replace the existing file, then click Yes to close and reopen the workbook**

   The title bar no longer displays "[Compatibility Mode]" and the file has changed to .xlsx format.

4. **Click cell A1, then save the workbook**

Saving a workbook in other formats

Excel data can be shared by **publishing**, the data on a network or on the web so that others can access it using a web browser. To publish an Excel document to an **intranet** (a company's internal website) or the web, you can save it in an HTML format. **HTML (Hypertext Markup Language)** is the coding format used for all web documents. You can also save your Excel file as a **single-file web page** that integrates all of the worksheets and graphical elements from the workbook into a single file. This file format is called MHTML, also known as MHT.

If you want to ensure that your workbook is displayed the same way on different computer platforms and screen settings, you can publish it in PDF format by clicking File, clicking Export, then clicking the Create PDF/XPS button. You can also save a workbook as a pdf file using the Save As dialog box and selecting PDF (*.pdf) in the Save as type list.

FIGURE 6-16: Compatibility Checker dialog box

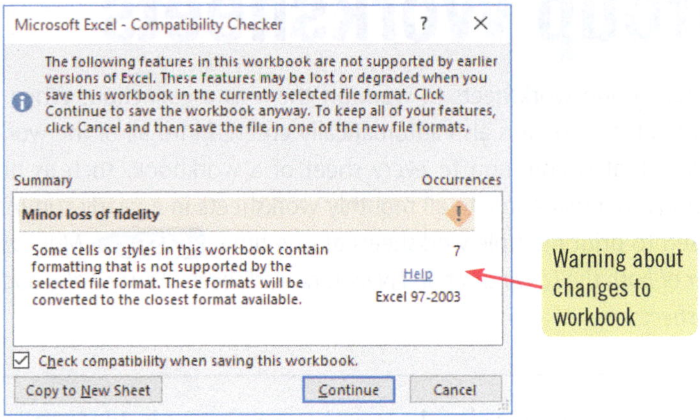

Warning about changes to workbook

FIGURE 6-17: Workbook in compatibility mode

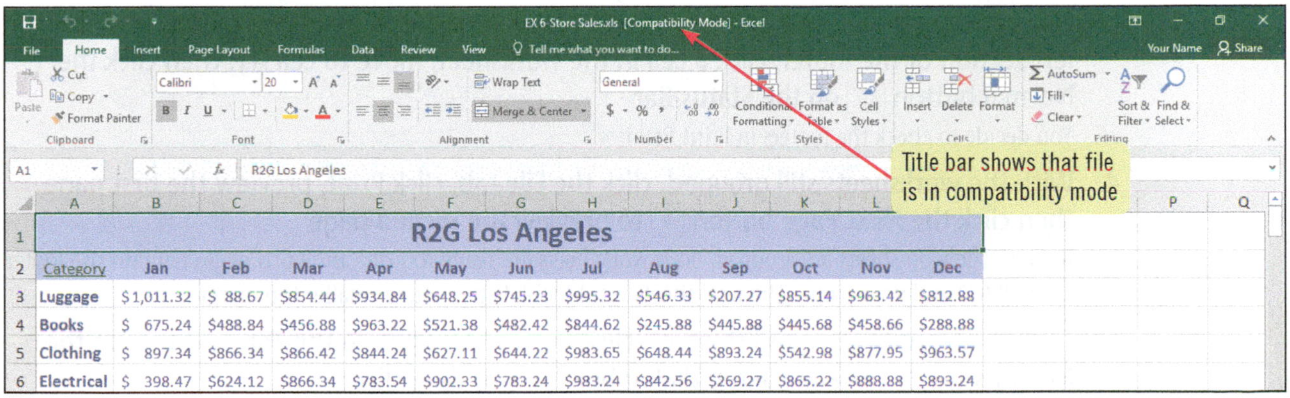

Title bar shows that file is in compatibility mode

TABLE 6-1: Workbook formats

type of file	file extension(s)	used for
Macro-enabled workbook	.xlsm	Files that contain macros
Excel 97 – 2003 workbook	.xls	Working with people using older versions of Excel
Single file webpage	.mht, .mhtml	Websites with multiple pages and graphics
webpage	.htm, .html	Simple single-page websites
Excel template	.xltx	Excel files that will be reused with small changes
Excel macro-enabled template	.xltm	Excel files that will be used again and contain macros
PDF (Portable document format)	.pdf	Files with formatting that needs to be preserved
XML paper specification	.xps	Files with formatting that needs to be preserved and files that need to be shared
OpenDocument spreadsheet	.ods	Files created with OpenOffice

Group Worksheets

You can group worksheets to work on them as a collection. When you enter data into one grouped worksheet, that data is also automatically entered into all of the worksheets in the group. This is useful for data that is common to every sheet of a workbook, such as headers and footers, or for column headings that will apply to all monthly worksheets in a yearly summary. Grouping worksheets can also be used to print multiple worksheets at one time. **CASE** *Mary asks you to add the text "R2G" to the footer of both the Los Angeles and New York worksheets. You will also add half-inch margins to the top of both worksheets.*

STEPS

1. **With the Los Angeles sheet active, press and hold [Shift], click the New York sheet, then release [Shift]**
   Both sheet tabs are selected, and the title bar now contains "[Group]", indicating that the worksheets are grouped together. Now any changes you make to the Los Angeles sheet will also be made to the New York sheet.

2. **Click the Insert tab, then click the Header & Footer button in the Text group**

3. **On the Header and Footer Tools Design tab, click the Go to Footer button in the Navigation group, type R2G in the center section of the footer, type your name in the left section of the footer, click a cell in the worksheet, move to cell A1, then click the Normal button on the Status Bar**
   You decide to check the footers in Print Preview.

4. **With the worksheets still grouped, click the File tab, click Print, preview the first page, then click the Next Page button to preview the second page**
   Because the worksheets are grouped, both worksheets are ready to print and both pages contain the footer with "R2G" and your name. The worksheets would look better with a smaller top margin.

5. **Click the Normal Margins list arrow, click Custom Margins, in the Top text box on the Margins tab of the Page Setup dialog box type .5, then click OK**
   You decide to ungroup the worksheets.

6. **Return to the worksheet, right-click the Los Angeles worksheet sheet tab, then click Ungroup Sheets**

7. **Save and close the workbook, exit Excel, then submit the workbook to your instructor**
   The completed worksheets are shown in FIGURES 6-18 and 6-19.

FIGURE 6-18: Los Angeles worksheet

R2G Los Angeles

Category	Jan	Feb	Mar	Apr	May	Jun	Jul	Aug	Sep	Oct	Nov	Dec
Luggage	$ 1,011.32	$ 88.67	$ 854.44	$ 934.84	$ 648.25	$ 745.23	$ 995.32	$ 546.33	$ 207.27	$ 855.14	$ 963.42	$ 812.88
Books	$ 675.24	$ 488.84	$ 456.88	$ 963.22	$ 521.38	$ 482.42	$ 844.62	$ 245.88	$ 445.88	$ 445.68	$ 458.66	$ 288.88
Clothing	$ 897.34	$ 866.34	$ 866.42	$ 844.24	$ 627.11	$ 644.22	$ 983.65	$ 648.44	$ 893.24	$ 542.98	$ 877.95	$ 963.57
Electrical	$ 398.47	$ 624.12	$ 866.34	$ 783.54	$ 902.33	$ 783.24	$ 983.24	$ 842.56	$ 269.27	$ 865.22	$ 888.88	$ 893.24

Your Name   R2G

FIGURE 6-19: New York worksheet

R2G New York

Category	Jan	Feb	Mar	Apr	May	Jun	Jul	Aug	Sep	Oct	Nov	Dec
Luggage	$ 912.68	$ 869.54	$ 844.32	$ 951.55	$ 877.34	$ 865.32	$ 951.53	$ 782.54	$ 445.32	$ 951.55	$ 963.54	$ 511.37
Books	$ 782.51	$ 863.54	$ 458.35	$ 874.21	$ 125.68	$ 799.39	$ 117.36	$ 185.67	$ 136.24	$ 536.54	$ 959.77	$ 999.99
Clothing	$ 899.30	$ 951.35	$ 752.21	$ 453.21	$ 933.35	$ 231.55	$ 745.21	$ 526.68	$ 158.69	$ 752.36	$ 422.31	$ 231.58
Electrical	$ 793.21	$ 532.54	$ 785.34	$ 423.36	$ 744.35	$ 401.23	$ 455.62	$ 953.57	$ 855.47	$ 975.11	$ 999.99	$ 963.24

Your Name   R2G

Practice

Concepts Review

1. Which element do you click to organize open worksheet windows in a specific configuration?
2. Which element points to a ScreenTip for a hyperlink?
3. Which element points to a hyperlink?
4. Which element do you click to name and save a set of display and/or print settings?
5. Which element do you click to open another instance of the active worksheet in a separate window?
6. Which element do you click to view and change the way worksheet data is distributed on printed pages?
7. Which element do you click to move between instances of a workbook?

FIGURE 6-20

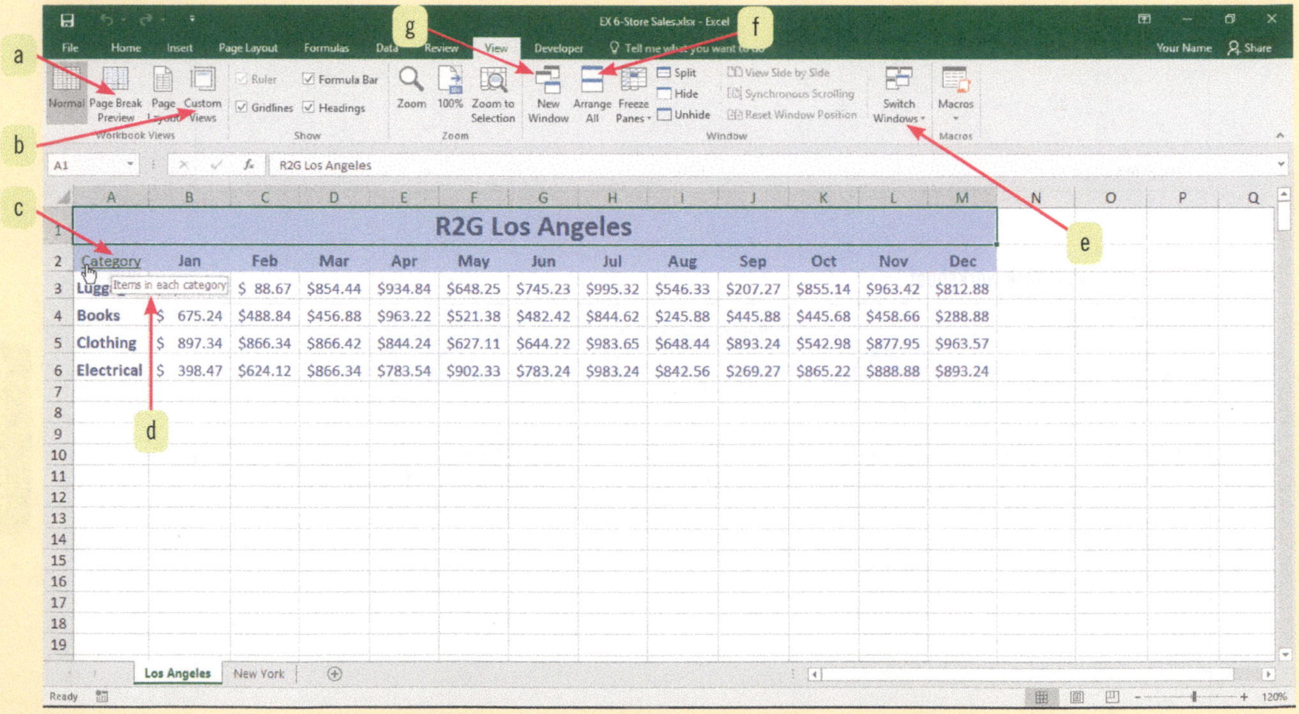

Match each term with the statement that best describes it.

8. Data entry area	a.	Webpage format
9. Watermark	b.	Portion of a worksheet that can be changed
10. Hyperlink	c.	Translucent background design on a printed worksheet
11. Dynamic page breaks	d.	An object that when clicked displays another worksheet or a webpage
12. HTML	e.	Adjust automatically when rows and columns are inserted or deleted

Select the best answer from the list of choices.

13. You can group contiguous worksheets by clicking the first sheet, and then pressing and holding _____ while clicking the last sheet tab that you want to group.
    - **a.** [Alt]
    - **b.** [Spacebar]
    - **c.** [Shift]
    - **d.** [F6]

14. A _____ is a set of display and/or print settings that you can save and access later.
    - **a.** View
    - **b.** Property
    - **c.** Data area
    - **d.** Keyword

15. Which of the following formats means that users can view but not change data in a workbook?
    - **a.** Macro
    - **b.** Read-only
    - **c.** Webpage
    - **d.** Template

Skills Review

1. **View and arrange worksheets.**
   a. Start Excel, open EX 6-2.xlsx from the location where you store your Data Files, then save it as **EX 6-Tea**.
   b. Open another instance of the workbook in a new window.
   c. Activate the East sheet in the EX 6-Tea.xlsx:1 workbook. Activate the West sheet in the EX 6-Tea.xlsx:2 workbook.
   d. View the EX 6-Tea.xlsx:1 and EX 6-Tea.xlsx:2 workbooks tiled horizontally. View the workbooks in a vertical arrangement.
   e. Hide the EX 6-Tea.xlsx:2 instance, then unhide the instance. Close the EX 6-Tea.xlsx:2 instance, and maximize the EX 6-Tea.xlsx workbook.

2. **Protect worksheets and workbooks.**
   a. On the East sheet, unlock the expense data in the range B12:F19.
   b. Protect the sheet without using a password.
   c. To make sure the other cells are locked, attempt to make an entry in cell D4 and verify that you receive an error message.
   d. Change the first-quarter mortgage expense in cell B12 to 6000.
   e. Protect the workbook's structure without applying a password. Right-click the East and West sheet tabs to verify that you cannot insert, delete, rename, move, copy, hide, or unhide the sheets, or change their tab color.
   f. Unprotect the workbook. Unprotect the East worksheet.
   g. Save the workbook.

3. **Save custom views of a worksheet.**
   a. Using the East sheet, create a custom view of the entire worksheet called **Entire East Budget**.
   b. Hide rows 10 through 23, then create a new view called **Income** showing only the income data.
   c. Use the Custom Views dialog box to display all of the data on the East worksheet.
   d. Use the Custom Views dialog box to display only the income data on the East worksheet.
   e. Use the Custom Views dialog box to return to the Entire East Budget view.
   f. Save the workbook.

4. **Add a worksheet background.**
   a. Use EX 6-3.jpg as a worksheet background for the East sheet, then delete it.
   b. Add EX 6-3.jpg to the East header, then preview the sheet to verify that the background will print.
   c. Add your name to the center section of the East worksheet footer, then save the workbook.

Skills Review (continued)

5. Prepare a workbook for distribution.

    a. Inspect the workbook and remove any properties, personal data, and header and footer information.

    b. Use the file's Properties dialog box to add a title of **Quarterly Budget**, the keyword **campus**, and the category **tea**.

    c. Mark the workbook as final and verify that "[Read-Only]" appears in the title bar.

    d. Remove the final status, then save the workbook.

6. Insert hyperlinks.

    a. On the East worksheet, make cell A11 a hyperlink to the file **EX 6-Expenses.xlsx** in your Data Files folder.

    b. Test the link and verify that Sheet1 of the target file displays expense details.

    c. Return to the EX 6-Tea.xlsx workbook, edit the hyperlink in cell A11 to add a ScreenTip that reads **Expense Details**, then verify that the ScreenTip appears.

    d. On the West worksheet, enter the text **East Campus Budget** in cell A25.

    e. Make the text in cell A25 a hyperlink to cell A1 in the East worksheet. (*Hint*: Use the Place in This Document button and note the cell reference in the Type the cell reference text box.)

    f. Test the hyperlink. Remove the hyperlink in cell A25 of the West worksheet, remove the text in the cell, then save the workbook.

7. Save a workbook for distribution.

    a. Save the EX 6-Tea.xlsx workbook as an Excel 97-2003 workbook, and review the results of the Compatibility Checker.

    b. Close the EX 6-Tea.xls file, then reopen EX 6-Tea.xls in Compatibility Mode.

    c. Convert the .xls file to .xlsx format, resaving the file with the same name and replacing the previously saved file. This requires the workbook to be closed and reopened.

    d. Save the workbook.

8. Grouping worksheets.

    a. Group the East and West worksheet.

    b. Add your name to the center footer section of the worksheets. Add 1.25" custom margins to the top of both worksheets.

    c. Preview both sheets, verify the tea cup will not print (it was removed when the file was inspected), then ungroup the sheets.

    d. Save the workbook, comparing your worksheets to **FIGURE 6-21**.

    e. Submit EX 6-Tea.xlsx and EX 6-Expenses (the linked file) to your instructor, close all open files, then exit Excel.

FIGURE 6-21

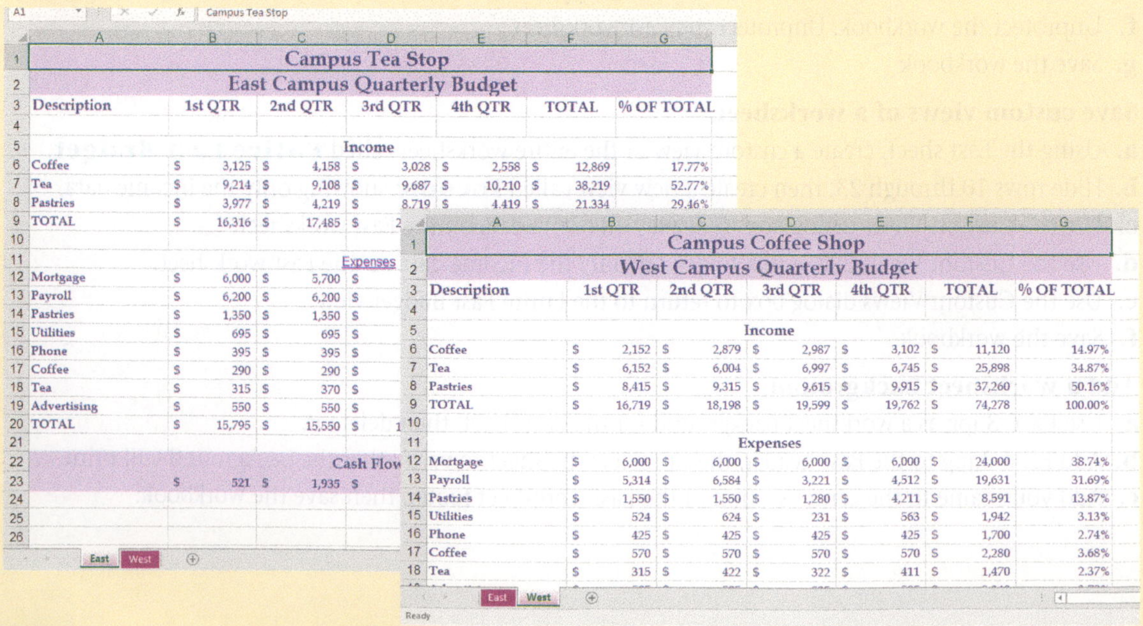

Independent Challenge 1

You manage American Pools, a pool supplier for the Florida home market. You are organizing your first-quarter sales in an Excel worksheet. Because the sheet for the month of January includes the same type of information you need for February and March, you decide to enter the headings for all of the first-quarter months at the same time. You use a separate worksheet for each month and create data for 3 months.

a. Start Excel, then save a new workbook as **EX 6-Pools.xlsx** in the location where you store your Data Files.

b. Name the first sheet **January**, name the second sheet **February**, and name the third sheet **March**.

c. Group the worksheets.

d. With the worksheets grouped, add the title **American Pools** centered across cells A1 and B1. Enter the labels **Type** in cell A2 and **Sales** in cell B2. Enter pool type labels in column A beginning in cell A3 and ending in cell A9. Use the following pool types in the range A3:A9: **Prefab**, **Masonry**, **Concrete**, **Vinyl**, **Gunite**, **Fiberglass**, and **Package**. Add the label **Total** in cell A10. Enter the formula to sum the Sales column in cell B10.

e. Ungroup the worksheets, and enter your own sales data for each of the sales categories in the range B3:B9 in the January, February, and March sheets.

f. Display each worksheet in its own window, then arrange the three sheets vertically.

g. Hide the window displaying the March sheet. Unhide the March sheet window.

h. Split the March window into two panes: the upper pane displaying rows 1 through 5, and the lower pane displaying rows 6 through 10. Scroll through the data in each pane, then remove the split. (*Hint*: Select row 6, click the View tab, then click Split in the Window group. Clicking Split again will remove the split.)

i. Close the windows displaying EX 6-Pools.xlsx:2 and EX 6-Pools.xlsx:3, then maximize the EX 6-Pools.xlsx workbook.

j. Add the keywords **pools custom** to your workbook, using the tags textbox in the Info place.

k. Group the worksheets again.

l. Add headers to all three worksheets that include your name in the left section and the sheet name in the center section. (*Hint*: You can add the sheet name to a header by clicking the Sheet Name button in the Header and Footer Elements group of the Header & Footer Tools Design tab.)

m. With the worksheets still grouped, format the worksheets using the fill and color buttons on the Home tab appropriately.

n. Ungroup the worksheets, then mark the workbook status as final. Close the workbook, reopen the workbook, and enable editing.

o. Save the workbook, submit the workbook to your instructor, then exit Excel.

Independent Challenge 2

As the payroll manager at National Solutions, a communications firm, you decide to organize the weekly timecard data using Excel worksheets. You use a separate worksheet for each week and track the hours for employees with different job classifications. A hyperlink in the worksheet provides pay rates for each classification, and custom views limit the information that is displayed.

a. Start Excel, open EX 6-4.xlsx from the location where you store your Data Files, then save it as **EX 6-Timecards**.

b. Compare the data in the workbook by arranging the Week 1, Week 2, and Week 3 sheets horizontally.

c. Maximize the Week 1 window. Unlock the hours data in the Week 1 sheet and protect the worksheet. Verify that the employee names, numbers, and classifications cannot be changed. Verify that the total hours data can be changed, but do not change the data.

d. Unprotect the Week 1 sheet, and create a custom view called **Complete Worksheet** that displays all the data.

Independent Challenge 2 (continued)

e. Hide column E and create a custom view of the data in the range A1:D22. Name the view **Employee Classifications**. Display each view, then return to the Complete Worksheet view.

f. Add a page break between columns D and E so that the Total Hours data prints on a second page. Preview the worksheet, then remove the page break. (*Hint*: Use the Breaks button on the Page Layout tab.)

g. Add a hyperlink to the Classification heading in cell D1 that links to the file EX 6-Classifications.xlsx. Add a ScreenTip that reads Pay Rates, then test the hyperlink. Compare your screen to FIGURE 6-22.

FIGURE 6-22

	A	B
1	National Solutions	
2	Classifications	Pay Rate
3	Project Manager	$70
4	Senior Project Manager	$85
5	Account Representative	$65
6	Senior Account Representative	$85
7		

h. Save the EX 6-Classifications workbook as an Excel 97-2003 workbook, reviewing the Compatibility Checker information. Close the EX 6-Classifications.xls file.

i. Group the three worksheets in the EX 6-Timecards.xlsx workbook, and add your name to the center footer section.

j. Save the workbook, then preview the grouped worksheets.

k. Ungroup the worksheets, and add 2-inch top and left margins to the Week 1 worksheet.

l. Hide the Week 2 and Week 3 worksheets, inspect the file and remove all document properties, personal information, and hidden worksheets. Do not remove header and footer information.

m. Add the keyword **hours** to the workbook, save the workbook, then mark it as final.

n. Close the workbook, submit the workbook to your instructor, then exit Excel.

Independent Challenge 3

One of your responsibilities as the office manager at South High School is to track supplies for the office. You decide to create a spreadsheet to track these orders, placing each month's orders on its own sheet. You create custom views that will focus on the categories of supplies. A hyperlink will provide a supplier's contact information.

a. Start Excel, open EX 6-5.xlsx from the location where you store your Data Files, then save it as **EX 6-South High**.

b. Arrange the sheets for the 3 months horizontally to compare expenses, then close the extra workbook windows and maximize the remaining window.

c. Create a custom view of the entire January worksheet named **All Supplies**. Hide the paper, pens, and miscellaneous supply data, and create a custom view displaying only the equipment supplies. Call the view **Equipment**.

d. Display the All Supplies view, group the worksheets, and create a total for the total costs in cell D32 on each month's sheet. If necessary, use the Format Painter to copy the format from cell D31 to cell D32.

e. With the sheets grouped, add the sheet name to the center section of all the sheets' headers and your name to the center section of all the sheets' footers.

f. Ungroup the sheets and use the Compatibility Checker to view the features that are unsupported in earlier Excel formats. (*Hint*: Click the File tab, on the Info tab, click the Check for Issues button, then click Check Compatibility.)

g. Add a hyperlink in cell A5 of the January sheet that opens the file EX 6-Equipment.xlsx. Add a ScreenTip of **Equipment Supplier**. Test the link, viewing the ScreenTip, then return to the EX 6-South High.xlsx workbook without closing the EX 6-Equipment.xlsx workbook. Save the EX 6-South High.xlsx workbook.

h. Hide the EX 6-Equipment.xlsx workbook, then unhide it.

Independent Challenge 3 (continued)

i. Freeze worksheet rows one through three on the January Sheet of the EX 6-South High.xlsx workbook. (*Hint*: Select row 4, click the View tab, click the Freeze Panes button in the Window group, then click Freeze Panes.) Scroll down in the worksheet to verify the top three rows remain visible.

j. Unfreeze rows one through three. (*Hint*: Click the View tab, click Freeze panes, then click Unfreeze Panes.)

k. Close both the EX 6-Equipment.xlsx and the EX 6-South High.xlsx workbooks.

l. Submit the workbooks to your instructor, then exit Excel.

Independent Challenge 4: Explore

As the assistant to the owner of an appliance store, you review the nonpayroll expense sheets submitted by employees for each job. You decide to create a spreadsheet to track these contract expenses.

a. Start Excel, open EX 6-6.xlsx from the location where you store your Data Files, then save it as **EX 6-Invoice** in the location where you store your Data Files.

b. Freeze rows 1 through 5 in the worksheet. Scroll vertically to verify rows 1 through 5 are visible at the top of the worksheet.

c. Research the steps necessary to hide a formula in the Formula Bar of a worksheet. Add a worksheet to the workbook. Record these steps in cell A1 on the new sheet of the workbook, then hide the display of the formula for cell B34 on Sheet1. Check the Formula Bar to verify the formula is hidden. Compare your worksheet to **FIGURE 6-23**.

FIGURE 6-23

B34	▼	:	×	✓	f_x	
◢	A				B	
1	**Expenses**					
2						
3	Activity:			Dishwasher Install		
4	Contract ID:			DW158		
5	Employee Number:			1002		
28	**Miscellaneous**					
29	Miscellaneous item 1					
30	Miscellaneous item 2					
31	Miscellaneous item 3					
32						
33						
34	Total Expenses			$		908.00
35						
36						

d. Save your workbook to your OneDrive folder. If you don't have a Microsoft account, research the steps for creating an account.

e. Share your workbook with a classmate. Give your classmate permission to edit the workbook. Enter the message **Please review and make necessary changes**.

f. Unprotect Sheet1. (Your formula will be displayed.) Add a header that includes your name on the left side of the worksheet (this will unfreeze rows 1 through 5). Using the Page Layout tab, scale Sheet1 to fit vertically on one page. Save the workbook, then preview the worksheet.

g. Save the workbook as a pdf file.

h. Close the pdf file, then close the workbook.

i. Submit the workbook and pdf file to your instructor, then exit Excel.

Visual Workshop

Start Excel, open EX 6-7.xlsx from the location where you store your Data Files, then save it as **EX 6-Listings**. Make your worksheet look like the one shown in FIGURE 6-24. The text in cell A4 is a hyperlink to the EX 6-Information workbook. The worksheet background is the Data File EX 6-8.jpg. Enter your name in the footer, save the workbook, submit the workbook to your instructor, close the workbook, then exit Excel.

FIGURE 6-24

	A	B	C	D	E	F
1	Ocean Side Realty					
2	Home Listings					
3	Listing Number	Location	Type	Bed	Bath	Garage
4	100_ (Price Information)	Waterfront	Condominium	2	1	No
5	12__	_erfront	Condominium	3	2	No
6	1597	1 block from water	House	4	2	Yes
7	1784	1 mile from water	House	5	3	No
8	2102	Waterfront	Condominium	4	2	No
9	2214	Village	House	2	1	No
10	2268	Waterfront	House	3	1	Yes
11	2784	Village	Condominium	3	2	No
12	3148	1 block from water	House	4	2	Yes
13	3364	1 mile from water	Condominium	2	2	No
14	3754	Waterfront	House	4	2	No
15	3977	Village	House	2	1	No
16	4102	Village	Condominium	2	1	No
17	4158	1 block from water	House	2	2	Yes
18						

Channarong Inthasaro/Shutterstock.com

Managing Data Using Tables

CASE Reason2Go uses tables to analyze project data. The vice president of sales and marketing, Mary Watson, asks you to help her build and manage a table of information about 2017 conservation projects. You will help by planning and creating a table; adding, changing, finding, and deleting table information; sorting table data; and performing calculations with table data.

Module Objectives

After completing this module, you will be able to:

- Plan a table
- Create and format a table
- Add table data
- Find and replace table data

- Delete table data
- Sort table data
- Use formulas in a table
- Print a table

Files You Will Need

EX 7-1.xlsx	EX 7-4.xlsx
EX 7-2.xlsx	EX 7-5.xlsx
EX 7-3.xlsx	EX 7-6.xlsx

Plan a Table

Learning
Outcomes
• Plan the data
  organization for
  a table
• Plan the data
  elements for
  a table

In addition to using Excel spreadsheet features, you can analyze and manipulate data in a table structure. An Excel **table** is an organized collection of rows and columns of similarly structured worksheet data. Tables are a convenient way to understand and manage large amounts of information. When planning a table, consider what information you want your table to contain and how you want to work with the data, now and in the future. As you plan a table, you should understand its most important components. A table is organized into rows called records. A **record** is a table row that contains data about an object, person, or other items. Records are composed of fields. **Fields** are columns in the table; each field describes one element of the record, such as a customer's last name or street address. Each field has a **field name**, which is a column label, such as "Address," that describes its contents. Tables usually have a **header row** as the first row, which contains the field names. To plan your table, use the guidelines below. **CASE** *Mary asks you to compile a table of the 2017 conservation projects. Before entering the project data into an Excel worksheet, you plan the table contents.*

DETAILS

As you plan your table, use the following guidelines:

- #### Identify the purpose of the table
  The purpose of the table determines the kind of information the table should contain. You want to use the conservation projects table to find all departure dates for a particular project and to display the projects in order of departure date. You also want to quickly calculate the number of available places for a project.

- #### Plan the structure of the table
  In designing your table's structure, determine the fields (the table columns) you need to achieve the table's purpose. You have worked with the sales department to learn the type of information they need for each project. **FIGURE 7-1** shows a layout sketch for the table. Each row will contain one project record. The columns represent fields that contain pieces of descriptive information you will enter for each project, such as the name, departure date, and duration.

- #### Plan your row and column structure
  You can create a table from any contiguous range of cells on your worksheet. Plan and design your table so that all rows have similar types of information in the same column. A table should not have any blank rows or columns. Instead of using blank rows to separate table headings from data, use a table style, which will use formatting to make column labels stand out from your table data. **FIGURE 7-2** shows a table, populated with data that has been formatted using a table style.

- #### Document the table design
  In addition to your table sketch, you should make a list of the field names to document the type of data and any special number formatting required for each field. Field names should be as short as possible while still accurately describing the column information. When naming fields it is important to use text rather than numbers because Excel could interpret numbers as parts of formulas. Your field names should be unique and not easily confused with cell addresses, such as the name D2. You want your table to contain eight field names, each one corresponding to the major characteristics of the 2017 conservation projects. **TABLE 7-1** shows the documentation of the field names in your table.

FIGURE 7-1: Table layout sketch

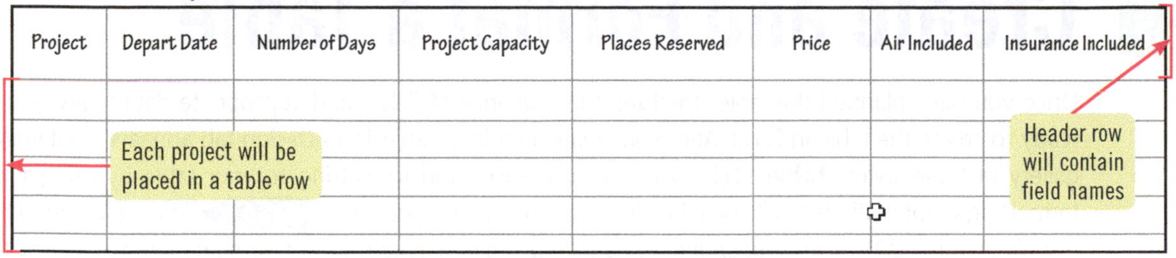

Project	Depart Date	Number of Days	Project Capacity	Places Reserved	Price	Air Included	Insurance Included
		Each project will be placed in a table row					Header row will contain field names

FIGURE 7-2: Formatted table with data

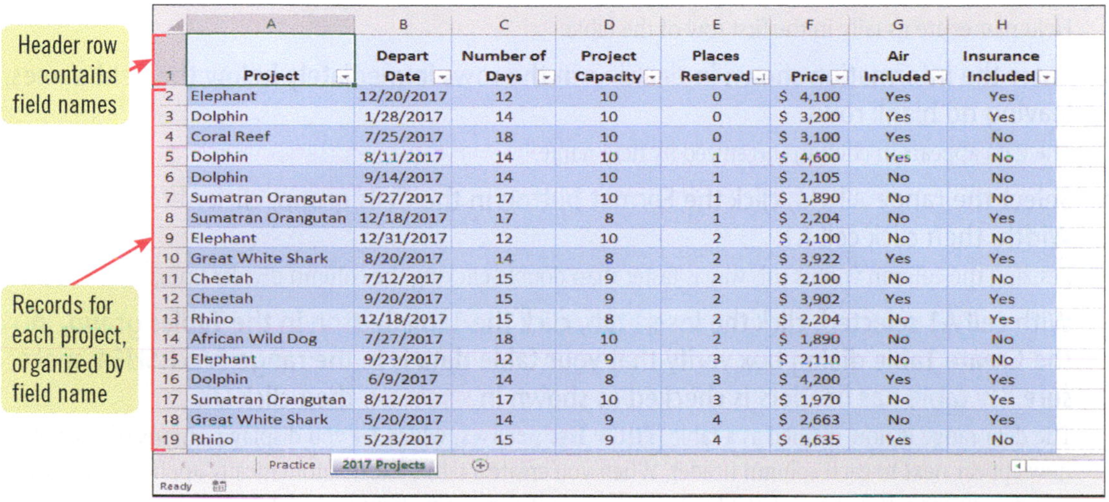

Header row contains field names

Records for each project, organized by field name

	Project	Depart Date	Number of Days	Project Capacity	Places Reserved	Price	Air Included	Insurance Included
2	Elephant	12/20/2017	12	10	0	$ 4,100	Yes	Yes
3	Dolphin	1/28/2017	14	10	0	$ 3,200	Yes	Yes
4	Coral Reef	7/25/2017	18	10	0	$ 3,100	Yes	No
5	Dolphin	8/11/2017	14	10	1	$ 4,600	Yes	No
6	Dolphin	9/14/2017	14	10	1	$ 2,105	No	No
7	Sumatran Orangutan	5/27/2017	17	10	1	$ 1,890	No	No
8	Sumatran Orangutan	12/18/2017	17	8	1	$ 2,204	No	Yes
9	Elephant	12/31/2017	12	10	2	$ 2,100	No	No
10	Great White Shark	8/20/2017	14	8	2	$ 3,922	Yes	Yes
11	Cheetah	7/12/2017	15	9	2	$ 2,100	No	No
12	Cheetah	9/20/2017	15	9	2	$ 3,902	Yes	Yes
13	Rhino	12/18/2017	15	8	2	$ 2,204	No	Yes
14	African Wild Dog	7/27/2017	18	10	2	$ 1,890	No	No
15	Elephant	9/23/2017	12	9	3	$ 2,110	No	No
16	Dolphin	6/9/2017	14	8	3	$ 4,200	Yes	Yes
17	Sumatran Orangutan	8/12/2017	17	10	3	$ 1,970	No	Yes
18	Great White Shark	5/20/2017	14	9	4	$ 2,663	No	Yes
19	Rhino	5/23/2017	15	9	4	$ 4,635	Yes	No

Practice | 2017 Projects

Ready

TABLE 7-1: Table documentation

field name	type of data	description of data
Project	Text	Name of project
Depart Date	Date	Date project departs
Number of Days	Number with 0 decimal places	Duration of the project
Project Capacity	Number with 0 decimal places	Maximum number of people the project can accommodate
Places Reserved	Number with 0 decimal places	Number of reservations for the project
Price	Accounting with 0 decimal places and $ symbol	Project price (This price is not guaranteed until a 30% deposit is received)
Air Included	Text	Yes: Airfare is included in the price No: Airfare is not included in the price
Insurance Included	Text	Yes: Insurance is included in the price No: Insurance is not included in the price

Create and Format a Table

Learning Outcomes
• Create a table
• Format a table

Once you have planned the table structure, the sequence of fields, and appropriate data types, you are ready to create the table in Excel. After you create a table, a Table Tools Design tab appears, containing a gallery of table styles. **Table styles** allow you to easily add formatting to your table by using preset formatting combinations of fill color, borders, type style, and type color. **CASE** *Mary asks you to build a table with the 2017 conservation project data. You begin by entering the field names. Then you enter the project data that corresponds to each field name, create the table, and format the data using a table style.*

STEPS

1. **Start Excel, open EX 7-1.xlsx from the location where you store your Data Files, then save it as EX 7-Conservation Projects**

2. **Beginning in cell A1 of the Practice sheet, enter each field name in a separate column, as shown in the first row of FIGURE 7-3**
   Field names are usually in the first row of the table.

3. **Enter the information shown in FIGURE 7-3 in the rows immediately below the field names, leaving no blank rows**
   The data appears in columns organized by field name.

4. **Select the range A1:H4, click the Format button in the Cells group, click AutoFit Column Width, then click cell A1**
   Resizing the column widths this way is faster than double-clicking the column divider lines.

5. **With cell A1 selected, click the Insert tab, click the Table button in the Tables group, in the Create Table dialog box verify that your table data is in the range $A$1:$H$4, make sure My table has headers is checked as shown in FIGURE 7-4, then click OK**
   The data range is now defined as a table. **Filter list arrows**, which let you display portions of your data, now appear next to each column header. When you create a table, Excel automatically applies a table style. The default table style has a dark blue header row and alternating light and dark blue data rows. The Table Tools Design tab appears, and the Table Styles group displays a gallery of table formatting options. You decide to choose a different table style from the gallery.

6. **Click the Table Styles More button ⬇, scroll to view all of the table styles, then move the mouse pointer over several styles without clicking**
   The Table Styles gallery on the Table Tools Design tab has three style categories: Light, Medium, and Dark. Each category has numerous design types; for example, in some of the designs, the header row and total row are darker and the rows alternate colors. The available table designs use the current workbook theme colors so the table coordinates with your existing workbook content. If you select a different workbook theme and color scheme in the Themes group on the Page Layout tab, the Table Styles gallery uses those colors. As you point to each table style, Live Preview shows you what your table will look like with the style applied. However, you only see a preview of each style; you need to click a style to apply it.

7. **Click Table Style Medium 23 to apply it to your table, then click cell A1**
   Compare your table to **FIGURE 7-5**.

FIGURE 7-3: Field names and three records entered in worksheet

	A	B	C	D	E	F	G	H
1	Project	Depart Date	Number of Days	Project Capacity	Places Reserved	Price	Air Included	Insurance Included
2	Elephant	42747	12	10	5	4255	Yes	No
3	Rhino	42748	15	8	8	1984	No	No
4	Cheetah	42754	15	10	8	1966	No	Yes
5								

FIGURE 7-4: Create Table dialog box

Table range

Verify that this box is checked

FIGURE 7-5: Formatted table with three records

	A	B	C	D	E	F	G	H
1	Project	Depart Date	Number of Days	Project Capacity	Places Reserved	Price	Air Included	Insurance Included
2	Elephant	1/12/2017	12	10	5	4255	Yes	No
3	Rhino	1/13/2017	15	8	8	1984	No	No
4	Cheetah	1/19/2017	15	10	8	1966	No	Yes

Changing table style options

You can change a table's appearance by using the check boxes in the Table Style Options group on the Table Tools Design tab, shown in FIGURE 7-6. For example, you can turn on or turn off the following options: Header Row, which displays or hides the header row; Total Row, which calculates totals for each column; **banding**, which creates different formatting for adjacent rows and columns; and special formatting for first and last columns. Use these options to modify a table's appearance either before or after applying a table style.

You can also create your own table style by clicking the Table Styles More button, then at the bottom of the Table Styles Gallery, clicking New Table Style. In the New Table Style dialog box, name the style in the Name text box, click a table element, then format selected table elements by clicking Format. You can also set a custom style as the default style for your tables by checking the Set as default table quick style for this document check box. You can click Clear at the bottom of the Table Styles gallery if you want to delete a table style from the currently selected table.

FIGURE 7-6: Table Style Options

	A	B	C	D	E	F	G	H	I
1	Project	Depart Date	Number of Days	Project Capacity	Places Reserved	Price	Air Included	Insurance Included	Places Available
2	African Wild Dog	1/21/2017	18	7	7	$ 3,850	Yes	Yes	0
3	African Wild Dog	3/23/2017	18	8	7	$ 2,450	No	No	1
4	African Wild Dog			7	5	$ 4,638	Yes	Yes	2
5	African Wild Dog	6/1	10		5	$ 2,190	No	No	5

Banded rows

Table Tools Design tab

Table Style Options group

Add Table Data

You can add records to a table by typing data directly below the last row of the table. After you press [Enter], the new row becomes part of the table and the table formatting extends to the new data. When the active cell is the last cell of a table, you can add a new row by pressing [Tab]. You can also insert rows in any table location. If you decide you need additional data fields, you can add new columns to a table. You can also expand a table by dragging the sizing handle in a table's lower-right corner; drag down to add rows and drag to the right to add columns. **CASE** ▸ *After entering all of the 2017 project data, Mary decides to offer two additional projects. She also wants the table to display the number of available places for each project and whether visas are required for the destination.*

STEPS

1. **Click the 2017 Projects sheet tab**

   The 2017 sheet containing the 2017 project data becomes active.

2. **Scroll down to the last table row, click cell A65, enter the data for the new Coral Reef project, as shown below, then press [Enter]**

Coral Reef	7/25/2017	18	10	0	$ 3,100	Yes	No

   As you scroll down, notice that the table headers are visible at the top of the table as long as the active cell is inside the table. The new Coral Reef project is now part of the table. You want to enter a record about a new January project above row 6.

3. **Scroll up to and click the inside left edge of cell A6 to select the table row data as shown in FIGURE 7-7, click the Insert list arrow in the Cells group, then click Insert Table Rows Above**

   Clicking the left edge of the first cell in a table row selects the entire table row, rather than the entire worksheet row. A new blank row 6 is available for the new record.

4. **Click cell A6, then enter the Dolphin record shown below**

Dolphin	1/28/2017	14	10	0	$ 3,200	Yes	Yes

   The new Dolphin project is part of the table. You want to add a new field that displays the number of available places for each project.

5. **Click cell I1, type the field name Places Available, then press [Enter]**

   The new field becomes part of the table, and the header formatting extends to the new field, as shown in FIGURE 7-8. The AutoCorrect menu allows you to undo or stop the automatic table expansion, but in this case you decide to leave this feature on. You want to add another new field to the table to display projects that require visas, but this time you will add the new field by resizing the table.

6. **Scroll down until cell I66 is visible, then drag the sizing handle in the table's lower-right corner one column to the right to add column J to the table, as shown in FIGURE 7-9**

   The table range is now A1:J66, and the new field name is Column1.

7. **Scroll up to and click cell J1, type Visa Required, then press [Enter]**

8. **Click the Insert tab, click the Header & Footer button in the Text group, enter your name in the center header text box, click cell A1, click the Normal button 🔲 on the status bar, then save the workbook**

FIGURE 7-7: Table row 6 selected

	A	B	C	D	E	F	G	H
1	Project	Depart Date	Number of Days	Project Capacity	Places Reserved	Price	Air Included	Insurance Included
2	Elephant	1/12/2017	12	10	5	$ 4,255	Yes	No
3	Rhino	1/13/2017	15	8	8	$ 1,984	No	No
4	Cheetah	1/19/2017	15	10	8	$ 1,966	No	Yes
5	African Wild Dog	1/21/2017	18	7	7	$ 3,850	Yes	Yes
6	Dolphin	2/22/2017	14	10	10	$ 2,134	No	No
7	Orangutan	2/28/2017	17	8	4	$ 4,812	Yes	No
8	Great White Shark	3/13/2017	14	10	5	$ 4,350	Yes	No
9	Coral Reef	3/19/2017	18	6	5	$ 2,110	No	Yes
10	Orangutan	3/20/2017	17	10	8	$ 1,755	No	Yes
11	African Wild Dog	3/23/2017	18	8	7	$ 2,450	No	No
12	Rhino	4/8/2017	15	10	10	$ 3,115	Yes	Yes
13	Elephant	4/11/2017	12	10	5	$ 4,255	Yes	No

Clicking here selects the entire worksheet row

Clicking here selects the table row

Row 6 of table selected

FIGURE 7-8: New table column

	A	B	C	D	E	F	G	H	I	J
1	Project	Depart Date	Number of Days	Project Capacity	Places Reserved	Price	Air Included	Insurance Included	Places Available	
2	Elephant	1/12/2017	12	10	5	$ 4,255	Yes	No		
3	Rhino	1/13/2017	15	8	8	$ 1,984	No	No		
4	Cheetah	1/19/2017	15	10	8	$ 1,966	No	Yes		
5	African Wild Dog	1/21/2017	18	7	7	$ 3,850	Yes	Yes		
6	Dolphin	1/28/2017	14	10	0	$ 3,200	Yes	Yes		
7	Dolphin	2/22/2017	14	10	10	$ 2,134	No	No		
8	Orangutan	2/28/2017	17	8	4	$ 4,812	Yes	No		
9	Great White Shark	3/13/2017	14	10	5	$ 4,350	Yes	No		
10	Coral Reef	3/19/2017	18	6	5	$ 2,110	No	Yes		

New record in row 6

New table column will show available places for each project

FIGURE 7-9: Resizing a table using the resizing handle

	Project	Depart Date	Number of	Project Cap	Places Reser	Price	Air Include	Insurance Ir	Places Avai	J	K	L
55	African Wild Dog	10/29/2017	18	10	6	$ 4,200	Yes	Yes				
56	Great White Shark	10/31/2017	14	9	8	$ 1,900	No	No				
57	African Wild Dog	10/31/2017	18	9	5	$ 3,908	Yes	No				
58	Great White Shark	11/18/2017	14	10	5	$ 2,200	No	Yes				
59	Rhino	12/18/2017	15	8	2	$ 2,204	No	Yes				
60	Orangutan	12/18/2017	17	8	1	$ 2,204	No	Yes				
61	Elephant	12/20/2017	12	10	0	$ 4,100	Yes	Yes				
62	Dolphin	12/20/2017	14	10	5	$ 2,100	No	Yes				
63	African Wild Dog	12/21/2017	18	9	8	$ 2,105	No	No				
64	Cheetah	12/30/2017	15	9	5	$ 3,922	Yes	Yes				
65	Elephant	12/31/2017	12	10	2	$ 2,100	No	No				
66	Coral Reef	7/25/2017	18	10	0	$ 3,100	Yes	No				
67												
68												

Drag sizing handle to add column J

Selecting table elements

When working with tables you often need to select rows, columns, and even the entire table. Clicking to the right of a row number, inside column A, selects the entire table row. You can select a table column by clicking the top edge of the header. Be careful not to click a column letter or row number, however, because this selects the entire worksheet row or column. You can select the table data by clicking the upper-left corner of the first table cell. When selecting a column or a table, the first click selects only the data in the column or table. If you click a second time, you add the headers to the selection.

Find and Replace Table Data

From time to time, you need to locate specific records in your table. You can use the Excel Find feature to search your table for the information you need. You can also use the Replace feature to locate and replace existing entries or portions of entries with information you specify. If you don't know the exact spelling of the text you are searching for, you can use wildcards to help locate the records. **Wildcards** are special symbols that substitute for unknown characters. **CASE** ▶ *Because the Sumatran Orangutans are critically endangered, Mary wants you to replace "Orangutan" with "Sumatran Orangutan" to avoid confusion with last year's Borneo projects. She also wants to know how many Cheetah projects are scheduled for the year. You begin by searching for records with the text "Cheetah".*

STEPS

1. **Click cell A1 if necessary, click the Home tab, click the Find & Select button in the Editing group, then click Find**

   The Find and Replace dialog box opens, as shown in **FIGURE 7-10**. In the Find what text box, you enter criteria that specify the records you want to find. You want to search for records whose Project field contains the label "Cheetah".

2. **Type Cheetah in the Find what text box, then click Find Next**

   A4 is the active cell because it is the first instance of Cheetah in the table.

3. **Click Find Next and examine the record for each Cheetah project found until no more matching cells are found in the table and the active cell is A4 again, then click Close**

   There are seven Cheetah projects.

4. **Return to cell A1, click the Find & Select button in the Editing group, then click Replace**

   The Find and Replace dialog box opens with the Replace tab selected and "Cheetah" in the Find what text box, as shown in **FIGURE 7-11**. You will search for entries containing "Orangutan" and replace them with "Sumatran Orangutan". To save time, you will use the asterisk (*) wildcard to help you locate the records containing Orangutan.

5. **Delete the text in the Find what text box, type Or* in the Find what text box, click the Replace with text box, then type Sumatran Orangutan**

   The asterisk (*) wildcard stands for one or more characters, meaning that the search text "Or*" will find words such as "orange", "cord", and "for". Because you notice that there are other table entries containing the text "or" with a lowercase "o" (Coral Reef), you need to make sure that only capitalized instances of the letter "O" are replaced.

6. **Click Options >>, click the Match case check box to select it, click Options <<, then click Find Next**

   Excel moves the cell pointer to the cell containing the first occurrence of "Orangutan".

7. **Click Replace All, click OK, then click Close**

   The dialog box closes. Excel made ten replacements. The Coral Reef projects remain unchanged because the "or" in "Coral" is lowercase.

8. **Save the workbook**

FIGURE 7-10: Find and Replace dialog box

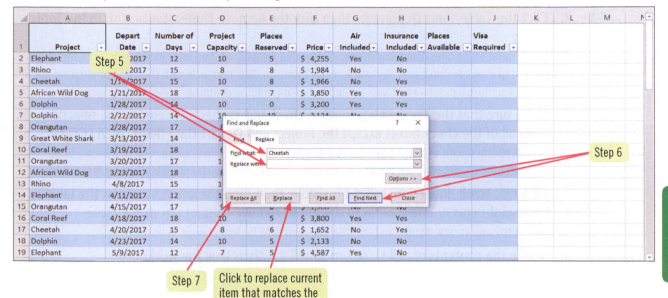

FIGURE 7-11: The Replace tab in the Find and Replace dialog box

Using Find and Select features

You can also use the Find feature to navigate to a specific place in a workbook by clicking the Find & Select button in the Editing group on the Home tab, clicking Go To, typing a cell address, then clicking OK. Clicking the Find & Select button also allows you to find comments and conditional formatting in a worksheet. You can use the Go to Special dialog box to select cells that contain different types of formulas or objects. Some Go to Special commands also appear on the Find & Select menu. Using this menu, you can also change the mouse pointer shape to the Select Objects pointer ℞ so you can quickly select drawing objects when necessary. To return to the standard Excel pointer ✚, press [Esc].

Delete Table Data

To keep a table up to date, you need to be able to periodically remove records. You may even need to remove fields if the information stored in a field becomes unnecessary. You can delete table data using the Delete button in the Cells group or by dragging the sizing handle at the table's lower-right corner. You can also easily delete duplicate records from a table. **CASE** *Mary is canceling the Rhino project that departs on 1/13/2017 and asks you to delete the record from the table. You will also remove any duplicate records from the table. Because the visa requirements are difficult to keep up with, Mary asks you to delete the field with visa information.*

STEPS

1. **Click the inside left edge of cell A3 to select the table row, click the Delete list arrow in the Cells group, then click Delete Table Rows**

   The Rhino project is deleted, and the Cheetah project moves up to row 3, as shown in **FIGURE 7-12**. You can also delete a table row or a column using the Resize Table button in the Properties group of the Table Tools Design tab, or by right-clicking the row or column, pointing to Delete on the shortcut menu, then clicking Table Columns or Table Rows. You decide to check the table for duplicate records.

2. **Click the Table Tools Design tab, then click the Remove Duplicates button in the Tools group**

   The Remove Duplicates dialog box opens, as shown in **FIGURE 7-13**. You need to select the columns that will be used to evaluate duplicates. Because you don't want to delete projects with the same destination but different departure dates, you will look for duplicate data in those columns.

3. **Make sure that the My data has headers check box is checked, remove the selection from all of the check boxes except the Project and Depart Date fields, then click OK**

   One duplicate record is found and removed, leaving 63 records of data and a total of 64 rows in the table, including the header row. You want to remove the last column, which contains space for visa information.

4. **Click OK, scroll down until cell J64 is visible, then drag the sizing handle of the table's lower-right corner one column to the left to remove column J from the table**

   The table range is now A1:I64, and the Visa Required field no longer appears in the table.

5. **Delete the contents of cell J1, return to cell A1, then save the workbook**

FIGURE 7-12: Table with row deleted

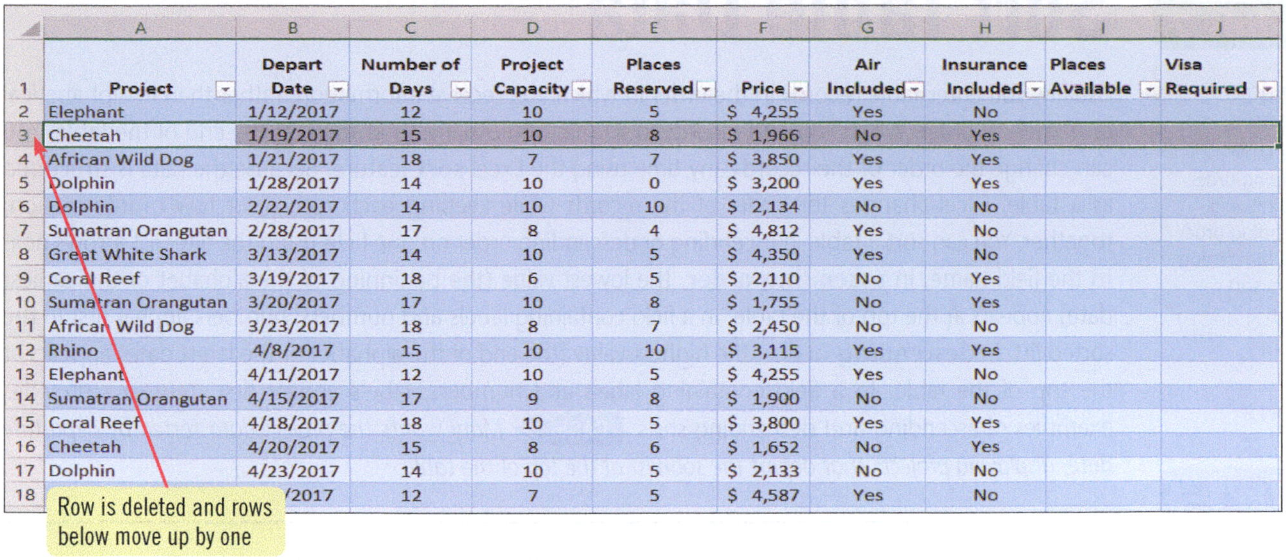

	Project	Depart Date	Number of Days	Project Capacity	Places Reserved	Price	Air Included	Insurance Included	Places Available	Visa Required
2	Elephant	1/12/2017	12	10	5	$ 4,255	Yes	No		
3	Cheetah	1/19/2017	15	10	8	$ 1,966	No	Yes		
4	African Wild Dog	1/21/2017	18	7	7	$ 3,850	Yes	Yes		
5	Dolphin	1/28/2017	14	10	0	$ 3,200	Yes	Yes		
6	Dolphin	2/22/2017	14	10	10	$ 2,134	No	No		
7	Sumatran Orangutan	2/28/2017	17	8	4	$ 4,812	Yes	No		
8	Great White Shark	3/13/2017	14	10	5	$ 4,350	Yes	No		
9	Coral Reef	3/19/2017	18	6	5	$ 2,110	No	Yes		
10	Sumatran Orangutan	3/20/2017	17	10	8	$ 1,755	No	Yes		
11	African Wild Dog	3/23/2017	18	8	7	$ 2,450	No	No		
12	Rhino	4/8/2017	15	10	10	$ 3,115	Yes	Yes		
13	Elephant	4/11/2017	12	10	5	$ 4,255	Yes	No		
14	Sumatran Orangutan	4/15/2017	17	9	8	$ 1,900	No	No		
15	Coral Reef	4/18/2017	18	10	5	$ 3,800	Yes	Yes		
16	Cheetah	4/20/2017	15	8	6	$ 1,652	No	Yes		
17	Dolphin	4/23/2017	14	10	5	$ 2,133	No	No		
18		2017	12	7	5	$ 4,587	Yes	No		

Row is deleted and rows below move up by one

FIGURE 7-13: Remove Duplicates dialog box

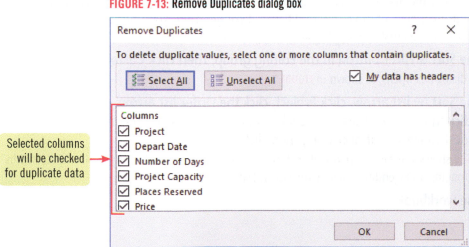

Selected columns will be checked for duplicate data

Sort Table Data

Usually, you enter table records in the order in which you receive information, rather than in alphabetical or numerical order. When you add records to a table, you usually enter them at the end of the table. You can change the order of the records any time using the Excel **sort** feature. Because the data is structured as a table, Excel changes the order of the records while keeping each record, or row of information, together. You can sort a table in ascending or descending order on one field using the filter list arrows next to the field name. In **ascending order**, the lowest value (the beginning of the alphabet or the earliest date) appears at the top of the table. In a field containing labels and numbers, numbers appear first in the sorted list. In **descending order**, the highest value (the end of the alphabet or the latest date) appears at the top of the table. In a field containing labels and numbers, labels appear first. **TABLE 7-2** provides examples of ascending and descending sorts. **CASE** *Mary wants the project data sorted by departure date, displaying projects that depart the soonest at the top of the table.*

STEPS

1. **Click the Depart Date filter list arrow, then click Sort Oldest to Newest**

   Excel rearranges the records in ascending order by departure date, as shown in **FIGURE 7-14**. The Depart Date filter list arrow has an upward pointing arrow indicating the ascending sort in the field. You can also sort the table on one field using the Sort & Filter button.

2. **Click the Home tab, click any cell in the Price column, click the Sort & Filter button in the Editing group, then click Sort Largest to Smallest**

   Excel sorts the table, placing records with higher prices at the top. The Price filter list arrow now has a downward pointing arrow next to the filter list arrow, indicating the descending sort order. You can also rearrange the table data using a **multilevel sort**. This type of sort rearranges the table data using more than one field, where each field is a different level, based on its importance in the sort. If you use two sort levels, the data is sorted by the first field, and the second field is sorted within each grouping of the first field. Since you have many groups of projects with different departure dates, you want to use a multilevel sort to arrange the table data first by projects and then by departure dates within each project.

3. **Click the Sort & Filter button in the Editing group, then click Custom Sort**

   The Sort dialog box opens, as shown in **FIGURE 7-15**.

4. **Click the Sort by list arrow, click Project, click the Order list arrow, click A to Z, click Add Level, click the Then by list arrow, click Depart Date, click the second Order list arrow, click Oldest to Newest if necessary, then click OK**

   FIGURE 7-16 shows the table sorted alphabetically in ascending order (A–Z) by Project and, within each project grouping, in ascending order by the Depart Date.

5. **Save the workbook**

Sorting conditionally formatted data

If conditional formats have been applied to a table, you can sort the table using conditional formatting to arrange the rows. For example, if cells are conditionally formatted with color, you can sort a field on Cell Color, using the color with the order of On Top or On Bottom in the Sort dialog box. If the data is not in a table, you can select a cell in the column of conditionally formatted data you want to sort by, or select the range of cells to be sorted, right-click the selection, point to Sort, then select the font color, highlighted color, or icon that you want to appear on top.

FIGURE 7-14: Table sorted by departure date

Up arrow indicates ascending sort in the field

Records are sorted by departure date in ascending order

	Project	Depart Date	Number of Days	Project Capacity	Places Reserved	Price	Air Included	Insurance Included	Places Available
2	Elephant	1/12/2017	12	10	5	$ 4,255	Yes	No	
3	Cheetah	1/19/2017	15	10		,966	No	Yes	
4	African Wild Dog	1/21/2017	18	7		,850	Yes	Yes	
5	Dolphin	1/28/2017	14	10		,200	Yes	Yes	
6	Dolphin	2/22/2017	14	10		,134	No	No	
	atran Orangutan	2/28/2017	17	8	4	$ 4,812	Yes	No	
	t White Shark	3/13/2017	14	10	5	$ 4,350	Yes	No	
	Reef	3/19/2017	18	6	5	$ 2,110	No	Yes	
	atran Orangutan	3/20/2017	17	10	8	$ 1,755	No	Yes	
	ican Wild Dog	3/23/2017	18	8	7	$ 2,450	No	No	
12	Rhino	4/8/2017	15	10	10	$ 3,115	Yes	Yes	
13	Elephant	4/11/2017	12	10	5	$ 4,255	Yes	No	
14	Sumatran Orangutan	4/15/2017	17	9	8	$ 1,900	No	No	
15	Coral Reef	4/18/2017	18	10	5	$ 3,800	Yes	Yes	
16	Cheetah	4/20/2017	15	8	6	$ 1,652	No	Yes	
17	Dolphin	4/23/2017	14	10	5	$ 2,133	No	No	
18	Elephant	5/9/2017	12	7	5	$ 4,587	Yes	No	

FIGURE 7-15: Sort dialog box

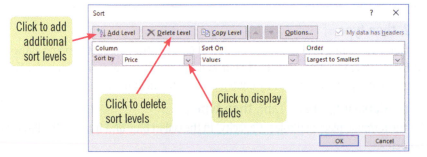

Click to add additional sort levels

Click to delete sort levels

Click to display fields

FIGURE 7-16: Table sorted using two levels

	Project	Depart Date	Number of Days	Project Capacity	Places Reserved	Price	Air Included	Insurance Included	Places Available
2	African Wild Dog	1/21/2017	18	7	7	$ 3,850	Yes	Yes	
3	African Wild Dog	3/23/2017	18	8	7	$ 2,450	No	No	
4	African Wild Dog	5/18/2017	18	7	5	$ 4,638	Yes	Yes	
5	African Wild Dog	6/10/2017	18	10	5	$ 2,190	No	No	
6	African Wild Dog	6/27/2017	18	10	7	$ 1,944	No	No	
7	African Wild Dog	7/27/2017	18	10	2	$ 1,890	No	No	
8	African Wild Dog	8/23/2017	18	7			No	No	
9	African Wild Dog	9/18/2017	18	10			Yes	Yes	
10	African Wild Dog	10/29/2017	18	9			Yes	Yes	
11	African Wild Dog	10/31/2017	18	9			Yes	No	
12	African Wild Dog	12/21/2017	18	9			No	No	
13	Cheetah	1/19/2017	15	10	8	$ 1,966	No	Yes	
14	Cheetah				6	$ 1,652	No	Yes	
15	Cheetah				8	$ 4,600	Yes	No	
16	Cheetah				2	$ 2,100	No	No	
17	Cheetah	9/20/2017	15	9	2	$ 3,902	Yes	Yes	

Second-level sort arranges records by departure date within each project grouping

First-level sort on project arranges records by project name

TABLE 7-2: Sort order options and examples

option	alphabetic	numeric	date	alphanumeric
Ascending	A, B, C	7, 8, 9	1/1, 2/1, 3/1	12A, 99B, DX8, QT7
Descending	C, B, A	9, 8, 7	3/1, 2/1, 1/1	QT7, DX8, 99B, 12A

Specifying a custom sort order

You can identify a custom sort order for the field selected in the Sort by box. Click the Order list arrow in the Sort dialog box, click Custom List, then click the desired custom order. Commonly used custom sort orders are days of the week (Sun, Mon, Tues, Wed, etc.) and months (Jan, Feb, Mar, etc.); alphabetic sorts do not sort these items properly.

Use Formulas in a Table

Learning Outcomes
- Build a table formula
- Use calculated columns to display formula results
- Use the table style options to add summary information to a table

Many tables are large, making it difficult to know from viewing them the "story" the table tells. The Excel table calculation features help you summarize table data so you can see important patterns and trends. After you enter a single formula into a table cell, the **calculated columns** feature fills in the remaining cells with the formula's results. The column continues to fill with the formula results as you enter rows in the table. This makes it easy to update your formulas because you only need to edit the formula once, and the change will fill in to the other column cells. The **structured reference** feature allows your formulas to refer to table columns by names that are automatically generated when you create the table. These names adjust as you add or delete table fields. An example of a table reference is =[Sales]–[Costs], where Sales and Costs are field names in the table. Tables also have a specific area at the bottom called the **table total row** for calculations using the data in the table columns. The cells in this row contain a dropdown list of functions that can be used for the column calculation. The table total row adapts to any changes in the table size. **CASE** ▶ *Mary asks you to calculate the number of available places for each project. You will also add summary information to the end of the table.*

STEPS

1. **Click cell I2, then type =[**
   A list of the table field names appears, as shown in **FIGURE 7-17**. Structured referencing allows you to use the names that Excel created when you defined your table to reference fields in a formula. You can choose a field by clicking it and pressing [Tab] or by double-clicking the field name.

2. **Click [Project Capacity], press [Tab], then type]**
   Excel begins the formula, placing [Project Capacity] in the cell in blue and framing the Project Capacity data in a blue border.

3. **Type -[, double-click [Places Reserved], then type]**
   Excel places [Places Reserved] in the cell in red and outlines the Places Reserved data in a red border.

4. **Press [Enter]**
   The formula result, 0, is displayed in cell I2. The table column also fills with the formula, displaying the number of available places for each project.

5. **Click the AutoCorrect Options list arrow [⊞▾] to view options for the column**
   Because the calculated columns option saves time, you decide to leave the feature on. You want to display the total number of available places on all of the projects.

6. **Press [Esc] to close the menu, click the Table Tools Design tab, then click the Total Row check box in the Table Style Options group to select it**
   A total row appears at the bottom of the table, and the sum of the available places, 268, is displayed in cell I65. You can include other formulas in the total row.

7. **Click cell C65 (the Number of Days column), then click the cell list arrow on the right side of the cell**
   The list of available functions appears, as shown in **FIGURE 7-18**. You want to find the average project length.

8. **Click Average, then save your workbook**
   The average project length, 15 days, appears in cell C65.

FIGURE 7-17: Table field names

	A	B	C	D	E	F	G	H	I	J	K	L	M	N
1	Project	Depart Date	Number of Days	Project Capacity	Places Reserved	Price	Air Included	Insurance Included	Places Available					
2	African Wild Dog	1/21/2017	18	7	7	$ 3,850	Yes	Yes	=[					
3	African Wild Dog	3/23/2017	18	8	7	$ 2,450	No	No						
4	African Wild Dog	5/18/2017	18	7	5	$ 4,638	Yes	Yes						
5	African Wild Dog	6/10/2017	18	10	5	$ 2,190	No	No						
6	African Wild Dog	6/27/2017	18	10	7	$ 1,944	No	No						
7	African Wild Dog	7/27/2017	18	10	2	$ 1,890	No	No						
8	African Wild Dog	8/23/2017	18	7	4	$ 2,877	No	No						
9	African Wild Dog	9/18/2017	18	10	5	$ 4,190	Yes	Yes						
10	African Wild Dog	10/29/2017	18	10	6	$ 4,200	Yes	Yes						
11	African Wild Dog	10/31/2017	18	9	5	$ 3,908	Yes	No						
12	African Wild Dog	12/21/2017	18	9	8	$ 2,105	No	No						
13	Cheetah	1/19/2017	15	10	8	$ 1,966	No	Yes						
14	Cheetah	4/20/2017	15	8	6	$ 1,652	No	Yes						
15	Cheetah	6/11/2017	15	10	8	$ 4,600	Yes	No						
16	Cheetah	7/12/2017	15	9	2	$ 2,100	No	No						
17	Cheetah	9/20/2017	15	9	2	$ 3,902	Yes	Yes						
18	Cheetah	12/30/2017	15	9	5	$ 3,922	Yes	Yes						

Field names list: Project, Depart Date, Number of Days, Project Capacity, Places Reserved, Price, Air Included, Insurance Included, Places Available

Field names list appears

FIGURE 7-18: Functions in the Total row

	Project	Depart Date	Number of	Project Cap	Places Reser	Price	Air Include	Insurance In	Places Ava
55	Sumatran Orangutan	2/28/2017	17	8	4	$ 4,812	Yes	No	4
56	Sumatran Orangutan	3/20/2017	17	10	8	$ 1,755	No	Yes	2
57	Sumatran Orangutan	4/15/2017	17	9	8	$ 1,900	No	No	1
58	Sumatran Orangutan	5/27/2017	17	10	1	$ 1,890	No	No	9
59	Sumatran Orangutan	6/18/2017	17	8	6	$ 4,204	Yes	Yes	2
60	Sumatran Orangutan	7/9/2017	17	8	5	$ 3,990	Yes	No	3
61	Sumatran Orangutan	8/12/2017	17	10	3	$ 1,970	No	Yes	7
62	Sumatran Orangutan	9/11/2017	17	8	5	$ 2,922	No	Yes	3
63	Sumatran Orangutan	10/23/2017	17	8	4	$ 2,450	No	No	4
64	Sumatran Orangutan	12/18/2017	17	8	1	$ 2,204	No	Yes	7
65	Total								268
66			None						
67			Average						
68			Count						
69			Count Numbers						
70			Max						
71			Min						
72			Sum						
73			StdDev						
74			Var						
			More Functions...						

Functions available in the Total row

Excel 2016

Print a Table

You can determine the way a table will print using the Page Layout tab. Because tables often have more rows than can fit on a page, you can define the first row of the table (containing the field names) as the **print title**, which prints at the top of every page. If your table does not include any descriptive information above the field names, you can use headers and footers to add identifying text, such as the table title or the report date. **CASE** ▶ *Mary asks you for a printout of the project information. You begin by previewing the table.*

STEPS

1. **Click the File tab, click Print, then view the table preview**

   Below the table you see 1 of 2, which indicates you are viewing page 1 of a 2-page document.

2. **In the Preview window, click the Next Page button ▶ in the Preview area to view the second page**

   All of the field names in the table fit across the width of page 1. Because the records on page 2 appear without column headings, you want to set up the first row of the table, which contains the field names, as a print title.

3. **Return to the worksheet, click the Page Layout tab, click the Print Titles button in the Page Setup group, click inside the Rows to repeat at top text box under Print titles, in the worksheet scroll up to row 1 if necessary, click any cell in row 1 on the table, then compare your Page Setup dialog box to FIGURE 7-19**

   When you select row 1 as a print title, Excel automatically inserts an absolute reference to the row that will repeat at the top of each page.

4. **Click the Print Preview button in the Page Setup dialog box, then click ▶ in the preview window to view the second page**

   Setting up a print title to repeat row 1 causes the field names to appear at the top of each printed page. The printout would be more informative with a header to identify the table information.

5. **Return to the worksheet, click the Insert tab, click the Header & Footer button in the Text group, click the left header section text box, then type 2017 Conservation Projects**

6. **Select the left header section text, click the Home tab, click the Increase Font Size button A˄ in the Font group twice to change the font size to 14, click the Bold button B in the Font group, click any cell in the table, then click the Normal button ▦ in the status bar**

7. **Save the table, preview it, close the workbook, exit Excel, then submit the workbook to your instructor**

   Compare your printed table with FIGURE 7-20.

FIGURE 7-19: Page Setup dialog box

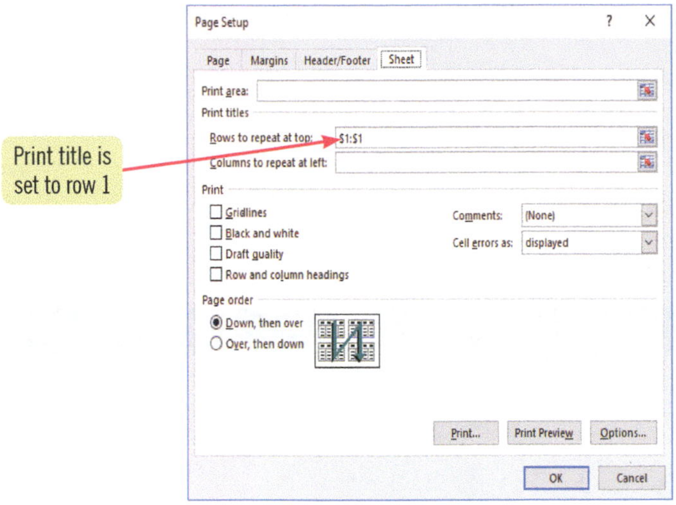

Print title is set to row 1

FIGURE 7-20: Printed table

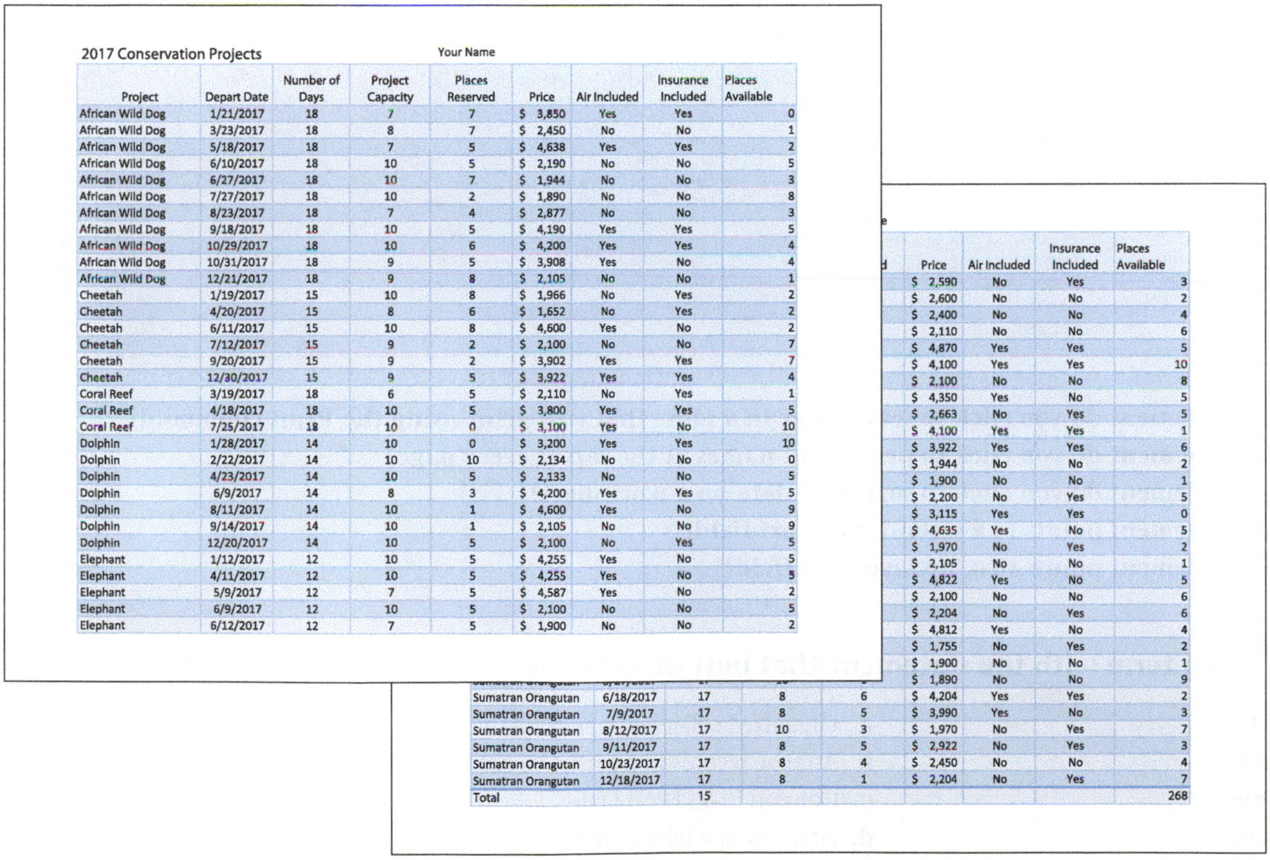

2017 Conservation Projects   Your Name

Project	Depart Date	Number of Days	Project Capacity	Places Reserved	Price	Air Included	Insurance Included	Places Available
African Wild Dog	1/21/2017	18	7	7	$ 3,850	Yes	Yes	0
African Wild Dog	3/23/2017	18	8	7	$ 2,450	No	No	1
African Wild Dog	5/18/2017	18	7	5	$ 4,638	Yes	Yes	2
African Wild Dog	6/10/2017	18	10	5	$ 2,190	No	No	5
African Wild Dog	6/27/2017	18	10	7	$ 1,944	No	No	3
African Wild Dog	7/27/2017	18	10	2	$ 1,890	No	No	8
African Wild Dog	8/23/2017	18	7	4	$ 2,877	No	No	3
African Wild Dog	9/18/2017	18	10	5	$ 4,190	Yes	Yes	5
African Wild Dog	10/29/2017	18	10	6	$ 4,200	Yes	Yes	4
African Wild Dog	10/31/2017	18	9	5	$ 3,908	Yes	No	4
African Wild Dog	12/21/2017	18	9	8	$ 2,105	No	No	1
Cheetah	1/19/2017	15	10	8	$ 1,966	No	Yes	2
Cheetah	4/20/2017	15	8	6	$ 1,652	No	Yes	2
Cheetah	6/11/2017	15	10	8	$ 4,600	Yes	No	2
Cheetah	7/12/2017	15	9	2	$ 2,100	No	No	7
Cheetah	9/20/2017	15	9	2	$ 3,902	Yes	Yes	7
Cheetah	12/30/2017	15	9	5	$ 3,922	Yes	Yes	4
Coral Reef	3/19/2017	18	6	5	$ 2,110	No	Yes	1
Coral Reef	4/18/2017	18	10	5	$ 3,800	Yes	Yes	5
Coral Reef	7/25/2017	18	10	0	$ 3,100	Yes	No	10
Dolphin	1/28/2017	14	10	0	$ 3,200	Yes	Yes	10
Dolphin	2/22/2017	14	10	10	$ 2,134	No	No	0
Dolphin	4/23/2017	14	10	5	$ 2,133	No	No	5
Dolphin	6/9/2017	14	8	3	$ 4,200	Yes	Yes	5
Dolphin	8/11/2017	14	10	1	$ 4,600	Yes	No	9
Dolphin	9/14/2017	14	10	1	$ 2,105	No	No	9
Dolphin	12/20/2017	14	10	5	$ 2,100	No	Yes	5
Elephant	1/12/2017	12	10	5	$ 4,255	Yes	No	5
Elephant	4/11/2017	12	10	5	$ 4,255	Yes	No	5
Elephant	5/9/2017	12	7	5	$ 4,587	Yes	No	2
Elephant	6/9/2017	12	10	5	$ 2,100	No	No	5
Elephant	6/12/2017	12	7	5	$ 1,900	No	No	2

Second printed page (partial):

Price	Air Included	Insurance Included	Places Available
$ 2,590	No	Yes	3
$ 2,600	No	No	2
$ 2,400	No	No	4
$ 2,110	No	No	6
$ 4,870	Yes	Yes	5
$ 4,100	Yes	Yes	10
$ 2,100	No	No	8
$ 4,350	Yes	No	5
$ 2,663	No	Yes	5
$ 4,100	Yes	Yes	1
$ 3,922	Yes	Yes	6
$ 1,944	No	No	2
$ 1,900	No	No	1
$ 2,200	No	Yes	5
$ 3,115	Yes	Yes	0
$ 4,635	Yes	No	5
$ 1,970	No	Yes	2
$ 2,105	No	No	1
$ 4,822	Yes	No	5
$ 2,100	No	No	6
$ 2,204	No	Yes	6
$ 4,812	Yes	No	4
$ 1,755	No	Yes	2
$ 1,900	No	No	1
$ 1,890	No	No	9

Project	Depart Date	Number of Days	Project Capacity	Places Reserved	Price	Air Included	Insurance Included	Places Available
Sumatran Orangutan	6/18/2017	17	8	6	$ 4,204	Yes	Yes	2
Sumatran Orangutan	7/9/2017	17	8	5	$ 3,990	Yes	No	3
Sumatran Orangutan	8/12/2017	17	10	3	$ 1,970	No	Yes	7
Sumatran Orangutan	9/11/2017	17	8	5	$ 2,922	No	Yes	3
Sumatran Orangutan	10/23/2017	17	8	4	$ 2,450	No	No	4
Sumatran Orangutan	12/18/2017	17	8	1	$ 2,204	No	Yes	7
Total		15						268

Setting a print area

Sometimes you will want to print only part of a worksheet. To do this, select any worksheet range, click the File tab, click Print, click the Print Active Sheets list arrow, then click Print Selection. If you want to print a selected area repeatedly, it's best to define a **print area**, the area of the worksheet that previews and prints when you use the Print command in Backstage view. To set a print area, select the range of data on the worksheet that you want to print, click the Page Layout tab, click the Print Area button in the Page Setup group, then click Set Print Area. You can add to the print area by selecting a range, clicking the Print Area button, then clicking Add to Print Area. A print area can consist of one contiguous range of cells, or multiple areas in different parts of a worksheet.

Practice

Concepts Review

FIGURE 7-21

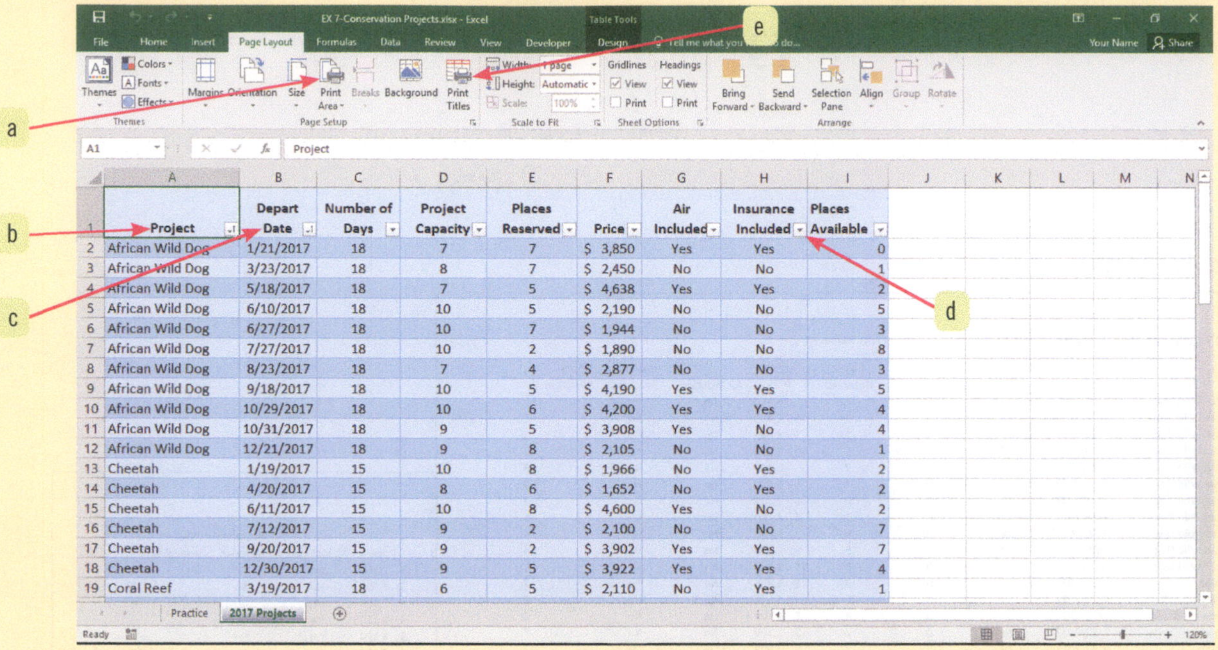

1. Which element do you click to set a range in a table that will print using the Print command?
2. Which element do you click to print field names at the top of every page?
3. Which element do you click to sort field data on a worksheet?
4. Which element points to a second-level sort field?
5. Which element points to a top-level sort field?

Match each term with the statement that best describes it.

6. Sort	a. Organized collection of related information in Excel
7. Field	b. Arrange records in a particular sequence
8. Table	c. Column in an Excel table
9. Record	d. First row of a table containing field names
10. Header row	e. Row in an Excel table

Select the best answer from the list of choices.

11. Which of the following series appears in descending order?
    a. 8, 6, 4, C, B, A
    b. 4, 5, 6, A, B, C
    c. 8, 7, 6, 5, 6, 7
    d. C, B, A, 6, 5, 4

12. Which of the following Excel options do you use to sort a table of employee names in order from Z to A?

a. Ascending
b. Absolute
c. Alphabetic
d. Descending

13. When printing a table on multiple pages, you can define a print title to:

a. Include the sheet name in table reports.
b. Include field names at the top of each printed page.
c. Exclude from the printout all rows under the first row.
d. Include gridlines in the printout.

14. You can easily add formatting to a table by using:

a. Table styles.
b. Print titles.
c. Print areas.
d. Calculated columns.

Skills Review

1. Create and format a table.

a. Start Excel, open EX 7-2.xlsx from the location where you store your Data Files, then save it as **EX 7-Employees**.

b. Using the Practice sheet, enter the field names in the first row and the first two records in rows two and three, as shown in the table below, adjusting column widths as necessary to fit the text entries.

Last Name	First Name	Years Employed	Department	Full/Part Time	Training Completed
Diamond	Irene	4	Support	P	Y
Mendez	Darryl	3	Sales	F	N

c. Define the data you entered as a table, then add a table style of Medium 9.

d. On the Staff sheet, define the cells containing data as a table with a header row. Adjust the column widths, if necessary, to display the field names. Enter your name in the center section of the worksheet footer, return to Normal view if necessary, then save the workbook.

e. Apply a table style of Light 19 to the table.

f. Enter your name in the center section of the worksheet footer, return to Normal view if necessary, then save the workbook.

2. Add table data.

a. Add a new record in row seven for **Holly Wallace**, a 5-year employee in the Support department. Holly works part time and has completed training. Adjust the height of the new row to match the other table rows.

b. Insert a table row above Julie Kosby's record, and add a new record for **Sally Alden**. Sally works full time, has worked at the company for 2 years in Sales, and has not completed training. Adjust the table formatting if necessary.

c. Insert a new data field in cell G1 with a label **Weeks Vacation**. Wrap the label in the cell to display the field name with **Weeks** above **Vacation**, and then widen the column as necessary to see both words. (*Hint:* Use the Wrap Text button in the Alignment group on the Home tab.)

d. Add a new column to the table by dragging the table's sizing handle, and give the new field a label of **Employee #**. Widen the column to fit the label.

e. Save the file.

3. Find and replace table data.

a. Return to cell A1.

b. Open the Find and Replace dialog box and, then if necessary uncheck the Match case option. Find the first record that contains the text **Support**.

c. Find the second and third records that contain the text **Support**.

d. Replace all **Support** text in the table with **Service**, then save the file.

Skills Review (continued)

4. Delete table data.

   a. Go to cell A1.

   b. Delete the record for Irene Diamond.

   c. Use the Remove Duplicates button to confirm that the table does not have any duplicate records.

   d. Delete the Employee # table column, then delete its column header, if necessary.

   e. Save the file.

5. Sort table data.

   a. Sort the table by Years Employed in largest to smallest order.

   b. Sort the table by Last Name in A to Z order.

   c. Perform a multilevel sort: Sort the table first by Full/Part Time in A to Z order and then by Last Name in A to Z order.

   d. Check the table to make sure the records appear in the correct order.

   e. Save the file.

6. Use formulas in a table.

   a. In cell G2, enter the formula that calculates an employee's vacation time; base the formula on the company policy that employees working at the company less than 4 years have 2 weeks of vacation. At 4 years of employment and longer, an employee has 3 weeks of vacation time. Use the table's field names where appropriate. (*Hint*: The formula is: **=IF([Years Employed]<4,2,3)**.)

   b. Check the table to make sure the formula filled into the cells in column G and that the correct vacation time is calculated for all cells in the column.

   c. Add a Total Row to display the total number of vacation weeks.

   d. Change the function in the Total Row to display the maximum number of vacation weeks. Change the entry in cell A8 from Total to **Maximum**.

   e. Compare your table to FIGURE 7-22, then save the workbook.

FIGURE 7-22

	A	B	C	D	E	F	G
1	Last Name	First Name	Years Employed	Department	Full/Part Time	Training Completed	Weeks Vacation
2	Alden	Sally	2	Sales	F	N	2
3	Green	Jane	1	Service	F	N	2
4	Kosby	Julie	4	Sales	F	Y	3
5	Mendez	Darryl	3	Sales	F	N	2
6	Ropes	Mark	1	Sales	P	Y	2
7	Wallace	Holly	5	Service	P	Y	3
8	Maximum						3

7. Print a table.

   a. Add a header that reads **Employees** in the left section, then format the header in bold with a font size of **16**.

   b. Add column A as a print title that repeats at the left of each printed page.

   c. Preview your table to check that the last names appear on both pages.

   d. Change the page orientation to landscape, preview the worksheet, then save the workbook.

   e. Submit your workbook to your instructor. Close the workbook, then exit Excel.

Independent Challenge 1

You are the clinical coordinator for an acupuncture clinic. Your administrative assistant created an Excel worksheet with client data including the results of a survey. You will create a table using the client data, and analyze the survey results to help focus the clinic's expenses in the most successful areas.

   a. Start Excel, open EX 7-3.xlsx from the location where you store your Data Files, then save it as **EX 7-Clients**.

   b. Create a table from the worksheet data, and apply Table Style Light 10.

Independent Challenge 1 (continued)

c. Add the two records shown in the table below:

Last Name	First Name	Street Address	City	State	Zip	Area Code	Ad Source
Ross	Kim	4 Ridge Rd.	San Francisco	CA	94177	415	Health Center
Jones	Kathy	512 17th St.	Seattle	WA	98001	206	Radio

d. Find the record for Mike Rondo, then delete it.

e. Click cell A1 and replace all instances of **TV** with **Social Media**.

f. Remove duplicate records where all fields are identical.

g. Sort the list by Last Name in A to Z order.

h. Sort the list again by Area Code in Smallest to Largest order.

i. Sort the table first by Survey Source in A to Z order, then by State in A to Z order. Compare your table to **FIGURE 7-23**.

FIGURE 7-23

	A	B	C	D	E	F	G	H
1	Last Name	First Name	Street Address	City	State	Zip	Area Code	Survey Source
2	Graham	Shelley	989 26th St.	Chicago	IL	60611	773	Education Website
3	Hogan	Andy	32 William St.	Concord	MA	01742	508	Education Website
4	Kelly	Shawn	22 Kendall St.	Cambridge	MA	02138	617	Education Website
5	Masters	Latrice	88 Las Puntas Rd.	Boston	MA	02205	617	Education Website
6	Nelson	Michael	229 Rally Rd.	Kansas City	MO	64105	816	Education Website
7	Dickenson	Tonia	883 E. 34th St.	New York	NY	10044	212	Education Website
8	Gonzales	Fred	5532 West St.	Houston	TX	77098	281	Education Website
9	Chelly	Yvonne	900 Sola St.	San Diego	CA	92106	619	Health Center
10	Worthen	Sally	2120 Central St.	San Francisco	CA	93772	415	Health Center
11	Malone	Kris	1 South St.	San Francisco	CA	94177	415	Health Center
12	Ross	Kim	4 Ridge Rd.	San Francisco	CA	94177	415	Health Center
13	Roberts	Bob	56 Water St.	Chicago	IL	60618	771	Health Center
14	Kim	Janie	9 First St.	San Francisco	CA	94177	415	Health Website
15	Oren	Scott	72 Yankee St.	Brookfield	CT	06830	203	Health Website
16	Duran	Maria	Galvin St.	Chicago	IL	60614	773	Health Website
17	Smith	Carolyn	921 Lopez St.	San Diego	CA	92104	619	Newspaper
18	Herbert	Greg	1192 Dome St.	San Diego	CA	93303	619	Newspaper
19	Kelly	Janie	9 First St.	San Francisco	CA	94177	415	Newspaper
20	Roberts	Bob	56 Water St.	Chicago	IL	60614	312	Newspaper
21	Miller	Hope	111 Stratton St.	Chicago	IL	60614	773	Newspaper
22	Warner	Salvatore	100 Westside St.	Chicago	IL	60620	312	Newspaper

j. Enter your name in the center section of the worksheet footer.

k. Add a centered header that reads **Client Survey** in bold with a font size of 16.

l. Add print titles to repeat the first row at the top of each printed page.

m. Save the workbook, preview it, then submit the workbook to your instructor.

n. Close the workbook, then exit Excel.

Independent Challenge 2

You manage Illuminate, a store that sells LED bulbs in bulk online. Your customers purchase items in quantities of 10 or more. You decide to plan and build a table that tracks recent sales, and includes customer information and transaction details.

a. Prepare a plan for a table that includes details about sales transactions, including the customer's name and what they purchased.

b. Sketch a sample table on a piece of paper, indicating how the table should be built. Create a table documenting the table design including the field names, type of data, and description of the data. Some examples of items are 60W Soft White, 65W Soft White, 60W Daylight, 65W Daylight, and 100W Daylight.

Independent Challenge 2 (continued)

c. Start Excel, create a new workbook, then save it as **EX 7-LED** in the location where you store your Data Files. Enter the field names shown in the table below in the designated cells:

cell	field name
A1	Customer Last
B1	Customer First
C1	Item
D1	Quantity
E1	Cost

d. Enter eight data records using your own data.

e. Define the data as a table using the data in the range A1:E9. Adjust the column widths as necessary.

f. Apply the Table Style Light 7 to the table.

g. Add a field named **Total** in cell F1.

h. Enter a formula in cell F2 that calculates the total by multiplying the Quantity field by the Cost field. Check that the formula was filled down in the column.

i. Format the Cost and Total columns using the Accounting number format. Adjust the column widths as necessary.

j. Add a new record to your table in row 10. Add another record above row 4.

k. Sort the table in ascending order by Cost.

l. Enter your name in the worksheet footer, then save the workbook.

m. Preview the worksheet, then submit your workbook to your instructor.

n. Close the workbook, then exit Excel.

Independent Challenge 3

You are a sales manager at a consulting firm. You are managing your accounts using an Excel worksheet and have decided that a table will provide additional features to help you keep track of the accounts. You will use the table sorting features and table formulas to analyze your account data.

a. Start Excel, open EX 7-4.xlsx from the location where you store your Data Files, then save it as **EX 7-Accounts**.

b. Create a table with the worksheet data, and apply a table style of your choice. Adjust the column widths as necessary.

c. Sort the table on the Budget field using the Smallest to Largest order.

d. Sort the table using two fields, first by Contact in A to Z order, then by Budget in Smallest to Largest order.

e. Add the new field label **Balance** in cell G1, and adjust the column width as necessary.

f. Enter a formula in cell G2 that uses structured references to table fields to calculate the balance on an account as the Budget minus the Expenses.

g. Add a new record with an account number of **4113** with a type of **Inside**, a code of **I5**, a budget of **$550,000**, expenses of **$400,000**, and a contact of **Maureen Smith**.

h. Verify that the formula accurately calculated the balance for the new record.

i. Replace all of the Maureen Smith data with **Maureen Lang**.

j. Find the record for the 2188 account number and delete it.

k. Delete the Type and code fields from the table.

Independent Challenge 3 (continued)

l. Add a total row to the table and display the totals for appropriate columns. Adjust the column widths as necessary. Compare your table to **FIGURE 7-24**. (Your table style may differ.)

FIGURE 7-24

	A	B	C	D	E
1	Account Number	Budget	Expenses	Contact	Balance
2	1084	$ 275,000	$ 215,000	Cindy Boil	$ 60,000
3	5431	$ 375,000	$ 250,000	Cindy Boil	$ 125,000
4	9624	$ 650,000	$ 550,000	Cindy Boil	$ 100,000
5	2117	$ 550,000	$ 525,000	Kathy Jenkins	$ 25,000
6	5647	$ 750,000	$ 600,000	Kathy Jenkins	$ 150,000
7	6671	$ 175,000	$ 150,000	Maureen Lang	$ 25,000
8	1097	$ 250,000	$ 210,000	Maureen Lang	$ 40,000
9	4301	$ 350,000	$ 210,000	Maureen Lang	$ 140,000
10	7814	$ 410,000	$ 320,000	Maureen Lang	$ 90,000
11	4113	$ 550,000	$ 400,000	Maureen Lang	$ 150,000
12	Total	$ 4,335,000	$ 3,430,000		$ 905,000
13					
14					

m. Enter your name in the center section of the worksheet footer, add a center section header of **Accounts** using formatting of your choice, change the page orientation to landscape, then save the workbook.

n. Preview your workbook, submit the workbook to your instructor, close the workbook, then exit Excel.

Independent Challenge 4: Explore

As the sales manager at a environmental supply firm, you track the sales data of the associates in the department using a table in Excel. You decide to highlight associates that have met the annual sales targets for the annual meeting.

a. Start Excel, open EX 7-5.xlsx from the location where you store your Data Files, then save it as **EX 7-Sales**.

b. Create a table that includes all the worksheet data, and apply the table style of your choice. Adjust the column widths as necessary.

c. Sort the table on the Balance field using the Largest to Smallest order.

d. Use conditional formatting to format the cells of the table containing positive balances with a light red fill.

e. Sort the table using the Balance field using the order of No Fill on top.

f. Format the table to emphasize the Balance column, and turn off the banded rows. (*Hint*: Use the Table Style Options on the Table Tools Design tab.)

g. Research how to print nonadjacent areas on a single page. (Excel prints nonadjacent areas of a worksheet on separate pages by default.) Add a new sheet to the workbook, then enter the result of your research on Sheet2 of the workbook.

h. Return to Sheet1 and create a print area that prints only the Employee Number, Associate, and Balance columns of the table on one page.

FIGURE 7-25

	A	B	E
1	Employee Number	Associate	Balance
2	6547	Larry Makay	$ (5,000)
3	2984	George Well	$ (10,000)
4	4874	George Well	$ (73,126)
5	6647	Kris Lowe	$ (95,000)
6	5512	Nancy Alden	$ 108,357
7	3004	Lou Colby	$ 95,000
8	4257	Bob Allen	$ 50,000
9	9821	Joe Wood	$ 45,000
10	8624	Judy Smith	$ 25,000
11	1005	Janet Casey	$ 17,790

i. Compare your table with **FIGURE 7-25**. Save the workbook.

j. Preview your print area to make sure it will print on a single page.

k. Enter your name in the worksheet footer, then save the workbook.

l. Submit the workbook to your instructor, close the workbook, then exit Excel.

Visual Workshop

Start Excel, open EX 7-6.xlsx from the location where you store your Data Files, then save it as **EX 7-Technicians**. Create a table and sort the data as shown in FIGURE 7-26. (*Hint*: The table is formatted using Table Style Medium 13.) Add a worksheet header with the sheet name in the center section that is formatted in bold with a size of 14. Enter your name in the center section of the worksheet footer. Save the workbook, preview the table, close the workbook, submit the workbook to your instructor, then exit Excel.

FIGURE 7-26

	Job Number	Employee Number	Amount Billed	Location	Technician Name
2	2257	69741	$ 109.88	Main	Eric Mallon
3	1032	65418	$ 158.32	Satellite	Eric Mallon
4	1587	10057	$ 986.34	Main	Jerry Thomas
5	1533	66997	$ 112.98	Satellite	Jerry Thomas
6	2187	58814	$ 521.77	Satellite	Jerry Thomas
7	2588	69784	$ 630.55	Main	Joan Rand
8	2001	48779	$ 478.24	Satellite	Joan Rand
9	1251	69847	$ 324.87	Main	Kathy Green
10	2113	36697	$ 163.88	Main	Kathy Green
11	2357	10087	$ 268.24	Main	Mark Eaton
12	1111	13987	$ 658.30	Satellite	Mark Eaton

Analyzing Table Data

CASE ▶ The vice president of sales and marketing, Mary Watson, asks you to display information from a table of scheduled projects to help the sales representatives with customer inquiries. She also asks you to summarize the project sales for a presentation at the international sales meeting. You will prepare these using various filters, subtotals, and Excel functions.

Module Objectives

After completing this module, you will be able to:

- Filter a table
- Create a custom filter
- Filter a table with the Advanced Filter
- Extract table data
- Look up values in a table
- Summarize table data
- Validate table data
- Create subtotals

Files You Will Need

EX 8-1.xlsx	EX 8-5.xlsx
EX 8-2.xlsx	EX 8-6.xlsx
EX 8-3.xlsx	EX 8-7.xlsx
EX 8-4.xlsx	

Filter a Table

Learning Outcomes
• Filter records using AutoFilter
• Filter records using search criteria

An Excel table lets you easily manipulate large amounts of data to view only the data you want, using a feature called **AutoFilter**. When you create a table, arrows automatically appear next to each column header. These arrows are called **filter list arrows**, **AutoFilter list arrows**, or **list arrows**, and you can use them to **filter** a table to display only the records that meet criteria you specify, temporarily hiding records that do not meet those criteria. For example, you can use the filter list arrow next to the Project field header to display only records that contain Cheetah in the Project field. Once you filter data, you can copy, chart, and print the displayed records. You can easily clear a filter to redisplay all the records. **CASE** *Mary asks you to display only the records for the Cheetah projects. She also asks for information about the projects that have the most reservations and the projects that depart in March.*

STEPS

1. **Start Excel, open EX 8-1.xlsx from where you store your Data Files, then save it as EX 8-Projects**

2. **Click the Project list arrow**

   Sort options appear at the top of the menu, advanced filtering options appear in the middle, and at the bottom is a list of the project data from column A, as shown in **FIGURE 8-1**. Because you want to display data for only the Cheetah projects, your **search criterion** (the text you are searching for) is Cheetah. You can select one of the Project data options in the menu, which acts as your search criterion.

3. **In the list of projects for the Project field, click Select All to clear the check marks from the projects, scroll down the list of projects, click Cheetah, then click OK**

   Only those records containing "Cheetah" in the Project field appear, as shown in **FIGURE 8-2**. The row numbers for the matching records change to blue, and the list arrow for the filtered field has a filter icon ⊤. Both indicate that there is a filter in effect and that some of the records are temporarily hidden.

4. **Move the pointer over the Project list arrow**

   The ScreenTip Project: Equals "Cheetah" describes the filter for the field, meaning that only the Cheetah records appear. You decide to remove the filter to redisplay all of the table data.

5. **Click the Project list arrow, then click Clear Filter From "Project"**

   You have cleared the Cheetah filter, and all the records reappear. You want to display the most popular projects, those that are in the top five percent of seats reserved.

6. **Click the Places Reserved list arrow, point to Number Filters, click Top 10, select 10 in the middle box, type 5, click the Items list arrow, click Percent, then click OK**

   Excel displays the records for the top five percent in the number of Places Reserved field, as shown in **FIGURE 8-3**. You decide to clear the filter to redisplay all the records.

7. **On the Home tab, click the Sort & Filter button in the Editing group, then click Clear**

   You have cleared the filter and all the records reappear. You can clear a filter using either the AutoFilter menu command or the Sort & Filter button on the Home tab. The Sort & Filter button is convenient for clearing multiple filters at once. You want to find all of the projects that depart in March.

8. **Click the Depart Date list arrow, point to Date Filters, point to All Dates in the Period, then click March**

   Excel displays the records for only the projects that leave in March. You decide to clear the filter and display all of the records.

9. **Click the Sort & Filter button in the Editing group, click Clear, then save the workbook**

Analyzing Table Data

FIGURE 8-1: Worksheet showing AutoFilter options

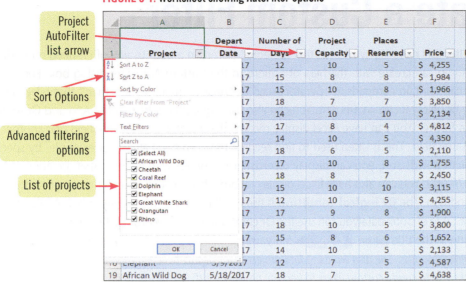

Project AutoFilter list arrow

Sort Options

Advanced filtering options

List of projects

FIGURE 8-2: Table filtered to show Cheetah projects

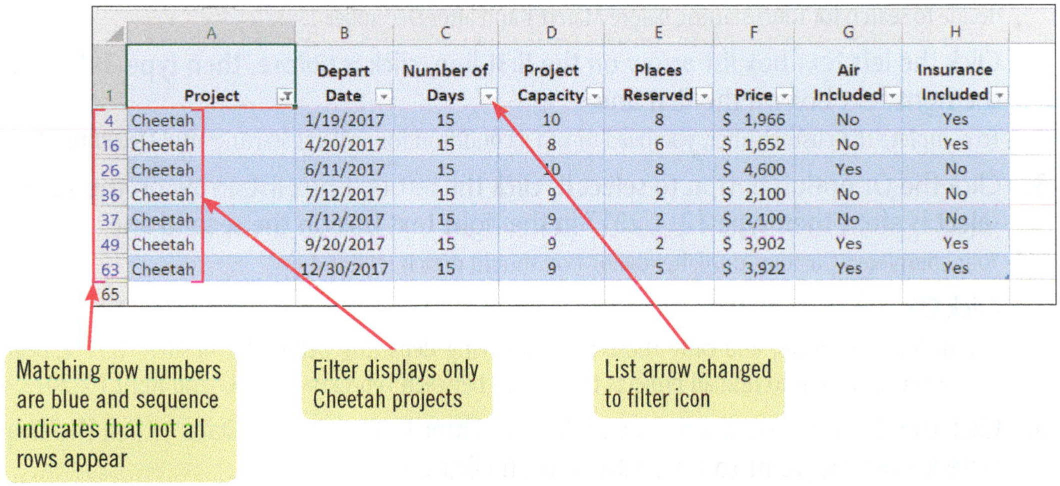

	A	B	C	D	E	F	G	H
1	Project	Depart Date	Number of Days	Project Capacity	Places Reserved	Price	Air Included	Insurance Included
4	Cheetah	1/19/2017	15	10	8	$ 1,966	No	Yes
16	Cheetah	4/20/2017	15	8	6	$ 1,652	No	Yes
26	Cheetah	6/11/2017	15	10	8	$ 4,600	Yes	No
36	Cheetah	7/12/2017	15	9	2	$ 2,100	No	No
37	Cheetah	7/12/2017	15	9	2	$ 2,100	No	No
49	Cheetah	9/20/2017	15	9	2	$ 3,902	Yes	Yes
63	Cheetah	12/30/2017	15	9	5	$ 3,922	Yes	Yes
65								

Matching row numbers are blue and sequence indicates that not all rows appear

Filter displays only Cheetah projects

List arrow changed to filter icon

FIGURE 8-3: Table filtered with top 5% of Places Reserved

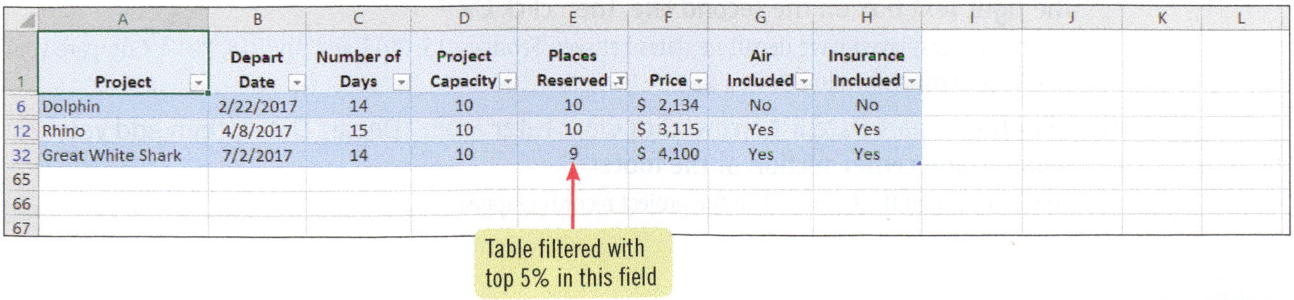

	A	B	C	D	E	F	G	H	I	J	K	L
1	Project	Depart Date	Number of Days	Project Capacity	Places Reserved	Price	Air Included	Insurance Included				
6	Dolphin	2/22/2017	14	10	10	$ 2,134	No	No				
12	Rhino	4/8/2017	15	10	10	$ 3,115	Yes	Yes				
32	Great White Shark	7/2/2017	14	10	9	$ 4,100	Yes	Yes				
65												
66												
67												

Table filtered with top 5% in this field

Create a Custom Filter

While AutoFilter lists can display records that are equal to certain amounts, you often need more detailed filters, which you can create with the help of options in the Custom AutoFilter dialog box. For example, your criteria can contain comparison operators such as "greater than" or "less than" that let you display values above or below a certain amount. You can also use **logical conditions** like And and Or to narrow a search even further. You can have Excel display records that meet a criterion in a field *and* another criterion in that same field. This is often used to find records between two values. For example, by specifying an **And logical condition**, you can display records for customers with incomes that are above $40,000 *and* below $70,000. You can also have Excel display records that meet either criterion in a field by specifying an Or condition. The **Or logical condition** is used to find records that satisfy either of two values. For example, in a table of book data you can use the Or condition to find records that contain either Beginning *or* Introduction in the title name. **CASE** *Mary wants to locate projects for customers who want to participate in the winter months. She also wants to find projects that depart between February 15, 2017 and April 15, 2017. She asks you to create custom filters to find the projects satisfying these criteria.*

STEPS

1. **Click the Depart Date list arrow, point to Date Filters, then click Custom Filter**

   The Custom AutoFilter dialog box opens. You enter your criteria in the text boxes. The left text box on the first line currently displays "equals." Because you want to find all projects that occur in the winter months, you decide to search for tours starting before March 1 and after December 1.

2. **Click the left text box list arrow on the first line, click is before, then type 3/1/2017 in the right text box on the first line**

   To complete the custom filter, you need to add a condition for projects starting after December 1.

3. **Click the Or option button to select it, click the left text box list arrow on the second line, select is after, then type 12/1/2017 in the right text box on the second line**

   Your completed Custom AutoFilter dialog box should match **FIGURE 8-4**.

4. **Click OK**

   The dialog box closes, and only those records having departing before 3/1 or after 12/1 appear in the worksheet. You want to find all projects that depart between February 15, 2017 and April 15, 2017.

5. **Click the Depart Date list arrow, click Clear Filter From "Depart Date", click the Depart Date list arrow, point to Date Filters, then click Custom Filter**

   You want to find the departure dates that are between February 15, 2017 and April 15, 2017 (that is, after February 15 *and* before April 15).

6. **Click the left text box list arrow on the first line, click is after, then type 2/15/2017 in the right text box on the first line**

   The And condition is selected, which is correct.

7. **Click the left text box list arrow on the second line, select is before, type 4/15/2017 in the right text box on the second line, then click OK**

   The records displayed have departure dates between February 15, 2017 and April 15, 2017. Compare your records to those shown in **FIGURE 8-5**.

8. **Click the Depart Date list arrow, click Clear Filter From "Depart Date", then add your name to the center section of the footer**

   You have cleared the filter, and all the project records reappear.

FIGURE 8-4: Custom AutoFilter dialog box

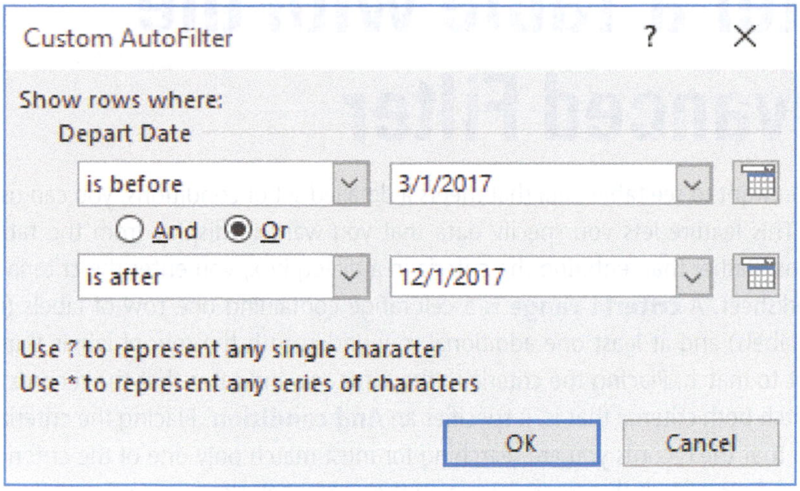

FIGURE 8-5: Results of custom filter

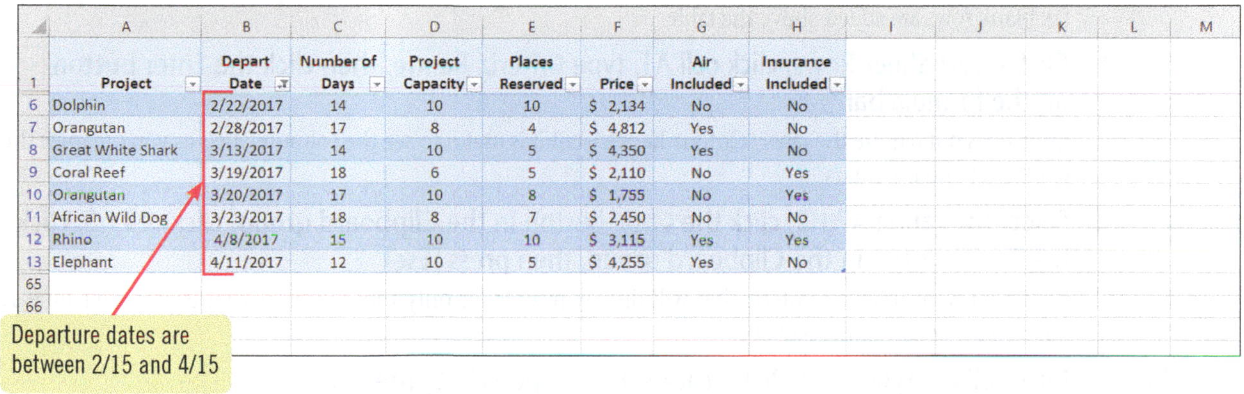

	A	B	C	D	E	F	G	H	I	J	K	L	M
1	Project	Depart Date	Number of Days	Project Capacity	Places Reserved	Price	Air Included	Insurance Included					
6	Dolphin	2/22/2017	14	10	10	$ 2,134	No	No					
7	Orangutan	2/28/2017	17	8	4	$ 4,812	Yes	No					
8	Great White Shark	3/13/2017	14	10	5	$ 4,350	Yes	No					
9	Coral Reef	3/19/2017	18	6	5	$ 2,110	No	Yes					
10	Orangutan	3/20/2017	17	10	8	$ 1,755	No	Yes					
11	African Wild Dog	3/23/2017	18	8	7	$ 2,450	No	No					
12	Rhino	4/8/2017	15	10	10	$ 3,115	Yes	Yes					
13	Elephant	4/11/2017	12	10	5	$ 4,255	Yes	No					
65													
66													

Departure dates are between 2/15 and 4/15

Using more than one rule when conditionally formatting data

You can apply conditional formatting to table cells in the same way that you can format a range of worksheet data. You can add multiple rules by clicking the Home tab, clicking the Conditional Formatting button in the Styles group, then clicking New Rule for each additional rule that you want to apply. You can also add rules using the Conditional Formatting Rules Manager, which displays all of the rules for a data range. To use the Rules Manager, click the Home tab, click the

Conditional Formatting button in the Styles group, click Manage Rules, then click New Rule for each rule that you want to apply to the data range. You can also use a function to conditionally format cells. For example, if you have a column of invoice dates and you want to format the dates that are overdue, open the Rules Manager, click Use a formula in the Select a Rule Type section, and then edit the rule description add a formula such as "<TODAY()."

Filter a Table with the Advanced Filter

Learning Outcomes
• Filter records using a criteria range and the And condition
• Filter records using a criteria range and the Or condition

When you want to see table data that meets a detailed set of conditions, you can use the Advanced Filter feature. This feature lets you specify data that you want to display from the table using And and Or conditions. Rather than entering the criteria in a dialog box, you enter the criteria in a criteria range on your worksheet. A **criteria range** is a cell range containing one row of labels (usually a copy of the column labels) and at least one additional row underneath the row of labels that contains the criteria you want to match. Placing the criteria in the same row indicates that the records you are searching for must match both criteria; that is, it specifies an **And condition**. Placing the criteria in the different rows indicates that the records you are searching for must match only one of the criterion; that is, it specifies an **Or condition**. With the criteria range on the worksheet, you can easily see the criteria by which your table is sorted. Another advantage of the Advanced Filter is that you can move filtered table data to a different area of the worksheet or to a new worksheet, as you will see in the next lesson. **CASE** ▸ *Mary wants to identify projects that depart after 6/1/2017 and that cost less than $2,000. She asks you to use the Advanced Filter to retrieve these records. You begin by defining the criteria range.*

STEPS

1. **Select table rows 1 through 6, then click the Insert list arrow in the Cells group**
   Six blank rows are added above the table.

2. **Click Insert Sheet Rows; click cell A1, type Criteria Range, then click the Enter button ☑ on the formula bar**
   Excel does not require the label "Criteria Range", but it is useful to see the column labels as you organize the worksheet and use filters.

QUICK TIP
You can apply multiple criteria by using AutoFilter a second time on the results of the previously filtered data. Each additional filter builds on the results of the filtered data and filters the data further.

3. **Select the range A7:H7, click the Copy button in the Clipboard group, click cell A2, click the Paste button in the Clipboard group, then press [Esc]**
   Next, you want to insert criteria that will display records for only those projects that depart after June 1, 2017 and that cost under $2,000.

4. **Click cell B3, type >6/1/2017, click cell F3, type <2000, then click ☑**
   You have entered the criteria in the cells directly beneath the Criteria Range labels, as shown in **FIGURE 8-6**.

5. **Click any cell in the table, click the Data tab, then click the Advanced button in the Sort & Filter group**
   The Advanced Filter dialog box opens, with the table (list) range already entered. The default setting under Action is to filter the table in its current location ("in-place") rather than copy it to another location.

TROUBLE
If your filtered records don't match the figure, make sure there are no spaces between the > symbol and the 6 in cell B3, and the < symbol and the 2 in cell F3.

6. **Click the Criteria range text box, select the range A2:H3 in the worksheet, then click OK**
   You have specified the criteria range and used the filter. The filtered table contains seven records that match both criteria—the departure date is after 6/1/2017 and the price is less than $2,000, as shown in **FIGURE 8-7**. You'll filter this table even further in the next lesson.

FIGURE 8-6: Criteria in the same row indicating an and condition

	A	B	C	D	E	F	G	H	I	J	K	L
1	Criteria Range											
2	Project	Depart Date	Number of Days	Project Capacity	Places Reserved	Price	Air Included	Insurance Included				
3		>6/1/2017				<2000						
4												
5												
6												
7	Project	...ber of Date	Number of Days	Project Capacity	Places Reserved	Price	Air Included	Insurance Included				
8	Elephant	1/12/2017	12	10	5	$ 4,255	Yes	No				
9	Rhino	1/13/2017	15	8	8	$ 1,984	No	No				

Filtered records will match these criteria

FIGURE 8-7: Filtered table

	A	B	C	D	E	F	G	H	I	J	K	L	M
1	Criteria Range												
2	Project	Depart Date	Number of Days	Project Capacity	Places Reserved	Price	Air Included	Insurance Included					
3		>6/1/2017				<2000							
4													
5													
6													
7	Project	Depart Date	Number of Days	Project Capacity	Places Reserved	Price	Air Included	Insurance Included					
33	Elephant	6/12/2017	12	7	5	$ 1,900	No	No					
34	Rhino	6/12/2017	15	8	6	$ 1,970	No	Yes					
37	African Wild Dog	6/27/2017	18	10	7	$ 1,944	No	No					
44	African Wild Dog	7/27/2017	18	10	2	$ 1,890	No	No					
46	Orangutan	8/12/2017	17	10	3	$ 1,970	No	Yes					
49	Great White Shark	8/27/2017	14	10	8	$ 1,944	No	No					
61	Great White Shark	10/31/2017	14	9	8	$ 1,900	No	No					
71													
72													

Depart dates are after 6/1/2017

Prices are less than $2000

Saving time with conditional formatting

You can emphasize top- or bottom-ranked values in a field using conditional formatting. To highlight the top or bottom values in a field, select the field data, click the Conditional Formatting button in the Styles group on the Home tab, point to Top/Bottom Rules, select a Top or Bottom rule, if necessary enter the percentage or number of cells in the selected range that you want to format, select the format for the cells that meet the top or bottom criteria, then click OK. You can also format your worksheet or table data using icon sets and color scales based on the cell values. A **color scale** uses a set of two, three, or four fill colors to convey relative values. For example, red could fill cells to indicate they have higher values and green could signify lower values. To add a color scale, select a data range, click the Home tab, click the Conditional Formatting

button in the Styles group, then point to Color Scales. On the submenu, you can select preformatted color sets or click More Rules to create your own color sets. **Icon sets** let you visually communicate relative cell values by adding icons to cells based on the values they contain. An upward-pointing green arrow might represent the highest values, and downward-pointing red arrows could represent lower values. To add an icon set to a data range, select a data range, click the Conditional Formatting button in the Styles group, then point to Icon Sets. You can customize the values that are used as thresholds for color scales and icon sets by clicking the Conditional Formatting button in the Styles group, clicking Manage Rules, clicking the rule in the Conditional Formatting Rules Manager dialog box, then clicking Edit Rule.

Extract Table Data

Whenever you take the time to specify a complicated set of search criteria, it's a good idea to extract the matching records, rather than filtering it in place. When you **extract** data, you place a copy of a filtered table in a range that you specify in the Advanced Filter dialog box. This way, you won't accidentally clear the filter or lose track of the records you spent time compiling. To extract data, you use an Advanced Filter and enter the criteria beneath the copied field names, as you did in the previous lesson. You then specify the location where you want the extracted data to appear. **CASE** ▶ *Mary needs to filter the table one step further to reflect only African Wild Dog or Great White Shark projects in the current filtered table. She asks you to complete this filter by specifying an Or condition, which you will do by entering two sets of criteria in two separate rows. You decide to save the filtered records by extracting them to a different location in the worksheet.*

STEPS

1. **In cell A3 enter African Wild Dog, then in cell A4 enter Great White Shark**

   The new sets of criteria need to appear in two separate rows, so you need to copy the previous filter criteria to the second row.

2. **Copy the criteria in cells B3:F3 to B4:F4**

   The criteria are shown in **FIGURE 8-8**. When you use the Advanced Filter this time, you indicate that you want to copy the filtered table to a range beginning in cell A75, so that Mary can easily refer to the data, even if you use more filters later.

3. **If necessary, click the Data tab, then click Advanced in the Sort & Filter group**

4. **Under Action, click the Copy to another location option button to select it, click the Copy to text box, then type A75**

   The last time you filtered the table, the criteria range included only rows 2 and 3. Now you have criteria in row 4, so you need to adjust the criteria range.

5. **Edit the contents of the Criteria range text box to show the range $A$2:$H$4, click OK, then if necessary scroll down until row 75 is visible**

   The matching records appear in the range beginning in cell A75, as shown in **FIGURE 8-9**. The original table, starting in cell A7, contains the records filtered in the previous lesson.

6. **Press [Ctrl][Home], then click the Clear button in the Sort & Filter group**

   The original table is displayed starting in cell A7, and the extracted table remains in A75:H79.

7. **Save the workbook**

FIGURE 8-8: Criteria in separate rows

	A	B	C	D	E	F	G	H	I	J	K
1	Criteria Range										
2	Project	Depart Date	Number of Days	Project Capacity	Places Reserved	Price	Air Included	Insurance Included			
3	African Wild Dog	>6/1/2017				<2000					
4	Great White Shark	>6/1/2017				<2000					

Criteria on two lines indicates an OR condition

FIGURE 8-9: Extracted data records

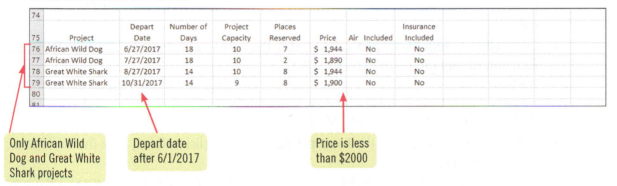

	Project	Depart Date	Number of Days	Project Capacity	Places Reserved	Price	Air Included	Insurance Included			
74											
75	Project	Depart Date	Number of Days	Project Capacity	Places Reserved	Price	Air Included	Insurance Included			
76	African Wild Dog	6/27/2017	18	10	7	$ 1,944	No	No			
77	African Wild Dog	7/27/2017	18	10	2	$ 1,890	No	No			
78	Great White Shark	8/27/2017	14	10	8	$ 1,944	No	No			
79	Great White Shark	10/31/2017	14	9	8	$ 1,900	No	No			
80											
81											

Only African Wild Dog and Great White Shark projects

Depart date after 6/1/2017

Price is less than $2000

Understanding the criteria range and the copy-to location

When you define the criteria range and the copy-to location in the Advanced Filter dialog box, Excel automatically creates the range names Criteria and Extract for these ranges in the worksheet. The Criteria range includes the field names and any criteria rows underneath them. The Extract range includes just the field names above the extracted table. You can select these ranges by clicking the Name box list arrow, then clicking the range name. If you click the Name Manager button in the Defined Names group on the Formulas tab, you will see these new names and the ranges associated with each one.

Look Up Values in a Table

The Excel VLOOKUP function helps you locate specific values in a table. VLOOKUP searches vertically (V) down the far left column of a table, then reads across the row to find the value in the column you specify, much as you might look up a number in a name and address list: You locate a person's name, then read across the row to find the phone number you want. **CASE** *Mary wants to be able to find a project by entering the project code. You will use the VLOOKUP function to accomplish this task. You begin by viewing the table name so you can refer to it in a lookup function.*

STEPS

1. **Click the Lookup sheet tab, click the Formulas tab in the Ribbon, then click the Name Manager button in the Defined Names group**

   The named ranges for the workbook appear in the Name Manager dialog box, as shown in **FIGURE 8-10**. The Criteria and Extract ranges appear at the top of the range name list. At the bottom of the list is information about the three tables in the workbook. Table1 refers to the table on the 2017 Projects sheet, Table2 refers to the table on the Lookup sheet, and Table3 refers to the table on the Subtotals worksheet. The Excel structured reference feature automatically created these table names when the tables were created.

2. **Click Close**

   You want to find the project represented by the code 754Q. The VLOOKUP function lets you find the project name for any project code. You will enter a project code in cell M1 and a VLOOKUP function in cell M2.

3. **Click cell M1, enter 754Q, click cell M2, click the Lookup & Reference button in the Function Library group, then click VLOOKUP**

   The Function Arguments dialog box opens, with boxes for each of the VLOOKUP arguments. Because the value you want to find is in cell M1, M1 is the Lookup_value. The table you want to search is the table on the Lookup sheet, so its assigned name, Table2, is the Table_array.

4. **With the insertion point in the Lookup_value text box, click cell M1, click the Table_array text box, then type Table2**

   The column containing the information that you want to find and display in cell M2 is the second column from the left in the table range, so the Col_index_num is 2. Because you want to find an exact match for the value in cell M1, the Range_lookup argument is FALSE.

5. **Click the Col_index_num text box, type 2, click the Range_lookup text box, then enter FALSE**

   Your completed Function Arguments dialog box should match **FIGURE 8-11**.

6. **Click OK**

   Excel searches down the far-left column of the table until it finds a project code that matches the one in cell M1. It then looks in column 2 of the table range and finds the project for that record, Dolphin, and displays it in cell M2. You use this function to determine the project for one other project code.

7. **Click cell M1, type 335P, then click the Enter button ✓ on the formula bar**

   The VLOOKUP function returns the value of Elephant in cell M2.

8. **Press [Ctrl][Home], then save the workbook**

FIGURE 8-10: Named ranges in the workbook

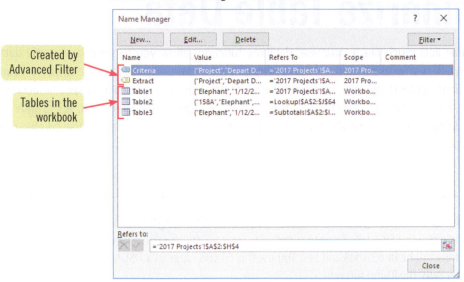

Created by Advanced Filter

Tables in the workbook

FIGURE 8-11: Completed Function Arguments dialog box for VLOOKUP

Range name of table to search

Location of value you want to search for

Search the second column

Finds exact match

Using other LOOKUP functions

When your data is arranged horizontally in rows instead of vertically in columns, use the HLOOKUP (Horizontal Lookup) function. HLOOKUP searches horizontally across the upper row of a table until it finds the matching value, then looks down the number of rows you specify. The arguments are identical to those for the VLOOKUP function, except that instead of a Col_index_number, HLOOKUP uses a Row_index_number, which indicates the location of the row you want to search. You can use the MATCH function when you want the position of an item in a range. The MATCH function uses the syntax: MATCH (lookup_value,lookup_array,match_ type) where the lookup_value is the value you want to match in the lookup_ array range. The match_type can be 0 for an exact match,

1 for matching the largest value that is less than or equal to lookup_value, or –1 for matching the smallest value that is greater than or equal to the lookup_value. The Transpose function is a LOOKUP function that can be used to rearrange a range of cells, which is also called an array. For example, a vertical range of cells will be arranged horizontally or vice versa. The Transpose array function is entered using the syntax: =TRANSPOSE(range array).

The LOOKUP function is used to locate information in a table. The syntax for the LOOKUP formula is LOOKUP(lookup_value, array). The lookup_value is the value that will be used in the search, the array is the range of cells that will be searched for the lookup_value.

Summarize Table Data

Because a table acts much like a database, database functions allow you to summarize table data in a variety of ways. When working with a sales activity table, for example, you can use Excel to count the number of client contacts by sales representative or to total the amount sold to specific accounts by month. **TABLE 8-1** lists database functions commonly used to summarize table data. **CASE** *Mary is considering adding projects for the 2017 schedule. She needs your help in evaluating the number of places available for scheduled projects.*

STEPS

1. **Review the criteria range for the Rhino project in the range L5:L6**

   The criteria range in L5:L6 tells Excel to summarize records with the entry "Rhino" in the Project column. The functions will be in cells M8 and M9. You use this criteria range in a DSUM function to sum the places available for only the Rhino projects.

2. **Click cell M8, click the Insert Function button in the Function Library group, in the Search for a function text box type database, click Go, scroll to and click DSUM under Select a function, then click OK**

   The first argument of the DSUM function is the table, or database.

3. **In the Function Arguments dialog box, with the insertion point in the Database text box, move the pointer over the upper-left corner of cell A1 until the pointer changes to ↘, click once, then click again**

   The first click selects the table's data range, and the second click selects the entire table, including the header row. The second argument of the DSUM function is the label for the column that you want to sum. You want to total the number of available places. The last argument for the DSUM function is the criteria that will be used to determine which values to total.

4. **Click the Field text box, then click cell G1, Places Available; click the Criteria text box and select the range L5:L6**

   Your completed Function Arguments dialog box should match **FIGURE 8-12**.

5. **Click OK**

   The result in cell M8 is 25. Excel totaled the information in the Places Available column for those records that meet the criterion of Project equals Rhino. The DCOUNT and the DCOUNTA functions can help you determine the number of records meeting specified criteria in a database field. DCOUNTA counts the number of nonblank cells. You will use DCOUNTA to determine the number of projects scheduled.

6. **Click cell M9, click the Insert Function button ƒx on the formula bar, in the Search for a function text box type database, click Go, then double-click DCOUNTA in the Select a function list**

7. **With the insertion point in the Database text box, move the pointer over the upper-left corner of cell A1 until the pointer changes to ↘, click once, click again to include the header row, click the Field text box, click cell B1, click the Criteria text box and select the range L5:L6, then click OK**

   The result in cell M9 is 8, and it indicates that there are eight Rhino projects scheduled for the year. You also want to display the number of places available for the Dolphin projects.

8. **Click cell L6, type Dolphin, then click the Enter button ☑ on the formula bar**

   The formulas in cells M8 and M9 are updated to reflect the new criteria. **FIGURE 8-13** shows that 33 places are available in the six scheduled Dolphin projects.

FIGURE 8-12: Completed Function Arguments dialog box for DSUM

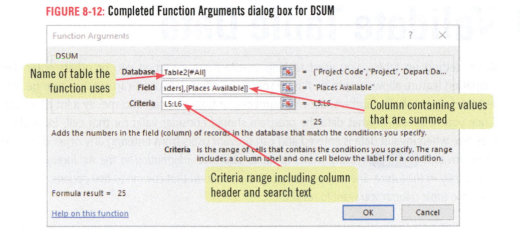

Name of table the function uses → Database

Column containing values that are summed

Criteria range including column header and search text

FIGURE 8-13: Result generated by database functions

	Project Capacity	Places Reserved	Places Available	Price	Air Included	Insurance Included			
1								Project Code	335P
2	10	5	5	$ 4,255	Yes	No		Project	Elephant
3	8	8	0	$ 1,984	No	No		*Project Information*	
4	10	8	2	$ 1,966	No	Yes			
5	7	7	0	$ 3,850	Yes	Yes		Project	
6	10	10	0	$ 2,134	No	No		Dolphin	
7	8	4	4	$ 4,812	Yes	No			
8	10	5	5	$ 4,350	Yes	No		Places Available	33
9	6	5	1	$ 2,110	No	Yes		Number of projects scheduled	6
10	10	8	2	$ 1,755	No	Yes			
11	8	7	1	$ 2,450	No	No			
12	10	10	0	$ 3,115	Yes	Yes			
13	10	5	5	$ 4,255	Yes	No			
14	9	8	1	$ 1,900	No	No			

Information for Dolphin projects

TABLE 8-1: Common database functions

function	result
DGET	Extracts a single record from a table that matches criteria you specify
DSUM	Totals numbers in a given table column that match criteria you specify
DAVERAGE	Averages numbers in a given table column that match criteria you specify
DCOUNT	Counts the cells that contain numbers in a given table column that match criteria you specify
DCOUNTA	Counts the cells that contain nonblank data in a given table column that match criteria you specify

Validate Table Data

When setting up tables, you want to help ensure accuracy when you or others enter data. The Data Validation feature allows you to do this by specifying what data users can enter in a range of cells. You can restrict data to whole numbers, decimal numbers, or text. You can also specify a list of acceptable entries. Once you've specified what data the program should consider valid for that cell, Excel displays an error message when invalid data is entered and can prevent users from entering any other data that it considers to be invalid. **CASE** *Mary wants to make sure that information in the Air Included column is entered consistently in the future. She asks you to restrict the entries in that column to two options: Yes and No. First, you select the table column you want to restrict.*

STEPS

1. **Click the top edge of the Air Included column header**
   The column data is selected.

2. **Click the Data tab, click the Data Validation button in the Data Tools group, in the Data Validation dialog box click the Settings tab if necessary, click the Allow list arrow, then click List**
   Selecting the List option lets you type a list of specific options.

3. **Click the Source text box, then type Yes, No**
   You have entered the list of acceptable entries, separated by commas, as shown in **FIGURE 8-14**. You want the data entry person to be able to select a valid entry from a drop-down list.

4. **Verify that the In-cell dropdown check box contains a check mark, then click OK**
   The dialog box closes, and you return to the worksheet.

5. **Click the Home tab, click any cell in the last table row, click the Insert list arrow in the Cells group, click Insert Table Row Below, click the Air Included cell in this row, then click its list arrow**
   A list of valid list entries opens, as shown in **FIGURE 8-15**. You could click an item in the list to enter in the cell, but you want to test the data restriction by entering an invalid entry.

6. **Click the list arrow to close the list, type Maybe, then press [Enter]**
   A warning dialog box appears and prevents you from entering the invalid data, as shown in **FIGURE 8-16**.

7. **Click Cancel, click the list arrow, then click Yes**
   The cell accepts the valid entry. The data restriction ensures that records contain only one of the two correct entries in the Air Included column. The table is ready for future data entry.

8. **Delete the last table row, add your name to the center section of the footer, then save the workbook**

Restricting cell values and data length

In addition to providing an in-cell drop-down list for data entry, you can use data validation to restrict the values that are entered into cells. For example, you might want to restrict cells in a selected range to values less than a certain number, date, or time. To do so, click the Data tab, click the Data Validation button in the Data Tools group, on the Settings tab click the Allow list arrow, select Whole number, Decimal, Date, or Time, click the Data list arrow, select less than, then in the bottom text box, enter the maximum value. You can also limit the length of data entered into cells by choosing Text length in the Allow list, clicking the Data list arrow and selecting less than, then entering the maximum length in the Maximum text box.

FIGURE 8-14: Creating data restrictions

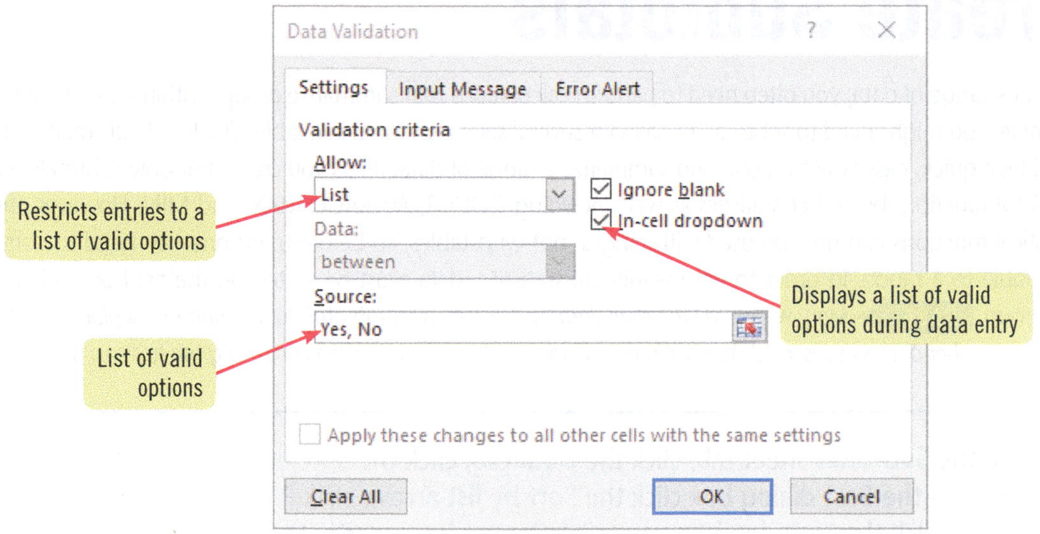

Restricts entries to a list of valid options →

List of valid options →

Displays a list of valid options during data entry

FIGURE 8-15: Entering data in restricted cells

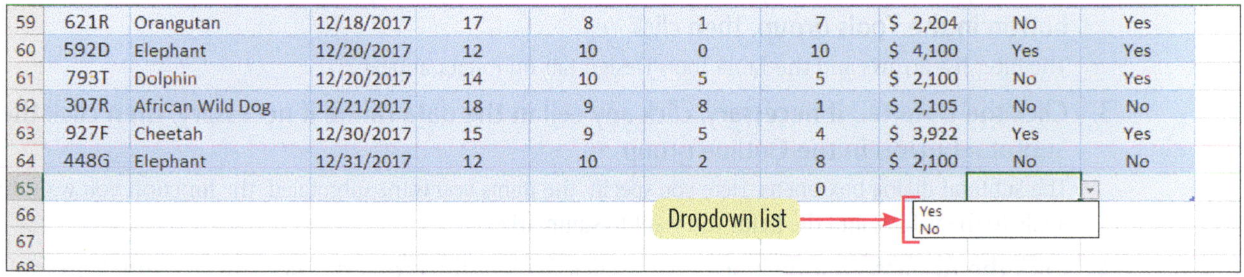

59	621R	Orangutan	12/18/2017	17	8	1	7	$ 2,204	No	Yes
60	592D	Elephant	12/20/2017	12	10	0	10	$ 4,100	Yes	Yes
61	793T	Dolphin	12/20/2017	14	10	5	5	$ 2,100	No	Yes
62	307R	African Wild Dog	12/21/2017	18	9	8	1	$ 2,105	No	No
63	927F	Cheetah	12/30/2017	15	9	5	4	$ 3,922	Yes	Yes
64	448G	Elephant	12/31/2017	12	10	2	8	$ 2,100	No	No
65							0			
66									Yes / No	
67										
68										

Dropdown list →

FIGURE 8-16: Invalid data warning

Microsoft Excel

⊗ This value doesn't match the data validation restrictions defined for this cell.

Retry   Cancel   Help

Adding input messages and error alerts

You can customize the way data validation works by using the two other tabs in the Data Validation dialog box: Input Message and Error Alert. The Input Message tab lets you set a message that appears when the user selects that cell. For example, the message might contain instructions about what type of data to enter. On the Input Message tab, enter a message title and message, then click OK. The Error Alert tab lets you set one of three alert styles if a user enters invalid data. The Information style displays your message with the information icon but allows the user to proceed with data entry. The Warning style displays your information with the warning icon and gives the user the option to proceed with data entry or not. The Stop style, which you used in this lesson, is the default; it displays your message and only lets the user retry or cancel data entry for that cell.

Create Subtotals

Learning Outcomes
- Summarize worksheet data using subtotals
- Use outline symbols
- Convert a table to a range

In a large range of data, you often need to perform calculations that summarize groups within a set of data. For example, you might need to subtotal the sales for several sales reps listed in a table. The Excel Subtotals feature provides a quick, easy way to group and summarize a range of data. It lets you create not only subtotals using the SUM function, but other statistics as well, including COUNT, AVERAGE, MAX, and MIN. However, these statistical functions can only be used with ranges, not with tables, so before using one you need to convert your table to a range. In order to get meaningful statistics, data must be sorted on the field on which you will group. **CASE** ▶ *Mary wants you to group data by projects, with subtotals for the number of places available and the number of places reserved. You begin by first sorting the table and then converting the table to a range.*

STEPS

1. **Click the Subtotals sheet tab, click the Data tab, click the Sort button in the Sort & Filter group, in the Sort dialog box click the Sort by list arrow, click Project, click the Add Level button, click the Then by list arrow, click Depart Date, verify that the order is Oldest to Newest, then click OK**

   You have sorted the table in ascending order, first by project, then by departure date within each project grouping.

2. **Click any cell in the table, click the Table Tools Design tab, click the Convert to Range button in the Tools group, then click Yes**

   The filter list arrows and the Table Tools Design tab no longer appear.

3. **Click the Data tab if necessary, click any cell in the data range if necessary, then click the Subtotal button in the Outline group**

   The Subtotal dialog box opens. Here you specify the items you want subtotaled, the function you want to apply to the values, and the fields you want to summarize.

4. **Click the At each change in list arrow, click Project if necessary, click the Use function list arrow, click Sum; in the "Add subtotal to" list click the Places Reserved and Places Available check boxes to select them if necessary, then click the Insurance Included check box to deselect it**

5. **If necessary, click the Replace current subtotals and Summary below data check boxes to select them**

   Your completed Subtotal dialog box should match **FIGURE 8-17**.

6. **Click OK, then scroll down so you can see row 73**

   The subtotaled data appears after each project grouping, showing the calculated subtotals and grand total in columns E and F. Excel displays an outline to the left of the worksheet, with outline buttons to control the level of detail that appears. The button number corresponds to the detail level that is displayed. You want to show the second level of detail, the subtotals and the grand total.

7. **Click the outline symbol [2]**

   Only the subtotals and the grand total appear. Your subtotals and grand total should match **FIGURE 8-18**.

8. **Add your name to the center section of the footer, preview the worksheet, then save the workbook**

9. **Close the workbook, exit Excel, then submit the workbook to your instructor**

FIGURE 8-17: Completed Subtotal dialog box

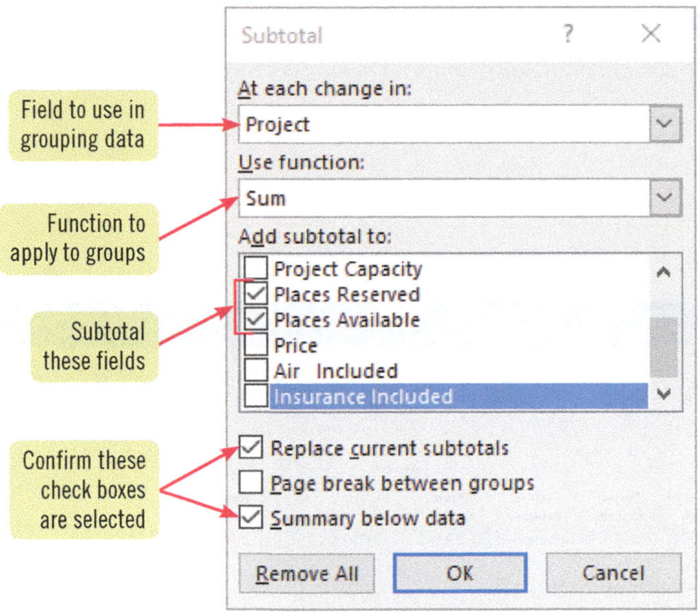

Field to use in grouping data

Function to apply to groups

Subtotal these fields

Confirm these check boxes are selected

FIGURE 8-18: Data with subtotals and grand total

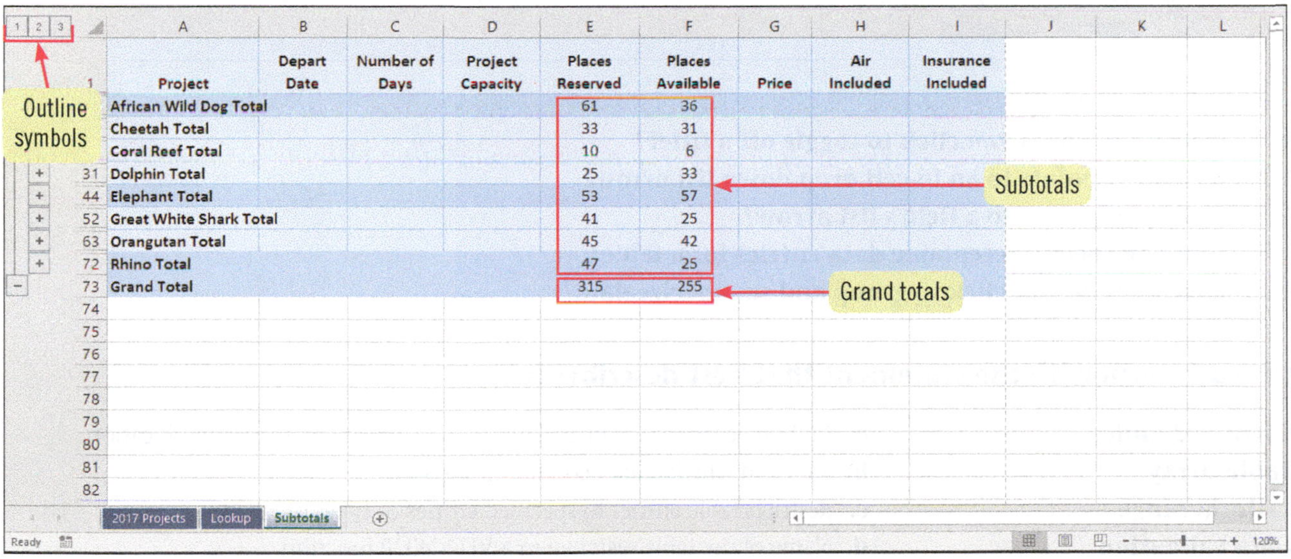

Outline symbols

Subtotals

Grand totals

Excel 2016

Practice

Concepts Review

FIGURE 8-19

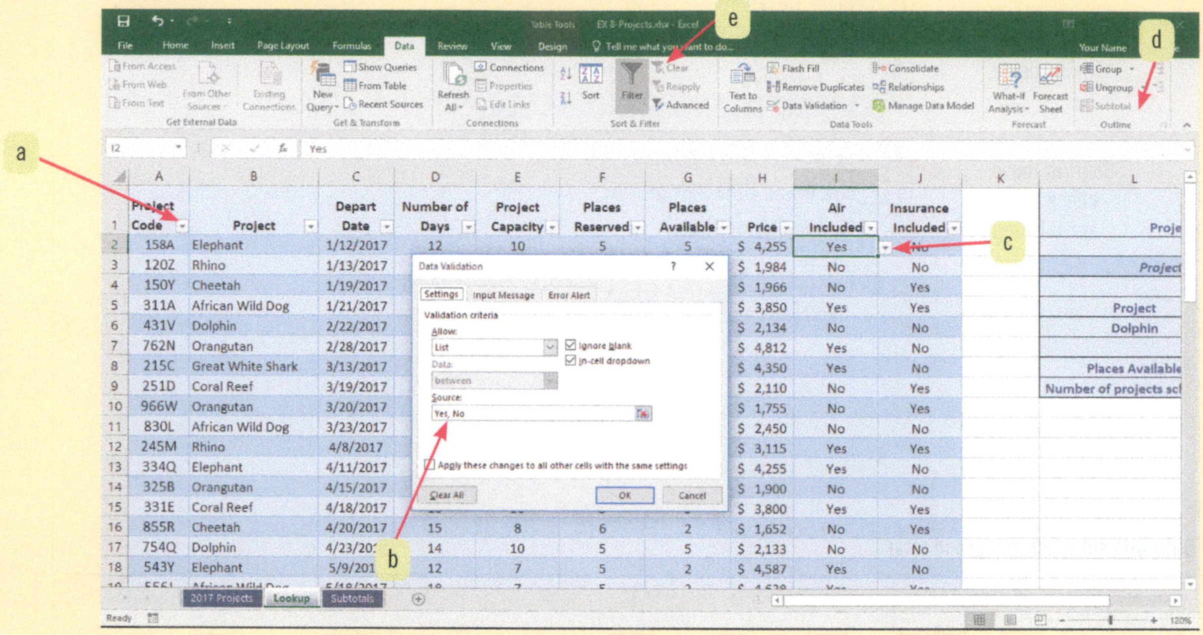

1. **Which element would you click to toggle off a filter?**
2. **Which element points to an in-cell drop-down list arrow?**
3. **Which element points to a field's list arrow?**
4. **Where do you specify acceptable data entries for a table?**
5. **Which element do you click to group and summarize data?**

Match each term with the statement that best describes it.

6. **Extracted table**
7. **Table_array**
8. **Criteria range**
9. **Data validation**
10. **DSUM**

a. Cell range when Advanced Filter results are copied to another location
b. Range in which search conditions are set
c. Restricts table entries to specified entries or types of entries
d. Name of the table searched in a VLOOKUP function
e. Function used to total table values that meet specified criteria

Select the best answer from the list of choices.

11. **What does it mean when you select the Or option when creating a custom filter?**
   a. Both criteria must be true to find a match.
   b. Neither criterion has to be 100% true.
   c. Either criterion can be true to find a match.
   d. A custom filter requires a criteria range.

12. **The _____ logical condition finds records matching both listed criteria.**
   a. True
   b. Or
   c. And
   d. False

13. Which function finds the position of an item in a table?

a. VLOOKUP   c. DGET

b. MATCH   d. HLOOKUP

14. What must a data range have before subtotals can be inserted?

a. Enough records to show multiple subtotals   c. Formatted cells

b. Sorted data   d. Grand totals

Skills Review

1. Filter a table.

a. Start Excel, open EX 8-2.xlsx from where you store your Data Files, then save it as **EX 8-HR**.

b. With the Compensation sheet active, filter the table to list only records for employees in the Dallas branch.

c. Clear the filter, then add a filter that displays the records for employees in the Dallas and LA branches.

d. Redisplay all employees, then use a filter to show the three employees with the highest annual salary.

e. Redisplay all the records.

2. Create a custom filter.

a. Create a custom filter showing employees hired before 1/1/2015 or after 12/31/2016.

b. Create a custom filter showing employees hired between 1/1/2014 and 12/31/2015.

c. Enter your name in the worksheet footer, then preview the filtered worksheet.

d. Redisplay all records.

e. Save the workbook.

3. Filter and extract a table with the Advanced Filter.

a. Retrieve a list of employees who were hired before 1/1/2017 and who have an annual salary of more than $75,000 a year. Define a criteria range by inserting six new rows above the table on the worksheet and copying the field names into the first row.

b. In cell D2, enter the criterion **<1/1/2017**, then in cell G2 enter **>75000**.

c. Click any cell in the table.

d. Open the Advanced Filter dialog box.

e. Indicate that you want to copy to another location, enter the criteria range **A1:J2**, verify that the List range is $A$7:$J$17, then indicate that you want to place the extracted list in the range starting at cell **A20**.

f. Confirm that the retrieved list meets the criteria as shown in FIGURE 8-20.

g. Save the workbook, then preview the worksheet.

FIGURE 8-20

	A	B	C	D	E	F	G	H	I	J	K
1	Employee Number	First Name	Last Name	Hire Date	Branch	Monthly Salary	Annual Salary	Annual Bonus	Benefits Dollars	Annual Compensation	
2				<1/1/2017			>75000				
3											
4											
5											
6											
7	Employee Number	First Name	Last Name	Hire Date	Branch	Monthly Salary	Annual Salary	Annual Bonus	Benefits Dollars	Annual Compensation	
8	1005	Molly	Lake	2/12/2015	LA	$ 4,850	$ 58,200	$ 1,470	$ 13,386	$ 73,056	
9	1778	Lynn	Waters	4/1/2016	Chicago	$ 5,170	$ 62,040	$ 5,125	$ 14,269	$ 81,434	
10	1469	Donna	Davie	5/6/2016	Dallas	$ 6,550	$ 78,600	$ 6,725	$ 18,078	$ 103,403	
11	1734	Martha	Mele	12/10/2016	Dallas	$ 7,450	$ 89,400	$ 5,550	$ 20,562	$ 115,512	
12	1578	Hank	Gole	2/15/2014	Chicago	$ 4,950	$ 59,400	$ 1,680	$ 13,662	$ 74,742	
13	1499	Peter	East	3/25/2015	LA	$ 1,750	$ 21,000	$ 1,630	$ 4,830	$ 27,460	
14	1080	Emily	Malone	6/23/2014	Chicago	$ 4,225	$ 50,700	$ 2,320	$ 11,661	$ 64,681	
15	1998	Mike	Magee	8/3/2017	Chicago	$ 5,750	$ 69,000	$ 5,900	$ 15,870	$ 90,770	
16	1662	Ted	Reily	9/29/2016	LA	$ 7,500	$ 90,000	$ 3,002	$ 20,700	$ 113,702	
17	1322	Jason	Round	5/12/2016	Dallas	$ 4,750	$ 57,000	$ 995	$ 13,110	$ 71,105	
18											
19											
20	Employee Number	First Name	Last Name	Hire Date	Branch	Monthly Salary	Annual Salary	Annual Bonus	Benefits Dollars	Annual Compensation	
21	1469	Donna	Davie	5/6/2016	Dallas	$ 6,550	$ 78,600	$ 6,725	$ 18,078	$ 103,403	
22	1734	Martha	Mele	12/10/2016	Dallas	$ 7,450	$ 89,400	$ 5,550	$ 20,562	$ 115,512	
23	1662	Ted	Reily	9/29/2016	LA	$ 7,500	$ 90,000	$ 3,002	$ 20,700	$ 113,702	
24											

Skills Review (continued)

4. Look up values in a table.

  a. Click the Summary sheet tab. Use the Name Manager to view the table names in the workbook, then close the dialog box.

  b. Prepare to use a lookup function to locate an employee's annual compensation; enter the Employee Number **1578** in cell A18.

  c. In cell B18, use the VLOOKUP function and enter **A18** as the Lookup_value, **Table2** as the Table_array, **10** as the Col_index_num, and **FALSE** as the Range_lookup; observe the compensation displayed for that employee number, then check it against the table to make sure it is correct.

  d. Replace the existing Employee Number in cell A18 with **1998**, and view the annual compensation for that employee.

  e. Format cell B18 with the Accounting format with the $ symbol and no decimal places.

  f. Save the workbook.

5. Summarize table data.

  a. Prepare to enter a database function to average the annual salaries by branch, using the LA branch as the initial criterion. In cell E18, use the DAVERAGE function, and click the upper-left corner of cell A1 twice to select the table and its header row as the Database, select cell G1 for the Field, and select the range D17:D18 for the Criteria. Verify that the average LA salary is 56400.

  b. Test the function further by entering the text **Dallas** in cell D18. When the criterion is entered, cell E18 should display 75000.

  c. Format cell E18 in Accounting format with the $ symbol and no decimal places.

  d. Save the workbook.

6. Validate table data.

  a. Select the data in column E of the table, and set a validation criterion specifying that you want to allow a list of valid options.

  b. Enter a list of valid options that restricts the entries to **LA**, **Chicago**, and **Dallas**. Remember to use a comma between each item in the list.

  c. Indicate that you want the options to appear in an in-cell drop-down list, then close the dialog box.

  d. Add a row to the table. Go to cell E12, then select Chicago in the drop-down list.

  e. Complete the new record by adding an Employee Number of **1119**, a First Name of **Cate**, a Last Name of **Smith**, a Hire Date of **10/1/2017**, a monthly salary of **$5000**, and an Annual Bonus of **$5000**. Format the range F12:J12 as Accounting with no decimal places and using the $ symbol. Compare your screen to FIGURE 8-21.

  f. Add your name to the center section of the footer, save the worksheet, then preview the worksheet.

FIGURE 8-21

	A	B	C	D	E	F	G	H	I	J	K
1	Employee Number	First Name	Last Name	Hire Date	Branch	Monthly Salary	Annual Salary	Annual Bonus	Benefits Dollars	Annual Compensation	
2	1005	Molly	Lake	2/12/2015	LA	$ 4,850	$ 58,200	$ 1,470	$ 13,386	$ 73,056	
3	1778	Lynn	Waters	4/1/2016	Chicago	$ 5,170	$ 62,040	$ 5,125	$ 14,269	$ 81,434	
4	1469	Donna	Davie	5/6/2016	Dallas	$ 6,550	$ 78,600	$ 6,725	$ 18,078	$ 103,403	
5	1734	Martha	Mele	12/10/2016	Dallas	$ 7,450	$ 89,400	$ 5,550	$ 20,562	$ 115,512	
6	1578	Hank	Gole	2/15/2014	Chicago	$ 4,950	$ 59,400	$ 1,680	$ 13,662	$ 74,742	
7	1499	Peter	East	3/25/2015	LA	$ 1,750	$ 21,000	$ 1,630	$ 4,830	$ 27,460	
8	1080	Emily	Malone	6/23/2014	Chicago	$ 4,225	$ 50,700	$ 2,320	$ 11,661	$ 64,681	
9	1998	Mike	Magee	8/3/2017	Chicago	$ 5,750	$ 69,000	$ 5,900	$ 15,870	$ 90,770	
10	1662	Ted	Reily	9/29/2016	LA	$ 7,500	$ 90,000	$ 3,002	$ 20,700	$ 113,702	
11	1322	Jason	Round	5/12/2016	Dallas	$ 4,750	$ 57,000	$ 995	$ 13,110	$ 71,105	
12	1119	Cate	Smith	10/1/2017	Chicago	$ 5,000	$ 60,000	$ 5,000	$ 13,800	$ 78,800	
13											
14											
15											
16											
17	Employee Number	Annual Compensation			Branch	Average Annual Salary					
18	1998	$ 90,770			Dallas	$ 75,000					
19											
20											

Skills Review (continued)

7. Create subtotals.

a. Click the Subtotals sheet tab.

b. Use the Branch field list arrow to sort the table in ascending order by branch.

c. Convert the table to a range.

d. Group and create subtotals of the Annual Compensation data by branch, using the SUM function.

e. Click the 2 outline button on the outline to display only the subtotals and the grand total. Compare your screen to FIGURE 8-22.

f. Enter your name in the worksheet footer, save the workbook, then preview the worksheet.

g. Save the workbook, close the workbook, exit Excel, then submit your workbook to your instructor.

FIGURE 8-22

	A	B	C	D	E	F	G	H	I	J
	Employee Number	First Name	Last Name	Hire Date	Branch	Monthly Salary	Annual Salary	Annual Bonus	Benefits Dollars	Annual Compensation
6					Chicago Total					$ 311,627
10					Dallas Total					$ 290,020
14					LA Total					$ 214,218
15					Grand Total					$ 815,865
16										
17										
18										

Independent Challenge 1

As the manager of Tampa Medical, a diagnostic supply company, you spend a lot of time managing your inventory. To help with this task, you have created an Excel table that you can extract information from using filters. You also need to add data validation and summary information to the table.

a. Start Excel, open EX 8-3.xlsx from where you store your Data Files, then save it as **EX 8-Diagnostic**.

b. Using the table data on the Inventory sheet, create a filter to display information about only the pulse monitors. Clear the filter.

c. Use a Custom Filter to generate a list of products with a quantity greater than 15. Clear the filter.

d. Copy the labels in cells A1:E1 into A16:E16. Type **Stethoscope** in cell A17, and type **<$275.00** in cell C17. Use the Advanced Filter with a criteria range of A16:E17 to extract a table of stethoscopes priced less than $275.00 to the range of cells beginning in cell A20. Enter your name in the worksheet footer, save the workbook, then preview the worksheet.

e. On the Summary sheet, select the table data in column B. Open the Data Validation dialog box, then indicate you want to use a validation list with the acceptable entries of **Lee**, **Rand**, **Barry**. Make sure the In-cell dropdown check box is selected.

f. Test the data validation by trying to change any cell in column B of the table to **Lane**.

g. Using FIGURE 8-23 as a guide, enter a function in cell E18 that calculates the total quantity of Stethoscopes available in your inventory. Enter your name in the worksheet footer, preview the worksheet, then save the workbook.

h. On the Subtotals sheet, sort the table in ascending order by product. Convert the table to a range. Insert subtotals by product using the Sum function, then select Quantity in the "Add Subtotal to" box. Remove the check box for the Total field, if necessary. Use the appropriate button on the outline to display only the subtotals and grand total. Save the workbook, then preview the worksheet.

i. Submit the workbook to your instructor. Close the workbook, then exit Excel.

FIGURE 8-23

Function Arguments	? X
DSUM	
Database Table2[#All]	= {"Product","Manufacturer","Unit Pric...
Field Table2[[#Headers],[Quantity]]	= "Quantity"
Criteria D17:D18	= "Stethoscope"
	= 64

Adds the numbers in the field (column) of records in the database that match the conditions you specify.

Database is the range of cells that makes up the list or database. A database is a list of related data.

Formula result = 64

Help on this function   OK   Cancel

Independent Challenge 2

As the senior accountant at Miami Plumbing Supply, you are adding new features to the company's accounts receivables workbook. The business supplies both residential and commercial plumbers. You have put together an invoice table to track sales for the month of June. Now that you have this table, you would like to manipulate it in several ways. First, you want to filter the table to show only invoices over a certain amount with certain order dates. You also want to subtotal the total column by residential and commercial supplies. To prevent data entry errors you will restrict entries in the Order Date column. Finally, you would like to add database and lookup functions to your worksheet to efficiently retrieve data from the table.

a. Start Excel, open EX 8-4.xlsx from where you store your Data Files, then save it as **EX 8-Invoices**.

b. Use the Advanced Filter to show invoices with amounts more than $300.00 ordered before 6/15/2017, using cells A27:B28 to enter your criteria and extracting the results to cell A33. (*Hint*: You don't need to specify an entire row as the criteria range.) Enter your name in the worksheet footer.

c. Use the Data Validation dialog box to restrict entries to those with order dates between 6/1/2017 and 6/30/2017. Test the data restrictions by attempting to enter an invalid date in cell B25.

d. Enter **23706** in cell G28. Enter a VLOOKUP function in cell H28 to retrieve the total based on the invoice number entered in cell G28. Make sure you have an exact match with the invoice number. Test the function with the invoice number 23699.

e. Enter the date **6/1/2017** in cell J28. Use the database function, DCOUNT, in cell K28 to count the number of invoices for the date in cell J28. Save the workbook, then preview the worksheet.

f. On the Subtotals worksheet, sort the table in ascending order by Type, then convert the table to a range. Create subtotals showing the totals for commercial and residential invoices. Display only the subtotals for the commercial and residential accounts, along with the grand total.

g. Save the workbook, preview the worksheet, close the workbook, then exit Excel. Submit the workbook to your instructor.

Independent Challenge 3

You are the manager of Fitness Now, a service company for fitness equipment. You have created an Excel table that contains your invoice data, along with the totals for each invoice. You would like to manipulate this table to display service categories and invoices meeting specific criteria. You would also like to add subtotals to the table and add database functions to total categories of invoices. Finally, you want to restrict entries in the Category column.

a. Start Excel, open EX 8-5.xlsx from where you store your Data Files, then save it as **EX 8-Equipment**.

b. On the Invoice sheet, use the headings in row 37 to create an advanced filter that extracts records with the following criteria to cell A42: totals greater than $1500 having dates either before 9/10/2017 or after 9/19/2017. (*Hint*: Recall that when you want records to meet one criterion or another, you need to place the criteria on separate lines.)

c. Use the DSUM function in cell G2 to let worksheet users find the total amount for the category entered in cell F2. Format the cell containing the total using the Accounting format with the $ symbol and no decimals. Verify the warranty category total is $8,228. Preview the worksheet.

d. Use data validation to create an in-cell drop-down list that restricts category entries to "Preventative Maintenance", "Warranty", and "Service". Use the Error Alert tab of the Data Validation dialog box to set the alert style to the Warning style with the message "Data is not valid." Test the validation in the table with valid and invalid entries. Save the workbook, enter your name in the worksheet footer, then preview the worksheet.

e. Using the Subtotals sheet, sort the table by category in ascending order. Convert the table to a range, and add Subtotals to the totals by category. Widen the columns, if necessary.

f. Use the outline to display only category names with subtotals and the grand total. Enter your name in the worksheet footer.

g. Save the workbook, then preview the worksheet.

h. Close the workbook, exit Excel, then submit the workbook to your instructor.

Independent Challenge 4: Explore

You are an inventory manager at East Coast Medical, a medical equipment distributor. You track your inventory of equipment in an Excel worksheet. You would like to use conditional formatting in your worksheet to help track the products that need to be reordered as well as your inventory expenses. You would also like to prevent data entry errors. Finally, you would like to add an area to quickly look up prices and quantities for customers.

a. Start Excel, open EX 8-6.xlsx from where you store your Data Files, then save it as **EX 8-East Coast Medical**.

b. Using FIGURE 8-24 as a guide, use conditional formatting to add icons to the quantity column using the following criteria: format quantities greater than or equal to 300 with a green circle, quantities greater than or equal to 100 but less than 300 with a yellow circle, and quantities less than 100 with a red circle. (*Hint*: You may need to click in the top Value text box for the correct value to display for the red circle.)

c. Conditionally format the Total data using Top/Bottom Rules to emphasize the cells containing the top 30 percent with red text.

d. Add another rule to format the bottom 20 percent in the Total column with purple text from the standard colors palette.

e. Restrict the Wholesale Price field entries to decimal values between 0 and 10000. Add an input message of **Prices must be less than $10,000**. Add an Information level error message of **Please check price**. Test the validation entering a price of $10,100 in cell C3 and allow the new price to be entered.

FIGURE 8-24

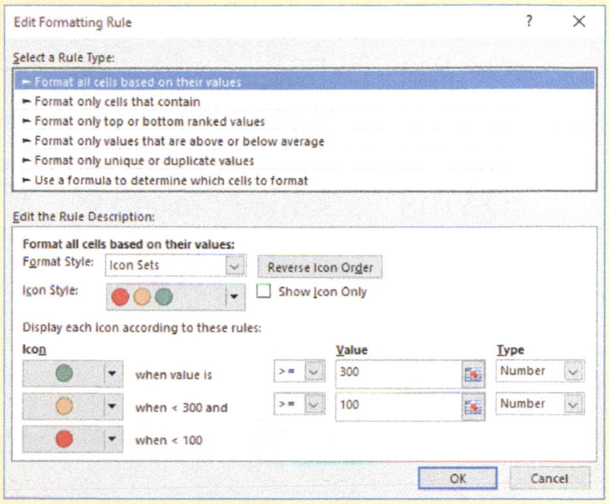

f. Below the table, create a product lookup area with the following labels in adjacent cells: **Product Number**, **Wholesale Price**, **Quantity**. Right align these labels in the cells.

g. Using the Table Tools Design tab, name the table "Inventory".

h. Enter 1445 under the label Product Number in your products lookup area.

i. In the product lookup area, enter lookup functions to locate the wholesale price and quantity information for the product number that you entered in the previous step. Use the assigned table name of Inventory and make sure you match the product number exactly. Format the wholesale price with the Accounting format and two decimal places.

j. Enter your name in the center section of the worksheet header, save the workbook, then preview the worksheet comparing it to FIGURE 8-25.

k. Close the workbook, exit Excel, then submit the workbook to your instructor.

FIGURE 8-25

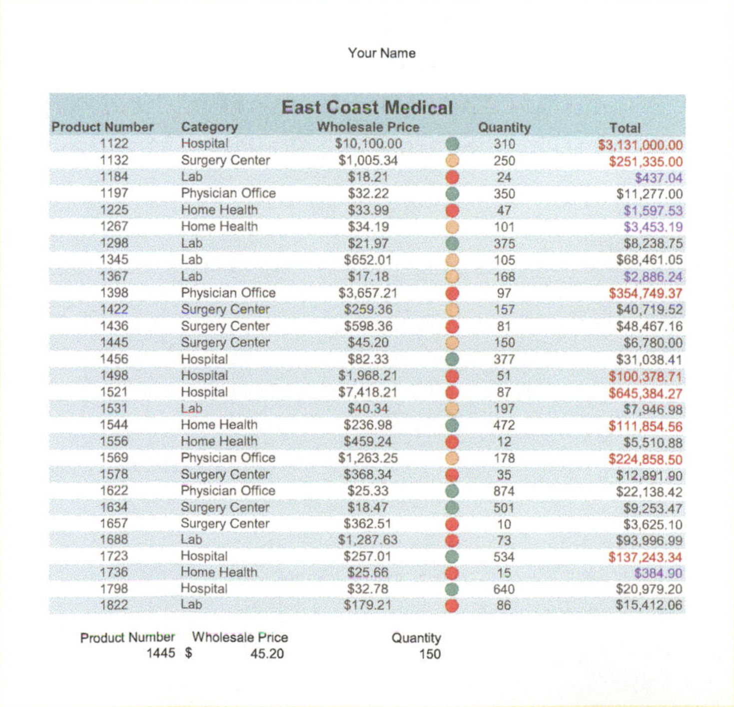

Your Name

East Coast Medical

Product Number	Category	Wholesale Price	Quantity	Total
1122	Hospital	$10,100.00	310	$3,131,000.00
1132	Surgery Center	$1,005.34	250	$251,335.00
1184	Lab	$18.21	24	$437.04
1197	Physician Office	$32.22	350	$11,277.00
1225	Home Health	$33.99	47	$1,597.53
1267	Home Health	$34.19	101	$3,453.19
1298	Lab	$21.97	375	$8,238.75
1345	Lab	$652.01	105	$68,461.05
1367	Lab	$17.18	168	$2,886.24
1398	Physician Office	$3,657.21	97	$354,749.37
1422	Surgery Center	$259.36	157	$40,719.52
1436	Surgery Center	$598.36	81	$48,467.16
1445	Surgery Center	$45.20	150	$6,780.00
1456	Hospital	$82.33	377	$31,038.41
1498	Hospital	$1,968.21	51	$100,378.71
1521	Hospital	$7,418.21	87	$645,384.27
1531	Lab	$40.34	197	$7,946.98
1544	Home Health	$236.98	472	$111,854.56
1556	Home Health	$459.24	12	$5,510.88
1569	Physician Office	$1,263.25	178	$224,858.50
1578	Surgery Center	$368.34	35	$12,891.90
1622	Physician Office	$25.33	874	$22,138.42
1634	Surgery Center	$18.47	501	$9,253.47
1657	Surgery Center	$362.51	10	$3,625.10
1688	Lab	$1,287.63	73	$93,996.99
1723	Hospital	$257.01	534	$137,243.34
1736	Home Health	$25.66	15	$384.90
1798	Hospital	$32.78	640	$20,979.20
1822	Lab	$179.21	86	$15,412.06

Product Number	Wholesale Price	Quantity
1445	$ 45.20	150

Visual Workshop

Open EX 8-7.xlsx from where you store your Data Files, then save it as **EX 8-Therapy**. Complete the worksheet as shown in FIGURE 8-26. An in-cell drop-down list has been added to the data entered in the Pool field. The range A18:F21 is extracted from the table using the criteria in cells A15:A16. Add your name to the worksheet footer, save the workbook, preview the worksheet, then submit the workbook to your instructor.

FIGURE 8-26

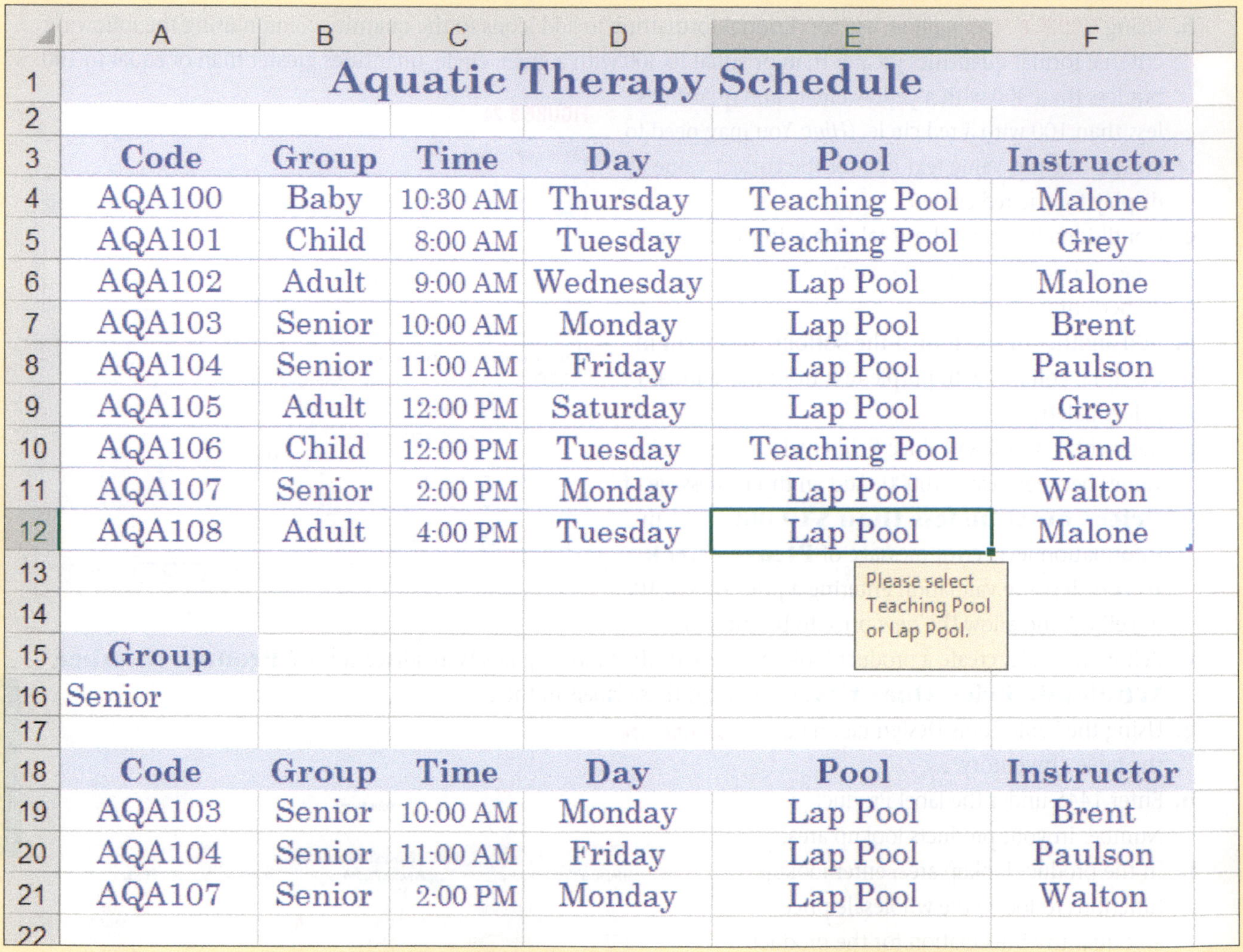

	A	B	C	D	E	F
1	Aquatic Therapy Schedule					
2						
3	Code	Group	Time	Day	Pool	Instructor
4	AQA100	Baby	10:30 AM	Thursday	Teaching Pool	Malone
5	AQA101	Child	8:00 AM	Tuesday	Teaching Pool	Grey
6	AQA102	Adult	9:00 AM	Wednesday	Lap Pool	Malone
7	AQA103	Senior	10:00 AM	Monday	Lap Pool	Brent
8	AQA104	Senior	11:00 AM	Friday	Lap Pool	Paulson
9	AQA105	Adult	12:00 PM	Saturday	Lap Pool	Grey
10	AQA106	Child	12:00 PM	Tuesday	Teaching Pool	Rand
11	AQA107	Senior	2:00 PM	Monday	Lap Pool	Walton
12	AQA108	Adult	4:00 PM	Tuesday	Lap Pool	Malone
13					Please select Teaching Pool or Lap Pool.	
14						
15	Group					
16	Senior					
17						
18	Code	Group	Time	Day	Pool	Instructor
19	AQA103	Senior	10:00 AM	Monday	Lap Pool	Brent
20	AQA104	Senior	11:00 AM	Friday	Lap Pool	Paulson
21	AQA107	Senior	2:00 PM	Monday	Lap Pool	Walton
22						

Automating Worksheet Tasks

CASE ▶ Jo Katz, director of operations for Africa at Reason2Go, asks you to help automate tasks so that staff at the Cape Town headquarters can work more efficiently. You start by creating a macro that will save people time when working in Excel. The macro will automatically insert text that identifies the worksheet as a Cape Town headquarters document.

Module Objectives

After completing this module, you will be able to:

- Plan a macro
- Enable a macro
- Record a macro
- Run a macro
- Edit a macro
- Assign keyboard shortcuts to macros
- Use the Personal Macro Workbook
- Assign a macro to a button

Files You Will Need

EX 9-1.xlsx
EX 9-2.xlsx
EX 9-3.xlsx

Plan a Macro

Learning
Outcomes
• Plan a macro
• Determine the
  storage location
  for a macro

A **macro** is a named set of instructions you can create that performs tasks automatically, in an order you specify. You create macros to automate Excel tasks that you perform frequently. For example, you can create a macro to enter and format text or to save and print a worksheet. To create a macro, you record the series of actions using the macro recorder built in to Excel, or you write the instructions in a special programming language. Because the sequence of actions in a macro is important, you need to plan the macro carefully before you record it. **CASE** ▸ *Jo likes your idea to create a macro for the Africa headquarters to place the location of the office in the upper-left corner of any worksheet. You work with Jo to plan the macro.*

DETAILS

To plan a macro, use the following guidelines:

• ### Assign the macro a descriptive name

  The first character of a macro name must be a letter; the remaining characters can be letters, numbers, or underscores. Letters can be uppercase or lowercase. Spaces are not allowed in macro names; use underscores in place of spaces. Press [Shift][-] to enter an underscore character. You decide to name the macro "HQStamp". See **TABLE 9-1** for a list of macros that could be created to automate other tasks at Reason2Go.

• ### Write out the steps the macro will perform

  This planning helps eliminate careless errors. After discussion with Jo, you write down a description of the new HQStamp macro, as shown in **FIGURE 9-1**.

• ### Decide how you will perform the actions you want to record

  You can use the mouse, the keyboard, or a combination of the two. For the new HQStamp macro, you want to use both the mouse and the keyboard.

• ### Practice the steps you want Excel to record, and write them down

  During your meeting with Jo, you write down the sequence of actions to include in the macro.

• ### Decide where to store the description of the macro and the macro itself

  Macros can be stored in an active workbook, in a new workbook, or in the **Personal Macro Workbook**, a special workbook used only for macro storage. You decide to store the macro in a new workbook.

FIGURE 9-1: Handwritten description of planned macro

Macro to create stamp with the Headquarters location

Name: HQStamp

Description: Adds a stamp to the top left of the worksheet, identifying it as a
                 Cape Town office worksheet

Steps: 1. Position the cell pointer in cell A1.
                 2. Type Cape Town, then click the Enter button.
                 3. Click the Format button, then click Format Cells.
                 4. Click the Font tab, under Font style, click Bold; under Underline, click
                    Single; under Color, click Blue; then click OK.

TABLE 9-1: Possible macros and their descriptive names

description of macro	descriptive name for macro
Enter a frequently used proper name, such as "Jo Katz"	JoKatz
Enter a frequently used company name, such as Reason2Go	Company_Name
Print the active worksheet on a single page, in landscape orientation	FitToLand
Add a footer to a worksheet	FooterStamp
Add totals to a worksheet	AddTotals

Using a macro to filter table data

You can create a macro using the Advanced Filter feature to automate the filtering process for table data that you filter frequently. To create a filtering macro, create a criteria range on the worksheet and determine the sheet location where the filtered records will be displayed. Then, record the macro by creating an advanced filter that uses the criteria range, the list range (table range), and the location where the filtered results will be displayed. As long as you keep the same ranges on the worksheet, you can change the data in either the criteria or table ranges and then run the macro to filter the table for that new data.

Enable a Macro

Learning
Outcomes
• Create a macro-
enabled workbook
• Enable macros by
changing a
workbook's
security level

Because a macro may contain a **virus**—destructive software that can damage your computer files—the default security setting in Excel disables macros from running. Although a workbook containing a macro will open, if macros are disabled they will not function. You can manually change the Excel security setting to allow macros to run if you know a macro came from a trusted source. When saving a workbook with a macro, you need to save it as a macro-enabled workbook with the extension .xlsm. **CASE** *Jo asks you to change the security level to enable all macros. As a courtesy to others who are sharing your computer in a classroom or lab, you will change the security level back to the default setting after you create and run your macros.*

STEPS

1. **Start Excel, open a blank workbook, click the Save button** 🖫 **on the Quick Access Toolbar, navigate to where you store your Data Files, in the Save As dialog box click the Save as type list arrow, click Excel Macro-Enabled Workbook (*.xlsm), in the File name text box type EX 9-Macro Workbook, then click Save**

   The security settings that enable macros are available on the Developer tab. The Developer tab does not appear by default, but you can display it by customizing the Ribbon.

QUICK TIP
If the Developer
tab is displayed on
your Ribbon, skip
steps 2 and 3.

2. **Click the File tab, click Options, then click Customize Ribbon in the category list**

   The Customize the Ribbon options open in the Excel Options dialog box, as shown in **FIGURE 9-2**.

3. **Click the Developer check box, if necessary, in the Main Tabs area on the right side of the screen to select it, then click OK**

   The Developer tab appears on the Ribbon. You are ready to change the security settings.

4. **Click the Developer tab, then click the Macro Security button in the Code group**

   The Trust Center dialog box opens.

QUICK TIP
For increased secu-
rity, you can click
the security setting
"Disable all macros
with notification"
instead. Using that
setting, you will
need to click Enable
Content to run mac-
ros in a .xlsm file.

5. **Click Macro Settings if necessary, click the Enable all macros (not recommended; potentially dangerous code can run) option button to select it, as shown in FIGURE 9-3, then click OK**

   The dialog box closes. Macros will remain enabled until you disable them by deselecting the Enable all macros option. As you work with Excel, you should disable macros when you are not working with them.

FIGURE 9-2: Excel Options dialog box

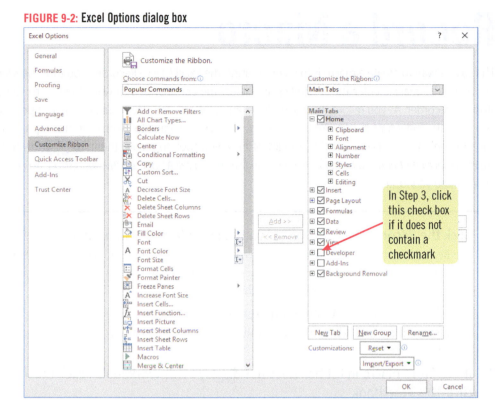

FIGURE 9-3: Trust Center dialog box

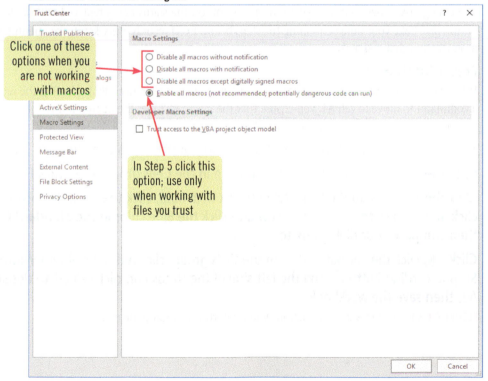

Disabling macros

To prevent viruses from running on your computer, you should disable all macros when you are not working with them. To disable macros, click the Developer tab then click the Macro Security button in the Code group. Clicking any of the first three options disables macros. The first option disables all macros without notifying you. The second option notifies you when macros are disabled, and the third option allows only digitally signed macros to run.

Record a Macro

The easiest way to create a macro is to record it using the Excel Macro Recorder. You turn the Macro Recorder on, name the macro, enter the keystrokes and select the commands you want the macro to perform, then stop the recorder. As you record the macro, Excel automatically translates each action into program code that you can later view and modify. You can take as long as you want to record the macro; a recorded macro contains only your actions, not the amount of time you took to record them. **CASE** ▸ *You are ready to create a macro that enters a headquarters location "stamp" in cell A1 of the active worksheet. You create this macro by recording your actions.*

STEPS

1. **Click the Record Macro button ⊞ on the left side of the status bar**
   The Record Macro dialog box opens, as shown in **FIGURE 9-4**. The default name Macro1 is selected. You can either assign this name or enter a new name. This dialog box also lets you assign a shortcut key for running the macro and assign a storage location for the macro.

2. **Type HQStamp in the Macro name text box**
   It is important to check where the macro will be stored because the default choice is the last location that was selected.

3. **If the Store macro in list box does not display "This Workbook", click the list arrow, then click This Workbook**

4. **Type your name in the Description text box, then click OK**
   The dialog box closes, and the Record Macro button on the status bar is replaced with a Stop Recording button ⊞. Take your time performing the steps below. Excel records every keystroke, menu selection, and mouse action that you make.

5. **Press [Ctrl][Home]**
   When you begin an Excel session, macros record absolute cell references. By beginning the recording with a command to move to cell A1, you ensure that the macro includes the instruction to select cell A1 as the first step, in cases where A1 is not already selected.

6. **Type Cape Town in cell A1, then click the Enter button ✓ on the formula bar**

7. **Click the Home tab, click the Format button in the Cells group, then click Format Cells**

8. **Click the Font tab, in the Font style list box click Bold, click the Underline list arrow and click Single, click the Color list arrow and click the Blue color in the Standard Colors row, then compare your dialog box to FIGURE 9-5**

9. **Click OK, click the Format button in the Cells group, click AutoFit Column Width, click the Stop Recording button ⊞ on the left side of the status bar, click cell D1 to deselect cell A1, then save the workbook**
   FIGURE 9-6 shows the result of the actions you took while recording the macro.

FIGURE 9-4: Record Macro dialog box

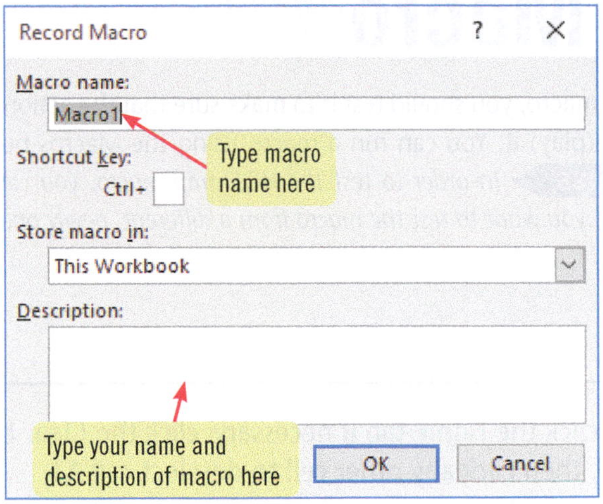

Record Macro

Macro name:
Macro1|

Type macro name here

Shortcut key:
Ctrl+ [ ]

Store macro in:
This Workbook

Description:
[ ]

Type your name and description of macro here

OK   Cancel

FIGURE 9-5: Font tab of the Format Cells dialog box

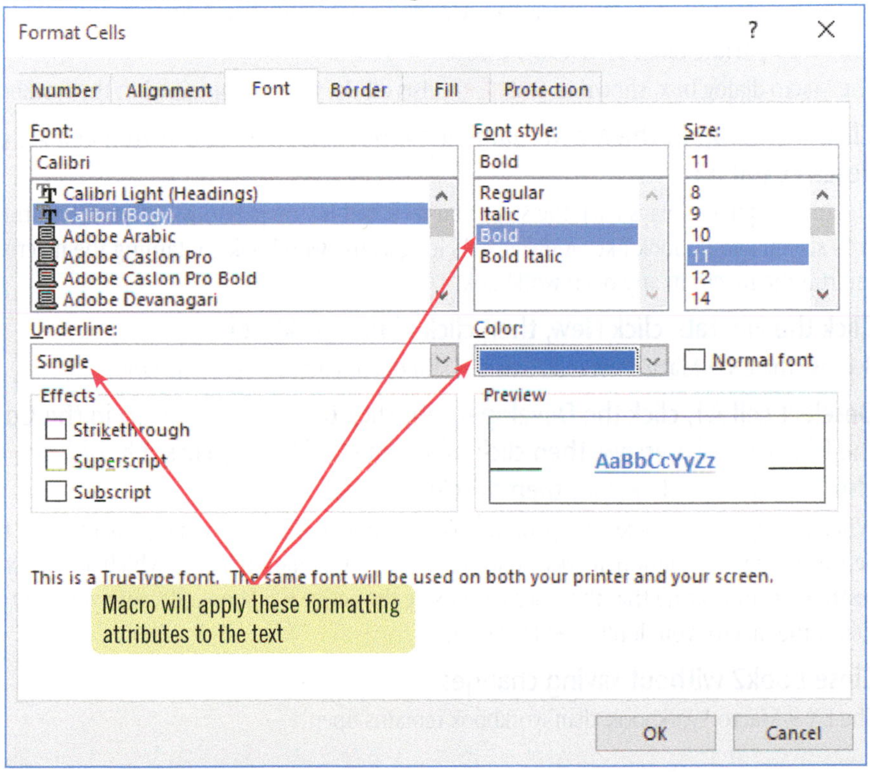

Format Cells

Number Alignment **Font** Border Fill Protection

Font:
Calibri

- Calibri Light (Headings)
- Calibri (Body)
- Adobe Arabic
- Adobe Caslon Pro
- Adobe Caslon Pro Bold
- Adobe Devanagari

Font style:
Bold

- Regular
- Italic
- Bold
- Bold Italic

Size:
11

- 8
- 9
- 10
- 11
- 12
- 14

Underline:
Single

Color:
[ ] ☐ Normal font

Effects
☐ Strikethrough
☐ Superscript
☐ Subscript

Preview

AaBbCcYyZz

This is a TrueType font. The same font will be used on both your printer and your screen.

Macro will apply these formatting attributes to the text

OK   Cancel

FIGURE 9-6: Headquarters stamp

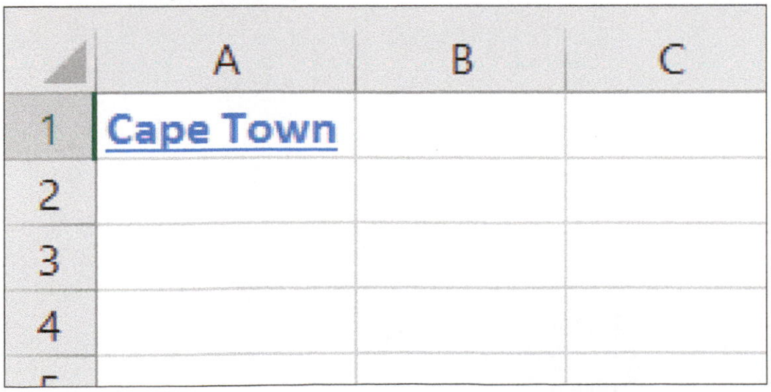

	A	B	C
1	Cape Town		
2			
3			
4			

Run a Macro

Learning Outcomes
- Display selected macros
- Run a macro using the Macro dialog box

Once you record a macro, you should test it to make sure that the actions it performs are correct. To test a macro, you **run** (play) it. You can run a macro using the Macros button in the Code group of the Developer tab. **CASE** *In order to test the HQStamp macro, you clear the contents of cell A1. After completing this test, you want to test the macro from a different, newly opened workbook.*

STEPS

1. **Click cell A1, click the Home tab if necessary, click the Clear button in the Editing group, click Clear All, then click any other cell to deselect cell A1**

   When you delete only the contents of a cell, any formatting still remains in the cell. By using the Clear All option you can be sure that the cell is free of contents and formatting.

2. **Click the Developer tab, click the Macros button in the Code group, click the Macros in list arrow, then click This Workbook**

   The Macro dialog box, shown in **FIGURE 9-7**, lists all the macros contained in the workbook.

3. **Click HQStamp in the Macro name list if necessary, as you watch cell A1 click Run, then deselect cell A1**

   The macro quickly plays back the steps you recorded in the previous lesson. When the macro is finished, your screen should look like **FIGURE 9-8**. As long as the workbook containing the macro remains open, you can run the macro in any open workbook.

4. **Click the File tab, click New, then click Blank workbook**

   Because the EX 9-Macro Workbook.xlsm is still open, you can use its macros.

QUICK TIP
To create a button on the Quick Access Toolbar that will run a macro, click the Customize Quick Access Toolbar button ⬇, click More Commands..., click the Choose commands from list arrow, click Macros, click the desired macro in the list, click Add, then click OK.

5. **Deselect cell A1, click the Developer tab, click the Macros button in the Code group, click the Macros in list arrow, then click All Open Workbooks, click 'EX 9-Macro Workbook. xlsm'!HQStamp, click Run, then deselect cell A1**

   When multiple workbooks are open, the macro name in the Macro dialog box includes the workbook name between single quotation marks, followed by an exclamation point which is an **external reference indicator**, indicating that the macro is outside the active workbook. Because you only used this workbook to test the macro, you don't need to save it.

6. **Close Book2 without saving changes**

   The EX 9-Macro Workbook.xlsm workbook remains open.

FIGURE 9-7: Macro dialog box

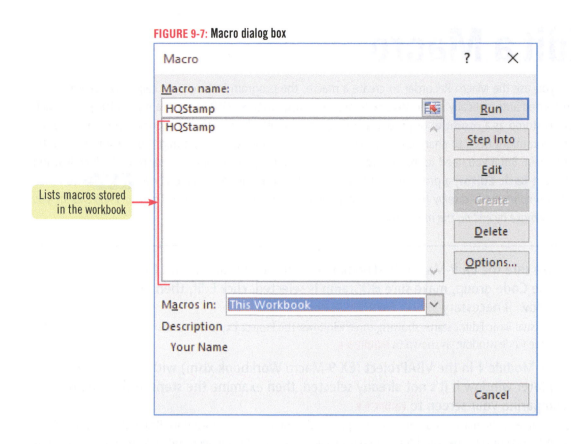

Lists macros stored in the workbook

FIGURE 9-8: Result of running HQStamp macro

Formatted text inserted into cell A1

Running a macro automatically

You can create a macro that automatically performs certain tasks when the workbook in which it is saved is opened. This is useful for actions you want to do every time you open a workbook. For example, you may import data from an external data source into the workbook or format the worksheet data in a certain way. To create a macro that will automatically run when the workbook is opened, you need to name the macro Auto_Open and save it in that workbook.

Edit a Macro

When you use the Macro Recorder to create a macro, the program instructions, called **program code**, are recorded automatically in the **Visual Basic for Applications (VBA)** programming language. Each macro is stored as a **module**, or program code container, attached to the workbook. After you record a macro, you might need to change it. If you have a lot of changes to make, it might be best to record the macro again. But if you need to make only minor adjustments, you can edit the macro code directly using the **Visual Basic Editor**, a program that lets you display and edit your macro code. **CASE** *Jo wants the HQStamp macro to display the department stamp in a slightly larger font size. This is a small change you can easily make by editing the macro code.*

STEPS

1. **Make sure the EX 9-Macro Workbook.xlsm workbook is open, click the Macros button in the Code group, make sure HQStamp is selected, click Edit, then maximize the Code window, if necessary**

   The Visual Basic Editor starts, showing three windows: the Project Explorer window, the Properties window, and the Code window, as shown in **FIGURE 9-9**.

2. **Click Module 1 in the VBAProject (EX 9-Macro Workbook.xlsm) within the Project Explorer window if it's not already selected, then examine the steps in the macro, comparing your screen to FIGURE 9-9**

   The name of the macro and your name appear at the top of the Code window. Below this area, Excel has translated your keystrokes and commands into macro code. When you open and make selections in a dialog box during macro recording, Excel automatically stores all the dialog box settings in the macro code. For example, the line .FontStyle = "Bold" was generated when you clicked Bold in the Format Cells dialog box. You also see lines of code that you didn't generate directly while recording the HQStamp macro, for example, .Name = "Calibri".

3. **In the line .Size = 11, double-click 11 to select it, then type 12**

   Because Module1 is attached to the workbook and not stored as a separate file, any changes to the module are saved automatically when you save the workbook.

4. **Review the code in the Code window**

5. **Click File on the menu bar, then click Close and Return to Microsoft Excel**

   You want to rerun the HQStamp macro to make sure the macro reflects the change you made using the Visual Basic Editor. You begin by clearing the headquarters location from cell A1.

6. **Click cell A1, click the Home tab, click the Clear button in the Editing group, then click Clear All**

7. **Click any other cell to deselect cell A1, click the Developer tab, click the Macros button in the Code group, make sure HQStamp is selected, click Run, then deselect cell A1**

   The headquarters stamp is now in 12-point type, as shown in **FIGURE 9-10**.

8. **Save the workbook**

FIGURE 9-9: Visual Basic Editor showing Module1

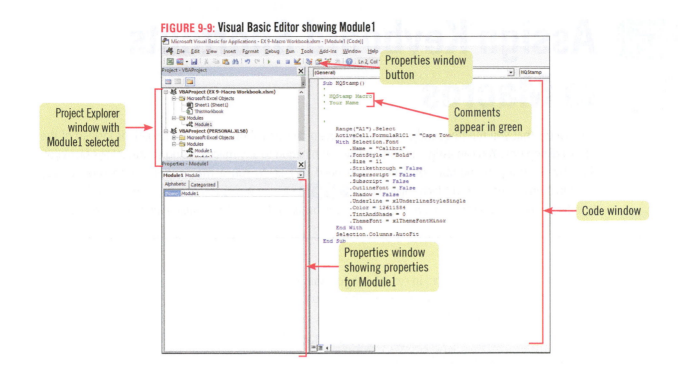

Project Explorer window with Module1 selected

Properties window button

Comments appear in green

Code window

Properties window showing properties for Module1

FIGURE 9-10: Result of running edited HQStamp macro

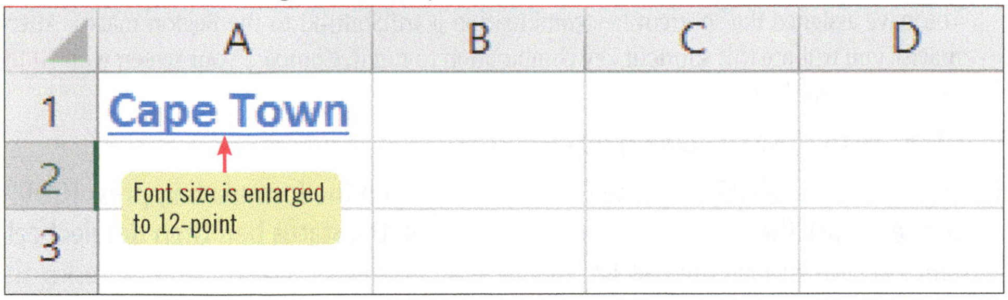

	A	B	C	D
1	Cape Town			
2				
3				

Font size is enlarged to 12-point

Adding comments to Visual Basic code

With practice, you will be able to interpret the lines of macro code. Others who use your macro, however, might want to review the code to, for example, learn the function of a particular line. You can explain the code by adding comments to the macro. **Comments** are explanatory text added to the lines of code. When you enter a comment, you must type an apostrophe (') before the comment text. Otherwise, the program tries to interpret it as a command. On the screen, comments appear in green after you press [Enter], as shown in **FIGURE 9-9**. You can also insert blank lines as comments in the macro code to make the code more readable. To do this, type an apostrophe, then press [Enter].

Assign Keyboard Shortcuts to Macros

For macros that you run frequently, you can run them by using shortcut key combinations instead of the Macro dialog box. You can assign a shortcut key combination to any macro. Using shortcut keys saves you time by reducing the number of actions you need to take to run a macro. You assign shortcut key combinations in the Record Macro dialog box. **CASE** *Jo also wants you to create a macro called Region to enter the headquarters region into a worksheet. You assign a shortcut key combination to run the macro.*

STEPS

1. **Click cell B2**

   You want to record the macro in cell B2, but you want the macro to enter the region of Africa anywhere in a worksheet. Therefore, you will not begin the macro with an instruction to position the cell pointer, as you did in the HQStamp macro.

2. **Click the Record Macro button [icon] on the status bar**

   The Record Macro dialog box opens.

3. **With the default macro name selected, type Region in the Macro name text box**

   Notice the option Shortcut key: Ctrl+ followed by a text box. You can type a letter (A–Z) in the Shortcut key text box to assign the key combination of [Ctrl] plus that letter to run the macro. Because some common Excel shortcuts use the [Ctrl][*letter*] combination, such as [Ctrl][C] for Copy, you decide to use the key combination [Ctrl][Shift] plus a letter to avoid overriding any of these shortcut key combinations.

4. **Click the Shortcut key text box, press and hold [Shift], type R, then in the Description box type your name**

   You have assigned the shortcut key combination [Ctrl][Shift][R] to the Region macro. After you create the macro, you will use this shortcut key combination to run it. Compare your screen with **FIGURE 9-11**. You are ready to record the Region macro.

5. **Click OK to close the dialog box**

6. **Type Africa in cell B2, click the Enter button [icon] on the formula bar, press [Ctrl][I] to italicize the text, click the Stop Recording button [icon] on the status bar, then deselect cell B2**

   Africa appears in italics in cell B2. You are ready to run the macro in cell A5 using the shortcut key combination.

7. **Click cell A5, press and hold [Ctrl][Shift], type R, then deselect the cell**

   The region appears in cell A5, as shown in **FIGURE 9-12**. The macro played back in the selected cell (A5) instead of the cell where it was recorded (B2) because you did not click cell B2 after you began recording the macro.

FIGURE 9-11: Record Macro dialog box with shortcut key assigned

Record Macro   **?   ✕**

Macro name:

Region

Shortcut key:

Ctrl+Shift+ R ← Shortcut to
                   run macro

Store macro in:

This Workbook

Description:

Your Name

OK   Cancel

FIGURE 9-12: Result of running the Region macro

	A	B	C	D	E	F	G	H
1	**Cape Town**							
2		*Africa* ← Result of recording macro in cell B2						
3								
4								
5	*Africa* ← Result of running macro in cell A5							
6								
7								
8								

Excel 2016

Using relative referencing when creating a macro

By default, Excel records absolute cell references in macros. You can record a macro's actions based on the relative position of the active cell by clicking the Use Relative References button in the Code group prior to recording the action. For example, when you create a macro using the default setting of absolute referencing, bolding the range A1:D1 will always bold that range when the macro is run. However, if you click the Use Relative References button when recording the macro before bolding the range, then running the macro will not necessarily result in bolding the range A1:D1. The range that will be bolded will depend on the location of the active cell when the macro is run. If the active cell is A4,

then the range A4:D4 will be bolded. Selecting the Use Relative References button highlights the button name, indicating it is active, as shown in FIGURE 9-13. The button remains active until you click it again to deselect it. This is called a toggle, meaning that it acts like an off/on switch: it retains the relative reference setting until you click it again to turn it off or you exit Excel.

FIGURE 9-13: Use Relative References button selected

Use the Personal Macro Workbook

Learning Outcomes
- Determine when to use the Personal Macro Workbook
- Save a macro in the Personal Macro Workbook

When you create a macro, it is automatically stored in the workbook in which you created it. But if you wanted to use that macro in another workbook, you would have to copy the macro to that workbook. Instead, it's easier to store commonly used macros in the Personal Macro Workbook. The **Personal Macro Workbook** is an Excel file that is always available, unless you specify otherwise, and gives you access to all the macros it contains, regardless of which workbooks are open. The Personal Macro Workbook file is automatically created the first time you choose to store a macro in it, and is named PERSONAL.XLSB. You can add additional macros to the Personal Macro Workbook by saving them in the workbook. By default, the PERSONAL.XLSB workbook opens each time you start Excel, but you don't see it because Excel designates it as a hidden file. When you exit Excel at the end of this module, you will not save any changes that you make to the Personal Macro Workbook in this lesson. **CASE** *You often print worksheets in landscape orientation with 1" left, right, top, and bottom margins. You decide to create a macro that automatically formats a worksheet for printing this way. Because you plan to use this macro in future workbooks, you will store the macro in the Personal Macro Workbook.*

STEPS

1. **Click the Record Macro button [icon] on the status bar**
   The Record Macro dialog box opens.

2. **Type FormatPrint in the Macro name text box, click the Shortcut key text box, press and hold [Shift], type F, then click the Store macro in list arrow**
   You have named the macro FormatPrint and assigned it the shortcut combination [Ctrl][Shift][F]. The "This Workbook" storage option is selected by default, indicating that Excel automatically stores macros in the active workbook, as shown in **FIGURE 9-14**. You can also choose to store the macro in a new workbook or in the Personal Macro Workbook.

3. **Click Personal Macro Workbook, in the Description text box enter your name, then click OK**
   The recorder is on, and you are ready to record the macro keystrokes.

4. **Click the Page Layout tab, click the Orientation button in the Page Setup group, click Landscape, click the Margins button in the Page Setup group, click Custom Margins, then enter 1 in the Top, Left, Bottom, and Right text boxes**
   Compare your margin settings to **FIGURE 9-15**.

5. **Click OK, then click the Stop Recording button [icon] on the status bar**
   You want to test the macro.

6. **Add a new worksheet, in cell A1 type Macro Test, press [Enter], press and hold [Ctrl][Shift], then type F**
   The FormatPrint macro plays back the sequence of commands.

7. **Preview Sheet2 in Backstage view and verify in the Settings that the orientation is landscape and the Last Custom Margins are 1" on the left, right, top, and bottom**

8. **Click the Back button [icon], then save the workbook**

FIGURE 9-14: Record Macro dialog box showing macro storage options

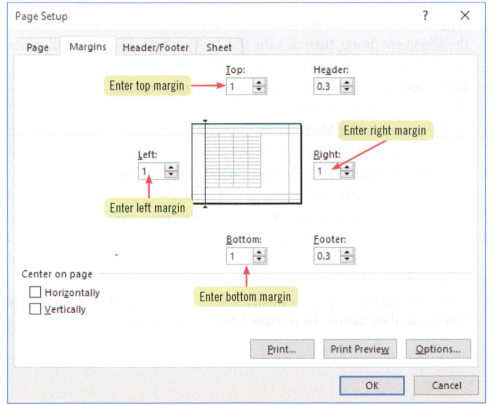

Record Macro   ?   ✕

Macro name:

FormatPrint

Shortcut key:

Ctrl+Shift+ F

Click to store in Personal Macro Workbook

Store macro in:

This Workbook

Personal Macro Workbook
Des New Workbook
This Workbook

Click to save in new blank workbook

Stores macro in active workbook

OK   Cancel

FIGURE 9-15: Margin settings for the FormatPrint macro

Page Setup   ?   ✕

Page   Margins   Header/Footer   Sheet

Top: Header:

Enter top margin → 1   0.3

Enter right margin

Left: Right:

1   1

Enter left margin

Bottom: Footer:

1   0.3

Enter bottom margin

Center on page
☐ Horizontally
☐ Vertically

Print...   Print Preview   Options...

OK   Cancel

Excel 2016

Working with the Personal Macro Workbook

Once you use the Personal Macro Workbook, it opens automatically each time you start Excel so you can add macros to it. By default, the Personal Macro Workbook is hidden in Excel as a precautionary measure so you don't accidentally delete anything from it. If you need to delete a macro from the Personal Macro Workbook, click the View tab click Unhide in the Window group, click PERSONAL.XLSB, then click OK. To hide the Personal Macro Workbook, make it the active workbook, click the View tab then click Hide in the Window group. If you should see a message that Excel is unable to record to your Personal Macro Workbook, check to make sure it is enabled: Click the File tab, click Options, click Add-ins, click the Manage list arrow, click Disabled Items, then click Go. If your Personal Macro Workbook is listed in the Disabled items dialog box, click its name, then click Enable.

Assign a Macro to a Button

Learning Outcomes
- Create a button shape in a worksheet
- Assign a macro to a button

When you create macros for others who will use your workbook, you might want to make the macros more visible so they're easier to use. In addition to using shortcut keys, you can run a macro by assigning it to a button on your worksheet. Then when you click the button the macro will run. **CASE** ▶ *To make it easier for people in the sales division to run the HQStamp macro, you decide to assign it to a button on the workbook. You begin by creating the button.*

STEPS

QUICK TIP
To format a macro button using 3-D effects, clip art, photographs, fills, and shadows, right-click it, select Format Shape from the shortcut menu, then select the desired options in the Format Shape pane.

1. **Add a new worksheet to the workbook, click the Insert tab, click the Shapes button ⬚ in the Illustrations group, then click the first rectangle in the Rectangles group**
   The mouse pointer changes to a + symbol.

2. **Click at the top-left corner of cell A8, then drag ╋ to the lower-right corner of cell B9**
   Compare your screen to **FIGURE 9-16**.

3. **Type HQ Macro to label the button, click the Home tab, click the Center button ▤ in the Alignment group, then click the Middle Align button ▤ in the Alignment group**
   Now that you have created the button, you are ready to assign the macro to it.

4. **Right-click the new button, then on the shortcut menu click Assign Macro**
   The Assign Macro dialog box opens.

5. **Click HQStamp under Macro name, then click OK**
   You have assigned the HQStamp macro to the button.

6. **Click any cell to deselect the button, then click the button**
   The HQStamp macro plays, and the text Cape Town appears in cell A1, as shown in **FIGURE 9-17**.

7. **Save the workbook, preview Sheet3 in Backstage view, then close the workbook**

8. **Click the Developer tab, click the Macro Security button in the Code group, click Macro Settings if necessary, click the Disable all macros with notification option button to select it, then click OK**

9. **Exit Excel, clicking Don't Save when asked to save changes to the Personal Macro Workbook, then submit the workbook to your instructor**

FIGURE 9-16: Button shape

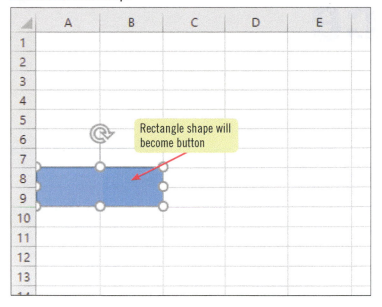

FIGURE 9-17: Sheet3 with the headquarters location text

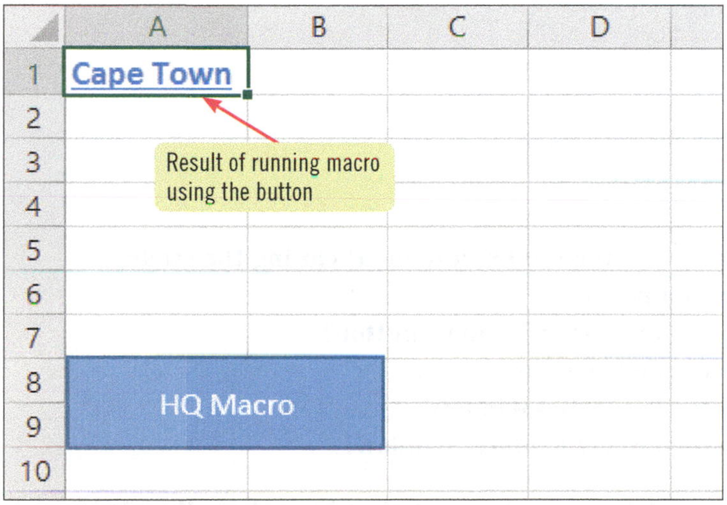

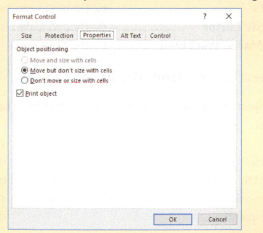

Creating and formatting a form control

You can add an object called a **form control** to an Excel work-sheet to make it easier for users to enter or select data. Click the Developer tab on the Ribbon, click the Insert button in the Controls group, click the desired control in the Form Controls area of the Insert gallery, then draw the shape on the worksheet. After adding a control to a worksheet, you need to link it to a cell or cells in the worksheet. To do this, right-click it, select Format Control, then click the Control tab if necessary. For example, if you add a list box form control, the input range is the location of the list box selections and the cell link is the cell with the numeric value for the current position of the list control. To edit the form control's positioning properties (such as moving, sizing, and printing) right-click the form control, select Format Control, then click the Properties tab. See **FIGURE 9-18**.

FIGURE 9-18: Properties tab of the Format Control dialog box

Practice

Concepts Review

FIGURE 9-19

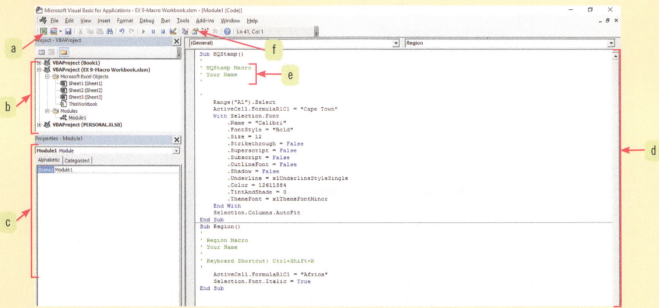

1. Which element do you click to return to Excel without closing the module?
2. Which element points to comments?
3. Which element points to the Properties Window button?
4. Which element points to the Code window?
5. Which element points to the Properties window?
6. Which element points to the Project Explorer window?

Match each term or button with the statement that best describes it.

7. Virus		a. Set of instructions that performs a task in a specified order
8. Macro		b. Statements that appear in green explaining the macro
9. Comments		c. Destructive software that can damage computer files
10. Visual Basic Editor		d. Used to make changes to macro code
11. Personal Macro Workbook		e. Used to store frequently used macros

Select the best answer from the list of choices.

12. You can open the Visual Basic Editor by clicking the _____ button in the Macro dialog box.
    - a. Edit
    - b. Programs
    - c. Modules
    - d. Visual Basic Editor

13. Which of the following is the best candidate for a macro?
    - a. An often-used sequence of commands or actions
    - b. A nonsequential task
    - c. A seldom-used command or task
    - d. A one-button or one-keystroke command

14. **Which of the following is *not* true about editing a macro?**
    a. You edit macros using the Visual Basic Editor.
    b. A macro cannot be edited and must be recorded again.
    c. You can type changes directly in the existing program code.
    d. You can make more than one editing change in a macro.

15. **A macro named _____ will automatically run when the workbook it is saved in opens.**
    a. Default
    b. Auto_Open
    c. Macro1
    d. Open_Macro

16. **Macros are recorded with relative references:**
    a. Only if the Use Relative References button is selected.
    b. In all cases.
    c. By default.
    d. Only if the Use Absolute References button is not selected.

17. **Why is it important to plan a macro?**
    a. Macros can't be deleted.
    b. Planning helps prevent careless errors from being introduced into the macro.
    c. It is impossible to edit a macro.
    d. Macros won't be stored if they contain errors.

18. **Macro security settings can be changed using the _____ tab.**
    a. Home
    b. Developer
    c. Security
    d. Review

19. **You can run macros:**
    a. From the Macro dialog box.
    b. From shortcut key combinations.
    c. From a button on the worksheet.
    d. Using all of the above.

Skills Review

1. **Plan and enable a macro.**
    a. You need to plan a macro that enters and formats your name and department in a worksheet, in the range A1:A2.
    b. Write out the steps the macro will perform.
    c. Write out how the macro could be used in a workbook.
    d. Start Excel, open a new workbook, then save it as a Macro-Enabled workbook named **EX 9-Macros** in the location where you store your Data Files. (*Hint*: The file will have the file extension .xlsm.)
    e. Use the Excel Options feature to display the Developer tab if it is not showing in the Ribbon.
    f. Using the Trust Center dialog box, enable all macros.

2. **Record a macro.**
    a. Open the Record Macro dialog box.
    b. Name the new macro **MyDept**, store it in the current workbook, and enter your name in the Description text box as the person who recorded the macro.
    c. Record the macro, entering your name in cell A1 and **Sales Department** in cell A2. (*Hint*: You need to press [Ctrl][Home] first to ensure cell A1 will be selected when the macro runs.)
    d. Resize column A to fit the information entirely in that column.
    e. Format the font using Purple from Standard Colors.
    f. Add bold formatting to the text in the range A1:A2.
    g. Stop the recorder, then save the workbook.

Skills Review (continued)

3. Run a macro.

a. Clear cell entries and formats in the range affected by the macro, resize the width of column A to 8.43, then select cell B3.

b. Run the MyDept macro. Confirm that your name and your sales department are entered in the range A1:A2.

c. On the worksheet, clear all the cell entries and formats generated by running the MyDept macro. Resize the width of column A to 8.43.

d. Save the workbook.

4. Edit a macro.

a. Open the MyDept macro in the Visual Basic Editor.

b. Change the line of code above the last line from Selection.Font.Bold = True to **Selection.Font.Bold = False**.

c. Use the Close and Return to Microsoft Excel command on the File menu to return to Excel.

d. Test the macro on Sheet1, click outside the range A1:A2, then compare your worksheet to **FIGURE 9-20**, verifying that the text is not bold.

e. Save the workbook.

FIGURE 9-20

▲	A	B	C
1	Your Name		
2	Sales Department		
3			
4			

5. Assign keyboard shortcuts to macros.

a. Create a macro named **DeptStamp** in the current workbook, assign your macro the shortcut key combination [Ctrl][Shift][D], enter your name in the description. (*Hint*: If you get an error when trying to use [Ctrl][Shift][D], select another key combination.)

b. Begin recording, starting in the current cell of the worksheet. Type **Sales Department**, format it in bold, italic, and with a font color of green, without underlining. Stop recording.

c. Clear the contents and formats from the cell containing the sales department text that you used to record the macro.

d. Use the shortcut key combination to run the DeptStamp macro in a cell other than the one in which it was recorded. Compare your macro result to **FIGURE 9-21**. The Sales Department text may appear in a different cell.

e. Save the workbook.

FIGURE 9-21

D	E	F	G	H
	Sales Department			

6. Use the Personal Macro Workbook.

a. Using Sheet1, record a new macro called **FitToLand** and store it in the Personal Macro Workbook with your name in the Description text box. If you already have a macro named FitToLand, replace that macro. The macro should set the print orientation to landscape.

b. After you record the macro, add a new worksheet, and enter **Test data for FitToLand macro** in cell A1.

c. Preview Sheet2 in Backstage view to verify the orientation is set to portrait.

d. Run the FitToLand macro. (You may have to wait a few moments.)

e. Add your name to the Sheet2 footer, then preview Sheet2 to verify that it is now in Landscape.

f. Save the workbook.

7. Assign a macro to a button.

a. Add a new worksheet, then enter **Landscape Button Test** in cell A1.

b. Using the rectangle shape, draw a rectangle in the range A7:B8.

c. Label the button with the text **Landscape Macro**, then center and middle align the text. Compare your worksheet to **FIGURE 9-22**.

d. Assign the macro PERSONAL.XLSB!FitToLand to the button.

e. Verify that the orientation of Sheet3 is set to portrait.

f. Run the FitToLand macro using the button.

Skills Review (continued)

g. Preview the worksheet, and verify that it is in Landscape.

h. Add your name to the Sheet3 footer, then save the workbook.

i. Click the Developer tab, click the Macro Security button in the Code group, click Macro Settings if necessary, click the Disable all macros with notification option button to select it, then click OK.

j. Close the workbook, exit Excel without saving the FitToLand macro in the Personal Macro Workbook, then submit your workbook to your instructor.

FIGURE 9-22

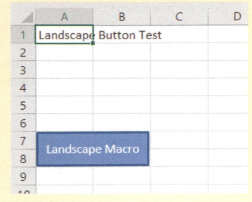

Independent Challenge 1

As the office manager of Cape Engineering, you need to develop ways to help your fellow employees work more efficiently. Employees have asked for Excel macros that can do the following:

- Adjust the column widths to display all column data in a worksheet.
- Place the company name of Cape Engineering in the header of a worksheet.

(Note: Remember to enable macros before beginning this independent challenge, and to disable them when you are finished.)

a. Plan and write the steps necessary for each macro.

b. Start Excel, open EX 9-1.xlsx from where you store your Data Files, then save it as a macro-enabled workbook called **EX 9-Engineering**.

c. Check your macro security on the Developer tab to be sure that macros are enabled.

d. Create a macro named **ColumnFit**, save it in the EX 9-Engineering.xlsm workbook, assign the ColumnFit macro a shortcut key combination of [Ctrl][Shift][F] (if this shortcut is already in use, choose a different keyboard combination), and add your name in the description area for the macro. Record the macro using the following instructions:

- Adjust a worksheet's column widths to display all data. (*Hint*: Select the entire sheet, click the Home tab, click the Format button in the Cells group, select AutoFit Column Width, then click cell A1 to deselect the worksheet.)
- End the macro recording.

e. Format the widths of columns A through G to 8.43, then test the ColumnFit macro with the shortcut key combination [Ctrl][Shift][F].

f. Create a macro named **CompanyName**, and save it in the EX 9-Engineering.xlsm workbook. Assign the macro a shortcut key combination of [Ctrl][Shift][N] (or a different keyboard combination if necessary), and add your name in the description area for the macro.

g. Record the CompanyName macro. The macro should place the company name of Cape Engineering in the center section of the worksheet header.

h. Enter **Cape Engineering Header test data** in cell A1 of Sheet2 and test the CompanyName macro using the shortcut key combination you set in Step f. Preview Sheet2 to view the header.

i. Edit the CompanyName macro in the Visual Basic Editor to change the company name from Cape Engineering to **Shore Engineering**. Close the Visual Basic Editor and return to Excel.

j. Add a rectangle button to Sheet3 in the range A6:D7. Label the button with the text **Company Name Header Macro**. Center and middle align the button text on the button.

k. Assign the CompanyName macro to the button.

Excel 2016

Independent Challenge 1 (continued)

l. Enter **Shore Engineering header test data** in cell A1. Compare your screen to **FIGURE 9-23**. Use the button to run the CompanyName macro. Preview the worksheet, checking the header to be sure it is displaying the new company name.

m. Enter your name in the footers of all three worksheets. Save the workbook, close the workbook, then submit the workbook to your instructor and exit Excel.

Independent Challenge 2

You are an assistant to the VP of Sales at Green Horizons, a landscape distributor. As part of your work, you create spreadsheets with sales projections for different regions of the company. You frequently have to change the print settings so that workbooks print in landscape orientation with custom margins of 1" on the top and bottom. You also add a header with the company name on every worksheet. You have decided that it's time to create a macro to streamline this process. *(Note: Remember to enable macros before beginning this independent challenge, and to disable them when you are finished.)*

a. Plan and write the steps necessary to create a macro that performs all of the tasks described above.

b. Check your macro security settings to confirm that macros are enabled.

c. Start Excel, create a new workbook, then save it as a macro-enabled file named **EX 9-Sales Macro** in the location where you store your Data Files.

d. Create a macro that changes the page orientation to landscape, adds custom margins of 1" at the top and bottom of the page, adds a header of **Green Horizons** in the center section, formatted in bold with a font size of 12 points. Name the macro **Format**, add your name in the description, assign it the shortcut key combination [Ctrl][Shift][F] (or a different combination if necessary), and store it in the current workbook.

e. Add a new worksheet and enter the text **Format Macro Test** in cell A1. Test the macro using the shortcut key combination you set in Step d. Preview Sheet2 to check the page orientation, margins, and header.

f. Add a new worksheet, enter the text **Format Worksheet Button Test** in cell A1, add a rectangular button with the text **Format Worksheet** that runs the Format macro, then test the macro using the button.

g. Preview the Visual Basic code for the macro.

h. Save the workbook, close the workbook, exit Excel, then submit the workbook to your instructor.

Independent Challenge 3

You are the Southeast regional sales manager of Atlantic Consulting, a technology consulting firm. You manage the Southeast operations and frequently create workbooks with data from three office locations. It's tedious to change the tab names and colors every time you open a new workbook, so you decide to create a macro that will add the office locations and colors to the three office location worksheet tabs, as shown in **FIGURE 9-24**. *(Note: Remember to enable macros before beginning this independent challenge, and to disable them when you are finished.)*

a. Plan and write the steps to create the macro described above.

b. Start Excel and open a new workbook.

c. Create the macro using the plan you created in Step a, name it **WBFormat**, assign it the shortcut key combination [Ctrl][Shift][W] (or a different combination if necessary), store it in the Personal Macro Workbook, and add your name in the description area. (*Hint:* The tab colors are red, green, and blue from the Standard Colors.)

d. After recording the macro, close the workbook without saving it. Save the changes to the Personal Macro workbook.

Independent Challenge 3 (continued)

e. Open a new workbook, then save it as a macro-enabled workbook named **EX 9-Atlantic Test** in the location where you store your Data Files. Use the shortcut key combination you created in Step c to test the macro in the new workbook.

f. Unhide the PERSONAL.XLSB workbook. (*Hint:* Click the View tab click the Unhide button in the Window group, click PERSONAL.XLSB, then click OK. You will hide PERSONAL.XLSB at the end of this exercise.)

g. Edit the WBFormat macro using FIGURE 9-25 as a guide, changing the Charlotte sheet name to Durham. (*Hint:* There are two instances of Charlotte that need to be changed.)

h. Open a new workbook, then save it as a macro-enabled workbook named **EX 9-Atlantic** in the location where you store your Data Files. Test the edited macro using the shortcut key combination you set in Step c.

i. Add a new sheet in the workbook, and name it **Code**. Copy the WBFormat macro code from the Personal Macro Workbook, and paste it in the Code sheet beginning in cell A1 (be careful to select only the code for this macro). Save the workbook, close the workbook, hide the Personal Macro Workbook, then submit EX 9-Atlantic to your instructor.

j. Hide the PERSONAL.XLSB workbook. (*Hint:* With the PERSONAL.XLSB workbook active, click the View tab, then click the Hide button in the Window group.)

k. Close the workbook without saving changes to the PERSONAL.XLSB workbook, then exit Excel.

FIGURE 9-25

```
Sub WBFormat()
'
' WBFormat Macro
' Your Name
'
' Keyboard Shortcut: Ctrl+Shift+W
'
    Sheets.Add After:=ActiveSheet
    Sheets.Add After:=ActiveSheet
    Sheets("Sheet1").Select
    Sheets("Sheet1").Name = "Miami"
    Sheets("Sheet2").Select
    Sheets("Sheet2").Name = "Atlanta"
    Sheets("Sheet3").Select
    Sheets("Sheet3").Name = "Durham"
    Sheets("Miami").Select
    With ActiveWorkbook.Sheets("Miami").Tab
        .Color = 255
        .TintAndShade = 0
    End With
    Sheets("Atlanta").Select
    With ActiveWorkbook.Sheets("Atlanta").Tab
        .Color = 5287936
        .TintAndShade = 0
    End With
    Sheets("Durham").Select
    With ActiveWorkbook.Sheets("Durham").Tab
        .Color = 12611584
        .TintAndShade = 0
    End With
End Sub
```

Independent Challenge 4: Explore

As the business manager for a hospital, you work with confidential information in a patient information workbook. To make sure your office colleagues understand the confidential nature of this workbook, you need to create a macro that provides a confidentiality message when this workbook is opened. *(Note: Remember to enable macros before beginning this independent challenge, and to disable them when you are finished.)*

FIGURE 9-26

```
Sub Auto_Open()
'
' Auto_Open Macro
' Your Name
'
MsgBox "Confidential"
'
End Sub
```

a. Start Excel, open EX 9-2.xlsx from where you store your Data Files, then save it as a Macro-Enabled workbook named **EX 9-Patient Information**.

b. Create a new macro with the name Auto_Open, store it in the Patient Information workbook, and add your name in the description area.

c. Stop the macro recording before completing any steps.

d. Open the Auto_Open macro in the Visual Basic Editor.

e. Use FIGURE 9-26 as a guide to add a message box to the Auto_Open macro.

f. Return to Excel and save the workbook.

g. Close, then reopen, the workbook.

h. Close the message box.

i. Enter your name in the footer. Save the workbook, close the workbook, then submit the workbook to your instructor and exit Excel.

Visual Workshop

Start Excel, open EX 9-3.xlsx from the location where you store your Data Files, then save it as a macro-enabled workbook called **EX 9-Accounts**. Create a macro with the name **TotalAccounts**, save the macro in the EX 9-Accounts workbook that does the following:

- Totals the weekly accounts for each employee by totaling the accounts for the first employee and copying that formula for the other employees
- Adds a row at the top of the worksheet and inserts a label of **Accounts** in a font size of 14 point, in bold font, centered across all columns
- Adds your name in the worksheet footer

Test the TotalAccounts macro by reopening EX 9-3.xlsx and running the macro. Compare your macro results to FIGURE 9-27. Close the Data File EX 9-3 without saving it, then save the EX 9-Accounts workbook. Submit the EX 9-Accounts workbook to your instructor. *(Note: Remember to enable macros before beginning this visual workshop, and to disable them when you are finished.)*

FIGURE 9-27

	A	B	C	D	E	F	G	H	I
1				**Accounts**					
2		Monday	Tuesday	Wednesday	Thursday	Friday	Saturday	Sunday	Total
3	John Smith	5	6	8	2	1	0	0	22
4	Paula Jones	6	8	8	7	7	6	2	44
5	Linda Kristol	4	3	7	6	3	5	0	28
6	Al Meng	7	6	6	5	5	1	0	30
7	Robert Delgado	7	6	5	8	7	7	0	40
8	Harry Degual	7	6	5	5	7	8	0	38
9	Jody Williams	8	6	2	6	8	5	3	38
10	Mary Abbott	7	8	8	6	7	2	0	38
11	Ken Yang	6	8	4	4	4	4	1	31
12	Cathy Martin	7	8	2	8	8	1	0	34
13									
14									
15									

Automating Worksheet Tasks

Enhancing Charts

CASE Reason2Go's manager of the Sydney office, Will Moss, has requested charts comparing sales and trends in the office's regions over the first two quarters. You will produce these charts and enhance them to improve their appearance, clarify the display, and make the worksheet data easier to interpret.

Module Objectives

After completing this module, you will be able to:

- Customize a data series
- Change a data source and add a chart style
- Add chart elements
- Format chart axes
- Create a combination chart
- Enhance a chart
- Summarize data with sparklines
- Identify data trends

Files You Will Need

EX 10-1.xlsx	EX 10-5.xlsx
EX 10-2.xlsx	EX 10-6.xlsx
EX 10-3.xlsx	EX 10-7.xlsx
EX 10-4.xlsx	

Customize a Data Series

A **data series** is the sequence of values that Excel uses to **plot**, or create, a chart. As with other Excel elements, you can change the data series presentation to get another view of your data. For example, you can reverse the data charted on the *x* and *y* axes. You can also format a chart's data series to make the chart more attractive and easier to read. **CASE** *Will wants a chart showing the sales for each region in January and February. You begin by creating a column chart, which you will customize to make it easier to compare the sales for each region.*

STEPS

1. **Start Excel, open EX 10-1.xlsx from the location where you store your Data Files, then save it as EX 10-Region Sales**

   To begin, Will wants to see how each region performed over January and February. The first step is to select the data you want to appear in the chart.

2. **Select the range A2:C5**

3. **Click the Quick Analysis tool** 📊 **at the lower right corner of the selected range, click the Charts tab, move the mouse pointer over the recommended charts to view your data in different chart types, then point to the Clustered Column option**

   A clustered column chart preview comparing the January and February sales for each branch appears, as shown in **FIGURE 10-1**. You decide to use this option to compare the monthly sales for each branch.

4. **Click Clustered Column, then on the Chart Tools Design tab on the Ribbon, click the Switch Row/Column button in the Data group**

   The legend now contains the region data, and the horizontal axis groups the bars by month. Will can now easily compare the region sales for each month. You want to see how the graph looks with the Australia data series plotted in a green color.

5. **Double-click the Jan Australia data series bar (the far-left bar on the graph), click the Fill & Line button** 🖍 **in the Format Data Series pane, click Fill, click the Solid fill option button, click the Fill Color list arrow** 🎨 **, click Dark Green, Accent 5 in the Theme Colors group, then close the Format Data Series pane**

6. **Point to the edge of the chart, then drag the chart to place its upper-left corner in the upper-left corner of cell A7**

7. **Drag the chart's lower-right corner sizing handle to fit the chart in the range A7:H20, then compare your chart to FIGURE 10-2**

   Dragging a corner sizing handle resizes the chart proportionally; dragging a side or top handle resizes it horizontally or vertically.

8. **Save the workbook**

Adding width and depth to data series

You can change the gap depth and the gap width in column charts by double-clicking one of the chart's data series, then dragging the Gap Width or depth sliders in the Format Data Series pane. Increasing the gap width adds space between each set of data on the chart by decreasing the width of the chart's data series. If you are working with 3-D charts, you also have the option to increase the gap depth to add depth to all categories of data.

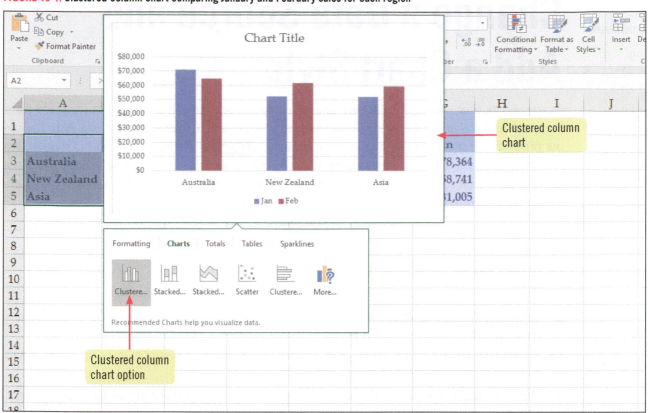

FIGURE 10-2: Chart comparing region sales in January and February

Change a Data Source and Add a Chart Style

As you update your workbooks with new data, you may also need to add data series to (or delete them from) a chart. Excel makes it easy to revise a chart's data source and to rearrange chart data. Also, you can use preformatted styles to make a chart more attractive. **CASE** ▶ *Will wants the chart to show branch sales for the first quarter, so you need to add the March data to your chart. You also want to add a chart style and modify the chart colors to make the chart more attractive. You begin by changing the data view to compare branch sales for each month.*

STEPS

1. **Click the Chart Tools Design tab if necessary, then click the Switch Row/Column button in the Data group**

   The region data again appears on the horizontal axis. You want to add the March data to the chart.

2. **In the worksheet, drag the lower-right corner of the data border in cell C5 to the right to include the data in column D**

   The March data series appears on the chart, as shown in **FIGURE 10-3**. You want to make the columns more attractive using one of the chart styles.

3. **With the chart selected, click the Chart Styles button 🖌 to the right of the chart, then scroll down to and click Style 14 (the last style)**

   The data bars have an appearance of depth and the January data bars are now a blue color again. The menu remains open. You want to change the colors of the data bars.

4. **Click Color at the top of the Chart Styles gallery**

   There are colorful and monochromatic color sets available.

5. **Point to the color galleries to preview them, click Color 2 (the second row from the top), then click 🖌 again to close the gallery**

   The data bars appear in the new color scheme. Compare your chart to **FIGURE 10-4**.

6. **Save the workbook**

FIGURE 10-3: Chart with March data series added

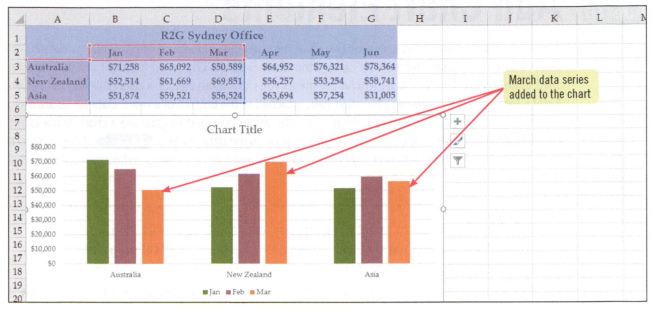

FIGURE 10-4: Chart with new Chart Style and color set

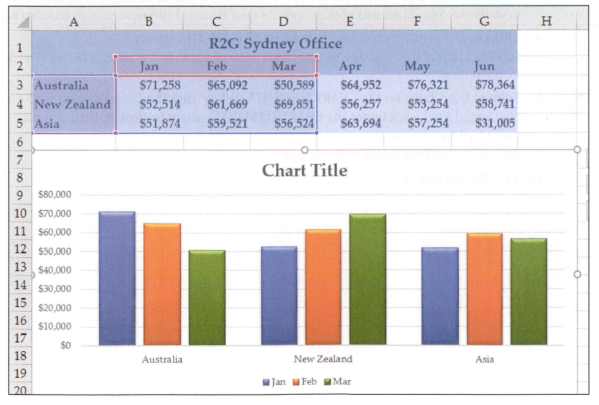

Add Chart Elements

When you create a chart, **chart elements** such as the chart title and legend often appear by default. You can add or remove chart elements by clicking the Chart Elements button on the right side of a selected chart to display an element list. Other chart elements you can choose include a data table and data labels. A **data table** is a grid containing the chart data, attached to the bottom of a chart. Data tables are useful because they display—directly on the chart itself—the values you used to generate a chart. **Data labels** also display series values, but value labels appear near or on the data markers. **CASE** *Will wants you to move the chart to its own worksheet, add a data table to emphasize the chart's first-quarter data, and add data labels.*

STEPS

1. **Click the chart object to select it if necessary, click the Chart Tools Design tab on the Ribbon if necessary, then click the Move Chart button in the Location group**

   The Move Chart dialog box opens. You want to place the chart on a new sheet named First Quarter.

2. **Click the New sheet option button, type First Quarter in the New sheet text box, then click OK**

   The chart moves to a separate sheet.

3. **Click the Chart Elements button [+], click the Data Table check box to select it, move the mouse pointer over the Data Table list arrow, click once, then verify that With Legend Keys is selected**

   A data table with the first-quarter data and a key to the legend appears at the bottom of the chart, as shown in **FIGURE 10-5**. You will add data labels to clarify the exact amount of sales represented by each data bar.

4. **Click the Data Labels check box in the CHART ELEMENTS gallery**

   Data labels appear above the data bars. You don't need the legend keys in the data table, so you decide to remove them.

5. **Point to Data Table on the CHART ELEMENTS gallery, click the Data Table list arrow, click No Legend Keys, click under the CHART ELEMENTS gallery to close it, then compare your chart to FIGURE 10-6**

   The data table no longer shows the legend keys.

6. **Save the workbook**

FIGURE 10-5: Chart with data table

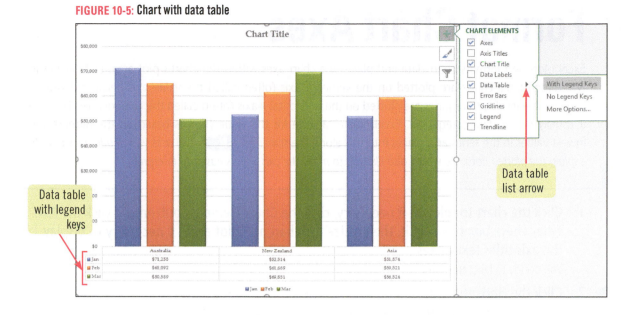

FIGURE 10-5: Chart with data table

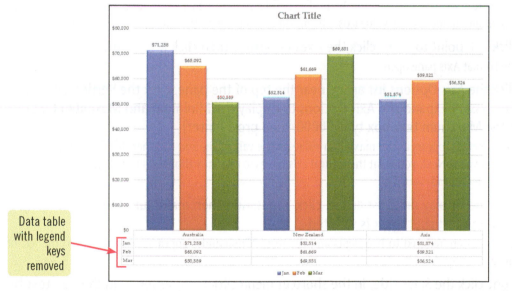

FIGURE 10-6: Chart with data table legend keys removed

Formatting legends

To format a legend's fill, border, color, or shadows, click the Chart Elements button ![+], point to Legend, click the Legend list arrow, then click More Options. Using the options in the Format Legend pane, you can use the Legend Options tab and Text Options tab to customize the legend. For example, you can add a picture to the legend by clicking the Fill & Line button, clicking Fill, clicking the Picture or texture fill option button, clicking the File, Clipboard, or Online button (depending on the picture source), then browsing to your image. The legend in **FIGURE 10-7** has a textured fill background. You can also drag a legend to any location. To change a legend's font size, color, or style, right-click the legend text, click Font on the shortcut menu, then adjust the settings in the Font dialog box.

FIGURE 10-7: Formatted legend

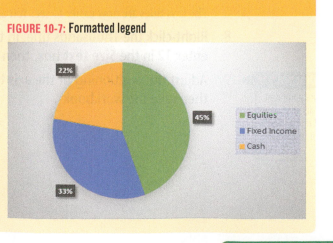

Excel 2016

Format Chart Axes

Learning Outcomes
• Add axis titles
• Change the vertical axis maximum value

Excel plots and formats chart data and places the chart axes within the chart's plot area. Data values in two-dimensional charts are plotted on the vertical *y*-axis (often called the value axis because it usually shows value levels). Categories are plotted on the horizontal *x*-axis (often called the category axis because it usually shows data categories). Excel creates a scale for the value (*y*) axis based on the highest and lowest values in the series and places intervals along the scale. **CASE** *Will asks you to add axes titles to explain the plotted data. He would also like you to make the axis values easier to interpret.*

STEPS

1. **Click the chart to select it if necessary, click the Chart Elements button ⊞, click the Axis Titles check box to select it, then resize the chart and plot areas if necessary to display the axis titles text boxes**
   You decide to label the axes.

2. **Click the Horizontal axis title text box, type Regions, then press [Enter]**
   The word "Regions" appears as the Horizontal axis title after you press [Enter].

3. **Click the Vertical axis title text box, type Sales, then press [Enter]**
   The word "Sales" appears in the Vertical axis title as shown in **FIGURE 10-8**. You decide to change the maximum number on the value axis. The maximum number on the value axis is currently $80,000.

4. **Click ⊞, point to Axes, click the Axes list arrow, then click More Options**
   The Format Axis pane opens.

5. **Click the Axis Options list arrow near the top of the pane, click the Vertical (Value) Axis, if necessary expand the Axis Options to display the Minimum and Maximum text boxes, in the Maximum text box type 90000, then press [Enter]**
   Now $90,000 appears as the maximum value on the value axis, and the chart bar heights adjust to reflect the new value. Next, you want the vertical axis values to appear without additional zeroes to make the chart data easier to read.

6. **Click the Display units list arrow, click Thousands, then make sure the Show display units label on chart check box is selected**
   The values are reduced to two digits and the word "Thousands" appears in a text box to the left of the values.

7. **Right-click the Sales title, in the shortcut menu click Font, enter 16 in the Size text box in the Font dialog box, click OK, right-click the Regions title, in the shortcut menu click Font, enter 16 in the Size text box in the Font dialog box, then click OK**
   The axis titles are now easier to see. You also want the unit label to be more legible.

8. **Right-click the Thousands title, in the shortcut menu click Font, in the Font dialog box enter 12 in the Size text box, then click OK**

9. **Adjust the positioning of the axis titles and/or unit label if necessary to match FIGURE 10-9, then save the workbook**

FIGURE 10-8: Chart with axis titles

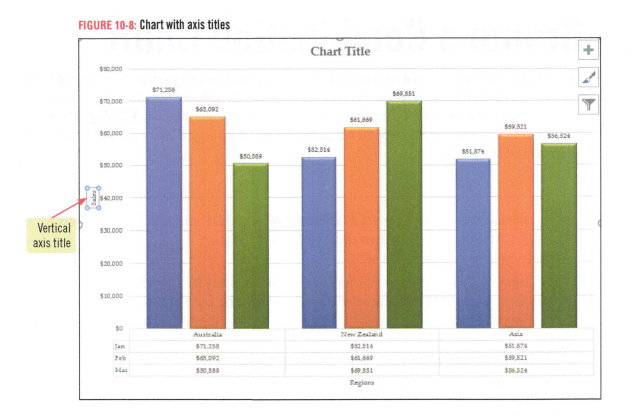

FIGURE 10-9: Chart with formatted axes and axis titles

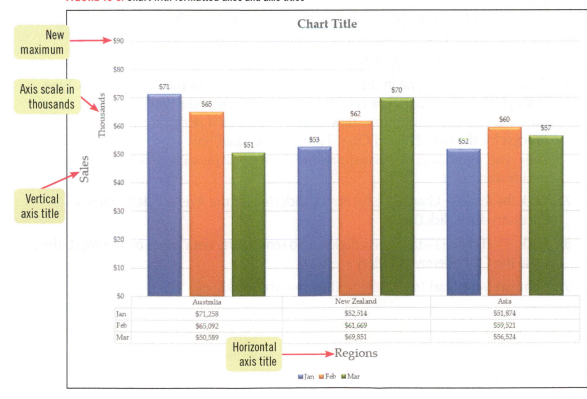

Excel 2016

Create a Combination Chart

Learning Outcomes
• Add chart data
• Create a chart with two types of graphs

A combination chart is a chart that combines two or more chart types in a single chart. This is helpful if you have different types of data in a chart and you want to emphasize the different data types. An example of a combination chart is a line and bar combination chart showing both profits and sales. **CASE** ▶ *Will wants the chart to also show sales averages for the first quarter months. To accomplish this, you decide to add a line chart to the existing column chart.*

STEPS

1. **Click the Sales sheet tab to select it, select the range A2:D5, click the Quick Analysis tool 📋, click the Totals tab, then click the Average button**
   Averages for the months appear in row 6.

2. **Click the First Quarter sheet tab, click the chart if necessary to select it, click the Chart Tools Design tab, then click the Select Data button in the Data group**
   The Select Data Source dialog box opens, where you can select worksheet data to include in the new chart element.

3. **Edit the Chart data range to =Sales!$A$2:$D$6, then click OK**
   The average data points are included in the chart as shown in **FIGURE 10-10**. Before you create the combination chart, you want to create more room on the chart. You can make more room by moving the legend into the data table.

4. **Click the Chart Elements button ⊞, click the Data Table list arrow, click With Legend Keys, click the Legend check box to remove the legend, then click ⊞ to close the gallery**
   You want to switch the axis data to show average amounts for each month.

5. **Click the Switch Row/Column button in the Data group**
   The average amounts for each month will be easier to distinguish if they are on a different type of graph.

QUICK TIP
You can plot two data sets on different axes by creating a combination chart, selecting the Secondary Axis checkbox next to one of the data series, then clicking OK.

6. **Click Change Chart Type in the Type group, click Combo in the Change Chart Type dialog box, in the Chart Type column near the bottom of the dialog box click the Australia Chart Type list arrow, click Clustered Column if necessary, then repeat this process for the New Zealand Chart Type and the Asia Chart Type**
   These values will appear in the clustered column chart format, but you want the average sales data to appear in a line chart format.

7. **Click the Average Chart Type list arrow, click Line for the Average data series if necessary, then click OK**

8. **Click ⊞, click the Data Labels check box to remove the data labels on the chart, then close the Chart Elements gallery**

9. **Compare your chart to FIGURE 10-11, then save the workbook**

Charting data accurately

The purpose of a chart is to help viewers interpret the worksheet data. When creating charts, make sure that your chart accurately portrays your data. Charts can sometimes misrepresent data and thus mislead people. For example, it is possible to change the y-axis units or its starting value to make charted sales values appear larger than they are. Even though you may have correctly labeled the sales values on the chart, the height of the data points will lead people viewing the chart to think the sales are higher than the labeled values. So use caution when you modify charts to make sure you accurately represent your data.

FIGURE 10-10: Chart with average data series

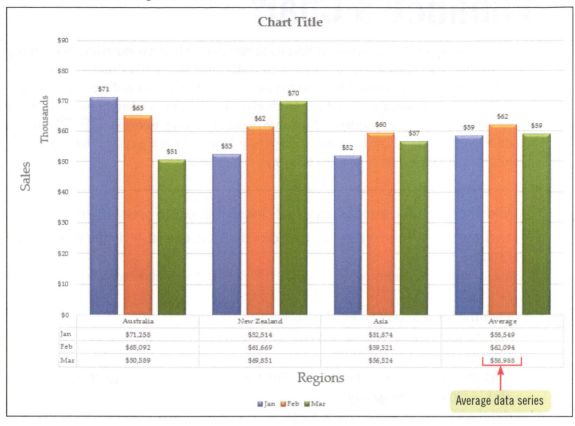

FIGURE 10-11: Combination chart with two types of graphs

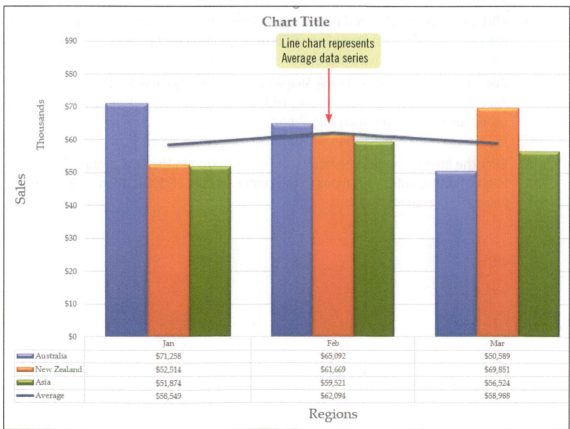

Excel 2016

Enhance a Chart

You can enhance your chart or worksheet titles using **WordArt**, which is preformatted text. Once you've added WordArt text, you can edit or format it by adding 3-D effects and shadows. WordArt text is a shape rather than text. This means that you cannot treat WordArt objects as if they were labels entered in a cell; that is, you cannot sort, use the spell checker, or use their cell references in formulas. You can further enhance your chart by adding a shape style to one of the chart elements. **CASE** ▶ *Will asks you to add a distinctive title to the chart. You decide to use WordArt for this purpose, and to achieve a more dimensional look for the chart by adding a shape style to the plot area.*

STEPS

1. **Click the Chart Title text box, type First Quarter Sales, then press [Enter]**

2. **Click the Chart Tools Format tab, then click the More button ⏷ in the WordArt Styles group**

   The Word Art styles gallery opens, as shown in **FIGURE 10-12**. This is where you select a WordArt style for your text.

3. **Click the Fill - Indigo - Accent 1, Shadow**

   The title text becomes formatted with blue letters. Next, you want to enhance the look of the plot area; you'll start by removing the gridlines.

4. **Click the Chart Elements button ⊞, click the Gridlines checkbox to deselect it, then click ⊞ to close the gallery**

   You also want to add a shape style to the plot area of the chart. Some chart elements cannot be selected using the CHART ELEMENTS gallery on the chart; instead, you need to use the Chart Elements list arrow on the Ribbon.

5. **Click the chart to select it if necessary, click the Chart Tools Format tab if necessary, click the Chart Elements list arrow in the Current Selection group, then click Plot Area**

   The plot area of the chart is selected, as shown by the four small circles on its corners.

6. **Click the More button ⏷ in the Shape Styles group, click the Subtle Effect - Indigo, Accent 1 button (in the fourth row), click the Shape Effects button in the Shape Styles group, point to Preset, then click Preset 5**

   The plot area of the chart is formatted in a light blue color with a slight 3-D effect.

7. **Click the Insert tab, click the Header & Footer button in the Text group, click the Custom Footer button, enter your name in the center section, click OK, then click OK again**

   Compare your chart to **FIGURE 10-13**.

FIGURE 10-12: WordArt Styles gallery

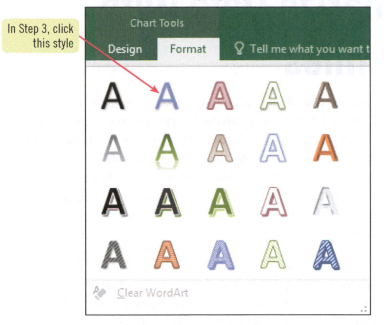

FIGURE 10-13: Chart with formatted title and plot area

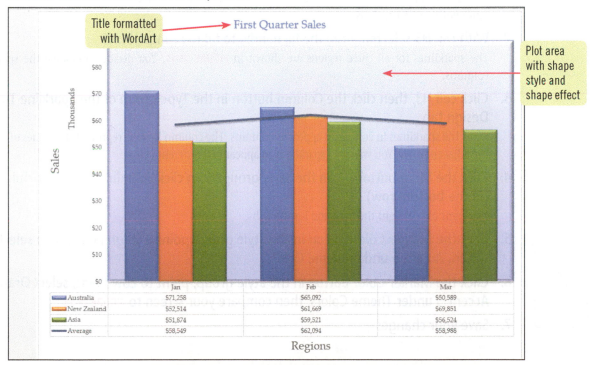

Working with hierarchical, waterfall, and statistical charts

In addition to common chart types such as column charts and pie charts, Excel includes chart types that are useful for illustrating more specific types of data. These include Waterfall, Histogram, Pareto, Box & Whisker; Treemap, and Sunburst. **Treemap** and **Sunburst** are hierarchical charts that are used to present data with many different levels. To insert one of these chart types, click the Insert tab, click the Insert Hierarchy Chart button 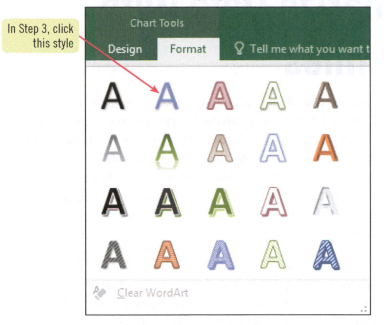 in the Charts group, then click the chart type. **Waterfall** charts help to visualize financial data or other data with positive and negative values. To insert a Waterfall chart, click the Insert tab, click the Insert Waterfall or Stock Chart button in the Charts group, then click Waterfall. **Histogram, Pareto,** and **Box & Whisker** charts are statistical chart types and can be added by clicking the Insert tab, clicking the Insert Statistic Chart button in the Charts group, then clicking the chart type. Pareto is one of the options in the Histogram category.

Excel 2016

Summarize Data with Sparklines

You can create a quick overview of your data by adding sparklines to the worksheet cells. **Sparklines** are miniature charts that show data trends in a worksheet range, such as sales increases or decreases. Sparklines are also useful for highlighting maximum and minimum values in a range of data. Sparklines usually appear close to the data they represent. Any changes that you make to a worksheet are reflected in the sparklines that represent the data. After you add sparklines to a worksheet, you can change the sparkline and color. You can also format high and low data points in special colors. **CASE** ▶ *As a supplement to the chart, Will wants the Sales worksheet to illustrate the sales trends for the first half of the year. You decide to add sparklines to tell a quick visual story about these trends.*

STEPS

1. **Click the Sales sheet, click cell H3, click the Insert tab if necessary, click the Line button in the Sparklines group, verify that the insertion point is in the Data Range text box, select the range B3:G3 on the worksheet, then click OK**

   A sparkline showing the sales trend for Australia appears in cell H3. You can copy the sparkline to cells representing other regions.

2. **With cell H3 selected, drag the fill handle to fill the range H4:H5**

   The sparklines for all three regions are shown in **FIGURE 10-14**. You decide to change the sparklines to columns.

3. **Click cell H3, then click the Column button in the Type group of the Sparkline Tools Design tab**

   All of the sparklines in column H appear as columns. The column heights represent the values of the data in the adjacent rows. You want the sparklines to appear in a different color.

4. **Click the More button ⏷ in the Style group, then click Sparkline Style Colorful #5 (in the bottom row)**

   You want to highlight the high and low months.

5. **Click the Marker Color button in the Style group, point to High Point, then select Dark Green, Accent 5 under Theme Colors**

6. **Click the Marker Color button in the Style group, point to Low Point, select Orange Accent 3 under Theme Colors, then compare your screen to FIGURE 10-15**

7. **Save your changes**

FIGURE 10-14: Sales trend sparklines

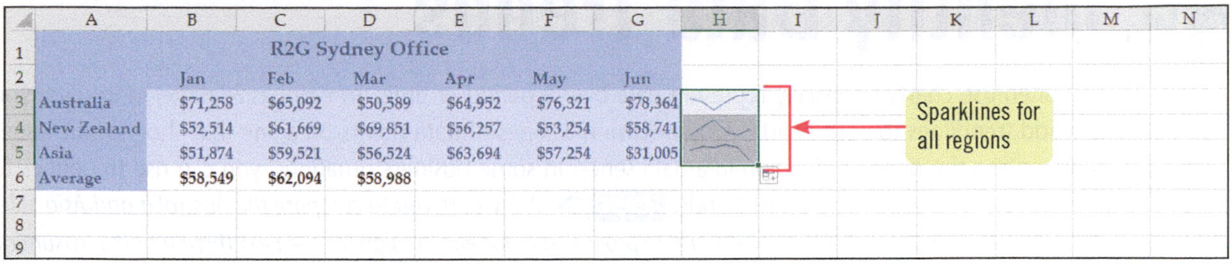

	A	B	C	D	E	F	G	H	I	J	K	L	M	N
1				R2G Sydney Office										
2		Jan	Feb	Mar	Apr	May	Jun							
3	Australia	$71,258	$65,092	$50,589	$64,952	$76,321	$78,364							
4	New Zealand	$52,514	$61,669	$69,851	$56,257	$53,254	$58,741							
5	Asia	$51,874	$59,521	$56,524	$63,694	$57,254	$31,005							
6	Average	$58,549	$62,094	$58,988										
7														
8														
9														

Sparklines for all regions

FIGURE 10-15: Formatted sparklines

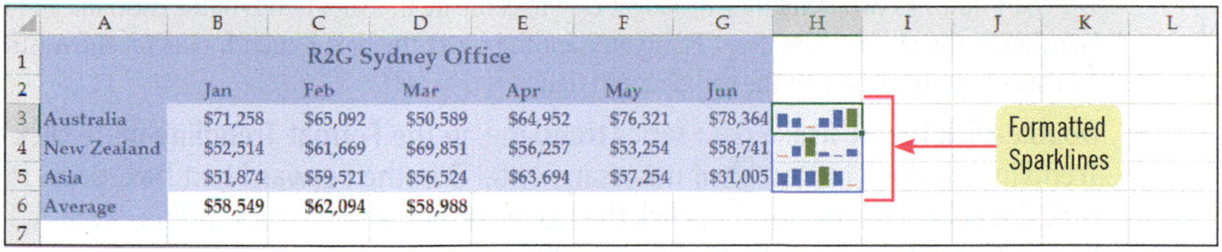

	A	B	C	D	E	F	G	H	I	J	K	L
1				R2G Sydney Office								
2		Jan	Feb	Mar	Apr	May	Jun					
3	Australia	$71,258	$65,092	$50,589	$64,952	$76,321	$78,364					
4	New Zealand	$52,514	$61,669	$69,851	$56,257	$53,254	$58,741					
5	Asia	$51,874	$59,521	$56,524	$63,694	$57,254	$31,005					
6	Average	$58,549	$62,094	$58,988								
7												

Formatted Sparklines

Identify Data Trends

Learning Outcomes
- Compare chart data using trendlines
- Format a trendline
- Forecast future trends using trendlines

You often use charts to visually represent data over a period of time. To emphasize patterns in data, you can add trendlines to your charts. A **trendline** is a series of data points on a line that shows data values representing the general direction in a data series. In some business situations, you can use trendlines to project future data based on past trends. **CASE** *Will wants you to compare the Australia and Asia sales performance over the first two quarters and to project sales for each region for the next three months, assuming past trends. You begin by charting the 6-months sales data in a 2-D Column chart.*

STEPS

1. **On the Sales sheet, select the range A2:G5, click the Quick Analysis tool 📧, click the Charts tab, then click the Clustered Column button**

2. **Drag the chart left until its upper-left corner is at the upper-left corner of cell A8, then drag the middle-right sizing handle right to the border between column G and column H**

   You are ready to add a trendline for the Australia data series.

3. **Click the Chart Elements button ⊞, click Trendline, verify that Australia is selected in the Add Trendline dialog box, then click OK**

   A linear trendline identifying Australia sales trends in the first 6 months is added to the chart, along with an entry in the legend identifying the line. You need to compare the Australia sales trend with the Asia sales trend.

4. **Make sure the Australia trendline is not selected, click ⊞ if necessary, point to Trendline, click the Trendline list arrow, click Linear, click Asia in the Add Trendline dialog box, then click OK**

   The chart now has two trendlines, making it easy to compare the sales trends of the Australia and the Asia branches as shown in **FIGURE 10-16**. Now you want to project the next 3-month sales for the Australia and Asia sales branches based on the past 6-month trends.

5. **Double-click the Australia data series trendline, in the Format Trendline pane click the Trendline Options button 📊 if necessary, enter 3 in the Forward text box, press [Enter], click the Fill & Line button 🔗, click the Color list arrow 🎨 ▾, click Indigo, Accent 1, Darker 50%, then close the Format Trendline pane**

   The formatted Australia trendline projects an additional 3 months of future sales trends for the region, assuming that past trends continue.

6. **Double-click the Asia data series trendline, enter 3 in the Forward text box in the Format Trendline pane, press [Enter], click 🔗, click the Color list arrow 🎨 ▾, click Orange, Accent 3, Darker 50%, then close the Format Trendline pane**

   The formatted Asia trendline also projects an additional 3 months of future sales trends for the region, assuming that past trends continue. The trends would be easier to spot if there were more room for the plot area.

7. **Click ⊞, then click the Chart Title checkbox to deselect it**

   Next you will change the Asia June data. When chart data is changed you will view the **chart animation** showing the resulting changes to the chart.

8. **Type 80,000 in cell G5, view the chart as you press [Enter], enter your name in the center section of the Sales sheet footer, save the workbook, preview the Sales sheet, close the workbook, submit the workbook to your instructor, then exit Excel**

   The completed worksheet is shown in **FIGURE 10-17**.

FIGURE 10-16: Chart with two trendlines

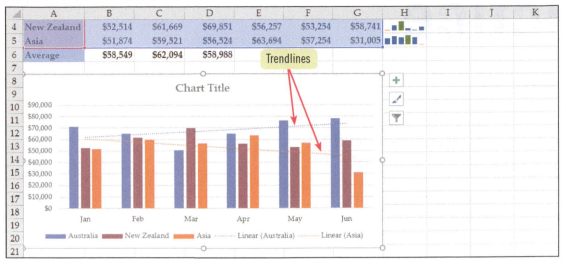

FIGURE 10-17: Sales chart with trendlines for Australia and Asia data

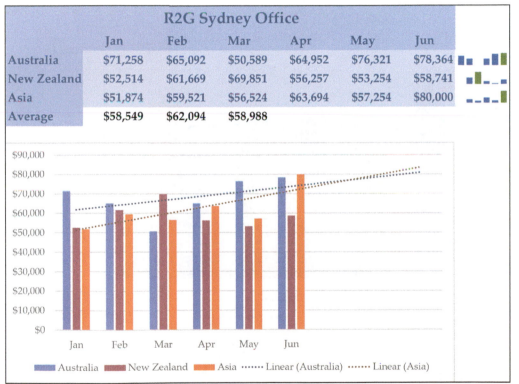

Choosing the right trendline options for your chart

Trendlines can help you forecast where your data is headed and understand its past values. You can choose from six types of trendlines: linear, exponential, logarithmic, power, polynomial, and moving average. A linear trendline is used for data series with data points that have the pattern of a line. An exponential or power trendline is a curved line that is used when data values increase or decrease in an arc shape. A polynomial trendline is also curved but changes direction more than one time. A moving average smooths out fluctuations in data by averaging the data points (two is the standard, but you can average more data points). Logarithmic trendlines are useful for data that increases or decreases before leveling out.

Excel 2016

Practice

Concepts Review

1. **Which element points to the vertical axis title?**
2. **Which element points to the vertical axis?**
3. **Which element points to the chart title?**
4. **Which element points to the chart legend?**
5. **Which element points to a data label?**
6. **Which element points to the horizontal axis?**

FIGURE 10-18

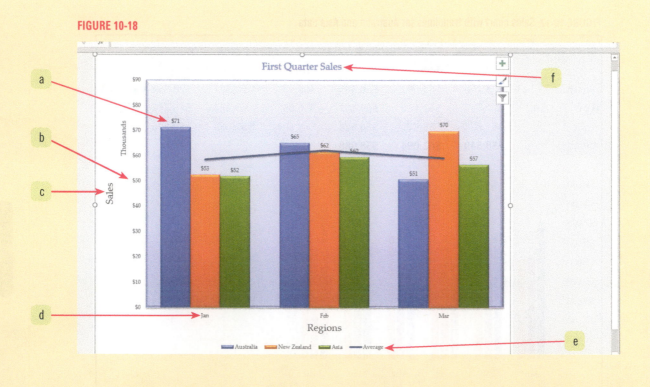

Match each term with the statement that best describes it.

7. **Plot area**
8. **Data series**
9. **X-axis**
10. **Sparklines**
11. **Trendlines**

a. Category axis
b. Miniature charts that show data trends
c. Line charts that can be used to project future data
d. Sequence of values plotted on a chart
e. Location holding data charted on the axes

Select the best answer from the list of choices.

12. Descriptive text that appears above a data marker is called a:
    a. Data series.
    c. High point.
    b. Data label.
    d. Period.

13. Which of the following is true regarding WordArt?
    a. Cell references to WordArt can be used in formulas.
    b. WordArt is a shape.
    c. Spelling errors in WordArt can be detected by the spell checker.
    d. Cells containing WordArt can be sorted.

14. Which Chart feature shows how a change in data values affects a chart?
    a. Visualization
    c. Update
    b. Animation
    d. Format

15. A chart's scale:
    a. Can be adjusted.
    c. Always has a minimum of 0.
    b. Always has a maximum of 80000.
    d. Always appears in units of 10.

16. A chart that combines two or more chart types is a:
    a. Combination chart.
    c. Clustered chart.
    b. Grouped chart.
    d. Complex chart.

17. What is a data table?
    a. A customized data series
    c. A grid with chart data displayed above a chart
    b. The data used to create a chart, displayed in a grid
    d. A three-dimensional arrangement of data on the *y*-axis

18. Which of the following is false regarding trendlines?
    a. Trendlines visually represent patterns in past data.
    c. Six types of trendlines can be added to a chart.
    b. Trendlines are used to project future data.
    d. Trendlines can be formatted to stand out on a chart.

Skills Review

1. **Customize a data series.**
   a. Start Excel, open EX 10-2.xlsx from the location where you save your Data Files, then save it as **EX 10-Campus Coffee**.
   b. Select the range A2:D6.
   c. Create a clustered column chart using the selected data.
   d. Move and resize the chart to fit in the range A8:G20.
   e. Change the fill color of the January data series to Tan, Accent 1, Darker 50% in the Theme Colors.
   f. Change the chart view by exchanging the row and column data.
   g. Save the workbook.

2. **Change a data source and add a chart style.**
   a. Add the April, May, and June data to the chart.
   b. Resize the chart to fill the range A8:J20 to display the new data.
   c. Change the chart view back to show the months in the legend by exchanging the row and column data.
   d. Apply Chart Style 14.
   e. Save the workbook.

3. **Add chart elements.**
   a. Move the chart to its own sheet named **Sales Chart**.
   b. Add a data table with legend keys.
   c. Add data labels to your chart.

Skills Review (continued)

   d. Remove the data table legend keys.

   e. Save the workbook, then compare your screen to **FIGURE 10-19**.

4. Format chart axes.

   a. Remove the data table.

   b. Set the value axis maximum to **5000**.

   c. Add a horizontal axis title and label it **Products**.

   d. Add a vertical axis title and label it **Sales**.

   e. Format both axes' titles in 12-point bold.

   f. Save the workbook.

5. Create a combination chart.

   a. On the Sales sheet, enter **Average** in cell A7.

   b. Select the range B3:G6 and use the Quick Analysis tool to place averages in row 7.

   c. Edit the data source for the chart to include the range **A2:G7**.

   d. Switch the row and column chart view.

   e. Change the chart type to a combination chart, with the coffee, tea, pastry, and juice data as clustered column charts and the average data as a line chart.

   f. Remove the data labels.

   g. Save the workbook.

6. Enhance a chart.

   a. Add a chart title of **Campus Coffee** to the top of the chart.

   b. Format the chart title with the WordArt style Fill – Blue, Accent 4, Soft Bevel.

   c. Remove the gridlines.

   d. Add a shape style of Subtle Effect - Aqua, Accent 3 to the plot area.

   e. Compare your chart to **FIGURE 10-20**.

   f. Add your name to the chart footer, then save the workbook.

7. Summarize data with sparklines.

   a. On the Sales worksheet, add a Line sparkline to cell H3 that represents the data in the range B3:G3.

   b. Copy the sparkline in cell H3 into the range H4:H6.

   c. Change the sparklines to columns.

   d. Apply the Sparkline style Colorful #2.

   e. Add high point markers with the color of Green from the Standard Colors.

   f. Save the workbook.

8. Identify data trends.

   a. Create a line chart using the data in the range A2:G6, then move and resize the chart to fit in the range A8:G20.

   b. Add linear trendlines to the Coffee and Tea data series.

   c. Change the Tea trendline color to red and the Coffee trendline color to purple.

   d. Set the forward option to six periods for both trendlines to view the future trend, increase the width of the chart to the border between columns J and K, remove the chart title, then compare your screen to **FIGURE 10-21**.

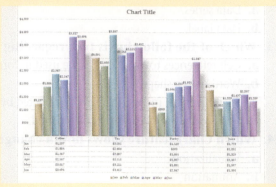

FIGURE 10-19

FIGURE 10-20

FIGURE 10-21

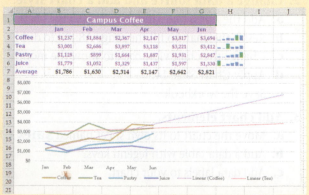

Skills Review (continued)

e. Add your name to the center footer section of the Sales sheet, save the workbook, preview the worksheet, close the workbook, then submit the workbook to your instructor.

f. Exit Excel.

Independent Challenge 1

You are the manager of a car rental company. You track the percentage of different types of vehicles rented from the lot using a worksheet. In preparation for an upcoming meeting with rental agents, you need to create two charts based on this data.

a. Start Excel, open EX 10-3.xlsx from the location where you store your Data Files, then save it as **EX 10-Vehicles**.

b. Using the data in A2:B7 of the Vehicles worksheet, create a pie chart on the worksheet.

c. Move the chart to a separate sheet named **Vehicles Pie Chart**. Format the chart using Chart Style 9.

d. Change the chart title to **Rental Percentages**. Format the title using WordArt Fill – Plum - Accent 3, Sharp Bevel. Change the chart title font to a size of 28. (*Hint*: Right-click the title and click Font on the shortcut menu.)

e. Add values to the data labels. (*Hint*: Double-click a data label and select the Value checkbox in the Format Data Labels pane.)

FIGURE 10-22

f. Select the Compact pie slice by clicking the chart, then clicking the Compact slice. Change the slice color to the Pink, Accent 2, Lighter 60% Theme color.

g. Add a shape style of Subtle Effect - Pink, Accent 2 to the chart area. Compare your chart to FIGURE 10-22.

h. Return to the Vehicles worksheet, then use the data in A1:B7 to create a clustered column chart.

i. Place the chart on a new sheet named **Vehicles Column Chart**. Format the chart using chart Style 7.

j. Change the chart title to **Rental Percentages** above the chart, and format the title using WordArt Style Fill - Pink, Accent 1, Shadow.

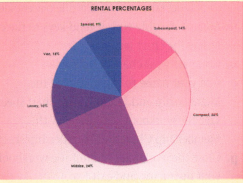

k. Format the title in 28-point font.

l. Add horizontal and vertical axis titles. Change the title of the horizontal axis to **Category**. Change the title of the vertical axis to **Percentage**. Format both axes' titles in 18-point bold.

m. Enter your name in the center sections of the footers of both chart sheets.

n. Save the workbook, then preview the charts.

o. Close the workbook, submit the workbook to your instructor, then exit Excel.

Independent Challenge 2

You manage the local YMCA branch, which offers different categories of memberships. The regional office has asked you to assemble a brief presentation on the membership data over the past 4 years. You decide to include a chart showing the memberships in each category as well as an analysis of trends in memberships.

a. Start Excel, open EX 10-4.xlsx from the location where you store your Data Files, then save it as **EX 10-Memberships**.

b. Create a clustered bar chart on the worksheet, comparing the membership enrollments in the four types of memberships over the years 2014–2017.

c. Change the row and column data so the years are shown in the legend.

d. Add a chart title of **Membership Data** above the chart, and format it using WordArt Style Gradient Fill - Dark Green, Accent 4, Soft Bevel.

Independent Challenge 2 (continued)

e. Move the chart to the region A9:H24.

f. Add Line sparklines to cells F4:F7 showing the membership trend from 2014 to 2017.

g. Format the sparklines using Sparkline Style Dark #5.

h. Add high point markers to the sparklines with the color Red, Accent 2 from the theme colors.

i. Add a new membership type of **Senior** in row 8 of the worksheet with the data in this table:

Year	Membership
2014	405
2015	499
2016	550
2017	690

j. Add the data to the chart. Copy the sparklines to cell F8.

k. Move the chart to a sheet named **Membership Chart**.

l. Add a horizontal axis title of **Number of Memberships**, and format it in 16-point bold font. Delete the vertical axis title placeholder.

m. Add a data table with legend keys to the chart. Delete the chart legend.

n. Compare your chart to FIGURE 10-23.

o. Add your name to the footers of the Membership and Membership Chart sheets, save the workbook, and preview the Membership Chart and Membership sheets.

p. Close the workbook, submit the workbook to your instructor, and exit Excel.

FIGURE 10-23

Independent Challenge 3

You manage the New England region of a home design store. You meet twice a year with the national sales manager to discuss store sales trends. You decide to use a chart to represent the sales trends for stores you manage. You begin by charting the sales for the first six months of the year. Then you add profit data to the chart and analyze the sales trend using a trendline. Lastly, you enhance the chart by adding a data table and titles.

a. Start Excel, open EX 10-5.xlsx from the location where you store your Data Files, then save the workbook as **EX 10-New England Home**.

b. Create a clustered column chart on the worksheet showing the January through March sales information, using the first Clustered Column suggestion in the chart recommendations. Move the upper-left corner of the chart to cell A8 on the worksheet.

c. Format the January data series using the Lime, Accent 1, Darker 50% color from the theme colors.

d. Add the Apr, May, and Jun data to the chart.

e. Move the chart to its own sheet named **Jan - Jun**.

f. Add the profit data shown in the table to the Sales sheet.

g. Add the new profit data to the chart, then change the row and column view so the store locations are in the legend.

h. Change the chart type to a combination chart placing all store locations in a clustered column chart and the profit data in a line chart.

Cell	Data
A7	Profit
B7	$2,510
C7	$1,870
D7	$2,350
E7	$1,970
F7	$1,005
G7	$1,855

Independent Challenge 3 (continued)

i. Add a chart title of **January - June Sales** in 28-point font above the chart. Format the chart title using the WordArt Style Fill - Lime, Accent1, Shadow.

j. Add a title of **Sales** in 20-point to the vertical axis. Format it in the same WordArt style as the chart title. Delete the horizontal axis title placeholder.

k. Change the value axis scale to a maximum of **6000**, then save your workbook.

l. Add data labels to the profit data series. (*Hint*: Select the profit line chart before adding data labels.)

m. Compare your chart to **FIGURE 10-24**.

n. Enter your name in the center footer section of the chart sheet, save the workbook, then preview the chart.

o. Close the workbook, submit the workbook to your instructor, then exit Excel.

FIGURE 10-24

Independent Challenge 4: Explore

As the sales manager of Atlantic Motors, you are interested in how average sales prices at your company correlate with customer satisfaction. The May sales and customer ratings data are in a worksheet and you will chart the data to visualize this relationship.

a. Start Excel, open EX 10-6.xlsx from the location where you store your Data Files, then save the workbook as **EX 10-Customer Satisfaction**.

b. Create a clustered column chart using the data in cells A3:B10. Move and resize your chart to fill the range D1:L20.

c. Link the chart title to cell A1. (*Hint*: With the chart title selected, type = in the formula bar, click cell A1, then press [Enter].)

d. Format the chart title text in WordArt style Fill - Blue, Accent 1, Shadow.

e. Add a vertical axis title and link it to cell A3. Format the axis title using a shape style of Subtle Effect - Blue, Accent 1. Add a shape effect of circle bevel.

f. Delete the horizontal axis title.

g. To improve the visibility of the Average Customer Rating series, place it on a line chart and assign it to a secondary axis. (*Hint*: Change the chart type to Combo and select Secondary Axis for the Average Customer Rating line chart.)

h. Change the text in cell B3 from Average Customer Rating to Customer Rating and verify that the legend changed.

i. Change the chart title link to cell A2 and verify the change in the chart title.

j. Edit cell B4 to 6.0 and view the chart animation of the second bar to reflect this data change.

k. Add data labels to the Customer Rating data series. (*Hint*: Select the Customer Rating line chart before adding data labels.)

l. Assign the same shape style to the chart title that you assigned to the vertical axis.

FIGURE 10-25

m. Compare your chart to **FIGURE 10-25**.

n. Change the worksheet orientation to Landscape, then scale the worksheet width to fit on 1 page. Enter your name in the center footer section of the worksheet, save the workbook, then preview the worksheet.

o. Close the workbook, submit the workbook to your instructor, then exit Excel.

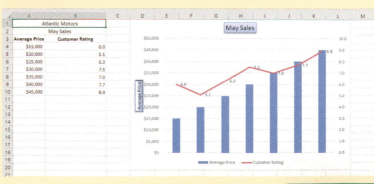

Excel 2016

Visual Workshop

Open EX 10-7.xlsx from the location where you store your Data Files, then create the custom chart shown in **FIGURE 10-26**. (*Hint*: The trendlines forecast three periods forward and use the standard line colors green and red.) Save the workbook as **EX 10-Footware Sales**. Study the chart and worksheet carefully to make sure you select the displayed chart type with all the enhancements shown. Enter your name in the center section of the worksheet footer, then preview the worksheet in landscape orientation on one page. Submit the workbook to your instructor.

FIGURE 10-26

Performing What-if Analysis

CASE Rae-Ann Schwartz, the manager of the head office for Reason2Go, is working on sales projections and targets for the first half of the year. In preparation for this project, Rae-Ann asks you to help analyze the sales data for the other four branch offices using what-if scenarios, data tables, Goal Seek, Solver, and the Analysis ToolPak.

Module Objectives

After completing this module, you will be able to:

- Define what-if analysis
- Track what-if analysis with Scenario Manager
- Generate a scenario summary
- Project figures using a data table

- Use Goal Seek
- Set up a complex what-if analysis with Solver
- Run Solver and summarize results
- Analyze data using the Analysis ToolPak

Files You Will Need

EX 11-1.xlsx	EX 11-5.xlsx
EX 11-2.xlsx	EX 11-6.xlsx
EX 11-3.xlsx	EX 11-7.xlsx
EX 11-4.xlsx	

Define What-if Analysis

Learning Outcomes
- Develop guidelines for performing what-if analysis
- Define what-if analysis terminology

By performing what-if analysis in a worksheet, you can get immediate answers to questions such as "What happens to profits if we sell 25 percent more of a certain product?" or "What happens to monthly payments if interest rates rise or fall?" A worksheet you use to produce what-if analysis is often called a **model** because it acts as the basis for multiple outcomes or sets of results. To perform a what-if analysis in a worksheet, you change the value in one or more **input cells** (cells that contain data rather than formulas), then observe the effects on dependent cells. A **dependent cell** usually contains a formula whose resulting value changes depending on the values in the input cells. A dependent cell can be located either in the same worksheet as the changing input value or in another worksheet. **CASE** *Rae-Ann Schwartz has received projected sales data from the other branch managers. She has created a worksheet model to perform an initial what-if analysis, as shown in* **FIGURE 11-1**. *She thinks the New York sales projections for the month of January should be higher. You first review the guidelines for performing what-if analysis.*

DETAILS

When performing what-if analysis, use the following guidelines:

- **Understand and state the purpose of the worksheet model**

  Identify what you want to accomplish with the model. What problem are you trying to solve? What questions do you want the model to answer for you? Rae-Ann's worksheet model is designed to total Reason2Go sales projections for the four branch offices during the first half of the year and to calculate the percentage of total sales for each branch. It also calculates the totals and percentages of total sales for each month.

- **Determine the data input value(s) that, if changed, affect(s) dependent cell results**

  In what-if analysis, changes in the content of the data input cells produce varying results in the output cells. You will use the model to work with one data input value: the January value for the New York branch, in cell B3.

- **Identify the dependent cell(s) that will contain results**

  The dependent cells usually contain formulas, and the formula results adjust as you enter different values in the input cells. The results of two dependent cell formulas (labeled Total and Percent of Total Sales) appear in cells H3 and I3, respectively. The total for the month of January in cell B7 is also a dependent cell, as is the percentage in cell B8.

- **Formulate questions you want what-if analysis to answer**

  It is important that you know the questions you want your model to answer. In the R2G model, you want to answer the following question: What happens to the New York branch percentage if the sales amount for the month of January increases to $114,110?

- **Perform what-if analysis**

  When you perform what-if analysis, you explore the relationships between the input values and the dependent cell formulas. In the R2G worksheet model, you want to see what effect an increase in sales for January has on the dependent cell formulas containing totals and percentages. Because the sales amount for this month is located in cell B3, any formula that references that cell is directly affected by a change in this sales amount—in this case, the total formula in cell H3. Because the formula in cell I3 references cell H3, a change in the sales amount affects this cell as well. The percentage formulas will also change because they reference the total formulas. **FIGURE 11-2** shows the result of what-if analysis described in this example.

FIGURE 11-1: Worksheet model for a what-if analysis

FIGURE 11-1: Worksheet model for a what-if analysis

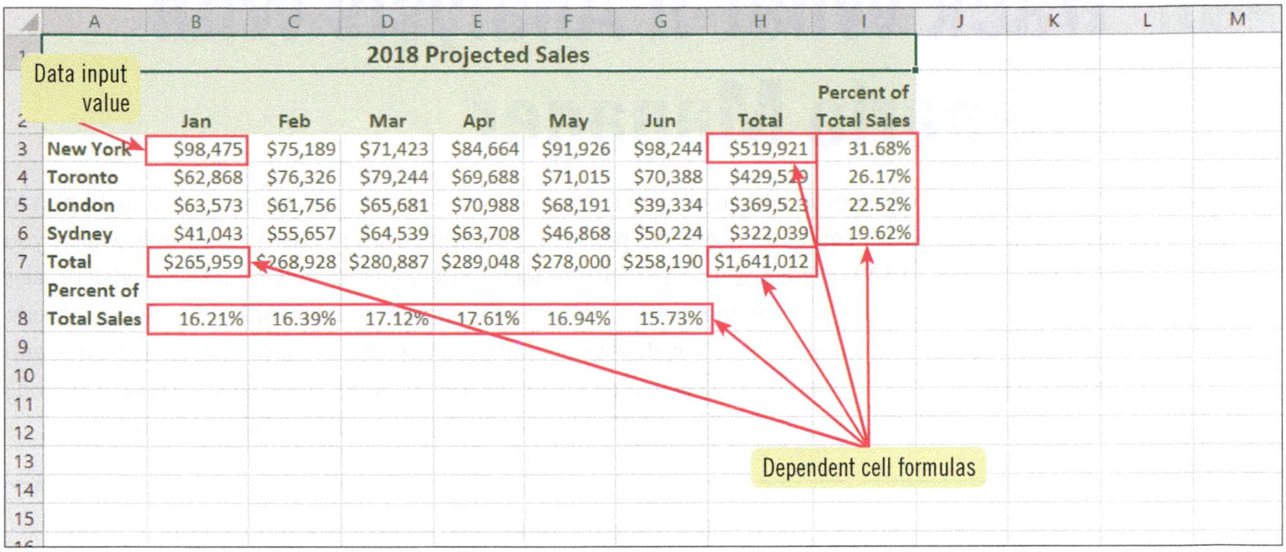

	A	B	C	D	E	F	G	H	I	J	K	L	M
1		2018 Projected Sales											
2		Jan	Feb	Mar	Apr	May	Jun	Total	Percent of Total Sales				
3	New York	$98,475	$75,189	$71,423	$84,664	$91,926	$98,244	$519,921	31.68%				
4	Toronto	$62,868	$76,326	$79,244	$69,688	$71,015	$70,388	$429,529	26.17%				
5	London	$63,573	$61,756	$65,681	$70,988	$68,191	$39,334	$369,523	22.52%				
6	Sydney	$41,043	$55,657	$64,539	$63,708	$46,868	$50,224	$322,039	19.62%				
7	Total	$265,959	$268,928	$280,887	$289,048	$278,000	$258,190	$1,641,012					
8	Percent of Total Sales	16.21%	16.39%	17.12%	17.61%	16.94%	15.73%						

Data input value

Dependent cell formulas

FIGURE 11-2: Changed input values and dependent formula results

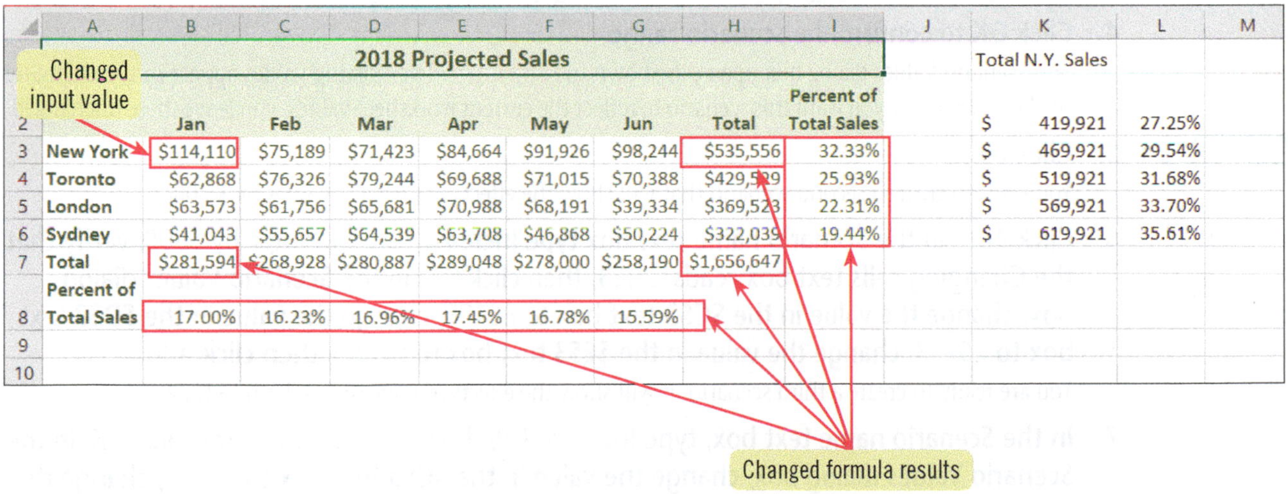

	A	B	C	D	E	F	G	H	I	J	K	L	M
1		2018 Projected Sales									Total N.Y. Sales		
2		Jan	Feb	Mar	Apr	May	Jun	Total	Percent of Total Sales				
3	New York	$114,110	$75,189	$71,423	$84,664	$91,926	$98,244	$535,556	32.33%		$ 419,921	27.25%	
4	Toronto	$62,868	$76,326	$79,244	$69,688	$71,015	$70,388	$429,529	25.93%		$ 469,921	29.54%	
5	London	$63,573	$61,756	$65,681	$70,988	$68,191	$39,334	$369,523	22.31%		$ 519,921	31.68%	
6	Sydney	$41,043	$55,657	$64,539	$63,708	$46,868	$50,224	$322,039	19.44%		$ 569,921	33.70%	
7	Total	$281,594	$268,928	$280,887	$289,048	$278,000	$258,190	$1,656,647			$ 619,921	35.61%	
8	Percent of Total Sales	17.00%	16.23%	16.96%	17.45%	16.78%	15.59%						

Changed input value

Changed formula results

Track What-if Analysis with Scenario Manager

Learning Outcomes
- Create scenarios to analyze Excel data
- Analyze scenarios using Scenario Manager

A **scenario** is a set of values you use to observe different worksheet results. For example, you might plan to sell 100 of a particular item, at a price of $5 per item, producing sales results of $500. But what if you reduced the price to $4 or increased it to $6? Each of these price scenarios would produce different sales results. A changing value, such as the price in this example, is called a **variable**. The Excel Scenario Manager simplifies the process of what-if analysis by allowing you to name and save multiple scenarios with variable values in a worksheet. **CASE** *You decide to use Scenario Manager to create scenarios showing how a New York sales increase can affect total R2G sales over the 3-month period of February through April.*

STEPS

1. **Start Excel, open EX 11-1.xlsx from the location where you store your Data Files, then save it as EX 11-Sales**

   The first step in defining a scenario is choosing the changing cells. **Changing cells** are those that will vary in the different scenarios.

2. **With the Projected Sales sheet active, select range C3:E3, click the Data tab, click the What-If Analysis button in the Forecast group, then click Scenario Manager**

   You want to be able to easily return to your original worksheet values, so your first scenario contains those figures.

3. **Click Add, drag the Add Scenario dialog box to the right if necessary until columns A and B are visible, then type Original Sales Figures in the Scenario name text box**

   The range in the Changing cells box shows the range you selected, as shown in **FIGURE 11-3**.

4. **Click OK to confirm the scenario range**

   The Scenario Values dialog box opens, as shown in **FIGURE 11-4**. The existing values appear in the changing cell boxes. Because you want this scenario to reflect the current worksheet values, you leave these unchanged.

5. **Click OK**

   You want to create a second scenario that will show the effects of increasing sales by $5,000.

6. **Click Add; in the Scenario name text box type Increase Feb, Mar, Apr by 5000; verify that the Changing cells text box reads C3:E3, then click OK; in the Scenario Values dialog box, change the value in the $C$3 text box to 80189, change the value in the $D$3 text box to 76423, change the value in the $E$3 text box to 89664, then click Add**

   You are ready to create a third scenario. It will show the effects of increasing sales by $10,000.

7. **In the Scenario name text box, type Increase Feb, Mar, Apr by 10000 and click OK; in the Scenario Values dialog box, change the value in the $C$3 text box to 85189, change the value in the $D$3 text box to 81423, change the value in the $E$3 text box to 94664, then click OK**

   The Scenario Manager dialog box reappears, as shown in **FIGURE 11-5**. You are ready to display the results of your scenarios in the worksheet.

8. **Make sure the Increase Feb, Mar, Apr by 10000 scenario is still selected, click Show, notice that the percent of New York sales in cell I3 changes from 31.68% to 32.91%; click Increase Feb, Mar, Apr by 5000, click Show, notice that the New York sales percent is now 32.30%; click Original Sales Figures, click Show to return to the original values, then click Close**

9. **Save the workbook**

FIGURE 11-3: Add Scenario dialog box

Cell range containing value that you will change

Your user name and date will be different

FIGURE 11-4: Scenario Values dialog box

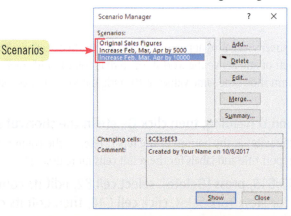

Changing cell boxes with original values

FIGURE 11-5: Scenario Manager dialog box with three scenarios listed

Scenarios

Merging scenarios

Excel stores scenarios in the workbook and on the worksheet in which you created them. To apply scenarios from another worksheet or workbook into the current worksheet, click the Merge button in the Scenario Manager dialog box. The Merge Scenarios dialog box opens, letting you select scenarios from other locations. When you click a sheet name in the sheet list, the text under the sheet list tells you how many scenarios exist on that sheet. To merge scenarios from another workbook, such as those sent to you in a workbook by a coworker, open the other workbook file, click the Book list arrow in the Merge Scenarios dialog box, then click the workbook name. When you merge workbook scenarios, it's best if the workbooks have the same structure, so that there is no confusion of cell values.

Generate a Scenario Summary

Although it may be useful to display the different scenario outcomes when analyzing data, it can be difficult to keep track of them. In most cases, you will want to refer to a single report that summarizes the results of all the scenarios in a worksheet. A **scenario summary** is an Excel table that compiles data from the changing cells and corresponding result cells for each scenario. For example, you might use a scenario summary to illustrate the best, worst, and most likely scenarios for a particular set of circumstances. Using cell naming makes the summary easier to read because the names, not the cell references, appear in the report. **CASE** ▶ *Now that you have defined multiple scenarios, you want to generate and print a scenario summary report. You begin by creating names for the cells in row 3 based on the labels in row 2, so that the report will be easier to read.*

STEPS

1. **Select the range B2:I3, click the Formulas tab, click the Create from Selection button in the Defined Names group, click the Top row check box to select it if necessary, then click OK**

   Excel creates the names for the data in row 3 based on the labels in row 2. You decide to review them.

2. **Click the Name Manager button in the Defined Names group**

   The eight labels appear, along with other workbook names, in the Name Manager dialog box, confirming that they were created, as shown in **FIGURE 11-6**. Now you are ready to generate the scenario summary report.

3. **Click Close in the Name Manager dialog box, click the Data tab, click the What-If Analysis button in the Forecast group, click Scenario Manager, then click Summary in the Scenario Manager dialog box**

   Excel needs to know the location of the cells that contain the formula results that you want to see in the report. You want to see the results for New York total and percentage of sales, and total R2G sales.

4. **With the contents of the Result cells text box selected, click cell H3 on the worksheet, type , (a comma), click cell I3, type , (a comma), then click cell H7**

   With the report type and result cells specified, as shown in **FIGURE 11-7**, you are now ready to generate the report.

5. **Click OK**

   A summary of the worksheet's scenarios appears on a new sheet titled Scenario Summary. The report shows outline buttons to the left of and above the worksheet so that you can hide or show report details. Because the Current Values column shows the same values as the Original Sales Figures column, you decide to delete column D.

6. **Right-click the column D heading, then click Delete in the shortcut menu**

   Next, you notice that the notes at the bottom of the report refer to the column that no longer exists. You also want to make the report title and labels for the result cells more descriptive.

7. **Select the range B13:B15, press [Delete], select cell B2, edit its contents to read Scenario Summary for New York Sales, click cell C10, then edit its contents to read Total New York Sales**

8. **Click cell C11, edit its contents to read Percent New York Sales, click cell C12, edit its contents to read Total R2G Sales, then click cell A1**

   The completed scenario summary is shown in **FIGURE 11-8**.

9. **Add your name to the center section of the Scenario Summary sheet footer, change the page orientation to landscape, then save the workbook and preview the worksheet**

FIGURE 11-6: Name Manager dialog box displaying new names

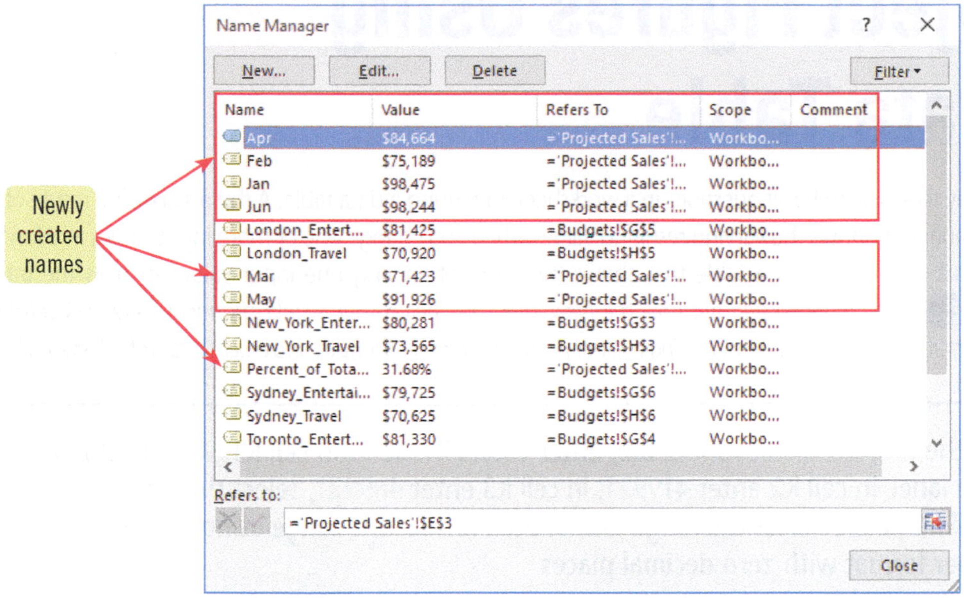

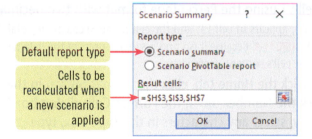

Newly created names

FIGURE 11-7: Scenario Summary dialog box

Default report type

Cells to be recalculated when a new scenario is applied

FIGURE 11-8: Completed Scenario Summary report

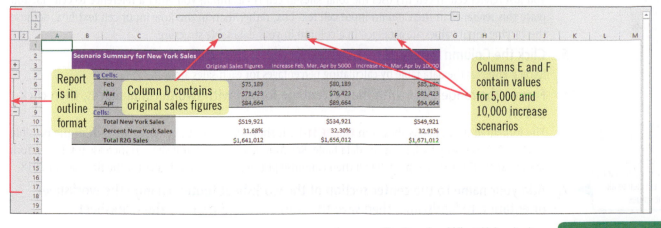

Report is in outline format

Column D contains original sales figures

Columns E and F contain values for 5,000 and 10,000 increase scenarios

Project Figures Using a Data Table

Another way to answer what-if questions in a worksheet is by using a data table. A **data table** is a range of cells that simultaneously shows the varying resulting values when you change one or more input values in a formula. A **one-input data table** is a table that shows the result of varying one input value, such as the interest rate. **CASE** *You want to find out how the New York sales percentage would change if New York total sales increased significantly. You begin by entering a set of possible values, in $50,000 increments, for total New York sales.*

STEPS

1. **Click the Projected Sales sheet tab, enter Total N.Y. Sales in cell K1, widen column K to fit the label, in cell K2 enter 419921, in cell K3 enter 469921, select the range K2:K3, drag the fill handle to select the range K4:K6, then format the range using the Accounting number format with zero decimal places**

   You begin setting up your data table by entering total New York sales lower and higher than the total in cell H3. You can choose any values for these totals but having a consistent variation between these values will help you understand the impact of the N.Y. total on the percent of total sales. You will use increasing amounts of $50,000. These possible totals constitute the **input values** in the data table. With the varying input values listed in column K, you enter a formula reference to cell I3 that you want Excel to use in calculating the resulting percentages (the **output values**) in column L, based on the possible totals in column K.

2. **Click cell L1, type =, click cell I3, click the Enter button ☑ on the formula bar, then format the value in cell L1 using the Percentage format with two decimal places**

   The value in cell I3, 31.68%, appears in cell L1, and the cell name =Percent_of_Total_Sales appears in the formula bar, as shown in **FIGURE 11-9**. Because it isn't necessary for users of the data table to see the value in cell L1, you want to hide the cell's contents from view.

3. **With cell L1 selected, click the Home tab, click the Format button in the Cells group, click Format Cells, click the Number tab in the Format Cells dialog box if necessary, click Custom under Category, select any characters in the Type box, type ;;; (three semicolons), then click OK**

   Applying the custom cell format of three semicolons hides the values in a cell. With the table structure in place, you can now generate the data table showing percentages for the varying sales amounts.

4. **Select the range K1:L6, click the Data tab, click the What-If Analysis button in the Forecast group, then click Data Table**

   The Data Table dialog box opens, as shown in **FIGURE 11-10**. Because the percentage formula in cell I3 (which you just referenced in cell L1) uses the total sales in cell H3 as input, you enter a reference to cell H3. You place this reference in the Column input cell text box, rather than in the Row input cell text box, because the varying input values are arranged in a column in your data table structure.

5. **Click the Column input cell text box, click cell H3, then click OK**

   Excel completes the data table by calculating percentages for each sales amount.

6. **Format the range L2:L6 with the Percentage format with two decimal places, then click cell A1**

   The formatted data table is shown in **FIGURE 11-11**. It shows the sales percentages for each of the possible levels of N.Y. sales. By looking at the data table, Rae-Ann determines that if she can increase total New York sales to $619,921, the N.Y. branch will then comprise just over 35% of total sales for the first half of 2018.

7. **Add your name to the center section of the worksheet footer, change the worksheet orientation to landscape, then save the workbook and preview the worksheet**

FIGURE 11-9: One-input data table structure

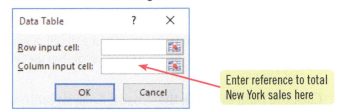

L1			fx	=Percent_of_Total_Sales									
	A	B	C	D	E	F	G	H	I	J	K	L	M
1	2018 Projected Sales										Total N.Y. Sales	31.68%	
2		Jan	Feb	Mar	Apr	May	Jun	Total	Percent of Total Sales		$		
3	New York	$98,475	$75,189	$71,423	$84,664	$91,926	$98,244	$519,921	31.68%		$	419,921	
4	Toronto	$62,868	$76,326	$79,244	$69,688	$71,015	$70,388	$429,529	26.17%		$	469,921	
5	London	$63,573	$61,756	$65,681	$70,988	$68,191	$39,334	$369,523	22.52%		$	519,921	
6	Sydney	$41,043	$55,657	$64,539	$63,708	$46,868	$50,224	$322,039	19.62%		$	569,921	
7	Total	$265,959	$268,928	$280,887	$289,048	$278,000	$258,190	$1,641,012			$	619,921	
8	Percent of Total Sales	16.21%	16.39%	17.12%	17.61%	16.94%	15.73%						
9													

Value displayed in cell I3

Varying sales totals

FIGURE 11-10: Data Table dialog box

Data Table   ? ✕

Row input cell: _____

Column input cell: _____

OK   Cancel

Enter reference to total New York sales here

FIGURE 11-11: Completed data table with resulting values

	A	B	C	D	E	F	G	H	I	J	K	L		P
1	2018 Projected Sales								Input values in column K		Total N.Y. Sales			
2		Jan	Feb	Mar	Apr	May	Jun	Total	Percent of Total Sales		$	419,921	27.25%	
3	New York	$98,475	$75,189	$71,423	$84,664	$91,926	$98,244	$519,921	31.68%		$	469,921	29.54%	
4	Toronto	$62,868	$76,326	$79,244	$69,688	$71,015	$70,388	$429,529	26.17%		$	519,921	31.68%	
5	London	$63,573	$61,756	$65,681	$70,988	$68,191	$39,334	$369,523	22.52%		$	569,921	33.70%	
6	Sydney	$41,043	$55,657	$64,539	$63,708	$46,868	$50,224	$322,039	19.62%		$	619,921	35.61%	
7	Total	$265,959	$268,928	$280,887	$289,048	$278,000	$258,190	$1,641,012						
8	Percent of Total Sales	16.21%	16.39%	17.12%	17.61%	16.94%	15.73%							
9														

Percentages (output values) in column L

Completed data table

Creating a two-input data table

A **two-input data table** shows the resulting values when two different input values are varied in a formula. You could, for example, use a two-input data table to calculate your monthly car payment based on varying interest rates and varying loan terms, as shown in **FIGURE 11-12**. In a two-input data table, different values of one input cell appear across the top row of the table, while different values of the second input cell are listed down the left column. You create a two-input data table the same way that you create a one-input data table, except you enter both a row and a column input cell. In the example shown in **FIGURE 11-12**, the two-input data table structure was created by first entering the number of payments in the range B6:D6 and rates in the range A7:A15. Then the data table values were created by selecting the range A6:D15, clicking the Data tab, clicking the What-If Analysis button in the Forecast group, then clicking Data Table. In the Data Table dialog box, the row input value is the term in cell C2. The column input value is the interest rate in cell B2. You can

check the accuracy of these values by cross-referencing the values in the data table with those in row 2 where you can see that an interest rate of 4.5% for 36 months has a monthly payment of $594.94.

FIGURE 11-12: Two-input data table

	A	B	C	D	E
1	Loan Amount	Interest Rate	# Payments	Monthly Payment	
2	$20,000.00	4.50%	36	$594.94	
3					
4		Car Payment for $20,000 Loan			
5			Term		
6		36	48	60	
7	4.00%	$590.48	$451.58	$368.33	
8	4.25%	$592.71	$453.82	$370.59	
9	4.50%	$594.94	$456.07	$372.86	
10	4.75%	$597.18	$458.32	$375.14	
11	5.00%	$599.42	$460.59	$377.42	
12	5.25%	$601.67	$462.85	$379.72	
13	5.50%	$603.92	$465.13	$382.02	
14	5.75%	$606.18	$467.41	$384.34	
15	6.00%	$608.44	$469.70	$386.66	
16					
17					

Use Goal Seek

Learning Outcomes
- Determine input values for a desired result using Goal Seek
- Answer questions about data using Goal Seek

You can think of goal seeking as what-if analysis in reverse. In what-if analysis, you might try many sets of values to achieve a certain solution. To **goal seek**, you specify a solution, then ask Excel to find the input value that produces the answer you want. "Backing into" a solution in this way, sometimes referred to as **backsolving**, can save a significant amount of time. For example, you can use Goal Seek to determine how many units must be sold to reach a particular sales goal or to determine what expense levels are necessary to meet a budget target. **CASE** *After reviewing the data table, Rae-Ann has a follow-up question: What January New York sales target is required to bring the overall January sales percentage to 17%, assuming the sales for the other branches don't change? You use Goal Seek to answer her question.*

STEPS

1. **Click cell B8**

   The first step in using Goal Seek is to select a goal cell. A **goal cell** contains a formula in which you can substitute values to find a specific value, or goal. You use cell B8 as the goal cell because it contains the percent formula.

2. **Click the Data tab, click the What-If Analysis button in the Forecast group, then click Goal Seek**

   The Goal Seek dialog box opens. The Set cell text box displays B8, the cell you selected in Step 1, which contains the formula that calculates January's percentage of sales. You need to indicate that the result in cell B8 should equal 17%.

3. **Click the To value text box, then type 17%**

   The value 17% represents the desired solution you want to reach by substituting different values in the By changing cell.

4. **Click the By changing cell text box, then click cell B3**

   You have specified that you want cell B3, the New York January amount, to change to reach the 17% solution, as shown in **FIGURE 11-13**.

5. **Click OK**

   The Goal Seek Status dialog box opens with the following message: "Goal Seeking with Cell B8 found a solution." In the worksheet, notice the new value in cell B3. By changing the amount in this cell to $114,110, Goal Seek achieves a January percentage of 17. If you click OK, the new value will be entered in the worksheet; if you click Cancel, the original value will be restored.

6. **Click OK, then click cell A1**

   Changing the sales amount in cell B3 changes the other dependent values in the worksheet (B7, H3, I3, and H7), as shown in **FIGURE 11-14**.

7. **Save the workbook, then preview the worksheet**

> **QUICK TIP**
> Before you select another command, you can return the worksheet to its status prior to the Goal Seek by pressing [Ctrl][Z].

FIGURE 11-13: Completed Goal Seek dialog box

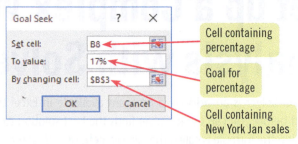

- Cell containing percentage
- Goal for percentage
- Cell containing New York Jan sales

FIGURE 11-14: Worksheet with new dependent values

	A	B	C	D	E	F	G	H	I	J
1	**2018 Projected Sales**									
2		**Jan**	**Feb**	**Mar**	**Apr**	**May**	**Jun**	**Total**	**Percent of Total Sales**	
3	**New York**	$114,110	$75,189	$71,423	$84,664	$91,926	$98,244	$535,556	32.33%	
4	**Toronto**	$62,868	$76,326	$79,244	$69,688	$71,015	$70,388	$429,529	25.93%	
5	**London**	$63,573	$61,756	$65,681	$70,988	$68,191	$39,334	$369,523	22.31%	
6	**Sydney**	$41,043	$55,657	$64,539	$63,708	$46,868	$50,224	$322,039	19.44%	
7	**Total**	$281,594	$268,928	$280,887	$289,048	$278,000	$258,190	$1,656,647		
8	**Percent of Total Sales**	17.00%	16.23%	16.96%	17.45%	16.78%	15.59%			
9										
13										
14										
15										
16										
17										

New target values calculated by Goal Seek

Using Excel's Data Analysis tools

Excel includes a set of data analysis features that work together and are referred to as Business Intelligence or BI. These tools include Power Query, Power Pivot, Power View, and Power Map. To make sure these tools are enabled, clicking File, click Options, click Advanced, then under Data make sure the Enable Data Analysis add ins: Power Pivot, Power View, and Power Map check box contains a checkmark. Power Query is used to import data into a workbook and manipulate it to a desired format. To access the Power Query features, click the Data tab, then click New Query, Show Queries, From Table, or Recent Sources in the Get & Transform group. To insert a Power Map into a worksheet, click the Insert tab, then click 3D Map in the Tours group. You can add data to the map by selecting the data on the worksheet, clicking the Insert tab, clicking 3D Map, then clicking Add Selected Data to 3D Maps. Power View uses the Power BI Desktop to explore and report data relationships using the dynamic dashboard. To use Power View you must insert a button on the Ribbon by clicking File, clicking Options, clicking Customize Ribbon, clicking the Popular Commands list arrow, clicking Commands Not in the Ribbon, clicking Insert a Power View Report, clicking New Tab on the right side of the Excel Options dialog box to place the Power View Reports button on a new tab, then clicking Add. The last of these BI tools, Power Pivot, is covered in the next module. If you download the Power BI Desktop, you can import Excel workbooks that contain Power Query queries, Power Pivot models, and Power View worksheets, as well as data from other sources, and then use the Power BI Desktop tools to create reports and charts. The BI Desktop has a query editor that is similar to Power Query and three views to work with data: Report view, Data view, and Relationships view.

Set up a Complex What-if Analysis with Solver

The Excel Solver is an **add-in**, a program available in Excel that provides optional features. It must be installed before you can use it. Solver finds the best solution to a problem that has several inputs. The cell containing the formula is called the **target cell**, or **objective**. Solver is helpful when you need to perform a complex what-if analysis involving multiple input values or when the input values must conform to specific limitations or restrictions called **constraints**. **CASE** ▶ *Rae-Ann decides to fund each branch with the same amount, $775,000, to cover expenses. She is willing to adjust the selected budget items to keep expenditures to this overall amount. You use Solver to help Rae-Ann find the best possible allocation. In this lesson you complete the Solver dialog box; in the next lesson you run Solver and generate solutions.*

STEPS

1. **Click the Budgets sheet tab**

   This worksheet is designed to calculate the travel, entertainment, and other budget categories for each branch. It assumes fixed costs for communications, equipment, advertising, salaries, and rent. You use Solver to change the entertainment and travel amounts in cells G3:H6 (the changing cells) to achieve your target of a total budget of $3,100,000 in cell I7 (the target cell). You want your solution to include a constraint on cells G3:H6 specifying that each branch is funded $775,000. Based on past budgets, you know there are two other constraints: the travel budgets must include at least $83,000, and the entertainment budgets must include at least $95,000. It is a good idea to enter constraints on the worksheet for documentation purposes, as shown in **FIGURE 11-15**.

2. **Click the Data tab, then click the Solver button in the Analyze group**

   In the Solver Parameters dialog box, you indicate the target cell with its objective, the changing cells, and the constraints under which you want Solver to work. You begin by entering your total budget objective.

3. **With the insertion point in the Set Objective text box, click cell I7 in the worksheet, click the Value Of option button if necessary, double-click the Value Of text box, then type 3,100,000**

   You have specified an objective of $3,100,000 for the total budget. In typing the total budget figure, be sure to type the commas.

4. **Click the By Changing Variable Cells text box, then select the range G3:H6 on the worksheet**

   You have told Excel which cells to vary to reach the goal of $3,100,000 total budget. You need to specify the constraints on the worksheet values to restrict the Solver's answer to realistic values.

5. **Click Add, with the insertion point in the Cell Reference text box in the Add Constraint dialog box, select the range I3:I6 in the worksheet, click the list arrow in the dialog box, click =, then with the insertion point in the Constraint text box click cell C9**

   As shown in **FIGURE 11-16**, the Add Constraint dialog box specifies that the values in cells in the range I3:I6, the total branch budget amounts, should be equal to the value in cell C9. Next, you need to add the constraint that the budgeted entertainment amounts should be at least $95,000.

6. **Click Add, with the insertion point in the Cell Reference text box select the range G3:G6 in the worksheet, click the list arrow, select >=, then with the insertion point in the Constraint text box click cell C11**

   Next, you need to specify that the budgeted travel amounts should be greater than or equal to $83,000.

7. **Click Add, with the insertion point in the Cell Reference text box select the range H3:H6, select >=, with the insertion point in the Constraint text box click cell C10, then click OK**

   The Solver Parameters dialog box opens with the constraints listed. Before proceeding, make sure your dialog box matches **FIGURE 11-17**.

Performing What-if Analysis

FIGURE 11-15: Worksheet set up for a complex what-if analysis

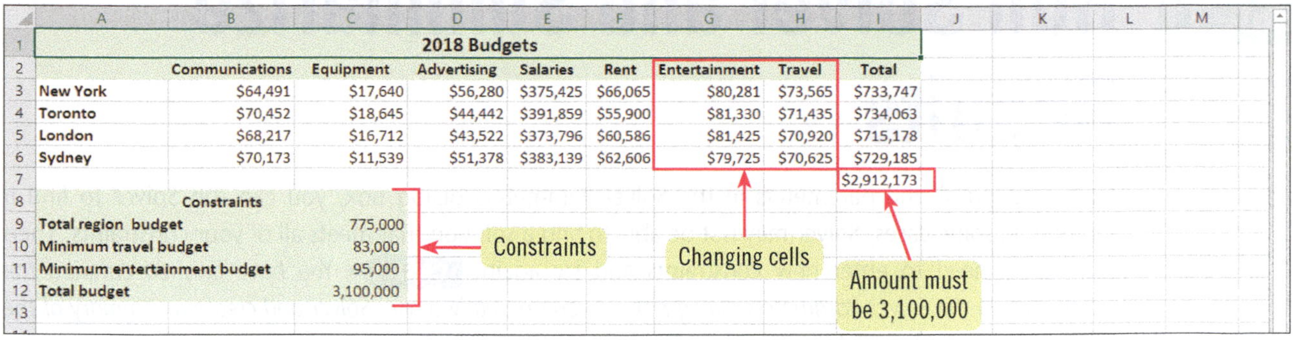

	A	B	C	D	E	F	G	H	I
1					2018 Budgets				
2		Communications	Equipment	Advertising	Salaries	Rent	Entertainment	Travel	Total
3	New York	$64,491	$17,640	$56,280	$375,425	$66,065	$80,281	$73,565	$733,747
4	Toronto	$70,452	$18,645	$44,442	$391,859	$55,900	$81,330	$71,435	$734,063
5	London	$68,217	$16,712	$43,522	$373,796	$60,586	$81,425	$70,920	$715,178
6	Sydney	$70,173	$11,539	$51,378	$383,139	$62,606	$79,725	$70,625	$729,185
7									$2,912,173
8		Constraints							
9	Total region budget		775,000						
10	Minimum travel budget		83,000						
11	Minimum entertainment budget		95,000						
12	Total budget		3,100,000						
13									

Constraints

Changing cells

Amount must be 3,100,000

FIGURE 11-16: Adding constraints

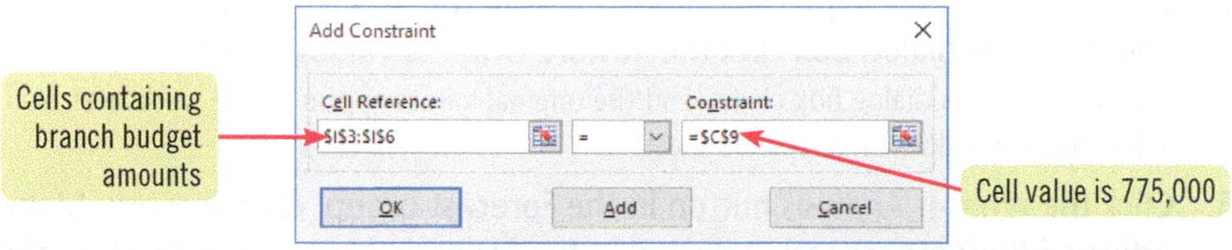

Cells containing branch budget amounts

Add Constraint

Cell Reference:
$I$3:$I$6   =   = $C$9

Constraint:

Cell value is 775,000

OK   Add   Cancel

FIGURE 11-17: Completed Solver Parameters dialog box

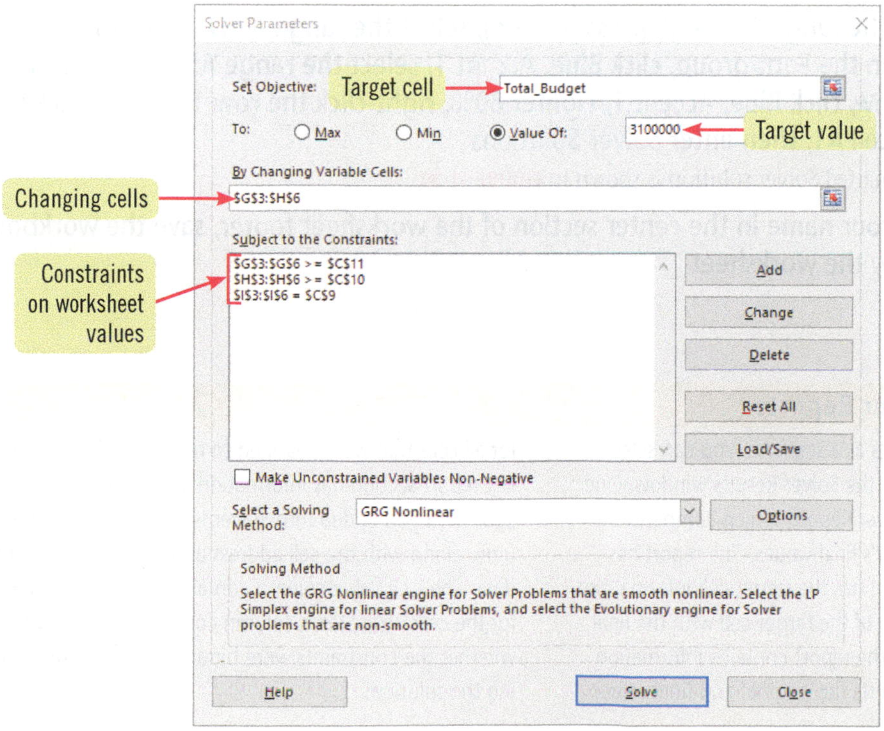

Solver Parameters

Set Objective: Target cell →   Total_Budget

To: ○ Max   ○ Min   ● Value Of: 3100000 ←   Target value

By Changing Variable Cells:
Changing cells → $G$3:$H$6

Subject to the Constraints:

Constraints on worksheet values →
$G$3:$G$6 >= $C$11
$H$3:$H$6 >= $C$10
$I$3:$I$6 = $C$9

Add
Change
Delete
Reset All
Load/Save

☐ Make Unconstrained Variables Non-Negative

Select a Solving Method: GRG Nonlinear   Options

Solving Method

Select the GRG Nonlinear engine for Solver Problems that are smooth nonlinear. Select the LP Simplex engine for linear Solver Problems, and select the Evolutionary engine for Solver problems that are non-smooth.

Help   Solve   Close

Run Solver and Summarize Results

Learning Outcomes
- Run Solver using the parameters in the Solver Parameters dialog box
- Create an answer report using solver

After entering all the parameters in the Solver Parameters dialog box, you can run Solver to find a solution. In some cases, Solver may not be able to find a solution that meets all of your constraints. Then you would need to enter new constraints and try again. **CASE** ▸ *You have finished entering the parameters in the Solver Parameters dialog box, so you are ready to run Solver and create a summary of the solution on a separate worksheet.*

STEPS

1. **Click Solve**

   The Solver Results dialog box opens, indicating that Solver has found a solution, as shown in **FIGURE 11-18**. The solution values appear in the worksheet, but you decide to save the solution values in a summary worksheet and display the original values in the worksheet.

2. **Click Save Scenario, type Adjusted Budgets in the Scenario Name text box, click OK, in the Solver Results dialog box click the Restore Original Values option button, then click OK**

   The Solver Results dialog box closes, and the original values appear in the worksheet. You will display the Solver solution values on a separate sheet.

3. **Click the What-If Analysis button in the Forecast group, click Scenario Manager, with the Adjusted Budgets scenario selected in the Scenario Manager dialog box click Summary, then click OK**

   The Solver results are displayed, as shown in **FIGURE 11-19**. You want to format the information so it is easier to interpret.

4. **Select Column A, click the Home tab if necessary, click the Delete button in the Cells group, right-click the Scenario Summary 2 sheet tab, click Rename on the shortcut menu, type Adjusted Budgets, then press [Enter]**

5. **Select the range A16:A18, press [Delete], select the range A2:D3, click the Fill Color list arrow in the Font group, click Blue, Accent 1, select the range A5:D15, click the Fill Color list arrow, click Blue, Accent 1, Lighter 80%, right-click the row 1 header, click Delete, select cell A1, then enter Solver Solutions**

   The formatted Solver solution is shown in **FIGURE 11-20**.

6. **Enter your name in the center section of the worksheet footer, save the workbook, then preview the worksheet**

Understanding Answer Reports

Instead of saving Solver results as a scenario, you can select from three types of reports in the Solver Results window. One of the most useful is the Answer Report, which compares the original values with the Solver's final values. The report has three sections. The top section has the target cell information; it compares the original value of the target cell with the final value. The middle section of the report contains information about the adjustable cells. It lists the original and final values for all cells that were changed to reach the target value. The last report section has information about the constraints. Each constraint you added into Solver is listed in the Formula column, along with the cell address and a description of the cell data. The Cell Value column contains the Solver solution values for the cells. The Status column contains information on whether the constraints were binding or not binding in reaching the solution.

FIGURE 11-18: Solver Results dialog box

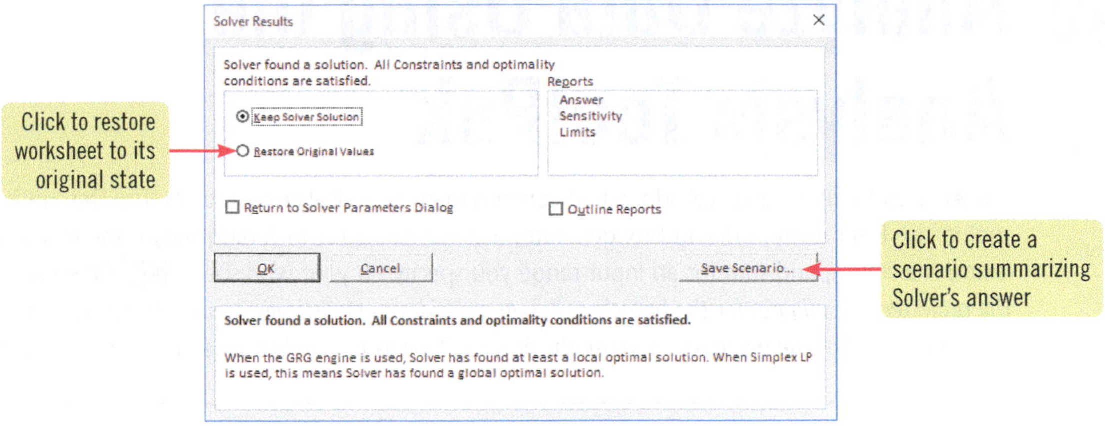

Click to restore worksheet to its original state

Click to create a scenario summarizing Solver's answer

FIGURE 11-19: Solver Summary

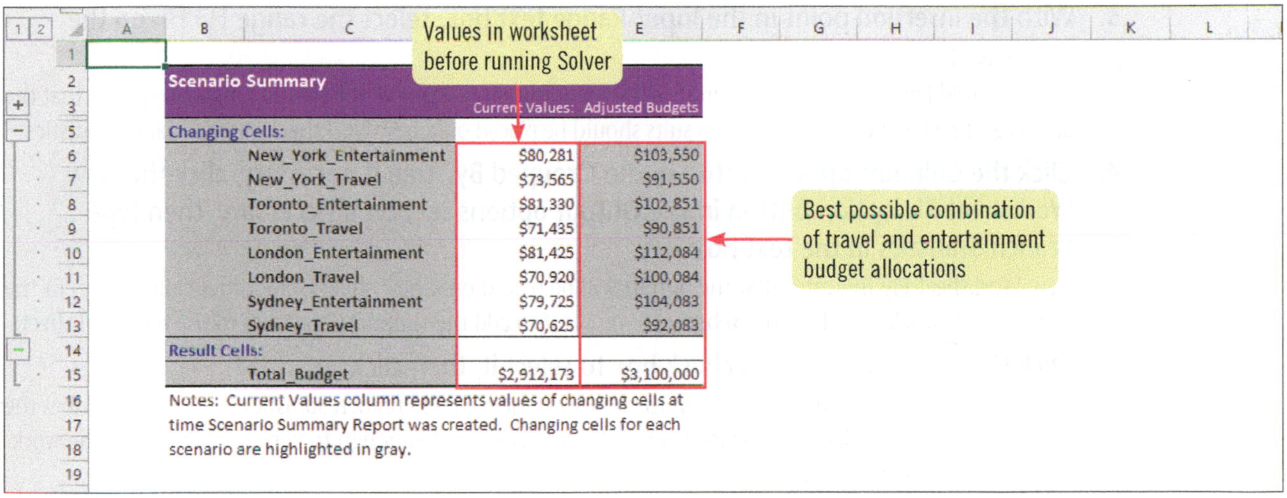

Values in worksheet before running Solver

Best possible combination of travel and entertainment budget allocations

FIGURE 11-20: Formatted Solver Summary

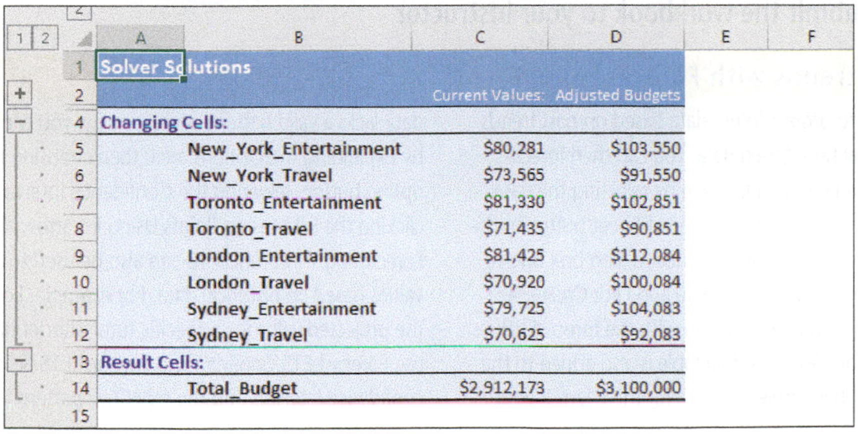

Learning
Outcomes
• Create a summary
statistics worksheet
• Analyze worksheet
data using
descriptive statistics

Analyze Data Using the Analysis ToolPak

The Analysis ToolPak is an Excel add-in that contains many statistical analysis tools. The Descriptive Statistics tool in the Data Analysis dialog box generates a statistical report including mean, median, mode, minimum, maximum, and sum for an input range you specify on your worksheet. **CASE** *After reviewing the projected sales figures for the branches, Rae-Ann decides to statistically analyze the projected branch sales totals submitted by the managers. You use the Analysis ToolPak to help her generate the sales statistics.*

STEPS

TROUBLE

If Data Analysis does not appear on your Data tab, click the File tab, click Options, click Add-ins, click Go, in the Add-ins dialog box click the Analysis ToolPak check box to select it, then click OK.

1. **Click the Projected Sales sheet tab, click the Data tab, then click the Data Analysis button in the Analyze group**

   The Data Analysis dialog box opens, listing the available analysis tools.

2. **Click Descriptive Statistics, then click OK**

   The Descriptive Statistics dialog box opens, as shown in **FIGURE 11-21**.

3. **With the insertion point in the Input Range text box, select the range H3:H6 on the worksheet**

   You have told Excel to use the total projected sales cells in the statistical analysis. You need to specify that the data is grouped in a column and the results should be placed on a new worksheet named Branch Statistics.

4. **Click the Columns option button in the Grouped By: area if necessary, click the New Worksheet Ply option button in the Output options section if necessary, then type Branch Statistics in the text box**

   New Worksheet Ply indicates that the output will be placed on a new sheet (sometimes called a ply) in the workbook. You selected this option because you want to add the summary statistics to the new worksheet.

5. **Click the Summary statistics check box to select it, then click OK**

   The statistics are generated and placed on the new worksheet named Branch Statistics. **TABLE 11-1** describes the statistical values provided in the worksheet. Column A is not wide enough to view the labels, and the worksheet needs a descriptive title.

6. **Widen column A to display the row labels, then edit the contents of cell A1 to read Total Projected Sales Jan – Jun**

   The completed report is shown in **FIGURE 11-22**.

7. **Enter your name in the center section of the Branch Statistics footer, preview the report, save the workbook, close the workbook, then exit Excel**

8. **Submit the workbook to your instructor**

Predicting data trends with Forecast Sheet

Forecast Sheet is a tool to project future data based on past trends when you have historical time-based data. You can then forecast the future of your data related to a timeline by selecting the data, clicking the Data tab, then clicking the Forecast Sheet button in the Forecast group. The Create Forecast Worksheet dialog box opens, where you can enter your Forecast End date and click Create. A chart is created, showing your values along with the forecast values and the related confidence levels. A data table is also added to the worksheet, showing the new projected data for the chart. If your data lacks a valid pattern or seasonality, you can manually set this by expanding the Options area, then choosing the Set Manually option button, lowering the Confidence Interval percentage, or clicking the Fill Missing Points Using list arrow and selecting Zeros. Forecasting sheet functions can also be used to predict future values based on historical data. For example, Forecast.ETS() returns the projected value for a specific future target date. You can also use Forecast.ETS.Confint() and Forecast.ETS.Seasonality() to find confidence intervals and the repetitive pattern length of data.

Performing What-if Analysis

FIGURE 11-21: Descriptive Statistics dialog box

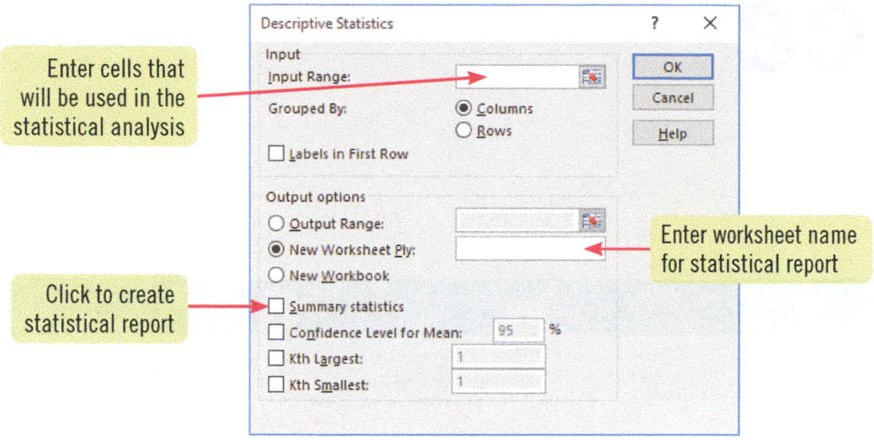

Enter cells that will be used in the statistical analysis →

Enter worksheet name for statistical report →

Click to create statistical report →

Descriptive Statistics	? ×

Input
Input Range: [   ] 🔢   OK
Grouped By: ● Columns   Cancel
                     ○ Rows   Help
☐ Labels in First Row

Output options
○ Output Range: [   ] 🔢
● New Worksheet Ply: [   ]
○ New Workbook
☐ Summary statistics
☐ Confidence Level for Mean: [95] %
☐ Kth Largest: [1]
☐ Kth Smallest: [1]

FIGURE 11-22: Completed report

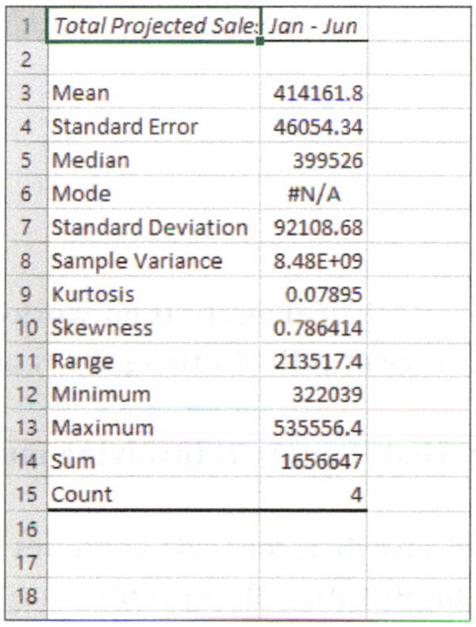

	Total Projected Sales	Jan - Jun
1	Total Projected Sales	Jan - Jun
2		
3	Mean	414161.8
4	Standard Error	46054.34
5	Median	399526
6	Mode	#N/A
7	Standard Deviation	92108.68
8	Sample Variance	8.48E+09
9	Kurtosis	0.07895
10	Skewness	0.786414
11	Range	213517.4
12	Minimum	322039
13	Maximum	535556.4
14	Sum	1656647
15	Count	4
16		
17		
18		

TABLE 11-1: Descriptive statistics

statistic	definition
Mean	The average of a set of numbers
Standard Error	The deviation of the mean of your data from the overall population
Median	The middle value of a set of numbers
Mode	The most common value in a set of numbers
Standard Deviation	The measure of how widely spread the values in a set of numbers are; if the values are all close to the mean, the standard deviation is close to zero
Sample Variance	The measure of how scattered the values in a set of numbers are from an expected value
Kurtosis	The measure of the peakedness or flatness of a distribution of data
Skewness	The measure of the asymmetry of the values in a set of numbers
Range	The difference between the largest and smallest values in a set of numbers
Minimum	The smallest value in a set of numbers
Maximum	The largest value in a set of numbers
Sum	The total of the values in a set of numbers
Count	The number of values in a set of numbers

Practice

Concepts Review

FIGURE 11-23

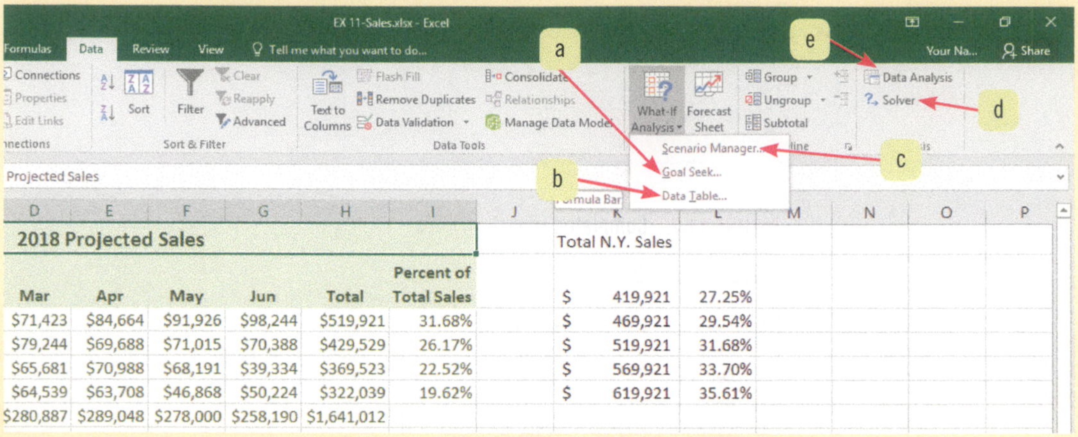

1. Which element do you click to perform a statistical analysis on worksheet data?
2. Which element do you click to create a range of cells showing the resulting values with varied formula input?
3. Which element do you click to perform what-if analysis involving multiple input values with constraints?
4. Which element do you click to name and save different sets of values to forecast worksheet results?
5. Which element do you click to find the input values that produce a specified result?

Match each term with the statement that best describes it.

6. One-input data table
7. Solver
8. Goal Seek
9. Scenario summary
10. Two-input data table

a. Add-in that helps you solve complex what-if scenarios with multiple input values
b. Separate sheet with results from the worksheet's scenarios
c. Generates values resulting from varying two sets of changing values in a formula
d. Helps you backsolve what-if scenarios
e. Generates values resulting from varying one set of changing values in a formula

Select the best answer from the list of choices.

11. The _____ button in the Scenario Manager dialog box allows you to bring scenarios from another workbook into the current workbook.
   a. Combine
   b. Add
   c. Merge
   d. Import
12. To hide the contents of a cell from view, which custom number format can you use?
   a. —
   b. ;;;
   c. Blank
   d. " "
13. In Solver, the cell containing the formula is called the:
   a. Target cell.
   b. Changing cell.
   c. Input cell.
   d. Output cell.

14. When you use Goal Seek, you specify a _____, then find the values that produce it.

a. Row input cell

b. Column input cell

c. Changing value

d. Solution

15. Which of the following Excel add-ins can be used to generate a statistical summary of worksheet data?

a. Solver

b. Lookup Wizard

c. Conditional Sum

d. Analysis ToolPak

Skills Review

1. Define what-if analysis.

a. Start Excel, open EX 11-2.xlsx from the location where you store your Data Files, then save it as **EX 11-Repair**.

b. Examine the Stair Stepper Repair worksheet to determine the purpose of the worksheet model.

c. Locate the data input cells.

d. Locate any dependent cells.

e. Examine the worksheet to determine problems the worksheet model can solve.

2. Track what-if analysis with Scenario Manager.

a. On the Stair Stepper Repair worksheet, select the range B3:B5, then use the Scenario Manager to set up a scenario called **Most Likely** with the current data input values.

b. Add a scenario called **Best Case** using the same changing cells, but change the Labor cost per hour in the $B$3 text box to **80**, change the Parts cost per job in the $B$4 text box to **70**, then change the Hours per job value in cell $B$5 to **2.5**.

c. Add a scenario called **Worst Case**. For this scenario, change the Labor cost per hour in the $B$3 text box to **95**, change the Parts cost per job in the $B$4 text box to **85**, then change the Hours per job in the $B$5 text box to **4**.

d. If necessary, drag the Scenario Manager dialog box to the right until columns A and B are visible.

e. Show the Worst Case scenario results, and view the total job cost.

f. Show the Best Case scenario results, and observe the job cost. Finally, display the Most Likely scenario results.

g. Close the Scenario Manager dialog box.

h. Save the workbook.

3. Generate a scenario summary.

a. Create names for the input value cells and the dependent cell using the range A3:B7.

b. Verify that the names were created. (You will see other names in the Name Manager dialog box.)

c. Create a scenario summary report, using the Cost to complete job value in cell B7 as the result cell.

d. Edit the title of the Summary report in cell B2 to read **Scenario Summary for Stair Stepper Repair**.

e. Delete the Current Values column.

f. Delete the notes beginning in cell B11. Compare your worksheet to FIGURE 11-24.

g. Return to cell A1, enter your name in the center section of the Scenario Summary sheet footer, save the workbook, then preview the Scenario Summary sheet.

FIGURE 11-24

		A	B	C	D	E	F	G
1 2	1							
	2		Scenario Summary for Stair Stepper Repair					
+	3				Most Likely	Best Case	Worst Case	
−	5		Changing Cells:					
	6			Labor_cost_per_hour	$85.00	$80.00	$95.00	
	7			Parts_cost_per_job	$75.00	$70.00	$85.00	
	8			Hours_per_job	3.00	2.50	4.00	
−	9		Result Cells:					
	10			Cost_to_complete_job	$330.00	$270.00	$465.00	
	11							
	12							

4. Project figures using a data table.

a. Click the Stair Stepper Repair sheet tab.

b. Enter the label **Labor $** in cell D3.

Skills Review (continued)

c. Format the label so that it is bold and right-aligned.

d. In cell D4, enter **80**; then in cell D5, enter **85**.

e. Select the range D4:D5, then use the fill handle to extend the series to cell D8.

f. In cell E3, reference the job cost formula by entering **=B7**.

g. Format the contents of cell E3 as hidden, using the ;;; Custom formatting type on the Number tab of the Format Cells dialog box.

h. Generate the new job costs based on the varying labor costs. Select the range D3:E8 and create a data table. In the data table dialog box, make cell B3 (the labor cost) the column input cell.

i. Format the range E4:E8 as currency with two decimal places. Compare your worksheet to **FIGURE 11-25**.

FIGURE 11-25

j. Enter your name in the center section of the worksheet footer, save the workbook, then preview the worksheet.

	A	B	C	D	E	F
1	Fitness Equipment Repair Model					
2						
3	Labor cost per hour	$85.00		Labor $		
4	Parts cost per job	$75.00		80	$315.00	
5	Hours per job	3.00		85	$330.00	
6				90	$345.00	
7	Cost to complete job:	$330.00		95	$360.00	
8				100	$375.00	
9						
10						

5. Use Goal Seek.

a. Click cell B7, and open the Goal Seek dialog box.

b. Assuming the labor rate and the hours remain the same, determine what the parts would have to cost so that the cost to complete the job is $300. (*Hint*: Enter a job cost of **300** as the To value, and enter **B4** (the Parts cost) as the By changing cell.) Write down the parts cost that Goal Seek finds.

c. Click OK, then use [Ctrl][Z] to reset the parts cost to its original value.

d. Enter the parts cost that you found in step 5b into cell A14.

e. Assuming the parts cost and hours remain the same, determine the labor so that the cost to complete the job is $300. Use [Ctrl][Z] to reset the labor cost to its original value. Enter the labor cost in cell A15.

f. Save the workbook, then preview the worksheet.

6. Set up a complex what-if analysis with Solver.

a. With the Equipment Repair sheet active, open the Solver Parameters dialog box.

b. Make B14 (the total repair costs) the objective cell, with a target value of 16,000.

c. Use cells B6:D6 (the number of all scheduled repairs) as the changing cells.

d. Specify that cells B6:D6 must be integers. (*Hint*: Select int in the Add Constraint dialog box.)

e. Specify a constraint that cells B6:D6 must be greater than or equal to 10.

7. Run Solver and summarize results.

a. Use Solver to find a solution.

b. Save the solution as a scenario named **Equipment Repair Solution**, and restore the original values to the worksheet.

c. Create a scenario summary using the Repair Solution scenario, delete the notes at the bottom of the solution, and change the title in cell B2 to **Repair Solution**. Compare your worksheet to **FIGURE 11-26**.

FIGURE 11-26

d. Enter your name in the center section of the worksheet footer, save the workbook, then preview the worksheet.

	A	B	C	D	E
1					
2					
3		Repair Solution			
				Current Values:	Equipment Repair Solution
5		Changing Cells:			
6			Number_Treadmill_Repairs	25	23
7			Number_Elliptical_Repairs	35	33
8			Number_Bike_Repairs	15	13
9		Result Cells:			
10			Total_Repair_Costs	$17,475.00	$16,000.00
11					

8. Analyze data using the Analysis ToolPak.

a. With the Equipment Repair sheet active, generate summary descriptive statistics for the repair cost per model, using cells B10:D10 as the input range. (*Hint*: The input is grouped in a row.) Place the statistics in a new worksheet named **Repair Cost Statistics**.

b. Widen columns as necessary to view the statistics.

Skills Review (continued)

c. Change the contents of cell A1 to **Repair Costs**. Delete row 6 containing the mode error (generated because you do not have any repeating data values). Also delete row 9 containing the kurtosis error information (generated because you only have three data values). Compare your worksheet to FIGURE 11-27.

d. Add your name to the center section of the worksheet footer, then preview the worksheet.

e. Save and close the workbook, submit the workbook to your instructor, then exit Excel.

FIGURE 11-27

	Repair Costs	
1		
2		
3	Mean	5825
4	Standard Error	1517.467737
5	Median	6500
6	Standard Deviation	2628.33122
7	Sample Variance	6908125
8	Skewness	-1.079453699
9	Range	5125
10	Minimum	2925
11	Maximum	8050
12	Sum	17475
13	Count	3
14		

Independent Challenge 1

You are the owner of Smith Landscaping, a landscaping and plowing company based in Boston. You are planning an equipment purchase of three new plows. You will research the monthly cost for a $150,000 equipment loan to purchase the new plows. You will create a worksheet model to determine the monthly payments based on several different interest rates and loan terms, using data from the company's bank. Using Scenario Manager, you will create the following three scenarios: a 4-year loan at 5 percent; a 3-year loan at 4.5 percent; and a 2-year loan at 4 percent. You will also prepare a scenario summary report outlining the payment details.

a. Start Excel, open EX 11-3.xlsx from the location where you store your Data Files, then save it as **EX 11-Equipment Loan**.

b. Create cell names for cells B4:B11 based on the labels in cells A4:A11, using the Create Names from Selection dialog box.

c. Use Scenario Manager to create scenarios that calculate the monthly payment on a $150,000 loan under the three sets of loan possibilities listed below. (*Hint*: Create three scenarios using cells B5:B6 as the changing cells.)

Scenario Name	Interest Rate	Term
5% 4 Yr	.05	48
4.5% 3 Yr	.045	36
4% 2 Yr	.04	24

d. Show each scenario to make sure it performs as intended, then display the 5% 4 Yr scenario.

e. Generate a scenario summary titled **Scenario Summary**. Use cells B9:B11 as the Result cells.

f. Delete the Current Values column in the report, and delete the notes at the bottom of the report. Rename the sheet **Equipment Purchase**.

g. Enter your name in the center section of the Equipment Purchase sheet footer. Save the workbook, then preview the scenario summary.

h. Close the workbook, exit Excel, then submit the workbook to your instructor.

Independent Challenge 2

You are a CFO at Locke & Rogers, a communications consulting company based in Michigan. The company president has asked you to prepare a loan summary report for a business expansion. You need to develop a model to show what the monthly payments would be for a $600,000 loan with a range of interest rates. You will create a one-input data table that shows the results of varying interest rates in 0.2% increments, then you will use Goal Seek to specify a total payment amount for this loan application.

a. Start Excel, open EX 11-4.xlsx from the location where you store your Data Files, then save it as **EX 11-Capital Loan**.

Independent Challenge 2 (continued)

b. Use FIGURE 11-28 as a guide to enter the data table structure. Reference the monthly payment amount from cell B9 in cell E4, then format the contents of cell E4 as hidden.

FIGURE 11-28

	A	B	C	D	E	F
1	**L & R Communications**					
2						
3				Interest Rate		
4	Loan Amount	$600,000.00				
5	Annual Interest Rate	7.60%		7.00%		
6	Term in Months	60		7.20%		
7				7.40%		
8				7.60%		
9	Monthly Payment:	$12,051.30		7.80%		
10	Total Payments:	$723,078.08		8.00%		
11	Total Interest:	$123,078.08		8.20%		
12				8.40%		
13				8.60%		

c. Using cells D4:E13, create a one-input data table with varying interest rates for the loan.

d. Generate the data table that shows the effect of varying interest rates on the monthly payments. Use cell B5, the Annual Interest Rate, as the column input cell. Format the range E5:E13 as currency with two decimal places. Widen Column E as necessary.

e. Select cell B10 and use Goal Seek to find the interest rate necessary for a total payment amount of $700,000. Use cell B5, the Annual Interest Rate, as the By changing cell. Note the interest rate, then cancel the solution found by Goal Seek. Enter the interest rate in cell B16.

f. Select cell B9 and use Goal Seek to find the interest rate necessary for a monthly payment amount of $11,000. Use cell B5, the Annual Interest Rate, as the By changing cell. Note the interest rate, then cancel the solution found by Goal Seek. Enter the interest rate in cell B17.

g. Enter your name in the center section of the worksheet footer, save the workbook, then preview the worksheet.

h. Close the workbook, exit Excel, then submit the workbook to your instructor.

Independent Challenge 3

You are the owner of Atlantic Mobile Storage, a residential storage company based in Boston. You are considering a purchase of new storage containers for your residential customers. You want to use Goal Seek to look at how the interest rate affects the monthly payments for two of each size of container. Next you want to look at options for expanding the storage service by purchasing a combination of differently sized containers that can store a total of 1500 cubic feet. As you review your expansion options, you need to keep the total monthly payments for all of the containers at or below $6,500. You use Solver to help find the best possible combination of containers and interest rates.

a. Start Excel, open EX 11-5.xlsx from the location where you store your Data Files, then save it as **EX 11-Atlantic Mobile**.

b. Use Goal Seek to find the interest rate that produces a monthly payment for the large container purchase of $1,850, and write down the interest rate that Goal Seek finds. Reset the interest rate to its original value, record the interest rate in cell A19, then enter **Interest rate for $1850 large container payment** in cell B19.

Independent Challenge 3 (continued)

c. Use Goal Seek to find the interest rate that produces a monthly payment for the medium container purchase of $1050. Reset the interest rate to its original value, record the interest rate in cell A20, then enter **Interest rate for $1050 medium container payment** in cell B20.

d. Use Goal Seek to find the interest rate that produces a monthly payment for the small container purchase of $675. Reset the interest rate to its original value, record the interest rate in cell A21, then enter **Interest rate for $675 small container payment** in cell B21.

e. Assign cell B8 the name **Quantity_Large**, name cell C8 **Quantity_Medium**, name cell D8 **Quantity_Small**, and name cell B15 **Total_Monthly_Payments**. Use Solver to set the total storage capacity of all containers to 1500. Use the quantity to purchase, cells B8:D8, as the changing cells. Specify that cells B8:D8 must be integers. Make sure that the total monthly payments amount in cell B15 is less than or equal to $6,500.

f. Generate a scenario named **Storage Container Solution** with the Solver values, and restore the original values in the worksheet. Create a scenario summary using the Storage Container Solution scenario and the Total Monthly Payments as the result cells, delete the notes at the bottom of the solution, and edit cell B2 to contain **Total Storage Capacity of 1500**.

g. Enter your name in the center footer section of both worksheets. Preview both worksheets, then save the workbook.

h. Close the workbook, then submit the workbook to your instructor.

Independent Challenge 4: Explore

You are researching various options for financing an RV loan. You haven't decided whether to finance the RV for 3, 4, or 5 years. Each loan term carries a different interest rate. To help with the comparison, you will create a two-input data table using interest rates and terms available at your credit union.

a. Start Excel, open the EX 11-6.xlsx from the location where you store your Data Files, then save it as **EX 11-RV Loan**.

b. Using **FIGURE 11-29** as a guide, enter the input values for a two-input data table with varying interest rates for 3-, 4-, and 5-year terms.

c. Reference the monthly payment amount from cell B9 in cell A13, and format the contents of cell A13 as hidden.

d. Generate the data table, using cells A13:D22, that shows the effect of varying interest rates and loan terms on the monthly payments. (*Hint*: Use cell B6, Term in Months, as the Row input cell, and cell B5, the Annual Interest Rate, as the Column input cell.)

e. Format the range B14:D22 as currency with two decimal places.

f. Enter your name in the center section of the Loan sheet footer, then preview the Loan sheet.

g. Save the workbook, close the workbook, then exit Excel and submit the workbook to your instructor.

FIGURE 11-29

	A	B	C	D	E
1	**RV Financing Options**				
2					
3					
4	Loan Amount	$16,500.00			
5	Annual Interest Rate	3.75%			
6	Term in Months	60			
7					
8					
9	Monthly Payment:	$302.01			
10	Total Payments:	$18,120.88			
11	Total Interest:	$1,620.88			
12					
13			36	48	60
14		3.00%			
15		3.25%			
16		3.50%			
17		3.75%			
18		4.00%			
19		4.25%			
20		4.50%			
21		4.75%			
22		5.00%			
23					

Visual Workshop

Open the file EX 11-7.xlsx from the location where you store your Data Files, then save it as **EX 11-Robotics**. Create the worksheet shown in FIGURE 11-30. (*Hint*: Use Goal Seek to find the Hourly labor cost to reach the total profit in cell H11 in the figure and accept the solution.) Then generate descriptive statistics for the four products' total profits on a worksheet named **Profits**, as shown in FIGURE 11-31. Add your name to the center footer section of each sheet, change the orientation of the Product Info sheet to landscape, then preview and print both worksheets.

FIGURE 11-30

	A	B	C	D	E	F	G	H	I	J
1	Pacific Robotics									
2	January Profit									
3	Hourly Labor Cost	$64.91								
4										
5										
6	Product Number	Hours	Parts Cost	Cost to Produce	Retail Price	Unit Profit	Units Produced	Total Profit		
7	23654	15	$896	$ 1,869.60	$ 2,854.00	$ 984.40	157	$ 154,550.54		
8	12574	17	$1,002	$ 2,105.42	$ 2,964.00	$ 858.58	87	$ 74,696.88		
9	35521	22	$1,421	$ 2,848.95	$ 3,964.00	$ 1,115.05	101	$ 112,620.14		
10	54496	84	$1,080	$ 6,532.17	$ 8,251.00	$ 1,718.83	92	$ 158,132.44		
11	Total Profit							$ 500,000.00		
12										
13										

FIGURE 11-31

	A	B	C	D
1	Profit Statistics			
2				
3	Mean	125000		
4	Standard Error	19694.87608		
5	Median	133585.3432		
6	Mode	#N/A		
7	Standard Deviation	39389.75215		
8	Sample Variance	1551552575		
9	Kurtosis	-1.877031404		
10	Skewness	-0.730953256		
11	Range	83435.55695		
12	Minimum	74696.87834		
13	Maximum	158132.4353		
14	Sum	500000		
15	Count	4		
16				

Analyzing Data with PivotTables

CASE ▶ Reason2Go uses PivotTables to analyze sales data. Dawn Parsons is preparing for the annual directors' meeting and asks you to analyze sales in Reason2Go's North American branches over the past year. You will create a PivotTable to summarize last year's sales data by quarter, product, and branch, and illustrate the information using a PivotChart.

Module Objectives

After completing this module, you will be able to:

- Plan and design a PivotTable report
- Create a PivotTable report
- Change a PivotTable's summary function and design
- Filter and sort PivotTable data

- Update a PivotTable report
- Explore PivotTable Data Relationships
- Create a PivotChart report
- Use the GETPIVOTDATA function

Files You Will Need

EX 12-1.xlsx   EX 12-5.xlsx
EX 12-2.xlsx   EX 12-6.xlsx
EX 12-3.xlsx   EX 12-7.xlsx
EX 12-4.xlsx

Plan and Design a PivotTable Report

Learning Outcomes
- Develop guidelines for a PivotTable
- Develop an understanding of PivotTable vocabulary

The Excel **PivotTable Report** feature lets you summarize large amounts of columnar worksheet data in a compact table format. Then you can freely rearrange, or "pivot", PivotTable rows and columns to explore the relationships within your data by category. Creating a PivotTable report (often called a PivotTable) involves only a few steps. Before you begin, however, you need to review the data and consider how a PivotTable can best summarize it. **CASE** ▶ *Dawn asks you to design a PivotTable to display Reason2Go's sales information for its branches in North America. You begin by reviewing guidelines for creating PivotTables.*

DETAILS

Before you create a PivotTable, think about the following guidelines:

- **Review the source data**

  Before you can effectively summarize data in a PivotTable, you need to understand the source data's scope and structure. The source data does not have to be defined as a table, but should be in a table-like format. That is, it should have column headings, should not have any blank rows or columns, and should have the same type of data in each column. To create a meaningful PivotTable, make sure that one or more of the fields have repeated information so that the PivotTable can effectively group it. Also be sure to include numeric data that the PivotTable can total for each group. The data columns represent categories of data, which are called **fields**, just as in a table. You are working with sales information that Dawn received from Reason2Go's North American branch managers, shown in **FIGURE 12-1**. Information is repeated in the Product ID, Category, Branch, and Quarter columns, and numeric information is displayed in the Sales column, so you will be able to summarize this data effectively in a PivotTable.

- **Determine the purpose of the PivotTable and write the names of the fields you want to include**

  The purpose of your PivotTable is to summarize sales information by quarter across various branches. You want your PivotTable to summarize the data in the Product ID, Category, Branch, Quarter, and Sales columns, so you need to include those fields in your PivotTable.

- **Determine which field contains the data you want to summarize and which summary function you want to use**

  The components of a Reason2Go project are organized into products, such as Insurance, Transportation, and Experience. You want to summarize sales information by summing the Sales field for each product in a branch by quarter. You'll do this by using the Excel SUM function.

- **Decide how you want to arrange the data**

  The PivotTable layout you choose is crucial to delivering the message you intend. Product ID values will appear in the PivotTable columns, Branch and Quarter numbers will appear in rows, and the PivotTable will summarize Sales figures, as shown in **FIGURE 12-2**.

- **Determine the location of the PivotTable**

  You can place a PivotTable in any worksheet of any workbook. Placing a PivotTable on a separate worksheet makes it easier to locate and prevents you from accidentally overwriting parts of an existing sheet. You decide to create the PivotTable as a new worksheet in the current workbook.

FIGURE 12-1: Sales worksheet

	A	B	C	D	E	F	G
1			Sales				
2	Product ID	Category	Branch	Quarter	Sales		
3	240	Transportation	Los Angeles	1	$ 1,115.33		
4	240	Transportation	Los Angeles	2	$ 1,974.21		
5	240	Transportation	Los Angeles	3	$ 822.87		
6	240	Transportation	Los Angeles	4	$ 1,089.24		
7	110	Insurance	Los Angeles	1	$ 975.50		
8	110	Insurance	Los Angeles	2	$ 2,566.41		
9	110	Insurance	Los Angeles	3	$ 2,355.78		
10	110	Insurance	Los Angeles	4	$ 3,117.22		
11	340	Experience	Los Angeles	1	$ 7,772.31		
12	340	Experience	Los Angeles	2	$ 7,655.21		
13	340	Experience	Los Angeles	3	$ 8,100.34		
14	340	Experience	Los Angeles	4	$ 8,566.14		
15	780	Transportation	Los Angeles	1	$ 1,027.25		
16	780	Transportation	Los Angeles	2	$ 2,231.47		
17	780	Transportation	Los Angeles	3	$ 2,136.11		
18	780	Transportation	Los Angeles	4	$ 1,117.36		
19	640	Insurance	Los Angeles	1	$ 1,499.31		
20	640	Insurance	Los Angeles	2	$ 6,321.22		
21	640	Insurance	Los Angeles	3	$ 6,002.11		
22	640	Insurance	Los Angeles	4	$ 6,211.87		
23	510	Experience	Los Angeles	1	$ 877.41		
24	510	Experience	Los Angeles	2	$ 1,889.35		
25	510	Experience	Los Angeles	3	$ 2,122.54		
26	510	Experience	Los Angeles	4	$ 2,556.74		
27	240	Transportation	New York	1	$ 1,897.51		
28	240	Transportation	New York	2	$ 2,374.32		
29	240	Transportation	New York	3	$ 1,032.57		
30	240	Transportation	New York	4	$ 1,230.41		
31	110	Insurance	New York	1	$ 4,921.45		
32	110	Insurance	New York	2	$ 3,319.92		

North America ⊕

Data with repeated information

Numeric data

FIGURE 12-2: PivotTable report based on Sales worksheet

Product ID values are column labels

	A	B	C	D	E	F	G	H
1								
2								
3	Sum of Sales	Column Labels ▼						
4	Row Labels ▼	110	240	340	510	640	780	Grand Total
5	⊟ Los Angeles	9014.91	5001.65	32094	7446.04	20034.51	6512.19	80103.3
6	1	975.5	1115.33	7772.31	877.41	1499.31	1027.25	13267.11
7	2	2566.41	1974.21	7655.21	1889.35	6321.22	2231.47	22637.87
8	3	2355.78	822.87	8100.34	2122.54	6002.11	2136.11	21539.75
9	4	3117.22	1089.24	8566.14	2556.74	6211.87	1117.36	22658.57
10	⊟ New York	15057.69	6534.81	29818.65	20039.58	8856.97	5056.28	85363.98
11	1	4921.45	1897.51	6258.21	2987.14	1305.47	1522.14	18891.92
12	2	3319.92	2374.32	7628.78	3880.78	2183.98	208.64	19596.42
13	3	4176.89	1032.57	8198.9	6728.9	2577.98	1324.14	24039.38
14	4	2639.43	1230.41	7732.76	6442.76	2789.54	2001.36	22836.26
15	⊟ Toronto	31883.87	3237.62	32350.46	9567.18	10106.56	4008.7	91154.39
16	1	6634.43	895.65	7790.34	2310.34	1376.34	781.14	19788.24
17	2	8100.14	921.32	6700.15	2524.87	3394.21	968.24	22608.93
18	3	8324.65	398.77	8883.54	2183.54	2412.58	1002.21	23205.29
19	4	8824.65	1021.88	8976.43	2548.43	2923.43	1257.11	25551.93
20	Grand Total	55956.47	14774.08	94263.11	37052.8	38998.04	15577.17	256621.67
21								
22								
23								

PivotTable summarizes sales figures by product ID, branch, and quarter

Branches and quarters are row labels

Excel 2016

Create a PivotTable Report

Once you've planned and designed your PivotTable report, you can create it. After you create the PivotTable, you **populate** it by adding fields to areas in the PivotTable. A PivotTable has four areas: the Report Filter, which is the field by which you want to filter the PivotTable; the Row Labels, which contain the fields whose labels will describe the values in the rows; the Column Labels, which appear above the PivotTable values and describe the columns; and the Values, which summarize the numeric data. **CASE** *With the planning and design stage complete, you are ready to create a PivotTable that summarizes sales information.*

STEPS

1. **Start Excel, open EX 12-1.xlsx from the location where you store your Data Files, then save it as EX 12-NA Sales**

   This worksheet contains last year's sales information for R2G's North American branches, including Product ID, Category, Branch, Quarter, and Sales. The records are sorted by branch. You first want to see what PivotTables Excel recommends for your data.

2. **Click the Insert tab, click the Recommended PivotTables button in the Tables group, then click each of the recommended layouts in the left side of the Recommended PivotTables dialog box, scrolling as necessary**

   The Recommended PivotTables dialog box displays recommended PivotTable layouts that summarize your data, as shown in **FIGURE 12-3**. You decide to create your own PivotTable.

3. **Click Blank PivotTable at the bottom of the dialog box**

   A new, blank PivotTable appears on the left side of the worksheet and the PivotTable Fields List appears in a pane on the right, as shown in **FIGURE 12-4**. You populate the PivotTable by clicking field check boxes in the PivotTable Fields List pane, often simply called the Field List. The diagram area at the bottom of the pane represents the main PivotTable areas and helps you track field locations as you populate the PivotTable. You can also drag fields among the diagram areas to change the PivotTable layout.

4. **Click the Branch field check box in the Field List**

   Because the Branch field is a text, rather than a numeric, field, Excel adds branch names to the rows area of the PivotTable, and adds the Branch field name to the ROWS area in the PivotTable Fields pane.

5. **Click the Product ID check box in the Field List**

   The Product ID information is automatically added to the PivotTable, and "Sum of Product ID" appears in the VALUES area in the diagram area. But because the data type of the Product ID field is numeric, the field is added to the VALUES area of the PivotTable and the Product ID values are summed, which is not meaningful. Instead, you want the Product IDs as column headers in the PivotTable.

6. **Click the Sum of Product ID list arrow in the VALUES area at the bottom of the PivotTable Fields List pane, then choose Move to Column Labels**

   The Product ID field becomes a column label, causing the Product ID values to appear in the PivotTable as column headers.

7. **Drag the Quarter field from the PivotTable Fields List pane and drop it below the Branch field in the ROWS area, select the Sales field check box in the PivotTable Fields List pane, then save the workbook**

   You have created a PivotTable that totals North American sales, with the Product IDs as column headers and Branches and Quarters as row labels. SUM is the Excel default function for data fields containing numbers, so Excel automatically calculates the sum of the sales in the PivotTable. The PivotTable tells you that Toronto sales of Product #110 (Insurance) were twice the New York sales level and more than three times the Los Angeles level. Product #340 (Experience) was the best selling product overall, as shown in the Grand Total row. See **FIGURE 12-5**.

FIGURE 12-3: Recommended PivotTables dialog box

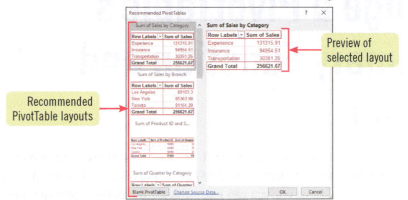

Recommended PivotTable layouts

Preview of selected layout

FIGURE 12-4: Empty PivotTable ready to receive field data

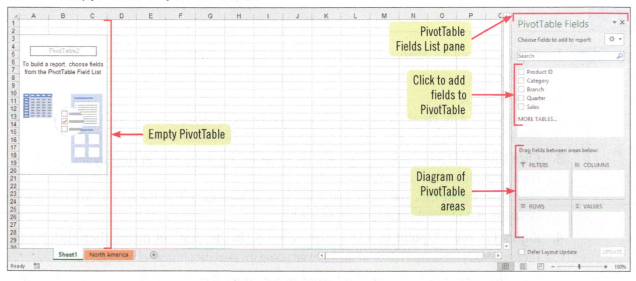

PivotTable Fields List pane

Click to add fields to PivotTable

Empty PivotTable

Diagram of PivotTable areas

FIGURE 12-5: New PivotTable with fields in place

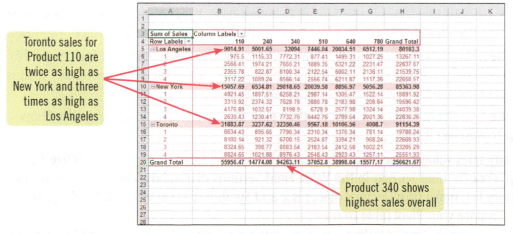

Toronto sales for Product 110 are twice as high as New York and three times as high as Los Angeles

Product 340 shows highest sales overall

Changing the PivotTable layout

The default layout for PivotTables is the compact form; the row labels are displayed in a single column, and the second-level field items (such as the quarters in the R2G example) are indented for readability. You can change the layout of your PivotTable by clicking the PivotTable Tools Design tab, clicking the Report Layout button in the Layout group, then clicking either Show in Outline Form or Show in Tabular Form. The tabular form and the outline form show each row label in its own column. The tabular and outline layouts take up more space on a worksheet than the compact layout.

Analyzing Data with PivotTables

Excel 2016

Change a PivotTable's Summary Function and Design

A PivotTable's **summary function** controls what calculation Excel uses to summarize the table data. Unless you specify otherwise, Excel applies the SUM function to numeric data and the COUNT function to data fields containing text. However, you can easily change the default summary functions to different ones. **CASE** *Dawn wants you to calculate the average sales for the North American branches using the AVERAGE function and to improve the appearance of the PivotTable for her presentation.*

STEPS

1. **Right-click cell A3, then point to Summarize Values By in the shortcut menu**
   The shortcut menu shows that the Sum function is selected by default, as shown in **FIGURE 12-6**.

2. **Click Average**
   The data area of the PivotTable shows the average sales for each product by branch and quarter, and cell A3 now contains "Average of Sales". You want to view the PivotTable data without the subtotals.

3. **Click the PivotTable Tools Design tab, click the Subtotals button in the Layout group, then click Do Not Show Subtotals**
   After reviewing the data, you decide that it would be more useful to sum the sales information than to average it. You also want to redisplay the subtotals.

4. **Right-click cell A3, point to Summarize Values By in the shortcut menu, then click Sum**
   Excel recalculates the PivotTable—in this case, summing the sales data instead of averaging it.

5. **Click the Subtotals button in the Layout group, then click Show all Subtotals at Top of Group**
   Just as Excel tables have styles that let you quickly format them, PivotTables have a gallery of styles to choose from. You decide to add a PivotTable style to the PivotTable to improve its appearance.

6. **Click the More button ⏷ in the PivotTable Styles gallery, then click Pivot Style Light 16**
   To further improve the appearance of the PivotTable, you decide to remove the unnecessary headers "Column Labels" and "Row Labels" and format the sales values as currency.

7. **Click the PivotTable Tools Analyze tab, then click the Field Headers button in the Show group to deselect it**

8. **Click any sales value in the PivotTable, click the Field Settings button in the Active Field group, click Number Format in the Value Field Settings dialog box, click Currency in the Category list, make sure Decimal places is 2 and Symbol is $, click OK, click OK again, then compare your PivotTable to FIGURE 12-7**
   You decide to give the PivotTable sheet a more descriptive name. When you name a PivotTable sheet, it is best to avoid using spaces in the name. If a PivotTable name contains a space, you must put single quotes around the name if you refer to it in a function.

9. **Rename Sheet1 PivotTable, add your name to the worksheet footer, save the workbook, then preview the sheet**

FIGURE 12-6: Shortcut menu showing Sum function selected

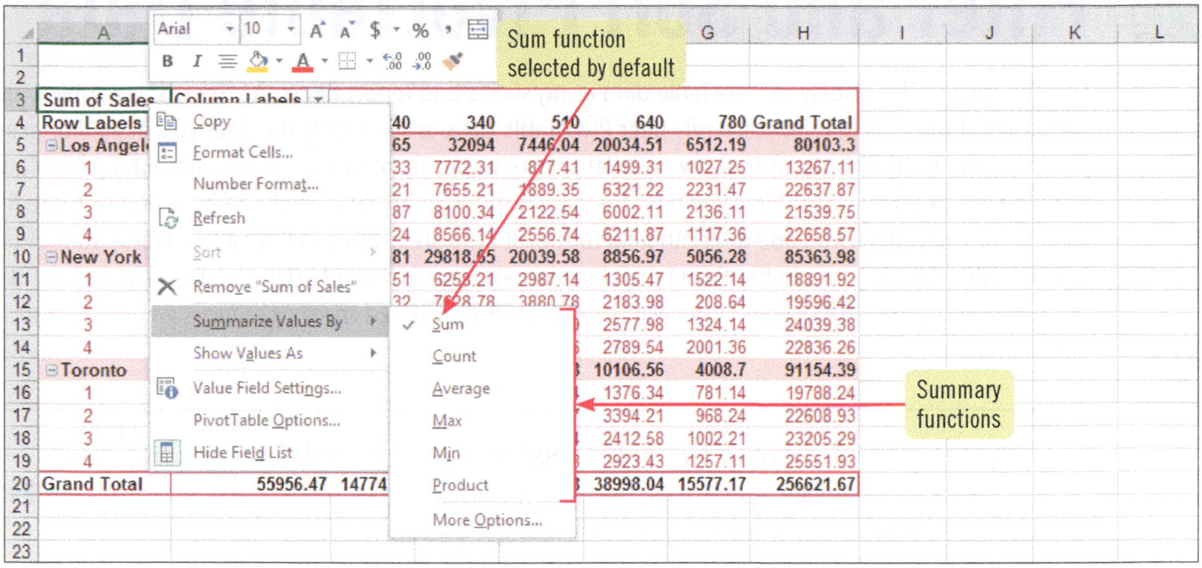

Sum function selected by default

Summary functions

FIGURE 12-7: Formatted PivotTable

	A	B	C	D	E	F	G	H	I	J
1										
2										
3	Sum of Sales									
4		110	240	340	510	640	780	Grand Total		
5	⊟Los Angeles	$9,014.91	$5,001.65	$32,094.00	$7,446.04	$20,034.51	$6,512.19	$80,103.30		
6	1	$975.50	$1,115.33	$7,772.31	$877.41	$1,499.31	$1,027.25	$13,267.11		
7	2	$2,566.41	$1,974.21	$7,655.21	$1,889.35	$6,321.22	$2,231.47	$22,637.87		
8	3	$2,355.78	$822.87	$8,100.34	$2,122.54	$6,002.11	$2,136.11	$21,539.75		
9	4	$3,117.22	$1,089.24	$8,566.14	$2,556.74	$6,211.87	$1,117.36	$22,658.57		
10	⊟New York	$15,057.69	$6,534.81	$29,818.65	$20,039.58	$8,856.97	$5,056.28	$85,363.98		
11	1	$4,921.45	$1,897.51	$6,258.21	$2,987.14	$1,305.47	$1,522.14	$18,891.92		
12	2	$3,319.92	$2,374.32	$7,628.78	$3,880.78	$2,183.98	$208.64	$19,596.42		
13	3	$4,176.89	$1,032.57	$8,198.90	$6,728.90	$2,577.98	$1,324.14	$24,039.38		
14	4	$2,639.43	$1,230.41	$7,732.76	$6,442.76	$2,789.54	$2,001.36	$22,836.26		
15	⊟Toronto	$31,883.87	$3,237.62	$32,350.46	$9,567.18	$10,106.56	$4,008.70	$91,154.39		
16	1	$6,634.43	$895.65	$7,790.34	$2,310.34	$1,376.34	$781.14	$19,788.24		
17	2	$8,100.14	$921.32	$6,700.15	$2,524.87	$3,394.21	$968.24	$22,608.93		
18	3	$8,324.65	$398.77	$8,883.54	$2,183.54	$2,412.58	$1,002.21	$23,205.29		
19	4	$8,824.65	$1,021.88	$8,976.43	$2,548.43	$2,923.43	$1,257.11	$25,551.93		
20	Grand Total	$55,956.47	$14,774.08	$94,263.11	$37,052.80	$38,998.04	$15,577.17	$256,621.67		
21										
22										
23										
24										

Using the Show buttons

To display and hide PivotTable elements, you can use the buttons in the Show group on the PivotTable Tools Analyze tab. For example, the Field List button will hide or display the PivotTable Fields List pane. The +/- buttons button will hide or display the Expand and Collapse Outline buttons, and the Field Headers button will hide or display the Row and Column Label headers on the PivotTable.

Analyzing Data with PivotTables

Filter and Sort PivotTable Data

Learning Outcomes
• Sort a PivotTable using the fields
• Filter a PivotTable using a slicer

You can restrict the display of PivotTable data using slicers and report filters. A **slicer** is a graphic object with a set of buttons that let you easily filter PivotTable data to show only the data you need. For example, you can use slicer buttons to show only data about a specific product. You can also filter a PivotTable using a **report filter**, which lets you filter the data using a list arrow to show data for one or more field values. For example, if you add a Month field to the FILTERS area, you can filter a PivotTable so that only January sales data appears in the PivotTable. You can also sort PivotTable data on any field in ascending or descending order. **CASE** ▶ *Dawn wants to see sales data about specific products for specific branches and quarters.*

STEPS

1. **Right-click cell H5, point to Sort in the shortcut menu, then click More Sort Options**

   The Sort By Value dialog box opens. As you select options in the dialog box, the Summary information at the bottom of the dialog box changes to describe the sort results using your field names.

2. **Click the Largest to Smallest option button to select it under Sort options, make sure the Top to Bottom option button is selected under Sort direction, review the sort description under Summary, then click OK**

   The branches appear in the PivotTable in decreasing order of total sales from top to bottom. You want to easily display the sales for specific product IDs at certain branches.

3. **Click any cell in the PivotTable, click the PivotTable Tools Analyze tab if necessary, click the Insert Slicer button in the Filter group, in the Insert Slicers dialog box, click the Product ID check box and the Branch check box to select both fields, click OK, then drag the slicers to the right of the PivotTable**

   The slicers contain buttons representing the Product ID numbers and Branch names, as shown in **FIGURE 12-8**. You want to filter the data to show only Product IDs 110 and 510 in the New York and Toronto branches.

4. **Click the 110 button in the Product ID slicer, press [CTRL], click the 510 button in the Product ID slicer, release [CTRL], click the New York button in the Branch slicer, press [CTRL], click the Toronto button in the Branch slicer, then release [CTRL]**

   The PivotTable displays only the data for Product IDs 110 and 510 in New York and Toronto, as shown in **FIGURE 12-9**. In the slicers, the Filter symbol changes, indicating the PivotTable is filtered to display the selected fields. You decide to clear the filter and remove the slicers.

5. **Click the Clear Filter button ▨ in the Product ID slicer, click ▨ in the Branch slicer, click the top of the Branch slicer, press [CTRL], click the top of the Product ID slicer, release [CTRL], right-click the Product ID slicer, then click Remove Slicers on the shortcut menu**

   You want to display the PivotTable data by quarter using a Report Filter.

6. **In the PivotTable Fields List pane, click the Quarter field list arrow in the ROWS area, then select Move to Report Filter in the list that opens**

   The Quarter field moves to cell A1, and a list arrow and the word "(All)" appear in cell B1. The list arrow lets you filter the data in the PivotTable by Quarter. "(All)" indicates that the PivotTable currently shows data for all quarters. You decide to filter the data to show only data for the fourth quarter.

7. **Click the cell B1 list arrow, click 4, click OK, then save your work**

   The PivotTable filters the sales data to display the fourth quarter only, as shown in **FIGURE 12-10**. The Quarter field list arrow changes to a filter symbol. A filter symbol also appears to the right of the Quarter field in the PivotTable Fields List pane, indicating that the PivotTable is filtered and summarizes only a portion of the PivotTable data.

FIGURE 12-8: Slicers for Product ID and Branch fields

Click a Product ID to view its data

Click a Branch to view its data

FIGURE 12-9: PivotTable filtered by Product ID and Branch

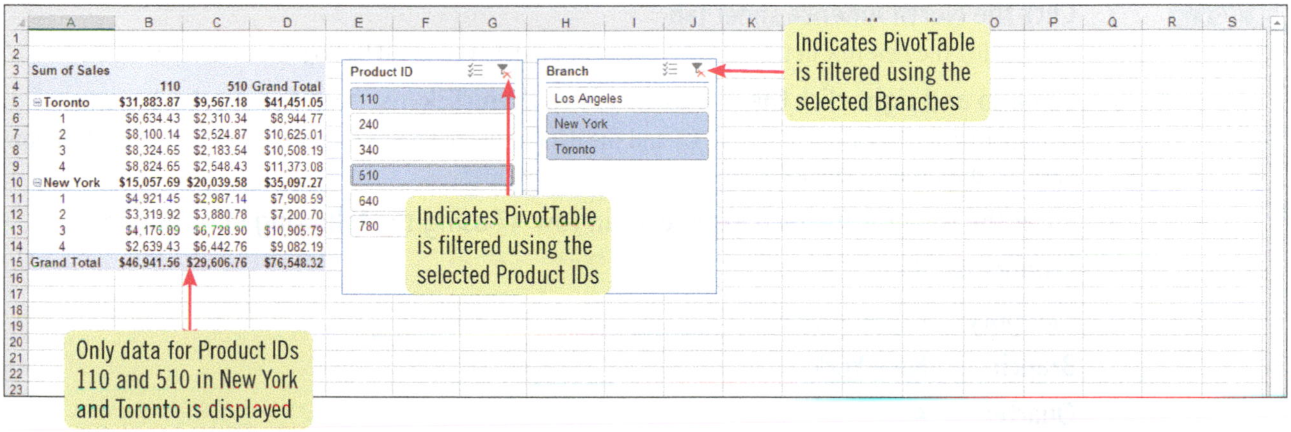

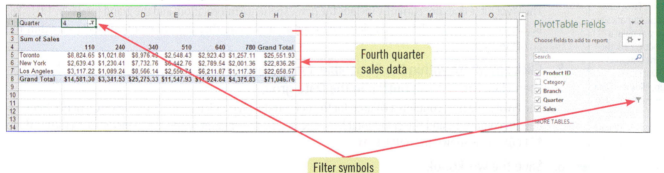

Indicates PivotTable is filtered using the selected Branches

Indicates PivotTable is filtered using the selected Product IDs

Only data for Product IDs 110 and 510 in New York and Toronto is displayed

FIGURE 12-10: PivotTable filtered by fourth quarter

Fourth quarter sales data

Filter symbols

Filtering PivotTables using multiple values

You can select multiple values when filtering a PivotTable report using a report filter. After clicking a field's report filter list arrow in the top section of the PivotTable Fields List pane or in cell B1 on the PivotTable itself, click the Select Multiple Items check box at the bottom of the filter selections. This lets you select multiple values for the filter. For example, selecting 1 and 2 as the report filter in a PivotTable with quarters would display all of the data for the first two quarters. You can also select multiple values for the row and column labels by clicking the PivotTable Tools Analyze tab, clicking the Field Headers button in the Show group, clicking the Row Labels list arrow or the Column Labels list arrow in cells A4 and B3 on the PivotTable, and selecting the data items that you want to display.

Analyzing Data with PivotTables

Update a PivotTable Report

Learning Outcomes
- Add data to a PivotTable data source
- Refresh a PivotTable

The data in a PivotTable report looks like typical worksheet data. However, because the PivotTable data is linked to a **data source** (the data you used to create the PivotTable), the results it displays are read-only. That means you cannot move or modify a part of a PivotTable by inserting or deleting rows, editing results, or moving cells. To change PivotTable data, you must edit the items directly in the data source, then update, or **refresh**, the PivotTable to reflect the changes. **CASE** *Dawn just learned that sales information for a custom group experience sold in New York during the fourth quarter was never entered into the Sales worksheet. Dawn asks you to add information about this experience to the data source and PivotTable. You start by inserting a row for the new information in the North America worksheet.*

STEPS

> **QUICK TIP**
> If you want to change the PivotTable's source data range, click the PivotTable Tools Analyze tab, then click the Change Data Source button in the Data group.

1. **Click the North America sheet tab**

   By inserting the new row in the correct position by branch, you avoid having to sort the data again.

2. **Scroll to and right-click the row 47 heading, then click Insert on the shortcut menu**

   A blank row appears as the new row 47, and the data in the old row 47, moves down to row 48. You now have room for the experience data.

3. **Enter the data for the new experience in row 47 using the following information**

Product ID	450
Category	Experience
Branch	New York
Quarter	4
Sales	3015.05

   The PivotTable does not yet reflect the additional data.

> **QUICK TIP**
> If you want Excel to refresh a PivotTable report automatically when you open a workbook, click the Options button in the PivotTable group, click the Data tab in the PivotTable Options dialog box, click the Refresh data when opening the file check box, then click OK.

4. **Click the PivotTable sheet tab, then verify that the Quarter 4 data appears**

   The PivotTable does not currently include the new experience information, and the grand total is $71,046.76. Before you refresh the PivotTable data, you need to make sure that the cell pointer is located within the PivotTable range.

5. **Click anywhere within the PivotTable if necessary, click the PivotTable Tools Analyze tab, then click the Refresh button in the Data group**

   The PivotTable now contains a column for the new product ID, which includes the new experience information, in column H, and the grand total has increased by the amount of the experience's sales ($3015.05) to $74,061.81, as shown in **FIGURE 12-11**.

6. **Save the workbook**

Grouping PivotTable data

You can group PivotTable data to analyze specific values in a field as a unit. For example, you may want to group sales data for quarters one and two to analyze sales for the first half of the year. To group PivotTable data, first select the rows and columns that you want to group, click the PivotTable Tools Analyze tab, then click the Group Selection button in the Group group. To summarize grouped data, click the Field Settings button in the Active Field group, click the Custom option button in the Field Settings dialog box, select the function that you want to use to summarize the data, then click OK. To collapse the group and show the function results, click the Collapse Outline button next to the group name. You can click the Expand Outline button next to the group name to display the rows or columns in the group. To ungroup data, select the Group name in the PivotTable, then click the Ungroup button in the Group group. If you add data with dates or times to a Pivot Table Time groups are automatically created that can be expanded and collapsed.

FIGURE 12-11: Updated PivotTable report

	A	B	C	D	E	F	G		H	I	J
1	Quarter	4	𝕋								
2											
3	**Sum of Sales**							New data is added			
4		110	240	340	510	640	780		450	**Grand Total**	
5	New York	$2,639.43	$1,230.41	$7,732.76	$6,442.76	$2,789.54	$2,001.36		$3,015.05	$25,851.31	
6	Toronto	$8,824.65	$1,021.88	$8,976.43	$2,548.43	$2,923.43	$1,257.11			$25,551.93	
7	Los Angeles	$3,117.22	$1,089.24	$8,566.14	$2,556.74	$6,211.87	$1,117.36			$22,658.57	
8	**Grand Total**	$14,581.30	$3,341.53	$25,275.33	$11,547.93	$11,924.84	$4,375.83		$3,015.05	$74,061.81	
9											
10											
11											

Totals are updated to include the new data

Adding a calculated field to a PivotTable

You can use formulas to analyze PivotTable data in a field by adding a calculated field. A calculated field appears in the Field List and can be manipulated like other PivotTable fields. To add a calculated field, click any cell in the PivotTable, click the PivotTable Tools Analyze tab, click the Fields, Items, & Sets button in the Calculations group, then click Calculated Field. The Insert Calculated Field dialog box opens. Enter the field name in the Name text box, click in the Formula text box, click a field name in the

Field list that you want to use in the formula, and click Insert Field. Use standard arithmetic operators to enter the formula you want to use. For example, **FIGURE 12-12** shows a formula to increase the Sales data by 20 percent. After entering the formula in the Insert Calculated Field dialog box, click Add, then click OK. The new field with the formula results appears in the PivotTable, and the field is added to the PivotTable Fields List pane, as shown in **FIGURE 12-13**.

FIGURE 12-12: Insert Calculated Field dialog box

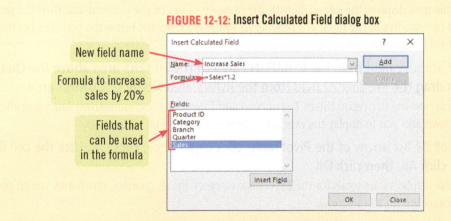

New field name
Formula to increase sales by 20%
Fields that can be used in the formula

FIGURE 12-13: PivotTable with calculated field

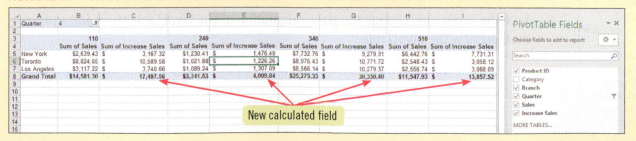

New calculated field

Explore PivotTable Data Relationships

Learning
Outcomes
• Change a
PivotTable's orga-
nization
• Add fields to a
PivotTable

What makes a PivotTable such a powerful analysis tool is the ability to change the way data is organized in the report. By moving fields to different positions in the report, you can explore relationships and trends that you might not see in the original report structure. **CASE** *Dawn asks you to include category information in the sales report. She is also interested in viewing the PivotTable in different arrangements to find the best organization of data for her presentation.*

STEPS

1. **Make sure that the PivotTable sheet is active, that the active cell is located anywhere inside the PivotTable, and that the PivotTable Fields List pane is visible**

2. **Click the Category check box in the Field List**
   The category data is added to the ROWS area below the corresponding branch data. As you learned earlier, you can move fields within an area of a PivotTable by dragging and dropping them to the desired location.

3. **In ROWS area of the PivotTable Fields List pane, drag the Category field up and drop it above the Branch field**
   As you drag, a green bar shows where the field will be inserted. The Category field is now the outer or upper field, and the Branch field is the inner or lower field. The PivotTable is restructured to display the sales data first by category and then by branch. The subtotals now reflect the sum of the categories, as shown in **FIGURE 12-14**. You can also move fields to different areas in the PivotTable.

4. **Drag the Category field from the ROWS area to anywhere in the COLUMNS area, then drag the Product ID field from the COLUMNS area to the ROWS area below the Branch field**
   The PivotTable now displays the sales data with the category values in the columns and then the product IDs grouped by branches in the rows. The product ID values are indented below the branches because the Product ID field is the inner row label.

5. **Drag the Category field from the COLUMNS area to the FILTERS area above the Quarter field, then drag the Product ID field from the ROWS area to the COLUMNS area**
   The PivotTable now has two report filters. The upper report filter, Category, summarizes data using all of the categories. Dawn asks you to display the experience sales information for all quarters.

6. **Click the cell B1 list arrow of the PivotTable, click Experience, click OK, click the cell B2 list arrow, click All, then click OK**
   The PivotTable displays sales totals for the Experience category for all quarters. Dawn asks you to provide the sales information for all categories.

7. **Click the cell B1 list arrow, click All, then click OK**
   The completed PivotTable appears as shown in **FIGURE 12-15**.

8. **Save the workbook, change the page orientation of the PivotTable sheet to Landscape, then preview the PivotTable**

FIGURE 12-14: PivotTable structured by branches within categories

	A	B	C	D	E	F	G	H	I
1	Quarter	4							
3	Sum of Sales								
4		110	240	340	510	640	780	450	Grand Total
5	Experience			$25,275.33	$11,547.93			$3,015.05	$39,838.31
6	New York			$7,732.76	$6,442.76			$3,015.05	$17,190.57
7	Toronto			$8,976.43	$2,548.43				$11,524.86
8	Los Angeles			$8,566.14	$2,556.74				$11,122.88
9	Insurance	$14,581.30				$11,924.84			$26,506.14
10	Toronto	$8,824.65				$2,923.43			$11,748.08
11	Los Angeles	$3,117.22				$6,211.87			$9,329.09
12	New York	$2,639.43				$2,789.54			$5,428.97
13	Transportation		$3,341.53				$4,375.83		$7,717.36
14	New York		$1,230.41				$2,001.36		$3,231.77
15	Toronto		$1,021.88				$1,257.11		$2,278.99
16	Los Angeles		$1,089.24				$1,117.36		$2,206.60
17	Grand Total	$14,581.30	$3,341.53	$25,275.33	$11,547.93	$11,924.84	$4,375.83	$3,015.05	$74,061.81

Category is outer field

Branch is inner field, values are indented

FIGURE 12-15: Completed PivotTable report

	A	B	C	D	E	F	G	H	I
1	Category	(All)							
2	Quarter	(All)							
4	Sum of Sales								
5		110	240	340	510	640	780	450	Grand Total
6	Toronto	$31,883.87	$3,237.62	$32,350.46	$9,567.18	$10,106.56	$4,008.70		$91,154.39
7	New York	$15,057.69	$6,534.81	$29,818.65	$20,039.58	$8,856.97	$5,056.28	$3,015.05	$88,379.03
8	Los Angeles	$9,014.91	$5,001.65	$32,094.00	$7,446.04	$20,034.51	$6,512.19		$80,103.30
9	Grand Total	$55,956.47	$14,774.08	$94,263.11	$37,052.80	$38,998.04	$15,577.17	$3,015.05	$259,636.72

Creating relationships with Power Pivot

Power Pivot is a data analysis tool included in most versions of Excel 2016. To make sure the Data Analysis add-ins are enabled, click the File tab, click Options, click Advanced, scroll to the bottom of the Advanced options, then click if necessary to add a checkmark to the Enable Data Analysis add-ins: Power Pivot, Power View, and Power Map checkbox. Power Pivot can be used to import data into Excel. For example, to use Power Pivot to import Access table data, click the Power Pivot tab on the Ribbon, click the Manage button in the Data Model group, click the Home tab in the Power Pivot for Excel window, click the Get External Data button, click From Database, click From Access, click Browse in the Table Import Wizard, navigate to the Access file, click Next, click Next again, select the table(s) for import, click Finish, then click Close after the import is completed. The imported table names are displayed at the bottom of the Power Pivot window along with the table data. You can expand the types of information you have access to by creating relationships between fields with similar data types in different data sources. This allows you to pull together columns from multiple tables in different sources into your PivotTable. To create a relationship in Power Pivot, click the Power Pivot tab if necessary, click the Manage button in the Data Model group, click the Design tab, in the Power Pivot for Excel window, click the

Create Relationship in the Relationships group, in the Create Relationship dialog box, select the Tables and Columns between which you want to create relationships, then click Create. **FIGURE 12-16** shows a relationship defined between fields in the Schedule and Employee tables of an Access database. A PivotTable can be created to display information about an employee from the Employee table and the number of hours worked from the Schedule table. Note that some versions of Excel, including Office 365 Home and Office 365 Personal, do not include Power Pivot. For more information, visit the Microsoft website.

FIGURE 12-16: Relationship between the Schedule and Employee tables

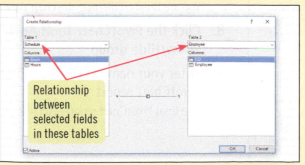

Relationship between selected fields in these tables

Create a PivotChart Report

A **PivotChart report** is a chart that you create from data or from a PivotTable report. **TABLE 12-1** describes how the elements in a PivotTable report correspond to the elements in a PivotChart report. When you create a PivotChart directly from data, Excel automatically creates a corresponding PivotTable report. If you change a PivotChart report by filtering or sorting the charted elements, Excel updates the corresponding PivotTable report to show the new data values. You can move the fields of a PivotChart using the PivotTable Fields List window; the new layout will be reflected in the PivotTable. **CASE** ▶ *Dawn wants you to chart the fourth quarter experience sales and the yearly experience sales average for her presentation. You create the PivotChart report from the PivotTable data.*

STEPS

1. **Click the cell B1 list arrow, click Experience, click OK, click the Quarter list arrow, click 4, then click OK**

   The fourth quarter experience sales information appears in the PivotTable. You want to create the PivotChart from the PivotTable information you have displayed.

2. **Click any cell in the PivotTable, click the PivotTable Tools Analyze tab, then click the PivotChart button in the Tools group**

   The Insert Chart dialog box opens and shows a gallery of chart types.

3. **Click the Clustered Column chart if necessary, then click OK**

   The PivotChart appears on the worksheet as shown in **FIGURE 12-17**. The chart has Field buttons that let you filter and sort a PivotChart in the same way you do a PivotTable. It will be easier to view the PivotChart if it is on its own sheet.

4. **Click the PivotChart Tools Design tab, click the Move Chart button in the Location group, click the New sheet option button, type PivotChart in the text box, then click OK**

   The chart represents the fourth quarter experience sales. Dawn asks you to change the chart to show the average sales for all quarters.

5. **Click the Quarter field button at the top of the PivotChart, click All, then click OK**

   The chart now represents the sum of experience sales for the year as shown in **FIGURE 12-18**. You can change a PivotChart's summary function to display averages instead of totals.

6. **Click the Sum of Sales list arrow in the VALUES area of the PivotTable Fields List pane, click Value Field Settings, click Average In the Value Field Settings dialog box, then click OK**

   The PivotChart report recalculates to display averages. The chart would be easier to understand if it had a title.

7. **Click the PivotChart Tools Design tab, click the Add Chart Element button in the Chart Layouts group, point to Chart Title, click Above Chart, type Average Experience Sales, press [Enter], then drag the chart title border to center the title over the columns**

   You are finished filtering the chart data and decide to remove the field buttons.

8. **Click the PivotChart Tools Analyze tab, then click the Field Buttons button in the Show/Hide group**

9. **Enter your name in the PivotChart sheet footer, save the workbook, then preview the PivotChart report**

   The final PivotChart report displaying the average experience sales for the year is shown in **FIGURE 12-19**.

FIGURE 12-17: PivotChart with fourth quarter experience sales

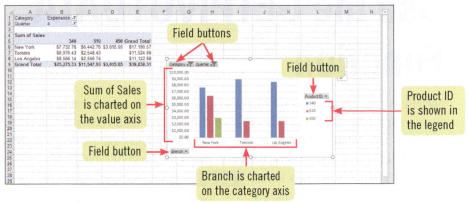

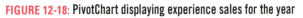

FIGURE 12-18: PivotChart displaying experience sales for the year

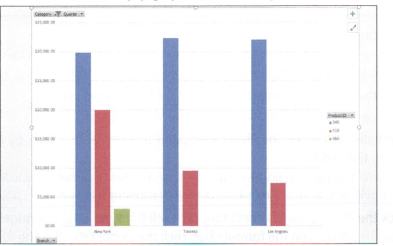

FIGURE 12-19: Completed PivotChart report

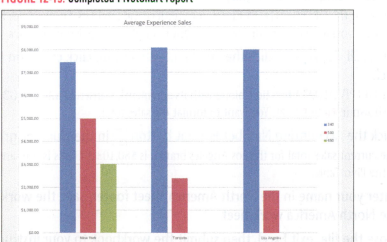

TABLE 12-1: PivotTable and PivotChart elements

PivotTable items	PivotChart items
Row labels	Axis fields
Column labels	Legend fields
Report filters	Report filters

Use the GETPIVOTDATA Function

Learning Outcomes
• Analyze the GETPIVOTDATA function
• Retrieve information from a PivotTable using the GETPIVOTDATA function

Because you can rearrange a PivotTable so easily, you can't use an ordinary cell reference when you want to reference a PivotTable cell in another worksheet. The reason is that if you change the way data is displayed in a PivotTable, the data moves, making an ordinary cell reference incorrect. Instead, to retrieve summary data from a PivotTable, you need to use the Excel GETPIVOTDATA function. See **FIGURE 12-20** for the GETPIVOTDATA function format. **CASE** *Dawn wants to include the yearly sales total for the Los Angeles branch in the North America sheet. She asks you to retrieve this information from the PivotTable and place it in the North America sheet. You use the GETPIVOTDATA function to retrieve this information.*

STEPS

1. **Click the PivotTable sheet tab**

   The sales figures in the PivotTable are average values for experiences. You decide to show sales information for all categories and change the summary information back to Sum.

2. **Click the Category filter arrow in cell B1, click All, then click OK**

   The PivotChart report displays sales information for all categories.

3. **Right-click cell A4 on the PivotTable, point to Summarize Values By on the shortcut menu, then click Sum**

   The PivotChart report recalculates to display sales totals. Next, you want to include the total for sales for the Los Angeles branch in the North America sheet by retrieving it from the PivotTable.

4. **Click the North America sheet tab, click cell G1, type Total Los Angeles Sales, click the Enter button** ✓ **on the formula bar, click the Home tab, click the Align Right button** ≡ **in the Alignment group, click the Bold button** B **in the Font group, then adjust the width of column G to display the new label**

   You want the GETPIVOTDATA function to retrieve the total Los Angeles sales from the PivotTable. Cell I8 on the PivotTable contains the data you want to display on the North America sheet.

5. **Click cell G2, type =, click the PivotTable sheet tab, click cell I8 on the PivotTable, then click** ✓

   The GETPIVOTDATA function, along with its arguments, is inserted into cell G2 of the North America sheet as shown in **FIGURE 12-21**. You want to format the sales total.

6. **Click the Accounting Number Format button** $ **in the Number group**

   The current sales total for the Los Angeles branch is $80,103.30. This is the same value displayed in cell I8 of the PivotTable.

7. **Enter your name in the North America sheet footer, save the workbook, then preview the North America worksheet**

8. **Close the file, exit Excel, then submit the workbook to your instructor**

   The North America worksheet is shown in **FIGURE 12-22**.

FIGURE 12-20: Format of GETPIVOTDATA function

=GETPIVOTDATA("Sales",PivotTable!$A$4,"Branch","Los Angeles")

Field where data is extracted from

PivotTable name and cell in the report that contains the data you want to retrieve

Field and value pair that describe the data you want to retrieve

FIGURE 12-21: GETPIVOTDATA function in the North America sheet

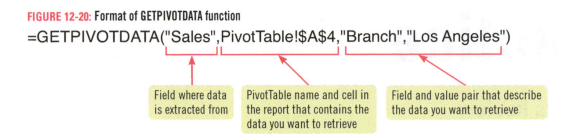

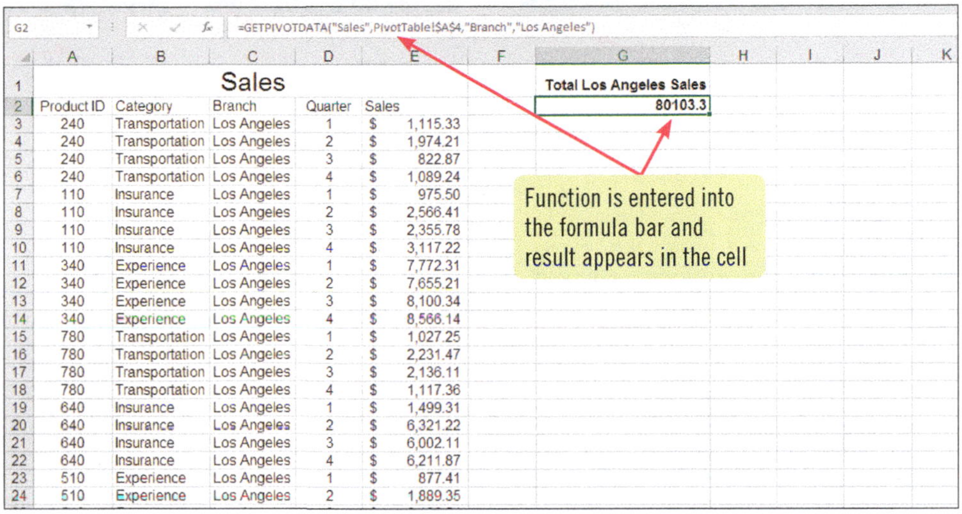

Function is entered into the formula bar and result appears in the cell

FIGURE 12-22: Completed North America worksheet showing total Los Angeles sales

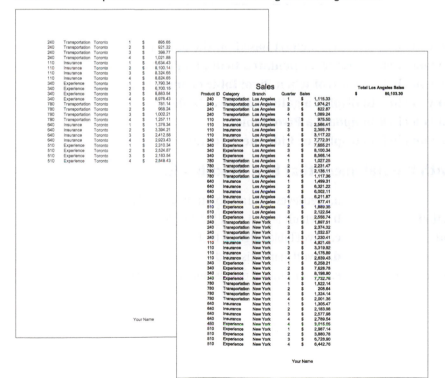

Practice

Concepts Review

FIGURE 12-23

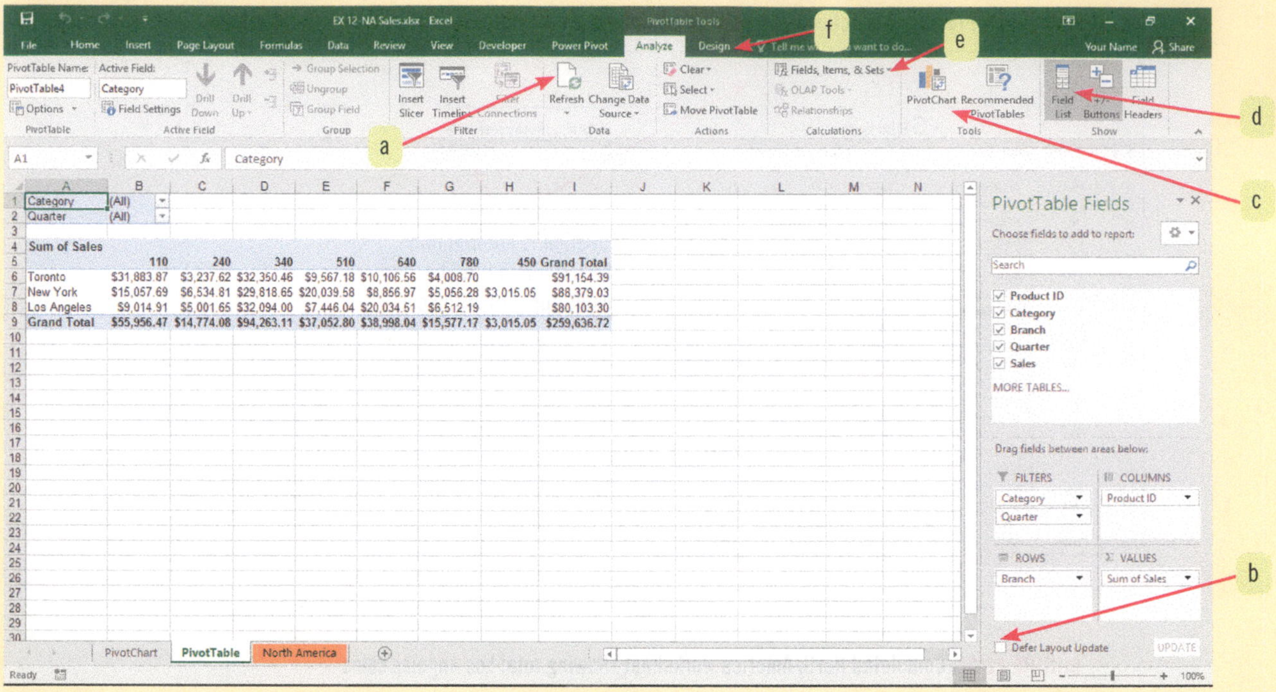

1. **Which element do you click to create a chart based on the data in a PivotTable?**
2. **Which element do you click to create a calculated field in a PivotTable?**
3. **Which element do you click to control when PivotTable changes will occur?**
4. **Which element do you click to display a gallery of PivotTable Styles?**
5. **Which element do you click to update a PivotTable?**
6. **Which element do you click to display or hide the PivotTable Fields List pane?**

Match each term with the statement that best describes it.

7. **Slicer**
8. **PivotTable Row Label**
9. **Summary function**
10. **Compact form**
11. **GETPIVOTDATA function**

a. Retrieves information from a PivotTable
b. Default layout for a PivotTable
c. PivotTable filtering tool
d. PivotChart axis field
e. Determines if data is summed or averaged

Select the best answer from the list of choices.

12. **Which PivotTable report area allows you to display only certain data using a list arrow?**
    - **a.** Values
    - **b.** Column Labels
    - **c.** Report Filter
    - **d.** Row Labels

13. **When a numeric field is added to a PivotTable, it is placed in the _____ area.**
    - **a.** VALUES
    - **b.** ROWS
    - **c.** COLUMNS
    - **d.** FILTERS

14. **When a nonnumeric field is added to a PivotTable, it is placed in the _____ area.**
    - **a.** VALUES
    - **b.** Report Filter
    - **c.** ROWS
    - **d.** COLUMNS

15. **To make changes to PivotTable data, you must:**
    - **a.** Drag a column header to the column area.
    - **b.** Create a page field.
    - **c.** Edit cells in the PivotTable, then refresh the source list.
    - **d.** Edit cells in the source list, then refresh the PivotTable.

Skills Review

1. **Plan and design a PivotTable report.**
   - **a.** Start Excel, open EX 12-2.xlsx from the location where you store your Data Files, then save it as **EX 12-US Sales**.
   - **b.** Review the fields and data values in the worksheet.
   - **c.** Verify that the worksheet data contains repeated values in one or more fields.
   - **d.** Verify that there are not any blank rows or columns in the range A1:E25.
   - **e.** Verify that the worksheet data contains a field that can be summed in a PivotTable.

2. **Create a PivotTable report.**
   - **a.** Create a blank PivotTable report on a new worksheet using the January Sales worksheet data in the range A1:E25.
   - **b.** Add the UPC field in the PivotTable Fields List pane to the COLUMNS area.
   - **c.** Add the Sales field in the PivotTable Fields List pane to the VALUES area.
   - **d.** Add the Store field in the PivotTable Fields List pane to the ROWS area.
   - **e.** Add the Sales Rep field in the PivotTable Fields List pane to the ROWS area below the Store field.

3. **Change a PivotTable's summary function and design.**
   - **a.** Change the PivotTable summary function to Average.
   - **b.** Rename the new sheet **Jan Sales PT**.
   - **c.** Change the PivotTable Style to Pivot Style Light 18. Format the sales values in the PivotTable as Currency with a $ symbol and two decimal places.
   - **d.** Enter your name in the center section of the PivotTable report footer, then save the workbook.
   - **e.** Change the Summary function back to Sum. Remove the headers "Row Labels" and "Column Labels."

4. **Filter and sort PivotTable data.**
   - **a.** Sort the stores in ascending order by total sales.
   - **b.** Use slicers to filter the PivotTable to display sales for the UPC 101548792461 in the Atlanta and Miami stores.
   - **c.** Clear the filters and delete the slicers.
   - **d.** Add the Region field to the FILTERS area in the PivotTable Fields List pane. Use the FILTERS list arrow to display sales for only the East region. Display sales for all regions.
   - **e.** Save the workbook.

5. **Update a PivotTable report.**
   - **a.** With the Jan Sales PT sheet active, note the Seattle total for UPC 101548792461.
   - **b.** Activate the January Sales sheet, and change L. Bartlet's sales of UPC 101548792461 in cell D8 to **$2,000**.
   - **c.** Refresh the PivotTable so it reflects the new sales figure.
   - **d.** Verify the Seattle total for UPC 101548792461 increased to $2,699. Save the workbook.

Skills Review (continued)

6. Explore PivotTable Data Relationships.

   a. In the PivotTable Fields List pane, drag the UPC field from the COLUMNS area to the ROWS area below the Sales Rep field. Drag the Sales Rep field from the ROWS area to the COLUMNS area.

   b. Drag the Store field from the ROWS area to the FILTERS area below the Region field. Drag the UPC field back to the COLUMNS area.

   c. Drag the Store field back to the ROWS area.

   d. Remove the Sales Rep field from the PivotTable.

   e. Compare your completed PivotTable to **FIGURE 12-24**, save the workbook.

FIGURE 12-24

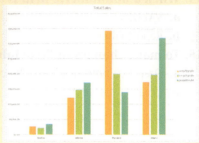

7. Create a PivotChart report.

   a. Use the existing PivotTable data to create a Clustered Column PivotChart report.

   b. Move the PivotChart to a new worksheet, and name the sheet **PivotChart**.

   c. Add the title **Total Sales** above the chart.

   d. Filter the chart to display only sales data for the east region. Display the sales data for all regions. Hide all of the Field Buttons.

   e. Add your name to the center section of the PivotChart sheet footer. Compare your PivotChart with **FIGURE 12-25**, and save the workbook.

FIGURE 12-25

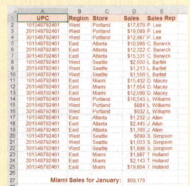

8. Use the GETPIVOTDATA function.

   a. In cell D27 of the January Sales sheet type =, click the Jan Sales PT sheet, click the cell that contains the grand total for Miami, then press [Enter].

   b. Review the GETPIVOTDATA function that was entered in cell D27.

   c. Enter your name in the January Sales sheet footer, compare your January Sales sheet to **FIGURE 12-26**, save the workbook, then preview the January Sales worksheet.

   d. Close the workbook and exit Excel. Submit the workbook to your instructor.

FIGURE 12-26

	A	B	C	D	E
1	UPC	Region	Store	Sales	Sales Rep
2	101548792461	West	Portland	$17,876	P. Lee
3	201548792461	West	Portland	$19,088	P. Lee
4	301548792461	West	Portland	$12,987	P. Lee
5	101548792461	East	Atlanta	$10,998	C. Berwick
6	201548792461	East	Atlanta	$12,322	C. Berwick
7	301548792461	East	Atlanta	$15,331	C. Berwick
8	101548792461	West	Seattle	$2,000	L. Bartlet
9	201548792461	West	Seattle	$1,213	L. Bartlet
10	301548792461	West	Seattle	$1,556	L. Bartlet
11	101548792461	East	Miami	$15,432	D. Macey
12	201548792461	East	Miami	$17,654	D. Macey
13	301548792461	East	Miami	$12,098	D. Macey
14	101548792461	West	Portland	$16,543	L. Williams
15	201548792461	West	Portland	$884	L. Williams
16	301548792461	West	Portland	$932	L. Williams
17	101548792461	East	Atlanta	$1,232	J. Allen
18	201548792461	East	Atlanta	$2,445	J. Allen
19	301548792461	East	Atlanta	$1,766	J. Allen
20	101548792461	West	Seattle	$699	S. Simpson
21	201548792461	West	Seattle	$1,003	S. Simpson
22	301548792461	West	Seattle	$1,898	S. Simpson
23	101548792461	East	Miami	$1,987	T. Holland
24	201548792461	East	Miami	$2,143	T. Holland
25	301548792461	East	Miami	$19,864	T. Holland
26					
27			Miami Sales for January:	$69,178	
28					

Independent Challenge 1

You are the accountant for the Service Department of an electrical services company. The Service Department employs three technicians that service business and residential accounts. Until recently, the owner had been tracking the technicians' hours manually in a log. You have created an Excel worksheet to track the following basic information: service date, technician name, job #, job category, hours, and billing information. The owner has asked you to analyze the data to provide information about the number of hours being spent on the various job categories. He also wants to find out how much of the technicians' work is on residential or business sites. You will create a PivotTable that sums the hours by category and technician. Once the table is completed, you will create a column chart representing the billing information.

   a. Start Excel, open EX 12-3.xlsx from the location where you store your Data Files, then save it as **EX 12-Service**.

   b. Create a PivotTable on a separate worksheet that sums hours by technician and category. Use **FIGURE 12-27** as a guide.

   c. Name the new sheet **PivotTable**, and apply the Pivot Style Light 20.

   d. Add slicers to filter the PivotTable using the category and technician data. Display only service data for Ryan's category Level 1 jobs. Remove the filters, and remove the slicers.

FIGURE 12-27

PivotTable Fields

Choose fields to add to report:

Search

☐ Date
☑ Technician
☐ Job #
☑ Category
☑ Hours
☐ Billing

MORE TABLES...

Drag fields between areas below:

▼ FILTERS	▥ COLUMNS
	Category ▼

▤ ROWS	Σ VALUES
Technician ▼	Sum of Hours ▼

☐ Defer Layout Update   UPDATE

Independent Challenge 1 (continued)

e. Add the Billing field to the FILTERS area of the PivotTable. Display only the PivotTable data for residential jobs.

f. Remove the headers of "Column Labels" and "Row Labels" from the PivotTable.

g. Create a clustered column PivotChart that shows the residential hours. Move the PivotChart to a new sheet named **PivotChart**.

h. Add the title **Residential Hours** above the chart.

i. Change the PivotChart filter to display hours for business sites. Edit the chart title to read **Business Hours**.

j. Hide the field buttons on the chart.

k. Add your name to the center section of the PivotTable and PivotChart footers, then save the workbook. Preview the PivotTable and the PivotChart. Close the workbook and exit Excel. Submit the workbook to your instructor.

Independent Challenge 2

You are the director of marketing for a fitness equipment company. The company sells new and used equipment as well as multi-year leases at stores as well as online. You also take orders by phone from your catalog customers. You have been using Excel to maintain a sales summary for the second quarter sales of the different categories of products sold by the company. You want to create a PivotTable to analyze and graph the sales in each product category by month and type of order.

a. Start Excel, open EX 12-4.xlsx from the location where you store your Data Files, then save it as **EX 12-Fitness Equipment**.

b. Create a PivotTable on a new worksheet named **PivotTable** that sums the sales amount for each category across the rows and each type of sale down the columns. Add the month field as an inner row label. Use FIGURE 12-28 as a guide.

c. Move the month field to the FILTERS area. Display the sum of sales data for the month of April.

d. Turn off the grand totals for the columns. (*Hint*: Use the Grand Totals button in the Layout group on the PivotTable Tools Design tab and choose On for Rows Only.)

e. Change the summary function in the PivotTable to Average.

f. Format the sales values using the Currency format with two decimal places and the $ symbol. Widen the columns as necessary to display the sales data.

g. On the Sales worksheet, change the April online used sales in cell D3 to $32,000. Update the PivotTable to reflect this increase in sales.

FIGURE 12-28

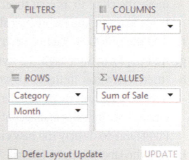

h. Sort the average sales of categories from smallest to largest using the grand total of sales.

i. Create a stacked column PivotChart report for the average April sales data for all three types of sales.

j. Change the PivotChart to display the June sales data.

k. Move the PivotChart to a new sheet, and name the chart sheet **PivotChart**.

l. Add the title **Average June Sales** above your chart.

m. On the PivotTable, move the Month field from the FILTERS area to the ROWS area of the PivotTable below the Category field.

n. Add a slicer to filter the PivotTable by month. Use the slicer to display the average sales in May and June.

o. Check the PivotChart to be sure that the filtered data is displayed.

p. Change the chart title to **Average Sales May and June** to describe the charted sales.

q. Add your name to the center section of the PivotTable and PivotChart worksheet footers, save the workbook, then preview the PivotTable and the PivotChart. Close the workbook and exit Excel. Submit the workbook to your instructor.

Independent Challenge 3

You are the North American sales manager for a medical equipment company with sales offices in the United States and Canada. You use Excel to keep track of the staff in the U.S. and Canadian offices. Management asks you to provide a summary table showing information on your sales staff, including their locations, status, and titles. You will create a PivotTable and PivotChart summarizing this information.

a. Start Excel, open EX 12-5.xlsx from the location where you store your Data Files, then save it as **EX 12-Sales Employees**.

b. Create a PivotTable on a new worksheet that shows the number of employees in each city, with the names of the cities listed across the columns, the titles listed down the rows, and the status indented below the titles. (*Hint*: Remember that the default summary function for cells containing text is Count.) Use **FIGURE 12-29** as a guide. Rename the new sheet **PivotTable**.

FIGURE 12-29

3	Count of Last Name	Column Labels								
4	Row Labels	Boston	Los Angeles	Miami	Montreal	San Francisco	St. Louis	Toronto	Vancouver	Grand Total
5	⊟ Sales Manager	1	1	2	3	3	2	3	1	16
6	Junior	1				1	1	1		4
7	Senior		1	2	3	2	1	2	1	12
8	⊟ Sales Representative	4	5	7	6	7	2	3	3	37
9	Junior	1	1	2	2	2	1	1	1	11
10	Senior	3	4	5	4	5	1	2	2	26
11	Grand Total	5	6	9	9	10	4	6	4	53
12										
13										

c. Change the structure of the PivotTable to display the data as shown in **FIGURE 12-30**.

d. Add a report filter using the Region field. Display only the U.S. employees.

e. Create a clustered column PivotChart from the PivotTable and move the chart to its own sheet named PivotChart. Rearrange the fields to create the PivotChart shown in **FIGURE 12-31**.

f. Add the title **U.S. Sales Staff** above the chart.

g. Add the Pivot Style Light 12 style to the PivotTable.

h. Insert a new row in the Employees worksheet above row 7. In the new row, add information reflecting the recent hiring of Cathy Olsen, a senior sales manager at the Boston office. Update the PivotTable to display the new employee information.

i. Add the label **Total Miami Staff** in cell G1 of the Employees sheet. Widen column G to fit the label.

j. Enter a function in cell H1 that retrieves the total number of employees located in Miami from the PivotTable. Change the page orientation of the Employees sheet to landscape.

k. Use a slicer to filter the PivotTable to display only the data for the cities of Boston, Miami, and Los Angeles.

l. Add another slicer for the Status field to display only the senior staff members.

m. Verify that the number of Miami staff in cell H1 of the Employees sheet is now 7.

FIGURE 12-30

3	Count of Last Name	Column Labels		
4	Row Labels	Junior	Senior	Grand Total
5	⊟ Sales Manager		4	12	16
6	Boston	1		1
7	Los Angeles		1	1
8	Miami		2	2
9	Montreal		3	3
10	San Francisco	1	2	3
11	St. Louis	1	1	2
12	Toronto	1	2	3
13	Vancouver		1	1
14	⊟ Sales Representative	11	26	37
15	Boston	1	3	4
16	Los Angeles	1	4	5
17	Miami	2	5	7
18	Montreal	2	4	6
19	San Francisco	2	5	7
20	St. Louis	1	1	2
21	Toronto	1	2	3
22	Vancouver	1	2	3
23	Grand Total	15	38	53
24				
25				

FIGURE 12-31

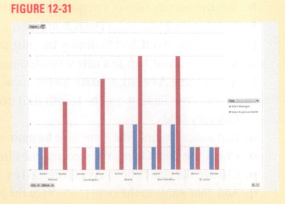

Independent Challenge 3 (continued)

n. Remove the slicers, but do not remove the filters.

o. Add your name to the center section of all three worksheet footers, save the workbook, then preview the PivotTable, the first page of the Employees worksheet, and the PivotChart.

p. Close the workbook and exit Excel. Submit the workbook to your instructor.

Independent Challenge 4: Explore

You are the Regional sales manager for a Massachusetts plumbing supplies company with offices in Boston, Worcester, and Springfield. You use Excel to keep track of the revenue generated by sales contracts in these offices. The CEO asks you to provide a summary table showing information on your offices' revenue over the past two years.

a. Start Excel, open EX 12-6.xlsx, then save it as **EX 12-Plumbing Revenue** in the location where you save your Data Files.

b. Create a PivotTable on a separate worksheet that sums revenue by office, year, and month. Use **FIGURE 12-32** as a guide.

FIGURE 12-32

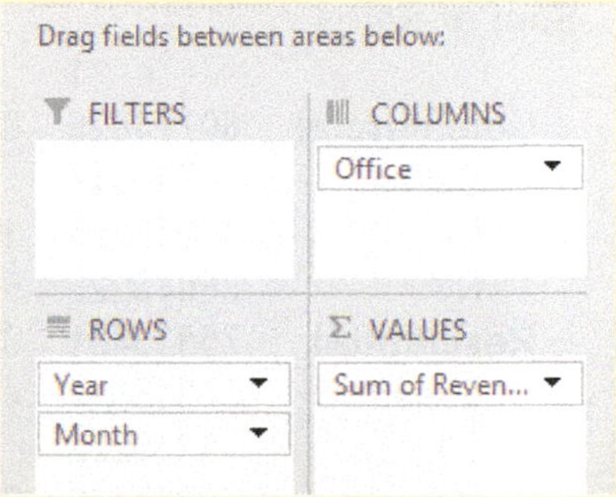

c. Name the new sheet **Summary**, and apply the Pivot Style Light 19.

d. Add slicers to filter the PivotTable using the Quarter and Office fields. Display only revenue data for Boston and Worcester for quarters 3 and 4. Remove the filters, but do not remove the slicers.

e. Format the Office slicer using the Slicer Style Light 5 in the Slicer Styles gallery on the Slicer Tools Options tab.

f. Change the Office slicer caption from Office to **Sales Office**. (*Hint*: Use the Slicer Caption text box in the Slicer group of the Slicer Tools Options tab.)

g. Change the Quarter slicer buttons to appear in two columns, with a button height of .3" and a button width of .56". (*Hint*: Use the options in the Buttons group of the Slicer Tools Options tab.)

h. Change the Quarter slicer shape to a height of 1.2" and width of 1.33". (*Hint*: Use the options in the Size group of the Slicer Tools Options tab.) Shorten the Sales Office slicer shape by dragging the lower slicer edge up to just below the bottom button.

i. Add a calculated field named **Average Sale** to the PivotTable to calculate the average sale using the formula =Revenue/Number of Contracts. Change the labels in cells C5, E5, and G5 to **Average** and format all of the Average labels as right justified.

j. Add the Quarter field to the PivotTable as a Report Filter.

k. Copy each quarter's data to a separate sheet. (*Hint*: Select the Quarter field in cell A1, click the Options list arrow in the PivotTable group of the PivotTable Tools Analyze tab, then select Show Report Filter Pages.) View the sheet for each quarter.

l. Remove the field headers, Group all of the worksheets, add your name to the center section of the footer for the worksheets, save the workbook, then preview the worksheets.

m. Close the workbook and exit Excel. Submit the workbook to your instructor.

Visual Workshop

Open EX 12-7.xlsx from the location where you store your Data Files, then save it as **EX 12-Quarterly Sales**. Using the data in the workbook, create the PivotTable shown in **FIGURE 12-33** on a worksheet named PivotTable, then generate a PivotChart on a new sheet named PivotChart as shown in **FIGURE 12-34**. (*Hint*: The PivotTable has been formatted using the Pivot Style Light 19. Note that the PivotChart has been filtered. The filtered data will be reflected in your PivotTable, which will no longer match **FIGURE 12-33**.) Add your name to the PivotTable and the PivotChart footers, then preview the PivotTable and the PivotChart. Save the workbook, close the workbook, exit Excel, then submit the workbook to your instructor.

FIGURE 12-33

	A	B	C	D	E	F	G
1							
2							
3	Sum of Sales						
4		1	2	3	4	Grand Total	
5	⊟Commercial	80774626	81505385	123475318	33314800	319070129	
6	Dallas	4715847	9489557	81027452	3250500	98483356	
7	LA	40015554	16505384	3942221	10018800	70481959	
8	NY	36043225	55510444	38505645	20045500	150104814	
9	⊟Residential	75533481	80665842	177575141	126661103	460435567	
10	Dallas	37515814	45048442	81020776	70504845	234089877	
11	LA	8015222	6605700	18045854	41025800	73692576	
12	NY	30002445	29011700	78508511	15130458	152653114	
13	Grand Total	156308107	162171227	301050459	159975903	779505696	
14							

FIGURE 12-34

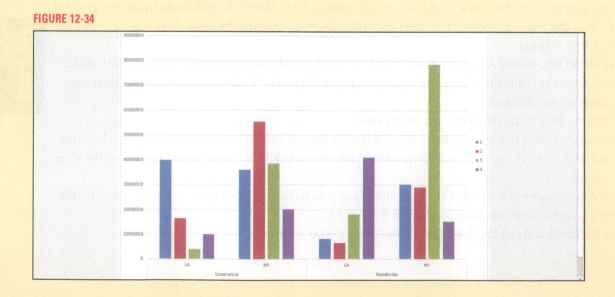

Exchanging Data with Other Programs

CASE Reason2Go's upper management has asked Mary Watson, the vice president of sales and marketing, to research the possible purchase of Service Adventures, a small company specializing in combining travel with volunteer work for corporate employees. Mary is reviewing the organization's files and developing a presentation on the feasibility of acquiring the company. She asks you to help set up the data exchange between Excel and other programs.

Module Objectives

After completing this module, you will be able to:

- Plan a data exchange
- Import a text file
- Import a database table
- Insert a graphic file in a worksheet
- Embed a workbook in a Word document
- Link a workbook to a Word document
- Link an Excel chart to a PowerPoint slide
- Import a table into Access

Files You Will Need

EX 13-1.txt	EX 13-12.xlsx
EX 13-2.accdb	EX 13-13.pptx
EX 13-3.jpg	EX 13-14.xlsx
EX 13-4.docx	EX 13-15.xlsx
EX 13-5.xlsx	EX 13-16.pptx
EX 13-6.pptx	EX 13-17.txt
EX 13-7.xlsx	EX 13-18.docx
EX 13-8.xlsx	EX 13-19.xlsx
EX 13-9.txt	EX 13-20.docx
EX 13-10.accdb	EX 13-21.xlsx
EX 13-11.jpg	EX 13-22.accdb

Plan a Data Exchange

Learning Outcomes
- Plan a data exchange between Office programs
- Develop an understanding of data exchange vocabulary

Because the tools available in Microsoft Office apps are designed to be compatible, exchanging data between Excel and other programs is easy. The first step involves planning what you want to accomplish with each data exchange. **CASE** ▶ *Mary asks you to use the following guidelines to plan data exchanges between Excel and other apps in order to complete the business analysis project.*

DETAILS

To plan an exchange of data:

- **Identify the data you want to exchange, its file type, and, if possible, the app used to create it**

  Whether the data you want to exchange is a graphics file, a database file, a worksheet, or consists only of text, it is important to identify the data's **source program** (the app used to create it) and file type. Once you identify the source program, you can determine options for exchanging the data with Excel. Mary needs to analyze a text file containing the Service Adventures sales data. Although she does not know the source program, Mary knows that the file contains unformatted text. A file that consists of text but no formatting is sometimes called an **ASCII** or **text** file. Because ASCII is a universally accepted file format, you can easily import an ASCII file into Excel. See **TABLE 13-1** for a partial list of other file formats that Excel can import.

- **Determine the app with which you want to exchange data**

  Besides knowing which program created the data you want to exchange, you must also identify which app will receive the data, called the **destination program**. This determines the procedure you use to perform the exchange. You might want to insert a graphic object into an Excel worksheet or add a spreadsheet to a Word document. Mary received a database table of Service Adventures' corporate customers created with the Access database app. After determining that Excel can import Access tables and reviewing the import procedure, you will import the database file into Excel so Mary can analyze it using Excel tools.

- **Determine the goal of your data exchange**

  Windows offers two ways to transfer data within and between apps that allow you to retain some connection with the source program. These data transfer methods use a Windows feature known as **object linking and embedding**, or **OLE**. The data to be exchanged, called an **object**, may consist of text, a worksheet, or any other type of data. You use **embedding** to insert a copy of the original object into the destination document and, if necessary, to then edit this data separately from the source document. This process is illustrated in **FIGURE 13-1**. You use **linking** when you want the information you inserted to be updated automatically if the data in the source document changes. This process is illustrated in **FIGURE 13-2**. You learn more about embedding and linking later in this module. Mary and you have determined that you need to use both object embedding and object linking for the analysis and presentation project.

- **Set up the data exchange**

  When you exchange data between two programs, it is often best to start both apps before starting the exchange. You might also want to tile the program windows on the screen either horizontally or vertically so that you can see both during the exchange. You will work with Excel, Word, Access, and PowerPoint when exchanging data for this project.

- **Execute the data exchange**

  The steps you use will vary, depending on the type of data you want to exchange. You are ready to start the data exchanges for the business analysis of Service Adventures.

FIGURE 13-1: Embedded object

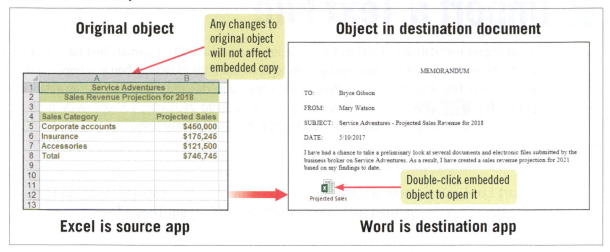

FIGURE 13-2: Linked object

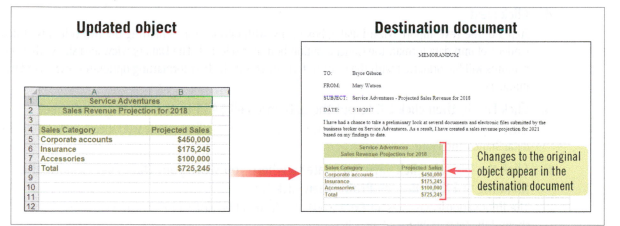

TABLE 13-1: File formats Excel can import

file format	file extension(s)	file format	file extension(s)
Access	.mdb, .accdb	All Data Sources	.odc, .udl, .dsn
Text	.txt, .prn, .csv, .dif, .sylk	OpenDocument Spreadsheet	.ods
Query	.iqy, .dqy, .oqy, .rqy	XML	.xml
Web page	.htm, .html, .mht, .mhtml	dBASE	.dbf

Import a Text File

Learning Outcomes
• Import a text file into an Excel workbook
• Format text data

You can import text data into Excel and save the imported data in Excel format. Text files use a tab or space as the **delimiter**, or column separator, to separate columns of data. When you import a text file into Excel, the Text Import Wizard automatically opens and describes how text is separated in the imported file. **CASE** ▶ *Now that you have planned the data exchange, you are ready to import a tab-delimited text file containing branch and profit data from Service Adventures.*

STEPS

1. **Start Excel, open a new blank workbook, click the Data tab, click From Text in the Get External Data group, then navigate to where you store your Data Files**
   The Import Text File dialog box shows only text files.

QUICK TIP
The data in the text file was separated, or delimited, by tabs, which is the default setting in the Text Import Wizard.

2. **Click EX 13-1.txt, then click Import**
   Step 1 of the Text Import Wizard dialog box opens, as shown in **FIGURE 13-3**. Under Original data type, the Delimited option button is selected. In the Preview of file box, line 1 indicates that the file contains two columns of data: Branch and Profit. No changes are necessary in this dialog box.

3. **Click Next**
   Step 2 of the Text Import Wizard dialog box opens. Under Delimiters, Tab is selected as the delimiter, indicating that tabs separate the columns of incoming data. The Data preview box contains a line showing where the tab delimiters divide the data into columns.

4. **Click Next**
   Step 3 of the Text Import Wizard dialog box opens, with options for formatting the two columns of data. Under Column data format, the General option button is selected. The Data preview area shows that both columns will be formatted with the General format. This is the best formatting option for text mixed with numbers.

5. **Click Finish, then click OK to put the data into cell $A$1 of the existing worksheet**
   Excel imports the text file into the blank workbook starting in cell A1 of the worksheet as two columns of data: Branch and Profit.

6. **Click the File tab, click Save, navigate to where you store your Data Files, change the filename to EX 13-Branch Profit, then click Save**
   The information is saved as an Excel workbook. It would be easier to read if it were formatted and if it showed the total profit for all branches.

7. **Click cell A8, type Total Profit, click cell B8, click the Home tab, click the AutoSum button in the Editing group, then click the Enter button ☑ on the formula bar**

8. **Rename the sheet tab Profit, center the column labels, apply bold formatting to them, format the data in column B using the Currency style with the $ symbol and no decimal places, then click cell A1**
   FIGURE 13-4 shows the completed worksheet, which analyzes the text file data you imported into Excel.

9. **Add your name to the center section of the worksheet footer, save the workbook, preview the worksheet, close the workbook, then submit the workbook to your instructor**

FIGURE 13-3: First Text Import Wizard dialog box

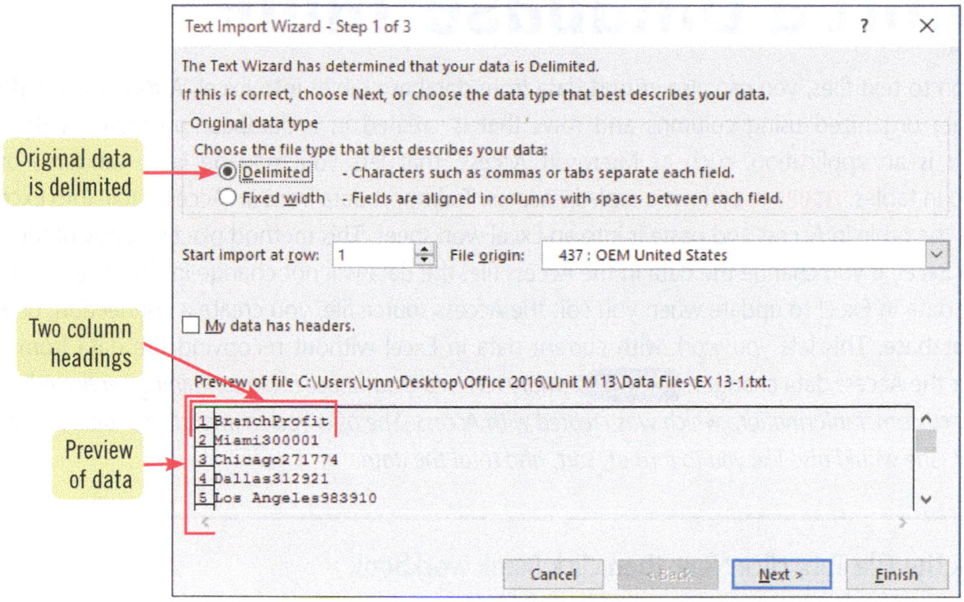

Original data is delimited

Two column headings

Preview of data

```
Text Import Wizard - Step 1 of 3                           ?    ×

The Text Wizard has determined that your data is Delimited.

If this is correct, choose Next, or choose the data type that best describes your data.
 Original data type
  Choose the file type that best describes your data:
   ⦿ Delimited   - Characters such as commas or tabs separate each field.
   ○ Fixed width  - Fields are aligned in columns with spaces between each field.

Start import at row:  1  ⬍   File origin:   437 : OEM United States  ⌄

☐ My data has headers.

Preview of file C:\Users\Lynn\Desktop\Office 2016\Unit M 13\Data Files\EX 13-1.txt.

 1 BranchProfit
 2 Miami300001
 3 Chicago271774
 4 Dallas312921
 5 Los Angeles983910

                        Cancel   < Back   Next >   Finish
```

FIGURE 13-4: Completed worksheet with imported text file

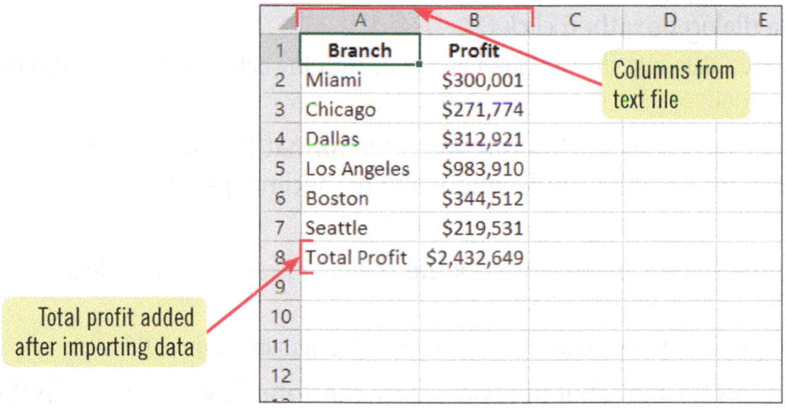

Columns from text file

Total profit added after importing data

	A	B	C	D	E
1	**Branch**	**Profit**			
2	Miami	$300,001			
3	Chicago	$271,774			
4	Dallas	$312,921			
5	Los Angeles	$983,910			
6	Boston	$344,512			
7	Seattle	$219,531			
8	Total Profit	$2,432,649			
9					
10					
11					
12					

Importing text files using other methods

Another way to open the Text Import Wizard to import a text file into Excel is to click the File tab, click Open, then navigate to the location where you store your Data Files. In the Open dialog box you will see only files that match the file types listed in the Files of type box—usually Microsoft Excel files. To import a text file, you need to change the file type: click All Excel Files (or the list arrow on the box to the right of the File name text box), click Text Files (*.prn; *.txt; *.csv), click the text file name, then click Open; the Text Import Wizard opens so you can complete the import. You can also drag the icon representing a text file on the Windows desktop into a blank worksheet window. Excel will create a worksheet from the data without opening the wizard.

Import a Database Table

In addition to text files, you can also import data from database tables into Excel. A **database table** is a set of data organized using columns and rows that is created in a database program. A **database program** is an application, such as Microsoft Access, that lets you manage large amounts of data organized in tables. **FIGURE 13-5** shows a table in Access. To import data from an Access table into Excel, you can copy the table in Access and paste it into an Excel worksheet. This method places a copy of the Access data into Excel; if you change the data in the Access file, the data will not change in the Excel copy. If you want the data in Excel to update when you edit the Access source file, you create a connection, or a **link**, to the database. This lets you work with current data in Excel without recopying the data from Access whenever the Access data changes. **CASE** *Mary received a database table containing Service Adventures' corporate customer information, which was created with Access. She asks you to import this table into an Excel workbook. She would also like you to format, sort, and total the data.*

STEPS

1. **Click the File Tab, click New, then click Blank workbook**
   A new workbook opens, displaying a blank worksheet for you to use to import the Access data.

2. **Click the Data tab, click the From Access button in the Get External Data group, then navigate to where you store your Data Files**

3. **Click EX 13-2.accdb, then click Open**
   The Import Data dialog box opens, so that you can select how you want the data to be used, and where you want to place it.

4. **Verify that the Table option button and the Existing worksheet button are selected in the Import Data dialog box, then click OK**
   Excel inserts the Access data into the worksheet as a table with the default Table Style Medium 2 format applied, as shown in **FIGURE 13-6**.

5. **Rename the sheet tab Customer Information, then format the data in columns F and G with the Currency format with the $ symbol and no decimal places**
   You are ready to sort the data using the values in column G.

6. **Click any cell in the table if necessary, click the cell G1 list arrow, then click Sort Smallest to Largest**
   The records are reorganized in ascending order according to the amount of the 2017 sales.

7. **Click the Table Tools Design tab if necessary, click the Total Row check box in the Table Style Options group to select it, click cell F19, click the cell F19 list arrow, click Sum in the drop-down function list, then click cell A1**
   Your completed worksheet should match **FIGURE 13-7**.

8. **Add your name to the center section of the worksheet footer, change the worksheet orientation to Landscape, save the workbook as EX 13-Customer Information, then preview the worksheet**

FIGURE 13-5: Access Table

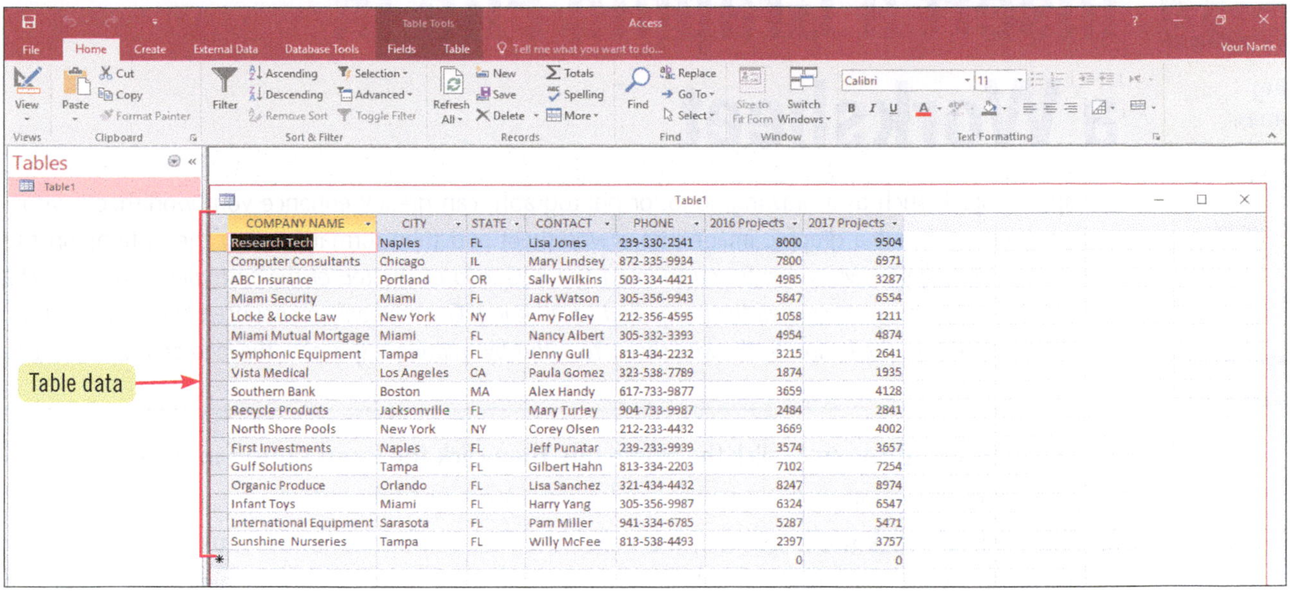

Table data

COMPANY NAME	CITY	STATE	CONTACT	PHONE	2016 Projects	2017 Projects
Research Tech	Naples	FL	Lisa Jones	239-330-2541	8000	9504
Computer Consultants	Chicago	IL	Mary Lindsey	872-335-9934	7800	6971
ABC Insurance	Portland	OR	Sally Wilkins	503-334-4421	4985	3287
Miami Security	Miami	FL	Jack Watson	305-356-9943	5847	6554
Locke & Locke Law	New York	NY	Amy Folley	212-356-4595	1058	1211
Miami Mutual Mortgage	Miami	FL	Nancy Albert	305-332-3393	4954	4874
Symphonic Equipment	Tampa	FL	Jenny Gull	813-434-2232	3215	2641
Vista Medical	Los Angeles	CA	Paula Gomez	323-538-7789	1874	1935
Southern Bank	Boston	MA	Alex Handy	617-733-9877	3659	4128
Recycle Products	Jacksonville	FL	Mary Turley	904-733-9987	2484	2841
North Shore Pools	New York	NY	Corey Olsen	212-233-4432	3669	4002
First Investments	Naples	FL	Jeff Punatar	239-233-9939	3574	3657
Gulf Solutions	Tampa	FL	Gilbert Hahn	813-334-2203	7102	7254
Organic Produce	Orlando	FL	Lisa Sanchez	321-434-4432	8247	8974
Infant Toys	Miami	FL	Harry Yang	305-356-9987	6324	6547
International Equipment	Sarasota	FL	Pam Miller	941-334-6785	5287	5471
Sunshine Nurseries	Tampa	FL	Willy McFee	813-538-4493	2397	3757
					0	0

FIGURE 13-6: Access table imported to Excel

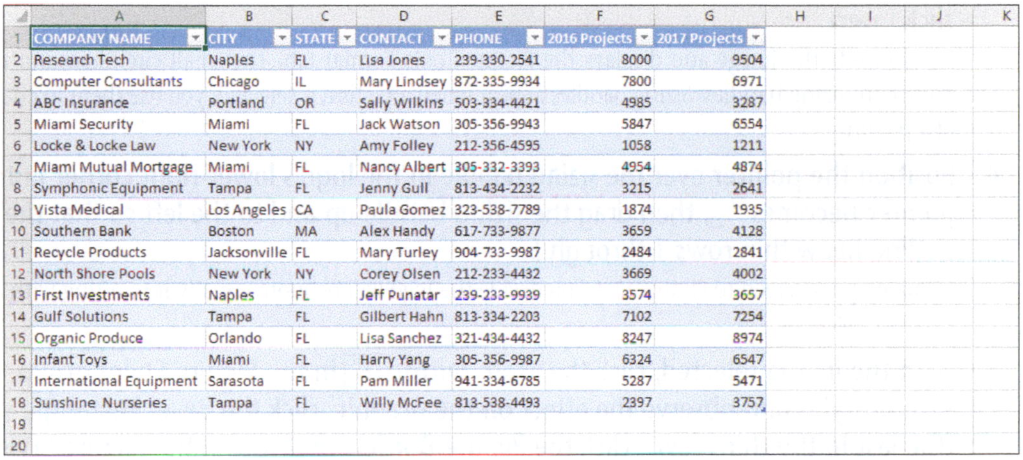

	A	B	C	D	E	F	G
1	COMPANY NAME	CITY	STATE	CONTACT	PHONE	2016 Projects	2017 Projects
2	Research Tech	Naples	FL	Lisa Jones	239-330-2541	8000	9504
3	Computer Consultants	Chicago	IL	Mary Lindsey	872-335-9934	7800	6971
4	ABC Insurance	Portland	OR	Sally Wilkins	503-334-4421	4985	3287
5	Miami Security	Miami	FL	Jack Watson	305-356-9943	5847	6554
6	Locke & Locke Law	New York	NY	Amy Folley	212-356-4595	1058	1211
7	Miami Mutual Mortgage	Miami	FL	Nancy Albert	305-332-3393	4954	4874
8	Symphonic Equipment	Tampa	FL	Jenny Gull	813-434-2232	3215	2641
9	Vista Medical	Los Angeles	CA	Paula Gomez	323-538-7789	1874	1935
10	Southern Bank	Boston	MA	Alex Handy	617-733-9877	3659	4128
11	Recycle Products	Jacksonville	FL	Mary Turley	904-733-9987	2484	2841
12	North Shore Pools	New York	NY	Corey Olsen	212-233-4432	3669	4002
13	First Investments	Naples	FL	Jeff Punatar	239-233-9939	3574	3657
14	Gulf Solutions	Tampa	FL	Gilbert Hahn	813-334-2203	7102	7254
15	Organic Produce	Orlando	FL	Lisa Sanchez	321-434-4432	8247	8974
16	Infant Toys	Miami	FL	Harry Yang	305-356-9987	6324	6547
17	International Equipment	Sarasota	FL	Pam Miller	941-334-6785	5287	5471
18	Sunshine Nurseries	Tampa	FL	Willy McFee	813-538-4493	2397	3757

FIGURE 13-7: Completed worksheet containing imported data

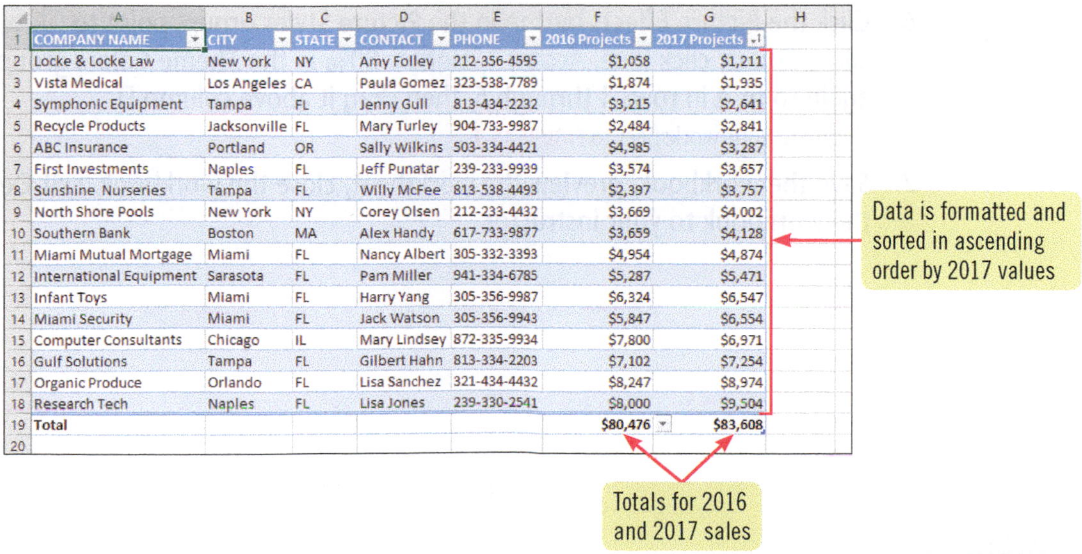

	A	B	C	D	E	F	G
1	COMPANY NAME	CITY	STATE	CONTACT	PHONE	2016 Projects	2017 Projects
2	Locke & Locke Law	New York	NY	Amy Folley	212-356-4595	$1,058	$1,211
3	Vista Medical	Los Angeles	CA	Paula Gomez	323-538-7789	$1,874	$1,935
4	Symphonic Equipment	Tampa	FL	Jenny Gull	813-434-2232	$3,215	$2,641
5	Recycle Products	Jacksonville	FL	Mary Turley	904-733-9987	$2,484	$2,841
6	ABC Insurance	Portland	OR	Sally Wilkins	503-334-4421	$4,985	$3,287
7	First Investments	Naples	FL	Jeff Punatar	239-233-9939	$3,574	$3,657
8	Sunshine Nurseries	Tampa	FL	Willy McFee	813-538-4493	$2,397	$3,757
9	North Shore Pools	New York	NY	Corey Olsen	212-233-4432	$3,669	$4,002
10	Southern Bank	Boston	MA	Alex Handy	617-733-9877	$3,659	$4,128
11	Miami Mutual Mortgage	Miami	FL	Nancy Albert	305-332-3393	$4,954	$4,874
12	International Equipment	Sarasota	FL	Pam Miller	941-334-6785	$5,287	$5,471
13	Infant Toys	Miami	FL	Harry Yang	305-356-9987	$6,324	$6,547
14	Miami Security	Miami	FL	Jack Watson	305-356-9943	$5,847	$6,554
15	Computer Consultants	Chicago	IL	Mary Lindsey	872-335-9934	$7,800	$6,971
16	Gulf Solutions	Tampa	FL	Gilbert Hahn	813-334-2203	$7,102	$7,254
17	Organic Produce	Orlando	FL	Lisa Sanchez	321-434-4432	$8,247	$8,974
18	Research Tech	Naples	FL	Lisa Jones	239-330-2541	$8,000	$9,504
19	Total					$80,476	$83,608

Data is formatted and sorted in ascending order by 2017 values

Totals for 2016 and 2017 sales

Exchanging Data with Other Programs

Excel 2016
Module 13

Learning
Outcomes
• Insert an image
  into an Excel
  worksheet
• Add a style to an
  image

Insert a Graphic File in a Worksheet

A graphic object, such as a drawing, logo, or photograph, can greatly enhance your worksheet's visual impact. You can insert a graphic image into a worksheet and then format it using the options on the Format tab. **CASE** *Mary wants you to insert the R2G logo at the top of the customer worksheet. The company's graphic designer created the image and saved it in JPG (commonly pronounced "jay-peg") format. You insert and format the image on the worksheet. You start by creating a space for the logo on the worksheet.*

STEPS

1. **Select rows 1 through 5, click the Home tab, then click the Insert button in the Cells group**
   Five blank rows appear above the header row, leaving space to insert the picture.

2. **Click cell A1, click the Insert tab, then click the Pictures button in the Illustrations group**
   The Insert Picture dialog box opens. Because you specified that you want to insert a picture, the dialog box displays only files that contain graphics file extensions, just as .jpg.

3. **Navigate to where you store your Data Files if necessary, click EX 13-3.jpg, then click Insert**
   Excel inserts the image and displays the Picture Tools Format tab. The small circles around the picture's border are sizing handles. Sizing handles appear when a picture is selected; you use them to change the size of a picture.

4. **Position the pointer over the sizing handle in the logo's lower-right corner until the pointer becomes ↖, then drag the sizing handle up and to the left so that the logo's outline fits within rows 1 through 5**
   Compare your screen to **FIGURE 13-8**. You decide the logo will be more visually interesting with a frame and a border color.

5. **With the image selected, click the More button ⤓ in the Picture Styles group, point to several styles and observe the effect on the graphic, click the Bevel Rectangle style (the last in the third row), click the Picture Border list arrow in the Picture Styles group, then click Blue, Accent 1, Lighter 40% in the Theme Colors group**
   You decide to add a glow to the image.

6. **Click the Picture Effects button in the Picture Styles group, point to Glow, point to More Glow Colors, click Blue, Accent 1, Lighter 80% in the Theme Colors group, resize the logo again to fit it in rows 1 through 5, then drag it above column D**
   Compare your worksheet to **FIGURE 13-9**.

7. **Save the workbook, preview the worksheet, close the workbook, exit Excel, then submit the workbook to your instructor**

FIGURE 13-8: Resized logo

In Step 4, drag
this sizing handle

FIGURE 13-9: Worksheet with formatted picture

Formatted
image

Formatting SmartArt graphics

SmartArt graphics provide another way to visually communicate information on a worksheet. Each SmartArt type communicates a kind of information or relationship, such as a list, process, or hierarchy. Each type has various layouts you can choose. To insert a SmartArt graphic into a worksheet, click the Insert tab, then click the Insert a SmartArt Graphic button in the Illustrations group. In the Choose a SmartArt Graphic dialog box, choose from eight SmartArt types: List, Process, Cycle, Hierarchy, Relationship, Matrix, Pyramid, and Picture. There is also a link for SmartArt available on Office.com. The dialog box describes the type of information that is appropriate for each selected layout. After you choose a layout and click OK, a SmartArt object appears on your worksheet. As you enter text in the text entry areas, the font automatically resizes to fit the graphic. The SmartArt Tools Design tab lets you choose color schemes and styles for your SmartArt. You can add shape styles, fills, outlines and other shape effects to SmartArt graphics using choices on the SmartArt Tools

Format tab. You can also add fills, outlines and other effects to text using this tab. **FIGURE 13-10** shows examples of SmartArt graphics. You can create a SmartArt graphic from an existing image by clicking the image, clicking the Picture Layout button in the Picture Styles group of the Picture Tools Format tab, then selecting the SmartArt type.

FIGURE 13-10: Examples of SmartArt graphics

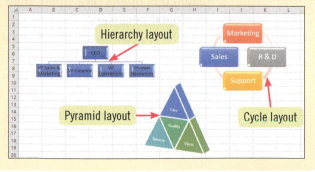

Embed a Workbook in a Word Document

Learning Outcomes
- Embed Excel data in a Word document
- Edit an embedded file icon caption

Microsoft Office programs work together to make it easy to copy an object (such as text, data, or a graphic) in a source program and then insert it into a document in a different program (the destination program). If you insert copied Excel data using a simple Paste command, however, you retain no connection to the source program. That's why it is often more useful to embed objects rather than simply paste them. Embedding allows you to edit an Excel workbook from within the source program using that program's commands and tools. If you send a Word document with an embedded workbook to another person, you do not need to send a separate Excel file with it. All the necessary information is embedded in the Word document. When you embed information, you can either display the data itself or an icon representing the data; users double-click the icon to view the embedded data. An icon is often used rather than the data when the worksheet data is too large to fit well on a Word document. **CASE** *Mary wants to update Bryce Gibson, the CEO of Reason2Go, on the project status. She asks you to prepare a Word memo that includes the projected sales workbook embedded as an icon. You begin by starting Word and opening the memo.*

STEPS

1. **Open a File Explorer window, navigate to the location where you store your Data Files, then double-click EX 13-4.docx to open the file in Word**

   The memo opens in Word.

2. **Click the File tab, click Save As, navigate to the location where you store your Data Files, change the file name to EX 13-Service Adventures Memo, then click Save**

   You want to embed the workbook below the last line of the document.

3. **Press [Ctrl][End], click the Insert tab, click the Object button in the Text group, then click the Create from File tab**

   FIGURE 13-11 shows the Create from File tab in the Object dialog box. You need to indicate the file you want to embed.

4. **Click Browse, navigate to the location where you store your Data Files, click EX 13-5.xlsx, click Insert, then select the Display as icon check box**

   You will change the icon caption to a more descriptive name.

5. **Click Change Icon, select the text in the Caption text box, type Projected Sales, click OK twice, then click anywhere in the Word document**

   The memo contains an embedded copy of the sales projection data, displayed as an icon, as shown in FIGURE 13-12.

6. **Double-click the Projected Sales icon on the Word memo, if the Open Package Contents dialog box opens click Open, then maximize the Excel window and the worksheet window if necessary**

   The Excel program starts and displays the embedded worksheet, with its location displayed in the title bar, as shown in FIGURE 13-13. Any changes you make to the embedded object using Excel tools are not reflected in the source document. Similarly, if you open the source document in the source program, changes you make are not reflected in the embedded copy.

7. **Click the File tab, click Close, exit Excel, click the Word File tab, then click Save**

   Your changes to the memo are saved, and the memo remains open.

FIGURE 13-11: Object dialog box

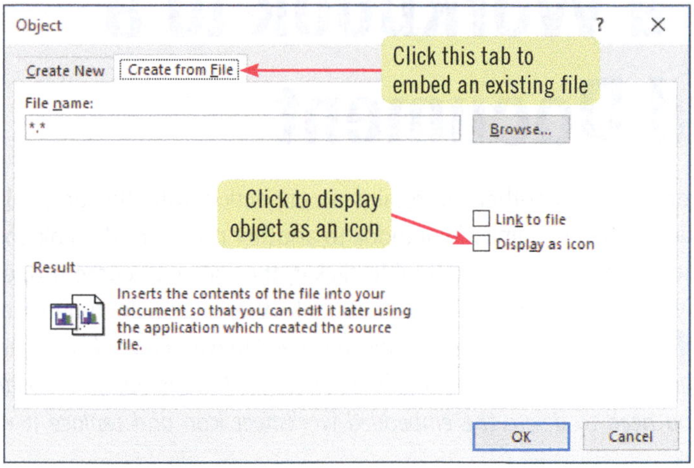

FIGURE 13-12: Memo with embedded worksheet displayed as an icon

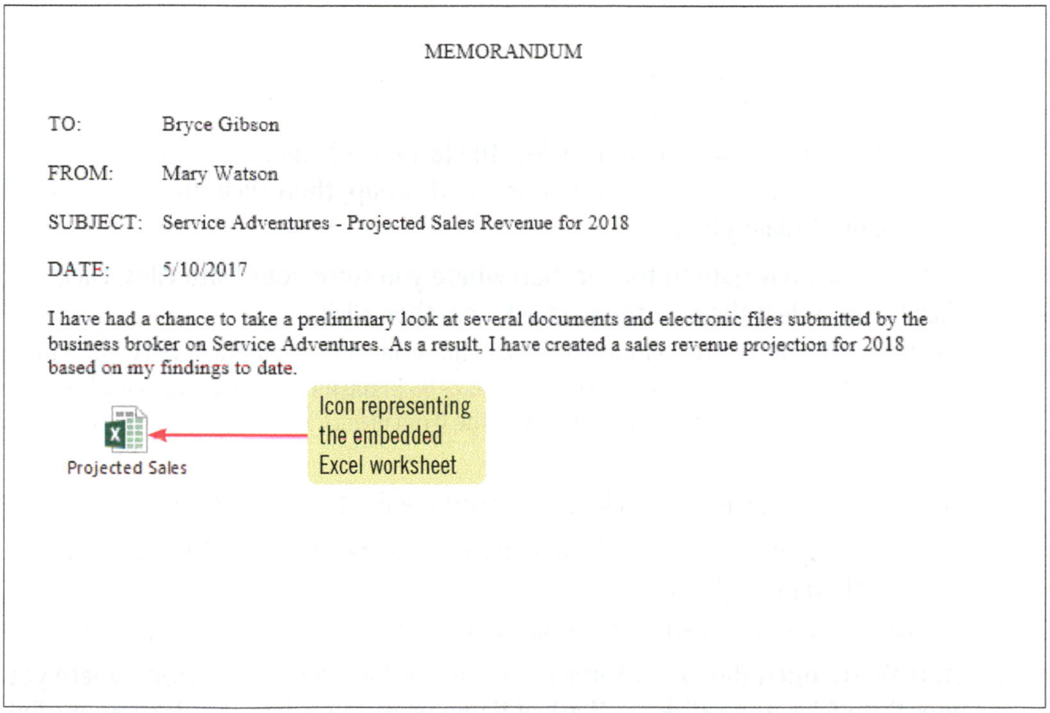

FIGURE 13-13: Embedded worksheet open in Excel

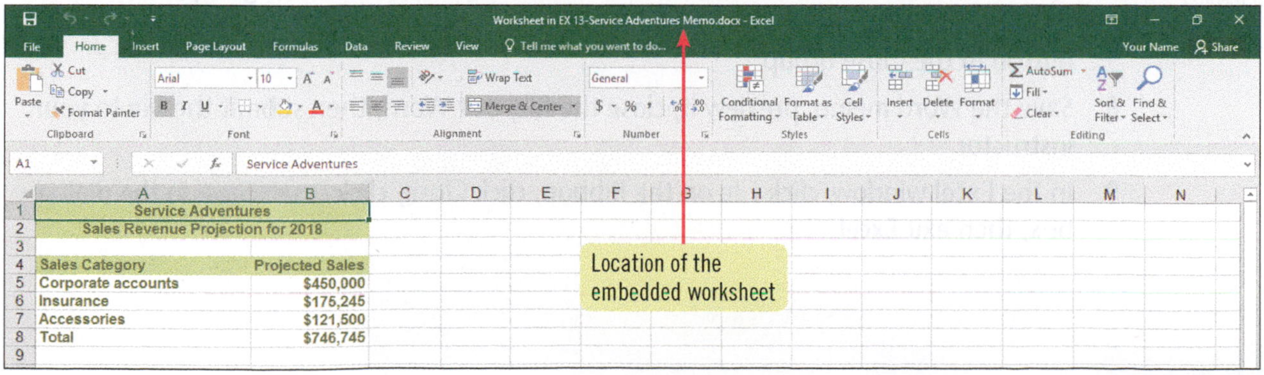

Link a Workbook to a Word Document

Learning Outcomes
• Link data from an Excel worksheet to a Word document
• Update links in a Word document

Linking a workbook to another file retains a connection with the original document as well as the original program. When you link a workbook to another program, the link contains a connection to the source document so that, when you double-click it, the source document opens for editing. In addition, any changes you make to the original workbook (the source document) are reflected in the linked object. **CASE** ▸ *Mary has just told you she may need to edit the workbook she embedded in the memo to Bryce. To ensure that these changes will be reflected in the memo, you decide to use linking instead of embedding. You need to delete the embedded worksheet icon and replace it with a linked version of the same workbook.*

STEPS

1. **With the Word memo still open, click the Projected Sales Worksheet icon to select it if necessary, then press [Delete]**

   The workbook is no longer embedded in the memo. The process of linking a file is similar to embedding, with a few important differences.

2. **Make sure the insertion point is below the last line of the memo, click the Insert tab if necessary, click the Object button in the Text group, then click the Create from File tab in the Object dialog box**

3. **Click Browse, navigate to the location where you store your Data Files, click EX 13-5.xlsx, click Insert, select the Link to file check box, then click OK**

   You didn't select the Display as icon check box so the memo now displays a linked copy of the sales projection data rather than an icon, as shown in **FIGURE 13-14**. In the future, any changes made to the source file, EX 13-5, will also be made to the linked copy in the Word memo. You verify this by making a change to the source file and viewing its effect on the memo.

4. **Click the File tab, click Save, close the Word memo, then exit Word**

5. **Start Excel, open EX 13-5.xlsx from where you store your Data Files, click cell B7, type 100000, then press [Enter]**

   You want to verify that the same change was made automatically to the linked copy of the workbook.

6. **Start Word, open the EX 13-Service Adventures Memo.docx file from where you store your Data Files, then click Yes if asked if you want to update the document's links**

   The memo displays the new value for Accessories, and the total has been updated as shown in **FIGURE 13-15**.

7. **Click the Insert tab, click the Header button in the Header & Footer group, click Edit Header, type your name in the Header area, then click the Close Header and Footer button in the Close group**

8. **Save the Word memo, preview it, close the file, exit Word, then submit the file to your instructor**

9. **In the Excel window, click File on the Ribbon, click Close, click Don't Save in the dialog box, then exit Excel**

FIGURE 13-14: Memo with linked worksheet

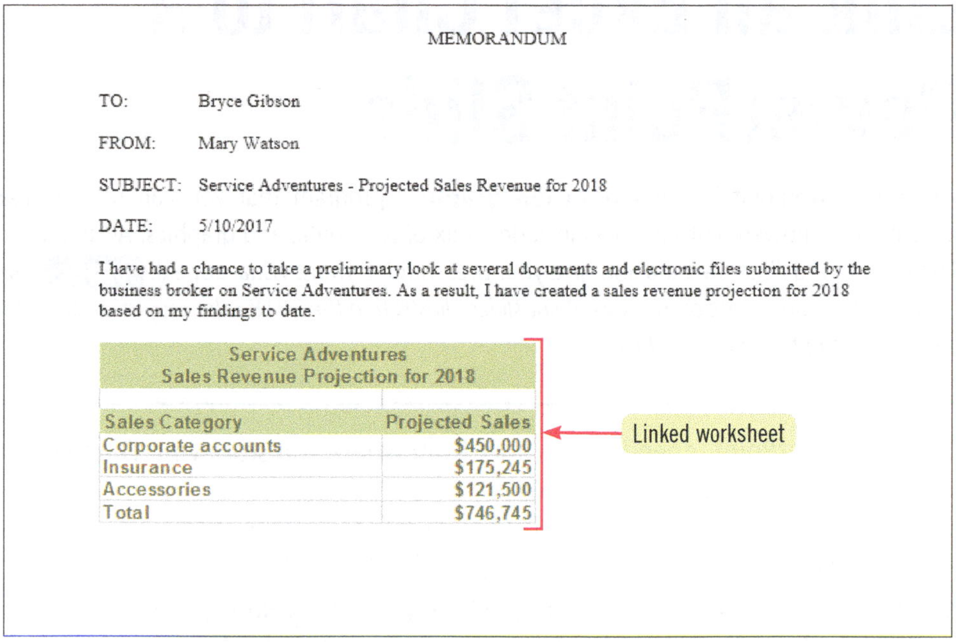

MEMORANDUM

TO: Bryce Gibson

FROM: Mary Watson

SUBJECT: Service Adventures - Projected Sales Revenue for 2018

DATE: 5/10/2017

I have had a chance to take a preliminary look at several documents and electronic files submitted by the business broker on Service Adventures. As a result, I have created a sales revenue projection for 2018 based on my findings to date.

Service Adventures Sales Revenue Projection for 2018	
Sales Category	**Projected Sales**
Corporate accounts	$450,000
Insurance	$175,245
Accessories	$121,500
Total	$746,745

← Linked worksheet

FIGURE 13-15: Memo with updated values

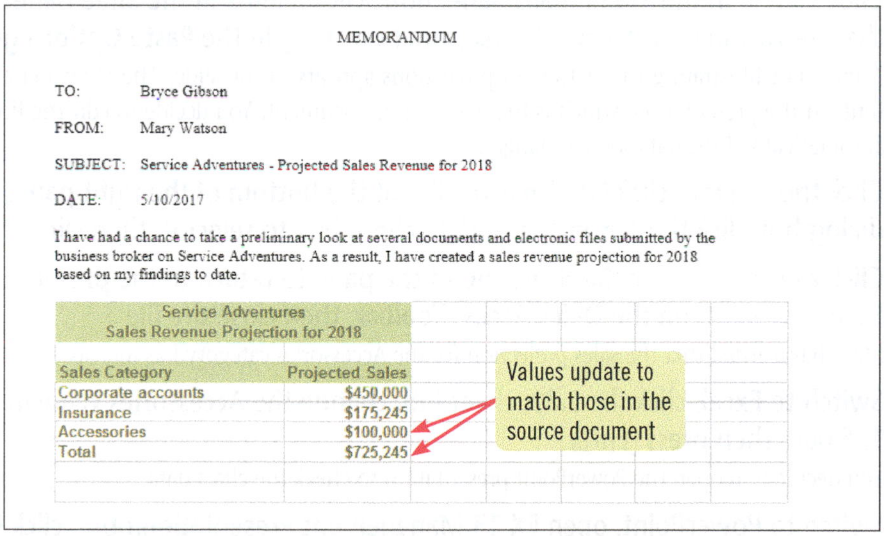

MEMORANDUM

TO: Bryce Gibson

FROM: Mary Watson

SUBJECT: Service Adventures - Projected Sales Revenue for 2018

DATE: 5/10/2017

I have had a chance to take a preliminary look at several documents and electronic files submitted by the business broker on Service Adventures. As a result, I have created a sales revenue projection for 2018 based on my findings to date.

Service Adventures Sales Revenue Projection for 2018	
Sales Category	Projected Sales
Corporate accounts	$450,000
Insurance	$175,245
Accessories	$100,000
Total	$725,245

Values update to match those in the source document

Managing links

When you open a document containing linked data, you are asked if you want to update the linked data. You can manage the updating of links by clicking the File tab, and clicking Edit Links to Files in the right pane. The Links dialog box opens, allowing you to change a link's update from the default setting of automatic to manual. The Links dialog box also allows you to change the link source, permanently break a link, open the source file, and manually update a link. If you send your linked files to another user, the links will be broken because the linked file path references the local machine where you inserted the links. Because the file path will not be valid on the recipient user's machine, the links will no longer be updated when the user opens the destination document. To correct this, recipients who have both the destination and source documents can use the Links dialog box to change the link's source in the destination document to their own machines. Then the links will be automatically updated when they open the destination document in the future.

Link an Excel Chart to a PowerPoint Slide

Learning Outcomes
- Link an Excel chart to a PowerPoint slide
- Configure automatic links in a PowerPoint file

Microsoft PowerPoint is a **presentation graphics** program that you can use to create slide show presentations. PowerPoint slides can include a mix of text, data, and graphics. Adding an Excel chart to a slide can help to illustrate data and give your presentation more visual appeal. **CASE** *Mary asks you to add an Excel chart to one of the PowerPoint slides, illustrating the 2018 sales projection data. She wants you to link the chart in the PowerPoint file.*

STEPS

1. **Start PowerPoint, open EX 13-6.pptx from where you store your Data Files, then save it as EX 13-Management Presentation**

   The presentation appears in Normal view and contains three panes, as shown in **FIGURE 13-16**. You need to open the Excel file and copy the chart that you will paste in the PowerPoint presentation.

   TROUBLE
   If you don't see Copy on the shortcut menu, you may have clicked the Plot area rather than the Chart area. Right-clicking the white area surrounding the pie will display the Copy command on the menu.

2. **Start Excel, open EX 13-7.xlsx from where you store your Data Files, right-click the Chart Area on the Sales Categories sheet, click Copy on the shortcut menu, then click the PowerPoint program button on the taskbar to display the presentation**

   To add the copied chart, you first need to select the slide on which it will appear.

3. **Click Slide 2 in the Thumbnails pane, right-click Slide 2 in the Slide pane, then click the Use Destination Theme & Link Data button 📋 in the Paste Options group**

   A pie chart illustrating the 2018 sales projections appears in the slide. The chart matches the colors and fonts in the presentation, which is the destination document. You decide to edit the link so it will update automatically if the data source changes.

   QUICK TIP
   The default setting for updating links in a PowerPoint file is Manual.

4. **Click the File tab, click Edit Links to Files at the bottom of the right pane, in the Links dialog box click the Automatic Update check box to select it, then click Close**

5. **Click the Back button ⬅ at the top of the pane to return to the presentation, click the Save button 💾 on the Quick Access Toolbar, then close the file**

   Mary has learned that the sales projection for the Accessories category has increased.

6. **Switch to Excel, click the Sales sheet tab, change the Accessories value in cell B7 to 125,000, then press [Enter]**

   You decide to reopen the PowerPoint presentation to check the chart data.

   QUICK TIP
   To update links in an open PowerPoint file, click the File tab, click Edit Links to Files in the right pane, click the link in the Links list, click Update now, then click Close.

7. **Switch to PowerPoint, open EX 13-Management Presentation.pptx, click Update Links, click Slide 2 in the Thumbnails pane, then point to the Accessories pie slice**

   The ScreenTip shows that the chart has updated to display the revised Accessories value, $125,000, you entered in the Excel workbook.

8. **Click the Slide Show button 🖵 on the status bar**

   Slide Show view shows the slide full screen, the way the audience will see it, as shown in **FIGURE 13-17**.

9. **Press [Esc] to return to Normal view; with Slide 2 selected click the Insert tab, click the Header & Footer button in the Text group, select the Footer check box, type your name in the Footer text box, click Apply to All, save and close the presentation, close the Excel file without saving it, exit PowerPoint and Excel, then submit the file to your instructor**

FIGURE 13-16: Presentation in Normal view

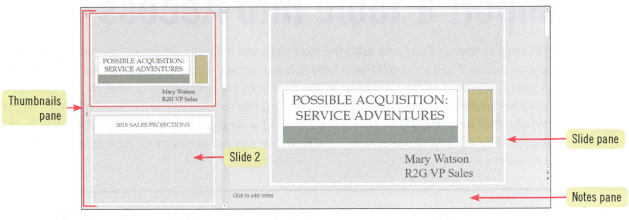

Thumbnails pane

Slide 2

Slide pane

Notes pane

FIGURE 13-17: Completed Sales Projections slide in Slide Show view

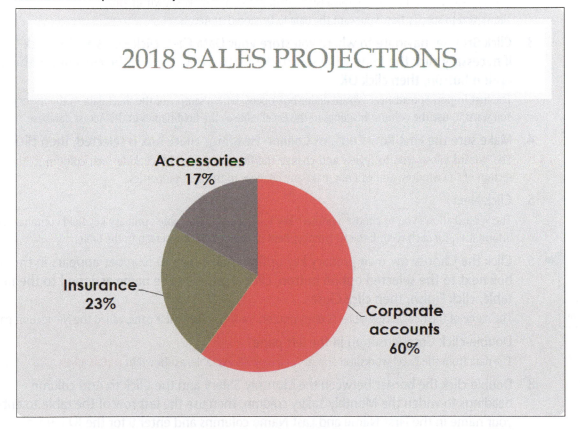

Import a Table into Access

If you need to analyze Excel data using the more extensive tools of a database, you can import it into Microsoft Access. When you import Excel table data into Access, the data becomes an Access table using the same field names as the Excel table. In the process of importing an Excel table, Access specifies a primary key for the new table. A **primary key** is the field that contains unique information for each record (row) of information. **CASE** *Mary has just received a workbook containing salary information for the managers at Service Adventures, organized in a table. She asks you to convert the Excel table to a Microsoft Access table.*

STEPS

1. **Start Access, click the Blank desktop database button, change the filename in the File Name text box to EX 13-SA Management, click the Browse button** 📁 **next to the filename, navigate to where you store your Data Files, click OK, click Create, then click the Close Table1 button** ☒ **on the right side of the Table1 pane (Do not close Access)**

   The empty table that opens in the EX 13-SA Management database is removed. You are ready to import the Excel table data.

2. **Click the External Data tab, then click the Excel button in the Import & Link group**

   The Get External Data - Excel Spreadsheet dialog box opens, as shown in **FIGURE 13-18**. This dialog box allows you to specify how you want the data to be stored in Access.

3. **Click Browse, navigate to where you store your Data Files, click EX 13-8.xlsx, click Open, if necessary click the Import the source data into a new table in the current database option button, then click OK**

   The first Import Spreadsheet Wizard dialog box opens, with a sample of the sheet data in the lower section. You want to use the column headings in the Excel table as the field names in the Access database.

4. **Make sure the First Row Contains Column Headings check box is selected, then click Next**

   The Wizard allows you to review and change the field properties by clicking each column in the lower section of the window. You will not make any changes to the field properties.

5. **Click Next**

   The Wizard allows you to choose a primary key for the table. The table's primary key field contains unique information for each record; the ID Number field is unique for each person in the table.

6. **Click the Choose my own primary key option, make sure ID Number appears in the text box next to the selected option button, click Next, note the name assigned to the new table, click Finish, then click Close**

   The name of the new Access table ("Compensation") appears in the left pane, called the Navigation pane.

7. **Double-click Compensation in the left pane**

   The data from the Excel worksheet appears in a new Access table, as shown in **FIGURE 13-19**.

8. **Double-click the border between the Monthly Salary and the Click to Add column headings to widen the Monthly Salary column, then use the last row of the table to enter your name in the First Name and Last Name columns and enter 0 for the ID Number**

9. **Click the Save button** 💾 **on the Quick Access Toolbar, close the file, then exit Access**

FIGURE 13-18: Get External Data - Excel Spreadsheet dialog box

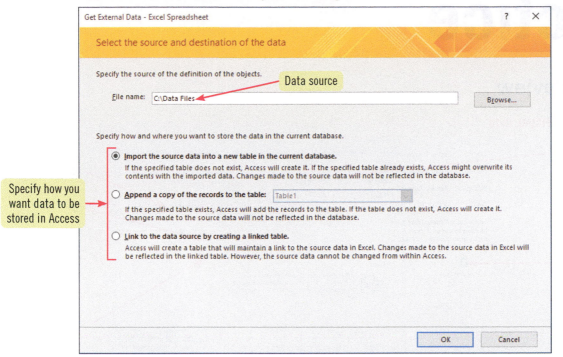

FIGURE 13-19: Completed Access table with data imported from Excel

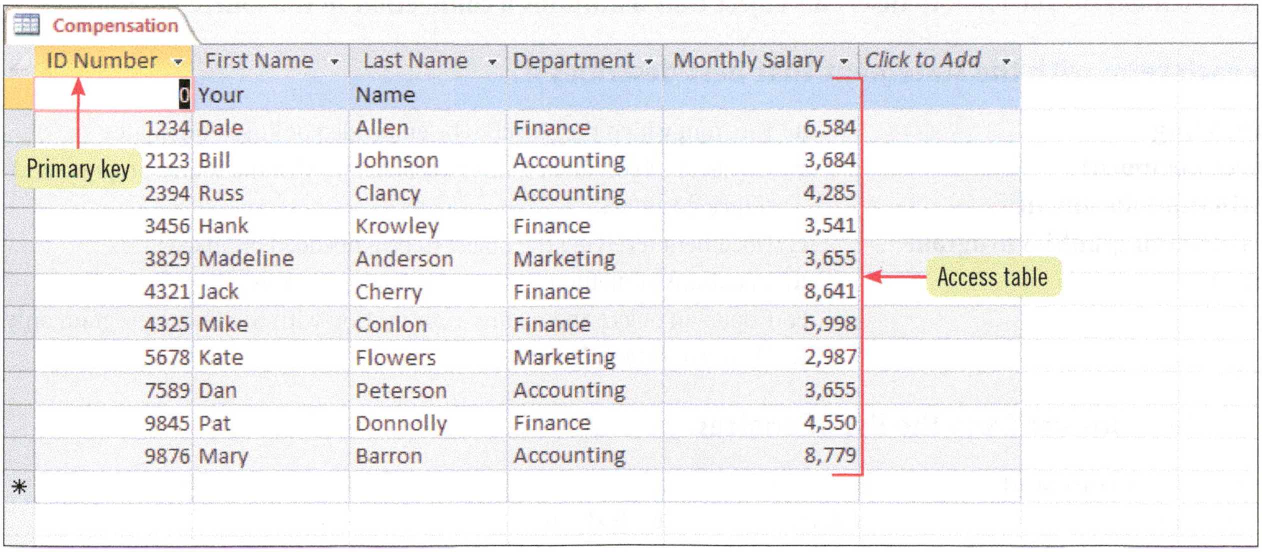

ID Number	First Name	Last Name	Department	Monthly Salary	Click to Add
0	Your	Name			
1234	Dale	Allen	Finance	6,584	
2123	Bill	Johnson	Accounting	3,684	
2394	Russ	Clancy	Accounting	4,285	
3456	Hank	Krowley	Finance	3,541	
3829	Madeline	Anderson	Marketing	3,655	
4321	Jack	Cherry	Finance	8,641	
4325	Mike	Conlon	Finance	5,998	
5678	Kate	Flowers	Marketing	2,987	
7589	Dan	Peterson	Accounting	3,655	
9845	Pat	Donnolly	Finance	4,550	
9876	Mary	Barron	Accounting	8,779	

Practice

Concepts Review

FIGURE 13-20

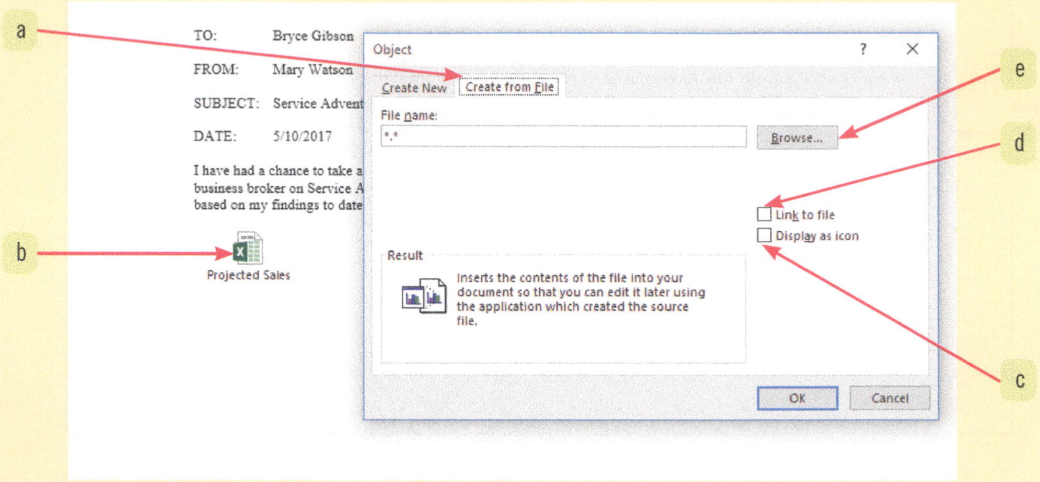

1. Which element do you click to insert an existing object into a Word document rather than creating a new file?
2. Which element do you click to embed information that can be viewed by double-clicking an icon?
3. Which element do you double-click to display an embedded Excel workbook?
4. Which element do you click to find a file to be embedded or linked?
5. Which element do you click to insert an object that maintains a connection to the source document?

Match each term with the statement that best describes it.

6. Embedding
7. Source document
8. Destination document
9. Presentation graphics program
10. Linking
11. OLE

a. File from which the object to be embedded or linked originates
b. Copies an object and retains a connection with the source program and source document
c. Document receiving the object to be embedded or linked
d. Data transfer method used in Windows programs
e. Copies an object and retains a connection with the source program only
f. Used to create slide shows

Select the best answer from the list of choices.

12. An object can consist of:
    a. Text, a worksheet, or any other type of data.
    b. A worksheet only.
    c. Text only.
    d. Database data only.
13. An ASCII file:
    a. Contains formatting but no text.
    b. Contains text but no formatting.
    c. Contains a PowerPoint presentation.
    d. Contains an unformatted worksheet.

14. To view a workbook that has been embedded as an icon in a Word document, you need to:

a. Double-click the icon.

b. Drag the icon.

c. Click View, then click Worksheet.

d. Click File, then click Open.

15. A column separator in a text file is called a(n):

a. Object.

b. Link.

c. Primary key.

d. Delimiter.

16. A field that contains unique information for each record in a database table is called a(n):

a. Primary key.

b. ID Key.

c. First key.

d. Header key.

Skills Review

1. Import a text file.

a. Start Excel, open a new blank workbook, import the tab-delimited text file EX 13-9.txt from where you store your Data Files, accepting the defaults in the Text Import Wizard, then save it as a Microsoft Office Excel workbook with the name **EX 13-Coffee Corner**.

b. Format the data in columns B and C using the Currency style with two decimal places.

c. Widen the columns if necessary so that all the data is visible.

d. Center the column labels and apply bold formatting, as shown in **FIGURE 13-21**.

e. Add your name to the center section of the worksheet footer, save the workbook, preview the worksheet, close the workbook, then submit the workbook to your instructor.

FIGURE 13-21

	A	B	C
1	Item	Cost	Price
2	Small	$0.59	$1.59
3	Medium	$0.80	$1.89
4	Large	$1.15	$2.09
5	X-Large	$1.30	$2.29
6	Latte, small	$1.50	$2.69
7	Latte, medium	$1.75	$3.19
8	Latte, large	$2.15	$3.69
9	Iced, small	$1.10	$1.99
10	Iced, medium	$1.70	$2.49
11	Iced, large	$2.10	$2.79
12			

2. Import a database table.

a. Open a blank workbook in Excel, use the From Access button in the Get External Data group on the Data tab to import the Access Data File EX 13-10.accdb from where you store your Data Files, then save it as a Microsoft Excel workbook named **EX 13-May Budget**.

b. Rename the sheet with the imported data **Budget**.

c. Delete the first data record in row 2.

d. Add a total row to the table to display the sum of the budgeted amounts in cell D25 (the Amount column).

e. Apply the Light 20 Table Style. Format range D2:D25 using the Currency style, the $ symbol, and two decimal places.

f. Save the workbook, and compare your screen to **FIGURE 13-22**.

FIGURE 13-22

	A	B	C	D	E
1	Category	Item	Month	Amount	
2	Compensation	Bonuses	May	$40,000.00	
3	Compensation	Commissions	May	$35,000.00	
4	Compensation	Conferences	May	$42,000.00	
5	Compensation	Promotions	May	$65,048.00	
6	Compensation	Payroll Taxes	May	$18,954.00	
7	Compensation	Salaries	May	$63,514.00	
8	Compensation	Training	May	$8,544.00	
9	Facility	Lease	May	$42,184.00	
10	Facility	Maintenance	May	$63,214.00	
11	Facility	Other	May	$11,478.00	
12	Facility	Rent	May	$80,214.00	
13	Facility	Telephone	May	$62,584.00	
14	Facility	Utilities	May	$57,964.00	
15	Supplies	Food	May	$61,775.00	
16	Supplies	Computer	May	$43,217.00	
17	Supplies	General Office	May	$47,854.00	
18	Supplies	Other	May	$56,741.00	
19	Supplies	Outside Services	May	$41,874.00	
20	Equipment	Computer	May	$49,874.00	
21	Equipment	Other	May	$43,547.00	
22	Equipment	Cash Registers	May	$55,987.00	
23	Equipment	Software	May	$63,147.00	
24	Equipment	Telecommunications	May	$58,779.00	
25	Total			$1,113,493.00	
26					
27					

3. Insert a graphic file in a worksheet.

a. Add four rows above row 1 to create space for an image.

b. In rows 1 through 4, insert the picture file EX 13-11.jpg from the location where you store your Data Files.

c. Resize and reposition the picture as necessary to make it fit in rows 1 through 4.

d. Apply the Beveled Matte, White Picture Style, and change the picture border color to Blue, Accent 5, Lighter 60%. Resize the picture to fit the image and the border in the first four rows. Move the picture to the center of the range A1:D4.

e. Compare your worksheet to **FIGURE 13-23**, add your name to the center section of the worksheet footer, preview the workbook, save and close the workbook, then submit the workbook to your instructor.

FIGURE 13-23

	A	B	C	D	E
1					
2					
3					
4					
5	Category	Item	Month	Amount	
6	Compensation	Bonuses	May	$40,000.00	
7	Compensation	Commissions	May	$35,000.00	
8	Compensation	Conferences	May	$42,000.00	
9	Compensation	Promotions	May	$65,048.00	
10	Compensation	Payroll Taxes	May	$18,954.00	
11	Compensation	Salaries	May	$63,514.00	
12	Compensation	Training	May	$8,544.00	
13	Facility	Lease	May	$42,184.00	
14	Facility	Maintenance	May	$63,214.00	
15	Facility	Other	May	$11,478.00	
16	Facility	Rent	May	$80,214.00	
17	Facility	Telephone	May	$62,584.00	
18	Facility	Utilities	May	$57,964.00	
19	Supplies	Food	May	$61,775.00	
20	Supplies	Computer	May	$43,217.00	
21	Supplies	General Office	May	$47,854.00	
22	Supplies	Other	May	$56,741.00	
23	Supplies	Outside Services	May	$41,874.00	
24	Equipment	Computer	May	$49,874.00	
25	Equipment	Other	May	$43,547.00	
26	Equipment	Cash Registers	May	$55,987.00	
27	Equipment	Software	May	$63,147.00	

Skills Review (continued)

4. **Embed a workbook in a Word document.**

   a. Start Word, type a memo addressed to your instructor, enter your name in the From line, enter **May Salaries** as the subject, and enter the current date in the Date line.

   b. In the memo body, enter **The May salaries are provided in the worksheet below**:

   c. At the bottom of the memo body, use the Object dialog box to embed the workbook EX 13-12.xlsx from where you store your Data Files, displaying it as an icon with the caption **Salary Details**.

   d. Save the document as **EX 13-May Salaries** in the location where you store your Data Files, then double-click the icon to verify that the workbook opens. (*Hint*: If the workbook does not appear after you double-click it, click the Excel icon on the taskbar.)

   e. Close the workbook and return to Word.

   f. Compare your memo to FIGURE 13-24.

FIGURE 13-24

To: Your Instructor

From: Your Name

Subject: May Salaries

Date: 11/1/2017

The May salaries are provided in the worksheet below:

Salary Details

5. **Link a workbook to a Word document.**

   a. Delete the icon in the memo body.

   b. In the memo body, link the workbook EX 13-12.xlsx, displaying the data, not an icon.

   c. Save the document, then note that Mark Glory's salary is $7000. Close the document.

   d. Open the EX 13-12.xlsx workbook in Excel, and change Mark Glory's salary to **$7500**.

   e. Open the **EX 13-May Salaries** document in Word, update the links, and verify that Mark Glory's salary has changed to $7,500 and that the new total salaries amount is $43,725, as shown in FIGURE 13-25. (*Hint*: If the dialog box does not open, giving you the opportunity to update the link, then right-click the worksheet object and click Update Link.)

   f. Save the **EX 13-May Salaries** document, preview the memo, close the document, exit Word, then submit the document to your instructor.

   g. Close the EX 13-12 workbook without saving changes, then exit Excel.

FIGURE 13-25

To: Your Instructor

From: Your Name

Subject: May Salaries

Date: 11/1/2017

The May salaries are provided in the worksheet below:

Coffee Corner Salary Summary			
First Name	Last Name	Position	Salary
Mark	Glory	Manager	$ 7,500
John	Crowley	Manager	$ 6,500
Melissa	Donolly	Manager	$ 5,954
Cathy	Wallace	Sales Associate	$ 6,325
Sandra	Jung	Custodian	$ 5,635
Karen	Aloitz	Sales Associate	$ 5,847
Gerry	Stimpson	Sales Associate	$ 5,964
		Total	$ 43,725

6. **Link an Excel chart to a PowerPoint slide.**

   a. Start PowerPoint.

   b. Open the PowerPoint file EX 13-13.pptx from where you store your Data Files, then save it as **EX 13-Budget Meeting**.

   c. Display Slide 2, May Expenditures.

   d. Start Excel, open EX 13-14 from where you store your data files, copy the chart, switch to PowerPoint, then link the chart on Slide 2, using the theme of the destination file. Edit the link to be updated automatically. Save and close the EX 13-Budget Meeting file.

   e. Change the Equipment amount on Sheet1 of EX 13-14 to $200,000, open the EX 13-Budget Meeting file, updating the links, and verify the Equipment percentage changed to 21% on Slide 2.

   f. View the slide in Slide Show view.

   g. Press [Esc] to return to Normal view. Resize and reposition the chart. Compare your slide to FIGURE 13-26.

FIGURE 13-26

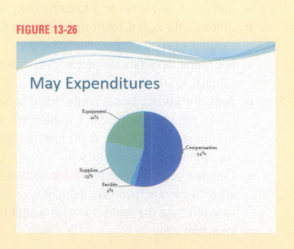

May Expenditures

Skills Review (continued)

h. Add a footer to all of the slides with your name.

i. Save the presentation, exit PowerPoint, close EX 13-14 without saving it, then submit the presentation to your instructor.

7. Import a table into Access.

a. Start Access.

b. Create a blank desktop database named **EX 13-Budget** in the location where you store your Data Files. Close Table1.

c. Use the External Data tab to import the Excel table in EX 13-15.xlsx from the location where you store your Data Files. Store the data in a new table, use the first row as column headings, let Access add the primary key, and use the default table name May Budget.

d. Open the May Budget table in Access, and widen the columns as necessary to fully display the field names and field information. Adjust the width of the Month column if necessary to more closely fit the May month data.

e. Enter your name in the Category column of row 24 in the table, save the database file, compare your screen to **FIGURE 13-27**, exit Access, then submit the database file to your instructor.

FIGURE 13-27

ID	Category	Item	Month	Amount	Click to Add
1	Compensation	Bonuses	May	$40,000.00	
2	Compensation	Commissions	May	$35,000.00	
3	Compensation	Conferences	May	$42,000.00	
4	Compensation	Promotions	May	$65,048.00	
5	Compensation	Payroll Taxes	May	$18,954.00	
6	Compensation	Salaries	May	$63,514.00	
7	Compensation	Training	May	$8,544.00	
8	Facility	Lease	May	$42,184.00	
9	Facility	Maintenance	May	$63,214.00	
10	Facility	Other	May	$11,478.00	
11	Facility	Rent	May	$80,214.00	
12	Facility	Telephone	May	$62,584.00	
13	Facility	Utilities	May	$57,964.00	
14	Supplies	Food	May	$61,775.00	
15	Supplies	Computer	May	$43,217.00	
16	Supplies	General Office	May	$47,854.00	
17	Supplies	Other	May	$56,741.00	
18	Supplies	Outside Services	May	$41,874.00	
19	Equipment	Computer	May	$49,874.00	
20	Equipment	Other	May	$43,547.00	
21	Equipment	Cash Registers	May	$55,987.00	
22	Equipment	Software	May	$63,147.00	
23	Equipment	Telecommunications	May	$58,779.00	
24	Your Name				

Independent Challenge 1

You are an agent for the LA office of West Coast Insurance. You have been asked to give a presentation to the regional manager about your sales in the past year. To illustrate your sales data, you will add an Excel chart to one of your slides, showing the different categories of insurance sales and the sales amounts for each category.

a. Start Excel, create a new workbook, then save it as **EX 13-Insurance Sales** in the location where you store your Data Files.

b. Starting in cell A1, enter the categories and the corresponding sales amounts shown below into the EX 13-Insurance Sales workbook. Name the sheet **Sales**.

Category	Sales
Homeowners	$10,500,000
Auto	$15,200,000
Umbrella	$7,000,000

c. Create a 3-D pie chart from the sales data. Format it using Chart Style 2.

d. Copy the chart to the Clipboard.

e. Start PowerPoint, open EX 13-16.pptx from where you store your Data Files, then save it as **EX 13-Sales Presentation**.

f. Link the Excel chart to Slide 2 using the destination theme. Use the sizing handles to change the size if necessary, and drag the edge of the chart to position it in the center of the slide if necessary.

FIGURE 13-28

g. View the slide in Slide Show view, then press [Esc] to end the show.

h. Add a footer to the slides with your name, then save the presentation. Slide 2 should look like **FIGURE 13-28**.

i. Change the status of links in the PowerPoint file to update automatically.

j. Close the presentation, exit PowerPoint, then submit the PowerPoint file to your instructor.

k. Save the workbook, then close the workbook, and exit Excel.

Independent Challenge 2

You are opening a new physical therapy clinic in Santa Barbara, California. The owner of a clinic in the area is retiring and has agreed to sell you a text file containing his list of supplier information. You need to import this text file into Excel so that you can manipulate the data. Later, you will convert the Excel file to an Access table so that you can give it to your business partner who is building a supplier database.

a. Start Excel, import EX 13-17.txt from where you store your Data Files, then save it as an Excel file named **EX 13-PT Suppliers**. (*Hint*: This is a tab-delimited text file, and the data has headers.)

b. Adjust the column widths as necessary. Rename the worksheet **Suppliers**.

c. Sort the worksheet data in ascending order by Supplier.

d. Add your name to the center section of the worksheet footer, save and close the workbook, then exit Excel.

e. Start Access, then create a new blank desktop database in the location where you store your Data Files. Name the new database **EX 13-Suppliers**. Close Table1.

f. Use the External Data tab to import the Excel file EX 13-PT Suppliers from where you store your Data Files. Store the data in a new table, use the column labels as the field names, let Access add the primary key, and accept the default table name.

g. Open the Suppliers table, then AutoFit the columns.

h. Enter your name in the Supplier column in row 13, then compare your database file to **FIGURE 13-29**.

i. Save and close the table, then exit Access.

j. Submit the database file to your instructor.

FIGURE 13-29

ID	Supplier	Address	City	State	Zip	Phone	Contact	Click to Add
1	Ace Equipment	45 Main St	Oakland	CA	94611	510-422-9923	R. Juan	
2	All Equipment	1157 East Rd	Daly City	CA	94623	415-465-7855	M. Lyons	
3	Elite Equipment	PO Box 1587	Milpitas	CA	94698	408-345-9343	P. Volez	
4	Equipment Plus	33 Jackson St	Fresno	CA	96899	608-332-8790	J. Jerry	
5	Holly Medial	44 West St	Brisbane	CA	94453	415-223-9912	H. Tran	
6	Jackson Equipment	394 19th Ave	San Francisco	CA	94554	415-444-9932	L. Solade	
7	Medical Pro	998 Little St	San Francisco	CA	94622	415-665-7342	W. Kitter	
8	Rehab Pro	223 Main St	Ventura	CA	93143	213-332-5568	A. Blume	
9	Rehab Unlimited	77 Sunrise St	Malibu	CA	93102	213-223-5432	J. Walsh	
10	West Coast Equipment	343 Upham St	Los Angeles	CA	93111	213-887-4456	P. Newhall	
11	West Coast Fitness	8 High St	San Jose	CA	94671	408-332-9981	K. McGuire	
12	West Medical	102 Lake Dr	San Diego	CA	93112	212-223-9934	S. Werthen	
13	Your Name							
(New)								

Independent Challenge 3

You are the newly hired sales manager at West Food Supplies. You would like to promote one of the account representatives, Caroline Walker, to a senior position. You have examined the sales of the other account representatives in the company and will present this information to the vice president of Human Resources, requesting permission to grant Caroline a promotion.

a. Start Word, open the Word file EX 13-18.docx from where you store your Data Files, then save it as **EX 13-Promotion**.

b. Add your name to the From line of the memo, and change the date to the current date.

c. At the end of the memo, embed the workbook EX 13-19.xlsx as an icon from the location where you store your Data Files. Change the caption for the icon to **Sales**. Double-click the icon to verify that the workbook opens.

d. Close the workbook, return to Word, delete the Sales icon, and link the workbook EX 13-19 to the memo, displaying the data, not an icon.

e. Save the EX 13-Promotion memo, then close the file.

f. Open the EX 13-19.xlsx workbook in Excel, then change Caroline Walker's sales to 800,000.

Independent Challenge 3 (continued)

g. Open the EX 13-Promotion memo, update the links, then make sure Caroline Walker's sales amount is updated.

h. Save and close the memo. Exit Word and submit the memo to your instructor.

i. Close EX 13-19 without saving the changes to Caroline Walker's information, then exit Excel.

Independent Challenge 4: Explore

You work as an account representative for a financial analyst. Each week you are required to submit your travel expenses to your supervisor in a Word document. You prefer to use Excel to track your expenses so you will link your worksheet to a Word document for your supervisor.

a. Open EX 13-20.docx from the location where you store your Data Files, then save it as **EX 13-Mileage**.

b. Replace the text "Your Name" in the FROM line with your own name.

c. Open EX 13-21.xlsx from where you store your Data Files, then copy the range A1:C6 to the Clipboard.

d. Return to the EX 13-Mileage document, then use the Paste Special command in the Paste Options to paste the copied range as a linked worksheet object with the destination style. (*Hint*: Using **FIGURE 13-30** as a guide, right-click below the line "My travel expenses for this week are shown below.", then click the Link & Use Destination Styles option in the Paste Options group. It is the 4th option from the left.) Save and close the memo.

FIGURE 13-30

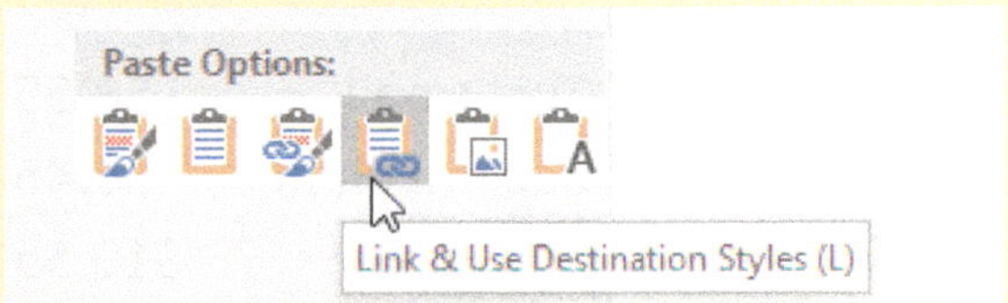

e. In the EX 13-21 workbook, change Monday's mileage to 80.

f. Return to Word, open the EX 13-Mileage memo, update links, then verify that Monday's reimbursement amount is now $46.00. Save and close the memo, then exit Word. Close the EX 13-21 workbook without saving the file, then exit Excel.

g. Using Access, create a new blank desktop database named **EX 13-Reimbursement** in the location where you store your Data Files. Open EX 13-21 and save it as EX 13-Report. Link the Excel data in the EX 13-Report.xlsx file to the EX 13-Reimbursement database file using **FIGURE 13-31** as a guide. View the data in the linked Mileage table by double-clicking the object's name.

h. Save and close the database file, open the EX 13-Report.xlsx file, then change the mileage for Friday to 10. Save and close the Excel file.

i. Open the EX 13-Reimbursement database, then verify that the mileage figure for Friday was updated in the linked Mileage table. Enter your name in the Description column of the Design View (*Hint*: Click the View button in the Views group, enter your name, then click the View button again to return to the Datasheet View, saving the table.). Close the database and exit Access.

j. Submit the EX 13-Mileage Word document, the EX 13-Report Excel file, and the EX 13-Reimbursement Access file to your instructor.

FIGURE 13-31

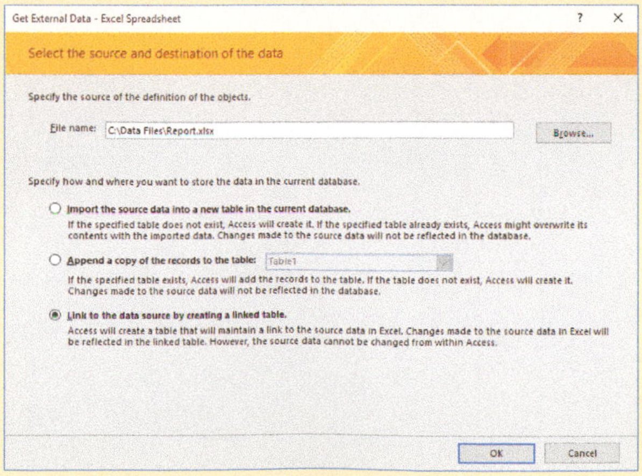

Excel 2016

Visual Workshop

Create the worksheet shown in FIGURE 13-32 by opening a blank workbook, importing the Access data in file EX 13-22.accdb, sorting the data in Excel, and formatting the price data. The image is EX 13-11.jpg and the picture border is the standard color blue. Add your name to the center section of the worksheet. Save the workbook as **EX 13-Prices**, close the workbook, then exit Excel. Submit the file to your instructor.

FIGURE 13-32

	A	B	C	D
1				
2				
3				
4				
5				
6	Item Code ▼	Product ▼	Price ▼	
7	A43	Cup, small	$8.55	
8	A53	Cup, medium	$9.45	
9	A37	Cup, large	$10.55	
10	A10	Mug, small	$10.75	
11	B98	Water bottle	$10.85	
12	B21	Cold cups	$11.75	
13	A51	Mug, medium	$11.95	
14	A67	Mug, large	$12.55	
15	B54	Tea infuser	$14.55	
16	B76	Travel mug	$18.55	
17	A41	Teapot	$22.75	
18	B11	Tea kettle	$38.75	
19				
20				

Topseller/shutterstock.com

Sharing Excel Files and Incorporating Web Information

CASE ▶ Dawn Parsons, the director of North and Central America at Reason2Go, asks you to share branch sales information with corporate office employees and branch managers using the company's intranet and the web. Dawn wants the North American branches to use shared workbooks to collaborate on sales worksheet data.

Module Objectives

After completing this module, you will be able to:

- Share Excel files
- Set up a shared workbook for multiple users
- Track revisions in a shared workbook
- Apply and modify passwords
- Work with XML schemas
- Import and export XML data
- Share web links
- Import and export HTML data

Files You Will Need

EX 14-1.xlsx	EX 14-9.xml
EX 14-2.xlsx	EX 14-10.htm
EX 14-3.xsd	EX 14-11.xlsx
EX 14-4.xml	EX 14-12.htm
EX 14-5.xml	EX 14-13.xsd
EX 14-6.htm	EX 14-14.xml
EX 14-7.xlsx	EX 14-15.htm
EX 14-8.xsd	

Share Excel Files

Learning Outcomes
- Determine the best way to share Excel workbooks
- Define XML and HTML terms

Microsoft Excel provides many different ways to share spreadsheets with people in your office, in your organization, or anywhere on the web. When you share workbooks, you have to consider how you will protect information that you don't want everyone to see and how you can control revisions others will make to your files. Also, some information you want to use might not be in Excel format. For example, there is a great deal of information published on the web in HTML format, so Excel allows you to import HTML to your worksheets. You can also export your worksheet data in HTML format. However, many companies find the XML format to be more flexible than HTML for storing and exchanging data, so they are increasingly using XML to store and exchange data both internally and externally. Excel allows you to easily import and export XML data. You can also share data using links to workbooks published on OneDrive. **FIGURE 14-1** shows methods of importing to and exporting from workbooks. **CASE** *You need to decide the best way to share Dawn's Excel workbooks with corporate office staff and branch managers.*

DETAILS

To share worksheet information, consider the following issues:

- **Allowing others to use a workbook**

  While many of your workbooks are for your own use, you will want to share some of them with other users. When users **share** your workbooks, they can simultaneously open them from a network server, modify them electronically, and return their revisions to you for incorporation with others' changes. You can view each user's name and the date each change was made. To share a workbook, you need to turn on the sharing feature for that workbook. Dawn wants to obtain feedback on R2G sales data from the branch managers, so you need to share the workbook so others can use it.

- **Controlling access to workbooks on a server**

  When you place a workbook on a network server, you will probably want to control who can open and change it. You can do this using Excel passwords. You decide to assign a password to the workbook, and then post the workbook on the R2G server. You can then give the corporate staff and branch managers the password, so only they can open the workbook and revise it.

- **HTML data**

  You can paste data from a web page into a worksheet and then manipulate and format it using Excel. You can also save Excel workbook information in HTML format so you can publish it on an intranet or on the web. You decide to publish the worksheet with the branch sales information in HTML format on the company intranet, as shown in **FIGURE 14-2**.

- **Working with XML data**

  Importing and storing data in XML format allows you to use it in different situations. For example, a company might store all of its sales data in an XML file and make different parts of the file available to various departments such as marketing and accounting. These departments can extract information that is relevant to their purposes from the file. A subset of the same XML file might be sent to vendors or other business associates who only require certain types of sales data stored in the XML file. You decide to import XML files that contain sales information from the Los Angeles and New York branches to get a sales summary for R2G's U.S. region, as shown in **FIGURE 14-3**.

- **Sharing workbooks in the cloud**

  After you save a workbook on your OneDrive, you can use Excel sharing tools to email links to your workbook, invite people to access the workbook using Excel Online, and even post a workbook link on a social networking site. You decide to share the branch sales results with the managers by saving the workbook in the cloud and sending the managers a link to access the information.

FIGURE 14-1: Importing and exporting data

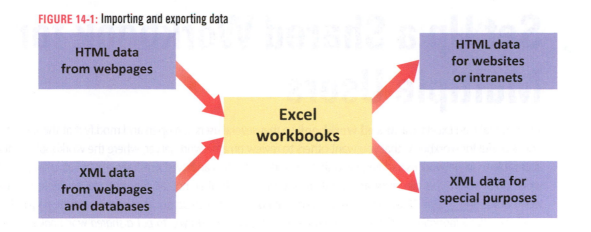

FIGURE 14-2: R2G sales information displayed in a web browser

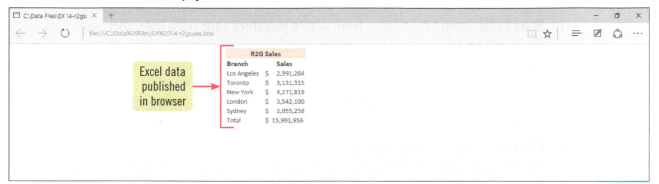

Excel data published in browser →

R2G Sales	
Branch	**Sales**
Los Angeles	$ 2,991,264
Toronto	$ 3,131,515
New York	$ 4,271,819
London	$ 3,542,100
Sydney	$ 2,055,258
Total	$ 15,991,956

FIGURE 14-3: Data imported from XML file

Excel worksheet with imported XML information →

	A	B	C	D	E
1	BRANCH	FNAME	LNAME	SALES	
2	Los Angeles	Kim	Maloney	$ 200,998	
3	Los Angeles	Dan	Green	$ 310,670	
4	Los Angeles	Lisa	Cane	$ 413,200	
5	Los Angeles	Bill	Nason	$ 210,400	
6	Los Angeles	Kathy	Deveney	$ 315,700	
7	Los Angeles	Meg	Lyons	$ 356,345	
8	Los Angeles	Elaine	Hansen	$ 211,345	
9	Los Angeles	Diane	Monroe	$ 215,300	
10	New York	Peg	Lane	$ 305,200	
11	New York	Brad	Bale	$ 150,400	
12	New York	Mary	Dealy	$ 412,200	
13	New York	Peter	Nally	$ 845,200	
14	New York	Julio	Sanchez	$ 312,300	
15	New York	Ann	Lane	$ 195,200	
16	New York	Jack	Bentz	$ 130,400	
17	New York	Paula	Hunt	$ 352,300	
18	New York	Keith	Glenn	$ 151,452	
19	New York	Lynn	McCarthy	$ 232,300	
20	New York	Paul	Reilly	$ 152,300	
21	New York	Rod	Stedman	$ 123,567	
22	New York	Al	Tessier	$ 218,200	
23	New York	Kathy	Vodel	$ 210,400	
24	New York	Ken	Perkins	$ 118,400	
25	**Total**			$ 6,143,777	

Set Up a Shared Workbook for Multiple Users

Learning Outcomes
- Share an Excel workbook
- Apply file sharing options

You can make an Excel file a **shared workbook** so that several users can open and modify it at the same time. This is useful for workbooks that you want others to review on a network server, where the workbook is equally accessible to all network users. When you share a workbook, you can have Excel keep a list of all changes to the workbook, which you can view and print at any time. Note that not all features are available in shared workbooks. **CASE** *Dawn wants to get feedback from selected corporate staff and branch managers before presenting the information at the next corporate staff meeting. She asks you to put a shared workbook containing sales data on the company's network. You begin by making her Excel file a shared workbook.*

STEPS

1. **Start Excel, open EX 14-1.xlsx from where you store your Data Files, then save it as EX 14-NA Sales**

   The workbook with the sales information opens, displaying two sheet tabs. The first contains sales data for R2G's North American branches; the second is a breakdown of the branch sales by sales rep.

2. **Click the Review tab, then click the Share Workbook button in the Changes group**

   The Share Workbook dialog box opens, as shown in **FIGURE 14-4**.

3. **Click the Editing tab if necessary**

   The dialog box lists the names of people who are currently using the workbook. You are the only user, so your name, or the name of the person entered as the computer user, appears, along with the current date and time.

4. **Click to select the check box next to Allow changes by more than one user at the same time. This also allows workbook merging., then click OK**

   A dialog box appears, asking if you want to save the workbook. This will resave it as a shared workbook.

5. **Click OK**

   Excel saves the file as a shared workbook. The title bar now reads EX 14-NA Sales.xlsx [Shared], as shown in **FIGURE 14-5**. This version replaces the unshared version.

Working with Office add-ins

To help manage information on your worksheets, you can insert an Office add-in to an Excel worksheet. The add-in will be available to use for all of your worksheets in the future. For example, there are maps, dictionaries, calendars and other tools that are helpful in working with Excel data. To insert an add-in into Excel, click the Insert tab, click the Store button in the Add-ins group, then select the add-in that you want to insert. To use an add-in that you inserted at an earlier time, click the Insert tab, then click the My Add-ins button in the Add-ins group.

FIGURE 14-4: Share Workbook dialog box

Select to allow multiple
users of the workbook
at the same time

Current users
of the workbook

Share Workbook   ? ✕

Editing | Advanced

☐ Allow changes by more than one user at the same time.
   This also allows workbook merging.

Who has this workbook open now:

Your Name (Exclusive) - 10/25/2017 1:57 PM

Remove User

OK   Cancel

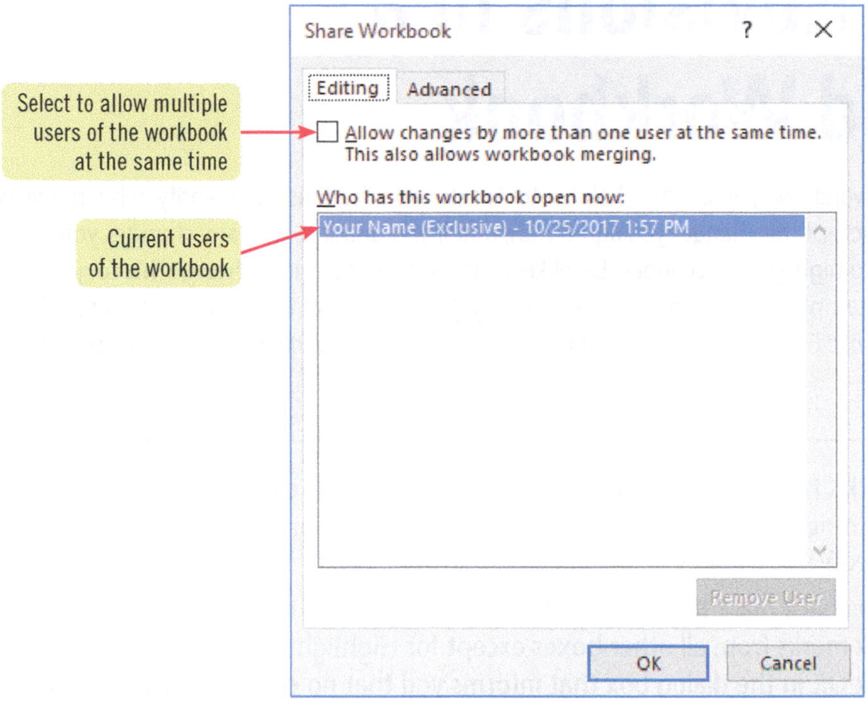

FIGURE 14-5: Shared workbook

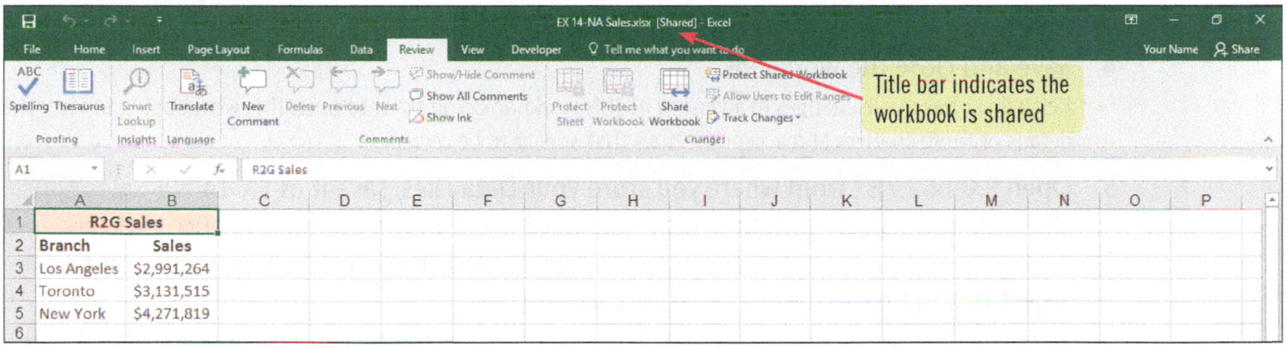

EX 14-NA Sales.xlsx [Shared] - Excel

File   Home   Insert   Page Layout   Formulas   Data   Review   View   Developer   ♀ Tell me what you want to do   Your Name   ♀ Share

Title bar indicates the
workbook is shared

A1   fx   R2G Sales

	A	B	C	D	E	F	G	H	I	J	K	L	M	N	O	P
1	R2G Sales															
2	Branch	Sales														
3	Los Angeles	$2,991,264														
4	Toronto	$3,131,515														
5	New York	$4,271,819														
6																

Merging workbooks

Instead of putting a shared workbook on a server to be shared simultaneously, you might want to distribute copies to your reviewers via e-mail. Once everyone has entered their changes and returned their workbook copies to you, you can merge the changed copies into one master workbook that contains everyone's changes. Each copy you distribute must be designated as shared, and the Change History feature on the Advanced tab of the Share Workbook dialog box must be activated. Occasionally a conflict occurs when two users are trying to edit the same cells in a shared workbook. In this case, the second person to save the file will see a Resolve Conflicts dialog box and need to choose Accept Mine or Accept Other. To merge workbooks, you first need to add the Compare and Merge Workbooks command to the Quick Access Toolbar by clicking the File tab, clicking Options, and clicking Quick Access Toolbar. Click All Commands in the Choose commands from list, click Compare and Merge Workbooks, click Add, then click OK. Once you get the changed copies back, open the master copy of the workbook, then click the Compare and Merge Workbooks button on the Quick Access Toolbar. The Select Files to Merge Into Current Workbook dialog box opens. Select the workbooks you want to merge (you can use the [Ctrl] key to select more than one workbook), then click OK.

Track Revisions in a Shared Workbook

Learning Outcomes
- Review changes to a shared workbook
- Create a change history worksheet

When you share workbooks, it is often helpful to **track** modifications, or identify who made which changes. You can accept the changes you agree with, and if you disagree with any changes you can reject them. In addition to highlighting changes, Excel keeps track of changes in a **change history**, a list of all changes that you can place on a separate worksheet. **CASE** ▶ *Dawn asks you to set up the shared NA Sales workbook so that Excel tracks all future changes. You then open a workbook and review its changes and the change history.*

STEPS

1. **Click the Track Changes button in the Changes group, then click Highlight Changes**

   The Highlight Changes dialog box opens, as shown in **FIGURE 14-6**, allowing you to turn on change tracking. You can also specify which changes to highlight and where you want to display changes.

2. **Click to add a check mark to the Track changes while editing check box if necessary, remove check marks from all other boxes except for Highlight changes on screen, click OK, then click OK in the dialog box that informs you that no changes have yet been made**

   Leaving the When, Who, and Where check boxes blank allows you to track all changes.

3. **Click the Sales by Rep sheet tab, change the sales figure for Sully in cell C3 to 250,000, press [Enter], then move the mouse pointer over the cell you just changed**

   A border with a small triangle in the upper-left corner appears around the cell you changed, and a ScreenTip appears with the date, the time, and details about the change, as shown in **FIGURE 14-7**.

4. **Save and close the workbook**

   Keith Silva has made changes to a version of this workbook. You want to open this workbook and view the details of these changes and accept the ones that appear to be correct.

5. **Open EX 14-2.xlsx from where you store your Data Files, save it as EX 14-NA Sales Edits, click the Review tab, click the Track Changes button in the Changes group, click Accept/Reject Changes, click the When check box in the Select Changes to Accept or Reject dialog box to deselect it, then click OK**

   You will accept the first four changes that Keith made to the workbook and reject his last change. You also want to see a list of all changes.

6. **Click Accept four times, click Reject to undo Keith's fifth change, click the Track Changes button in the Changes group, click Highlight Changes, click the When check box in the Highlight Changes dialog box to deselect it, click to select the List changes on a new sheet check box, then click OK**

   A new sheet named History opens, as shown in **FIGURE 14-8**, with Keith's changes in a filtered list. Because saving the file closes the History sheet, you need to copy the information to a new worksheet.

7. **Copy the range A1:I6 on the History sheet, click the New sheet button ⊕ next to the History sheet tab, on the new sheet click the Home tab, click the Paste button in the Clipboard group, widen the worksheet columns where necessary, then rename the new sheet tab Saved History**

8. **Add a footer with your name to the Saved History sheet, save and close the workbook, then submit the workbook to your instructor**

FIGURE 14-6: Highlight Changes dialog box

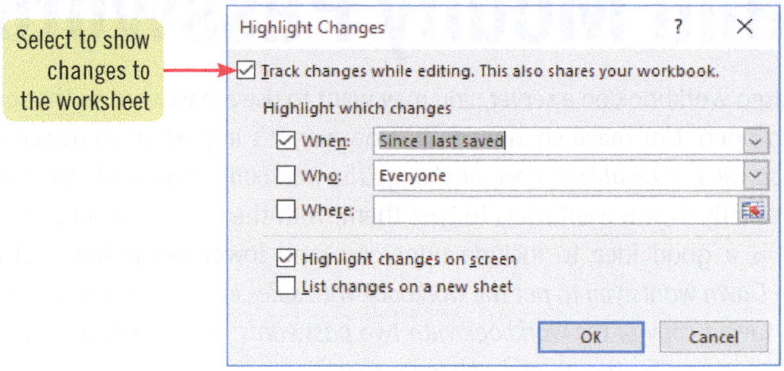

Select to show changes to the worksheet →

FIGURE 14-7: Tracked change

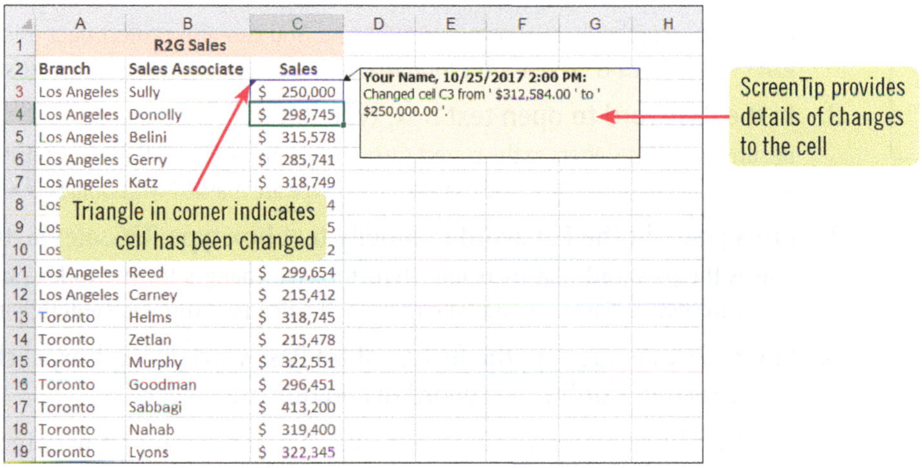

ScreenTip provides details of changes to the cell

Triangle in corner indicates cell has been changed

FIGURE 14-8: History sheet tab with change history

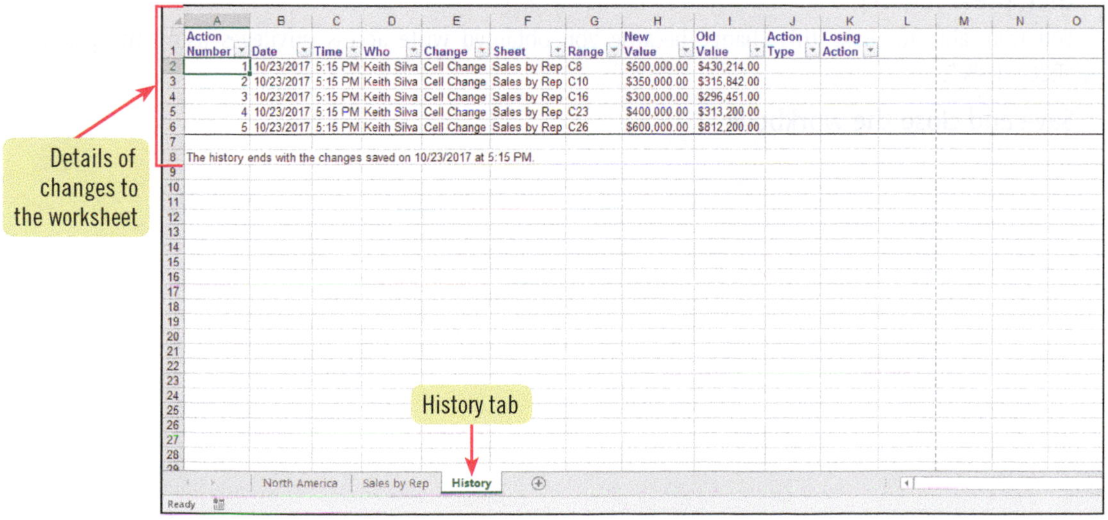

Details of changes to the worksheet

History tab

Apply and Modify Passwords

**Learning
Outcomes**
• Create a password
  to open a workbook
• Create a password
  to modify a
  workbook

When you place a shared workbook on a server, you may want to use a password so that only authorized people will be able to open it or make changes to it. However, it's important to remember that *if you lose your password, you will not be able to open or change the workbook.* Passwords are case sensitive, so you must type them exactly as you want users to type them, with the same spacing and using the same case. For security, it is a good idea to include uppercase and lowercase letters and numbers in a password. **CASE** ▶ *Dawn wants you to put the workbook with sales information on one of the company's servers. You decide to save a copy of the workbook with two passwords: one that users will need to open it, and another that they must use in order to make changes to it.*

STEPS

QUICK TIP
You can also use a password to encrypt the contents of a workbook: click the File tab, click Protect Workbook in the Info pane, click Encrypt with Password, then enter a password.

1. **Re-open EX 14-1.xlsx from where you store your Data Files, click the File tab, click Save As, navigate to where you store your Data Files, click the Tools list arrow at the bottom of the Save As dialog box, then click General Options**

   The General Options dialog box opens, with two password boxes: one to open the workbook, and one to modify the workbook, as shown in **FIGURE 14-9**. You can also protect data using a password to encrypt it. **Encrypted data** is encoded in a form that only authorized people with a password can decode.

2. **In the Password to open text box, type R2Gmanager#**

   Be sure to type the letters in the correct cases. This is the password that users must type to open the workbook. When you enter passwords, the characters you type are masked with bullets (• • •) for security purposes.

3. **Press [Tab], in the Password to modify text box type R2Gsales%, then click OK**

   This is the password that users must type to make changes to the workbook, also referred to as having **write access**. A dialog box asks you to verify the first password by reentering it.

4. **Enter R2Gmanager# in the first Confirm Password dialog box, click OK, enter R2Gsales% in the second Confirm Password dialog box, then click OK**

5. **Change the filename to EX 14-NA Sales PW, if necessary navigate to where you store your Data Files, click Save, then close the workbook**

QUICK TIP
To delete a password, reopen the General Options dialog box, highlight the symbols for the existing password, press [Delete], click OK, change the filename, then click Save.

6. **Reopen EX 14-NA Sales PW, enter the password R2Gmanager# when prompted for a password, click OK, then enter R2Gsales% to obtain write access**

   The Password dialog box is shown in **FIGURE 14-10**.

7. **Click OK, change the sales figure for the Los Angeles branch in cell B3 to 3,500,000, then press [Enter]**

   You were able to make this change because you obtained write access privileges using the password "R2Gsales%".

8. **Save and close the workbook**

FIGURE 14-9: General Options dialog box

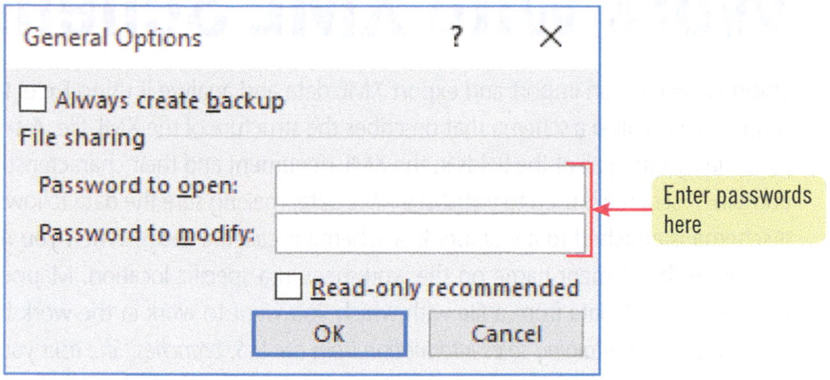

General Options ? ✕

☐ Always create backup

File sharing

Password to open: [   ] } ← Enter passwords here

Password to modify: [   ]

☐ Read-only recommended

[OK] [Cancel]

FIGURE 14-10: Password entry prompt

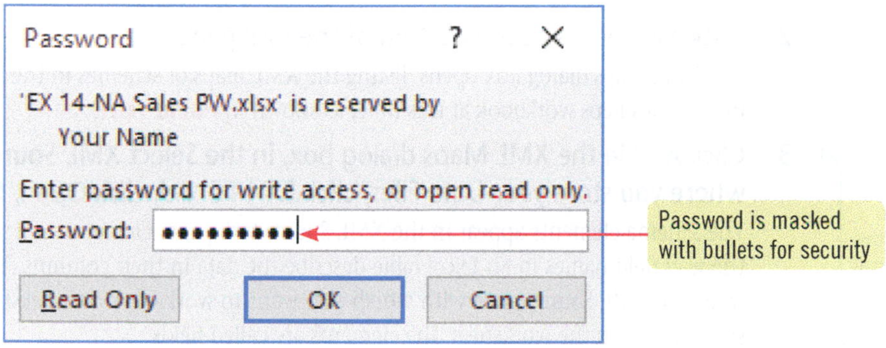

Password ? ✕

'EX 14-NA Sales PW.xlsx' is reserved by
    Your Name

Enter password for write access, or open read only.

Password: [••••••••••|] ← Password is masked with bullets for security

[Read Only] [OK] [Cancel]

Creating strong passwords for Excel workbooks

Strong passwords will help to protect your workbooks from security threats. A **strong password** has at least 14 characters that are not commonly used. Although your password needs to be easy to remember, it should be difficult for other people to guess. Avoid using your birthday, your pet's name, or other personal information in your password. Also avoid dictionary words and repeated characters. Instead, mix the types of characters using uppercase and lowercase letters, numbers, and special characters such as @ and %. See **TABLE 14-1** for rules and examples for creating strong passwords.

TABLE 14-1: Rules for creating strong passwords

rule	example
Include numbers	5qRyz8O6w
Add symbols	lQx!u%z7q9
Increase complexity	4!%5Zq^c6#
Use long passwords	Z7#l%2!q9!6@i9&Wb

Work with XML Schemas

Learning Outcomes
- Apply an XML schema to a workbook
- Map XML properties to a workbook

Using Excel you can import and export XML data and analyze it using Excel tools. To import XML data, Excel requires a file called a schema that describes the structure of the XML file. A **schema** contains the rules for the XML file by listing all of the fields in the XML document and their characteristics, such as the type of data they contain. A schema is used to **validate** XML data, making sure the data follows the rules given in the file. Once a schema is attached to a workbook, a schema is called a **map**. When you map an element to a worksheet, you place the element name on the worksheet in a specific location. Mapping XML elements allows you to choose the XML data from a file with which you want to work in the worksheet. **CASE** *Dawn has been given XML files containing sales information from the U.S. branches. She asks you to prepare a workbook to import the sales representatives' XML data. You begin by adding a schema to a worksheet that describes the XML data.*

STEPS

1. Create a new workbook, save it as EX 14-Sales Reps in the location where you store your Data Files, click the Developer tab, then click the Source button in the XML group

QUICK TIP
If the Developer tab does not appear, click the File tab, click Options, click Customize Ribbon, and select the Developer check box.

The XML Source pane opens. This is where you specify a schema, or map, to import. A schema has the extension .xsd. Dawn has provided you with a schema she received from the IT Department describing the XML file structure.

2. Click XML Maps at the bottom of the task pane

The XML Maps dialog box opens, listing the XML maps or schemas in the workbook. There are no schemas in the Sales Reps workbook at this time, as shown in **FIGURE 14-11**.

3. Click Add in the XML Maps dialog box, in the Select XML Source dialog box navigate to where you store your Data Files, click EX 14-3.xsd, click Open, then click OK

QUICK TIP
You can delete a map from a workbook by clicking the XML Maps button at the bottom of the XML Source task pane to open the XML Maps dialog box. In the dialog box select the map that you want to delete, click Delete, then click OK.

The schema elements appear in the XML Source task pane. Elements in a schema describe data similarly to the way field names in an Excel table describe the data in their columns. You choose the schema elements from the XML Source pane with which you want to work on your worksheet and map them to the worksheet. Once on the worksheet, the elements are called fields.

4. Click the BRANCH element in the XML Source task pane and drag it to cell A1 on the worksheet, then use FIGURE 14-12 as a guide to drag the FNAME, LNAME, SALES, and ENUMBER fields to the worksheet

The mapped elements appear in bolded format in the XML Source pane. The fields on the worksheet have filter arrows because Excel automatically creates a table on the worksheet as you map the schema elements. You decide to remove the ENUMBER field from the table.

5. Right-click the ENUMBER element in the XML Source task pane, then click Remove element

TROUBLE
Make sure that you right-click the ENUMBER element in the XML Source task pane and not the field on the worksheet.

ENUMBER is no longer formatted in bold because it is no longer mapped to the worksheet. This means that when XML data is imported, the ENUMBER field will not be populated with data. However, the field name remains in the table on the worksheet.

6. Drag the table resizing arrow to the left to remove cell E1 from the table

Because you plan to import XML data from different files, you want to be sure that data from one file will not overwrite data from another file when it is imported into the worksheet. You also want to be sure that Excel validates the imported data against the rules specified in the schema.

7. Click any cell in the table, click the Developer tab, then click the Map Properties button in the XML group

The XML Map Properties dialog box opens, as shown in **FIGURE 14-13**.

8. Click the Validate data against schema for import and export check box to select it, click the Append new data to existing XML tables option button to select it, then click OK

You are ready to import XML data into your worksheet.

FIGURE 14-11: XML Maps dialog box

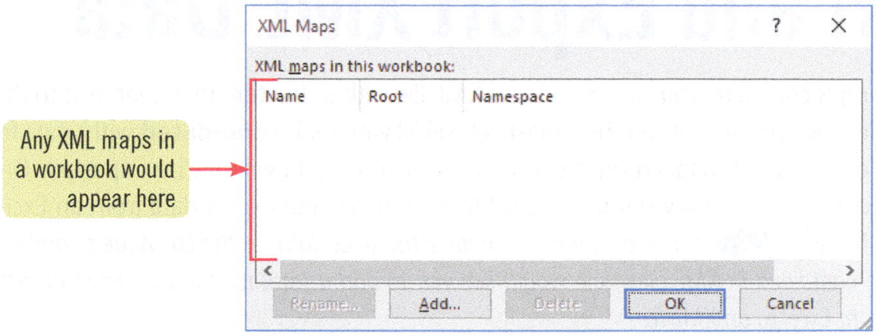

Any XML maps in a workbook would appear here

XML Maps

XML maps in this workbook:

Name	Root	Namespace

Rename... Add... Delete OK Cancel

FIGURE 14-12: XML elements mapped to the worksheet

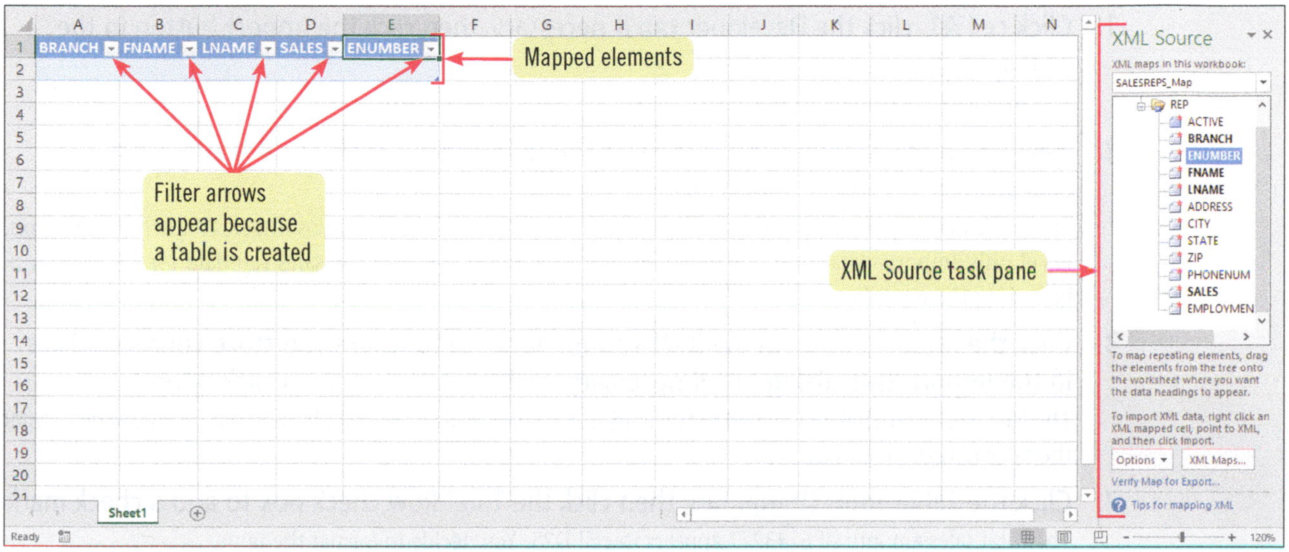

Mapped elements

Filter arrows appear because a table is created

	A	B	C	D	E
1	BRANCH	FNAME	LNAME	SALES	ENUMBER

XML Source task pane

XML Source

XML maps in this workbook:

SALESREPS_Map

REP
- ACTIVE
- BRANCH
- ENUMBER
- FNAME
- LNAME
- ADDRESS
- CITY
- STATE
- ZIP
- PHONENUM
- SALES
- EMPLOYMEN

To map repeating elements, drag the elements from the tree onto the worksheet where you want the data headings to appear.

To import XML data, right click an XML mapped cell, point to XML, and then click Import.

Options ▼   XML Maps...

Verify Map for Export...

Tips for mapping XML

Sheet1

Ready   120%

FIGURE 14-13: XML Map Properties dialog box

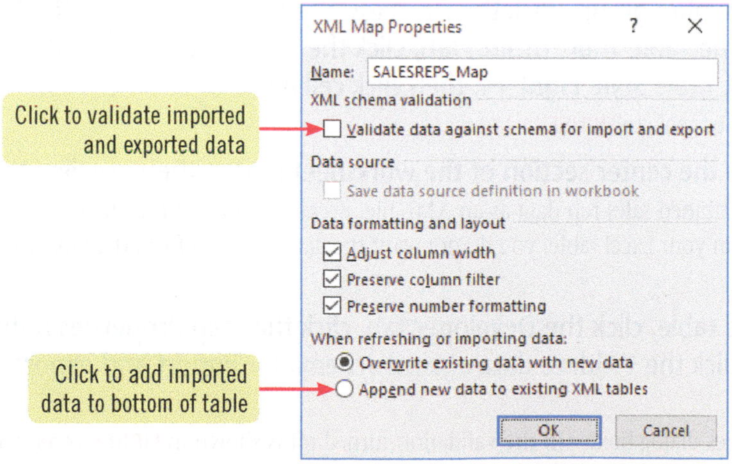

XML Map Properties

Name: SALESREPS_Map

XML schema validation

Click to validate imported and exported data

☐ Validate data against schema for import and export

Data source

☐ Save data source definition in workbook

Data formatting and layout

☑ Adjust column width
☑ Preserve column filter
☑ Preserve number formatting

When refreshing or importing data:
◉ Overwrite existing data with new data

Click to add imported data to bottom of table

○ Append new data to existing XML tables

OK   Cancel

Excel 2016

Learning more about XML

XML is a universal data format for business and industry information sharing. Using XML, you can store structured information related to services, products, or business transactions and easily share and exchange the information with others. XML provides a way to express structure in data. Structured data is tagged, or marked up, to indicate its content. For example, an XML data marker (tag) that contains an item's cost might be named COST. Excel's capability to work with XML data lets you access the large amount of information stored in the XML format. For example, organizations have developed many XML applications with a specific focus, such as MathML (Mathematical Markup Language) and RETML (Real Estate Transaction Markup Language).

Import and Export XML Data

Learning Outcomes
- Import XML data into a workbook
- Export Excel data into an XML file

After XML mapping is complete, you can import any XML file with a structure that conforms to the workbook schema. The mapped elements on the worksheet will fill with (or be **populated** with) data from the XML file. If an element is not mapped on the worksheet, then its data will not be imported. Once you import the XML data, you can analyze it using Excel tools. You can also export data from an Excel workbook to an XML file. **CASE** *Dawn asks you to combine the sales data for the Los Angeles and New York branches that are contained in XML files. She would like you to add a total for the combined branches and export the data from Excel to an XML file.*

STEPS

1. **Click cell A1, click the Developer tab if necessary, then click the Import button in the XML group**

   The Import XML dialog box opens.

2. **Navigate to where you store your Data Files if necessary, click EX 14-4.xml, then click Import**

   The worksheet is populated with data from the XML file that contains the Los Angeles branch information. Excel only imports data for the mapped elements. You decide to add the sales rep data for the New York branch to the worksheet.

3. **Click the Import button in the XML group, navigate to where you store your Data Files in the Import XML dialog box if necessary, click EX 14-5.xml, then click Import**

   The New York branch data is added to the worksheet, below the Los Angeles branch data. You decide to total the sales figures for all sales reps.

4. **Click the Table Tools Design tab, then click the Total Row check box to add a check mark**

   The total sales amount of 6143777 appears in cell D25. You decide to format the table.

5. **Select the range D2:D25, click the Home tab, click the Accounting Number Format button $ in the Number group, click the Decrease Decimal button ⬓ in the Number group twice, click the Table Tools Design tab, click the More button ⬓ in the Table Styles group, select Table Style Light 14, then click cell A1**

   Compare your completed table to **FIGURE 14-14**.

6. **Enter your name in the center section of the worksheet footer, then preview the table**

   You will export the combined sales rep data as an XML file. Because not all of the elements in the schema were mapped to fields in your Excel table, you do not want the data exported from the table to be validated against the schema.

7. **Click any cell in the table, click the Developer tab, click the Map Properties button in the XML group, then click the Validate data against schema for import and export check box to deselect it**

   The XML Map Properties dialog box with the validation turned off is shown in **FIGURE 14-15**. You are ready to export the XML data.

8. **Click OK, click the Export button in the XML group, navigate to where you store your Data Files in the Export XML dialog box, enter the name EX 14-US Reps in the File name text box, click Export, then save and close the workbook**

   The sales data is saved in XML format, in the file called EX 14-US Reps.xml.

FIGURE 14-14: Completed table with combined sales rep data

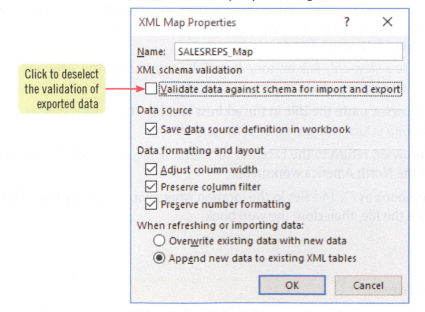

	A	B	C	D	E	F
1	BRANCH	FNAME	LNAME	SALES		
2	Los Angeles	Kim	Maloney	$ 200,998		
3	Los Angeles	Dan	Green	$ 310,670		
4	Los Angeles	Lisa	Cane	$ 413,200		
5	Los Angeles	Bill	Nason	$ 210,400		
6	Los Angeles	Kathy	Deveney	$ 315,700		
7	Los Angeles	Meg	Lyons	$ 356,345		
8	Los Angeles	Elaine	Hansen	$ 211,345		
9	Los Angeles	Diane	Monroe	$ 215,300		
10	New York	Peg	Lane	$ 305,200		
11	New York	Brad	Bale	$ 150,400		
12	New York	Mary	Dealy	$ 412,200		
13	New York	Peter	Nally	$ 845,200		
14	New York	Julio	Sanchez	$ 312,300		
15	New York	Ann	Lane	$ 195,200		
16	New York	Jack	Bentz	$ 130,400		
17	New York	Paula	Hunt	$ 352,300		
18	New York	Keith	Glenn	$ 151,452		
19	New York	Lynn	McCarthy	$ 232,300		
20	New York	Paul	Reilly	$ 152,300		
21	New York	Rod	Stedman	$ 123,567		
22	New York	Al	Tessier	$ 218,200		
23	New York	Kathy	Vodel	$ 210,400		
24	New York	Ken	Perkins	$ 118,400		
25	Total			$ 6,143,777		
26						
27						

Imported data is formatted

Total sales

Sheet1

FIGURE 14-15: XML Map Properties dialog box

XML Map Properties ? ✕

Name: SALESREPS_Map

XML schema validation

☐ Validate data against schema for import and export

Click to deselect the validation of exported data

Data source

☑ Save data source definition in workbook

Data formatting and layout

☑ Adjust column width
☑ Preserve column filter
☑ Preserve number formatting

When refreshing or importing data:

○ Overwrite existing data with new data
◉ Append new data to existing XML tables

OK   Cancel

Importing XML data without a schema

You can import XML data without a schema, and Excel will create one for you. If you choose this method, all of the XML elements are mapped to the Excel worksheet, and the data in all of the fields is populated using the XML file. When a schema is not used, you are unable to validate the data that is imported. You also need to delete all of the fields in the table that you will not use in the worksheet, which can be time consuming.

Share Web Links

Learning Outcomes
- Save a workbook on OneDrive
- Copy a workbook web link

Often you'll want to share your Excel workbooks with co-workers. You can do this by sending them a link to your workbook. When you send a link to your workbook that is saved on your OneDrive, your co-workers can use Excel Online to work with your file in the cloud. When you create the link, you can allow users to view the workbook, or to view and edit it. **CASE** ▶ *Dawn is working on the sales results with the branch managers. She asks you to save the sales information in the cloud and give her a link that she can share with the managers.*

STEPS

1. **Re-open EX 14-1.xlsx from where you store your Data Files, then save it as EX 14-Sales**
   You need to save the file to your OneDrive account before you can send a link to it.

2. **Click the File tab, click Share, then click Share with People if necessary**
   The Share screen shows the steps to invite people to use your workbook as shown in **FIGURE 14-16**.

3. **Click Save to Cloud, navigate to your OneDrive location, then click Save in the Save As dialog box**
   The workbook is now saved to your OneDrive, and you can invite other people to work with it.

4. **Click the File tab, click Share, then click the Share with People button**
   The Share pane opens on the right side of the worksheet. In this pane, you can invite people to either view or edit your workbook by entering their email addresses in the Invite people text box and selecting Can edit or Can view from the drop down list. You can also add a message to your invitations before clicking the Share button. Rather than sending invitations, you will get a link to the workbook to share with the branch managers.

5. **Click Get a sharing link**
   You will see link options in the Share pane as shown in **FIGURE 14-17**. You can choose to get a **View-only link** which allows people to view your Excel file, or you can select an **Edit link** which allows people to edit the file. You decide to create a View-only Link.

6. **Click the Create a view-only link button, then click Copy to copy the view-only Link URL**
   You decide to test the web link address by pasting it in your browser.

7. **Open your browser, paste the URL in the address text box, then press [Enter]**
   The workbook opens in Excel Online as shown in **FIGURE 14-18**.

8. **Close your browser, return to the Excel EX 14-Sales.xlsx file, then paste the copied link in cell A7 of the North America worksheet**

9. **Save the workbook as EX 14-Sales in the location where you store your Data Files, click Yes to replace the file, then close the workbook**

Creating your own web queries

The easiest way to retrieve data from a particular webpage on a regular basis is to create a customized web query. Click the Data tab, click the From Web button in the Get External Data group. In the Address text box in the New Web Query dialog box, type the address of the web page from which you want to retrieve data, then click Go. Click the yellow arrows next to the information you want to bring into a worksheet or click the upper-left arrow to import the entire page, verify that the information that you want to import has a blue checkmark next to it, then click Import. The Import Data dialog box opens and allows you to specify where you want the imported data to appear in the worksheet or workbook. You can save a query for future use by clicking the Save Query button 📇 in the New Web Query dialog box before you click Import. The query is saved as a file with an .iqy file extension.

FIGURE 14-16: Share window with invite options

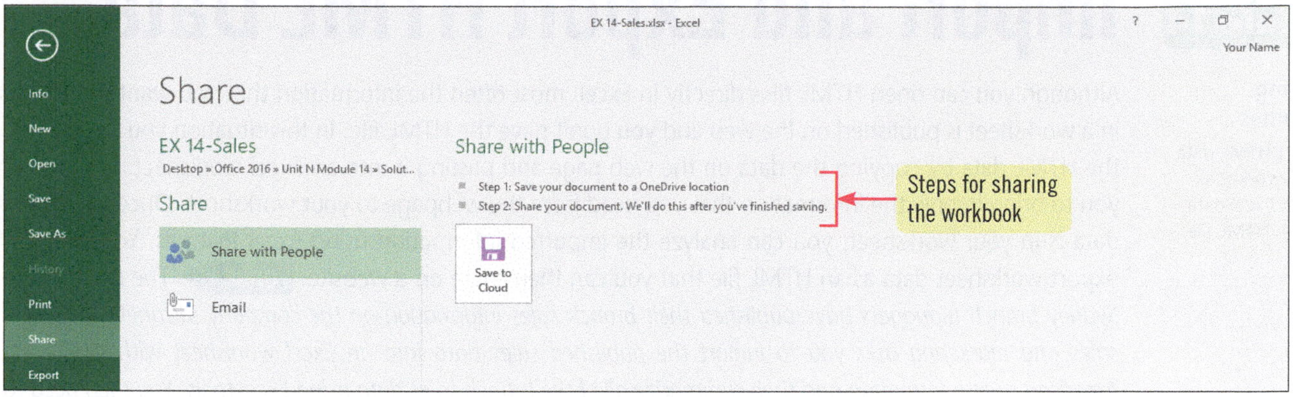

Share

EX 14-Sales
Desktop » Office 2016 » Unit N Module 14 » Solut...

Share

Share with People

Email

Share with People

Step 1: Save your document to a OneDrive location
Step 2: Share your document. We'll do this after you've finished saving.

Steps for sharing the workbook

Save to Cloud

FIGURE 14-17: Share pane with link options

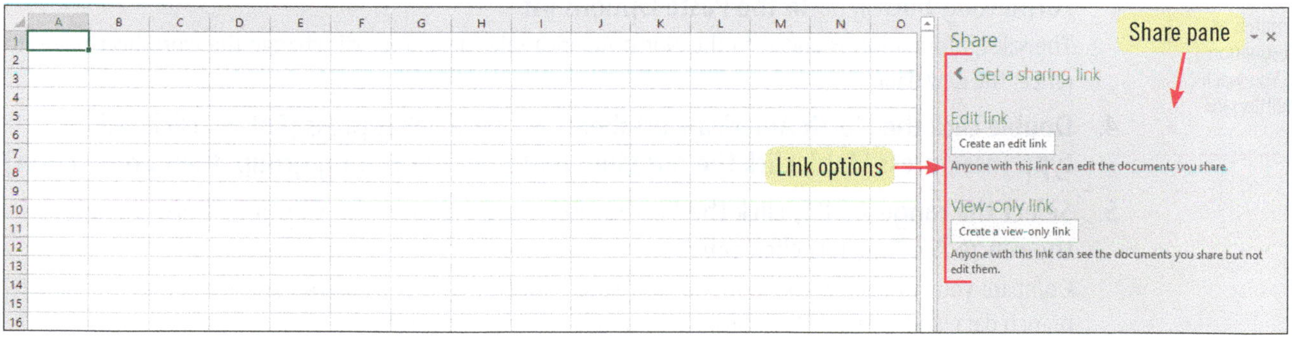

Share pane

Share

← Get a sharing link

Edit link

Create an edit link

Anyone with this link can edit the documents you share.

Link options

View-only link

Create a view-only link

Anyone with this link can see the documents you share but not edit them.

FIGURE 14-18: Workbook in Excel Online

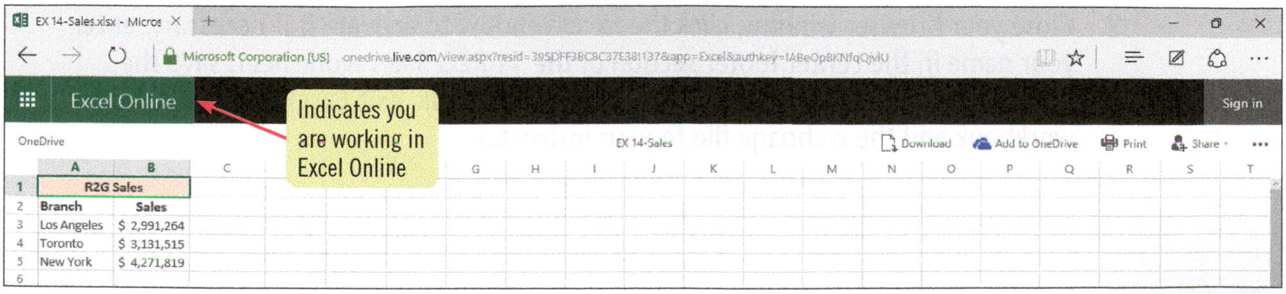

Excel Online

Indicates you are working in Excel Online

OneDrive

Sign in

EX 14-Sales

Download   Add to OneDrive   Print   Share ▾   •••

	A	B
1	R2G Sales	
2	Branch	Sales
3	Los Angeles	$ 2,991,264
4	Toronto	$ 3,131,515
5	New York	$ 4,271,819
6		

Import and Export HTML Data

Although you can open HTML files directly in Excel, most often the information that you want to include in a worksheet is published on the web and you don't have the HTML file. In this situation you can import the HTML data by copying the data on the web page and pasting it into an Excel worksheet. This allows you to bring in only the information that you need from the webpage to your worksheet. Once the HTML data is in your worksheet, you can analyze the imported information using Excel features. You can also export worksheet data as an HTML file that you can then share on a website. **CASE** ▶ *The London and Sydney branch managers have published their branch sales information on the company intranet. The VP of sales and marketing asks you to import the published sales data into an Excel worksheet with the North American sales information and then summarize all of the branch sales data using Excel tools. You then need to export the summarized data to an HTML file for posting on the company intranet.*

STEPS

1. **In File Explorer, navigate to the location where you store your Data Files, double-click EX 14-6.htm to open it in your browser, then copy the two table rows on the web page containing the London and Sydney sales information**

   You are ready to paste the information from the web page into an Excel worksheet.

2. **Re-open EX 14-1.xlsx from where you store your Data Files, then save it as EX 14-R2G Sales**

3. **Right-click cell A6 on the North America sheet, then click the Match Destination Formatting button 📋 in the Paste Options list**

   The sales information is added to the North America sales data. You will change the worksheet name to reflect the new data.

4. **Double click the North America worksheet tab, type Sales, press [Enter], click cell A8, type Total, press [Tab], click the AutoSum button in the Editing group, then press [Enter]**

5. **Select the range A5:B5, click the Format Painter button in the Clipboard group, select the range A6:B8, then click cell A1**

   Compare your worksheet to **FIGURE 14-19**. You are finished with the analysis and formatting of the R2G branch data, and are ready to publish this information in a web page.

6. **Click the File tab, click Save As, then browse to where you store your Data Files**

   The Save As dialog box lets you specify what workbook parts you want to publish.

7. **Click the Save as type list arrow, click Web Page (*.htm;*.html), edit the filename to read EX 14-r2gsales.htm, click the Selection: Sheet option button, click Publish, then click Publish again**

   The HTML file, containing only Sales worksheet, is saved in your Data Files location.

8. **In File Explorer, navigate to where you store your Data Files, then double-click the file EX 14-r2gsales.htm**

   The HTML version of your worksheet opens in your default browser, similar to **FIGURE 14-20**.

9. **Close your browser window, click the Excel window to activate it if necessary, enter your name in the center footer section of the 14-R2G Sales worksheet, save the workbook, preview the worksheet, close the workbook, exit Excel, then submit the workbook and the webpage file to your instructor**

FIGURE 14-19: Worksheet with R2G sales data

Formatted table with data added from HTML file →

	A	B	C
1	R2G Sales		
2	Branch	Sales	
3	Los Angeles	$ 2,991,264	
4	Toronto	$ 3,131,515	
5	New York	$ 4,271,819	
6	London	$ 3,542,100	
7	Sydney	$ 2,055,258	
8	Total	$15,991,956	
9			
10			
11			

← Two added rows

FIGURE 14-20: R2G Sales as webpage

C:\Data Files\EX 14-r2gs

file:///C:/Data%20Files/EX%2014-r2gsales.htm

Excel worksheet data displayed in a browser →

R2G Sales	
Branch	Sales
Los Angeles	$ 2,991,264
Toronto	$ 3,131,515
New York	$ 4,271,819
London	$ 3,542,100
Sydney	$ 2,055,258
Total	$ 15,991,956

Adding web hyperlinks to a worksheet

In Excel worksheets, you can create hyperlinks to information on the web. Every webpage is identified by a unique web address called a Uniform Resource Locator (URL). To create a hyperlink to a webpage, click the cell for which you want to create a hyperlink, click the Insert tab, click the Hyperlink button in the Links group, under Link to: make sure Existing File or Web Page is selected, specify the target for the hyperlink (the URL) in the Address text box, then click OK. If there is text in the cell, the text format changes to become a blue underlined hyperlink or the color the current workbook theme uses for hyperlinks. If there is no text in the cell, the website's URL appears in the cell.

Practice

Concepts Review

FIGURE 14-21

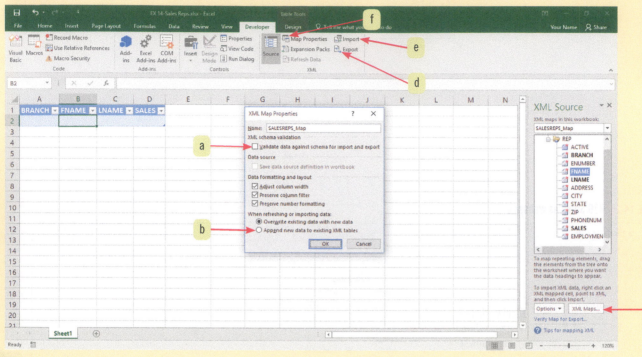

1. Which element do you click to add imported XML data below existing data in a table?
2. Which element do you click to save workbook data to an XML file?
3. Which element do you click to change the way XML data is imported and exported?
4. Which element do you click to check imported XML data using the schema rules?
5. Which element do you click to bring in XML data to a workbook table?
6. Which element do you click to add a schema to an Excel workbook?

Match each item with the statement that best describes it.

7. Change history
8. Password
9. xsd
10. Shared workbook
11. iqy

a. The file extension for an XML schema
b. A record of edits others have made to a worksheet
c. Used to protect a workbook from unauthorized use
d. The file extension for a web query
e. A file used by many people on a network

Select the best answer from the list of choices.

12. **Which of the following sharing links allows people to make changes to your Excel data?**
    a. Change Link
    b. Edit Link
    c. View-only Link
    d. Import Link

13. **Which of the following is the best example of a strong password for a workbook?**
    a. myfile
    b. MollY
    c. MYFILE
    d. my%File95gz

14. **A file that describes the structure of XML data is called a:**
    a. Query.
    b. Schema.
    c. Layout.
    d. Detail File.

15. **The process of selecting XML elements to include on a worksheet is called:**
    a. Sharing.
    b. Selecting.
    c. Mapping.
    d. Loading.

Skills Review

1. **Set up a shared workbook for multiple users.**
   a. Start Excel, open EX 14-7.xlsx from where you store your Data Files, then save it as **EX 14-Store Sales**.
   b. Use the Share Workbook command on the Review tab to set up the workbook so that more than one person can use it at one time.
   c. Save the workbook when prompted.
   d. Verify the workbook is marked as Shared in the title bar.
   e. Review the regional sales data for the first two quarters of the year.

2. **Track revisions in a shared workbook.**
   a. Change the Seattle sales to **$40,000** for the first quarter and **$47,000** for the second quarter.
   b. Save the file.
   c. Display the History sheet by opening the Highlight Changes dialog box, deselecting the When check box, then selecting the option for List changes on a new sheet.
   d. Compare your History sheet to **FIGURE 14-22**.
   e. Copy the range A1:I3 in the History sheet, add a new worksheet and paste the range in the new worksheet. Widen the columns

   FIGURE 14-22

	A	B	C	D	E	F	G	H	I	J	K	L	M	N	O	P	Q	R
1	Action Number	Date	Time	Who	Change	Sheet	Range	New Value	Old Value	Action Type	Losing Action							
2	1	10/26/2017	10:50 AM	Your Name	Cell Change	Sales	C2	$40,000.00	$31,988.00									
3	2	10/26/2017	10:50 AM	Your Name	Cell Change	Sales	D2	$47,000.00	$27,845.00									
4																		
5	The history ends with the changes saved on 10/26/2017 at 10:50 AM.																	
6																		
7																		
8																		

   to display all of the information, then rename the new worksheet to **History Sheet**.
   f. Enter your name in the History Sheet footer, then preview the History Sheet.
   g. Save the workbook, close it, then submit the workbook to your instructor.

3. **Apply and modify passwords.**
   a. Re-open EX 14-7.xlsx from where you store your Data Files, open the Save As dialog box, then open the General Options dialog box.
   b. Set the password to open the workbook as **Sales20** and the password to modify it as **FirstHalf20**.
   c. Save the password-protected file as **EX 14-Store Sales PW** in the location where you store your Data Files.
   d. Close the workbook.
   e. Use the assigned passwords to reopen the workbook and verify that you can change it by adding your name in the center section of the Sales sheet footer, save the workbook, preview the Sales worksheet, close the workbook, then submit the workbook to your instructor.

4. **Work with XML schemas.**

   a. Open a new blank workbook, then save it as **EX 14-Contact Information** in the location where you store your Data Files.

   b. Open the XML Source pane, and add the XML schema EX 14-8.xsd to the workbook.

   c. Map the FNAME element to cell A1 on the worksheet, LNAME to cell B1, PHONENUM to cell C1, and EMPLOYMENT_DATE to cell D1.

   d. Remove the EMPLOYMENT_DATE element from the map, then drag the table border to delete the field from it.

   e. Use the XML Map Properties dialog box to make sure imported XML data is validated using the schema, and that new data will be appended to existing XML tables.

5. **Import and export XML data.**

   a. Import the XML file EX 14-9.xml into the workbook.

   b. Sort the worksheet list in ascending order by LNAME.

   c. Apply the Table Style Light 10 to the table, then compare your screen to **FIGURE 14-23**.

   d. Enter your name in the center section of the worksheet footer, save the workbook, then preview the worksheet.

   e. Use the XML Map Properties dialog box to turn off the validation for imported and exported worksheet data, export the worksheet data to an XML file named **EX 14-Contact**, then save and close the workbook.

FIGURE 14-23

	A	B	C
1	FNAME	LNAME	PHONENUM
2	Keith	Conway	503-215-9214
3	Jess	Gold	503-222-3251
4	Ellen	Johnson	503-221-2661
5	Larry	Mendez	503-220-6525
6	Kyle	Menzie	503-203-8854
7	Beth	Norris	503-226-6321
8	Peter	Reilly	503-220-3647
9	Mary	Saunders	503-215-6336
10			

6. **Share web links.**

   a. Open EX 14-7.xlsx from the location where you store your Data Files, then save it as **EX 14-Region Sales**.

   b. Save the EX-Region Sales file to your OneDrive.

   c. Add a new worksheet to the workbook with the name **Share Links**. In the new sheet, enter **View-only link** in cell A1. Get a sharing link that allows the recipient to only view the workbook. Paste the link in cell B1.

   d. Enter **Edit link** in cell A2. Get a sharing link that allows the recipient to edit the workbook. Paste the link in cell B2. Widen columns A and B to fit the labels and links, then change the page orientation to landscape.

   e. Compare your screen to **FIGURE 14-24**. (Your links will be different.)

   f. Enter your name in the center section of the Share Links worksheet header, preview the worksheet, then save the workbook in the location where you store your Data Files.

FIGURE 14-24

	A	B
1	View-only link	https://onedrive.live.com/redir?page=view&resid=395DFF3BC8C37E38!145&authkey=!ANTveTEUFNWlce8
2	Edit link	https://onedrive.live.com/redir?page=view&resid=395DFF3BC8C37E38!145&authkey=!ANkh4-UOQbZqUCg
3		

   g. Save a copy of the workbook where you store your Data Files as **EX 14-Region Sales**, clicking Yes to replace the existing file, close the workbook, and submit the workbook to your instructor.

7. **Import and export HTML data.**

   a. Re-open EX 14-7.xlsx from the location where you store your Data Files, then save it as **EX 14-Sales2**.

   b. Open EX 14-10.htm in your browser from the location where you store your Data Files. Copy the data in the four rows of the webpage (not the column headings), and paste it below the data in the Sales sheet of the EX 14-Sales2 workbook.

   c. On the Sales sheet, enter **Total** in cell A27, and use **AutoSum** in cells C27 and D27 to total the values in columns C and D.

   d. Adjust the formatting for the new rows to match the other rows on the Sales sheet, add your name to the center section of the worksheet footer, save the workbook, then preview the Sales sheet.

Skills Review (continued)

e. Save the data on the Sales sheet as an HTML file with the name **sales2.htm**.

f. Close the workbook, exit Excel, open the sales2.htm file in your browser, compare your screen to FIGURE 14-25, close your browser, then submit the sales2.htm file to your instructor.

Independent Challenge 1

You are the aquatics manager at a local health center. One of your responsibilities is to work with the center's director on the water aerobics schedule. You use shared Excel workbooks to help you with this scheduling by sharing the workbook containing your first draft schedule with the director. You have received the shared workbook from the director with her changes and you will review the workbooks and accept the changes which have your approval.

a. Start Excel, open EX 14-11.xlsx from where you store your Data Files, then save it as **EX 14-Winter Schedule**.

b. Use the Accept or Reject Changes dialog box to accept the first three changes and reject the fourth change to the workbook.

c. Use the Highlight Changes dialog box to view each change on the screen. Review the ScreenTip details.

d. Use the Highlight Changes dialog box to create a History worksheet detailing the changes to the workbook.

e. In the History sheet, copy the information about the changes in the range A1:I5, and paste it in a new worksheet.

f. Widen the columns as necessary, and rename the new sheet **History Sheet**. Compare your History Sheet to FIGURE 14-26.

g. Add your name to the center section of the History sheet footer, change the sheet orientation to landscape, then preview the History worksheet.

h. Remove the Shared status of the workbook. (*Hint*: In the Share Workbook dialog box, deselect the "Allow changes by more than one user at the same time." checkbox.)

i. Add a password of **Winter%2017** to open the workbook and **Pool%2017** to modify it.

j. Save and close the workbook. Submit the EX 14-Winter Schedule.xlsx workbook to your instructor.

FIGURE 14-25

Region	Store	Quarter 1	Quarter 2
North	Seattle	$31,988	$27,845
North	Portland	$28,954	$22,415
North	Minneapolis	$30,250	$20,582
North	Madison	$30,158	$24,158
North	Billings	$29,574	$24,511
North	Columbus	$30,158	$21,877
North	Boston	$40,125	$26,647
North	Hartford	$30,215	$22,541
North	Concord	$19,548	$32,145
North	New York	$26,541	$32,451
North	Newark	$18,479	$29,365
North	San Francisco	$19,105	$20,100
South	Nashville	$17,511	$19,584
South	Savannah	$15,428	$17,558
South	Miami	$20,524	$22,125
South	Austin	$17,995	$18,995
South	Charleston	$19,025	$20,214
South	Atlanta	$20,123	$22,148
South	Charlotte	$19,887	$20,236
South	Raleigh	$28,625	$29,884
South	New Orleans	$27,541	$30,001
West	San Diego	$41,521	$47,556
West	Boise	$32,110	$37,584
West	Cheyenne	$31,220	$32,114
West	Phoenix	$30,154	$32,114
Total		$656,759	$654,750

FIGURE 14-26

Action Number	Date	Time	Who	Change	Sheet	Range	New Value	Old Value
1	10/26/2017	11:05 AM	Your Name	Cell Change	Winter	D3	9:50 a.m.	8:50 a.m.
2	10/26/2017	11:05 AM	Your Name	Cell Change	Winter	E5	Wednesday	Thursday
3	10/26/2017	11:05 AM	Your Name	Cell Change	Winter	D11	5:15 p.m.	4:15 p.m.
4	10/26/2017	11:05 AM	Your Name	Cell Change	Winter	E13	Saturday	Wednesday

Independent Challenge 2

As the office manager of a cleaning supplies company you are responsible for organizing sales information and publishing the information for the district managers. Your assistant has published the preliminary January sales information on the company website. You will copy that information from the webpage and work with it in Excel to calculate bonuses and totals. You will save the new sales information as an HTML file so it can be published on the web.

a. Use File Explorer to open EX 14-12.htm from where you store your Data Files to display it in your browser.

b. Start Excel, create a new workbook, then save it as **EX 14-January Sales** where you store your Data Files.

Excel 2016

Independent Challenge 2 (continued)

c. Return to the browser, copy the five rows of data, including the column headings from the table in the EX 14-12 file, and paste them in the EX 14-January Sales workbook. Adjust the column widths as necessary. Close the EX 14-12.htm file.

d. Add the new sales data from the table below in rows 6 and 7 of the worksheet.

Membership	Price
Fiona Silver	2500
Kathy Johnson	1750

e. Remove the borders around the cells in columns A and B. (*Hint*: Select the range A1:B7, click the Border list arrow, then click No Border.)

f. Enter **Bonus** in cell C1, and calculate each bonus in column C by multiplying the Sales values in column B by 10%.

g. Format the price information in columns B and C with the Accounting format, using the $ symbol with two decimal places. Widen the columns as necessary.

h. Add the passwords **January17** to open the EX 14-Rates workbook and **Bonus17** to modify it. Save the workbook, replacing the existing file, close the workbook, then reopen it by entering the passwords.

i. Verify that you can modify the workbook by adding totals in cells B8 and C8.

j. Format the label in cell C1 as bold and center the label in the cell. Compare your worksheet data to **FIGURE 14-27**.

k. Add your name to the center footer section of the worksheet, save the workbook, then preview the worksheet.

l. Save the worksheet data in HTML format using the name **EX 14-jansales.htm**. Close the workbook and exit Excel.

m. Open the EX 14-jansales.htm page in your browser and print the page.

n. Close your browser. Submit the EX 14-jansales.htm and the EX 14-January Sales file to your instructor.

FIGURE 14-27

	A	B	C	D
1	**Sales Rep**	**Sales**	**Bonus**	
2	John Flood	$ 1,500.00	$ 150.00	
3	Ken Tucker	$ 1,985.00	$ 198.50	
4	Jose Sanchez	$ 2,075.00	$ 207.50	
5	Caroline Doe	$ 2,080.00	$ 208.00	
6	Fiona Silver	$ 2,500.00	$ 250.00	
7	Kathy Johnson	$ 1,750.00	$ 175.00	
8		$11,890.00	$1,189.00	
9				

Independent Challenge 3

You are the sales manager for a manufacturing software firm. You are preparing customer lists for your sales associates. The sales history information for the firm is in an XML file, which you will bring into Excel to organize. You will use an XML schema to map only the customers' names and phone numbers to the worksheet. This will allow you to import the customer data and limit the information that is distributed to the sales associates. You will export your worksheet data as XML for future use.

a. Start Excel, create a new workbook, then save it as **EX 14-Customers** in the location where you store your Data Files.

b. Add the map EX 14-13.xsd from the location where you store your Data Files to the workbook.

c. Map the FNAME element to cell A1, LNAME to cell B1, and PHONENUM to cell C1. Make sure that imported XML data will be validated using the schema rules.

d. Import the XML data in file EX 14-14.xml from the location where you store your Data Files. Add the Table Style Light 21 to the table. Change the field name in cell A1 to **First Name**, change the field name in cell B1 to **Last Name**, and change the field name in cell C1 to **Phone Number**. Widen the columns as necessary to accommodate the full field names.

Independent Challenge 3 (continued)

e. Sort the table in ascending order by Last Name. Compare your sorted table to **FIGURE 14-28**.

f. Open the XML Map Properties dialog box to verify the Overwrite existing data with new data option button is selected. Map the ACTIVE element to cell D1. Import the XML data in file EX 14-14.xml again. (Your data will no longer be sorted.)

g. Map the PUR_DATE element to cell E1. Import the XML data in file EX 14-14.xml a third time. Change the field name in cell E1 to **Last Purchase**, and widen the column to accommodate the full field name.

h. Change the field name in cell D1 to **Active**. Filter the table to show only active donors. Compare your filtered table to **FIGURE 14-29**.

i. Export the worksheet data to an XML file named **EX 14-Phone List**.

j. Enter your name in the center section of the worksheet footer, preview the worksheet then save the workbook.

k. Close the workbook, exit Excel, then submit the workbook and the XML file to your instructor.

FIGURE 14-28

	A	B	C	D
1	First Name	Last Name	Phone Number	
2	Ann	Allen	773-248-6524	
3	Ken	Bush	708-412-5824	
4	Sandra	Cox	312-322-3163	
5	Bob	Dash	312-322-3163	
6	Paul	Dern	312-765-8756	
7	Kelly	Gonzales	773-379-0092	
8	Jean	Herandez	312-765-8756	
9	Allen	Lord	312-299-4298	
10	Lisa	McNeal	312-365-4789	
11	Molly	Turner	312-765-8756	
12				
13				

FIGURE 14-29

	A	B	C	D	E	F
1	First Name	Last Name	Phone Number	Active	Last Purchase	
2	Ken	Bush	708-412-5824	TRUE	Jan-16	
4	Lisa	McNeal	312-365-4789	TRUE	Jan-16	
7	Kelly	Gonzales	773-379-0092	TRUE	Nov-16	
9	Molly	Turner	312-765-8756	TRUE	Dec-16	
10	Paul	Dern	312-765-8756	TRUE	Nov-16	
11	Jean	Herandez	312-765-8756	TRUE	Dec-16	
12						

Independent Challenge 4: Explore

You will explore the add-ins available to use in worksheets and save your results in the cloud, on your OneDrive space.

a. Start Excel, create a new blank workbook, then save it as **EX 14-Add-in** in the location where you store your Data Files.

b. View the featured add-ins for Excel. (*Hint*: Click the Insert tab, click the Store button in the Add-ins group, then click a category that interests you.)

c. Insert a free add-in. (*Hint*: Click the add-in name, read the privacy policy and terms of use, then click Trust It.)

d. Explore the app to develop an understanding of its purpose.

e. In cell A1 of your worksheet enter the name of your app.

f. In row 2 enter the category of the add-in from the store. In row 3 of the worksheet enter information about the purpose of the app.

g. Enter your name in the center section of the worksheet footer.

h. Save your EX 14-Add-in workbook on your OneDrive.

i. Get sharing links to edit the workbook and to only view it.

j. Copy the sharing links and paste them into rows 5 and 6 of the worksheet with labels identifying each one. Change the orientation to landscape and scale the width to fit on one page.

k. Preview the worksheet then save the workbook to where you store your Data Files, replacing the previously saved workbook.

l. Close the workbook, exit Excel, then submit the workbook to your instructor.

Visual Workshop

Start Excel, create a new workbook, then save it as **EX 14-Events.xlsx** in the location where you store your Data Files. Open EX 14-15.htm in your browser from the location where you store your Data Files. Create the worksheet shown in **FIGURE 14-30** by pasting the information from the webpage into your EX 14-Events.xlsx file, formatting it, adding the fourth quarter information, adding the totals, and replacing the text Your Name with your name. (*Hint:* The colors are in the Office theme, the font size of the first three rows is 14, and the remaining font size is 12.) Preview the worksheet, then save the workbook. Submit the EX 14-Events.xlsx workbook to your instructor.

FIGURE 14-30

	A	B	C	D	E	F
1	NE Events					
2	Sales					
3	Your Name					
4	Category	1st Quarter	2nd Quarter	3rd Quarter	4th Quarter	Totals
5	Conferences	$ 98,004	$ 120,524	$ 158,475	$ 145,000	$ 522,003
6	Weddings	$ 8,500	$ 130,521	$ 165,147	$ 150,000	$ 454,168
7	Holiday Celebrations	$ 2,500	$ 9,350	$ 10,253	$ 80,000	$ 102,103
8	Sports Events	$ 9,658	$ 11,523	$ 12,365	$ 15,000	$ 48,546
9	Charity	$ 125,201	$ 99,521	$ 78,951	$ 80,000	$ 383,673
10	Totals	$ 243,863	$ 371,439	$ 425,191	$ 470,000	$1,510,493
11						

Customizing Excel and Advanced Worksheet Management

CASE ▶ Reason2Go's VP of sales and marketing, Mary Watson, asks you to review sales worksheet formulas, customize Excel workbooks, and create a sales template for the U.S. branches. You will use Excel tools and options to help Mary and the sales staff work quickly and efficiently in a customized environment.

Module Objectives

After completing this module, you will be able to:

- Audit a worksheet
- Control worksheet calculations
- Group worksheet data
- Work with cell comments

- Create a custom AutoFill list
- Create and apply a template
- Customize an Excel workbook
- Customize the Excel screen

Files You Will Need

EX 15-1.xlsx	EX 15-5.xlsx
EX 15-2.xlsx	EX 15-6.xlsx
EX 15-3.xlsx	EX 15-7.xlsx
EX 15-4.xlsx	

Audit a Worksheet

Learning Outcomes
- Locate formula errors
- Correct formula errors

Because errors can occur at any stage of worksheet development, it is important to include auditing as part of your workbook-building process. The Excel **auditing** feature helps you track errors and check worksheet logic to make sure your worksheet is error free and the data is arranged sensibly. The Formula Auditing group on the Formulas tab contains several error-checking tools to help you audit a worksheet. **CASE** ▶ *Mary asks you to help identify errors in the worksheet that tracks sales for the two U.S. branches, to verify the accuracy of year-end totals and percentages.*

STEPS

1. **Start Excel, open EX 15-1.xlsx from the location where you store your Data Files, then save it as EX 15-US Sales**

2. **Click the Formulas tab, then click the Error Checking button in the Formula Auditing group**

   The Error Checking dialog box opens and alerts you to a Divide by Zero Error in cell O5, as shown in **FIGURE 15-1**. The formula reads =N5/N8, indicating that the value in cell N5 will be divided by the value in cell N8. To correct the error, you must edit the formula so that it references cell N7, the Total.

   QUICK TIP

   In Excel formulas, blank cells have a value of zero. This error means the value in cell N5 cannot be divided by the value in cell N8 (zero) because division by zero is not mathematically possible.

3. **Click Edit in Formula Bar in the Error Checking dialog box, edit the formula in the formula bar to read =N5/N7, click the Enter button ☑ in the formula bar, then click Resume in the Error Checking dialog box**

   The edited formula produces the correct result, 0.47532, in cell O5. The Error Checking dialog box indicates another error in cell N6, the total New York sales. The formula reads =SUM(B6:L6) and should be =SUM(B6:M6). The top button in the Error Checking dialog box changes to "Copy Formula from Above". Since this formula in cell N5 is correct, you will copy it.

4. **Click Copy Formula from Above**

   The New York total changes to $518,010 in cell N6. The Error Checking dialog box finds another division-by-zero error in cell O6. You decide to use another tool to investigate this error.

   QUICK TIP

   You can use the Trace Error tool to highlight the cells used to calculate a formula by clicking the Formulas tab on the Ribbon, clicking the Error Checking list arrow in the Formula Auditing group, then clicking Trace Error to view the cells used in the formula calculations.

5. **Close the Error Checking dialog box, then click the Trace Precedents button in the Formula Auditing group**

   Blue arrows called **tracer arrows** point from the cells referenced by the formula to the active cell, as shown in **FIGURE 15-2**. The arrows help you determine if these cell references might have caused the error. The tracer arrows extend from the error to cells N6 and N8. To correct the error, you can see that you must edit the formula so that it references cell N7 in the denominator, the sales total, not cell N8.

6. **Edit the formula in the formula bar to read =N6/N7, then click ☑**

   The result of the formula, 0.52468, appears in cell O6. The November sales for the New York branch in cell L6 is high compared with sales posted for the other months. In the event that this is the result of an input error, you want to investigate the other cells in the sheet that are affected by the value of cell L6 as they would also be incorrect. You can do this by tracing the cell's **dependents**—the cells that contain formulas referring to cell L6.

   QUICK TIP

   To locate invalid data that may lead to errors in formula calculations, click the Data tab, click the Data Validation list arrow, then click Circle Invalid Data. Red circles appear around cells that are not consistent with data validation criteria.

7. **Click cell L6, then click the Trace Dependents button in the Formula Auditing group**

   The tracer arrows run from cell L6 to cells L7 and N6, indicating that the value in cell L6 affects the total November sales and the total New York sales. You decide to remove the tracer arrows and format the percentages in cells O5 and O6.

8. **Click the Remove Arrows button in the Formula Auditing group, select the range O5:O6, click the Home tab, format the cells in the Percent style with two decimal places, return to cell A1, then save the workbook**

FIGURE 15-1: Error Checking dialog box

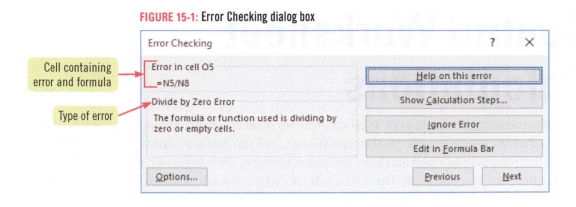

Cell containing error and formula

Type of error

FIGURE 15-2: Worksheet with traced error

▲	A	B	C	D	E	F	G	H	I	J	K	L	M	N	O
1							R2G U.S.								
2							2017 Sales Summary								
3															
4	Branch	Jan	Feb	Mar	Apr	May	Jun	Jul	Aug	Sep	Oct	Nov	Dec	Total	Percent
5	Los Angeles	$41,348	$39,882	$40,842	$41,880	$25,232	$37,557	$35,790	$42,786	$42,992	$40,102	$39,022	$41,852	$469,285	0.47532
6	New York	$45,698	$41,741	$46,349	$39,843	$41,791	$41,801	$40,941	$39,812	$37,341	$41,841	$51,711	$49,141	$518,010	#DIV/0!
7	Total	$87,046	$81,623	$87,191	$81,723	$67,023	$79,358	$76,731	$82,598	$80,333	$81,943	$90,733	$90,993	$987,295	
8															
9															

Tracer arrows

Watching and evaluating formulas

As you edit your worksheet, you can watch the effect that cell changes have on selected worksheet formulas. Select the cell or cells that you want to watch, click the Formulas tab, click the Watch Window button in the Formula Auditing group, click Add Watch in the Watch Window, then click Add. The Watch Window lists the workbook name, worksheet name, the cell address you want to watch, the current cell value, and its formula. As cell values that "feed into" the formula change, the resulting formula value in the Watch Window changes. To delete a watch, select the cell information in the Watch Window, then click Delete Watch. You can also step through a formula, and its results: Select a cell that contains a formula, then click the Evaluate Formula button in the Formula Auditing group. The formula appears in the Evaluation Window of the Evaluate Formula dialog box. As you click the Evaluate button, the cell references are replaced with their values and the formula result.

Control Worksheet Calculations

Learning Outcomes
- Control formula calculations
- Calculate worksheet formulas

Whenever you change a value in a cell, Excel automatically recalculates all the formulas in the worksheet based on that cell. This automatic calculation is efficient until you create a worksheet so large that the recalculation process slows down data entry and screen updating. Worksheets with many formulas, data tables, or functions may also recalculate slowly. In these cases, you might want to selectively determine if and when you want Excel to perform calculations. You do this by applying the **manual calculation** option. Once you change the calculation mode to manual, Excel applies manual calculation to all open worksheets. **CASE** *Because Mary knows that using specific Excel calculation options can help make worksheet building more efficient, she asks you to review the formula settings in the workbook and change the formula calculations from automatic to manual calculation.*

STEPS

QUICK TIP
You can also change the formula calculation to manual by clicking the Formulas tab, clicking the Calculation Options button in the Calculation group, then clicking Manual.

1. **Click the File tab, click Options, then click Formulas in the list of categories**

   The options related to formula calculation and error checking appear, as shown in **FIGURE 15-3**.

2. **Under Calculation options, click to select the Manual option button**

   When you select the Manual option, the Recalculate workbook before saving check box automatically becomes active and contains a check mark. Because the workbook will not recalculate until you save or close and reopen the workbook, you must make sure to recalculate your worksheet before you print it and after you finish making changes.

3. **Click OK**

   Mary informs you that the December total for the Los Angeles branch is incorrect. You adjust the entry in cell M5 to reflect the actual sales figure.

4. **Click cell M5**

   Before changing cell M5, notice that in cell N5 the total for the Los Angeles branch is $469,285, and the Los Angeles percent in cell O5 is 47.53%.

QUICK TIP
The Calculate Now command recalculates the entire workbook. To manually recalculate the workbook, press [F9] or press [Shift][F9] to recalculate only the active sheet.

5. **Type 40,000, then click the Enter button ☑ on the formula bar**

   The total and percent formulas are *not* updated. The total in cell N5 is still $469,285 and the percentage in cell O5 is still 47.53%. The word "Calculate" appears in the status bar to indicate that a specific value in the worksheet did indeed change and that the worksheet must be recalculated.

6. **Click the Formulas tab, click the Calculate Sheet button in the Calculation group, click cell A1, then save the workbook**

   The total in cell N5 is now $467,433 and the percentage in cell O5 is now 47.43%. The other formulas in the worksheet affected by the value in cell M5 changed as well, as shown in **FIGURE 15-4**. Because this is a relatively small worksheet that recalculates quickly, you will return to automatic calculation.

QUICK TIP
To automatically recalculate all worksheet formulas except one- and two-input data tables, click Automatic Except for Data Tables.

7. **Click the Calculation Options button in the Calculation group, then click Automatic**

   Now any additional changes you make will automatically recalculate the worksheet formulas.

8. **Enter your name in the center section of the worksheet footer, then save the workbook**

FIGURE 15-3: Excel formula options

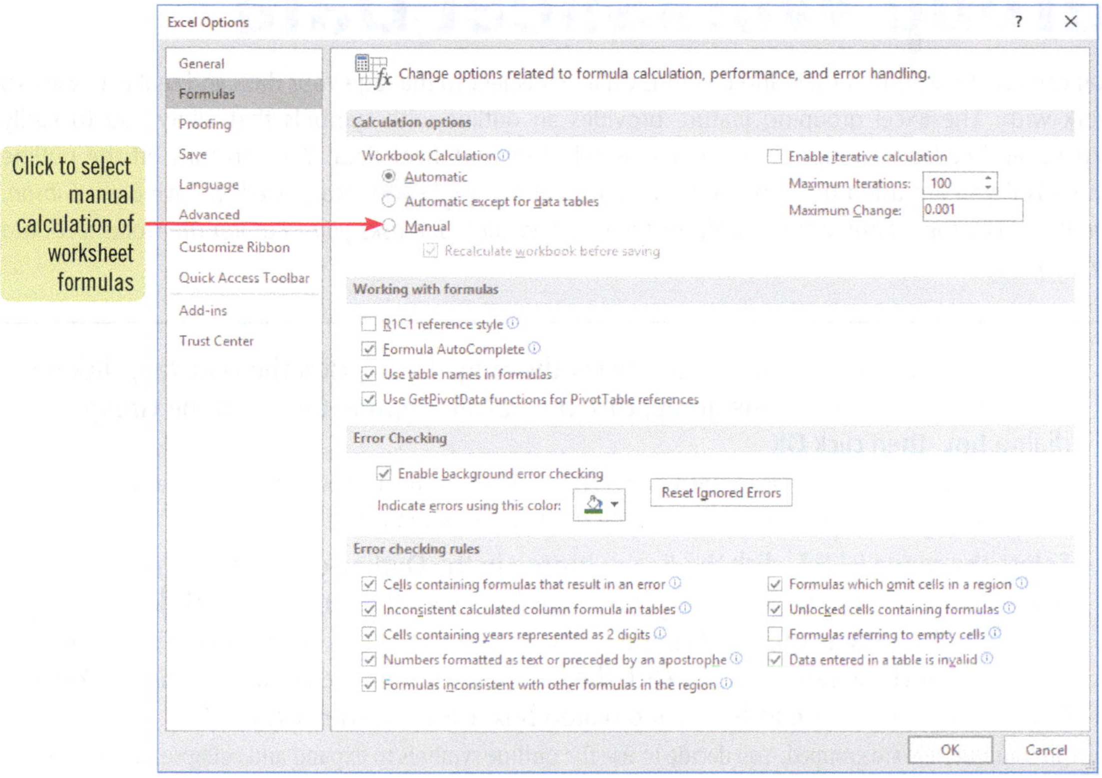

FIGURE 15-4: Worksheet with updated values

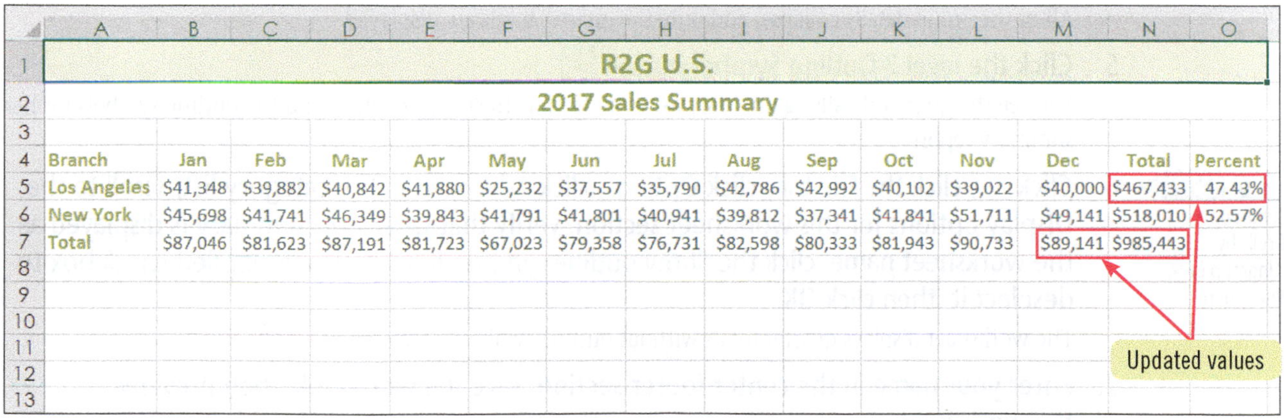

R2G U.S.

2017 Sales Summary

Branch	Jan	Feb	Mar	Apr	May	Jun	Jul	Aug	Sep	Oct	Nov	Dec	Total	Percent
Los Angeles	$41,348	$39,882	$40,842	$41,880	$25,232	$37,557	$35,790	$42,786	$42,992	$40,102	$39,022	$40,000	$467,433	47.43%
New York	$45,698	$41,741	$46,349	$39,843	$41,791	$41,801	$40,941	$39,812	$37,341	$41,841	$51,711	$49,141	$518,010	52.57%
Total	$87,046	$81,623	$87,191	$81,723	$67,023	$79,358	$76,731	$82,598	$80,333	$81,943	$90,733	$89,141	$985,443	

Group Worksheet Data

You can create groups of rows and columns on a worksheet to manage your data and make it easier to work with. The Excel grouping feature provides an outline with symbols that allow you to easily expand and collapse groups to show or hide selected worksheet data. You can turn off the outline symbols if you are using the condensed data in a report. **CASE** *Mary needs to give Bryce Gibson, the R2G CEO, the quarterly sales totals for the U.S. branches. She asks you to group the worksheet data by quarters.*

STEPS

1. **Click the Quarterly Summary sheet, select the range B4:D7, click the Data tab, click the Group button in the Outline group, click the Columns option button in the Group dialog box, then click OK**

   The first quarter information is grouped, and **outline symbols** that let you hide and display details appear over the columns, as shown in **FIGURE 15-5**. You continue to group the remaining quarters.

2. **Select the range F4:H7, click the Group button in the Outline group, click the Columns option button in the Group dialog box, click OK, select the range J4:L7, click the Group button in the Outline group, click the Columns option button in the Group dialog box, click OK, select the range N4:P7, click the Group button in the Outline group, click the Columns option button in the Group dialog box, click OK, then click cell A1**

   All four quarters are grouped. You decide to use the outline symbols to expand and collapse the first quarter information.

3. **Click the Collapse Outline button ⊟ above the column E label, then click the Expand Outline button ⊞ above the column E label**

   Clicking the (-) symbol temporarily hides the Q1 detail columns, and the (-) symbol changes to a (+) symbol. Clicking the (+) symbol expands the Q1 details and redisplays the hidden columns. The numbered Outline symbols in the upper-left corner of the worksheet are used to display and hide levels of detail across the entire worksheet.

4. **Click the level 1 Outline Symbol button 1**

   All of the group details collapse, and only the quarter totals are displayed.

5. **Click the level 2 Outline Symbol button 2**

   You see the quarter details again. Mary asks you to hide the quarter details and the outline symbols for her summary report.

6. **Click 1, click the File tab, click Options, click Advanced in the category list, scroll to the Display options for this worksheet section, verify that Quarterly Summary is displayed as the worksheet name, click the Show outline symbols if an outline is applied check box to deselect it, then click OK**

   The worksheet displays quarter totals without outline symbols, as shown in **FIGURE 15-6**.

7. **Enter your name in the center footer section, save the workbook, then preview the worksheet**

FIGURE 15-5: First quarter data grouped

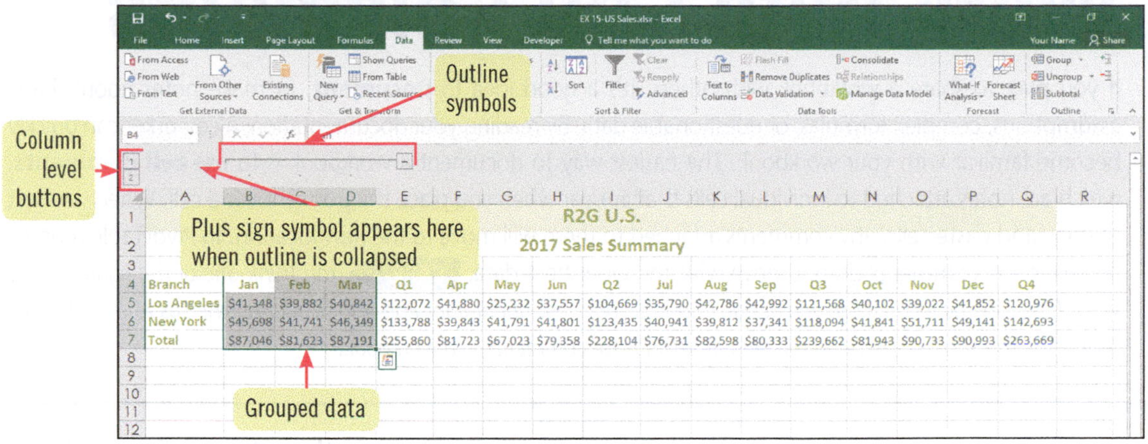

FIGURE 15-6: Quarterly summary

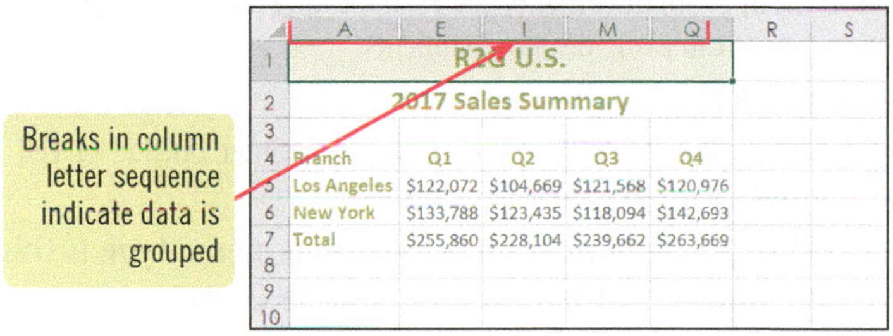

Applying and viewing advanced workbook properties

You can add summary information to your workbook, such as a subject, manager name, company name, or a category, using advanced properties. To view a workbook's advanced properties, click the File tab, click Info if necessary, click the Properties list arrow on the right side of Backstage view, then click Advanced Properties. The General tab displays file information. Use the Summary tab to add additional properties to the workbook. The Statistics tab displays file information and the Contents tab lists the file's worksheets. You can create and enter additional information fields on the Custom tab.

Work with Cell Comments

**Learning
Outcomes**
- Insert a new
  comment
- Show worksheet
  comments
- Print worksheet
  comments

If you plan to share a workbook with others, it's a good idea to **document**, or make notes about, basic assumptions, complex formulas, or questionable data. By reading your documentation, a coworker can quickly become familiar with your workbook. The easiest way to document a workbook is to use **cell comments**, which are notes attached to individual cells that appear when you place the pointer over a cell. When you sort or copy and paste cells, any comments attached to them will move to the new location. In PivotTable reports, however, the comments do not move with the worksheet data. **CASE** *You think one of the figures in the worksheet may be incorrect so you decide to add a comment about it for Rae-Ann Schwartz, the Los Angeles branch manager. You start by checking the default settings for comments in a workbook.*

STEPS

1. **Click the File tab if necessary, click Options, click Advanced in the category list, scroll to the Display section, click the Indicators only, and comments on hover option button to select it in the "For cells with comments, show:" section if necessary, then click OK**

   The other options in the "For cells with comments, show:" area allow you to display the comment and its indicator or no comments.

2. **Click the Sales sheet tab, click cell F5, click the Review tab, then click the New Comment button in the Comments group**

   The Comment box opens, as shown in **FIGURE 15-7**. Excel automatically includes the computer's username at the beginning of the comment. The **username** is the name that appears in the User name text box of the Excel Options dialog box. The white sizing handles on the border of the Comment box let you resize it.

3. **Type Is this figure correct? It looks low to me., then click outside the Comment box**

   A red triangle appears in the upper-right corner of cell F5, indicating that a comment is attached to the cell. People who use your worksheet can easily display comments.

4. **Place the pointer over cell F5**

   The comment appears next to the cell. When you move the pointer outside of cell F5, the comment disappears. You have a question about the value in Cell L6.

5. **Right-click cell L6, click Insert Comment on the shortcut menu, type Is this increase due to the new marketing campaign?, then click outside the Comment box**

   You've received some new information, and now need to delete one comment and edit another. You start by displaying all worksheet comments.

6. **Click cell A1, then click the Show All Comments button in the Comments group**

   The two worksheet comments are displayed on the screen, as shown in **FIGURE 15-8**.

7. **Click the Next button in the Comments group, with the comment in cell F5 selected click the Delete button in the Comments group, click the Next button, click the Edit Comment button, type Rae-Ann - at the beginning of the comment in the Comment box, click cell A1, then click the Show All Comments button in the Comments group**

   The Show All Comments button is a toggle button: You click it once to display comments, then click it again to hide comments. You decide to fit the worksheet to print on one page and preview the worksheet and the cell comment along with its associated cell reference on separate pages.

8. **Click the File tab, click Print, click Page Setup at the bottom of the Print pane, click the Fit to option button on the Page tab, click the Sheet tab, under Print click the Comments list arrow, click At end of sheet, click OK, then click the Next Page arrow ▶ at the bottom of the preview pane**

   Your comment appears on a separate page after the worksheet.

9. **Save the workbook**

FIGURE 15-7: Comment box

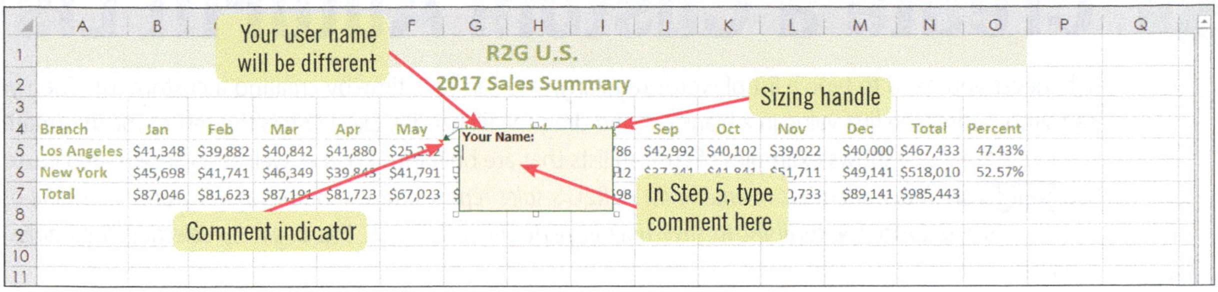

FIGURE 15-8: Worksheet with comments displayed

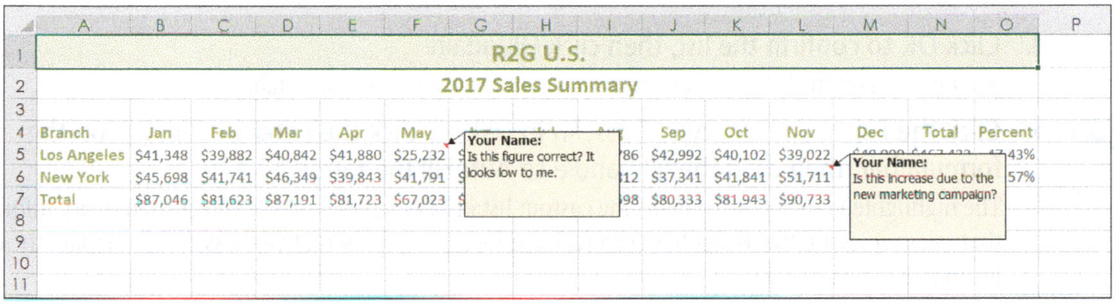

Working with Excel files

To increase your productivity, you can personalize the way recently used files and folders appear in Backstage view. For example, you can keep a workbook displayed in the Recent list of workbooks by clicking the File tab, clicking Open, right-clicking the file you want to keep, then clicking Pin to list. You can unpin the file by clicking the pin button ![pin] to the right of the workbook name. If you want to clear the unpinned workbooks from the Recent list, click the File tab, click Open, click Recent Workbooks, right-click a file you want to remove from the list, click Clear unpinned Workbooks, then click Yes.

If you accidently close a file without saving it, if an unstable program causes Excel to close abnormally, or if the power fails, you can recover your workbook, provided the AutoRecover feature is enabled. To enable AutoRecover, click the File tab, click Options, click Save in the Excel Options dialog box, verify that the Save AutoRecover information check box is selected; if necessary, modify the number of minutes AutoRecover saves your files by clicking the up or down arrow to adjust the number, then click OK. The AutoSave feature automatically saves your work at predetermined intervals, while the AutoRecover feature allows you to recover an AutoSaved file. If you need to restore an AutoRecovered file, click the File tab, click Info if necessary, click Manage Workbook, then click Recover Unsaved Workbooks to see a list of any AutoRecovered files.

Create a Custom AutoFill List

Learning
Outcomes
• Create a custom
  list
• Use a custom list

Whenever you need to type a list of words regularly, you can save time by creating a custom list. Then you can simply enter the first value in a blank cell and drag the fill handle. Excel enters the rest of the information for you. **FIGURE 15-9** shows examples of custom lists that are built into Excel as well as a user-created custom list. **CASE** *Mary often has to enter a list of R2G's sales representatives' names in her worksheets. She asks you to create a custom AutoFill list to save time in performing this task. You begin by selecting the names in the worksheet.*

STEPS

1. Click the **Jan sheet tab**, then select the range **A5:A24**

TROUBLE
If a list of sales
representatives
already appears in
the Custom lists box,
click the list, click
Delete, click OK,
then proceed with
Step 3.

2. Click the **File tab**, click **Options**, click **Advanced**, scroll down to the General section, then click **Edit Custom Lists**

   The Custom Lists dialog box displays the custom lists that are already built into Excel, as shown in **FIGURE 15-10**. You want to define a custom list containing the sales representatives' names you selected in column A. The Import list from cells text box contains the range you selected in Step 1.

3. Click **Import**

   The list of names is highlighted in the Custom lists box and appears in the List entries box.

4. Click **OK** to confirm the list, then click **OK** again

   You need to add the list of sales representatives' names in the Feb sheet tab.

QUICK TIP
You can also drag the
fill handle to the
right to enter a
custom list.

5. Click the **Feb sheet tab**, type **Gosselin** in cell A1, click the **Enter button** ☑ on the formula bar, then drag the **fill handle** to AutoFill the range **A2:A20**

   The highlighted range now contains the custom list of sales representatives you created. Mary informs you that sales representative Bolles has been replaced by a new representative, Hassan. You update the custom list to reflect this change.

6. Click the **File tab**, click **Options**, click **Advanced**, scroll down to the General section, click **Edit Custom Lists**, click the list of sales representatives names in the Custom lists box, change Bolles to **Hassan** in the List entries box, click **OK** to confirm the change, then click **OK** again

   You decide to check the new list to be sure it is accurate.

7. Click cell **C1**, type **Gosselin**, click ☑ on the formula bar, then drag the **fill handle** to fill the range **C2:C20**

   The highlighted range contains the updated custom list of sales representatives, as shown in **FIGURE 15-11**. You've finished creating and editing your custom AutoFill list, and you need to delete it from the Custom Lists dialog box in case others will be using your computer.

8. Click the **File tab**, click **Options**, click **Advanced**, scroll down to the General section, click **Edit Custom Lists**, click the list of sales representatives' names in the Custom lists box, click **Delete**, click **OK** to confirm the deletion, then click **OK** two more times

9. Save the workbook

Customizing Excel and Advanced Worksheet Management

FIGURE 15-9: Sample custom lists

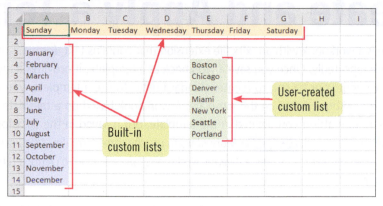

FIGURE 15-10: Custom Lists dialog box

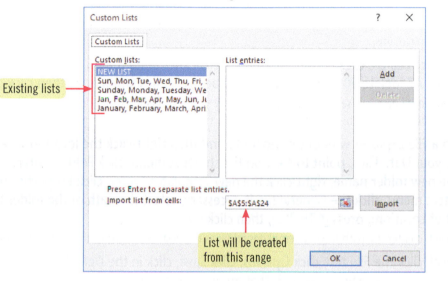

FIGURE 15-11: Custom lists with sales rep names

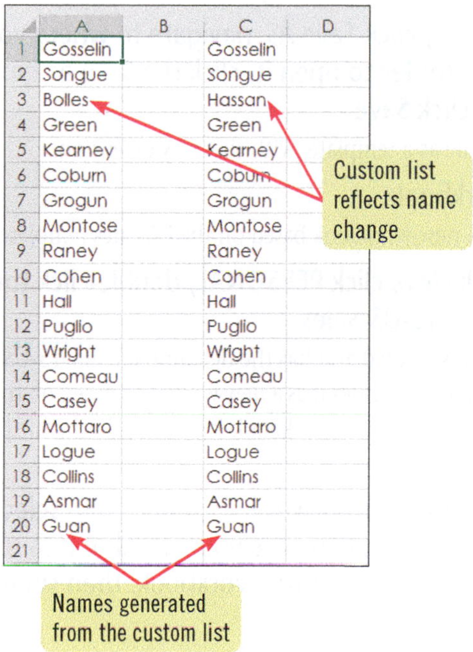

	A	B	C	D
1	Gosselin		Gosselin	
2	Songue		Songue	
3	Bolles		Hassan	
4	Green		Green	
5	Kearney		Kearney	
6	Coburn		Coburn	
7	Grogun		Grogun	
8	Montose		Montose	
9	Raney		Raney	
10	Cohen		Cohen	
11	Hall		Hall	
12	Puglio		Puglio	
13	Wright		Wright	
14	Comeau		Comeau	
15	Casey		Casey	
16	Mottaro		Mottaro	
17	Logue		Logue	
18	Collins		Collins	
19	Asmar		Asmar	
20	Guan		Guan	
21				

Custom list reflects name change

Names generated from the custom list

The right side tab says "Excel 2016"

Excel 2016

Customizing Excel and Advanced Worksheet Management

Create and Apply a Template

Learning
Outcomes
• Create a template
• Apply a template

A template is a workbook with an .xltx file extension that contains text, formulas, macros, and formatting that you use repeatedly. Once you save a workbook as a template, it provides a model for creating a new workbook without your having to reenter standard data. To use a template, you **apply** it, which means you create a workbook *based on* the template. A workbook based on a template has the same content, formulas, and formatting you defined in the template, but is saved in the .xlsx format. The template file itself remains unchanged. **CASE** ▶ *Mary plans to use the same formulas, titles, and row and column labels from the Sales worksheet for subsequent yearly worksheets. She asks you to create a template that will allow her to quickly prepare these worksheets.*

STEPS

1. **Delete the Quarterly Summary, Jan, and Feb sheets**

   The workbook now contains only the Sales sheet. You decide to use the Sales sheet structure and formulas as the basis for your new template. First you need to delete the data specific to this workbook, so that only the reusable information remains.

2. **Right-click cell L6, click Delete Comment, select the range B5:M6, press [Delete], double-click cell A2, delete 2017, delete the space before "Sales Summary", then click cell A1**

   The remaining data can serve as the basis for future yearly worksheets. See **FIGURE 15-12**. You will create a folder named Templates to save the template.

3. **Open a File Explorer window, navigate to and then right-click the location where you store your Data Files, point to New on the shortcut menu, click Folder, enter Templates as the new folder name, right-click the new Templates folder, click Properties on the shortcut menu, click the General tab if necessary, select the path of the folder to the right of Location:, press [CTRL][C], then click OK**

   You need to enter the path to your Templates folder as the destination for your saved templates.

4. **In Excel, click the File tab, click Options, click Save, click in the Default personal templates location text box, delete any path that appears in the text box, press [CTRL][V], scroll to the end of the path, type \Templates\, then click OK**

   New templates will now be saved to your Templates folder. You are now ready to create the template.

5. **Click the File tab, click Save As, navigate to where you store your Data Files, double-click the Templates folder to open it, click the Save as type list arrow, click Excel Template (*.xltx), then click Save**

   Excel saves the file as a template, with the .xltx extension.

6. **Close the workbook**

   Now you open a new workbook based on the US Sales template.

7. ▶ **Click File, click New, click PERSONAL, double-click the Templates folder if necessary, then double-click EX 15-US Sales**

   A new workbook is created and has the default name EX 15-US Sales1, as shown in **FIGURE 15-13**. The "1" at the end of the name identifies it as a new workbook based on the 15-US Sales template, just as "1" at the end of "Book1" identifies a new workbook based on the blank Excel template. You want to make sure the formulas are working correctly.

8. **Click cell B5, enter 200, click cell B6, enter 300, select the range B5:B6, copy the data into the range C5:M6, compare your workbook to FIGURE 15-14, save the workbook as EX 15-Template Test, close the workbook, then submit the workbook to your instructor**

FIGURE 15-12: Completed template

	Branch	Jan	Feb	Mar	Apr	May	Jun	Jul	Aug	Sep	Oct	Nov	Dec	Total	Percent
1							R2G U.S.								
2							Sales Summary								
3															
4	Branch	Jan	Feb	Mar	Apr	May	Jun	Jul	Aug	Sep	Oct	Nov	Dec	Total	Percent
5	Los Angeles													$0	#DIV/0!
6	New York													$0	#DIV/0!
7	Total	$0	$0	$0	$0	$0	$0	$0	$0	$0	$0	$0	$0	$0	
8															

Temporary divide-by-zero error messages

FIGURE 15-13: Workbook based on template

Default filename indicates workbook is based on template EX 15-US Sales

Workbook based on template contains the template's content, formatting, and formulas

Excel 2016

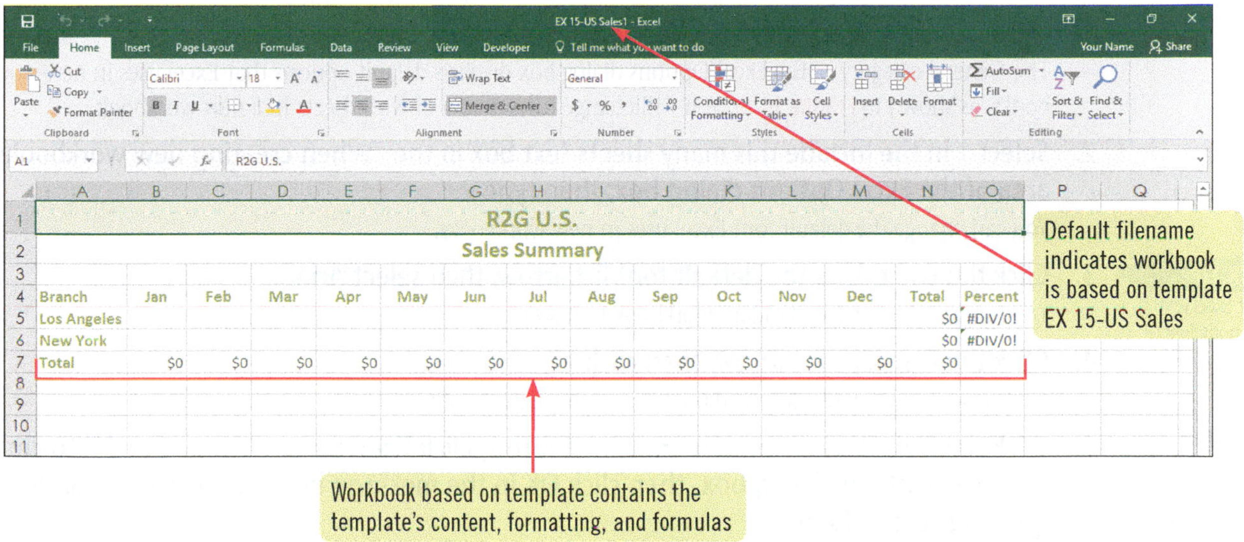

FIGURE 15-14: Completed template test

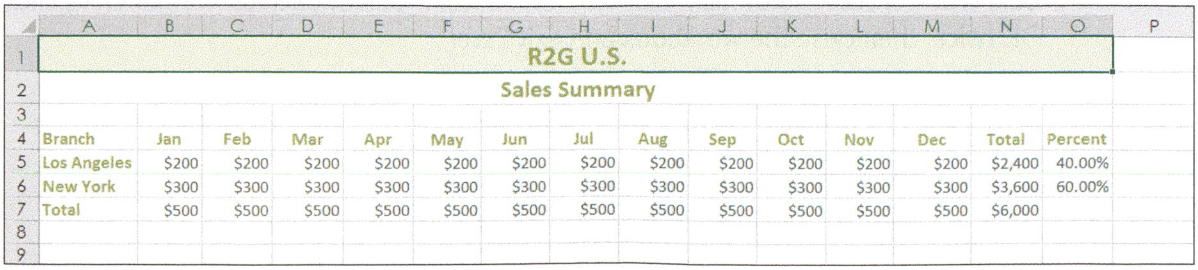

	Branch	Jan	Feb	Mar	Apr	May	Jun	Jul	Aug	Sep	Oct	Nov	Dec	Total	Percent
1							R2G U.S.								
2							Sales Summary								
3															
4	Branch	Jan	Feb	Mar	Apr	May	Jun	Jul	Aug	Sep	Oct	Nov	Dec	Total	Percent
5	Los Angeles	$200	$200	$200	$200	$200	$200	$200	$200	$200	$200	$200	$200	$2,400	40.00%
6	New York	$300	$300	$300	$300	$300	$300	$300	$300	$300	$300	$300	$300	$3,600	60.00%
7	Total	$500	$500	$500	$500	$500	$500	$500	$500	$500	$500	$500	$500	$6,000	
8															
9															

Customizing Excel and Advanced Worksheet Management

Customize an Excel Workbook

Learning Outcomes
• Change the number of default worksheets
• Change the default workbook font and view

The Excel default settings for editing and viewing a worksheet are designed to meet the needs of the majority of Excel users. You may find, however, that a particular setting doesn't always fit your particular needs, such as the default number of worksheets in a workbook, the default worksheet view, or the default font. You have already used the Advanced category in the Excel Options dialog box to create custom lists and the Formulas category to switch to manual calculation. The General category contains features that are commonly used by a large number of Excel users, and you can use it to further customize Excel to suit your work habits and needs. The most commonly used categories of the Excel Options are explained in more detail in **TABLE 15-1**. **CASE** *Mary is interested in customizing workbooks to allow her to work more efficiently. You decide to use a blank workbook to explore features that will help her better manage her data. In the last workbook you prepared for Mary you had to add a second worksheet. You would like to have two worksheets displayed rather than one when a new workbook is opened.*

STEPS

1. **Open a new blank workbook, click the File tab, then click Options**
   The General category of the Excel Options dialog box displays default options that Excel uses in new workbooks, as shown in **FIGURE 15-15**. You will change the number of worksheets in a new workbook.

2. **Select 1 in the Include this many sheets text box in the "When creating new workbooks" area of the Excel Options dialog box, then type 2**
   You can change the default font Excel uses in new workbooks.

3. **Click the Use this as the default font list arrow, then select Arial**
   You can also change the standard workbook font size.

4. **Click the Font size list arrow, then click 12**
   Mary would rather have new workbooks open in Page Layout view.

5. **Click the Default view for new sheets list arrow, click Page Layout View, click OK to close the Excel Options dialog box, then click OK in the message box that instructs you to quit and restart Excel**
   These default settings take effect after you exit and restart Excel.

6. **Close the workbook, exit Excel, start Excel again, then open a new blank workbook**
   A new workbook opens with two sheet tabs in Page Layout view and a 12-point Arial font, as shown in **FIGURE 15-16**. Now that you have finished exploring the Excel workbook Options, you need to restore the original Excel settings.

7. **Click the File tab, click Options, in the When creating new workbooks area of the General options, select 2 in the Include this many sheets text box and enter 1, click the Use this as the default font list arrow, select Body Font, select 12 in the Font size text box, type 11, click the Default view for new sheets list arrow, select Normal View, click OK twice, then close the workbook and exit Excel**

Customizing Excel and Advanced Worksheet Management

FIGURE 15-15: General category of Excel options

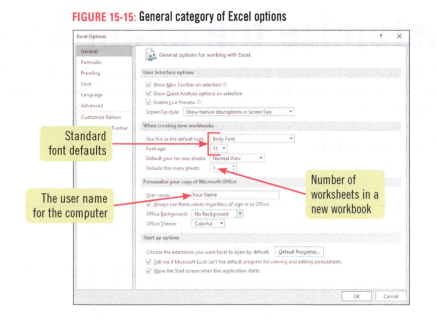

Standard font defaults

The user name for the computer

Number of worksheets in a new workbook

FIGURE 15-16: Workbook with new default settings

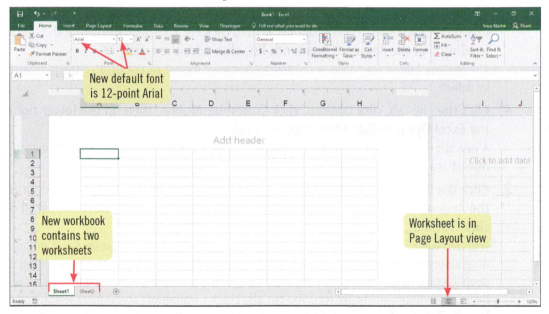

New default font is 12-point Arial

New workbook contains two worksheets

Worksheet is in Page Layout view

TABLE 15-1: Categories of Excel options

category	allows you to
General	Change the user name and the workbook screen display
Formulas	Control how the worksheet is calculated, how formulas appear, and error checking settings and rules
Proofing	Control AutoCorrect and spell-checking options
Save	Select a default format and location for saving files, and customize AutoRecover settings
Language	Control the languages displayed and allows you to add languages
Advanced	Create custom lists as well as customize editing and display options
Customize Ribbon	Add tabs and groups to the Ribbon
Quick Access Toolbar	Add commands to the Quick Access Toolbar
Add-Ins	Install Excel Add-in programs such as Solver and Analysis ToolPak
Trust Center	Change Trust Center settings to protect your Excel files

Customize the Excel Screen

Learning
Outcomes
• Customize the
  Quick Access
  Toolbar
• Customize the
  Ribbon

While the Quick Access Toolbar and the Ribbon give you easy access to many useful Excel features, you might have other commands that you want to have readily available to speed up your work. The Excel Options dialog box allows you to customize the Quick Access Toolbar and Ribbon, either for all workbooks (the default) or for a specific workbook. **CASE** *You are interested in customizing the Quick Access Toolbar to include spell checking. You also want to add a new tab to the Ribbon with accessibility tools.*

STEPS

1. **Start Excel, open a new, blank workbook, then save the file as EX 15-Customized in the location where you store your Data Files**

2. **Click the Customize Quick Access Toolbar button ▼ on the Quick Access Toolbar, then click More Commands**

    The Excel Options dialog box opens with the Quick Access Toolbar category selected, as shown in **FIGURE 15-17**. You want to add the spell checking feature to the Quick Access Toolbar for the EX 15-Customized workbook.

3. **Make sure Popular Commands is displayed in the Choose commands from list, click the Customize Quick Access Toolbar list arrow, click For EX 15-Customized.xlsx, click Spelling... in the Popular Commands list, click Add, then click OK**

    The Spelling button now appears on the Quick Access Toolbar to the right of the buttons that appear by default.

4. **Click the File tab, click Options, click Customize Ribbon, then on the lower-right side of the Excel Options dialog box click New Tab**

    A new tab named New Tab (Custom) appears in the listing of Main Tabs below the Home tab. Under the new tab is a new group named New Group (Custom).

5. **Click the Choose commands from list arrow, click Commands Not in the Ribbon, click the Accessibility Checker command, click Add, click Alt Text..., click Add, scroll down, click Zoom In, click Add, click Zoom Out, then click Add**

    Four accessibility tools now appear in the custom group on the new custom tab. Clicking the Check Accessibility button inspects your worksheet for features that need additional description for people with disabilities. Warnings are issued for worksheets with the default names as well as objects such as images and hyperlinks without alternative text. You can also check a worksheet's accessibility features by clicking the File tab, clicking Info, clicking the Check for Issues list arrow, then clicking Check Accessibility.

6. **Click New Tab (Custom) in the Main Tabs area, click Rename, in the Rename dialog box type Accessibility, click OK, click New Group (Custom) below the Accessibility tab, click Rename, in the Rename dialog box type Accessibility Tools in the Display name text box, click OK, then click OK again**

    The new custom tab appears in the Ribbon, just to the right of the Home tab. You can change the order of the tabs using the Move Up ▲ and Move Down ▼ buttons in the Excel Options dialog box. You decide to check it to verify it contains the buttons you want.

7. **Click the Accessibility tab, compare your tab to FIGURE 15-18, click the Zoom In button, then click the Zoom Out button**

    As a courtesy to other users of this computer, you will reset the Ribbon to the default settings.

8. **Click the File tab, click Options, click Customize Ribbon, on the lower-right side of the Excel Options dialog box click Reset, click Reset all customizations, click Yes, click OK, save the workbook, then close it and exit Excel**

Customizing Excel and Advanced Worksheet Management

FIGURE 15-17: Quick Access Toolbar category of Excel options

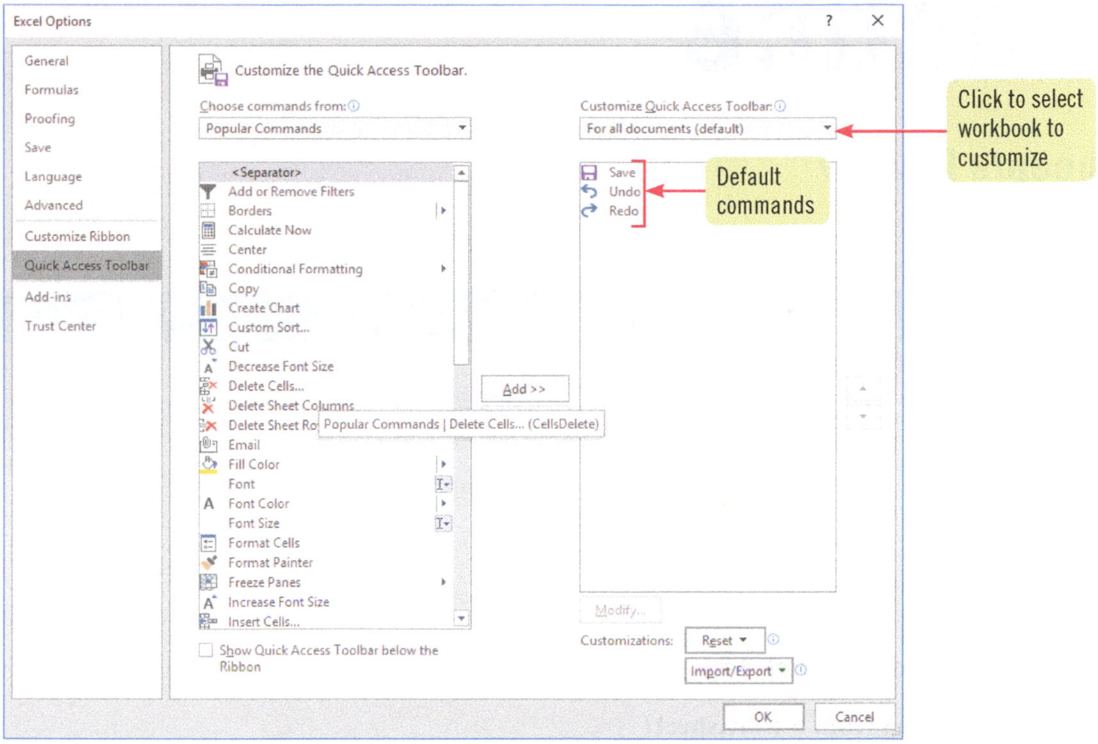

FIGURE 15-18: Workbook with new toolbar button and Accessibility Tab

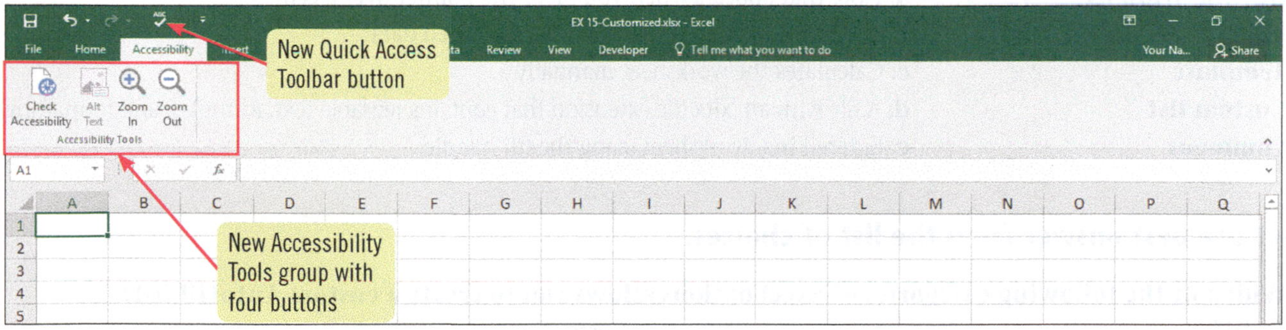

Customizing the Quick Access Toolbar

You can quickly add a button from the Ribbon to the Quick Access Toolbar by right-clicking it and selecting Add to Quick Access Toolbar. Right-clicking a Ribbon button also allows you to quickly customize the Ribbon and the Quick Access Toolbar. You can also move the Quick Access Toolbar from its default position and collapse the Ribbon.

Practice

Concepts Review

FIGURE 15-19

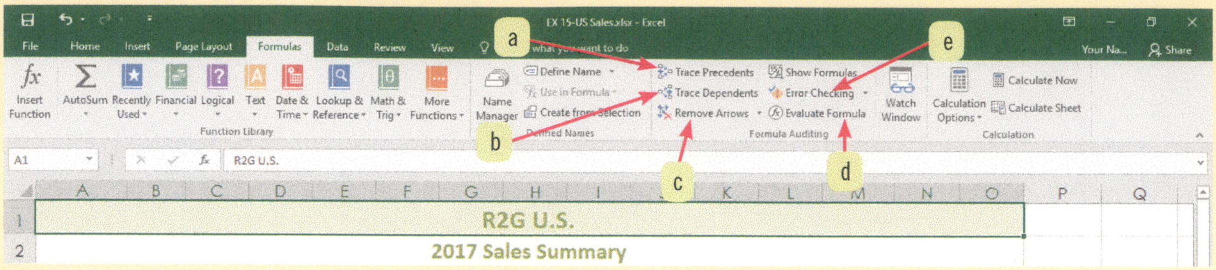

Which element do you click to:

1. Eliminate tracers from a worksheet?
2. Locate cells that reference the active cell?
3. Locate formula errors in a worksheet?
4. Step through a formula in a selected cell?
5. Find cells that may have caused a formula error?

Match each term with the statement that best describes it.

6. Outline symbols
7. [Shift][F9]
8. Template
9. Custom list
10. Comment

a. Note that appears when you place the pointer over a cell
b. Used to hide and display details in grouped data
c. Calculates the worksheet manually
d. A file with an .xltx file extension that contains reusable text, formulas, and formatting
e. Entered in a worksheet using the fill handle

Select the best answer from the list of choices.

11. Which of the following categories of Excel options allows you to create a custom AutoFill list?
    a. Add-Ins
    b. Advanced
    c. Customize
    d. Formulas

12. Which of the following categories of Excel options allows you to change the number of default worksheets in a workbook?
    a. General
    b. Proofing
    c. Advanced
    d. Formulas

13. To apply a custom list, you:
    a. Click the Fill tab in the Edit dialog box.
    b. Complete the first cell entry, then drag the fill handle.
    c. Press [Shift][F9].
    d. Select the list in the worksheet.

14. The _____ displays the fewest details in grouped data.
    a. Level 2 Outline button
    b. Level 1 Outline button
    c. Level 3 Outline button
    d. Level 4 Outline button

Skills Review

1. **Audit a worksheet.**
   a. Start Excel, open EX 15-2.xlsx from the location where you store your Data Files, then save it as **EX 15-Nashville**.
   b. Select cell B10, then use the Trace Dependents button to locate all the cells that depend on this cell.
   c. Clear the arrows from the worksheet.
   d. Select cell B19, use the Trace Precedents button to find the cells on which that figure is based, then correct the formula in cell B19. (*Hint*: It should subtract Total Expenses from Net Sales.)
   e. Use the Error Checking button to check the worksheet for any other errors. Correct any worksheet errors using the formula bar. (*Hint*: If you get an inconsistent formula error for cell F18, make sure it is totaled vertically or horizontally, then ignore the error.)

2. **Control worksheet calculations.**
   a. Open the Formulas category of the Excel Options dialog box.
   b. Change the worksheet calculations to manual.
   c. Change the figure in cell B6 to **22,000**.
   d. Recalculate the worksheet manually, using an appropriate key combination or button.
   e. Change the worksheet calculations back to automatic using the Calculation Options button, then save the workbook.

3. **Group worksheet data.**
   a. Group the income information as rows in the range A5:G6.
   b. Group the expenses information as rows in the range A10:G17.
   c. Hide the income details in rows 5 and 6.
   d. Hide the expenses details in rows 10 through 17.
   e. Enter your name in the center section of the worksheet footer, then preview the worksheet with the income and expenses detail hidden.
   f. Redisplay the income and expenses details.
   g. Remove the row grouping for the income and expenses details. (*Hint*: With the grouped rows selected, click the Data tab, then click the Ungroup button in the Outline group.)
   h. Save the workbook.

4. **Work with cell comments.**
   a. Insert a comment in cell E12 that reads **Does this include online advertising?**.
   b. Click anywhere outside the Comment box to close it.
   c. Display the comment by moving the pointer over cell E12, then check it for accuracy.
   d. Edit the comment in cell E12 to read **Does this include online and print advertising?**.
   e. Preview the worksheet and your comment, with the comment appearing at the end of the sheet.
   f. Save the workbook.

5. **Create a custom AutoFill list.**
   a. Select the range A4:A19.
   b. Open the Custom Lists dialog box, and import the selected text.
   c. Close the dialog box.
   d. Add a worksheet to the workbook. On Sheet2, enter **Income** in cell A1.
   e. Use the fill handle to enter the list through cell A15.
   f. Enter your name in the center section of the Sheet2 footer, then preview the worksheet.
   g. Open the Custom Lists dialog box again, delete the custom list you just created, then save the workbook.

6. **Create and apply a template.**
   a. Delete Sheet2 from the workbook.
   b. Delete the comment in cell E12 on Sheet1.
   c. Delete the income and expense data for all four quarters. Leave the worksheet formulas intact.

Skills Review (continued)

d. Save the workbook as a template with the name **EX 15-Nashville.xltx** in the template folder in the location where you store your Data Files. (*Hint*: If you haven't created a template folder in the location where you store your Data Files you will need to create one.)

e. Close the template, then open a new workbook based on the template by using the PERSONAL link, then double-clicking the EX 15-Nashville template in the template folder.

f. Test the template by entering the data for all four quarters and in every budget category shown in FIGURE 15-20.

g. Save the workbook as **EX 15-Nashville1.xlsx** in the location where you store your Data Files.

h. Preview the worksheet, close the workbook, then submit the workbook to your instructor.

FIGURE 15-20

	A	B	C	D	E	F	G	H
1	Nashville Café							
2								
3		Q1	Q2	Q3	Q4	Total	% of Total	
4	**Income**							
5	Beverages	$3,000	$3,000	$3,000	$3,000	$12,000	43%	
6	Food	$4,000	$4,000	$4,000	$4,000	$16,000	57%	
7	**Net Sales**	$7,000	$7,000	$7,000	$7,000	$28,000		
8								
9	**Expenses**							
10	Salaries	$100	$100	$100	$100	$400	3%	
11	Rent	$200	$200	$200	$200	$800	6%	
12	Advertising	$300	$300	$300	$300	$1,200	8%	
13	Cleaning	$400	$400	$400	$400	$1,600	11%	
14	Food	$500	$500	$500	$500	$2,000	14%	
15	Beverages	$600	$600	$600	$600	$2,400	17%	
16	Paper Products	$700	$700	$700	$700	$2,800	19%	
17	Insurance	$800	$800	$800	$800	$3,200	22%	
18	**Total Expenses**	$3,600	$3,600	$3,600	$3,600	$14,400	100%	
19	**Net Profit**	$3,400	$3,400	$3,400	$3,400	$13,600		

7. Customize an Excel workbook.

a. Open a new workbook, then open the General options of the Excel Options dialog box.

b. Change the number of sheets in a new workbook to **3**.

c. Change the default font of a new workbook to 14-point Times New Roman.

d. Close the workbook and exit Excel.

e. Start Excel and verify that the new workbook's font is 14-point Times New Roman and that it has three worksheets.

f. Reset the default number of worksheets to **1** and the default workbook font to 11-point Body Font.

8. Customize the Excel screen.

a. Use the Customize Ribbon category to add a tab named **Symbols** to the Ribbon with a group named **Math Symbols** containing the buttons Exponentiation Sign and Fraction. (*Hint*: These buttons are in the All Commands list.)

b. Use the Quick Access Toolbar category of the Excel Options dialog box to add the New and Open buttons to the Quick Access Toolbar.

c. Compare your Quick Access Toolbar and Ribbon to FIGURE 15-21.

d. Reset all customizations of the workbook, close the workbook, then exit Excel.

FIGURE 15-21

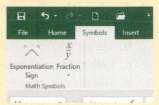

Independent Challenge 1

You are the VP of Human Resources at TechTest, an electronics testing company with offices in the east and the west regions of the United States. You are tracking the overtime hours for workers using total and percentage formulas. Before you begin your analysis, you want to check the worksheet for formula errors. Then, you group the first quarter data, add a comment to the worksheet, and create a custom list of the east and west locations and total labels.

a. Start Excel, open EX 15-3.xlsx from where you store your Data Files, then save it as **EX 15-Hours**.

b. Audit the worksheet, ignoring warnings that aren't errors and correcting the formula errors in the formula bar.

c. Select cell R5 and use the Trace Precedents button to show the cells used in its formula.

d. Select cell B10 and use the Trace Dependents button to show the cells affected by the value in the cell.

Customizing Excel and Advanced Worksheet Management

Independent Challenge 1 (continued)

e. Remove all arrows from the worksheet.

f. Group the months Jan, Feb, and March, then use the Outline symbols to hide the first quarter details.

g. Add the comment **This looks high for Miami.** to cell P5. Display the comment on the worksheet so it is visible even when you are not hovering over the cell.

h. Create a custom AutoFill list by importing the range A5:A15. Add a new worksheet to the workbook, then test the list in cells A1:A11 of the new worksheet. Delete the custom list.

i. Change the comment display to show only the comment indicators and the comments when hovering over the cell with the comment.

j. Add your name to the center section of the worksheet footer, preview the worksheet with the comment on a separate page, then save the workbook.

k. Close the workbook, exit Excel, then submit the workbook to your instructor.

Independent Challenge 2

You are the CFO of a pet supply company located in Providence. One of your responsibilities is to keep track of the company's regular monthly expenses. You have compiled a list of fixed expenses in an Excel workbook. Because the expense categories don't change from month to month, you want to create a custom AutoFill list including each expense item to save time in preparing similar worksheets in the future. You will also temporarily switch to manual formula calculation, check the total formula, and document the data.

a. Start Excel, open EX 15-4.xlsx from where you store your Data Files, then save it as **EX 15-Expenses**.

b. Select the range of cells A4:A15 on the Fixed Expenses sheet, then import the list to create a custom AutoFill list.

c. Add a new worksheet named Custom List to the workbook, then use the fill handle to insert your list in cells A1:A12 in the new sheet (*Hint:* the first word in the custom list is Utilities).

d. Add your name to the center section of the new worksheet footer, save the workbook, then preview the worksheet.

e. Delete your custom list, then return to the Fixed Expenses sheet.

f. Switch to manual calculation for formulas. Change the expense for Utilities to $9,500.00. Calculate the worksheet formula manually. Turn on automatic calculation again.

g. Add the comment **This may increase.** to cell B4. Display the comment on the worksheet so it is visible even when the mouse pointer is not hovering over the cell.

h. Use the Error Checking dialog box for help in correcting the error in cell B16. Verify that the formula is correctly totaling the expenses in column B.

i. Trace the precedents of cell B16. Compare your worksheet to **FIGURE 15-22**.

j. Remove the arrow and the comment display from the worksheet, leaving only the indicator displayed. Do not delete the comment from the worksheet cell.

k. Trace the dependents of cell B4. Remove the arrow from the worksheet.

l. Edit the comment in cell B4 to **This shouldn't change much with rate lock.**, and add the comment **This seems low.** to cell B10.

FIGURE 15-22

	A	B	C	D
1	**Ocean State Pet Supply**			
2	Monthly Expenses			
3	Category	Budget	Your Name:	
4	Utilities	$9,500.00	This may increase.	
5	Landscaping	$1,058.00		
6	Equipment	$3,011.00		
7	Taxes	$1,159.00		
8	Maintenance	$1,923.00		
9	Security	$1,032.00		
10	Cleaning	$277.00		
11	Recycling & Trash	$840.00		
12	Payroll	$7,311.00		
13	Supplies	$2,209.00		
14	Legal	$2,500.00		
15	Insurance	$1,795.00		
16	Total	$32,615.00		
17				

Independent Challenge 2 (continued)

m. Use the Next and Previous buttons in the Comments group of the Review tab to move between comments on the worksheet. Delete the comment in cell B10.

n. Add your name to the center section of the Fixed Expenses worksheet footer, save the workbook, then preview the Fixed Expenses worksheet with the comment appearing at the end of the sheet.

o. Close the workbook, exit Excel, then submit your workbook to your instructor.

Independent Challenge 3

As the business manager of the local health center you are responsible for the annual budget. You use Excel to track income and expenses using formulas to total each category and to calculate the net cash flow for the center. You want to customize your workbooks and settings in Excel so you can work more efficiently. You are also interested in grouping your data and creating a template that you can use to build next year's budget.

a. Start Excel, open EX 15-5.xlsx from where you store your Data Files, then save it as **EX 15-Budget**.

b. Add an icon to the Quick Access Toolbar for the EX 15-Budget.xlsx workbook to print preview and print a worksheet.

c. Add a tab to the Ribbon named Shapes with a group named Shape Tools. Add the buttons Elbow Arrow Connector, Elbow Connector, Freeform, and Right Arrow from the Commands Not in the Ribbon list to the new group. Compare your Ribbon and Quick Access Toolbar to **FIGURE 15-23**.

FIGURE 15-23

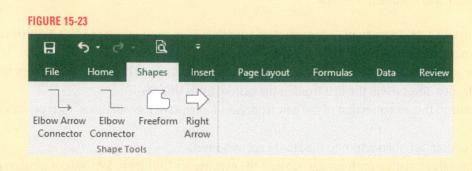

d. Add a new worksheet to the workbook, then name the new sheet Shapes. Test the new Shape Tools buttons on the Shapes worksheet by clicking each one and dragging an area to test the shapes. Add your name to the center footer section of the Shapes sheet.

e. Test the Print Preview button on the Quick Access Toolbar by previewing the Shapes sheet.

f. On the Budget sheet, group rows 4–6 and 9–14, then use the appropriate row-level Outline Symbol button to hide the expense and income details, as shown in **FIGURE 15-24**.

FIGURE 15-24

	A	B	C	D	E	F	G
1	Annual Budget						
2	Description	1st Qtr	2nd Qtr	3rd Qtr	4th Qtr	Total	
3	Income						
7	Income Total	$560,455	$515,750	$561,570	$556,788	$2,194,563	
8	Expenses						
15	Expenses Total	$459,508	$489,992	$560,659	$551,324	$2,061,483	
16	Net Cash Flow	$100,947	$25,758	$911	$5,464	$133,080	
17							
18							

Independent Challenge 3 (continued)

g. Add your name to the center section of the worksheet footer, save the workbook, then use the Print Preview button on the Quick Access Toolbar to preview the Budget worksheet. Redisplay all rows, using the Outline symbols, then save the workbook.

h. Delete the Shapes worksheet and all data in the Budget sheet, leaving the formulas and labels.

i. Save the workbook as a template named **EX 15-Budget** in the Templates folder in the location where you store your Data Files. Close the template file, and open a workbook based on the template. Save the workbook as **EX 15-New Budget**.

j. Test the template by entering data of your choice for the four quarters. Save the workbook, then preview the worksheet using the Print Preview button on the Quick Access Toolbar.

k. Customize Excel so that your workbooks will open with two worksheets in Page Layout view and use 12-point Trebuchet MS font.

l. Reset the Ribbon, close your workbook, exit Excel, and then open a new workbook to confirm the new default workbook settings. Reset the default Excel workbook to open with one sheet in Normal view and the 11-point Body Font. Close the new workbook.

m. Exit Excel, then submit the EX 15-Budget and EX 15-New Budget workbooks and the template to your instructor.

Independent Challenge 4: Explore

As the east coast sales manager of East Coast Food, you monitor the sales of each office. Your assistant has created an Excel workbook tracking the sales of the offices in your region with percentages of total sales. You will check the workbook for errors and add features before sending it back to your assistant for his review.

a. Start Excel, open EX 15-6.xlsx from the location where you store your Data Files, then save it as **EX 15-Sales**.

b. Audit the worksheet, ignoring warnings that aren't errors and correcting the formula errors in the formula bar.

c. Select cell S5 on the Sales sheet, then open the Evaluate Formula dialog box.

d. In the Evaluate Formula dialog box, click Evaluate three times to see the process of substituting values for cell addresses in the formula and the results of the formula calculations. Close the Evaluate Formula window.

e. Select cell S6, open the Watch Window. (*Hint*: Click the Watch Window button in the Formula Auditing group on the Formulas tab.)

f. Click Add Watch to add cell S6 to the Watch Window, and observe its value in the window as you change cell G6 to $1000. Close the Watch Window.

g. Add the comment **Is this correct?** to cell K7. Copy the comment in cell K7 and paste it in cell P5. (*Hint*: After copying cell K7, use the Paste Special option to copy the comment into cell P5.) Set your worksheet to display comment indicators only and comments on hover.

h. Using the Summary tab of the EX 15-Sales.xlsx Properties dialog box, add your name as the author, and **East Coast Food Annual Sales** as the Category. (*Hint*: Click the File tab, click Info, click the Properties list arrow, then click Advanced Properties.) Create a custom property of **Forward to** with a value of **Lisa Roberts**.

i. Pin the **EX 15-Sales** workbook to the Recent list. Unpin the workbook. Clear all unpinned workbooks from the Recent list.

j. Save the workbook. View any unsaved workbooks.

k. Add your name to the center section of the worksheet footer, scale the worksheet to fit on one page, save the workbook, then preview the worksheet. Close the workbook, exit Excel, then submit the workbook to your instructor.

Visual Workshop

Open EX 15-7.xlsx from the location where you store your Data Files, then save it as **EX 15-Supply**. Group the data as shown after removing any errors in the worksheet. Your grouped results should match **FIGURE 15-25**. (*Hint*: The Outline symbols have been hidden for the worksheet.) The new buttons on the Quick Access Toolbar have been added only to the EX 15-Supply workbook. Add your name to the center section of the worksheet footer, save the workbook, then preview the worksheet. Close the workbook, exit Excel, then submit the workbook to your instructor.

FIGURE 15-25

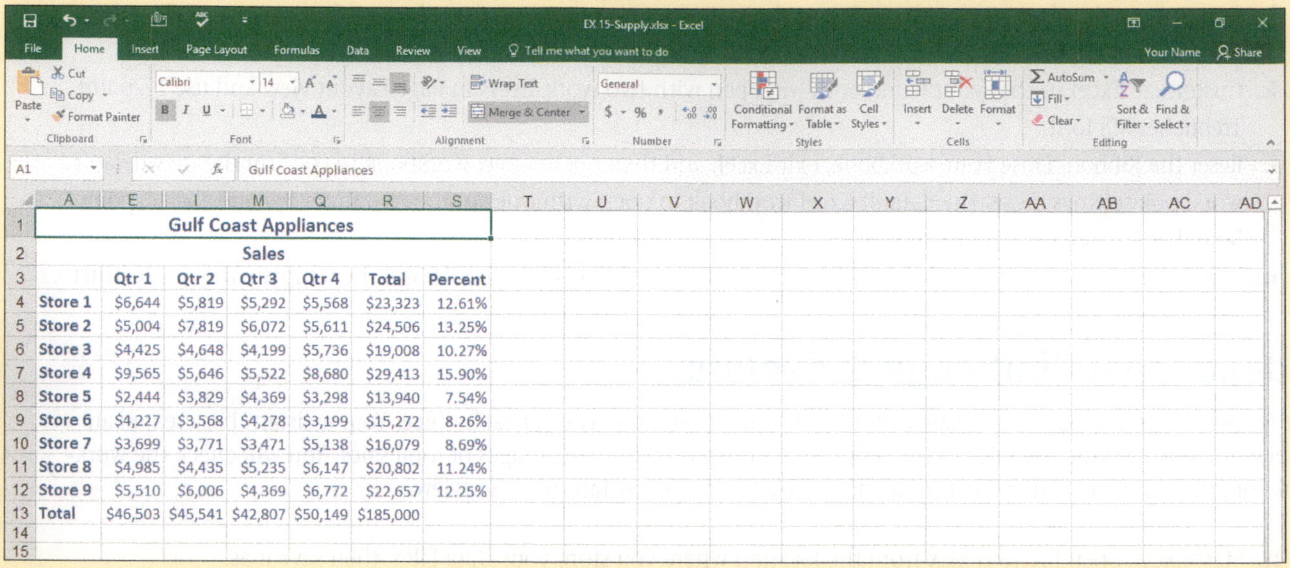

	A	E	I	M	Q	R	S
1	Gulf Coast Appliances						
2	Sales						
3		Qtr 1	Qtr 2	Qtr 3	Qtr 4	Total	Percent
4	Store 1	$6,644	$5,819	$5,292	$5,568	$23,323	12.61%
5	Store 2	$5,004	$7,819	$6,072	$5,611	$24,506	13.25%
6	Store 3	$4,425	$4,648	$4,199	$5,736	$19,008	10.27%
7	Store 4	$9,565	$5,646	$5,522	$8,680	$29,413	15.90%
8	Store 5	$2,444	$3,829	$4,369	$3,298	$13,940	7.54%
9	Store 6	$4,227	$3,568	$4,278	$3,199	$15,272	8.26%
10	Store 7	$3,699	$3,771	$3,471	$5,138	$16,079	8.69%
11	Store 8	$4,985	$4,435	$5,235	$6,147	$20,802	11.24%
12	Store 9	$5,510	$6,006	$4,369	$6,772	$22,657	12.25%
13	Total	$46,503	$45,541	$42,807	$50,149	$185,000	

Programming with Excel

CASE ▶ Reason2Go's vice president of sales and marketing, Mary Watson, would like to automate some of the time-consuming tasks for the sales group. She asks you to create macros, using the Visual Basic for Applications (VBA) programming language, that format worksheet data, calculate sales totals, evaluate whether sales quotas are met, and insert user information in a worksheet footer.

Module Objectives

After completing this module, you will be able to:

- View VBA code
- Analyze VBA code
- Write VBA code
- Add a conditional statement

- Prompt the user for data
- Debug a macro
- Create a main procedure
- Run a main procedure

Files You Will Need

EX 16-1.xlsm	EX 16-5.xlsm
EX 16-2.xlsx	EX 16-6.xlsm
EX 16-3.xlsm	EX 16-7.xlsm
EX 16-4.xlsm	EX 16-8.xlsm

View VBA Code

Learning
Outcomes
• Identify the VBA
  windows
• Define VBA
  procedure terms

As you learned in Module 9, you can create macros using the Excel macro recorder, which automatically writes Visual Basic for Applications (VBA) instructions for you as you perform actions. For additional flexibility, you can also create entire Excel macros by typing VBA program code. To enter and edit VBA code, you work in the **Visual Basic Editor**, a tool you can start from within Excel. A common method of learning any programming language is to view existing code. In VBA macro code, a sequence of VBA statements is called a **procedure**. The first line of a procedure, called the **procedure header**, defines the procedure's type, name, and arguments. **Arguments** are variables used by other procedures that the main procedure might run. **CASE** ➤ *Each month, Mary receives text files containing sales information from the Reason2Go branches. Mary has already imported the text file for the Toronto January sales into a worksheet, but it still needs to be formatted. She asks you to work on a macro to automate the process of formatting the imported information.*

STEPS

1. **Start Excel if necessary, open a blank workbook, click the Developer tab, then click the Macro Security button in the Code group**

   The Trust Center dialog box opens, as shown in **FIGURE 16-1**. You know the Reason2Go branch files are from a trusted source, so you decide to allow macros to run in the workbook.

2. **Click the Enable all macros option button if necessary, then click OK**

   You are ready to open a file and view its VBA code. A macro-enabled workbook has the extension .xlsm. Although a workbook containing a macro will open if macros are disabled, they will not function.

3. **Open EX 16-1.xlsm from the location where you store your Data Files, save it as EX 16-Monthly Sales, click the Developer tab then click the Macros button in the Code group**

   The Macro dialog box opens, showing the FormatFile macro procedure in the list box. If you have any macros saved in your Personal Macro workbook, they are also listed in the Macro dialog box.

4. **If it is not already selected click the FormatFile macro, then click Edit**

   The Microsoft Visual Basic for Applications window opens, containing three windows, shown in **FIGURE 16-2**. See **TABLE 16-1** to make sure your screen matches the ones shown in this module. You may need to select the Format module in the Project Explorer window. See also the yellow box on the next page for more information about the VBA window.

5. **Make sure both the Visual Basic window and the Code window are maximized to match FIGURE 16-2**

   In the Code window, the different parts of the FormatFile procedure appear in various colors. Comments explaining the code are displayed in green.

6. **Examine the top three lines of code, which contain comments, and the first line of code beginning with Sub FormatFile( )**

   The first two comment lines give the procedure name and tell what the procedure does. The third comment line explains that the keyboard shortcut for this macro procedure is Ctrl+Shift+F. Items that appear in blue are **keywords**, which are words Excel recognizes as part of the VBA programming language. The keyword Sub in the procedure header indicates that this is a **Sub procedure**, or a series of Visual Basic statements that perform an action but do not return (create and display) a value. An empty set of parentheses after the procedure name means the procedure doesn't have any arguments. In the next lesson, you analyze the procedure code to see what each line does.

FIGURE 16-1: Macro settings in the Trust Center dialog box

Select to allow macros to run →

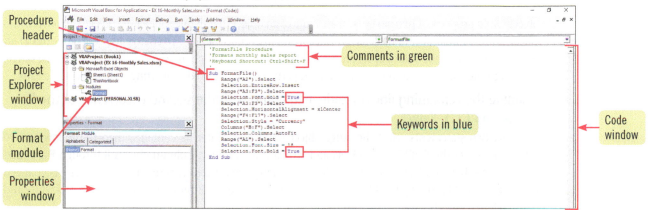

FIGURE 16-2: Procedure displayed in the Visual Basic Editor

Procedure header

Project Explorer window

Format module

Properties window

Comments in green

Keywords in blue

Code window

TABLE 16-1: Matching your screen to the module figures

if...	do this...
The Properties window is not displayed	Click the Properties Window button [icon] on the toolbar
The Project Explorer window is not displayed	Click the Project Explorer button [icon] on the toolbar
You see only the Code window	Click Tools on the menu bar, click Options, click the Docking tab, then make sure the Project Explorer and Properties Window options are selected
You do not see folders in the Explorer window	Click the Toggle Folders button [icon] on the Project Explorer window Project toolbar

Understanding the Visual Basic Editor

In Excel, a **module** is the Visual Basic equivalent of a worksheet. In it, you store macro procedures, just as you store data in worksheets. Modules, in turn, are stored in workbooks (or projects), along with worksheets. A **project** is the collection of all procedures in a workbook. You view and edit modules in the Visual Basic Editor, which is made up of the Project Explorer window (also called the Project window), the Code window, and the Properties window. **Project Explorer** displays a list of all open projects (or workbooks) and the worksheets and modules they contain. To view the procedures stored in a module, you must first select the module in Project Explorer (just as you would select a file in Windows Explorer). The **Code window** then displays the selected module's procedures. The **Properties window** displays a list of characteristics (or properties) associated with the module. A newly inserted module has only one property, its name.

Excel 2016

Programming with Excel

Analyze VBA Code

You can learn a lot about the VBA language simply by analyzing the code generated by the Excel macro recorder. The more VBA code you analyze, the easier it is for you to write your own programming code. **CASE** ▶ *Before writing any new procedures, you analyze a previously written procedure that applies formatting to a worksheet. Then you open a worksheet that you want to format and run the macro.*

STEPS

1. **With the FormatFile procedure still displayed in the Code window, examine the next four lines of code, beginning with Range("A2"). Select**

   Refer to **FIGURE 16-3** as you analyze the code in this lesson. Every Excel element, including a range, is considered an **object**. A **range object** represents a cell or a range of cells. The statement Range("A2").Select selects the range object cell A2. Notice that several times in the procedure, a line of code (or **statement**) selects a range, and then subsequent lines act on that selection. The next statement, Selection.EntireRow. Insert, inserts a row above the selection, which is currently cell A2. The next two lines of code select range A3:F3 and apply bold formatting to that selection. In VBA terminology, bold formatting is a value of an object's Bold property. A **property** is an attribute of an object that defines one of the object's characteristics (such as size) or an aspect of its behavior (such as whether it is enabled). To change the characteristics of an object, you change the values of its properties. For example, to apply bold formatting to a selected range, you assign the value True to the range's Bold property. To remove bold formatting, assign the value False.

2. **Examine the remaining lines of code, beginning with the second occurrence of the line Range("A3:F3"). Select**

   The next two statements select the range object A3:F3 and center its contents, then the following two statements select the F4:F17 range object and format it as currency. Column objects B through F are then selected, and their widths set to AutoFit. Finally, the range object cell A1 is selected, its font size is changed to 20, and its Bold property is set to True. The last line, End Sub, indicates the end of the Sub procedure and is also referred to as the **procedure footer**.

3. **Click the View Microsoft Excel button ▣ on the Visual Basic Editor toolbar to return to Excel**

   Because the macro is stored in the EX 16-Monthly Sales workbook, you can open this workbook and repeatedly use the macro stored there each month after you receive that month's sales data. You want to open the workbook containing data for Toronto's January sales and run the macro to format the data. You must leave the EX 16-Monthly Sales workbook open to use the macro stored there.

4. **Open EX 16-2.xlsx from the location where you store your Data Files, then save it as EX 16-January Sales**

   This is the workbook containing the data you want to format.

5. **Press [Ctrl][Shift][F] to run the procedure**

   The FormatFile procedure formats the text, as shown in **FIGURE 16-4**.

6. **Save the workbook**

   Now that you've successfully viewed and analyzed VBA code and run the macro, you will learn how to write your own code.

FIGURE 16-3: VBA code for the FormatFile procedure

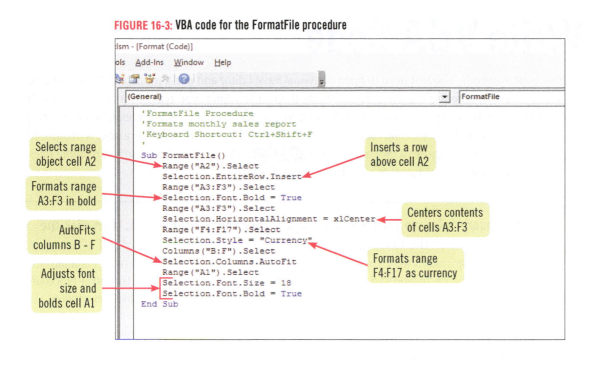

Selects range object cell A2

Formats range A3:F3 in bold

AutoFits columns B - F

Adjusts font size and bolds cell A1

Inserts a row above cell A2

Centers contents of cells A3:F3

Formats range F4:F17 as currency

```
lsm - [Format (Code)]
ols  Add-Ins  Window  Help

(General)                                        FormatFile

      'FormatFile Procedure
      'Formats monthly sales report
      'Keyboard Shortcut: Ctrl+Shift+F
      '
      Sub FormatFile()
          Range("A2").Select
          Selection.EntireRow.Insert
          Range("A3:F3").Select
          Selection.Font.Bold = True
          Range("A3:F3").Select
          Selection.HorizontalAlignment = xlCenter
          Range("F4:F17").Select
          Selection.Style = "Currency"
          Columns("B:F").Select
          Selection.Columns.AutoFit
          Range("A1").Select
          Selection.Font.Size = 18
          Selection.Font.Bold = True
      End Sub
```

FIGURE 16-4: Worksheet formatted using the FormatFile procedure

Formatted title

Row inserted

Formatted column headings

Range formatted as currency

Columns widened

	A	B	C	D	E	F	G	H
1	R2G Toronto January Sales							
2								
3	Code	Air Included	Insurance Included	New Project	Sales Rep #	Sales		
4	457R	Yes	Yes	Yes	15248	$101,400.00		
5	556J	Yes	No	Yes	13548	$ 77,875.00		
6	675Y	Yes	No	No	69541	$ 80,300.00		
7	446R	Yes	Yes	No	36654	$ 56,958.00		
8	251D	No	Yes	No	95478	$ 38,520.00		
9	335P	Yes	No	No	12532	$100,270.00		
10	431V	No	No	Yes	51241	$ 64,390.00		
11	215C	No	Yes	N	32145	$ 97,663.00		
12	325B	No	Yes	Yes	12584	$ 48,600.00		
13	311A	Yes	Yes	Yes	63344	$ 92,887.00		
14	422R	Yes	No	No	87454	$ 55,600.00		
15	331E	No	No	No	25469	$ 99,557.00		
16	831P	Yes	Yes	No	51487	$ 56,698.00		
17	337Q	No	Yes	No	35824	$ 29,574.00		
18								

Excel 2016

Write VBA Code

Learning Outcomes
- Create a VBA module
- Enter VBA code

To write your own code, you first need to open the Visual Basic Editor and add a module to the workbook. You can then begin entering the procedure code. In the first few lines, you typically include comments indicating the name of the procedure, a brief description, and shortcut keys, if applicable. When entering code, you must follow the formatting rules, or **syntax**, of the VBA programming language. A misspelled keyword or variable name causes a procedure to fail. **CASE** *Mary would like to total the monthly sales. You help her by writing a procedure that automates this routine task.*

STEPS

TROUBLE
If the Code window is empty, verify that the workbook that contains your procedures (EX 16-Monthly Sales) is open.

1. **With the January Sales worksheet still displayed, click the Developer tab, then click the Visual Basic button in the Code group**

   Two projects are displayed in the Project Explorer window, EX 16-Monthly Sales.xlsm (which contains the FormatFile macro) and EX 16-January Sales.xlsx (which contains the monthly data). The FormatFile procedure is again displayed in the Visual Basic Editor. You may have other projects in the Project Explorer window.

2. **Click the Modules folder in the EX 16-Monthly Sales.xlsm project**

   You need to store all of the procedures in the EX 16-Monthly Sales.xlsm project, which is in the EX 16-Monthly Sales.xlsm workbook. By clicking the Modules folder, you have activated the workbook, and the title bar changes from EX 16-January Sales to EX 16-Monthly Sales.

3. **Click Insert on the Visual Basic Editor menu bar, then click Module**

   A new, blank module with the default name Module1 appears in the EX 16-Monthly Sales.xlsm project, under the Format module. You think the property name of the module could be more descriptive.

4. **Click (Name) in the Properties window, type Total, then press [ENTER]**

   The module name is Total. The module name should not be the same as the procedure name (which will be AddTotal). In the code shown in **FIGURE 16-5**, comments begin with an apostrophe, and the lines of code under Sub AddTotal( ) have been indented using the Tab key. When you enter the code in the next step, after you type the procedure header Sub AddTotal( ) and press [Enter], the Visual Basic Editor automatically enters End Sub (the procedure footer) in the Code window.

TROUBLE
In some installations, clicking the Save button 🖫 on the Visual Basic toolbar causes Excel to stop working; if necessary, instead of using this button you can return to the worksheet and use the Save button 🖫 on the Quick Access Toolbar.

5. **Click in the Code window, then type the procedure code exactly as shown in FIGURE 16-5, entering your name in the second line, and pressing [Tab] to indent text and [Shift][Tab] to move the insertion point to the left**

   The lines that begin with ActiveCell.Formula insert the information enclosed in quotation marks into the active cell. For example, ActiveCell.Formula = "Total Sales:" inserts the words "Total Sales:" into cell E18, the active cell. As you type each line, Excel adjusts the spacing.

6. **Compare the code you entered in the Code window with FIGURE 16-5, make any corrections if necessary, then click the Save button 🖫 on the Visual Basic Editor toolbar**

7. **Click the View Microsoft Excel button 🗷 on the toolbar, click EX 16-January Sales.xlsx on the taskbar to activate the workbook if necessary, with the January worksheet displayed click the Developer tab if necessary, then click the Macros button in the Code group**

   Macro names have two parts. The first part ('EX 16-Monthly Sales.xlsm'!) indicates the workbook where the macro is stored. The second part (AddTotal or FormatFile) is the name of the procedure, taken from the procedure header.

TROUBLE
If an error message appears, click Debug. Click the Reset button 🔲 on the toolbar, correct the error, then repeat Steps 6–8.

8. **Click 'EX 16-MonthlySales.xlsm'!AddTotal to select it if necessary, then click Run**

   The AddTotal procedure inserts and formats the total sales in cell F18, as shown in **FIGURE 16-6**.

9. **Save the workbook**

FIGURE 16-5: VBA code for the AddTotal procedure

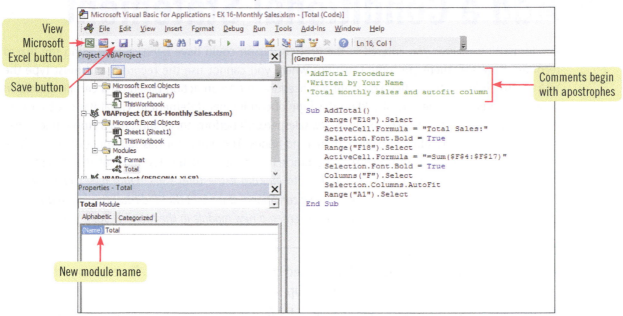

```
Microsoft Visual Basic for Applications - EX 16-Monthly Sales.xlsm - [Total (Code)]
```

View Microsoft Excel button →

Save button →

Project - VBAProject

Microsoft Excel Objects
  Sheet1 (January)
  ThisWorkbook
VBAProject (EX 16-Monthly Sales.xlsm)
  Microsoft Excel Objects
    Sheet1 (Sheet1)
    ThisWorkbook
  Modules
    Format
    Total

Properties - Total

Total Module
Alphabetic | Categorized
(Name) Total ← New module name

(General)

```
'AddTotal Procedure
'Written by Your Name
'Total monthly sales and autofit column
'
Sub AddTotal()
    Range("E18").Select
    ActiveCell.Formula = "Total Sales:"
    Selection.Font.Bold = True
    Range("F18").Select
    ActiveCell.Formula = "=Sum($F$4:$F$17)"
    Selection.Font.Bold = True
    Columns("F").Select
    Selection.Columns.AutoFit
    Range("A1").Select
End Sub
```

Comments begin with apostrophes →

FIGURE 16-6: Worksheet after running the AddTotal procedure

	A	B	C	D	E	F	G
1	R2G Toronto January Sales						
2							
3	Code	Air Included	Insurance Included	New Project	Sales Rep #	Sales	
4	457R	Yes	Yes	Yes	15248	$ 101,400.00	
5	556J	Yes	No	Yes	13548	$ 77,875.00	
6	675Y	Yes	No	No	69541	$ 80,300.00	
7	446R	Yes	Yes	No	36654	$ 56,958.00	
8	251D	No	Yes	No	95478	$ 38,520.00	
9	335P	Yes	No	No	12532	$ 100,270.00	
10	431V	No	No	Yes	51241	$ 64,390.00	
11	215C	No	Yes	N	32145	$ 97,663.00	
12	325B	No	Yes	Yes	12584	$ 48,600.00	
13	311A	Yes	Yes	Yes	63344	$ 92,887.00	
14	422R	Yes	No	No	87454	$ 55,600.00	
15	331E	No	No	No	25469	$ 99,557.00	
16	831P	Yes	Yes	No	51487	$ 56,698.00	
17	337Q	No	Yes	No	35824	$ 29,574.00	
18					Total Sales:	$ 1,000,292.00	

Result of AddTotal procedure ←

Entering code using AutoComplete

To assist you in entering the VBA code, the Editor uses **AutoComplete**, a list of words that can be used in the macro statement and match what you type. The list usually appears after you press [.] (period). To include a word from the list in the macro statement, select the word in the list, then double-click it or press [Tab]. For example, to enter the Range("E12").Select instruction, type Range("E12"), then press [.] (period). Type s to bring up the words beginning with the letter "s", select the Select command in the list, then press [Tab] to enter the word "Select" in the macro statement.

Add a Conditional Statement

Learning
Outcomes
• Enter a VBA condi-
tional statement
• Run a VBA condi-
tional statement

The formatting macros you entered in the previous lesson could have been created using the macro recorder. However, there are some situations where you cannot use the recorder and must type the VBA macro code, such as when you want a procedure to take an action based on a certain condition or set of conditions. One way of adding this type of conditional statement in Visual Basic is to use an **If...Then...Else statement**. For example, *if* a salesperson's performance rating is a 5 (top rating), *then* calculate a 10% bonus; otherwise (*else*), there is no bonus. The syntax for this statement is: "If *condition* Then *statements* Else [*else statements*]." The brackets indicate that the Else part of the statement is optional. **CASE** *Mary wants the worksheet to indicate if the total sales figure meets or misses the $1,000,000 monthly quota. You use Excel to add a conditional statement that indicates this information. You start by returning to the Visual Basic Editor and inserting a new module in the Monthly Sales project.*

STEPS

1. **With the January worksheet still displayed click the Developer tab if necessary, then click the Visual Basic button in the Code group**

2. **Verify that the Total module in the Modules folder of the EX 16-Monthly Sales VBAProject is selected in the Project Explorer window, click Insert on the Visual Basic Editor menu bar, then click Module**

   A new, blank module named Module1 is inserted in the EX 16-Monthly Sales workbook.

3. **In the Properties window click (Name), then type Sales**

   There is no need to press [Enter] after typing "Sales" because the new name will be entered once you click in the Code window.

QUICK TIP
The If...Then...Else
statement is similar
to the Excel
IF function.

4. **Click in the Code window, then type the code exactly as shown in FIGURE 16-7, entering your name in the second line**

   Notice the green comment lines in the middle of the code. These lines help explain the procedure.

5. **Compare the procedure you entered with FIGURE 16-7, make any corrections if necessary, click the Save button 🖫 on the Visual Basic Editor toolbar, then click the View Microsoft Excel button 🖾 on the Visual Basic Editor toolbar**

TROUBLE
If you get an error
message check your
code for errors, cor-
rect the errors, save
your macro, click the
Reset button ▣ on
the Visual Basic
Editor toolbar, then
rerun the macro.

6. **If necessary, click EX 16-January Sales.xlsx on the taskbar to display it, click the Macros button in the Code group, in the Macro dialog box click 'EX 16-Monthly Sales.xlsm'!SalesStatus, then click Run**

   The SalesStatus procedure indicates the status "Met Quota", as shown in **FIGURE 16-8**.

7. **Save the EX 16-January Sales workbook, then save the EX 16-Monthly Sales.xlsm workbook**

FIGURE 16-7: VBA code for the SalesStatus procedure

```
'SalesStatus Procedure
'Written by Your Name
'Tests whether total sales meet the monthly quota
'
Sub SalesStatus()
     Range("E20").Select
     ActiveCell.Formula = "Sales Status:"
     Selection.Font.Bold = True
     'If the total is less than 1000000 then
     'insert "Missed Quota" in cell F20
     If Range("F18") <= 1000000 Then
          Range("F20").Select
          ActiveCell.Formula = "Missed Quota"
     'otherwise, insert "Met Quota" in cell F20
     Else
          Range("F20").Select
          ActiveCell.Formula = "Met Quota"
     End If
     Range("A1").Select
End Sub
```

If ... Then ... Else statement

FIGURE 16-8: Result of running the SalesStatus procedure

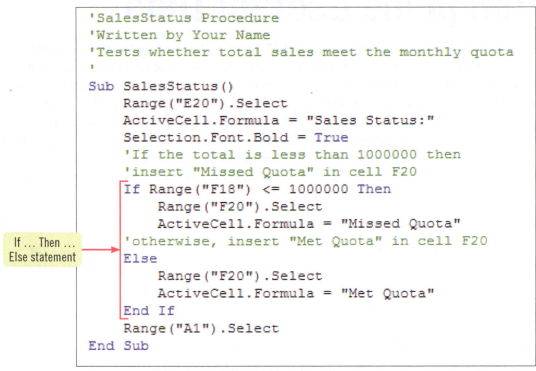

	A	B	C	D	E	F	G
1	**R2G Toronto January Sales**						
2							
3	**Code**	**Air Included**	**Insurance Included**	**New Project**	**Sales Rep #**	**Sales**	
4	457R	Yes	Yes	Yes	15248	$ 101,400.00	
5	556J	Yes	No	Yes	13548	$ 77,875.00	
6	675Y	Yes	No	No	69541	$ 80,300.00	
7	446R	Yes	Yes	No	36654	$ 56,958.00	
8	251D	No	Yes	No	95478	$ 38,520.00	
9	335P	Yes	No	No	12532	$ 100,270.00	
10	431V	No	No	Yes	51241	$ 64,390.00	
11	215C	No	Yes	N	32145	$ 97,663.00	
12	325B	No	Yes	Yes	12584	$ 48,600.00	
13	311A	Yes	Yes	Yes	63344	$ 92,887.00	
14	422R	Yes	No	No	87454	$ 55,600.00	
15	331E	No	No	No	25469	$ 99,557.00	
16	831P	Yes	Yes	No	51487	$ 56,698.00	
17	337Q	No	Yes	No	35824	$ 29,574.00	
18					**Total Sales:**	$ 1,000,292.00	
19							
20					**Sales Status** Met Quota		
21							
22							

Indicates status of monthly total

Prompt the User for Data

Another situation where you must type, not record, VBA code is when you need to pause a macro to allow user input. You use the VBA InputBox function to display a dialog box that prompts the user for information. A **function** is a predefined procedure that returns (creates and displays) a value; in this case the value returned is the information the user enters. The required elements of an InputBox function are as follows: *object*.InputBox("*prompt*"), where "*prompt*" is the message that appears in the dialog box. For a detailed description of the InputBox function, use the Visual Basic Editor's Help menu. **CASE** *You decide to create a procedure that will insert the user's name in the left footer area of the worksheet. You use the InputBox function to display a dialog box in which the user can enter his or her name. You also type an intentional error into the procedure code, which you will correct in the next lesson.*

STEPS

1. **With the January worksheet displayed click the Developer tab if necessary, click the Visual Basic button in the Code group, verify that the Sales module is selected in the EX 16-Monthly Sales VBAProject Modules folder, click Insert on the Visual Basic Editor menu bar, then click Module**

   A new, blank module named Module1 is inserted in the EX 16-Monthly Sales workbook.

2. **In the Properties window click (Name), then type Footer**

3. **Click in the Code window, then type the procedure code exactly as shown in FIGURE 16-9, entering your name in the second line**

   Like the SalesStatus procedure, this procedure also contains comments that explain the code. The first part of the code, Dim LeftFooterText As String, **declares**, or defines, LeftFooterText as a text string variable. In Visual Basic, a **variable** is a location in memory in which you can temporarily store one item of information. Dim statements are used to declare variables and must be entered in the following format: Dim *variablename* As *datatype*. The datatype here is "string." In this case, you plan to store the information received from the input box in the temporary memory location called LeftFooterText. Then you can place this text in the left footer area. The remaining statements in the procedure are explained in the comment line directly above each statement. Notice the comment pointing out the error in the procedure code. You will correct this in the next lesson.

4. **Review your code, make any necessary changes, click the Save button 💾 on the Visual Basic Editor toolbar, then click the View Microsoft Excel button ☒ on the Visual Basic Editor toolbar**

5. **With the January worksheet displayed, click the Macros button in the Code group, in the Macro dialog box click 'EX 16-Monthly Sales.xlsm'!FooterInput, then click Run**

   The procedure begins, and a dialog box generated by the InputBox function opens, prompting you to enter your name, as shown in FIGURE 16-10.

6. **With the cursor in the text box, type your name, then click OK**

7. **Click the File tab, click Print, then view the worksheet preview**

   Although the customized footer with the date is inserted on the sheet, because of the error your name does *not* appear in the left section of the footer. In the next lesson, you will learn how to step through a procedure's code line by line. This will help you locate the error in the FooterInput procedure.

8. **Click the Back button ⊙, save the EX 16-January Sales workbook, then save the EX 16-Monthly Sales.xlsm workbook**

TROUBLE

If your macro doesn't prompt you for your name, it may contain an error. Return to the Visual Basic Editor, click the Reset button ◻ correct the error by referring to **FIGURE 16-9**, then repeat Steps 4 and 5. You learn more about how to correct errors in the next lesson.

FIGURE 16-9: VBA code for the FooterInput procedure

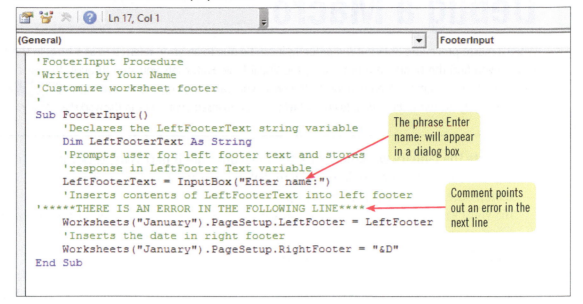

```
                  Ln 17, Col 1

(General)                                    FooterInput

    'FooterInput Procedure
    'Written by Your Name
    'Customize worksheet footer
    '
    Sub FooterInput()
        'Declares the LeftFooterText string variable
        Dim LeftFooterText As String
        'Prompts user for left footer text and stores
        'response in LeftFooter Text variable
        LeftFooterText = InputBox("Enter name:")
        'Inserts contents of LeftFooterText into left footer
    '*****THERE IS AN ERROR IN THE FOLLOWING LINE****
        Worksheets("January").PageSetup.LeftFooter = LeftFooter
        'Inserts the date in right footer
        Worksheets("January").PageSetup.RightFooter = "&D"
    End Sub
```

The phrase Enter name: will appear in a dialog box

Comment points out an error in the next line

FIGURE 16-10: InputBox function's dialog box

Dialog box showing user prompt

Microsoft Excel
Enter name:
OK
Cancel

	A	B	C	D		
1	R2G Toronto Januar					
2						
3	Code	Air Included	Insuran		Project	Sal
4	457R	Yes	Yes		152	
5	556J	Yes	No	Yes	135	
6	675Y	Yes	No	No	69541	$ 80,300.00
7	446R	Yes	Yes	No	36654	$ 56,958.00

Excel 2016

Naming variables

Variable names in VBA must begin with a letter. Letters can be uppercase or lowercase. Variable names cannot include periods or spaces, and they can be up to 255 characters long. Each variable name in a procedure must be unique. Examples of valid and invalid variable names are shown in **TABLE 16-2**.

TABLE 16-2: Variable names

valid	invalid
Sales_Department	Sales Department
SalesDepartment	Sales Department
Quarter1	1stQuarter

Debug a Macro

When a macro procedure does not run properly, it can be due to an error, referred to as a **bug**, in the code. To help you find the bug(s) in a procedure, the Visual Basic Editor lets you step through the procedure's code, one line at a time. When you locate the error, you can then correct, or **debug**, it. **CASE** ▶ *You decide to debug the macro procedure to find out why it failed to insert your name in the worksheet footer.*

QUICK TIP

A common mistake is to confuse the module name with the procedure name. remember that the module is the container that holds the procedure. To run a macro, always use the procedure name, not the module name.

1. **Activate the January worksheet click the Developer tab if necessary, click the Macros button in the Code group, in the Macro dialog box click 'EX 16-Monthly Sales. xlsm'!FooterInput, then click Step Into**

   The Visual Basic Editor opens with the yellow statement selector positioned on the first statement of the procedure, as shown in **FIGURE 16-11**.

2. **Press [F8] to step to the next statement**

   The statement selector skips over the comments and the line of code beginning with Dim. The Dim statement indicates that the procedure will store your name in a variable named LeftFooterText. Because Dim is a declaration of a variable and not a procedure statement, the statement selector skips it and moves to the line containing the InputBox function.

3. **Press [F8] again, with the cursor in the text box in the Microsoft Excel dialog box type your name, then click OK**

   The Visual Basic Editor opens. The statement selector is now positioned on the statement that reads Worksheets("January").PageSetup.LeftFooter = LeftFooter. This statement should insert your name (which you just typed in the text box) in the left section of the footer. This is the instruction that does not appear to be working correctly.

4. **If necessary scroll right until the end of the LeftFooter instruction is visible, then point to LeftFooter**

   The value of the LeftFooter variable is displayed as shown in **FIGURE 16-12**. Rather than containing your name, the variable LeftFooter at the end of this line is empty. This is because the InputBox function assigned your name to the LeftFooterText variable, not to the LeftFooter variable. Before you can correct this bug, you need to turn off the Step Into feature.

5. **Click the Reset button ▣ on the Visual Basic Editor toolbar to turn off the Step Into feature, click at the end of the statement containing the error, then replace the variable LeftFooter with LeftFooterText**

   The revised statement now reads Worksheets("January").PageSetup.LeftFooter = LeftFooterText.

6. **Delete the comment line pointing out the error, then click the Save button 🖫 on the Visual Basic Editor toolbar, then click the View Microsoft Excel button 🖾 on the Visual Basic Editor toolbar**

7. **With the January worksheet displayed click the Macros button in the Code group, in the Macro dialog box click 'EX 16-Monthly Sales.xlsm'!FooterInput, click Run to rerun the procedure, when prompted type your name, then click OK**

8. **Click the File tab, click Print, then view the worksheet preview**

   Your name now appears in the left section of the footer.

9. **Click the Back button ◉, save the EX 16-January Sales workbook, then save the EX 16-Monthly Sales.xlsm workbook**

FIGURE 16-11: Statement selector positioned on first procedure statement

```
(General)                                                    ▼   FooterInput

    'FooterInput Procedure
    'Written by Your Name
    'Customize worksheet footer
    '
    Sub FooterInput()
        'Declares the LeftFooterText string variable
        Dim LeftFooterText As String
        'Prompts user for left footer text and stores
        'response in LeftFooter Text variable
        LeftFooterText = InputBox("Enter name:")
        'Inserts contents of LeftFooterText into left footer
    '*****THERE IS AN ERROR IN THE FOLLOWING LINE****
        Worksheets("January").PageSetup.LeftFooter = LeftFooter
        'Inserts the date in right footer
        Worksheets("January").PageSetup.RightFooter = "&D"
    End Sub
```

Statement selector ➝ (points to `Sub FooterInput()`)

FIGURE 16-12: Value contained in LeftFooter variable

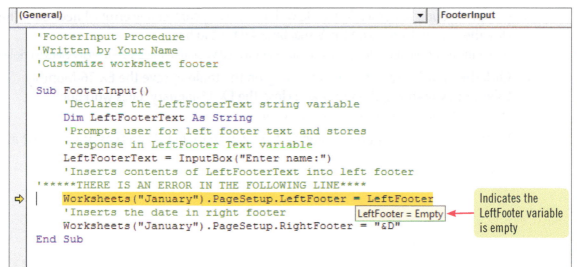

```
(General)                                                    ▼   FooterInput

    'FooterInput Procedure
    'Written by Your Name
    'Customize worksheet footer
    '
    Sub FooterInput()
        'Declares the LeftFooterText string variable
        Dim LeftFooterText As String
        'Prompts user for left footer text and stores
        'response in LeftFooter Text variable
        LeftFooterText = InputBox("Enter name:")
        'Inserts contents of LeftFooterText into left footer
    '*****THERE IS AN ERROR IN THE FOLLOWING LINE****
⇨ |     Worksheets("January").PageSetup.LeftFooter = LeftFooter
        'Inserts the date in right footer       LeftFooter = Empty
        Worksheets("January").PageSetup.RightFooter = "&D"
    End Sub
```

Indicates the LeftFooter variable is empty

Excel 2016

Create a Main Procedure

Learning Outcome
• Enter a VBA main procedure

When you routinely need to run several macros one after another, you can save time by combining them into one procedure. The resulting procedure, which processes (or calls) multiple procedures in sequence, is referred to as the **main procedure**. To create a main procedure, you type a **Call statement** for each procedure you want to run. The syntax of the Call statement is Call *procedurename*, where *procedurename* is the name of the procedure you want to run. **CASE** ▶ *To avoid having to run each of the macros you've created, one after another, every month, you want to create a main procedure that will call each of them in sequence in the EX 16-Monthly Sales workbook.*

STEPS

1. With the January worksheet displayed, click the Developer tab if necessary, then click the Visual Basic button in the Code group

2. Verify that EX 16-Monthly Sales is the active project, click Insert on the menu bar, then click Module

   A new, blank module named Module1 is inserted in the EX 16-Monthly Sales workbook.

3. In the Properties window click (Name), then type MainProc

4. In the Code window enter the procedure code exactly as shown in FIGURE 16-13, entering your name in the second line

5. Compare your main procedure code with FIGURE 16-13, correct any errors if necessary, then click the Save button 🖫 on the Visual Basic Editor toolbar

   To test the new main procedure, you need an unformatted version of the EX 16-January Sales worksheet.

6. Click the View Microsoft Excel button 🖾 on the toolbar, save the EX 16-Monthly Sales.xlsm workbook, then save and close the EX 16-January Sales workbook

   The EX 16-Monthly Sales workbook remains open.

7. Open EX 16-2.xlsx from the location where you store your Data Files, then save it as EX 16-January Sales 2

   In the next lesson, you'll run the main procedure.

Copying a macro to another workbook

If you would like to use a macro in another workbook, you can copy the module to that workbook using the Visual Basic Editor. Open both the source and destination Excel workbooks, then open the Visual Basic Editor and verify that macros are enabled. In Project Explorer, drag the module that will be copied from the source workbook to the destination workbook.

FIGURE 16-13: VBA code for the MainProcedure procedure

FIGURE 16-13: VBA code for the MainProcedure procedure

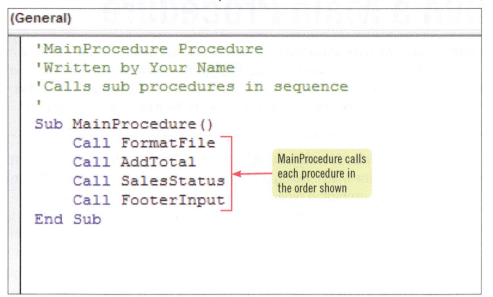

Writing and documenting VBA code

When you write VBA code in the Visual Basic Editor, you want to make it as readable as possible. This makes it easier for you or your coworkers to edit the code when changes need to be made. The procedure statements should be indented, leaving the procedure name and its End statement easy to spot in the code. This is helpful when a module contains many procedures. It is also good practice to add comments at the beginning of each procedure that describe its purpose and any assumptions made in the procedure, such as the quota amounts. You should also explain each code statement with a comment. You have seen comments inserted into VBA code by beginning the statement with an apostrophe. You can also add comments to the end of a line of VBA code by placing an apostrophe before the comment, as shown in **FIGURE 16-14**.

FIGURE 16-14: VBA code with comments at the end of statements

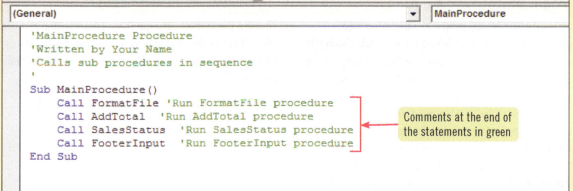

Excel 2016

Run a Main Procedure

Running a main procedure allows you to run several macros in sequence. You can run a main procedure just as you would any other macro procedure. **CASE** ▶ *You have finished creating a main procedure, and you are ready to run it. If the main procedure works correctly, it should format the worksheet, insert the sales total, insert a sales status message, and add your name and the date to the worksheet footer.*

STEPS

1. **In the January Sales 2 workbook click the Developer tab, click the Macros button in the Code group, in the Macro dialog box click 'EX 16-Monthly Sales.xlsm'!MainProcedure, click Run, when prompted type your name, then click OK**

   The MainProcedure runs the FormatFile, AddTotal, SalesStatus, and FooterInput procedures in sequence. You can see the results of the FormatFile, AddTotal, and SalesStatus procedures in the worksheet window, as shown in **FIGURE 16-16**. To view the results of the FooterInput procedure, you need to preview the worksheet.

2. **Click the File tab, click Print, view the worksheet preview and verify that your name appears in the left footer area and the date appears in the right footer area, click the Back button ⬅, then click the Developer tab if necessary**

3. **Click the Visual Basic button in the Code group**

   You need to add your name to the Format module.

4. **In the Project Explorer window, double-click the Format module, add a comment line after the procedure name that reads Written by [Your Name], then click the Save button 💾**

   You want to see the options for printing VBA code.

5. **Click File on the Visual Basic Editor menu bar, then click Print**

   The Print - VBAProject dialog box opens, as shown in **FIGURE 16-17**. The Current Module is selected which will print each procedure separately. It is faster to print all the procedures in the workbook at one time by clicking the Current Project option button to select it. You can also create a file of the VBA code by selecting the Print to File check box. You do not want to print the modules at this time.

6. **Click Cancel in the Print - VBAProject dialog box**

7. **Click the View Microsoft Excel button 🗖 on the toolbar**

8. **Save the EX 16-Monthly Sales.xlsm workbook, save the EX 16-January Sales 2 workbook, then preview the worksheet**

   Compare your formatted worksheet to **FIGURE 16-18**.

9. **Close the EX 16-January Sales 2 workbook, close the EX 16-Monthly Sales workbook, exit Excel, then submit the EX 16-January Sales 2 workbook to your instructor**

Running a macro using a button

You can run a macro by assigning it to a button on your worksheet. Create a button by clicking the Insert tab, clicking the Shapes button 🔲 ▾ in the Illustrations group, choosing a shape, then drawing the shape on the worksheet. After you create the button, right-click it, click Assign Macro, then click the macro the button will run and click OK. It is a good idea to label the button with descriptive text; select it and begin typing. You can also format macro buttons using clip art, photographs, fills, and shadows. You format a button using the buttons on the Drawing Tools Format tab. To add a fill to the button, click the Shape Fill list arrow and select a fill color, picture, texture, or gradient.

To add a shape effect, click the Shape Effects button and select an effect. You can also use the WordArt styles in the WordArt Styles group. **FIGURE 16-15** shows a button formatted with a gradient, bevel and WordArt.

FIGURE 16-15: Formatted macro button

Date Stamp

FIGURE 16-16: Result of running MainProcedure procedure

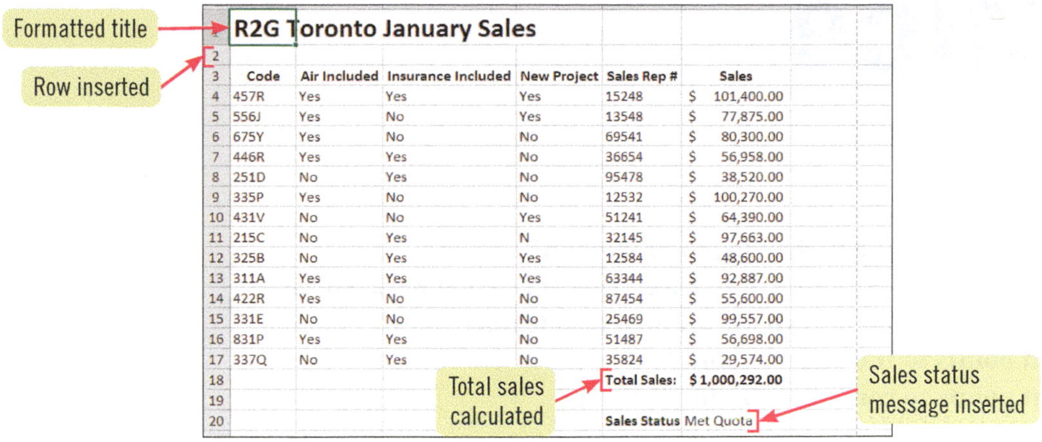

Formatted title →

Row inserted →

	Code	Air Included	Insurance Included	New Project	Sales Rep #	Sales
1	**R2G Toronto January Sales**					
2						
3	Code	Air Included	Insurance Included	New Project	Sales Rep #	Sales
4	457R	Yes	Yes	Yes	15248	$ 101,400.00
5	556J	Yes	No	Yes	13548	$ 77,875.00
6	675Y	Yes	No	No	69541	$ 80,300.00
7	446R	Yes	Yes	No	36654	$ 56,958.00
8	251D	No	Yes	No	95478	$ 38,520.00
9	335P	Yes	No	No	12532	$ 100,270.00
10	431V	No	No	Yes	51241	$ 64,390.00
11	215C	No	Yes	N	32145	$ 97,663.00
12	325B	No	Yes	Yes	12584	$ 48,600.00
13	311A	Yes	Yes	Yes	63344	$ 92,887.00
14	422R	Yes	No	No	87454	$ 55,600.00
15	331E	No	No	No	25469	$ 99,557.00
16	831P	Yes	Yes	No	51487	$ 56,698.00
17	337Q	No	Yes	No	35824	$ 29,574.00
18					Total Sales:	$ 1,000,292.00
19						
20					Sales Status	Met Quota

Total sales calculated →

Sales status message inserted →

FIGURE 16-17: Printing options for macro procedures

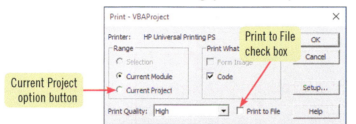

Print to File check box

Current Project option button

FIGURE 16-18: Formatted January worksheet

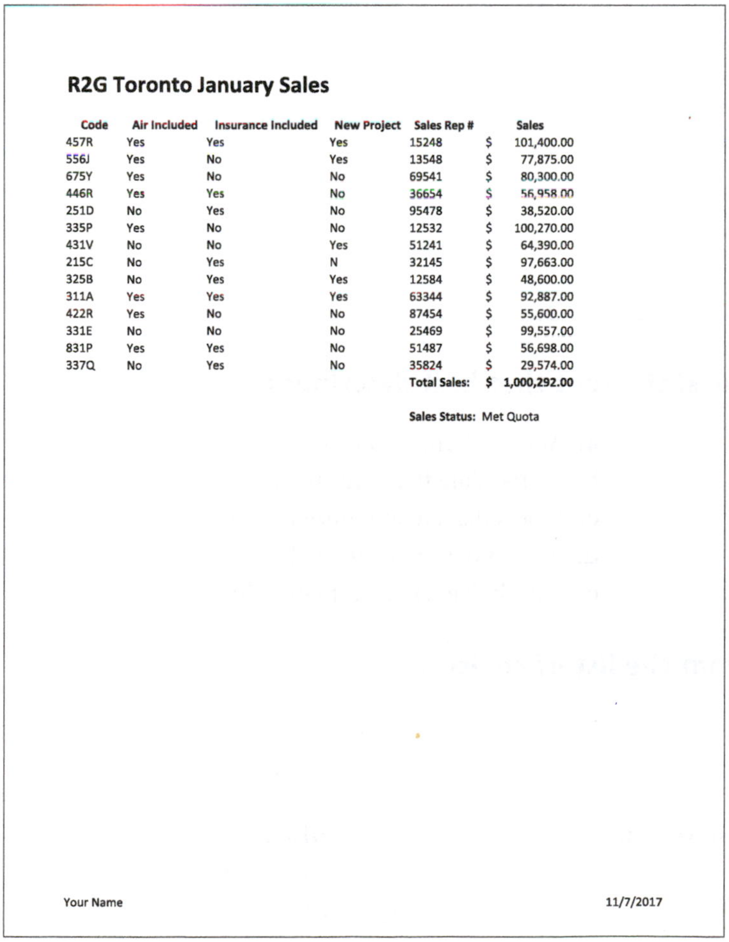

R2G Toronto January Sales

Code	Air Included	Insurance Included	New Project	Sales Rep #	Sales
457R	Yes	Yes	Yes	15248	$ 101,400.00
556J	Yes	No	Yes	13548	$ 77,875.00
675Y	Yes	No	No	69541	$ 80,300.00
446R	Yes	Yes	No	36654	$ 56,958.00
251D	No	Yes	No	95478	$ 38,520.00
335P	Yes	No	No	12532	$ 100,270.00
431V	No	No	Yes	51241	$ 64,390.00
215C	No	Yes	N	32145	$ 97,663.00
325B	No	Yes	Yes	12584	$ 48,600.00
311A	Yes	Yes	Yes	63344	$ 92,887.00
422R	Yes	No	No	87454	$ 55,600.00
331E	No	No	No	25469	$ 99,557.00
831P	Yes	Yes	No	51487	$ 56,698.00
337Q	No	Yes	No	35824	$ 29,574.00
				Total Sales:	$ 1,000,292.00

Sales Status: Met Quota

Your Name   11/7/2017

Practice

Concepts Review

1. Which element points to the Project Explorer window?
2. Which element do you click to return to Excel from the Visual Basic Editor?
3. Which element do you click to turn off the Step Into feature?
4. Which element points to the Code window?
5. Which element points to comments in the VBA code?

FIGURE 16-19

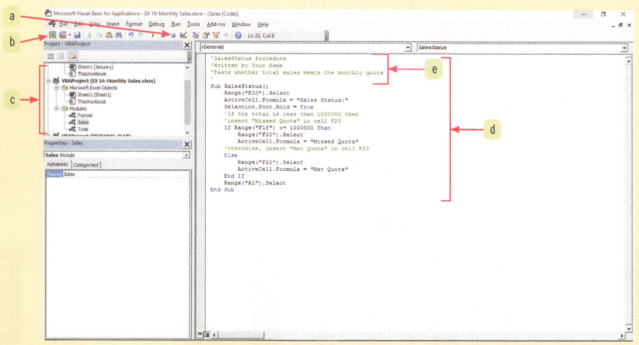

Match each term with the statement that best describes it.

6. Function   **a.** Another term for a macro in Visual Basic for Applications (VBA)

7. Sub procedure   **b.** A procedure that returns a value

8. Procedure   **c.** Words that are recognized as part of the programming language

9. Keywords   **d.** A series of statements that perform an action but don't return a value

10. Comments   **e.** Descriptive text used to explain parts of a procedure

Select the best answer from the list of choices.

11. **You enter the statements of a macro in:**
    - **a.** The Macro dialog box.
    - **b.** Any blank worksheet.
    - **c.** The Properties window of the Visual Basic Editor.
    - **d.** The Code window of the Visual Basic Editor.

12. **A location in memory where you can temporarily store information is a:**
    - **a.** Variable.
    - **b.** Procedure.
    - **c.** Sub procedure.
    - **d.** Function.

13. Comments are displayed in _____ in VBA code.

    a. Black   **c.** Red

    b. Blue   **d.** Green

14. If your macro doesn't run correctly, you should:

    a. Select the macro in the Macro dialog box, click Step Into, then debug the macro.

    b. Create an If...Then...Else statement.

    c. Click the Project Explorer button.

    d. Click the Properties button.

15. Keywords are displayed in _____ in VBA code.

    a. Black   **c.** Green

    b. Blue   **d.** Red

Skills Review

1. View and analyze VBA code.

    a. Start Excel, open EX 16-3.xlsm from the location where you store your Data Files, enable macros, then save it as **EX 16-HVAC**.

    b. Review the unformatted December worksheet.

    c. Open the Visual Basic Editor.

    d. Select the DataFormat module, and review the Format procedure.

    e. Insert comments in the procedure code describing what action you think each line of code will perform. (*Hint*: One of the statements will sort the list by Store #.) Add comment lines to the top of the procedure to describe the purpose of the macro and to enter your name.

    f. Save the macro, return to the worksheet, then run the Format macro.

    g. Compare the results with the code and your comments.

    h. Save the workbook.

2. Write VBA code.

    a. Open the Visual Basic Editor, and insert a new module named **Total** in the EX 16-HVAC project.

    b. Enter the code for the SalesTotal procedure exactly as shown in **FIGURE 16-20**. Enter your name in the second line.

    c. Save the macro, return to the December worksheet, then run the SalesTotal macro.

    d. Save the workbook.

FIGURE 16-20

```
'SalesTotal Procedure
'Written by Your Name
'Totals December sales
Sub SalesTotal()
    Range("E17").Select
    ActiveCell.Formula = "=SUM($E$3:$E$16)"
    Selection.Font.Bold = True
    With Selection.Borders(xlTop)
        .LineStyle = xlSingle
    End With
    Columns("E").Select
    Selection.Columns.AutoFit
    Range("A1").Select
End Sub
```

3. Add a conditional statement.

    a. Open the Visual Basic Editor, and insert a new module named **Goal** in the EX 16-HVAC project.

    b. Enter the SalesGoal procedure exactly as shown in **FIGURE 16-21**. Enter your name on the second line.

    c. Save the macro, return to the December worksheet, and run the SalesGoal macro. The procedure should enter the message **Missed goal** in cell E18. Save the workbook.

FIGURE 16-21

```
'SalesGoal Procedure
'Written by Your Name
'Tests whether sales goal was met
Sub SalesGoal()
    'If the total is >=100000, then insert "Met Goal"
    'in cell E18
    If Range("E17") >= 100000 Then
        Range("E18").Select
        ActiveCell.Formula = "Met goal"
    'otherwise, insert "Missed goal" in cell E18
    Else
        Range("E18").Select
        ActiveCell.Formula = "Missed goal"
    End If
    Range("A1").Select
End Sub
```

Skills Review (continued)

4. Prompt the user for data.

   a. Open the Visual Basic Editor, and insert a new module named **Header** in the EX 16-HVAC project.

   b. Enter the HeaderFooter procedure exactly as shown in **FIGURE 16-22**. You are entering an error in the procedure that will be corrected in Step 5.

   c. Save the macro, then return to the December worksheet, and run the HeaderFooter macro.

   d. Preview the December worksheet. Your name should be missing from the left section of the footer.

   e. Save the workbook.

FIGURE 16-22

```
(General)                                                          ▼   HeaderFooter

    'HeaderFooter Procedure
    'Written by Your Name
    'Procedure to customize the header and footer
    Sub HeaderFooter()
        'Inserts the filename in the header
        Worksheets("December").PageSetup.CenterHeader = "&F"
        'Declares the variable FooterText as a string
        Dim FooterText As String
        'Prompts user for footer text
        Footer = InputBox("Enter your full name:")
        'Inserts response into left footer
        Worksheets("December").PageSetup.LeftFooter = FooterText
        'Inserts the date into right footer
        Worksheets("December").PageSetup.RightFooter = "&D"
    End Sub
```

5. Debug a macro.

   a. Return to the Visual Basic Editor and use the Step Into feature to locate where the error occurred in the HeaderFooter procedure. Use the Reset button to turn off the debugger.

   b. Edit the procedure in the Visual Basic Editor to correct the error. (*Hint*: The error occurs on the line: Footer = InputBox("Enter your full name:"). The variable that will input the response text into the worksheet footer is FooterText. The line should be: FooterText = InputBox("Enter your full name:").)

   c. Save the macro, return to the December worksheet, then run the HeaderFooter macro again.

   d. Verify that your name now appears in the left section of the footer, then save the file.

6. Create and run a main procedure.

   a. Return to the Visual Basic Editor, insert a new module, then name it **MainProc**.

   b. Begin the main procedure by entering comments in the code window that provide the procedure's name (MainProcedure) and explain that its purpose is to run the Format, SalesTotal, SalesGoal, and HeaderFooter procedures. Enter your name in a comment.

   c. Enter the procedure header **Sub MainProcedure()**.

   d. Enter four Call statements that will run the Format, SalesTotal, SalesGoal, and HeaderFooter procedures in sequence.

   e. Save the procedure and return to Excel.

   f. Open EX 16-3.xlsm, then save it as **EX 16-HVAC 2**.

   g. Run the MainProcedure macro, entering your name when prompted. (*Hint*: In the Macro dialog box, the macro procedures you created will now have EX 16-HVAC.xlsm! as part of their names. This is because the macros are stored in the EX 16-HVAC workbook, not in the EX 16-HVAC 2 workbook.)

   h. Verify that the macro ran successfully by comparing your worksheet to **FIGURE 16-23**.

   i. Save the EX 16-HVAC 2 workbook, preview the December worksheet to check the header and footer, then close the EX 16-HVAC 2 workbook.

   j. Save the EX 16-HVAC workbook, close the workbook, exit Excel, then submit the EX 16-HVAC workbook to your instructor.

FIGURE 16-23

	A	B	C	D	E	F
1	Texas HVAC					
2	Store #	City	State	Manager	Sales	
3	157	Lubbock	TX	Golly	$ 5,534.34	
4	241	Beaumont	TX	Lin	$ 4,643.93	
5	312	Dallas	TX	Hall	$ 7,225.22	
6	336	Galveston	TX	Holland	$ 7,715.68	
7	367	Midland	TX	Nason	$ 7,654.32	
8	457	Corpus Christi	TX	Mores	$ 5,987.36	
9	527	San Antonio	TX	Dally	$ 8,228.33	
10	547	Arlington	TX	Pearcy	$ 5,251.22	
11	627	Houston	TX	Early	$ 8,583.66	
12	634	Austin	TX	Ebson	$ 6,594.22	
13	641	Alpine	TX	Hornsby	$ 8,001.34	
14	756	El Paso	TX	Carnes	$ 6,645.93	
15	963	Waco	TX	Cleaver	$ 8,656.83	
16	998	Fort Worth	TX	Dover	$ 4,442.90	
17					$95,165.28	
18					Missed goal	
19						

Independent Challenge 1

You are the sales manager for a plumbing supply company with offices in Miami, Boston, and Chicago. You have been given a macro written by the previous sales manager that you need to document and test. You will first run the macro procedure to see what it does, then add comments to the VBA code to document it. You will also enter data to verify that the formulas in the macro work correctly.

a. Start Excel, open EX 16-4.xlsm from the location where you store your Data Files, then save it as **EX 16-First Quarter**.

b. Run the First macro, noting anything that you think should be mentioned in your documentation.

c. Review the First procedure in the Visual Basic Editor. It is stored in the FirstQtr module.

d. Document the procedure by adding comments to the code, indicating the actions the procedure performs.

e. Enter your name in a comment line, then save the procedure.

f. Return to the Jan-Mar worksheet, and use FIGURE 16-24 as a guide to enter data in cells B4:D6. The totals will appear as you enter the income data.

g. Format the range B4:D8 using the Accounting Number format with no decimal places, as shown in FIGURE 16-24.

FIGURE 16-24

	A	B	C	D
1		January	February	March
2	Sales			
3				
4	Miami	$ 5,000	$ 4,000	$ 7,000
5	Boston	$ 6,000	$ 5,000	$ 8,000
6	Chicago	$ 7,000	$ 6,000	$ 9,000
7				
8	Total Sales	$ 18,000	$ 15,000	$ 24,000

h. Check the total income calculations in row 8 to verify that the macro is working correctly.

i. Save the workbook, then preview the worksheet.

j. Close the workbook, exit Excel, then submit the workbook to your instructor.

Independent Challenge 2

You manage a car dealership that sells Volvos, Toyotas, and Subarus. Each month you are required to produce a report stating whether sales quotas were met for the three models of automobiles. The quotas for each month are as follows: Volvo 15, Toyota 12, and Subaru 10. You decide to create a procedure to automate your monthly task of determining the sales quota status for the three models. You would like your assistant to take this task over when you go on vacation next month. Because he has little experience with Excel, you decide to create a second procedure that prompts a user with input boxes to enter the actual placement results for the month.

FIGURE 16-25

```
Sub SalesQuota()

    If Range("C4") >= 15 Then
        Range("D4").Select
        ActiveCell.Formula = "Yes"
    Else
        Range("D4").Select
        ActiveCell.Formula = "No"
    End If


    If Range("C5") >= 12 Then
        Range("D5").Select
        ActiveCell.Formula = "Yes"
    Else
        Range("D5").Select
        ActiveCell.Formula = "No"
    End If


    If Range("C6") >= 10 Then
        Range("D6").Select
        ActiveCell.Formula = "Yes"
    Else
        Range("D6").Select
        ActiveCell.Formula = "No"
    End If

End Sub
```

a. Start Excel, open EX 16-5.xlsm from the location where you store your Data Files, then save it as **EX 16-Car Sales**.

b. Use the Visual Basic Editor to insert a new module named **Quotas** in the EX 16-Car Sales workbook. Create a procedure in the new module named **SalesQuota** that determines the quota status for each category and enters Yes or No in the Status column. The VBA code is shown in FIGURE 16-25.

c. Add comments to the SalesQuota procedure, including the procedure name, your name, and the purpose of the procedure.

Independent Challenge 2 (continued)

d. Insert a new module named **MonthlySales**. Create a second procedure named **Sales** that prompts a user for placement data for each car model, enters the input data in the appropriate cells, then calls the SalesQuota procedure. The VBA code is shown in **FIGURE 16-26**. (*Hint*: The procedure's blank lines group the macro code in related modules. These blank lines are optional and their purpose is to make the procedure easier to understand.)

e. Add a comment noting the procedure name on the first line. Add a comment with your name on the second line. Add a third comment line at the top of the procedure describing its purpose. Enter comments in the code to document the macro actions.

f. Run the Sales macro, and enter **13** for Volvo sales, **14** for Toyota sales, and **11** for Subaru sales. Correct any errors in the VBA code.

g. Return to the worksheet, save the workbook, then preview the worksheet. Close the workbook, exit Excel, then submit your workbook to your instructor.

FIGURE 16-26

```
Sub Sales()

    Dim Volvo As String
    Volvo = InputBox("Enter Number of Volvos Sold")
    Range("C4").Select
    Selection = Volvo

    Dim Toyota As String
    Toyota = InputBox("Enter Number of Toyotas Sold")
    Range("C5").Select
    Selection = Toyota

    Dim Subaru As String
    Subaru = InputBox("Enter Number of Subarus sold")
    Range("C6").Select
    Selection = Subaru

    Call SalesQuota

End Sub
```

Independent Challenge 3

You are the business manager for Boston Pilates. Every month you prepare a report showing the income by studio. You decide to create a macro that will format the monthly reports. You add the same footers on every report, so you will create another macro that adds a footer to a document. Finally, you will create a main procedure that calls the macros to format the report and adds a footer, and then run it. You begin by opening a workbook with the January data. You will save the macros you create in this workbook.

a. Start Excel, open EX 16-6.xlsm from the location where you store your Data Files, then save it as **EX 16-Pilates**.

b. Insert a module named **Format**, then create a procedure named **Formatting** that:
   - Selects cells A1 and A2, and formats that range in bold font and 14 pt font size.
   - Selects the range containing fee data in column C, and formats it as currency.
   - Selects cell A1 before ending.

c. Save the Formatting procedure.

d. Insert a module named **Foot**, then create a procedure named **Footer** that:
   - Declares a string variable for text that will be placed in the left footer.
   - Uses an input box to prompt the user for his or her name, and places the name in the left footer.
   - Places the date in the right footer.

e. Save the Footer procedure.

f. Insert a module named **Main**, then create a procedure named **MainProc** that calls the Footer procedure and the Formatting procedure.

Independent Challenge 3 (continued)

g. Save the procedure, return to the January worksheet, then run the MainProc procedure. Debug each procedure as necessary. Your worksheet should look like FIGURE 16-27.

h. Document each procedure by inserting a comment line with the procedure name, your name, and a description of the procedure.

i. Preview the January worksheet, save the workbook, close the workbook, exit Excel, then submit the workbook to your instructor.

FIGURE 16-27

	A	B	C	D
1	Boston Pilates			
2	January Income			
3	Studio	Type	Fees	
4	North	Equipment	$ 825.00	
5	Center	Mat	$1,725.00	
6	East	Equipment	$ 650.00	
7	West	Equipment	$ 775.00	
8	South	Mat	$1,050.00	
9				

Independent Challenge 4: Explore

As the business manager of a florist shop, you decide to create a log of your non-payroll monthly expenses in an effort to budget the shop's expenses. You have a workbook with a macro that tracks the major expenses for the first three months of the year. You want to expand this macro to track six months of expenses.

a. Start Excel, open EX 16-7.xlsm from the location where you store your Data Files, then save it as **EX 16-Expenses**.

b. Run the MonthExpenses macro and enter expense numbers of your choosing to verify the macro is working properly.

c. Edit the MonthExpenses procedure to add the abbreviated month entries of Apr, May, and Jun in cells E1, F1, and G1, and the totals for these months in cells E8, F8, and G8.

d. Run the macro and debug the procedure as necessary. Enter expense numbers to verify the macro is working properly. Widen columns where necessary.

e. Save your work.

f. Verify that the totals are correct for each month.

g. Enter your name as a comment in the second line of the procedure.

h. Insert a module named **Format** with a procedure named **Formatting** that formats cells B2:G8 as currency, formats the total label and totals in cells A8:G8 in bold, widens the width of columns A through G to AutoFit the formatted data, and then selects cell A1. The VBA code is shown in FIGURE 16-28.

i. Save the macro, return to the worksheet, then without running the macro, assign the macro Formatting to a button on the worksheet. (*Hint*: Use the Rectangle tool to create the button, label the button **Format**, then right-click the button to assign the macro.)

j. Format the button and its label with styles and attributes of your choice.

k. Test the button and debug the Formatting macro if necessary.

l. Save the workbook, close the workbook, exit Excel, then submit the workbook to your instructor.

FIGURE 16-28

```
'Formatting Procedure
'Your Name
'Formats Expenses
'
Sub Formatting()
    Range("B2:G8").Select
    Selection.Style = "Currency"
    Range("A8:G8").Select
    Selection.Font.Bold = True
    Range("A1").Select
    Columns("A:G").Select
    Selection.Columns.AutoFit
End Sub
```

Visual Workshop

Open EX 16-8.xlsm from the location where you store your Data Files, then save it as **EX 16-Events**. Create a macro procedure named **Format** in a module named **FormatTotal** that will format the worksheet as shown in FIGURE 16-29. (*Hints*: The font size of the first two rows is 14 pt and the other rows are 12 pt. Notice that a total row has been added.) Run the macro and debug it as necessary to make the worksheet match FIGURE 16-29. Insert your name in a comment line under the procedure name, then preview the worksheet. Submit the workbook to your instructor.

FIGURE 16-29

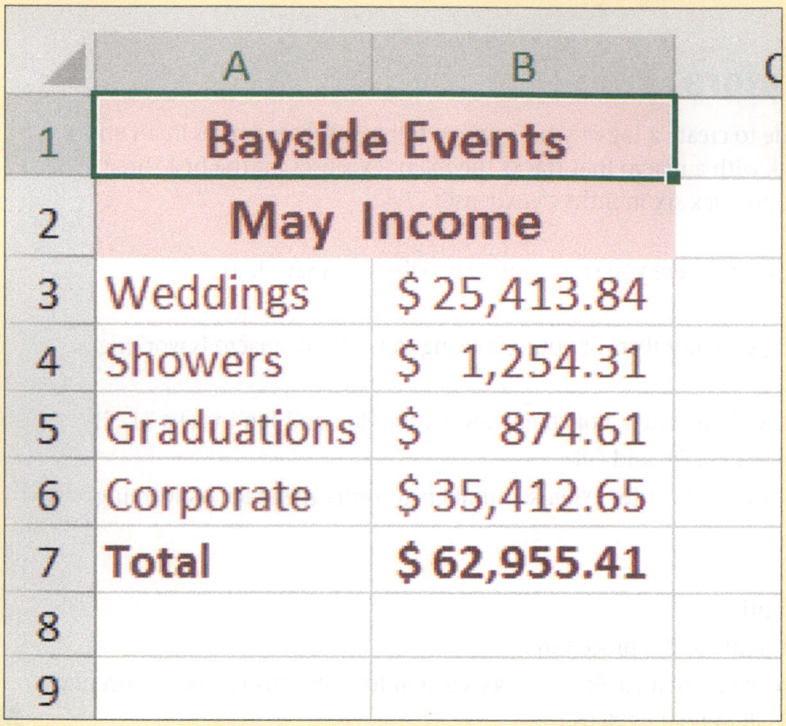

	A	B
1	**Bayside Events**	
2	**May Income**	
3	Weddings	$ 25,413.84
4	Showers	$ 1,254.31
5	Graduations	$ 874.61
6	Corporate	$ 35,412.65
7	**Total**	**$ 62,955.41**
8		
9		

Glossary

3-D reference A worksheet reference that uses values on other sheets or workbooks, effectively creating another dimension to a workbook.

Absolute cell reference In a formula, a cell address that refers to a specific cell and does not change when you copy the formula; indicated by a dollar sign before the column letter and/or row number. *See also* Relative cell reference.

Active The currently available document, program, or object; on the taskbar, when more than one program is open, the button for the active program appears slightly lighter.

Active cell The cell in which you are currently working.

Add-in An extra program, such as Solver, that provides optional Excel features.

Alignment The placement of cell contents in relation to a cell's edges; for example, left-aligned, centered, or right-aligned.

And logical condition A filtering feature that searches for records by specifying that all entered criteria must be matched.

Animation emphasis effect In Sway, a special effect you can apply to an object to animate it.

Argument Information necessary for a formula or function to calculate an answer. In the Visual Basic for Applications (VBA) programming language, variable used in procedures that a main procedure might run. *See also* Main procedure.

Arithmetic operators In a formula, symbols that perform mathematical calculations, such as addition (+), subtraction (–), multiplication (*), division (/), or exponentiation (^).

Ascending order In sorting an Excel field (column), the lowest value (the beginning of the alphabet, or the earliest date) appears at the beginning of the sorted data.

ASCII file A text file that contains data but no formatting; instead of being divided into columns, ASCII file data are separated, or delimited, by tabs or commas.

Auditing Track errors and check worksheet logic in Excel.

AutoComplete In the Visual Basic for Applications (VBA) programming language, a list of words that appears as you enter code; helps you automatically enter elements with the correct syntax.

AutoFill Feature activated by dragging the fill handle; copies a cell's contents or continues a series of entries into adjacent cells.

AutoFill Options button Button that appears after using the fill handle to copy cell contents; enables you to choose to fill cells with specific elements (such as formatting) of the copied cell if desired.

AutoFilter A table feature that lets you click a list arrow and select criteria by which to display certain types of records; *also called* filter.

AutoFilter list arrows *See* Filter List arrows.

AutoFit A feature that automatically adjusts the width of a column or the height of a row to accommodate its widest or tallest entry.

Backsolving A problem-solving method in which you specify a solution and then find the input value that produces the answer you want; sometimes described as a what-if analysis in reverse. In Excel, the Goal Seek feature performs backsolving.

Backstage view View that appears when the File tab is clicked. The navigation bar on the left side contains commands to perform actions common to most Office programs, such as opening a file, saving a file, and closing the file.

Backward-compatible Software feature that enables documents saved in an older version of a program to be opened in a newer version of the program.

Banding Worksheet formatting in which adjacent rows and columns are formatted differently.

Box and Whisker A statistical chart that presents the distribution of data emphasizing the mean as well as data outside the mean.

Bug In programming, an error that causes a procedure to run incorrectly.

Business Intelligence tools Excel features for gathering and analyzing data to answer sophisticated business questions.

Calculated columns In a table, a column that automatically fills in cells with formula results, using a formula entered in only one other cell in the same column.

Calculation operators Symbols in a formula that indicate what type of calculation to perform on the cells, ranges, or values.

Call statement A Visual Basic statement that retrieves a procedure that you want to run, using the syntax Call *procedurename*.

Card A section for a particular type of content in a Sway presentation.

Category axis Horizontal axis of a chart, usually containing the names of data groups; in a 2-dimensional chart, also known as the x-axis.

Cell The intersection of a column and a row in a worksheet or table.

Cell address The location of a cell, expressed by cell coordinates; for example, the cell address of the cell in column A, row 1 is A1.

Cell comment Note you add to a worksheet cell; appears when you place the pointer over the cell.

Cell pointer Dark rectangle that outlines the active cell.

Cell styles Predesigned combinations of formats based on themes that can be applied to selected cells to enhance the look of a worksheet.

Change history A worksheet containing a list of changes made to a shared workbook.

Changing cells In what-if analysis, cells that contain the values that change in order to produce multiple sets of results.

Chart animation The movement of a chart element after the relevant worksheet data is changed.

Chart elements Parts of a chart, such as its title or its legend, which you can add, remove, or modify.

Chart sheet A separate sheet in a workbook that contains only a chart, which is linked to the workbook data.

Charts Pictorial representations of worksheet data that make it easier to see patterns, trends, and relationships; *also called* graphs.

Clip A media file, such as a graphic, sound, animation, or movie; also, a short segment of audio or video.

Clip art A graphic image, such as a corporate logo, a picture, or a photo, that can be inserted into a document.

Clipboard A temporary Windows storage area that holds the selections you copy or cut.

Cloud computing Work done in a virtual environment using data, applications, and resources stored on servers and accessed over the Internet or a company's internal network rather than on users' computers.

Code window In the Visual Basic Editor, the window that displays the selected module's procedures, written in the Visual Basic programming language.

Color scale In conditional formatting, a formatting scheme that uses a set of two, three, or four fill colors to convey relative values of data.

Column heading Box that appears above each column in a worksheet; identifies the column letter, such as A, B, etc.

Combination chart A chart that combines two or more chart types in a single chart.

Comments In a Visual Basic procedure, notes that explain the purpose of the macro or procedure; they are preceded by a single apostrophe and appear in green.

Comparison operators In a formula, symbols that compare values for the purpose of true/false results.

Compatibility The ability of different programs to work together and exchange data.

Complex formula A formula that uses more than one arithmetic operator.

Conditional formatting A type of cell formatting that changes based on the cell's value or the outcome of a formula.

Consolidate To combine data on multiple worksheets and display the result on another worksheet.

Constraints Limitations or restrictions on input data in what-if analysis.

Contextual tab A tab that is displayed only when a specific task can be performed; appears in an accent color.

Cortana The Microsoft Windows virtual assistant that integrates with Microsoft Edge to find and provide information.

Creative Commons license A public copyright license that allows the free distribution of an otherwise copyrighted work.

Criteria range In advanced filtering, a cell range containing one row of labels and at least one additional row underneath it that contains the criteria you want to match.

Data entry area The unlocked portion of a worksheet where users are able to enter and change data.

Data label Descriptive text that appears above a data marker in a chart.

Data marker A graphical representation of a data point in a chart, such as a bar or column.

Data point Individual piece of data plotted in a chart.

Data series A column or row in a datasheet. Also, the selected range in a worksheet that Excel converts into a chart.

Data source Worksheet data used to create a chart or PivotTable.

Data table A range of cells that shows the resulting values when one or more input values are varied in a formula; when one input value is changed, the table is called a one-input data table, and when two input values are changed, it is called a two-input data table. In a chart, it is a grid containing the chart data.

Database program An application, such as Microsoft Access, that lets you manage large amounts of data organized in tables.

Database table A set of data organized using columns and rows that is created in a database program.

Debug In programming, to find and correct an error in code.

Declare In the Visual Basic programming language, to assign a type, such as numeric or text, to a variable.

Delimiter A separator such as a space, comma, or semicolon between elements in imported data.

Dependent cell A cell, usually containing a formula, whose value changes depending on the values in the input cells. For example, a payment formula or function that depends on an input cell containing changing interest rates is a dependent cell.

Dependents In auditing, cells that contain formulas referring to the selected cell.

Descending order In sorting an Excel field (column), the order that begins with the letter Z, the highest number, or the latest date of the values in a field.

Destination program In a data exchange, the program that will receive the data.

Dialog box launcher An icon you can click to open a dialog box or task pane from which to choose related commands.

Digital signature An electronic signature that can be added to a VBA project to guarantee it hasn't been changed.

Docs.com A Microsoft website designed for sharing Sway sites.

Document To make notes about basic worksheet assumptions, complex formulas, or questionable data.

Document window Most of the screen in any given program, where you create a document, slide, or worksheet.

Drawing canvas In OneNote, a container for shapes and lines.

Dynamic page breaks In a larger workbook, horizontal or vertical dashed lines that represent the place where pages print separately. They also adjust automatically when you insert or delete rows or columns, or change column widths or row heights.

Edit To make a change to the contents of an active cell.

Edit Link A link to a workbook on a OneDrive that can be edited by users.

Electronic spreadsheet A computer program used to perform calculations and analyze and present numeric data.

Element An XML component that defines the document content.

Embed To insert a copy of data into a destination document; you can double-click the embedded object to modify it using the tools of the source program.

Embedded chart A chart displayed as an object in a worksheet.

Encrypted data Data protected by use of a password, which encodes it in a form that only authorized people with a password can decode.

Exploding Visually pulling a slice of a pie chart away from the whole pie chart in order to add emphasis to the pie slice.

Extensible Markup Language (XML) A system for defining languages using tags to structure data.

External reference indicator In a macro name, an exclamation point (!) that indicates that a macro is outside the active workbook.

Extract To place a copy of a filtered table in a range you specify in the Advanced Filter dialog box.

Field In a table, a column that describes a characteristic about records, such as first name or city. In a PivotTable, you can drag field names to PivotTable row, column, data, or report filter areas to explore data relationships.

Field name A column label that describes a field.

File A stored collection of data.

Filter list arrows List arrows that appear next to field names in an Excel table; used to display portions of your data. *Also called* AutoFilter list arrows.

Flash Fill An Excel feature that automatically fills in column or row data based on calculations you enter.

Font The typeface or design of a set of characters (letters, numbers, symbols, and punctuation marks).

Font size The size of characters, measured in units called points.

Font style Format such as bold, italic, and underlining that can be applied to change the way characters look in a worksheet or chart.

Form control An object that can be added to a worksheet to help users enter data. An example is a list box form control.

Format The appearance of a cell and its contents, including font, font styles, font color, fill color, borders, and shading. *See also* Number format.

Formula A set of instructions used to perform one or more numeric calculations, such as adding, multiplying, or averaging, on values or cells.

Formula bar The area above the worksheet grid where you enter or edit data in the active cell.

Formula prefix An arithmetic symbol, such as the equal sign (=), used to start a formula.

Free response quiz A type of Office Mix quiz containing questions that require short answers.

Freeze To hold in place selected columns or rows when scrolling in a worksheet that is divided in panes. *See also* Panes.

Function A predefined formula that provides a shortcut for a common or complex calculation, such as SUM (for calculating a sum) or FV (for calculating the future value of an investment). In the Visual Basic for Applications (VBA) programming language, a predefined procedure that returns a value, such as the InputBox function which prompts the user to enter information.

Gallery A visual collection of choices you can browse through to make a selection. Often available with Live Preview.

Goal cell In backsolving, a cell containing a formula in which you can substitute values to find a specific value, or goal.

Goal Seek A problem-solving method in which you specify a solution and then find the input value that produces the answer you want; sometimes described as a what-if analysis in reverse; *also called* backsolving.

Gridlines Evenly spaced horizontal and/or vertical lines used in a worksheet or chart to make it easier to read.

Groups Each tab on the Ribbon is arranged into groups to make features easy to find.

Header row In an Excel table, the first row; it contains field (column) names.

Histogram A statistical column chart that presents the frequency data.

HTML (Hypertext Markup Language) The coding format used for web documents.

Hub A pane in Microsoft Edge that provides access to favorite websites, a reading list, browsing history, and downloaded files.

Hyperlink An object (a filename, a word, a phrase, or a graphic) in a worksheet that, when you click it, displays another worksheet or a Webpage called the target. *See also* Target.

Icon sets In conditional formatting, groups of images used to visually communicate relative cell values based on the values they contain.

If...Then...Else statement In the Visual Basic programming language, a conditional statement that directs Excel to perform specified actions under certain conditions; its syntax is "If *condition* Then *statements* Else [*elsestatements*].

Ink to Math tool The OneNote tool that converts handwritten mathematical formulas to formatted equations or expressions.

Ink to Text tool The OneNote tool that converts inked handwriting to typed text.

Inked handwriting In OneNote, writing produced when using a pen tool to enter text.

Inking toolbar In Microsoft Edge, a collection of tools for annotating a webpage.

Input cells Spreadsheet cells that contain data instead of formulas and that act as input to a what-if analysis; input values often change to produce different results. Examples include interest rates, prices, or other data.

Input values In a data table, the variable values that are substituted in the table's formula to obtain varying results, such as interest rates.

Insertion point A blinking vertical line that appears when you click in the formula bar or in an active cell; indicates where new text will be inserted.

Instance A worksheet in its own workbook window.

Integrate To incorporate a document and parts of a document created in one program into another program; for example, to incorporate an Excel chart into a PowerPoint slide, or an Access table into a Word document.

Interface The look and feel of a program; for example, the appearance of commands and the way they are organized in the program window.

Intranet An internal network site used by a group of people who work together.

Keyword (Macros) In a macro procedure, a word that is recognized as part of the Visual Basic programming language.

Keywords Terms added to a workbook's Document Properties that help locate the file in a search.

Labels Descriptive text or other information that identifies data in rows, columns, or charts, but is not included in calculations.

Landscape Page orientation in which the contents of a page span the length of a page rather than its width, making the page wider than it is tall.

Launch To open or start a program on your computer.

Legend In a chart, information that identifies how data is represented by colors or patterns.

Link To insert an object into a destination program; the information you insert will be updated automatically when the data in the source document changes.

Linking The dynamic referencing of data in the same or in other workbooks, so that when data in the other location is changed, the references in the current location are automatically updated.

List arrows *See* AutoFilter list arrows.

Live Preview A feature that lets you point to a choice in a gallery or palette and see the results in the document without actually clicking the choice.

Lock To secure a row, column, or sheet so that data in that location cannot be changed.

Logical conditions Using the operators And and Or to narrow a custom filter criteria.

Logical formula A formula with calculations that are based on stated conditions.

Logical test The first part of an IF function; if the logical test is true, then the second part of the function is applied; if it is false, then the third part of the function is applied.

Macro A named set of instructions, written in the Visual Basic programming language, that performs tasks automatically in a specified order.

Main procedure A macro procedure containing several macros that run sequentially.

Major gridlines In a chart, the gridlines that represent the values at the tick marks on the value axis.

Manual calculation An option that turns off automatic calculation of worksheet formulas, allowing you to selectively determine if and when you want Excel to perform calculations.

Map An XML schema that is attached to a workbook.

Map an XML element A process in which XML element names are placed on an Excel worksheet in specific locations.

Metadata Information that describes data and is used in Microsoft Windows document searches.

Microsoft OneNote Mobile app The lightweight version of Microsoft OneNote designed for phones, tablets, and other mobile devices.

Minor gridlines In a chart, the gridlines that represent the values between the tick marks on the value axis.

Mixed reference Cell reference that combines both absolute and relative cell addressing.

Mode indicator An area on the left end of the status bar that indicates the program's status. For example, when you are changing the contents of a cell, the word 'Edit' appears in the mode indicator.

Model A worksheet used to produce a what-if analysis that acts as the basis for multiple outcomes.

Module In Visual Basic, contains macros procedures; is stored in a workbook.

Multilevel sort A reordering of table data using more than one column (field) at a time.

Name box Box to the left of the formula bar that shows the cell reference or name of the active cell.

Navigate To move around in a worksheet; for example, you can use the arrow keys on the keyboard to navigate from cell to cell, or press [Page Up] or [Page Down] to move one screen at a time.

Normal view Default worksheet view that shows the worksheet without features such as headers and footers; ideal for creating and editing a worksheet, but may not be detailed enough when formatting a document.

Note In OneNote, a small window that contains text or other types of information.

Notebook In OneNote, the container for notes, drawings, and other content.

Number format A format applied to values to express numeric concepts, such as currency, date, and percentage.

Object Independent element on a worksheet (such as a chart or graphic) that is not located in a specific cell or range; can be moved and resized and displays handles when selected. In object linking and embedding (OLE), the data to be exchanged between another document or program. In Visual Basic, every Excel element, including ranges.

Object Linking and Embedding (OLE) A Microsoft Windows feature that allows you to transfer data from one document and program to another using embedding or linking.

Objective *See* Target cell.

OLE *See* Object Linking and Embedding.

OneDrive An online storage and file sharing service; access to OneDrive is through a Microsoft account.

One-input data table A range of cells that shows resulting values when one input value in a formula is changed.

Online collaboration The ability to incorporate feedback or share information across the Internet or a company network or intranet.

Or logical condition A filtering feature that searches for records by specifying that only one entered criterion must be matched.

Order of precedence Rules that determine the order in which operations are performed within a formula containing more than one arithmetic operator.

Outline symbols In Outline view, the buttons that, when clicked, change the amount of detail that appears in the outlined worksheet.

Output values In a data table, the calculated results that appear in the body of the table.

Page In OneNote, a workspace for inserting notes and other content, similar to a page in a physical notebook.

Page Break Preview A view that displays a reduced view of each page in a worksheet, along with page break indicators that you can drag to include more or less information on a page.

Page Layout view Provides an accurate view of how a worksheet will look when printed, including headers and footers.

Panes Sections into which you can divide a worksheet when you want to work on separate parts of the worksheet at the same time; one pane freezes, or remains in place, while you scroll in another pane until you see the desired information.

Pareto A sorted histogram chart.

Paste Options button Button that appears onscreen after pasting content; enables you to choose to paste only specific elements of the copied selection, such as the formatting or values, if desired.

Personal macro workbook A workbook that can contain macros that are available to any open workbook. By default, the personal macro workbook is hidden.

PivotChart report An Excel feature that lets you summarize worksheet data in the form of a chart in which you can rearrange, or "pivot," parts of the chart structure to explore new data relationships.

PivotTable Field List A window containing fields that can be used to create or modify a PivotTable.

PivotTable Report (PivotTable) An Excel feature that allows you to summarize worksheet data in the form of a table in which you can rearrange, or "pivot," parts of the table structure to explore new data relationships; *also called* a PivotTable.

Plot The Excel process that converts numerical information into data points on a chart.

Plot area In a chart, the area inside the horizontal and vertical axes.

Point A unit of measure used for font size and row height. One point is equal to 1/72nd of an inch.

Populate The process of importing an XML file and filling the mapped elements on the worksheet with data from the XML file. Also the process of adding data or fields to a table, PivotTable, or a worksheet.

Portrait Page orientation in which the contents of a page span the width of a page, so the page is taller than it is wide.

PowerPivot A data analysis tool that can be used to create relationships between fields in tables from different data sources.

Presentation graphics program A program such as Microsoft PowerPoint that you can use to create slide show presentations.

Previewing Prior to printing, seeing onscreen exactly how the printed document will look.

Primary key The field in a database that contains unique information for each record.

Print area A portion of a worksheet that you can define using the Print Area button on the Page Layout tab; after you select and define a print area, the Quick Print feature prints only that worksheet area.

Print title In a table that spans more than one page, the field names that print at the top of every printed page.

Procedure A sequence of Visual Basic statements contained in a macro that accomplishes a specific task.

Procedure footer In Visual Basic, the last line of a Sub procedure.

Procedure header The first line in a Visual Basic procedure, it defines the procedure type, name, and arguments.

Program code Macro instructions, written in the Visual Basic for Applications (VBA) programming language.

Project In the Visual Basic Editor, the equivalent of a workbook; a project contains Visual Basic modules.

Project Explorer In the Visual Basic Editor, a window that lists all open projects (or workbooks) and the worksheets and modules they contain.

Properties File characteristics, such as the author's name, keywords, or the title, that help others understand, identify, and locate the file.

Properties window In the Visual Basic Editor, the window that displays a list of characteristics, or properties, associated with a module.

Property In Visual Basic, an attribute of an object that describes its character or behavior.

Publish To share Excel workbook data on a network or on the web so that others can access it using a web browser.

Quick Access toolbar A small toolbar on the left side of a Microsoft application program window's title bar, containing icons that you click to quickly perform common actions, such as saving a file.

Quick Analysis tool An icon that is displayed below and to the right of a range that lets you easily create charts and other elements.

Range A selection of two or more cells, such as B5:B14.

Range object In Visual Basic, an object that represents a cell or a range of cells.

Reading view In Microsoft Edge, the display of a webpage that removes ads and most graphics and uses a simple format for the text.

Read-only format Describes cells that display data but that cannot be changed in a protected worksheet.

Record In a table, data concerning an object or a person.

Reference operators In a formula, symbols which enable you to use ranges in calculations.

Refresh To update a PivotTable so it reflects changes to the underlying data.

Relative cell reference In a formula, a cell address that refers to a cell's location in relation to the cell containing the formula and that automatically changes to reflect the new location when the formula is copied or moved; default type of referencing used in Excel worksheets. *See also* Absolute cell reference.

Report filter A feature that allows you to filter PivotTable data to show one or more fields.

Responsive design A way to provide content so that it adapts appropriately to the size of the display on any device.

Return In a function, to display a result.

Ribbon Appears beneath the title bar in every Office app window and displays likely commands for the current task.

Run To play, as a macro.

Sandbox A computer security mechanism that helps to prevent attackers from gaining control of a computer.

Scenario A set of values you use to forecast results; the Excel Scenario Manager lets you store and manage different scenarios.

Scenario summary An Excel table that compiles data from various scenarios so that you can view the scenario results next to each other for easy comparison.

Schema In an XML document, a list of the fields, called elements or attributes, and their characteristics.

Scope In a named cell or range, the worksheet(s) in which the name can be used.

Screen capture An electronic snapshot of your screen, which you can paste into a document.

Screen clipping In OneNote, an image copied from any part of a computer screen.

Screen recording In Office Mix, a video you create by capturing your desktop and any actions performed on it.

Screenshot An image of an open file that is pasted into an Excel document; you can move, copy, and edit the image.

Scroll bars Bars on the right edge (vertical scroll bar) and bottom edge (horizontal scroll bar) of a window that allow you to move around in a document that is too large to fit on the screen at once.

Search criterion In a workbook or table search, the text you are searching for.

Secondary axis In a combination chart, an additional axis that supplies the scale for one of the chart types used.

Section tab In OneNote, a divider for organizing a notebook.

Share *See* Shared workbook.

Shared workbook An Excel workbook that several users can open and modify.

Sheet tab scrolling buttons Allow you to navigate to additional sheet tabs when available; located to the left of the sheet tabs.

Sheet tabs Identify the sheets in a workbook and let you switch between sheets; located below the worksheet grid.

Single-file webpage Format that integrates all of the worksheets and graphical elements from a workbook into a single file, in the format MHTML, also known as MHT.

Sizing handles Small series of dots at the corners and edges of a chart indicating that the chart is selected; drag to resize the chart.

Slicer A graphic object used to filter a PivotTable.

Slide Notes In Office Mix, the written and displayed version of notes typically used to recite narration while creating a slide recording.

Slide recording In Office Mix, a video you create by recording action with a webcam, a camera attached or built in to a computer.

SmartArt graphics Predesigned diagram types for specific types of data, including List, Process, Cycle, and Hierarchy.

Source program In a data exchange, the program used to create the data you are embedding or linking.

Sparkline A quick, simple chart located within a cell that serves as a visual indicator of data trends.

Stated conditions In a logical formula, criteria you create.

Statement In Visual Basic, a line of code.

Status bar Bar at the bottom of the Excel window that provides a brief description about the active command or task in progress.

Storyline In Sway, the workspace for assembling a presentation.

Strong password A password that is difficult to guess and that helps to protect your workbooks from security threats; has at least 14 characters that are a mix of upper- and lowercase letters, numbers, and special characters.

Structured reference Allows table formulas to refer to table columns by names that are automatically generated when the table is created.

Sub procedure A series of Visual Basic statements that performs an action but does not return a value.

Suite A group of programs that are bundled together and share a similar interface, making it easy to transfer skills and program content among them.

Summary function In a PivotTable, a function that determines the type of calculation applied to the PivotTable data, such as SUM or COUNT.

Sunburst A circular hierarchical chart used to present data with many different levels.

Sway site A website Sway creates to share and display a Sway presentation.

Sync In OneNote, to save a new or updated notebook so that all versions of the notebook, such as a notebook on OneDrive and a copy on a hard drive, have the same contents.

Syntax In the Visual Basic programming language, the formatting rules that must be followed so that a procedure will run successfully.

Table An organized collection of rows and columns of similarly structured data on a worksheet.

Table styles Predesigned formatting that can be applied to a range of cells or even to an entire worksheet; especially useful for those ranges with labels in the left column and top row, and totals in the bottom row or right column. *See also* Table.

Table total row A row you can add to the bottom of a table for calculations using the data in the table columns.

Tabs Organizational unit used for commands on the Ribbon. The tab names appear at the top of the Ribbon and the active tab appears in front.

Target The location that a hyperlink displays after you click it.

Target cell In what-if analysis (specifically, in Excel Solver), the cell containing the formula. *Also called* objective.

Template In Excel, a predesigned, formatted file that serves as the basis for a new workbook; in OneNote, a page design you can apply to new pages to provide an appealing background, a consistent layout, or elements suitable for certain types of notes, such as meeting notes or to-do lists.

Text annotations Labels added to a chart to draw attention to or describe a particular area.

Text concatenation operators In a formula, symbols used to join strings of text in different cells.

Text file *See* ASCII file.

Theme A predefined set of colors, fonts, line and fill effects, and other formats that can be applied to an Excel worksheet and give it a consistent, professional look.

Tick marks Notations of a scale of measure on a chart axis.

Title bar Appears at the top of every Office program window; displays the document name and program name.

To Do tag In OneNote, an icon that helps you keep track of your assignments and other tasks; in Microsoft Edge, an annotation on a webpage.

Toggle A button with two settings, on and off.

Tracer arrows In Excel worksheet auditing, arrows that point from cells that might have caused an error to the active cell containing an error.

Track To identify and keep a record of who makes which changes to a workbook.

Treemap A rectangular hierarchical chart used to present data with many different levels.

Trendline A series of data points on a line that shows data values that represent the general direction in a series of data.

Two-input data table A range of cells that shows resulting values when two input values in a formula are changed.

User interface A term for all the ways you interact with an app.

Username The name that appears in the User name text box of the Excel Options dialog box. This name is displayed at the beginning of comments added to a worksheet.

Validate A process in which an xml schema makes sure the xml data follows the rules outlined in the schema.

Value axis In a chart, vertical axis that contains numerical values; in a 2-dimensional chart, also known as the y-axis.

Values Numbers, formulas, and functions used in calculations.

Variable In what-if analysis, a changing input value, such as price or interest rate, that affects a calculated result; in Visual Basic, an area in memory in which you can temporarily store an item of information.

VBA *See* Visual Basic for Applications.

View A method of displaying a document window to show more or fewer details or a different combination of elements that makes it easier to complete certain tasks, such as formatting or reading text.

View-only Link A link to a workbook on a OneDrive that can be viewed by users.

Virus Destructive software that can damage your computer files.

Visual Basic Editor A program that lets you display and edit macro code.

Visual Basic for Applications (VBA) A programming language used to create macros in Excel.

Waterfall A chart used to present data with positive and negative values.

Watermark A translucent background design on a worksheet that is displayed when the worksheet is printed. A watermark is a graphic file that is inserted into the document header.

Web query An Excel feature that lets you obtain data from a webpage and place it in an Excel workbook for analysis.

What-if analysis A decision-making tool in which data is changed and formulas are recalculated, in order to predict various possible outcomes.

Wildcard A special symbol that substitutes for unknown characters in defining search criteria in the Find and Replace dialog box. The most common types of wildcards are the question mark (?), which stands for any single character, and the asterisk (*), which represents any group of characters.

WordArt Specially formatted text, created using the WordArt button on the Drawing toolbar.

Workbook A collection of related worksheets contained within a single file which has the file extension xlsx.

Worksheet A single sheet within a workbook file; also, the entire area within an electronic spreadsheet that contains a grid of columns and rows.

Worksheet window Area of the program window that displays part of the current worksheet; the worksheet window displays only a small fraction of the worksheet, which can contain a total of 1,048,576 rows and 16,384 columns.

Write access The ability to make changes to a workbook; with read access, a user can only read the workbook contents and cannot make changes.

X-axis The horizontal axis in a chart; often shows data categories, such as months or locations.

XML Acronym that stands for eXtensible Markup Language, which is a language used to structure, store, and send information.

Y-axis The vertical axis in a chart; often shows numerical values.

Z-axis The third axis in a true 3-D chart, lets you compare data points across both categories and values.

Zooming in A feature that makes a document appear larger but shows less of it on screen at once; does not affect actual document size.

Zooming out A feature that shows more of a document on screen at once but at a reduced size; does not affect actual document size.

Index